Cold Warriors

ALSO BY DUNCAN WHITE

*Nabokov and His Books: Between Late Modernism
and the Literary Marketplace*

ch.
CUSTOM
HOUSE

DUNCAN WHITE

COLD WARRIORS

Writers Who Waged the Literary Cold War

HarperCollins books may be purchased for educational, business, or sales promotional use. For information, please e-mail the Special Markets Department at SPsales@harpercollins.com.

FIRST EDITION

Designed by Bonni Leon-Berman

Library of Congress Cataloging-in-Publication Data has been applied for.

ISBN 978-0-06-244981-8

19 20 21 22 23 LSC 10 9 8 7 6 5 4 3 2 1

To Eden, Bella, and Luke

CONTENTS

Cold Warriors

INTRODUCTION

BETWEEN FEBRUARY AND May 1955, a group secretly funded by the Central Intelligence Agency launched a secret weapon into Communist territory. Gathering at launch sites in West Germany, operatives inflated ten-foot balloons, armed them with their payload, waited for favorable winds, and launched them into Poland.[1] They then watched as the balloons were carried deep behind the Iron Curtain, where they would eventually disgorge their contents. These, though, were not explosive or incendiary weapons: they were books. At the height of the Cold War, the CIA made copies of George Orwell's *Animal Farm* rain down from the Communist sky.

The scheme was part of a larger effort to penetrate the wall of censorship the Soviet Union had erected around its Warsaw Pact allies. Western radio broadcasts were jammed, letters were censored, and only state-run newspapers were published. The CIA disguised its role in the campaign to get banned materials into these countries by secretly channeling funds through front organizations that produced the tens of millions of books, leaflets, pamphlets, posters, and the hundreds of thousands of balloons needed to fly them into enemy territory. In response, the authorities in Czechoslovakia, Hungary, and Poland warned its citizens that possession of this material was illegal and even sought to shoot down the balloons with fighter planes and antiaircraft guns.

Dropping *Animal Farm* into Poland proved challenging. It was one thing to send over hundreds of leaflets in a balloon, but another to send over large numbers of books. The Free Europe Press (one of the CIA's front organizations) produced a special compact forty-eight-page edition of the novel printed on lightweight paper stock so that as many as thirty copies could be loaded onto a balloon at a time.[2] From the vantage of the twenty-first century, when ISIS fighters in the Syrian desert are targeted by a Reaper drone operated from a trailer thousands of miles away in the Nevada desert, the idea of dropping books on the enemy by balloon may seem quaint, even absurd. Yet in the Cold War both superpowers poured vast resources into overt and covert means to undermine the enemy with the printed word on a massive scale.

How effective literature was in winning over hearts and minds is hard to measure, but what is indisputable is how seriously it was taken by both superpowers. Secretive agencies established propaganda networks to amplify the voices of those writers whose work found ideological favor, and both Western and Communist secret services sought ways to censor, intimidate, or silence those writers whose work was critical of their countries. This book tells the story of the writers on both sides of the Iron Curtain who found themselves locked in this exhilarating, dangerous conflict, and how the literature they made took shape under this shadow.

The Cold War may have been a conflict of ideas, but imposing those ideas on the enemy through military means was not an option. As Kenneth Osgood writes in *Total Cold War*, the existence of nuclear weapons meant that "the Cold War, more than any other conflict in human history, was channeled into nonmilitary modes of combat, particularly ideological and symbolic ones."[3] Each side therefore used various forms of propaganda and disinformation as a way to undermine the way its enemy organized its own society. Some of this propaganda was crude and, as such, ineffective. But literature was another matter, for it had a more sophisticated power to persuade. In reading *Animal Farm,* with its allegory of a revolution gone awry, exploited by corrupt and self-serving leaders interested only in consolidating their own power, Polish citizens might begin to question the received truths of their rulers. That was why it was worth sending batches of the novel through the air into enemy territory.

BY THE TIME THE COLD WAR BEGAN in the late 1940s, the Soviet Union's leaders were already old hands at cultural warfare. In the aftermath of the revolution they sought to use literature as a means of legitimating their power and as a tool by which to remake society. Part of this project involved educating the populace, and in the twenty years after the revolution, literacy rates in the country rose from below 30 percent to above 75 percent. What these new readers should be reading was another matter. While the Bolsheviks argued among themselves about how much autonomy writers should be allowed, they all agreed that literature was political, and that the literature produced in the Soviet Union should light the path to socialism. The number of books published per year tripled by the late 1920s as editions of the writings of Friedrich Engels, Karl Marx, Vladimir Lenin, and Joseph Stalin were published in huge numbers. (There were also large runs of editions of Russian classics including works by Anton Chekhov, Nikolai Gogol, Alexander Pushkin, and Ivan Turgenev.)[4] To ensure that the new books being published followed the Party line, all publishing houses came under the control of the state publisher Gosizdat, to which they had to submit their manuscripts for censorship. Works that espoused "bourgeois" or "reactionary" values were banned and its authors punished, sometimes jailed. Literary production was further consolidated in 1932 when, under Joseph Stalin, all the different writers' groups were disbanded and a new organization, the

Union of Soviet Writers, was formed. Its members were mandated to write books that adhered to the tenets of "socialist realism." The consequences of deviance became much more serious, with a nonconforming writer facing the gulag or the executioner's bullet. As the poet Osip Mandelstam pointed out, this suppression of literature actually granted it a perverse power. "If they're killing people for poetry that means they honor and esteem it, they fear it," he said, "that means poetry is power." Mandelstam, who dared to write a poem mocking Stalin, died in the camps.

At the same time as the Kremlin imposed ideological rigor on literature at home, it staged an ambitious and sophisticated propaganda campaign abroad. One of the goals was to win the sympathy of the literary elite of the West and, by implication, the sympathy of their readership. It was not necessary to convert these intellectuals to ardent Communists, but to convince them that the Soviet Union was a force for good in the world against the evils of exploitative capitalism and imperialism. This was partly about self-preservation: the Kremlin knew its enemies in the West wanted the Communist project to fail and would seize any opportunity to chip away at its legitimacy. Western intellectuals seemed like ideal targets for persuasion. With the Great Depression appearing to augur the failure of capitalism, Communism was, in historian David Priestland's words, "a rational system" that drew upon "the laws of historical development" to lead to a kind of secular utopia.[5] Furthermore, Marxism-Leninism cast them as potential heroes in this story, the vanguard who would lead the proletariat into revolution. With fascism rising in Germany, Italy, and Japan, intellectuals felt an urgent need to find a path to a better society, to slough off the inequalities that racism, misogyny, and imperialism made manifest in Western societies. The socialist model offered by the Soviet Union was understandably appealing, especially as the truth about its authoritarianism was carefully masked by the Kremlin's disinformation.

The organization responsible for cultural propaganda was the Communist International (Comintern), which had been founded in 1919.[6] Its propaganda impresario was Willi Münzenberg, a charismatic German revolutionary who had been part of Vladimir Lenin's coterie during his period of exile in Zurich, a man with a genius for establishing front organizations that the Comintern could use to get its message out without revealing its hand. Münzenberg set up "charities, publishers, newspapers, magazines, theaters, film studios, and cinema houses" all over the globe, and sought to involve famous writers—including Henri Barbusse, Bertolt Brecht, John Dos Passos, Ernest Hemingway, and Romain Rolland—in petitions, protests, conferences, and other ventures.[7] The Comintern also housed the Department of International Communication, which, despite its bland name, was highly secretive and collaborated with the Soviet intelligence service on clandestine operations.[8] By the mid-1930s, these methods were used to help drum up support for the Republican cause in the Spanish Civil War (the Comintern processed volunteers who fought in the International Brigades) and to try to persuade the rest of the world that the defendants in the Moscow Show Trials were indeed guilty of the outlandish crimes of which they were accused.

The United States realized the value of cultural warfare much later, only during the Second World War. The Office of War Information (OWI), established in 1942, made literature a central plank of its propaganda operations, as it worked with the U.S. Army, the Psychological Warfare Branch, and the newly founded Office of Strategic Services intelligence agency (forerunner of the CIA) to develop new programs. One OWI poster carried the slogan, "Books Are Weapons in the War of Ideas," and depicted a Nazi book burning in the foreground. In the background loomed a giant book the size of a building, on the cover of which was written a quotation from President Franklin D. Roosevelt: "Books cannot be killed by fire. People die, but books never die. No man and no force can put thought in a concentration camp forever. No man and no force can take from the world the books that embody man's eternal fight against tyranny. In this war, we know, books are weapons."[9] The OWI distributed more than 120 million books to American soldiers during the war as a means of bolstering morale.[10] The Armed Services Editions helped popularize many books that are now considered classics, including Betty Smith's *A Tree Grows in Brooklyn* and F. Scott Fitzgerald's *The Great Gatsby*.[11] As the Allies approached victory, plans were made for using books as propaganda to re-educate the defeated enemy, including prisoners of war.[12] From 1944 the OWI began producing books translated into French, German, and Italian (the Overseas Editions), which were distributed in liberated towns and cities. Some of the 3.6 million books circulated in this way were nakedly pro-American tracts but included among them was material that the OWI hoped reflected well on American literary achievement, such as Hemingway's *For Whom the Bell Tolls* (described as "a representative novel by an American writer").[13] A parallel program run by the OWI's London office produced the Transatlantic Editions, which were even more literary in content, distributing French and Dutch anthologies that included the work of Willa Cather, T. S. Eliot, Hemingway, John Steinbeck, and Edmund Wilson.[14] Even though vast numbers of books were distributed, the strategy was not only to reach a wide audience but also to exert influence over the independent thinkers who would shape politics and society. "Books do not have their impact upon the mass mind but upon the minds of those who would mold the mass mind—upon leaders of thought and formulators of public opinion," read one OWI memo. "The impact of a book may last six months or several decades. Books are the most enduring propaganda of all."[15]

With the war won, and tension escalating with the Soviet Union, the United States prepared itself for a different kind of conflict. While it had the technological advantage of nuclear weapons (which the Russians did not develop until 1949), in terms of espionage, propaganda, psychological warfare, and cultural warfare it lagged far behind its rival. The Harry S. Truman administration was warned by its Psychological Strategy Board that *The Short History of the Communist Party* was the best-selling book in the world, "with the possible exception of the Bible," and that the Kremlin was orchestrating a "massive, comprehensive, worldwide campaign of ideological indoctrination."[16] Washington felt the pressing need to catch up as relations with Moscow deteriorated.

While the rival superpowers embarked on an arms race and competed over technologies of space flight, the first decades of the Cold War were also marked by an escalating "book race." In Moscow, a vast administration (more than three hundred thousand people by the 1970s) was employed by the centralized publishing industry.[17] The International Book Publishing Corporation produced huge numbers of books in "free-world languages" (40 million books by 1950, and 40 million per year by 1961).[18] As literary scholar Greg Barnhisel points out, one of the reasons for producing books in such numbers was to undermine the idea of the market itself—these books were cheaply mass-produced and sold at a loss. And while most of these books were Communist political tracts, they also produced editions of novels, including one of Stalin's favorites: Mikhail Sholokhov's *And Quiet Flows the Don*. In fact, during the Cold War, the production of literature in the Soviet Union escalated dramatically: between 1928 and 1940, novels, poetry, and plays accounted for

10–12 percent of the total printed output; between 1956 and 1970 it rose to 30–33 percent.[19]

The United States instituted its own book programs, including one by which the government helped with currency exchange to incentivize the publication of American books in many foreign markets, including Germany, Poland, and Yugoslavia, and later Pakistan, Burma, the Philippines, Taiwan, and Indonesia. While the publishers chose which books were to be published, the State Department made sure these contained nothing harmful to U.S. interests.[20] More directly anti-Communist was the State Department–funded Books in Translation Program, which purchased foreign rights of suitable books, such as Czeslaw Milosz's *The Captive Mind,* Arthur Koestler's *Darkness at Noon,* and Orwell's *Animal Farm* and *Nineteen Eighty-Four,* paid for their translation, and then helped find local publishers and distributors. Working in Europe, Asia, the Middle East, and Latin America, the program placed 50 million books into circulation, editions of which gave no indication that they had been subsidized by an American agency. The State Department also established a network of reading rooms around the world. The Information Center Service, as this program was known, had been established in the Second World War and by 1946 boasted 67 libraries and a total of three million visitors. By 1962 it was up to 181 centers in 80 countries (plus 85 other reading rooms).[21] While these centers offered a large selection of books, some even critical of the United States, they sought to avoid stocking anything deemed pro-Communist or dealing with one of the favorite topics the Soviets used to point to America's moral failings—its continuing racist treatment of its African American population.[22]

Literary prizes were another way of contesting prestige. No award produced more desire—or anxiety—than the Nobel Prize for Literature. The Soviet Union felt slighted when Maxim Gorky, the doyen of Soviet writers, lost out in 1933 to

Ivan Bunin, a Russian émigré who had fled the revolution to live in Paris. When first William Faulkner (1949) and then Ernest Hemingway (1954) won the award, America's literary superiority appeared to have been recognized in front of the rest of the world. The wound reopened when Boris Pasternak, a critic of the regime, was awarded the prize in 1958 at the expense of his rival Mikhail Sholokhov, a Kremlin favorite. The 1970 award to Aleksandr Solzhenitsyn prompted a major diplomatic incident.[23]

While the "book race" was unfolding, the Americans also sought to catch up in other areas. With much of Europe seeking to rebuild itself after the devastation of war, the Cold War was initially contested over states in which a strong Communist Party (including Italy, Germany, and France) threatened to expand Soviet influence. Winning over intellectuals in those countries—something in which the Soviets had excelled—was seen as essential to shaping public opinion. The Psychological Strategy Board, made up of representatives of the State Department, the Department of Defense, and the CIA, argued that the best way to do this was through the promotion of literature, as a 1953 report made clear: "In most parts of the world, the radio and television are still novelties; magazines have low circulation; and newspapers circulate mostly among political groups whose opinions are already formed . . . Books—permanent literature— are by far the most powerful means of influencing the attitudes of intellectuals."[24]

The campaign to influence intellectuals and writers was both overt and covert. There were the publicly acknowledged programs run by the State Department, but then there was also the hidden hand of the CIA, which secretly invested in conventions, prizes, publishing houses, and literary magazines through a series of supposedly charitable foundations it used as front organizations—an approach indebted to the strategies of the Comintern. What was perhaps surprising is the way the U.S.

government and its various agencies ended up as champions of the experimental literature of the early twentieth century's avant-garde—those writers who gathered under the name of "modernism"—despite its seeming complexity or elitism. At the twenty-fifth-anniversary celebrations of the Museum of Modern Art in New York City, President Dwight D. Eisenhower said that "freedom of the arts is a basic freedom, one of the pillars of liberty in our land." In case the audience missed the point, Eisenhower went on: "my friends, how different it is in tyranny. When artists are made the slaves and tools of the state; when artists become chief propagandists of a cause, progress is arrested and creation and genius are destroyed."[25] The dynamics of the Cold War made the government the champion of difficult elitist art—that of James Joyce, Jackson Pollock, and William Faulkner—in large part because it was banned in Moscow. This meant that the kinds of magazines and publishers these front organizations supported often supported the most challenging and innovative literature. To a writer who valued the artistic goals of modernism, it must have felt like validation instead of collaboration. It is perhaps unsurprising, therefore, that by the 1960s so many prominent American and British writers had at one point taken a paycheck for a piece of writing that was indirectly paid for by the CIA.[26]

COLD WARRIORS IS THE STORY of the writers who dealt with the consequences of having literature become a Cold War battleground. In the United States, depending on your politics, you could find your voice silenced, or it could be amplified in publications all around the world. In the Soviet Union, if your work was considered ideologically orthodox, you could find yourself a national hero, published by the millions, with a dacha in the countryside and a cushy lifestyle. However, if you deviated, or dissented, you could find your books disappearing from libraries, your name excised from encyclopedias, and end up yourself in the labor camps or executed by the secret police in the basement of the Lubyanka prison. Around the world, authors were directly involved in how the global conflict played out. They led double lives as spies, volunteered in foreign wars, engaged in guerrilla insurgencies, churned out propaganda, exposed official hypocrisy, and risked their lives to write books that defied the Cold War consensus. And just as writers were involved in the most intense moments of the Cold War, they also played a crucial role in bringing it to an end, with some even emerging from the wreckage of Communism as leaders of a new, changed world.

To grapple with this history, this book takes the form of a group biography, tracing the interconnected lives and works of writers on both sides of the Iron Curtain from the origins of the Cold War to its final unraveling. My aim is to tell the story of the literary Cold War from *both* sides of the Iron Curtain, as, just like the larger Cold War itself, the fight over literature was one locked in interdependence. If Soviet "socialist realism" was established in opposition to Western "modernism," then one of the reasons that the U.S. government and the CIA became such staunch champions of modernism was the very fact that it was excoriated and banned in the Soviet Union. Literary betrayal, therefore, was not just a matter of content, it was also a matter of style. Where a writer was published also mattered, of course: during the Red Scare in the 1940s and 1950s, any American writer who was praised in *Pravda* became a target for the FBI, the House Un-American Activities Committee (HUAC), and Senator Joseph McCarthy's investigators, and, by the same token, any American writer who criticized U.S. policies was sure to find a large readership in the Soviet Union. Even after Soviet cultural policies became less draconian in the decades after Stalin's death in 1953, there were still very serious consequences for an author who dared publish in the West without official sanction. This book suggests that to understand how literature took shape and developed in the twentieth century, we have to pay attention to how writers in both blocs responded to and negotiated these enmeshed dynamics.

One of the biggest challenges of this book was deciding which writers to focus on. Some selections seemed obvious for the indisputable influence they exercised over the Cold War: George Orwell, Arthur Koestler, Boris Pasternak, and Aleksandr Solzhenitsyn, for example. Another criterion for selection was writers who had lived through various stages of the Cold War and therefore could provide a throughline to the book: Graham Greene, Mary McCarthy, and Stephen Spender fit this profile. Others have less space dedicated to them but have compelling, essential stories to tell: Ernest Hemingway and the end of the Second World War; Anna Akhmatova under late Stalinism; Howard Fast during the Red Scare; Richard Wright at the Bandung Conference; John le Carré at the Berlin Wall; Vaclav Havel leading the Velvet Revolution. Some of the writers and books featured here will be readily familiar, but I hope seeing them in the context of the Cold War will prompt readers to return to their work with fresh eyes. Others, like Isaac Babel, Gioconda Belli, and Andrei Sinyavsky, are perhaps less well known but are at the center of crucial stories in the unfolding of the literary Cold War. Finally, there is Kim Philby, the infamous KGB double agent, who is not a literary figure at all (although his memoir is elegantly written). I have included his story in this book to help clarify the way espionage and literature became so fascinatingly intertwined during the Cold War—Philby did not *write* fiction; he *lived* it.

While this book ranges across several continents from the 1930s to the 1990s, it does not pretend to give a comprehensive account of the Cold War. The focus here is predominately on American, British, and Russian writers, although never forgetting that the Cold War was a conflict of truly global scope. Still, so far-reaching and so pervasive was the conflict that many stories are inevitably untold. There is, for example, another version of this book that could focus on writers of the Global South and how they became enmeshed in the way the Cold War fostered and suppressed independence movements as the European empires collapsed. I hope that this book might inspire readers to explore some of these stories.

The decision to tell the literary history of the Cold War through writers (and the books they wrote) is also a way of making an argument. This book is profoundly indebted to the work of those who explore the cultural Cold War through its institutions on both sides of the Iron Curtain; this book is built on the foundations of their painstaking archival work (much of it having to find imaginative ways around the fact that the intelligence agencies on both sides refuse to declassify their files).[27] However, the risks of this approach are that writers can too easily be characterized as passive purveyors of propaganda, ciphers for ideology, or puppets of secretive intelligence organizations. The truth is often a lot less straightforward than that, with writers leading lives of messy contradiction, in which they asserted their own autonomy in surprising ways. In this regard the title of this book carries a note of irony. Stephen Spender, reflecting on his role in the conflict later in life, said he always resented being called a "Cold Warrior," though, he reluctantly admitted, "I suppose it is what I was."[28] Others might have embraced the label—certainly the Koestler of the 1950s would have—but, for the most part, writers did not consider themselves to be soldiers in an ideological conflict. Even Alexander Fadeyev, the Soviet novelist and bureaucrat who cracked his ideological whip with devastating consequences for many fellow writers, still had moments when his ideological commitments gave way to a messier—and redemptive—humanity.

The issue of complicity is at the center of this book. Every writer in these pages had to grapple with it in one form or another—such was the price to be paid for writing at a time when literature had become so pervasively politicized, when, to paraphrase historian Giles Scott-Smith, to be apolitical was itself a form of politics.[29] Even the most courageous and stubborn of writers, such as Solzhenitsyn, were forced into making accommodations with the power of the state. At the same time, the cultural policies on both sides of the Iron Curtain lent great power to literature—this was a force strong enough to merit dropping books like bombs from the sky. On both sides of the Iron Curtain, writers exploited that power in ways that the White House, the Kremlin, the CIA, and the KGB never expected. There is no question that the Cold War shaped literature, but in the pages that follow, I also want to tell the story of how literature shaped the Cold War.

Part One

SPAIN

ONE

Orwell

HUESCA & BARCELONA, 1937

THE BULLET THAT ENTERED GEORGE ORWELL'S NECK was a fraction of an inch from changing the way we think about the Cold War. He had been back at the front lines of fighting in Huesca only ten days when a fascist sniper hit him, the bullet ripping through his throat. Orwell was an acting officer, in charge of some thirty soldiers, both Spanish and English, and at daybreak he had got up early to speak with his sentries. This was Orwell's second stint at the front, and his experiences of Spanish marksmanship had made him somewhat cavalier. As he spoke to Harry Milton, the sentry on duty, he had the dawn at his back. This made his silhouette an inviting target to the enemy, who were encamped in trenches 150 yards away across a deserted orchard, and who had the advantage of higher ground. "Gosh! Are you hit?" said Milton as Orwell collapsed in front of him while in midsentence.[1] Orwell later recalled the bullet's impact as feeling as if he were at the center of an explosion: "There seemed to be a loud bang and a blinding flash of light all around me, and I felt a tremendous shock—no pain, only a violent shock, such as you get from an electric terminal; with it a sense of utter weakness, a feeling of being stricken and shrivelled up to nothing."[2]

Lying in the trench, Orwell could not feel his right arm and, as his comrades lifted him onto a stretcher, an alarming quantity of blood poured out of his mouth. Milton was convinced Orwell was "a goner."[3] The bullet had passed clean through his neck. One of the stretcher-bearers, Harry Webb, poured alcohol into the wound. Orwell said he felt a "pleasant coolness."[4] As he was bundled along on the stretcher, he felt leaves brushing against his face. "What a good thing it was to be alive in a world where silver poplars grow," he remembered thinking.[5] If he breathed too hard, blood bubbled out of his mouth. He presumed the artery had been hit and that he was dying. He thought of his wife, Eileen, and became angry at the idea of dying in a "stale corner of the trenches" through some "stupid mischance."[6] It was not the way his Spanish adventure was supposed to end.

In fact, it was far from over; a sinister new chapter was about to begin. Had the bullet opened his carotid artery he would have bled out on that stretcher and he would have been remembered as an unfulfilled writer who became a martyr in the war with fascism, like the poet John Cornford, who was killed by a sniper on the Cordoba front in December 1936. Since he was hit but not killed, Orwell entered a new trajectory, into a confrontation with a force he would come to despise as deeply as fascism: Stalinism. The coming weeks and months offered up an unexpected education in the virulent spread of totalitarianism. It infected those Orwell thought he was fighting alongside, and before long, it came after him.

ORWELL FIRST ARRIVED in the bustling, cosmopolitan city of Barcelona on Boxing Day, 1936, with the uncomplicated goal of fighting fascists.[7] To his own later embarrassment, he confessed to having little understanding of the complexities of the war and the various factions that were fighting it. To progressive intellectuals of his generation, this was a rallying point against rising fascism, which had already defeated left-wing movements in Italy (1922), Germany (1933), and Austria (1934). On July 17,

1936, high-ranking officers in the Spanish army staged a coup to seize power from the Popular Front government, which had won a narrow majority in elections the previous February.[8] The coup appeared stillborn: the plotters needed to transport the battle-hardened troops of the Army of Africa, called such because it was made up of colonial soldiers garrisoned in Morocco, across the Straits of Gibraltar, but the Republic retained control of the navy. Fearing the coup would fail, they looked to fascist allies abroad. The Italian leader Benito Mussolini, a long-standing backer of the Spanish far right, including the Carlists and the Falange, initially wavered in his support but eventually decided to throw his weight behind the insurgency, sending money, planes, pilots, officers, and finally ground troops to Spain.[9] Two of the first batch of Italian planes crashed over French Algeria, alerting the world to Mussolini's direct support of the insurgents. The Nationalists, as they styled themselves, also sent a delegation to Germany to seek support from the Nazis. Adolf Hitler received them at Bayreuth, fresh from a performance of Richard Wagner's *Siegfried*. Fired up by the opera and ranting about Bolshevism, Hitler agreed to intervene, launching Operation Magic Fire. German fighter planes (including the elite Condor Legion) were soon patrolling the Spanish skies, shortly to be followed by arms and ammunition. Crucially, German transport planes were provided to airlift the Army of Africa to Seville, with General Francisco Franco at its head.[10]

Franco had not been the leader of the Nationalist forces at the coup's inception. That role was supposed to be played by José Sanjurjo, a general who had failed in a previous coup attempt in 1932 and was living in exile in neighboring Portugal, which had itself succumbed to a military coup in 1926 and was ruled by the dictator António Salazar. Two days after the Nationalists rose up, a plane arrived in Portugal to fly Sanjurjo to Spain. The problem was that this plane was a de Havilland Puss Moth two-seater, not designed for heavy cargo. Sanjurjo was a big man and ill-advisedly hauled a large suitcase on board. On takeoff from a racetrack near Cascais, the plane clipped the top of the tree-line, crashed, and burst into flames. With the other credible candidates locked in Republican prisons, Franco emerged as leader by process of elimination. Within a week, foreign embassies were referring to the Nationalist forces as Francoist, and he soon thereafter assumed the title of Caudillo, the equivalent of Duce or Führer. The coalition of conservative forces that welcomed the coup—including the military, the monarchists, the church, and the wealthy landowners—were motivated by opposition to socialist reform and stirred up by fear of "Judeo-Masonic-Bolshevism." Under Franco the reactionary right crystallized into fascism, determined to win back Spain through a campaign of terror.

Thanks to the intervention of Germany and Italy, the coup had gathered momentum and the situation looked bleak for the Republicans by the end of the summer of 1936. Having arrived in the southern town of Algeciras, in August and September Franco's forces made their way north, marching toward Madrid, leaving a trail of atrocity in their wake. Fearing Madrid would not be able to resist, the Republican government, a coalition of left-wing parties led by socialist Prime Minister Francisco Largo Caballero, fled the capital for Valencia.

In their hour of need, the Republicans finally received help from abroad. On October 15 the Republican forces took delivery of the first batch of arms from the Soviet Union; shortly after, the first of the International Brigades began arriving to reinforce the Republicans.[11] The brigades were made up of left-wing volunteers from around the world, including German and Italian exiles, and American, Belgian, British, Canadian, Cuban, French, and Polish anti-fascists, recruited by the Communist International (Comintern) and transported across the

French-Spanish border. The Comintern was an organization ostensibly dedicated to the cause of spreading Communism around the world but was often in practice prepared to go to any lengths, including propaganda, espionage, and assassinations, to enforce the Party line as laid down in Moscow. The import of Soviet weapons and Communist-organized volunteers greatly increased the political leverage of the Spanish Communist Party, who sought to incrementally increase their power over the Republican coalition government. But at the same time, Moscow ordered them not to go too far. Stalin was playing realpolitik: he wanted to preserve the Popular Front, so as not to make Britain and France fear that Spain was about to turn Communist, and he wanted to keep Hitler tied up in an expensive and debilitating war. For the most part the volunteers were not professional soldiers, but they had been given some military training at the headquarters in Albacete before moving on to Madrid just in time to help repel Franco's November assault. The foreign volunteers played a key role in holding the city and, to sympathizers like Orwell, reading about it in the newspapers in London, this heroic resistance offered the "thrill of hope."[12]

At thirty-three, Orwell wanted to fight the good fight while he still could. He was a writer with a growing reputation in Britain. *Down and Out in Paris and London,* published in 1933, a memoir of his experiences living as a dishwasher in a hotel in Paris and as a tramp on the streets of London, had made "George Orwell" into a literary hero of the British Left (Orwell was his pen name, his real name being Eric Blair).[13] The three novels he had written since—*Burmese Days* (1934), *A Clergyman's Daughter* (1935), and *Keep the Aspidistra Flying* (1936)—had not enjoyed as much success, failing to sell out their three-thousand-copy print runs, but he had high hopes for his latest book, a return to nonfiction.[14] He left for Spain with the manuscript of *The Road to Wigan Pier,* his account of time spent among working people in the north of

England, entrusted to his publisher. For now, though, Orwell's priority was not writing but fighting.

Getting to Spain was not straightforward. Orwell initially sought the help of Harry Pollitt, the general secretary of the British Communist Party. When Pollitt asked whether he was going to join the International Brigades, Orwell said he wanted to see what was going on himself before committing to anything. This convinced an already suspicious Pollitt of Orwell's political unreliability, and he instead advised Orwell to get a passage of safe conduct from the Spanish Embassy in Paris. Just before leaving for Paris, Orwell got in touch with the Independent Labour Party (ILP), where he had some friends, and they sent him a letter of introduction to John McNair, their representative in Barcelona.[15] A group of ILP volunteers were preparing to travel to Spain and set up their own fighting unit but Orwell, impatient to get going, set out ahead of them. In Paris, Orwell visited with Henry Miller, whose novels were still banned in the United States. Miller told Orwell any ideals he had of fighting for democracy and freedom were "baloney," but he was undeterred by this pessimism.[16] Arriving at the border in a train packed with Czech, French, and German volunteers, Orwell found that the Anarchist guards seemed impressed by his ILP letter (they did not care about the embassy documents), so he decided, for pragmatic reasons, he would make McNair his first port of call. It was a fateful decision.

"I had come to Spain with some notion of writing newspaper articles," he recalled, "but I had joined the militia almost immediately, because at that time and in that atmosphere it seemed the only conceivable thing to do."[17] Orwell was exhilarated. Barcelona was in the grip of revolution: many churches had been destroyed, the buildings were draped in Communist and Anarchist flags, and the walls were covered with slogans and posters. The use of formal pronouns had disappeared, as had formal dress, and when Orwell tried to tip the elevator operator in his hotel, the manager told him that tipping was illegal, as everyone received a fair wage. "It was the first time I had ever been in a town where the working class was in the saddle," he wrote.[18] While the coalition Republican government was technically in charge, the city was effectively run by the CNT, an anarcho-syndicalist labor union with militia forces exceeding their rivals, and Barcelona seemed alive with possibility.

Orwell's excitement revealed significant naivete about the political reality on the ground. The Popular Front government included a whole spectrum of left-wing parties, from the moderate Republicans, to the Socialists, the Communists, and the Anarchists, all of which contained factions and were allied to different trade unions. Taking his bearings in Barcelona, Orwell was "exasperated" by the "kaleidoscope of political parties and trade unions" and felt like all of Spain was suffering "from a plague of initials." "I was not only uninterested in the political situation but unaware of it," he wrote. "I knew there was a war on but I had no notion of what kind of war. If you had asked me why I had joined the militia I should have answered: 'To fight against Fascism,' and if you had asked me what I was fighting *for,* I should have answered: 'Common decency.'"[19] Jennie Lee, a former ILP member of Parliament who was agitating for the Republican cause, recalled Orwell approaching her in a hotel lounge with a pair of size twelve boots slung over his shoulder offering "to drive a car or do anything else" but "preferably to fight in the front line."[20]

McNair, a veteran socialist from Tyneside, did not know what to make of this gangling man with "a distinctly bourgeois accent," but when it dawned on him that this Eric Blair was in fact George Orwell, whose work he had read and admired, he made sure to sign him up immediately.[21] The ILP were connected to a group of independent Marxists using the acronym

POUM (Partido Obrero de Unificación Marxista); both groups had refused to join the Comintern because they did not want to be subject to the Party line from Moscow.[22] When Orwell insisted that he wanted to fight, McNair took him to the POUM's Lenin barracks. Securing Orwell was a coup for the ILP and the POUM, and much was made of his fighting for them in their political literature.[23] What Orwell did not realize was that by joining the POUM, he had made an enemy of more than the fascists.

THREE MONTHS BEFORE ORWELL ARRIVED IN BARCELONA, the Soviet spy Alexander Mikhailovich Orlov also traveled via Paris to Spain, flying from Toulouse to Barcelona before driving up to Madrid, where he took up his cover as an attaché of the embassy.[24] Orlov was an experienced agent of the NKVD (the People's Commissariat for Internal Affairs).[25] He worked as a roving "illegal resident" around Western Europe; illegals adopted nonofficial cover, often foreign identities. In London, Orlov posed as a refrigerator salesman, while acting as a point of contact for another illegal, Arnold Deutsch, who had recruited three young British spies: Kim Philby, Don Maclean, and Guy Burgess.[26]

Orlov's arrival was part of a strategy of intervention by the Kremlin in Spain. The Soviet Union had ostensibly signed a non-intervention pact with Britain and France, but on September 18, 1936, Stalin and his Politburo had secretly launched Operation X, to begin clandestine operations led by the NKVD and the GRU (Soviet military intelligence).[27] Orlov had a wide-ranging brief: he supervised NKVD training camps in Argen, Barcelona, Bilbao, and Valencia, and he was to report on the situation directly to Moscow while also helping the Spanish Communists build up a secret police force of their own, ostensibly to identify Fifth Columnists—that is, secret fascists who pretended to support the Republican cause only to engage in acts of sabotage. At the same time, the Soviets bled their supposed allies dry. While Mexico also offered financial support, the Republican government was heavily reliant on the Soviet Union, who sold their weapons and vehicles at a staggering markup.[28] To pay for this materiel the Republican government arranged for the Spanish gold reserves, which they had secreted in the port city of Cartagena, to be shipped to Odessa. Orlov later claimed to have masterminded this operation, but his role was probably limited to handling the security of loading the crates of gold onto the ship that would take them to the Soviet Union.[29]

Fascist collaborators were not the only enemy, however. In the Soviet Union, Stalin was in the process of asserting his power through a campaign of purges and terror, claiming that his old rival, Leon Trotsky, was responsible for conspiracies to assassinate the Soviet leadership, and implicating his political rivals in these concocted plots. The Great Terror, as it became known, spread to all corners of Soviet life, with arbitrary arrests and summary executions resulting in the "largest scale peacetime political persecution and blood-letting in European history."[30] In October, the head of the NKVD, Genrikh Yagoda, was sacked by telegram for his failures to uncover these plots and, with the perfect logic of the secret police, was eventually executed for being a conspirator in them. Yagoda's replacement, Nikolai Yezhov, pursued Stalin's agenda with zeal. Orlov, plump, well groomed, and menacing, brought the purge to Spain, intent on defeating the Trotskyist enemy within. The POUM were obvious targets. They had both historical connections with Trotsky—their leader, Andrés Nin, had served as Trotsky's secretary—and were outspoken critics of Stalin and his Show Trials.[31] Furthermore, they demanded social revolution within the Republic, arguing that it would help win the war; the Soviet line was that the priority was to win the war first, and then to implement changes. Orlov knew what Stalin and Yezhov expected of him and what would happen if he did not deliver.[32] In October 1936, Orlov informed Moscow Center that the "Trotskyist organization POUM can be easily liquidated."[33] By December, the Comintern informed the Spanish Communist Party that they endorsed "the complete and final crushing of Trotskyism in Spain."[34]

ORWELL SPENT THE EARLY MONTHS of 1937 fighting on the front lines in the mountainous region of Alcubierre. He soon discovered that the Catalan recruits, many of them teenagers, were appallingly equipped and had no sense of military discipline. He had worried before heading out to Spain that he would not be in good enough shape, or have enough experience, to join up. Instead, he found himself a leader. His training in the Indian Imperial Police soon marked him out as officer material and, despite his nonexistent Catalan and poor Spanish, he did his best to instill some basic principles, drilling the troops on the Barcelona barracks square. He also won respect by drinking his men under the table.[35]

Without rifles to train with, there was only so much that could be done. They paraded down the main avenue in central Barcelona, Las Ramblas—a photograph from the time shows Orwell towering a full head taller than the rest of his unit—before being sent to the Aragón front, where they occupied filthy, freezing trenches. Orwell was promoted to *cabo* (corporal), serving under Georges Kopp, a charismatic and courageous Belgian adventurer who became a close friend.[36] With old guns, poor marksmanship, no artillery, and heavy mists swirling, there was little danger of being hit by the enemy; more threatening were the hungry rats, of whom Orwell had an almost phobic fear. While recovering from an infected hand behind the front lines,

Orwell found the rats lurking near the food supplies to be almost as big as cats: "great bloated brutes that waddled over the beds of muck, too impudent even to run away unless you shot at them."[37] Inescapable were the lice: Orwell managed to change out of his clothes only three times in his eighty days at the front, and he could feel them swarming on his body.

When the ILP's thirty-strong British contingent arrived at the front, Orwell left his POUM troops to join his countrymen, who were entrenched in a more westerly position at Monte Irazo, opposite the fascists defending Zaragoza. The head of the ILP militia, Bob Edwards, recalled Orwell's striking appearance when he showed up:

> All six foot three of him was striding towards me and his clothing was grotesque to say the least. He wore corduroy riding breeches, khaki puttees and huge boots, I've never seen boots that were so large, clogged in mud. He had a yellow pigskin jerkin, a coffee coloured balaclava hat and he wore the longest scarf I've ever seen, khaki scarf wound round his neck right up to his ears, on his shoulder he carried an old-fashioned German rifle, I think it must have been fifty years old; and hanging to his belt were two hand grenades.[38]

Orwell spent much of his time in the trenches writing while smoking the black pipe tobacco he favored. While his first weeks with the ILP were just as cold, wet, and miserable as those he had spent with the POUM troops—relieved by occasional deliveries of tea, tobacco, and biscuits from his wife, Eileen, who had been newly installed in Barcelona as secretary to McNair—in early April he finally experienced real combat, leading an attack on a fascist redoubt.

The purpose of the attack was to create a diversion for a more substantial assault further down the line. The night was pitch-black, it was raining, and they were forced to wade through waist-deep irrigation ditches; by the time they were ready for the assault everyone was coated in mud. Orwell was ready for the fight: he had oiled his cartridges and dirtied his bayonet to prevent it catching any light. They crawled through the sludge of no-man's-land until they got within grenade-throwing distance of the enemy trench. Orwell flung three grenades, the last of which landed in a parapet concealing a machine-gun position. They stormed the position successfully—Orwell fruitlessly trying to bayonet one of the fleeing fascists—but could not hold it for long. The enemy rallied and soon closed in. When they were only twenty yards away, one of the ILP men, Bob Smillie, streaming blood from a head wound, flung a grenade at them. It failed to go off. Orwell shouted for someone to hand him a "bomb." Another ILP man, Douglas Moyle, quickly passed him one. "I flung it and threw myself on my face. By one of those strokes of luck that happen about once in a year I had managed to drop the bomb almost exactly where the rifle had flashed. There was the roar of the explosion and then, instantly, a diabolical outcry of screams and groans. We had got one of them, anyway; I don't know whether he was killed but certainly he was badly hurt. Poor wretch, poor wretch! I felt a vague sorrow as I heard him screaming."[39] Taking whatever weapons and ammo they could pilfer, they retreated to their lines. The diversion had worked. Afterward, Orwell celebrated the success of their operation by smoking a cigar Eileen brought for him from England.

WHEN ORWELL RETURNED TO BARCELONA, in April 1937, after three and a half months at the front, he found that "the revolutionary atmosphere had vanished."[40] As he made his way through the streets, his tattered leather jacket and ill-fitting woolen hat caked in mud, he noticed that people were dressed smartly again, that they seemed indifferent to the war, and, whereas previously the anarchist CNT had been in control, there were now visibly more government troops on the street. And with the Soviet supplies pouring in, the Spanish Communists were increasingly influential in the government's decisions. Even detecting the change in atmosphere, Orwell still did not quite grasp how perilous it was being associated with the POUM. In what, in retrospect, seemed an astonishingly naive move, he sought help from the Communists in getting to Madrid. Having read about the resistance to the attack on Madrid and the continuing siege, he wanted to see it for himself and thought the only way to do so was to join the International Brigades.[41] Edwards, his ILP commanding officer, tried to persuade him that this was foolhardy. He warned him about André Marty, who was in charge at the International Brigade headquarters in Albacete. Marty was a Frenchman working for the Comintern and, covertly, for Soviet military intelligence, a Stalinist doctrinaire, and fervent in his hunt for Trotskyist "elements"; he freely admitted having five hundred of his own men shot, many for purported espionage.[42] Milton, the only American serving in the ILP and an avowed Trotskyist, told Orwell that the Communists running the International Brigades would kill him. Non-Communist foreigners who volunteered for the International Brigades were interviewed by NKVD agents and, on arrival at Albacete, their passports were taken and sent by diplomatic bag to Moscow (where they were recycled for use in future missions by NKVD illegals). Many foreigners were recruited in Albacete to work as spies. Milton was surely right: things would have not gone well under Marty for someone as independent and forthright as Orwell. Still, Orwell was set on Madrid, and he sought the help of a Communist friend who was attached to Spanish Medical Aid. While this friend thought it should be possible to secure a position in the Brigades, Orwell postponed committing so that he could recover his strength and, crucially, have a new pair of boots made. It was, he recalled, "the kind of detail that's always deciding one's destiny."[43]

As Orwell tried to rest up, he began noticing that "under the surface-aspect of the town . . . there was the unmistakable feeling of political rivalry and hatred."[44] The rivalry was, in simplified terms, a power struggle between the Communists and the Anarchists; there had been violent clashes between the two groups all across the country in previous weeks. In May, the rivalry turned into open conflict on the streets of Barcelona. The Republican government, now effectively controlled by the Communists, had been steadily building up its police force in the city (from which Anarchist union members were excluded) and had ordered all private weapons to be surrendered. On May 3 the government ordered the seizure of the telephone exchange, which had been in CNT-Anarchist hands since its capture in the fighting that followed the coup the previous summer. The exchange was crucial, as it allowed the CNT to monitor the government's communications, and the threat of closing down those communications gave them political leverage. It was a carefully designed provocation, and, in Orwell's words, it was "the match that fired an already existing bomb."[45] Orlov and his Spanish Communist allies encouraged and exploited the factional conflict; under its cover the purge of the "Trotskyists" in Spain began in earnest.

The afternoon of May 3, Orwell was making his way down Las Ramblas, Barcelona's tree-lined central avenue, when he heard bullets fizzing through the air. He saw a group of Anarchists on a side street exchanging fire with the government's elite Assault Guards, in a church tower. "I thought instantly: 'It's started!'" Orwell wrote. "But I thought it without any very great feeling of surprise—for days everyone had been expecting 'it' to start at any moment. I realized that I must get back at once to the hotel to see if my wife was all right."[46] That was far from straight-forward. The Anarchist fighters were blocking the path back up Las Ramblas, and a panicking crowd of pedestrians surged toward the entrance to the metro, seeking cover. Orwell feared getting trapped underground and went the other way. An American doctor he had known at the front swept by at that moment, taking Orwell by the arms and ushering him toward the Hotel Falcón, where the POUM's forces were stationed. As they made their way to the hotel, a truck load of armed Anarchists raced in the opposite direction. The streets of Barcelona were about to descend into chaotic fighting: a civil war within the civil war.

At the POUM headquarters, a former cabaret theater opposite the Falcón, rifles and ammo were handed out. Orwell thought about trying to make his way back to the Continental, the hotel where he and Eileen were staying, but decided against it, given the rumors that the Assault Guards would soon attack the POUM headquarters. After a couple of hours, Orwell managed to get through to his hotel on the phone. While he could not get hold of Eileen, he did speak to McNair, who assured him that she was safe. A state of general confusion pervaded the city. There was a shortage of rifles, and Orwell had his stolen by one of the militia youths. He managed to procure a couple of crude grenades, but as he tried to sleep (wrapped in one of the theater's stage curtains) he worried that they would go off if he rolled on them. In the middle of the night, one of Orwell's comrades woke him up, handed him a new rifle, and placed him on guard duty.

In the morning, as Orwell made his way back up Las Ramblas, he saw barricades being erected out of cobblestones and sandbags. The Assault Guards from the day before were still in the church tower on the side street. "I paused and then crossed the opening at a run; sure enough, a bullet cracked right past me, uncomfortably close."[47] After checking on Eileen at the

Continental he returned to the POUM headquarters, where he found Kopp, his commander at the front. The orders came down to guard the headquarters but only to fire if fired upon. Orwell was stationed on the roof of a cinema across the road, affording a magnificent view of the city:

> From the little windows in the observatory you could see for miles around—vista after vista of tall slender buildings, glass domes and fantastic curly roofs with brilliant green and copper tiles; over to eastward the glittering pale blue sea—the first glimpse of the sea I had had since coming to Spain. And the whole huge town of a million people was locked in a sort of violent inertia, a nightmare of noise without movement. The sunlit streets were quite empty. Nothing was happening except the streaming of bullets from barricades and sandbagged windows.[48]

Orwell spent three days on the roof, battling boredom and hunger, just as he had in the trenches. There were some Assault Guards barricaded in a café opposite, but, thanks to a diplomatic intervention from Kopp, it was determined that they had no appetite for a fight.

Back at the Continental, where Orwell still took his meals, "a horrible atmosphere of suspicion had grown up."[49] Among the new guests was a large Russian, nicknamed Charlie Chan, who Orwell felt certain worked for Soviet intelligence. "Various people were infected with spy mania and were creeping around whispering that everyone else was a spy for the Communists, or the Trotskyists, or the Anarchists, or what-not. The fat Russian agent was cornering all the foreign refugees in turn and explaining plausibly that this whole affair was an Anarchist plot."[50]

The evidence hardly bore this out: the conflict was winding down and it did not look good for the Anarchists. The telephone exchange was in the hands of government forces, the various barricaded factions were running out of food, and there was desire on both sides for a truce. Assault Guards brought up from Valencia, armed with Soviet-issued rifles, flooded the streets. The Communists ramped up their propaganda by declaring the POUM a secretly fascist organization.

When his Communist friend approached him to see if he was still interested in joining the International Brigades, Orwell told him the events of the previous days had changed his mind. He now had a clearer picture of what was going on. All over Barcelona foreigners who were not members of the Communist Party were being denounced to the secret police. Orwell was no longer under any illusions about where this was coming from: the actions of the Spanish Communist Party, he deduced, could only come "under orders from the USSR."[51] Some three days after the end of the Barcelona fighting, Orwell headed back to the front lines, but it was now "difficult to think about this war in the same naively idealistic manner as before."[52]

WHEN ORWELL ARRIVED for his second stint at the front, he heard that his friend Smillie, the English journalist with whom he had fought in the ILP militia, had been arrested attempting to leave the country. He had been thrown into a Valencia prison and nobody was allowed to see him, not even a lawyer. Orwell now believed that even if Franco were beaten, Spain would be ruled by a dictatorship, because the Republican government had allowed the Communists too much power.[53] What would follow, Orwell believed, was Stalinism and the secret police. Orwell was no longer sure he was fighting wholly on the side of the angels; he could console himself only with the knowledge that Franco was the greater devil.

And with that sniper's bullet, Franco's men almost finished

him. It was only the onset of pain that convinced him he was not going to die just yet. He needed proper medical care urgently; at Sietamo Hospital (a rather grand name for a series of wooden huts not far from the front lines), a nurse tried to force soup, eggs, and stew down his throat. He was transferred to Lerida, which was halfway between the front and Barcelona. For the first part of the one-hundred-kilometer journey, taken by truck, someone had forgotten to strap the patients down. As the truck struggled over the rutted country roads, men were thrown to the floor, howling in agony and vomiting from the pain. Orwell clung to his stretcher with his good left arm. He spent five or six days recovering in Lerida, and while he began to walk (with his arm in a sling) he had completely lost his voice. At another hospital, in Tarragona, a doctor told him one of his vocal cords was paralyzed and he would never get his voice back.[54] This was not true—after two months speaking in a whisper his other vocal cord compensated—but he did end up speaking with a distinct rasp.

Once he was strong enough to travel, at the end of May, Orwell returned to Barcelona only to find that the sense of menace he had previously found in the lobby of the Hotel Continental now pervaded the city. There was, he wrote, "a peculiar evil feeling in the air—an atmosphere of suspicion, fear, uncertainty, and veiled hatred."[55] Orwell was always sharpest—as a thinker and a writer—when he was working from direct experience. For *Down and Out in Paris and London* he had lived in destitution in order to begin to understand what it meant to be poor. His devastating critique of the cruelties and hypocrisies of the British Empire, delivered in *Burmese Days* and in some of his finest essays, drew on his time as an officer in the Indian Imperial Police. What he experienced in Barcelona during these days sharpened his thinking again. He had always planned to write about Spain, but faced with the menace of Stalinism, larger, more ambitious projects started to germinate. And there was no question who was now running things. The May Days fighting had precipitated a government crisis and Largo Caballero, who resisted Communist attempts to take control, resigned as prime minister. On May 17, 1937, Juan Negrín, another socialist but one with strong Communist connections, replaced him. As Orwell put it, "The 'Stalinists' were in the saddle, and therefore it was a matter of course that every 'Trotskyist' was in danger."[56] The newspapers were being heavily censored, and those known to be associated with the Anarchists or the POUM were being thrown in jail. Wounded and disillusioned, Orwell knew it was time to leave:

> Nothing was happening as yet, I myself had not even any mental picture of what was going to happen; and yet there was a perpetual vague sense of danger, a consciousness of some evil thing that was impending. However little you were actually conspiring, the atmosphere forced you to feel like a conspirator. You seemed to spend all your time holding whispered conversations in corners of cafés and wondering whether that person at the next table was a police spy.[57]

Orwell was right to be paranoid; spies *were* everywhere. In fact, they were even closer than he thought.

TWO
Koestler

MALAGA, 1937

IN FEBRUARY 1937, the Republicans suffered a heavy defeat in Andalusia, in the south of Spain. The previous November the International Brigades had helped hold Madrid while on the Aragon front, where Orwell was battling the rats and the cold, the conflict was locked in stalemate. In the south, however, the Republicans were routed: the battle of Malaga was so one-sided as to barely qualify as such. As the city fell, Arthur Koestler, a thirty-one-year-old Hungarian reporter accredited to the liberal British daily *News Chronicle*, cautiously made his way through the darkening streets. The sun was setting on the life Koestler thought he knew; like Orwell he was about to be launched on a new trajectory, one that would bring the two writers together as the most important novelists of the early Cold War.

At the time, though, Koestler was simply scared. The street-lights had gone out and the trams had stopped running. Much of the city had been left ruined by bombs and shells. Members of the militia, supposedly preparing for the defense of the city, ran around in confusion. Shots and cries rang out sporadically as night descended. This, Koestler thought, is what the death of a city looks like: "There is no longer anyone in control, anyone in authority; there are no public services left in the city; its very bones have gone soft, its nerves sinews and muscles are decomposing, the highly developed organism has degenerated into an

amorphous jelly-fish."[1] Earlier in the day, Koestler had spurned
an opportunity to escape before the enemy occupied the city,
impulsively jumping out of a car that was part of the evacuation
of Republican forces to Valencia. His motivations for doing so
were not clear even to himself, although he was very anxious not
to be thought of as a coward and recognized that reporting on
the Republican occupation of the city would constitute a genuine scoop. In order to write the story, he needed to survive, and
he knew, from his previous reporting of the conflict, that when
the fascists arrived there would be a bloodbath. His journalist's
accreditation would only offer so much protection, and if he was
caught in the streets, he was likely to be shot.

Koestler made for the one friend he had left in Malaga, at the
Villa Santa Lucia, up on a hill half a mile out of town. He found
it hard going in the dark, stumbling through fields. Then came
the humming from the night sky above, a noise he knew well. As
the bombs fell he threw himself into the mud. Eventually he arrived at the gate of a large villa, a building Koestler remembered
being used as a temporary hospital. A porter, holding a revolver,
told Koestler that, yes, it *used* to be a hospital but now, with the
fascists at the gates it had reverted to being the house of Señor
Bolín. The name sent a chill down Koestler's spine.

Koestler told the porter that he was looking for Don Pedro's
house and was told it was just next door. Don Pedro was Sir
Peter Chalmers-Mitchell, a seventy-three-year-old Englishman
who retired to Malaga after founding Whipsnade Zoo, just north
of London. Despite being four decades his junior, Koestler became good friends with Sir Peter, who sympathized with the
Republican cause and refused to leave Malaga, hoping that if
he remained as a witness, he might mitigate some of the fascist
excesses in the coming days. He was a little irked when a dishev-
eled Koestler stumbled in; he was late for dinner (sardines, jam,
and fine white wine). When Sir Peter learned that Koestler had

given up the opportunity to leave he called his guest a "perfect fool." On the terrace after dinner they watched as in the darkened hills around Malaga "a row of shining points of light, like a chain of fairy lamps at a fete" descended slowly: these were the tanks rumbling into the city.[2]

In charge of this invading force was General Gonzalo Queipo de Llano, Nationalist commander in the south. He was a braggart and a narcissist who claimed to have captured Seville with just fourteen troops during the initial coup. He made these claims in his wild, ranting radio broadcasts, in which he exulted in his triumphs and promised that his soldiers would not only brutally kill all Republican enemies but also rape their wives and daughters. Under his command the Falangist Black Squad conducted summary executions in Granada. Among those murdered was the poet Federico García Lorca, falsely accused of being a Soviet spy.[3]

With Franco's advance on Madrid having ground to a halt, repelled by a combination of Republican troops and the International Brigades, a new influx of Italian troops arrived in the south to help Queipo de Llano finish off Andalusia. For the five days preceding the fall of Malaga, the Italian motorized columns, with their *guerra celera* shock tactics, easily cut through underequipped Republican defenses. Malaga, softened up by Italian bombing raids, was in no shape to repeat the last-ditch defiance shown by Madrid. The only thing in question was the scale of the coming massacre.[4]

As Koestler and Sir Peter watched the lights of the Italian tanks slowly make their way down the hillsides, they both nursed the private fear that they might well be among those killed. Sir Peter had recently published a letter in the *Times* condemning Franco's forces and was known to sympathize with the Republicans. Koestler's situation was even more serious: he was, by his own description, the "best-hated journalist" at Franco's Nationalist headquarters. The previous month Koestler's damning account of the Nationalist terror was published in German as *Menschenopfer Unerhört* (roughly translated as *Unprecedented Human Sacrifice*) and in French as *L'Espagne ensanglantée* (roughly *Bloodstained Spain*), a work that documented atrocities by Franco's forces, replete with photographs of victims of bombings and firing squads. The book ended with thirteen close-up portraits of children killed in the bombing of Getafe. Sir Peter had read Koestler's book and knew the cruelties of which the fascists were capable. That evening he produced two small metal cases containing a hypodermic syringe, a spare needle, and a tube of morphine tablets. Giving the second case to Koestler, he told his guest he did not want to be taken alive. Koestler went to the bathroom to practice injecting himself. The following day, they watched through binoculars as Malaga surrendered with a whimper.

THERE WAS ANOTHER REASON the fascists wanted to get their hands on Koestler: they were still furious with him for the stunt he had pulled in Seville the previous September. He had arrived in Lisbon at the end of August as an accredited reporter with the *News Chronicle* and with *Pester Lloyd*, a Hungarian German-language newspaper (Koestler was born in Budapest but raised in Austria so spoke German). He worked his way into Franco-sympathizing circles in the Portuguese capital and managed to secure a letter of safe passage into rebel territory from Franco's brother. Having succeeded in getting to Seville, he discovered that foreign journalists who failed to toe the Nationalist line were being arrested, including a French reporter the previous night. Posing as a Franco sympathizer, he persuaded Captain Luís Bolín, the press chief, to grant him an interview with his boss, Queipo de Llano, and the "Radio General" provided rich material for a poison portrait. This, though, was not the only scoop Koestler was after. In the summer of 1936, the Soviet Union, France, Britain, Italy, and Germany had agreed to a policy of nonintervention, and Koestler wanted proof that the Germans were breaking this agreement. At the Hotel Cristina he found it.

On August 28, he spotted four German pilots drinking sherry in the lobby. With them was a fifth man. To Koestler's horror he recognized the man in civilian dress: Hans Strindberg, son of the famous playwright and a former colleague from Koestler's days as a journalist for the Ullstein Press in Weimar Berlin. Strindberg knew Koestler to be a Communist supporter. With two of the pilots moving across the lobby to cut off his exit, Koestler realized he needed to do something fast. He approached Strindberg and tried to shake his hand, causing a scene when Strindberg refused to take it. Captain Bolín, whom Koestler described as a "tall, weak-faced, tough-acting officer of Scandinavian descent," arrived in the lobby as the dispute became heated.[5] Koestler saw an opportunity and ran up to Bolín to make a scene. Believing this to be a petty dispute between foreign reporters, he lost his temper with them and told them all "to go to hell."[6] Koestler pretended to storm off in a huff, rushed back to his hotel, packed his bags, and fled. A warrant for his arrest was issued an hour after he had crossed the border to Gibraltar. Having been duped into giving a Republican sympathizer an interview with Queipo de Llano, Bolín swore that if he got hold of Koestler he would "shoot him like a mad dog." That was why the name of Bolín so disconcerted Koestler when he knocked at the door of the neighboring villa. It was not a common name in Spain.[7]

His fears had foundation. Late in the morning after the fall of Malaga on February 9, Koestler was fortifying himself with a brandy when three fascist officers burst into the library. Koestler tried to make it up the next flight of stairs, thinking of the syringe in his pocket. Before he could make it, a voice shouted: "Hands up!" He turned to find three revolvers pointed at him. Worse still, one of the men taking aim at his chest was Colonel Luís Bolín. According to Koestler's account, Sir Peter walked in, hearing the commotion. The Fascists ordered him to raise his hands, too (in Sir Peter's account, he was caught first, Koestler after). Bolín called in the gardener and ordered him to find some rope. It was typical of the Nationalist forces to bind those whom they planned to execute; the photographs of atrocities in Koestler's book testified to that. Koestler was also terrified that they would simply hang him there and then. Desperate to slow things down, he said, "Look here, Bolín, if you are going to shoot me, take me upstairs; don't do it in Sir Peter's presence."[8] Bolín looked momentarily discomfited. It might have saved Koestler's life.

Sir Peter realized the only hope was Tomas Bolín, the owner of the next-door villa and Luís's cousin. He had one of his staff run over to fetch him. Tomas was a Franco supporter, and when the military coup failed to take in Malaga, he had thrown himself on Sir Peter's mercy, despite knowing his political sympathies lay with the Republicans. Sir Peter had sheltered Tomas and his family in his villa and, when an Anarchist militia patrol came to the property, even saved his neighbor's life. The young officer in charge had demanded to see Tomas's paperwork, and Sir Peter had no choice but to give him an envelope of papers. In it was Tomas's membership card to the Falange and a collection of pornographic postcards. The Englishman cut the young Anarchist a deal: you keep the postcards and I'll keep the membership card. Tomas was eventually arrested anyway, but Sir Peter secured his release and then smuggled him and his family to safety in Gibraltar. By any standards, Tomas Bolín owed Sir Peter a debt.

When Tomas entered the library, wearing a red beret, the officers were binding Koestler's hands with electrical wire (the gardener could not find any rope). As one officer struggled to bend the wire into shape, another stuck his gun painfully into Koestler's ribs. Koestler described him as a "fat, bald-headed fellow with incredibly bestial features. During the whole proceeding he has a grin on his face and literally snorts with pleasure. He snorts through his nose as though he has asthma; I can feel his breath on my ear. Up till now I have only come across such sadistic types in political cartoons, and have never really believed that they actually exist. The fellow grins, and snorts and snorts. He is obviously a pathological sex case. My physical disgust is almost stronger than my fear."[9] Sir Peter persuaded Tomas Bolín to speak with him next door and Luís followed them in shortly after. Voices were raised but Koestler could not make out what was being said, stuck as he was next to the officer pressing the gun into his rib cage. Whatever was said, Sir Peter bought Koestler some time. "It is an elevating thought that one should owe one's life to a set of dirty postcards," Koestler wrote.[10]

The danger was far from over. Led from the house with his hands bound, Koestler presented an inviting target to the Nationalist troops. Only Luís Bolín's authority prevented him from being lynched. The soldiers bundled him into the back of a car and drove him to the police station. There they left him in the back seat for two hours in the pounding Andalusian sun. Eventually, the police hauled him out, photographed him in the street while a crowd jeered, dragged him into the station, and left him in a huge room with two guards. He sat in silence, sweating. Screams rang out in the courtyard and a man was dragged in, blood pouring from his face and chest. The man's wounds were so severe that Koestler thought he "must have been run over by a steam engine."[11] They dragged him out through another door. There were more screams, then quiet, and finally one last scream in "an unnaturally high-pitched shrill voice" before the silence returned.[12] Two more men were dragged through in succession to be tortured. Each time Koestler feared he would be next. For some reason he had not yet been searched and he began stealthily to conceal the different parts of his suicide kit around his person: syringe into his cigarette packet, tablets into his breast-pocket handkerchief, needles into the lining of his coat. He persuaded the guards to let him use the toilet and to his dismay, he discovered there was no running water in which to dissolve the morphine. He started to fill the syringe from a puddle on the floor but disgust overcame him.

At nightfall Bolín returned. Koestler was taken to the courtyard and searched. Inevitably, one of the guards pricked his hand on one of the concealed needles. Koestler was forced to deposit his suicide kit onto a plate—none of the soldiers wanted to touch the needle—and had his money and pen confiscated. After a few more hours in a dark room he was put in the back of a truck and driven off into the night. Again, it seemed execution was imminent until one of the soldiers in the truck reassured him he was going first to prison.

On arrival at Malaga prison his captors marched him down a long corridor and forced him to strip to his underwear. His shoes were hit with an iron hammer, and the guard ran his hand through Koestler's hair. The concealed needle had rattled them. The prison officer was also disconcerted by Koestler's long golf socks, and asked him if he had ever disguised himself as a woman. They took away his belt and led him into an empty cell, and for the first time in his life he "heard the sound of a cell door being slammed from outside."[13] It did not last long, as minutes later he was led down a corridor toward an iron grille, behind which lay the isolation cells. As they passed steel door after steel door, one of the prison guards escorting Koestler told him that all of the "reds" being held would be dead by the morning. The guard assured him that he, too, would be killed, and Koestler felt his knees turn "to flabby jelly."[14] The isolation cell was similar to the first one except the window was smaller and higher up. He saw blood spattered on the wall above his bed, fresh blood, and could smell its sour tang. The toilet hole was stopped up, and when he tried the tap nothing came out. He sat on the wire bedstead and heard shots ring out and isolated cries. He vomited. Would not his status as an accredited journalist with a British newspaper protect him? But while he was being searched, Koestler had caught a glimpse of Bolín's official report. He was being held as a *caso internacional*. An international case. A spy. The problem was not that there had been some misunderstanding. The problem was it was true.

THREE

Spender

CÁDIZ, VALENCIA, MADRID & ALBACETE, 1937

FOR THE BRITISH COMMUNIST PARTY, recruiting Stephen Spender represented a real coup. Spender was not just a famous poet, he was a *fashionable* one, and his relative youth—he was still only twenty-seven—fostered a connection with a generation of undergraduates who admired the way he fused his poetic sensibility with *engagé* politics. It helped that he was tall, slim, handsome, sexually adventurous, and posh: he was a romantic rebelling against the establishment from which he came, and he was doing it in style. His anti-fascist credentials were strong. He had seen firsthand what the National Socialists were capable of on the streets of Berlin during the final days of the Weimar Republic. Sunbathing on the beaches of Rügen, on the north German coast, Spender and his friends had heard the barking of orders and the reports of shots as stormtroopers conducted their training.[1] As early as 1929 he had heard reports of a compelling demagogue from Austria drawing crowds of the angry and the disenfranchised, and in 1934, on holiday on the Dalmatian coast, a car carrying Hermann Göring almost ran him over as it sped past.[2] His poetry and journalism reflected his commitment to fighting this emerging enemy. He was part of a group of British writers, including W. H. Auden, Christopher Isherwood, Louis MacNeice and Cecil Day-Lewis, who rejected the unofficial doctrine of the Bloomsbury mandarins that politics had no place in literature. Virginia Woolf might find it vulgar—and she told Spender as much—but he felt he had no choice other than to put his art into the service of his politics. "We anti-Fascist writers of what has been called the Pink Decade were not, in any obvious sense, a lost generation," he recalled years later. "But we were divided between our literary vocation and an urge to save the world from Fascism. We were the Divided Generation of Hamlets who found the world out of joint and failed to set it right."[3] Standing in the British Communist Party's headquarters in Covent Garden, just a few days into the new year of 1937, the urge was proving stronger than the vocation: he wanted to go to Spain to serve the Republican cause.

Harry Pollitt, who had been so suspicious of Orwell when they had met a few weeks previously, knew that Spender had significant propaganda value. It is hard to imagine Pollitt, a Mancunian boilermaker, had much personal sympathy for this earnest, Oxford-educated poet, but he knew that the Left Book Club was about to publish Spender's *Forward from Liberalism,* a book that advocated for Communism even as it refused to follow the Party line.[4] The club, founded by Victor Gollancz the previous year, had attracted more than forty thousand members and was preparing to publish Orwell's *The Road to Wigan Pier* (later the same year it would publish Koestler's *Spanish Testament).* In the meeting Pollitt cheerfully upbraided Spender for misunderstanding the circumstances of the first of the Moscow Show Trials and called him out on various other "deviations."[5] Nevertheless, this was the time of the Popular Front and all antifascists were supposed to be in it together. Spender joined the Party and wrote an article for the front page of its mouthpiece, the *Daily Worker.*[6] As to Spain, Pollitt mused, what about joining the International Brigades? Spender could be naive but he was not a fool. He knew he'd make a hopeless soldier. It is not clear that this mattered too much to Pollitt: Spender had the makings of an attractive martyr. There is a story—most likely apocryphal—that Pollitt even joked that if only Spender would get himself killed, he'd "give the party its Byron."[7]

It turned out Spender was to be put to more sustainable use. Not long after his meeting with Pollitt he was contacted by the *Daily Worker* and asked to go to Spain and report on the fallout from the sinking of the Russian supply ship *Komsomol* by the Italians. This was no ordinary reporting gig: the Russians did not know what had happened to the crew and wanted information on where they were being held. Spender, who spoke decent Spanish, was charged with finding out: a request that "both disturbed and astonished" him. "It raised the question whether to supply such information would be spying," he wrote. "However, it certainly did not involve betraying my country, nor obtaining military secrets, nor indeed anything outside the run of ordinary journalism."[8] Still, he knew he would be filing copy for some very particular readers. He agreed, despite his misgivings, assuaging his conscience by refusing payment and asking that his friend Cuthbert Worsley be allowed to come along as sidekick.[9]

While he was sincere in his desire to fight fascism, there was another motivation for Spender wanting to go to Spain: anxiety over his former lover, Tony Hyndman. Spender had split with Hyndman in September after four years together. To compound the rejection, the following month he began seeing Inez Pearn, a twenty-two-year-old Oxford postgraduate student. On December 15, Spender and Pearn were married at a Hammersmith registry office. When Hyndman found out, he was furious and set out for Spain to fight in the International Brigades. This was a deliberately self-destructive act, as Hyndman was not cut out for military life and he knew it. He was the son of a hotelier from

Cardiff, and his father, worried that his son was not made for life in the army or down the pits, had sent him off to secretarial college to learn typing and shorthand.[10] After working for a spell as a clerk in Cardiff he'd ended up joining the Coldstream Guards. Despite shipping out to Khartoum for a spell, he managed to avoid any actual fighting and left after three years of largely inept soldiering. After a couple of years of drifting he'd met Spender in the spring of 1933. They were soon living together, Hyndman working as Spender's secretary. Spender fell in love with Hyndman's "background, his soldiering, his working-class home." Since his youth Spender had been fascinated by "working men," a fascination that in adulthood manifested itself in a penchant for rough trade. With Hyndman, though, this initial attraction developed into an intense, combative relationship. They both resented Hyndman's dependence on Spender, and eventually Spender came to realize there was more than excesses of passion to this pattern of behavior: "gradually I came to see that in the moments of our quarrels and the making up of them, when we were most completely and terribly together, there was something in each which wanted to destroy the other."[11] To Spender it now appeared that Hyndman, by going to Spain, was bent on destroying himself.

Spender saw off Hyndman at Victoria Station, handing him £30 in case he changed his mind and wanted to come back. The former secretary was heading first to Brussels, where he was to spend Christmas with Isherwood, traveling with Giles Romilly, an Oxford undergraduate and Winston Churchill's nephew. After a drunken night with his guests, Isherwood wrote to Spender to try to reassure him that Hyndman was not heading to Spain in consequence of his marriage to Pearn. As much as he wanted to believe Isherwood, Spender knew better: "Someone I loved had gone into this war as a result of my influence and of my having abandoned him." It was, Spender claimed, the "greatest distress of my life in this decade."[12]

It was not long before he was making for Spain himself, under his journalistic cover, seeking the location of the missing crew of the *Komsomol*. The whole "mission" had an element of the absurd to it. He and Worsley arrived in Barcelona on January 6, a week after Orwell and a week before Koestler. The pair made their way to Gibraltar but were prevented from entering Nationalist Cádiz, where the Russian sailors were rumored to be held. Instead of kicking their heels they made day trips across the Mediterranean to Algiers, Marrakesh, Oran, and Tangiers, looking for leads and tasked with reporting any evidence of Italian or German influence in southern Spain.[13] Spender finally got confirmation that they were being held in Cádiz from Lord Marley, a British official who was allowed into the city. Spender realized he could have easily found out the information from London.[14] What he was doing was not without risk, though, as foreign journalists suspected of spying, like Koestler in Malaga, were being arrested. It was probably for the best that Spender had not managed to talk his way into Cádiz: the idea of the handsome, lanky poet searching out the Russian crew behind enemy lines was not a promising one. Discretion was not among Spender's virtues.

HYNDMAN'S EARLY POSTCARDS and letters from Spain had been breezy, so when Spender arrived back in London on February 5 he was not particularly concerned. These high spirits did not last. Despite his time in the Coldstream Guards, Hyndman was not good at taking orders and spent a few days in a cell for insubordination during basic training. On release he was given a Soviet rifle and, along with the rest of the British brigade, dispatched to Madrid. They were heading to the Jarama Valley to defend the capital from Franco.

The battle was a bloodbath. The Army of Africa was battle hardened and supported by a huge artillery bombardment. The Republicans held out, but the price they paid was a heavy one: as many as twenty-five thousand killed in the fighting, including large numbers of men in the International Brigades.[15] Hyndman later estimated that three hundred of the nearly four hundred in his battalion died on the first day. He spent it desperately trying to rescue machine guns from an overturned truck while planes swooped down and raked them with bullets.[16] He spent four days cowering in an olive grove while the moans of the wounded and dying rung out around him.[17] Two weeks later, in the hills of Pingarrón, Hyndman refused an order to advance and was taken back to Albacete under armed escort. He was suffering from a stomach ulcer that made him vomit frequently, but the Commissars of the Brigades, fearful that letting him go would set a bad example to the other men, overruled the medical officer's recommendation of an honorable discharge. There was little sympathy for psychological trauma among the Stalinist officers running the Red Brigades.

While the Battle of Jarama was raging, Spender left London for Spain a second time, on February 20. The British Communist Party had a new task for him: to broadcast propaganda for a trade union radio station in Valencia. Having made his way to the city, via Barcelona, Spender discovered he had just missed W. H. Auden, his poetic mentor and a close friend. Auden had gone to Spain initially planning to join the International Brigades, with Wilfred Owen's poetry from the trenches of the Great War ringing in his ears, but like Spender, he realized he was not cut out for combat and sought to drive an ambulance instead.[18] In Valencia he found little to do; the tawdry highlight was getting riotously drunk with Koestler before he left for Malaga. On his return to Britain he wrote "Spain 1937," one of the defining poems of the war. Spender, too, found Valencia a dead end: the radio station he was supposed to work for was closed due to "the unification of political parties."[19] Freed from his responsibilities, Spender realized there was nothing stopping him from going to Albacete to find Hyndman.

IT HAD TAKEN SPENDER A DAY of wandering the streets of Albacete, but he eventually found the right café. First impressions were deceptive: Hyndman looked good, "fit and bronzed and young in his uniform." As soon as the pair got out of earshot of the other soldiers, Hyndman opened up and Spender realized that his "physical fitness concealed an extreme nervousness." He wanted desperately to go back to England, to be an "ordinary chap."[20] He hated war and had decided he was a pacifist. All his left-wing militancy had evaporated.

"You must get me out of here!" Hyndman whispered.[21] No sooner did Spender have a moment of privacy with his former lover than he was being implored to rescue him. Spender knew it would be difficult to get him transferred out of the Brigades but thought he might intervene on his part and try to get him excused from fighting in the front line. There must, Spender reasoned, be a noncombatant position Hyndman could fill. He patiently persuaded Hyndman that this was the best course of action.

Just as Spender had anticipated, the Political Commissar of the British Battalion, Peter Kerrigan, said there was no possibility of a discharge. Kerrigan was a Glaswegian who had led workers' strikes back in the mid-1920s and completed his political education at the International Lenin School in Moscow. He was a hard-liner. There appeared to be some horse trading: Kerrigan guaranteed Hyndman would be kept in a noncombatant position, but Spender was expected to visit the front lines near Madrid. Perhaps Kerrigan saw genuine propaganda value in this, or perhaps he simply wanted to be rid of this posh poet making a fuss about a useless soldier. Spender was pleased with the deal and left for Madrid with Captain George Nathan as an escort. (Hyndman had been Nathan's courier at Jarama.)

In Madrid, Spender got his first taste of the war proper. The Indian novelist Mulk Raj Anand accompanied him to the trenches in a ridge outside the city, and both momentarily panicked as "bullets spat round us like shrieking starlings in the olive trees." From the safety of the trench, Spender saw "corpses lying in No Man's Land like ungathered waxy fruit."[22] Led to a machine-gun emplacement, Spender was encouraged to fire off a burst into the enemy lines (he privately prayed that he did not hit anyone). Speaking to the troops over lunch, Spender detected their hostility when Hyndman's name came up and returned to Madrid in a hurry. The city was under siege. It was freezing cold, and the journalists and intellectuals gathered in the same cafés every day trying to fight off the shivers with heavy greatcoats and bad cognac. Reports came in of a comprehensive defeat for the Republicans northeast of the city only for later reports to tell of an unlikely victory; the Italian troops that Koestler had watched walk into Malaga almost unopposed two months previous had been humiliated at the Battle of Guadalajara.

When Spender returned to Albacete from Madrid, he discovered Hyndman was in prison. With news of the Italian advance toward Guadalajara, the International Brigades had been mobilized. Despite Kerrigan's assurances to Spender, Hyndman had been told he was going to be sent into battle. The prospect forced him into desperate action: along with a friend, John Lepper, he fled for Valencia, hoping to get repatriated by the British Consulate or find a way of smuggling himself out of the country. Hyndman later believed he was betrayed by a local woman who had seemed sympathetic to his plight but was in all likelihood a member of the Spanish Communist Party. Hyndman and Lepper spent several days in a Valencia prison before being sent back to Albacete, where Hyndman was questioned by a young Polish officer who suspected him of being a spy. He was sentenced to two months in a labor camp.

Spender was distraught. He went back to Valencia and wrote to the Judicial Commission of the International Brigades, appealing on Hyndman's behalf. As he waited for a response, he wandered the city with a new friend, the celebrated novelist Ernest Hemingway, whom he described as a "black-haired, bushy-moustached, hairy-handed giant."[23] It was a curious friendship under the circumstances. Spender was fretting about a male lover who had behaved like a coward—not exactly Hemingway's scene. Yet the self-consciously macho American took to Spender, even protecting him when Communists baited him for his association with Hyndman.

When the Commission got back to Spender, he was told that, as a good Communist, he should be "pleased that [Hyndman] is going to be disciplined by us."[24] He tried every avenue he could think of, appealing, via the British Embassy, to the Republican minister of foreign affairs, Julio Álvarez del Vayo, and to his fellow poet Edgell Rickword, who had clout in the upper echelons of the British Communist Party. All he wanted was an assurance that once the two months in the labor camp were up, Hyndman would be allowed to return home. When Spender returned to Albacete he was met by a furious Kerrigan, angered by the fuss Spender was stirring up, and who, as a consequence, refused to let him even see Hyndman. What Spender feared was that, once released, the Communists would send Hyndman back into battle, where he would be "accidentally" shot. That was how difficult soldiers were dealt with.

Again and again, Spender came up against the same cold

logic. What was the life of this one soldier compared to the larger struggle? How could one deserter distract you from the cause? Spender could not bring himself to "give up a life which might be saved, and which was of no value in this war, in order to satisfy a state of mind with which I sympathized [. . .] This was a turning point in my affairs. It was the first time I had acted without hesitation and without being obsessed by the need to justify my actions. I was simply determined to do everything in my power to prevent him dying in Spain."[25] He was forced to leave his former lover behind, in the hands of men he felt sure would kill him. Spender had entered the Spanish War a Communist, striding toward a socialist future. Faced with the brutal reality of placing ends over means, he began shuffling backward to liberalism.

FOUR

Orwell

BARCELONA, 1937

WHEN GEORGE ORWELL RETURNED to Barcelona for the third time, on June 20, 1937, he discovered that the Spanish secret police were after him.[1] He had been forced to return to the front in order to have his discharge papers countersigned and, in his absence, the Communists had initiated a purge of their perceived enemies. Orwell was on the list. As he arrived in the lobby of the Hotel Continental, Eileen approached him calmly, placed her arm around his neck, and smiled for the benefit of anyone watching. Once they were close enough she hissed in his ear:

"Get *out!*"
"What?"
"Get out *at once.*"
"What?"
"Don't keep standing here! You must get outside quickly!"[2]

Eileen guided a bewildered Orwell toward the hotel exit. Marceau Pivert, a French friend of Orwell's who was just entering the lobby, seemed distressed to see him and told him he needed to hide before the hotel called the police. A sympathetic member of the staff joined in, urging Orwell to leave in his broken

English. Eileen managed to get him to a café on a discreet side street, where she explained the seriousness of the situation.

DAVID CROOK, a young Englishman working for the ILP's Barcelona office, had become friends with both Orwell and his wife over the last few months. He was not what he seemed. He had arrived in Spain in January 1937, the month after Orwell, eager to join up with the International Brigades and fight the Fascists.[3] He was descended from Russian-Jewish immigrants and grew up in Hampstead, attending the prestigious Cheltenham College. Like many young men who grew up after the First World War, he was attracted to left-wing causes. He moved to New York City, where he attended Columbia University and embraced radical politics, joining the Young Communist League. As a student delegate he traveled down to Kentucky to support the famous miners' strike in Harlan County, witnessing its brutal suppression by the National Guard. On his return to London he became a member of the British Communist Party. At one meeting, the doomed poet John Cornford spoke about the Republican cause in Spain, and Crook was inspired to enlist. Like Hyndman, Crook was thrust straight into the action at the Battle of Jarama, taking three bullets to the leg. Recovering in Madrid, he socialized with the literary set, including the brilliant war correspondent Martha Gellhorn, her lover Ernest Hemingway, Mulk Raj Anand, and Spender. At this point he came to the attention of Soviet intelligence agents. After recruiting him, the NKVD sent him to a training camp in Albacete, where he was given a crash course in sabotage and surveillance techniques. There he became a Communist spy.[4]

Crook's mission was to infiltrate the ILP and report on all their activities. The Soviets already had one agent in place, David Wickes, who volunteered as an interpreter with the ILP and passed what information he found on to his handlers.[5] Now Crook was to infiltrate deeper and get hold of documents. Orwell was his most prestigious target. As cover Crook pretended to be a stringer for a British newspaper, with credentials on headed paper secured from "a comrade in London."[6] The NKVD arranged for him to be discharged from the International Brigade with "lung trouble." The day after Orwell returned from the front for the first time, before the outbreak of the May fighting, Crook installed himself at the Continental, befriended Eileen, and insinuated his way into the ILP office.[7] During the long Spanish lunch breaks, when the office was deserted, he took documents to a safe house on Calle Muntaner and photographed them. He compiled reports on the Orwells, Kopp, and McNair and, at meetings in a local café, delivered them folded up in a newspaper to his handler, Hugh O'Donnell (code name "Sean O'Brien"). Sometimes he secreted the reports in the hotel bathroom if more discretion was needed. Crook reported that Kopp and Eileen were having an affair, the kind of information the NKVD valued for blackmail purposes. Kopp professed to be in love with Eileen, and while Orwell recuperated from his wound, their "association" developed "in little leaps" (these are her words; Orwell and Eileen had an unconventional relationship, and she was clear with Kopp that he could never replace his friend and rival).[8] Also among the documents Crook apparently lifted was a report from Orwell's doctor about his neck wound, which ended up in Orwell's KGB file in Moscow. He was compiling evidence that could be used as justification for the coming purge.[9]

Nobody suspected Crook, but there were plenty of other reasons to be fearful. Orwell knew it was pointless to remain in Spain; he could no longer serve the cause to which he had committed himself. Any foreign fighters seeking to leave the country were considered deserters, so it was important that Orwell got his discharge papers in order. For that, he needed to return to the front one last time. It took him five days. Time was running out.

THE RAID ON EILEEN'S ROOM came early in the hours of June 16, the same day that the Communist-controlled Republican government declared the POUM an illegal organization. The NKVD and the Spanish secret police (the SIM) moved swiftly on their targets. The NKVD assassin Iosif Grigulevich led the hit squad. Nin, POUM's leader, had previously served as Trotsky's private secretary in Moscow and, even though the two had split over political differences, argued that Catalonia should have given Trotsky asylum. Those associations proved fatal. He was "arrested, brutally tortured, then flayed alive when he refused to confess to imaginary crimes."[10] Irwin Wolf, another of Trotsky's former secretaries, was kidnapped and executed. Kurt Landau, a prominent Austrian Trotskyist, went into hiding, but thanks to information gathered by Crook, the death squad kidnapped and murdered him, too.[11] Landau's wife spent five months in prison, all the while vainly trying to discover what had happened to her husband. Kopp was arrested at the Continental and thrown in prison. Crook, in order to maintain the integrity of his cover and to continue his spying, was "arrested" by two plainclothes policemen and thrown into the same jail as Kopp.

In the raid on Eileen's room agents of the SIM confiscated every piece of paper they could find, including Orwell's diaries, papers, and photographs. They also seized Orwell's books, including his French edition of Hitler's *Mein Kampf* and, ironically, Stalin's *Ways of Liquidating Trotskyists and Other Double Dealers*. For two hours the policemen sounded the walls, checked behind the radiators, sifted through the trash, and held every item of clothing up to the light, searching for hidden letters or pamphlets. They went through every single one of Orwell's cigarette papers looking for hidden messages, yet for some reason, perhaps a perverse sense of decency, they failed to search the bed in which Eileen had concealed their passports and checkbooks. "The Spanish secret police had some of the spirit of the Gestapo, but not much of its competence," he wrote.[12]

Orwell arrived back in Barcelona on June 20, having secured his discharge papers. It became clear he needed to get out quickly if he were to avoid the same fate as others associated with the POUM. Eileen told him McNair and an eighteen-year-old ILP volunteer, Stafford Cottman, were already in hiding. Eileen feared the only reason she remained free was as bait for her husband. She told him to destroy his militia card and incriminating photographs. On no account could he return to the hotel. He would have to go into hiding, as there was almost certainly a warrant out for his arrest. Orwell suddenly felt like "a hunted fugitive."[13] The Orwells now had to find a way to get out of Barcelona and across the French border undetected. This was easier said than done. Suspicious as Orwell was, he had no idea just how closely the Communists were having him watched.

Eileen arranged for them all to meet the following morning at the British Consulate. Orwell spent the night in the ruins of an old church. After learning that it would take the consulate three days to get their passports ready, he and his friends did their best to remain inconspicuous. That night, in the bitter cold, Orwell, McNair, and Cottman slept, or at least tried to, "in some long grass at the edge of a derelict building lot."[14] They spent the following morning restless for the cafés to open so that they could revive themselves with a coffee. After that Orwell went to the barber for a shave and then for a shoeshine. He took care to avoid any of the hotels or cafés associated with the POUM. Instead he began frequenting the city's most exclusive restaurants, where no one knew him. Orwell took care not to be stopped as the streets "were thronged by local and Valencia assault guards,

Carabineros and ordinary police, besides God knows how many spies in plain clothes."[15]

The morning after going into hiding, Orwell learned that Smillie, the young journalist alongside whom he had fought on the front, had died in a Valencia prison. The official verdict was appendicitis, but Smillie was only twenty-two, and Orwell had seen just how tough he was. At best, Orwell thought, Smillie had been allowed to die "like a neglected animal."[16] Kopp later claimed he saw a police file that said Smillie had died from heavy kicks to the stomach.[17] Orwell never forgave Smillie's death.

By day the Englishmen pretended to be in the city on business, by night they slept rough. To get some respite, Orwell spent one day at the public baths. "It was an extraordinary, insane existence we were leading," he wrote. "By night we were criminals, but by day we were prosperous English visitors—that was our pose, anyway."[18] Needing an outlet, Orwell took the opportunity of an unobserved moment to scrawl political slogans on the walls. While on the run, Orwell persisted in the "ineradicable English belief that 'they' cannot arrest you unless you have broken the law," even though "practically everyone we knew was in jail by this time."[19] He tried to do something for his friend Kopp, taking a great risk of his own arrest in twice visiting him in the filthy, overcrowded prison. Eileen offered to help Crook by smuggling letters out. But in the end there was nothing they could do for Kopp, and he spent the next year and a half being shuttled from prison to prison, from interrogation to interrogation, from prison ship to labor camp. Even years later, Orwell kept among his papers a report detailing how when Kopp refused to sign a confession he was "put in a coal bin without light, air, or food where enormous rats ran in and out of his legs."[20] The use of rats in torture stuck with Orwell and became the subject of an iconic scene in *Nineteen Eighty-Four*. When Kopp was finally released eighteen months later, he had lost ninety-eight pounds in weight, and was suffering from scurvy and blood poisoning.[21]

In the prison, Orwell had also seen Milton, who had tried to leave the country only to be arrested at the frontier despite having all his papers in order. The American had helped carry Orwell to the ambulance when he was wounded, and they had served together for months on the front line. But fearful of discovery, they "walked past each other as though [they] had been total strangers."[22] Milton's failure to get out was a warning to Orwell and his friends: even jumping through the right hoops was no guarantee of a successful escape.

Finally Orwell discovered his papers were ready. The group hatched an escape plan. A train was leaving for Port Bou, on the French border, at half past eight in the evening. It was important the secret police did not get wind of their planned escape. Eileen was to give no indication that she was leaving or they would pounce. They would order a taxi ahead of time but Eileen should pack her bags and pay the bill only at the last possible moment. To his horror, when Orwell arrived at the station he discovered that the train had left early. Fortunately, it had done so in time for him to warn his wife. It was a close call.

Orwell managed to ascertain that the manager of a local restaurant was an Anarchist and therefore sympathetic to their cause. He put Orwell and his two friends up in a spare room, a great relief after sleeping rough. A train left early the next morning, June 23, and, joined by Eileen, the group took seats in the dining car. "Two detectives came round the train taking the names of foreigners," he wrote, "but when they saw us in the dining-car they seemed satisfied that we were respectable."[23]

At the border crossing the guards looked up their names in a card index of suspects. It was a tense moment, but for some reason their names were not listed. (Orwell suspected police inefficiency.) Everyone was searched thoroughly, but nothing incriminating was found. The guards pored over Orwell's discharge papers and, in another stroke of luck, failed to make the connection that the Twenty-Ninth Division was in fact the POUM. The Orwells and their friends made it to France and safety (the first newspaper they read contained a premature report announcing McNair's arrest for espionage). A secret police file, dated July 13 and prepared for the Tribunal for Espionage and High Treason in Valencia, denounced Orwell and Eileen as "confirmed Trotskyists."[24] The report was compiled with information from Wickes (and almost certainly Crook). Orwell had fled just in time.

Orwell's tenure in Spain, he later wrote, "was a queer business. We started off by being heroic defenders of democracy and ended by slipping over the border with the police panting on our heels."[25] His wounds hurt and his health, as always, was poor. He needed time to recover. But when his strength returned he knew what he needed to do: he needed to tell the world, and most importantly his fellow left-wingers, the truth about what was going on in Spain. The Communists had perhaps mistaken Orwell for another naive volunteer, there to be pushed around, but they had in fact made a powerful enemy, an enemy who now prepared to fight back with his trusted weapons, the typewriter and the pen.

FIVE

Koestler

SEVILLE, 1937

SITTING IN HIS ISOLATION CELL, what Koestler needed at all costs to conceal from his captors was his status as an agent of the Comintern. Koestler had joined the Communist Party in 1931, when he was twenty-six years old. He had been born in to what he described as a "Continental middle-middle class family" but the advent of the First World War led to the collapse of his father's business, and they left Budapest for Vienna.[1] His father worked in textiles before the war, but in the following years he failed at a number of business ventures, eventually losing what remained of his savings in the Austrian hyperinflation of 1922. Koestler became the sole provider for his family, resentful of the way the fluctuations of capitalism ruined his comfortable life. All around him the "pauperized bourgeois" were becoming "rebels of the Right or Left."[2] Koestler, by then a respected journalist with the influential Ullstein newspaper group in Berlin, turned to the left. He read Marx, Feuerbach, Engels, and Lenin, triggering a "mental explosion": "the new light seems to pour from all directions across the skull; the whole universe falls into a pattern like the stray pieces of a jigsaw puzzle assembled by magic at one stroke."[3]

In 1931, Koestler joined the German Communist Party. One of his new comrades instructed this fervent convert to meet an official whom he only later discovered to be Ernst Schneller, head of "Agitprop" in Germany and a member of the intelligence "Apparat," run by a combination of the German Communist Party and the NKVD. Schneller was a skinny, shabby-looking individual who claimed to survive on raw vegetables, and Koestler was impressed by his ascetic mien. Schneller instructed Koestler to keep his new Party membership secret (within the Party Koestler was to be known as Ivan Steinberg) and to stay in his job at Ullstein, where he could be useful. All went smoothly for Koestler as he passed on political gossip to his contacts until he recruited a younger colleague. This young man, after a bout of initial enthusiasm, was overcome by guilt at betraying his co-workers at Ullstein and gave Koestler an ultimatum: the two of them had to either confess or he would be forced to kill himself. The truth came out, and Ullstein fired Koestler.

Over the following years he threw himself into life as a Party activist, canvassing door to door: "We sold the World Revolution like vacuum cleaners."[4] He learned to follow the Party line even when it seemed patently self-defeating—including the way the Party attacked the more moderate socialists, helping facilitate the rise of the National Socialists—and became wary of "Trotskyist" infiltration. In 1932, he traveled to the Soviet Union for eighteen months on the understanding that afterward he would write a book celebrating how his journey broke down his bourgeois skepticism. The trip transformed him from a relatively obscure journalist into a financially secure author, as he received an advance for not only the Russian and German editions but also for the Armenian, Georgian, and Ukrainian rights (only the German edition, *Von Weissen Nächten und Roten Tagen,* was actually published, in 1934). He traveled extensively and saw firsthand the skeletal victims of the Holodomor, the enforced famine in Ukraine in which more than five million are estimated to have died, but he allowed officials to explain it away ("these were kulaks who had resisted collectivization of the land").[5] He allowed himself to believe in the necessity of wildly deceitful propaganda about the West, about the need to "liquidate" opposition groups, and to control all published material. At times his faith was shaken but it held.

At the end of his travels Koestler, both Jewish and Communist, could not return to Berlin with Hitler in power, so he made his way to Paris to join up with fellow exiled Party members. Living on the Left Bank, Koestler worked for the indefatigable Willi Münzenberg, head of Agitprop for the Comintern in Western Europe. Since the declaration of the Popular Front policy at the Seventh Congress of the Comintern in December 1935, Münzenberg had relentlessly established front organizations in the anti-fascist cause. Koestler threw himself into this work. When Franco staged his coup, Koestler went straight to Münzenberg and asked for help in getting to Spain to fight. Münzenberg had a different idea. He devised a plan for Koestler to pose as a right-wing journalist in order to gather evidence of German and Italian involvement. Otto Katz, Münzenberg's deputy, had contacts at the *News Chronicle,* which had taken an anti-Franco position, and Koestler had easily secured accreditation as cover. Koestler was given cash and booked on a boat to Lisbon. As he'd crossed the border from Portugal to Spain, entering Nationalist territory, he wondered what would happen to him if he were caught. "I was certainly a paid agent, travelling under false pretenses," he wrote; "on the other hand, I was not working for any military organisation, merely for a propaganda department, albeit the Comintern's."[6]

Koestler's mission in Seville had been a success, and his reports about German pilots secretly flying missions in Spain made the front page of the *News Chronicle.* That he had almost been caught added to the frisson. In October 1936, the Comintern sent him back to Spain on another "special assignment." This time his destination had been Madrid, a city under siege.

Several right-wing politicians had fled the city in the immediate aftermath of the uprising, leaving behind paperwork that might demonstrate Nazi involvement in planning the coup. It had been Koestler's job to sift through these archives for anything incriminating. He had to tread carefully to negotiate the various feuding factions—Anarchists, Communists, Socialists—behind the Republican lines. He was in Madrid for four weeks and, to his embarrassment, ferried around in an Isotta Fraschini, an ostentatious Italian luxury car. "Never had a smaller man," Koestler wrote, "travelled in a bigger car."[7]

He had worked fast. Franco's forces were closing on Madrid, and few believed the city could long withstand a siege, including the government who had fled for Valencia. Koestler decided to flee too. He met pilots from the Escuadrilla España, the squadron of mercenaries and volunteers assembled by the French novelist André Malraux, who offered him a ride to Valencia, where they were due to collect their newly arrived planes. Accepting the offer, Koestler brought with him two suitcases of documents from fascist sympathizers. Although the Comintern was delighted by the papers Koestler had managed to smuggle out, he was ashamed for having fled Madrid with the cowardly politicians while the Republican soldiers and International Brigade volunteers had stayed behind and halted Franco's advance. Perhaps it was his shame about running that led him to stubbornly refuse to leave Malaga, landing him in an isolation cell.

KOESTLER SPENT FOUR TRAUMATIC DAYS in Malaga prison. Every moment he feared he was to be executed, but if his captors discovered that he was a Comintern agent, he would be tortured first. He tried to distract himself by scratching mathematical formulae on the wall and making plans to learn a new language, but the sound of screams followed by shots followed by silence swiftly eroded his resolve. He stopped eating and drinking, crumbling bread down the toilet and pouring away his coffee, hoping that he would thereby faint more quickly if tortured. He soon came up with a more radical plan: suicide. He planned to hang himself with his tie, but the only hook in the room was too low to the ground. He discovered a shard of glass in the window and resolved to slit his wrists instead. No longer worried about torture, he ate corned beef and bread and sought comfort in a straw mattress that had been brought to his cell. That night, the guards threw another man into his prison. Koestler knew something was gravely wrong with his new blood-drenched cellmate but could not put his finger on it. He eventually realized that his jaw was dislocated from its socket. He could not speak or eat. Shortly before he was taken out and shot, the man gave Koestler his last two cigarette stumps. Faced with the man's suffering and overcome by a wave of apathy, Koestler abandoned his plan to kill himself.

That he had survived the first round of mass executions seemed a promising sign. Nearly four thousand Republicans had been shot in the immediate aftermath of the fall of Malaga, and Koestler estimated that six hundred had been killed in his prison alone.[8] He hoped that his status as an accredited journalist for a British newspaper was protecting him; he did not know that he had already been sentenced to death in absentia by a court-martial in Malaga. On day four of his incarceration, Civil Guards with bayonets on their rifles entered his cell. Once more he feared his time had come, only to be overcome with relief when he was placed in handcuffs; those they planned to shoot were bound with cord.

The guards led Koestler out of the prison and the fresh air made him lightheaded. They loaded him into the back of a heavy truck with about forty other prisoners, their hands all tied with cord. He asked where he was being taken. The answer: Seville—

Queipo de Llano's Seville. It had been only six months since he had tricked his way into that city, written a nasty profile of Queipo de Llano, and escaped arrest. This news gave him a "feeling akin to that of a roamer in the jungle who has inadvertently trodden on the tail of a tiger."[9]

After a long train journey Koestler arrived in Seville late at night. As he was driven through the city he noticed the Hotel Cristina, where he had seen the German pilots and been recognized by Strindberg. After brief stop at the police station, he was taken to the Seville prison, which had been built in 1931. Everything was made of steel; Koestler thought it looked "like the engine room of a warship."[10] On being locked in his cell he could not believe his luck: running water! A functioning toilet! A woolen blanket! A window he could look out of! He fell asleep and woke to the sound not of gunfire but of prisoners playing football in the courtyard. After four days amid the stench of blood and shit of Malaga prison, this felt to Koestler like a "luxury hotel."[11] A few days later, the guards granted him a visit from a barber.

Something was amiss, however. Koestler importuned the inmates in the yard for a cigarette, but despite his shouts, everyone ignored him. After some time, he noticed a faded white line painted on the floor of the courtyard between his cell window and where the other prisoners gathered. Nobody crossed it. The cells on his side of the line were clearly off-limits. "And now at last," Koestler wrote, "I admitted to myself what had gradually been dawning on me from the start. I had been put into one of the condemned cells."[12] The hotel seemed a lot less luxurious. The bare bulb hanging from the ceiling burned all night, although this at least spared him from waking from his nightmares into the dark. He tried to stay sane by scratching diary entries onto the wall with a wire he snapped off the bed frame, crossing out the entries after he had written them.

On February 19, ten days after his arrest in Malaga, Koestler received his first official deputation. At 5 P.M. the door to his cell unexpectedly opened, and in strode three Falangists in full uniform. Leading this delegation was a woman who introduced herself as Helena. She had a slight American accent and said she was a correspondent for the Hearst Press.

"Are you Koestler?"
"Yes."
"Do you speak English?"
"Yes."
"Are you a Communist?"
"No."
"But you are a red, aren't you?"
"I am in sympathy with the Valencia government but do not
    belong to any party."
"Do you know the consequences of your activities?"
"No, I do not."
"Well, it means death."
"Why?"
"Because you are suspected of being a spy."

Koestler denied it. He asked what kind of spy put his byline to articles attacking one side in a war only to walk into their territory carrying his passport. Helena said the authorities would look into this. She told him that both the *News Chronicle* and William Randolph Hearst himself had intervened on his behalf with General Franco. He "might possibly" get a commutation. In light of this, Helena asked, would Koestler consider making a statement? Koestler said something to the effect that General Franco seemed a man of "humanitarian outlook" whom he could "trust implicitly." Helena wrote it all down and gave him the statement to sign. "I realized," Koestler wrote, "that I was about to sign my own moral death sentence, and that this sentence no one could commute." He crossed out what Helena had written and instead wrote that were Franco to commute his sentence that he "could only suppose that it is mainly out of political considerations."[13] The interview did not last much longer. As she left, Helena told Koestler that she was a colleague of Bolín's, that Madrid was about to fall, and that she would try to get him moved to a better prison. When she left the room all that remained was the scent of her perfume.

In the following days those two words—"might possibly"—began to obsess Koestler. "Doubt is a bacillus that eats slowly but surely into the brain; the patient positively feels the dirty little beast grazing on his grey matter."[14] Nothing happened, and the days resolved into monotony. Koestler could feel himself atrophying: "my brain was drained and the few drops of thought that I squeezed out of it were pale, like thrice-brewed tea."[15] He stared at the arms of his watch going around until his eyes watered.

As the hours turned into days and the days into weeks, Koestler prized anything that broke the tedium. He managed to get a copy of the Spanish translation of John Stuart Mill's autobiography from the prison librarian, and more books followed thereafter. He made demands that were ignored until he forced the issue by going on a hunger strike. Once given a pencil and paper, he began to record a diary as well as reconstructing the circumstances of his arrest. He noticed in himself a growing feeling of inferiority regarding his captors. "I had never believed the saying that a dictatorship or a single person or a minority can maintain its ascendancy by the sword alone," he wrote. "But I had not known how living and real were those atavistic forces that paralyze the majority from within."[16] With these thoughts a heresy was germinating. At one stage a guard, Don Ramon, asked him how an intelligent man like himself had got mixed up with the

Communists. Koestler told the guard he was no longer "a *rojo*." Reflecting on this moment later, Koestler believed he "had spoken the truth with the intention of telling a lie. Inwardly, I was no longer a Communist, but the break was neither conscious nor definite; and my intention in uttering that phrase was, of course, that Don Ramon should report it."[17]

It was not until March 27, more than six weeks since his arrest, that Koestler received his first word from the outside world, when a letter arrived from his wife, Dorothy. The contents were general and vague, clearly designed to get past the censor but the last sentence was telling: she asked him to respond in his own handwriting. She clearly did not know if he was alive or dead and wanted proof. The letter did not answer many of his questions, but it did include one hundred pesetas, allowing him to buy better food rations, wine, and cigarettes. He lurched between happiness and apathy. At the beginning of April, he decided he must do something. Repeated requests to see the British consul had got him nowhere. He began secretly starving himself, hoping to make himself weak and increase his heart rate. He then faked a heart attack, hoping that his captors would be forced to do something, perhaps move him to a hospital. The prison doctor counseled rest. After a week without food he was reading a Spanish translation of Leo Tolstoy's *War and Peace* when he came to the passage about the shooting of the Russian prisoners after Moscow had fallen to Napoleon. He vomited into the toilet but all he could bring up was bile. He had brought himself dangerously close to death.

On April 12 a young Falangist came to his cell and stuck a gun under his nose. The man informed Koestler he would be shot, only to then spend two hours in the cell talking away. After the initial shock, it slowly dawned on Koestler what this young fascist was telling him: his solitary confinement was over. He would be allowed to exercise in the yard and write letters. When he stepped outside the following afternoon, he took a huge gulp of fresh air and promptly fainted. Everything seemed to be getting better. Koestler could talk to the other three inmates from the condemned wing during their time in the yard and, with pen and ink, he began to write letters.

Then they started shooting the prisoners again. April 17 was the anniversary of the declaration of the Republic, and in celebration the Nationalists began another round of executions. For five nights in a row at 10 P.M. the phone rang in the warder's office, a sound that resonated around the prison. A list of names was communicated. Then the night bell rung, the signal that the firing squad was on its way to gather its victims, a priest leading the procession. One night the priest fumbled with the lock on Koestler's door but was instructed to go on. He had the wrong cell. By this stage, Koestler was suffering from nervous trembling in his sleep, the whole bed shaking. Listening to the executions took Koestler to the brink. In desperation he cut his gums and asked for cotton wool to stanch the bleeding, using it instead to block up his ears at night. By his calculation forty-seven men were shot that week. Koestler, though, survived.

Three things happened in quick succession: first, a letter from the British Consul in which he wrote that he was trying to visit; second, another letter from Dorothy in which she told him a major campaign was being run in Britain for his release; third, a visit from the Consul himself, bearing good news. Koestler's case had provoked questions in the House of Commons, he was told. His advocates had framed it as an issue of press freedom. The Foreign Office had written to Franco and different options were being pursued, the most promising of which was a potential prisoner exchange. By this stage, Koestler's covert fasting had taken its toll. He struggled to get out of bed on some days and when he was inspected by the prison doctor he was asked to undress. He was shocked by his own emaciation: he looked like "a walking skeleton from a Walt Disney cartoon."[18]

On May 8, he was taken before a military examiner and questioned for two hours, finding most of the questions idiotic as the examiner seemed preoccupied with proving that the *News Chronicle* was a Communist newspaper. To Koestler's relief, he saw in his file that he was no longer charged with being a spy but rather with aiding the Republican militia, making it much more likely the Francoists would agree to a prisoner exchange. His membership in the Comintern remained a secret. His optimism was short-lived, though. The consul grimly told him negotiations were getting nowhere. "There is nothing in the tenet of even the gloomiest monastic order," he wrote, "which condemns a man to endure purgatory, and then, when it is all over, sends him back to hell."[19] He became convinced, again, that he would be executed.

Four days later, on May 12, "between the siesta and the evening meal the cell door flew open and freedom was thrown at me like a club."[20] He was taken from his cell, which by now he shared with Carlos, an Italian prisoner, to the prison warden's office. Sitting in the warden's chair was a stranger in a black shirt and no tie. The stranger bowed with exaggerated formality and told Koestler he was going to take him away. Koestler returned to his cell, shook Carlos by the hand, and departed, the door slamming shut behind him. As they walked down the corridor, Koestler's diary fell out of his pocket and the leaves of paper scattered on the floor. "What have you got there?" the stranger asked. "Private letters," Koestler answered. The stranger helped him gather them up. Back in the warden's office, Koestler signed a document declaring that he would no longer meddle in Spanish affairs. Before he could prepare himself, he was led out of the front gate and was stunned by the simple sights of the outside world: a donkey cart creaking by, a man reading a newspaper, a child eating grapes, local girls flirting with the prison guards.

There was time for one last scare. Koestler was ushered into a car, in the back of which sat two police officers. He was told they were driving "to another town" but when the car stopped, Koestler panicked. The car idled by an empty field. To his relief, he heard the approaching sound of an engine and a monoplane, a tiny Baby Douglas, appeared from behind a thicket. They were on the outskirts of an airfield. The stranger in the black shirt was one of the Nationalist's finest pilots and his wife, held hostage by Republican forces, was being exchanged for Koestler. The flight was bumpy, and the pilot shouted Francoist propaganda at Koestler the whole way. They landed at La Linea, on the border with Gibraltar, where Koestler was held for forty-eight hours. On May 14 he crossed the border and set foot on the safety of British soil. He was a free man again. He was also a changed man. He had gone into a prison a fervent Communist, but he came out with his faith in the cause shaken. The prison diary, clutched in his hand, was testament to that.

SIX

Spender, Orwell & Koestler

MADRID & LONDON, 1937

WITH HYNDMAN STUCK IN A LABOR CAMP outside Albacete, Spender returned to London in April 1937 to campaign for his release. He had been back home just three days when he met again with Harry Pollitt, still the general secretary of the British Communist Party. The meeting was heated. In a letter to his friend Wogan Phillips, Spender recounted how Pollitt refused to help "until right at the end of the interview when he said, 'Tell me, is there any sex in this.' I said yes. He said, 'I know.' Then he went off the deep end and said people like me were no use at the Front, no use in the revolution, no use anywhere, so Tony would be brought home and then would be 'in the mud.'"[1] Spender was being blackmailed: if he wrote critically about the Party then, Pollitt intimated, he would be exposed as "a bloody homosexual intellectual worrying about his boyfriend."[2] Spender enlisted everyone he could think of to write letters on Hyndman's behalf, including Leonard Woolf and E. M. Forster. Spender wrote to the mother of Giles Romilly, with whom Hyndman had traveled to Spain, and she in turn appealed to her brother-in-law, Winston Churchill, the influential Conservative politician and former First Lord of the Admiralty.

Churchill thundered about sending a battleship after his

nephew (although not, alas, Hyndman).[3] Spender received assurances that Hyndman would return, only to be disappointed again and again. He sought consolation in his poetry, writing about Spain, the war, and Hyndman.

In *The Still Centre,* the collection in which he eventually published these poems in 1939, he wrote a short foreword in which he apologized for the failure of his poems about the war in Spain to "strike a more heroic note."[4] In several poems he meditated on the death of young men; in "Ultima Ratio Regum," he wrote about a boy "lying dead under the olive trees," who was "too young and too silly" to deserve such a fate. "He was a better target for a kiss," Spender wrote.[5] Hyndman's presence flickers throughout the collection, such as in "The Coward," which reflects on the posthumous reputation of those whose courage failed them in the field. The strongest poem in *The Still Centre* is "Port Bou," in which Spender wrote about experiencing a moment of heightened aesthetic perception while sitting on a bridge on the hillside above the border town's harbor. He notices the way "the earth-and-rock flesh arms" of the headlands "embrace but do not enclose the sea" in a way that resembles how he cradles the newspaper he is reading. It is a moment of tranquility and security and, as he contemplates the scene, a truckload of earnest militiamen stops and they ask him what news there is of the fighting in the newspaper. They depart for the front, shouting and saluting. But then the poem turns; Spender is left alone, as quiet descends on Port Bou, only to be jolted out of his reverie by firing practice down at the sea front: "my body seems a cloth which the machine-gun stitches / Like a sewing machine, neatly, with cotton from a reel; And the solitary, irregular, thin 'paffs' from the carbines / Draw on long needles white threads through my navel."[6] It is a poem that describes the arc of Spender's experience in Spain: first the optimism, the comradeship, the sense of purpose, then the sudden interruption into the realities of violence.

In May, he reunited with Hemingway in Paris, where they gave a reading together at Sylvia Beach's famous bookshop, Shakespeare & Company. Among those in the audience was James Joyce, who listened to Hemingway read (somewhat falteringly; Hemingway was a nervous public speaker) from the novel that would become *For Whom the Bell Tolls*, while Spender read from poems that would make up *The Still Centre*.

There were complications in Hyndman's case. He had been accused of being involved in a Trotskyist plot and had been sent back from the labor camp to the barracks prison. He was held in a filthy cell with nine other men. As the days wore on, some of his fellow prisoners were removed without warning. Hyndman feared they were being sent to the front to be shot and that he might be next.

Spender was in a curious position. He had effectively left the Communist Party, and the Hyndman situation now kept him from going public with his criticism of what he had seen in Spain. Moreover, the Republicans were losing the war, and Spender still felt loyal to the non-Communist partners in the Popular Front. One of the concessions he made to Pollitt and the Party was to return to Spain for the Second International Congress of Writers for the Defense of Culture in July 1937 (the first had been held in Paris two years previously). The gathering of more than two hundred writers from thirty different countries was ostensibly an expression of anti-fascist intellectual solidarity in the literary world, but it was in fact a propaganda event organized by the Comintern, whose activities in Spain were directed by the NKVD.[7] This was developing into an effective strategy. Using front groups to disguise their involvement, the Soviet Union clandestinely funded gatherings of sympathetic intellectuals (with travel and accommodation paid) in the hope that these intellectuals would help sway public opinion in their own countries. A few knew that money was coming from Moscow and did not care; the majority were in the dark. These meetings were also an opportunity to acquaint writers, artists, and thinkers with what the "correct" thinking was on current issues. It was a means of weaponizing culture that would persist into the Cold War.

Getting to Madrid was difficult. The Foreign Office refused Spender a visa, so he got over the border using forged documents (Spender's Spanish alter ego was "Ramos Ramos"), procured by André Malraux. The Congress opened in Valencia on July 4, then moved to besieged Madrid for four days, then one day in Barcelona, before culminating in Paris. There was a large delegation of Communist-sympathizing Spanish writers (Spender was particularly taken with Rafael Alberti, José Bergamin, Miguel Hernandez, and Antonio Machado), as well as celebrated foreign writers like Langston Hughes, Malcolm Cowley, Pablo Neruda, Octavio Paz, Alejo Carpentier, Julien Benda, and Tristan Tzara.[8] Hemingway sent his apologies and a message of solidarity. The Russians were also represented, with Spanish War stalwarts Ilya Ehrenburg and Mikhail Koltsov in attendance. Alexei Tolstoy was chairman. For Spender, though, the star was Malraux, who in his tweed suit "had an air of battered youth, with face jutting pallidly over his intently crouching body as he looked at his audience."[9] Malraux was a charismatic self-mythologizer and later that year would publish *L'Espoir*, his novel of the Spanish Civil War. Politically Malraux was in favor. While he had previously admired Trotsky, he had since broken with him and become an ardent fellow traveler.

The talk of the conference was not Malraux, however, but another French writer, André Gide, who had presided over the previous International Congress of Writers two years before. Having been such a champion of the Communist cause, Gide had been invited to Moscow by the Union of Soviet Writers to attend the funeral of Maxim Gorky and tour the country. On his return he had the temerity to write *Retour de l'URSS,* in which he attacked the totalitarian strain in Stalinism. "What is wanted now is compliance, conformism," he wrote. "What is desired and demanded is approval that is not mere resignation, but a sincere and enthusiastic approval. What is most astounding is that this attempt is successful. On the other hand the smallest protest, the least criticism, is liable to the severest penalties, and in fact is immediately stifled. And I doubt whether in any other country in the world, even Hitler's Germany, thought be less free, more bowed down, more fearful (terrorized), more vassalized."[10] Shortly before the Congress began, Gide published a follow-up, *Retouches à mon Retour de l'URSS,* which stood by these criticisms. What happened in Madrid proved Gide's point: because he dared to criticize the Soviet Union, the Stalinists went after him. Gide's work was, according to Spender, "constantly discussed in private and almost as often dragged onto the open platform."[11] Spender had met Gide earlier that summer and was shocked at the vitriol with which he was denounced as both a Trotskyist and a fascist. Fellow French writer Louis Aragon called him a traitor. The consequences of Gide's heresy were a clear warning: if you broke with Stalin, you were a target. From the Soviet perspective, the main purpose of the Congress was as a platform with which to denounce Gide (it has even been speculated that Stalin personally organized these attacks).[12] To Spender, who had already secretly broken with the Communists, this was a sobering glimpse into the future.

To Spender, the experience of being part of this "circus of intellectuals" was deeply uncomfortable. The writers were whisked from banquet to banquet in Rolls-Royces, toasted with champagne, and celebrated in song, and a "kind of hysterical conceitedness seized certain delegates."[13] Spender found particularly appalling the Communist novelist Sylvia Townsend Warner, who "behaved like a vicar's wife presiding over a tea party given on a vicarage lawn as large as the whole of Republican Spain."[14] On the drive back from Barcelona to the French border, the driver gleefully informed his English passengers that he had participated in the purge of the POUM in Barcelona, personally having killed six men. Having safely arrived at the French border and sitting in the sunshine on the quay in Port Bou, Spender recalled Warner blithely remarking: "And what is so nice is that we didn't see or hear of a single act of violence on the Republican side." When Spender raised the "cheerful confession" of their driver, Warner and her partner simply turned away.

Spender was ready to turn away himself. Finally, there was good news from Albacete. Taking pity on Hyndman, a medical officer had x-rayed him and pronounced him unfit for action. That, combined with the pressure Spender had brought to bear on the International Brigades, was enough to warrant his repatriation. Hyndman returned to London at the end of July, as Spender returned from the Congress. To Spender's immense relief, the Communists had given up their leverage over him.[15]

FOR ORWELL, a new fight was brewing. While still resting up in Banyuls, just over the French border, he began work on his essay "Eyewitness in Barcelona," in which he gave his account of the May riots and the suppression of the POUM, contradicting the official Communist line.[16] He submitted it to the left-wing magazine the *New Statesman* but it was rejected. To, in his words, "sugar the pill" they sent him a book to review, Franz Borkenau's *The Spanish Cockpit*. If they were hoping this might result in Orwell taking a different tack, they were naive; Borkenau was a former Comintern agent turned hardened critic of Stalinism, and his book was an indictment of Soviet behavior in Spain. Like Orwell, he had been marked by the secret police. In his review, Orwell called *Spanish Cockpit* "the best book yet written" on the war, as it showed that "far from pushing the Spanish Government further towards the Left, the Communist influence has pulled it violently towards the Right."[17] Kingsley Martin, the editor of the *New Statesman,* rejected the review, telling Orwell that it "too far controverts the political policy of the paper." That they offered to pay only made this worse. To Orwell this showed "the mentality of a whore."[18] It was a sign of things to come.

Such a powerful hold did the Communists have on left-wing institutions that Orwell struggled to find an outlet. In July, he began to get his side of the story out when the first instalment of his essay "Spilling the Spanish Beans" was published in the *New English Weekly.*[19] Yet he was unmistakably being targeted. One of the first things he'd seen on return to his home in Wallington was an edition of the *News Chronicle* that featured an extract from *The Road to Wigan Pier,* part of a series to give critically acclaimed writers more exposure to the public. (The writer featured in the previous issue had been Spender.) Yet the reception of his book was far from laudatory. Orwell was repeatedly attacked in the left-wing press and in the *Daily Worker* especially; Pollitt even authored a review in which he dismissed Orwell as a "disillusioned little middle-class boy" who is obsessed with the "'smell' of the working class."[20] So perturbed was Orwell that he wrote to his publisher, Victor Gollancz, who enjoyed great influence in left-wing circles, to intercede on his behalf. Orwell felt he was being targeted as part of a "campaign of organized libel" being directed against anyone who had served with the POUM.[21]

While he asked Gollancz for help, he also thought of the publisher as part of the "Communist racket." Back in May, in the immediate aftermath of the battle for Barcelona, Orwell had written to Gollancz proposing a book about his experiences. Within a week of being back in England, Orwell spoke on the phone to one of Gollancz's editors, Norman Collins, describing the book he planned to write. Collins relayed this to Gollancz, who rejected it before even speaking to Orwell, telling him in a letter of July 5 that the book "would harm the fight against fascism."[22] If Orwell was going to tell his Spanish story, he needed a new publisher.

It was under this cloud that Orwell received an appeal from *Left Review* to contribute to a book entitled *Authors Take Sides on the Spanish War.* In early August, Orwell wrote to Nancy Cunard, the shipping heiress and political radical who was organizing the volume, in a rage. "Will you please stop sending me this bloody rubbish," he wrote. "This is the second or third time I have had it. I am not one of your fashionable pansies like Auden and Spender, I was six months in Spain, most of the time fighting, I have a bullet-hole in me at present and I am not going to write blah about defending democracy and gallant little anybody."[23] *Authors Take Sides on the Spanish War* featured 148 contributors, including W. H. Auden, T. S. Eliot, and Ezra Pound, as well as Arthur Koestler and Sir Peter Chalmers-Mitchell.[24] It was Spender who riled Orwell, though. Spender had spent the previous month at the Writers' Congress in Madrid and seemed to Orwell to be typical of the Communist dilettante (he called them "Parlour Bolsheviks"), providing intellectual cover for the Stalinists as they imprisoned and murdered his friends. Kopp was in jail, as was Milton, and Smillie had been killed. This perhaps explains, but does not excuse, the ugliness of Orwell's homophobia in his letter to Cunard. Orwell could not know that Spender had broken with the Communists over their treatment of Hyndman. At the end of the letter, with no little menace, Orwell told Cunard to deliver a message to "your pansy friend Spender": "I am preserving specimens of his war-heroics and that when the time comes when he squirms for shame at having written it, as the people who wrote the war-propaganda in the Great War are squirming now, I shall rub it in good and hard."[25]

It is all the more astonishing that, in light of these unpromising beginnings, Spender and Orwell became friends. They were introduced by their mutual friend, the writer Cyril Connolly, and when Orwell was laid up in a sanatorium in Kent the following March (a tubercular lesion in his left lung had begun bleeding), Spender traveled down to visit him. In one letter to Spender, Orwell confided that "I sometimes feel I hadn't been properly alive since the beginning of 1937." In the same letter, Orwell brought up the fact that both he and Spender were sponsors of the International Anti-Fascist Solidarity organization and that Cunard was one, too, an opportunity for Orwell to apologize for being rude about Spender in response to *Authors Takes Sides in the Spanish War*. It seems Spender was unaware of the insults or politely pretended to be.

In April *Homage to Catalonia* was published by Fredric Warburg, who championed books that challenged left-wing orthodoxies. It was a masterful work, rendered in elegant, spare prose and fusing memoir with reportage. Having read an advance copy, Spender assured Orwell that the book would have a positive impact on the Republican cause, assuming it was not treated "à la Gide." While some reviewers were enthusiastic, there was predictable pushback from many critics on grounds of Orwell's suspect politics: an anonymous reviewer in the *Listener* accused him of effectively being a Fifth Columnist.[26]

In writing *Homage to Catalonia*, Orwell felt particular pressure to be scrupulous, knowing that any errors or indulgences would be seized upon. He was aware that in trying to do justice to the full complexity of the Spanish War, he needed to go into the kind of detail that could be off-putting. In the first edition of the book, Orwell advised readers at the beginning of chapter 11 to "please skip" it if they were "not interested in political controversy and the mob of parties and sub-parties with their confusing names." It is, he wrote, "a horrible thing to have to enter into the details of inter-party polemics; it is like diving into a cesspool. But it is necessary to try and establish the truth, so far as it is possible. This squalid brawl in a distant city is more important than might appear at first sight."[27]

Here was the bind Orwell found himself in. He wanted to bring his message from Spain to as many readers as possible, but the complexity of delivering that message and the need for exactitude and detail made that delivery a challenge, especially when so many did not want to hear the message in the first place. Then there was the context of impending war, anxieties over which were obsessing British readers, causing interest in the Spanish Civil War to wane. Of the 1,500 copies of *Homage to Catalonia* printed, only 683 copies sold in the first six months of publication. This was a necessary failure, though. It taught Orwell that if he were to fight back against Stalinism, he would need different literary weapons.

Two MONTHS BEFORE *Homage to Catalonia* was published, Orwell reviewed a book about the Spanish War that would be better received and reach a much larger audience: *Spanish Testament* by Arthur Koestler. It allowed Orwell to gauge the costs of his heresy: with the support of the Left Book Club, support that had been withdrawn from his own book, Koestler's memoir sold in the region of sixty thousand copies. Despite the fact that the first half of the book was thinly disguised Communist propaganda, Orwell was compelled by what he read, especially Koestler's account of his time in prison in Seville, which he felt was of "the greatest psychological interest." *Spanish Testament* was, to Orwell's mind, "one of the most honest and unusual documents that have been produced by the Spanish War."[28] Like *Homage to Catalonia*, it presaged greater works to come.

Koestler's break with Communism was not immediate, but in the months after his release "the inner change that had taken place in cell No. 40" began "gradually percolating through to the surface."[29] On arriving in London he discovered that it had been Sir Peter who had alerted the outside world to his plight, having himself been rescued by the captain of a British destroyer that had docked in Malaga the day after they had both been arrested. Hearing of Koestler's internment, Dorothy, herself a Communist activist, had persuaded the Comintern to pay for her to go to London to campaign on her husband's behalf. She did so with tireless courage, all the more creditable as she and Koestler had effectively separated two years before. Koestler felt keenly the debt of gratitude he owed them both. He also felt profoundly uncomfortable with his public reception, as a heroic reporter who had been unjustly imprisoned by Franco; the need to deceive those who had fought for his release about his true status as a Comintern agent was becoming "unbearably odious."[30] Something was going to break.

That summer Koestler and Dorothy made one last go of living together, and he dictated *Spanish Testament* to her in the small house they had found in quiet Shepperton, on the outskirts of London. The relationship could not be revived, though. As a way of getting Koestler back to work, the *News Chronicle* sent him on what was supposed to be a cushy assignment to Palestine.

His first stop was in Paris, where he was debriefed by members of the Comintern. In theory, he had nothing to fear. He had made no deal with his captors, so there should have been no suspicion of his having been "turned." Yet he was not deaf to the stories filtering out of the Soviet Union. In Valencia, in the days before he made that fateful trip to Malaga, he had heard the Soviet journalist Mikhail Koltsov talk about the impending trial of Koestler's old friend Karl Radek, a former confidant of Lenin and an influential Communist activist. Dorothy's brother Ernst Ascher, a doctor in the Volga region, had been arrested on charges of having injected syphilis into his patients. At the end of the meeting, which took place with two Comintern agents at a cafe, Koestler noticed his hands were shaking. "The Terror was roaring across Russia, like a tidal wave drowning everyone in its way," he wrote, "and even a small, distant ripple of it made the cup tremble in one's hands in a Paris café."[31]

After a disappointing visit with Thomas Mann in Switzerland (a writer he idolized and whose *Buddenbrooks* helped keep him sane in prison), Koestler met his parents in Belgrade (they traveled down from Budapest by train); it was the last time he saw his father. After that he was back into the thick of it, arriving in new places as violence erupted. He met with members of the Communist underground in Greece, a country under the dictatorial control of General Ioannis Metaxas since a coup the previous year. From there he sailed for Alexandria, where riots had recently erupted, before going on to witness the resumption of the Arab Uprising in Palestine, with its bombings and ambushes. Koestler found Jerusalem under curfew reminded him of "the silence of Malaga, the last night before its fall."[32]

The publication of *Spanish Testament* made his reputation as an important writer. On his return to Britain, in the first months of 1938, Koestler went on a lecture tour for the Left Book Club, talking about his experiences in Spain. Koestler found the English Communists and fellow travelers to be an odd bunch. Compared to the intensity of Communist meetings on the continent, these gatherings were more like "tea parties in the vicarage" and "the cranks and eccentrics" he met were "certainly closer to the Pickwick Club than the Comintern."[33] There was one question that threw him, however. The first time a member of the audience asked him about the POUM, Koestler's mind went blank. He knew what he *should* say, which was that the POUM had divided the Popular Front and therefore had become *objectively* fascist no matter what the subjective motivation of its members had been. Instead, though, Koestler blurted out what he really thought: he disagreed with the POUM's political goals but he believed "Andres Nin and his comrades had been acting in good faith, and to call them traitors was both stupid and a desecration of the dead."[34] It was Koestler's first public heresy, committed, unknown to him, in defense of his future friend George Orwell.

Koestler waited for the response that did not come. "At every meeting," he wrote, "I pressed a figurative revolver to my head, pulled the trigger, heard a faint click, and found to my astonishment that I was still alive and a valued member of the Communist Party."[35] Back in Paris after the tour, he was horrified by the latest and most spectacular of the Moscow Show Trials, as prestigious Communists, including the old Bolshevik Nikolai Bukharin, were charged with, and confessed to, being part of an improbable conspiracy with the exiled Leon Trotsky.

Shortly after the trial, Eva Striker, with whom Koestler had been friends since they were five (her mother had been their kindergarten teacher), was freed after eighteen months in prison in Moscow and Leningrad. Striker, a design director at a porcelain factory outside of Moscow, had been accused of placing concealed swastikas in the patterns on the teacups she was producing and, even more fancifully, of hiding a pistol for the purpose of assassinating Stalin. She told Koestler of how she, like him, had struggled to retain her sanity during her solitary confinement, living under fear of an imminent execution. She, too, had tried to kill herself, cutting her wrist with a wire. An interrogator had tricked her into signing a false confession but had then himself been swept up in the purges. To her surprise, she had been released, but her ex-husband, the physicist Alexander Weissberg, also a friend of Koestler's, was still in prison.

The resonances between their experiences affected Koestler profoundly. His incarceration in Spain, Striker's stories about her time in the NKVD's Lubyanka prison, and the reports of the latest show trial all told different versions of the same story.

Koestler could not get over "the fuss that had been made about me" in comparison with "the unsung end of my friends in Russia." He became "increasingly aware of a crushing debt that must somehow be repaid. *Darkness at Noon,* which I started writing the next year, was the first instalment towards it."[36]

KOESTLER FINALLY LEFT THE PARTY in the spring of 1938 but, even then, in his initial letter of resignation, he asked the Comintern to keep it secret and said he was doing it to prevent his exposure as a Communist from damaging the cause in England. It was, in the words of his biographer Michael Scammell, both "ethically dubious and confused in its reasoning."[37] A second letter was more strongly worded. "It is a logical contradiction," Koestler wrote, "when with uncanny regularity the leadership sees itself obliged to undertake more and more bloody operations within the movement, and in the same breath insists that the movement is healthy. Such an accumulation of grave surgical interventions points with much greater likelihood to the existence of a much more serious illness." He said that, after his time in prison in Spain, he had "the elementary need to breathe, to think, and to write freely again, and to speak my mind."[38] Even this letter broke only with Stalinism, not with the ideals of the Soviet Union; it was not until August of the following year, with the Molotov-Ribbentrop Pact of nonaggression between Nazi Germany and the Soviet Union, that Koestler's faith in the Communist project finally left him.[39]

In July 1938, having finished his first novel, *The Gladiators,* Koestler traveled with his new girlfriend, the English sculptor Daphne Hardy, down to Roquebrune on the French Riviera and began work on *Darkness at Noon.* The subject of *The Gladiators* was the Spartacus slave revolt against the Roman Empire, which gave Koestler the opportunity to write about means and ends, and the justification for revolutionary violence. The book ended up confused and pessimistic, and somewhat clunkily executed, possibly because he had been working on it off and on for three years. He began work on a new novel that would address more directly his political crisis. His working title was *The Vicious Circle*, and the story was to be about a group of prisoners sentenced to death in a totalitarian country, but when he started writing it, he realized that it was really going to be about just one character: an old Bolshevik, Nikolai Salmanovich Rubashov. Koestler knew how it would begin, with Rubashov asleep, dreaming of when he was arrested working as an underground agent in a hostile country, then waking, confused, to the sounds of policemen banging at the door. This time his own people were coming for him. Koestler later claimed that while he had not intended it, this opening served as "a symbolic assertion of the basic sameness of the two totalitarian regimes."[40]

Koestler also knew how the book would end, with Rubashov confessing to his guilt. This was his effort to explain one of "the great enigmas of our time"[41]—that is, why hardened revolutionaries like Bukharin and Ivan Smirnov, many of whom had been imprisoned or tortured under the Tsar, should confess to outlandish crimes. What Koestler showed was how Rubashov was not broken by threats or torture but persuaded to see how his own ideology demanded he sacrifice himself to the needs of the Party, however perverted those needs had become. Whatever his *subjective* culpability, his actions in disagreeing with Party policy made him *objectively* guilty, and the interrogators used Rubashov's own political writings to force him to understand that his own abasement and liquidation were what the internal logic of his ideology demanded. The means, however terrible, were always justified by the end, which was the distant but inevitable socialist utopia prophesized by Karl Marx.

Koestler said that Rubashov was modelled on Bukharin in his

"manner of thinking" and on a synthesis of Trotsky and Radek for his "personality and physical appearance," but there is much of Koestler himself in the character, too.[42] He drew heavily on his own experiences of solitary confinement in his Seville prison cell, borrowing from Eva Striker's account to Russify some of the details. Most important, though, the novel was a way for Koestler to write about his own struggles with ends and means: having deliberately ignored or speciously justified many crimes and cruelties over the previous seven years. In the early 1930s in the USSR he had witnessed the consequences of collectivization, effectively a state-imposed famine, in Ukraine; he knew that dissent within the Soviet Union was brutally stamped out by the secret police; he knew how cynically the Comintern manipulated people to their own ends; he knew that the defendants in the Moscow trials were not the fascist agents they confessed to being. Yet with all that knowledge he had remained a loyal Communist. Writing *Darkness at Noon* was an act of heresy, though the book itself is about a man whose faith in Communism and revolution is absolute.

He worked on the draft at a furious pace, the words pouring out of him, and to get away from any distractions he and Hardy moved to a tiny alpine village so he could finish the novel. There, however, he read about the pact of nonaggression between Nazi Germany and the Soviet Union, and he made straight for Paris as France mobilized for war, hoping to get to safety in London. He had reason to panic. The French police suspected he was a Communist, and with the new alliance between Stalin and Hitler, he feared arrest. The problem for Koestler was that the British also knew about his political past, and MI5 rejected his appeal for a visa to move to Britain. As he searched for a way out, he kept a bag packed by his bedside.

The Paris police came for him on October 2, 1939. His connections to members of the Comintern had convinced them he was a Soviet propagandist. He was interned first in a local prison and then in the Roland Garros tennis stadium. After nine days in cramped, wet conditions, Koestler learned he was being sent to an internment camp for undesirable aliens and told Hardy to notify friends, including Malraux, what had happened to him.

Koestler was shipped off to Le Vernet, near Toulouse. The camp was surrounded by trenches and barbed wire, and the prisoners slept two hundred to a hut. Koestler had his head shaved and was put to manual work, but he used the wiles he had acquired in Spanish prison to secure privileges. He pleaded a heart problem to get off the hard labor and, through carefully distributed bribes, managed to get food, books, a lamp, and a more comfortable bed. Most important, though, he got permission from the camp officials to write and, sitting outside under an umbrella during the day and working by a lamp rigged from sardine cans at night, he resumed work on *Darkness at Noon*.

Koestler's release was secured through a bizarre series of connections. His estranged wife, Dorothy, who had been such an effective advocate for him when he was imprisoned in Spain, got the right people on the case (Daphne Hardy did not have Dorothy's connections or experience), including Paul Willert, a British diplomat who knew Münzenberg and Katz, Koestler's former Comintern bosses, and who was now working for MI5. Willert got Malraux involved, and he sought to get Koestler passage to Mexico. It also seems Willert used MI5 colleague Noël Coward's friendship with Jean Giraudoux, French minister for information, to help secure Koestler's release.[43] Coward, a hugely successful playwright, was recruited to British intelligence by high-ranking diplomat Robert Vansittart, and he used his celebrity and personal flamboyance as cover to infiltrate high society and report on Nazi sympathizers.

Back in Paris Koestler's troubles were far from over. He was warned he was going to be arrested again but told he could avoid that fate if he became an informer. He refused. His apartment was raided, books and papers seized, but the manuscript of *Darkness at Noon* piled neatly on his desk was untouched. He kept writing, while Hardy translated his work into English. By May 1940 the draft was done, and Koestler sent a copy of it by post to London. Ten days later the Nazis swept into France.

The police came for him again on May 22. He asked Walter Benjamin, the Marxist philosopher and his neighbor, to fetch Hardy from the post office. Koestler gave her instructions before he was whisked off to the Stade Buffalo cycling venue, which was being used to intern enemy aliens. At the stadium, he used his Hungarian passport and an invented story to talk himself out of being locked up and went into hiding. Per Koestler's instructions, Hardy packed up the manuscript of *Darkness at Noon* with some other possessions, and the pair fled south to Limoges. The next few days passed in chaos and confusion as Koestler and Hardy sought to get out of France before the Germans arrived. In a moment of desperation Koestler signed up with the Foreign Legion. Before he officially enlisted, he had a furious fight with Hardy about his decision, and when a plan to escape by boat from Bordeaux fell apart, they agreed to part. A distraught Koestler swallowed a cyanide pill, acquired from a friend in Paris, but vomited it up before it could take effect.

The Legion sent Koestler to Marseille, which was packed with those seeking to flee the Nazis. He bumped into Benjamin, who gave Koestler, terrified of falling into Nazi hands, some morphine tablets from his supply before he fled for the Spanish border. Benjamin crossed to Port Bou days later, but after being told he would be deported back to France and knowing this would mostly likely result in his being handed over to the Nazis, he killed himself with an overdose of the tablets.

Koestler had more luck, though. He heard about a small group of soldiers from the British Expeditionary Force who planned to escape to North Africa. Koestler persuaded them to take him with them, making himself useful by bribing a port official to give them Foreign Legion papers and uniforms. Together with four British soldiers he got on a boat to Oran and, with a bit more bribery, on a train to Casablanca. There the five fugitives met a man who called himself "Ellerman" (in fact Rüdiger von Etzdorf, a German-born agent of British intelligence), who got the group on a fishing boat to Lisbon. Having made it to Portugal, Koestler thought he was safe, but once again MI5 denied him a visa to enter Britain. He was stuck in Lisbon, crawling with German and Spanish spies, and fell into despair. Again attempting suicide, he took Benjamin's morphine pills, but he must have misjudged the dosage because he awoke vomiting from his drugged stupor.

Finally, Koestler's luck turned. He managed to inveigle his way onto a flight to England and, on landing, dramatically told the immigration official at Whitchurch airport in Bristol to arrest him. Clearly manic and desperate, after his initial interrogation in Bristol it appeared he would be sent straight back to Lisbon, but a superior officer made the decision to send him to London for further questioning first. Koestler knew he had to do everything in his power not to be deported, and so decided to go on a hunger strike. As a result, he was interrogated by an officer from the intelligence services who disguised his identity under a black hood. But Koestler—talking for his life—did enough to persuade the authorities to keep him in Britain. A member of the secret service who witnessed this interrogation described Koestler as "one third genius, one third blackguard, and one third lunatic."[44]

The worst was over. Koestler spent six weeks in solitary confinement in London's Pentonville Prison, which he described as a "three-star prison."[45] He had regular visits from Hardy, who told him that *Darkness at Noon* was about to be published.[46] A novel that had its origins in a prison in Seville was, in December

1940, finally ready to be printed and bound while its author was incarcerated in a prison in London.

The initial impact of the book was modest, garnering good reviews but selling only 2,500 copies—much better than *Homage to Catalonia* but nothing compared to *Spanish Testament*. The aftershocks were much stronger: six months later, on publication in the United States it sold in huge numbers after being selected for the Book of the Month Club; five years later, the French translation (*Le Zéro et l'Infini*) detonated at a crucial moment in the incipient Cold War, creating a literary sensation for a people who were tempted by Communism as a way of rebuilding a shattered country. In the week of publication, readers lined up in the street to get their copy, and more than half a million were sold in France in the two years after its publication.

There were also profound impacts that are harder to quantify. One of the first reviewers of *Darkness at Noon* was Orwell. Writing in the January 4, 1941, edition of the *New Statesman*, he stressed that while the book was "brilliant" as a novel it was "probably most valuable as an interpretation of the Moscow 'confessions' by someone with an inner knowledge of totalitarian methods." Orwell used the review to rage against the "eagerness of Western intellectuals" who had justified the trials and that the "simultaneous cases in Spain" had been "sedulously covered up or lied about in the Left-wing press."[47] At this first reading he found it a "notable advance" on Koestler's previous work but years later he felt it deserved to be called a "masterpiece." *Darkness at Noon* showed him that fiction, rather than journalism or memoir, however scrupulous, was the most effective way to communicate the essence of totalitarianism. He needed to reimagine his Spanish experiences as Koestler had imagined his. When he found a way to do so, he sent the manuscript to Koestler, who sent back his "envious congratulations" for this "glorious and heart-breaking allegory."[48] The book, of course, was *Animal Farm*.

Part Two

TRIALS

SEVEN

Babel

MOSCOW, 1934

"A HEAP OF DUNG, crawling with worms, photographed by a cinema apparatus through a microscope—such is James Joyce's work," bellowed Karl Radek. With his chin-strap beard, thick, round glasses and unkempt, receding hair, the Soviet propagandist cut a faintly comical figure as he ranted into the microphone. Sitting in the audience, surrounded by his fellow writers, Isaac Babel listened with dismay. Radek's words echoed around the vast Hall of Columns in the House of Unions building in Moscow, a grand venue befitting the First Congress of the Union of Soviet Writers. This was where Lenin had lain in state. Now, for two weeks in August 1934, more than seven hundred delegates gathered in the largest assembly of writers in Russian history, presided over by the first man of Russian letters, the walrus-moustached Maxim Gorky. It was Gorky who had asked Babel to return from Paris the previous year to help him organize the Congress. Despite his misgivings, Babel could not refuse his mentor.

On the walls of the hall hung posters depicting Shakespeare and Cervantes, Gogol and Pushkin, and every time Babel entered and left the building, he was confronted by a giant banner suspended on the facade of the building opposite carrying the slogan: "Writers are the engineers of human souls." It was a phrase of Stalin's coinage.

There were many souls waiting to be engineered in the Soviet Union: in the years after the revolution Russian literacy rose
from 20 percent to 80 percent. The Congress began with a series
of open-air readings in the Moscow Park of Culture and Rest,
attended by tens of thousands. During the subsequent proceedings, the Hall of Columns was visited by delegation upon
delegation from every corner of the Soviet Union, from young
pioneers to miners and engineers.[1] The proceedings, two sessions a day of speeches, were covered exhaustively in *Pravda*.
This was a major event, an attempt to jolt Soviet literature back
to life in its cultural war with the West.

For a writer like Babel, the preceding years had been miserable. After a period of relative freedom in the 1920s, Soviet literature came under the sway of hard-line factions who believed
writers should form themselves into "artistic brigades" of "shock
workers" and be attached to the large-scale construction projects or collective farms that were part of Stalin's Five-Year Plan
to industrialize the Soviet Union.[2] These brigades of writers
were encouraged to write collective novels about the factory or
canal to which they had been assigned. The Russian Association
of Proletarian Writers, who were the dominant faction from
1929, were not tolerant of those who did not follow their line,
and many writers who charted their own course were bullied,
censored, and denounced. Babel, who never joined the Party, was
considered suspiciously independent. Those who, like Boris Pilnyak and Evgeny Zamyatin, dared to publish their work abroad
were either humiliated or cast out and denied the opportunity
to publish at all.[3] Pilnyak, who enjoyed a huge readership and
critical acclaim, made the mistake of publishing his novel *Mahogany* in Berlin after it had failed to pass the Soviet censors. He
had to grovel his way back into favor. Zamyatin refused to apologize after his dystopian masterwork, *We,* was published abroad

and was banned from publishing until, with the help of Gorky, Stalin permitted him to go into exile in France.

The problem for those directing Soviet cultural policy was that the books produced by the "artistic brigades" were mostly terrible. Even as committed a revolutionary writer as Gorky was embarrassed by what his country was producing. And Stalin listened to Gorky. In 1932, without warning, Stalin killed off the idea of "proletarian literature," forcibly disbanding all the factions and forming one large new collective: the Union of Soviet Writers. This was an historic moment, the dawn of a new kind of literature, to be called "socialist realism," a state-mandated aesthetic built into the statute book of the new writers' union. It was different from realism in that it did not depict "objective reality" but rather reality "in its revolutionary development." What reality in its revolutionary development looked like was one of the problems that the Congress was supposed to solve.[4]

What became clear was that it was easier to define socialist realism by what it was not rather than what it was, and one of the things it most certainly was not was modernism. That is why Radek was ranting about Joyce in the session dedicated to "international" literature. In the conclusion to his speech, he told the audience that world literature was defined by a fundamental opposition: socialist realism versus *Ulysses*.[5] Joyce's novel had been first published in 1922, but it was cleared of obscenity in the United States only in December 1933. By the time of the Congress it was an unlikely best seller in the United States, shipping thirty-three thousand copies by April.[6] For Radek, Joyce's novel was the ultimate expression of experimental, modernist individualism, the death spasm of "bourgeois literature" drawn out over one thousand pages. It wasn't just Joyce. "In the pages of Proust," Radek said, "the old world, like a mangy dog, no longer capable of any action whatever, lies basking in the sun and endlessly licks its sores."[7] Modernism was a literature for navel-gazing when what the moment demanded was political urgency. The previous summer, the Nazis had burned books on the streets of Germany and, in this climate, literature was not something to be idly composed by an artist in their garret, detached from society. "On May 10, 1933," Radek said, "all the world's writers were told: There is no such thing as neutrality in that struggle which is now taking place on the arena of history."[8] Radek argued that the foundations of Western literary culture were being threatened by fascism. "Hundreds, if not thousands, of writers have been forced to flee from Germany as from an earthquake, leaving their books for the hangman to destroy," he said.[9] The kind of literature needed to fight fascism could not afford to be apolitical; it had to be engaged. "Trying to present a picture of revolution by the Joyce method," Radek said, "would be like trying to catch a dreadnought with a shrimping net."[10] Under the Nazis, Radek warned, the message to the writer was simple: "He who is not for us is against us."[11]

It did not take a writer as sharp as Babel to catch the irony. What was to happen to those who cared more for the literature of Marcel Proust and James Joyce than for the edicts of socialist realism? What was to happen to a writer like Babel who could write only about the reality he saw around him, not about an idealized version of the reality as socialist realism demanded? Those who listened closely heard some ominous caveats in Radek's speech. "It goes without saying that the revolution and the Party do not exist in order to ensure to all members complete liberty," he said.[12]

As packed as the Hall of Columns was, there were faces missing. Radek brought up the case of Nikolai Gumilev, the poet who was arrested by the Cheka, the secret police established by Lenin in the immediate aftermath of the revolution, and shot in 1921. Here, Radek explained, was a writer of talent who had given himself to counterrevolutionary causes. Radek did not mention the many others who were not there. Gumilev's ex-wife, the great poet Anna Akhmatova, was absent, as was the writer Mikhail Bulgakov. These two were fortunate only to have been ostracized. The predicament of the poet Osip Mandelstam, arrested four months previously, was more serious. He had composed an epigram mocking Stalin that he was careful enough not to transcribe but not careful enough about to whom he recited it. Someone had made a copy and given it to the secret police, and he confessed to its authorship in a cell of the Lubyanka prison. He almost certainly owed his life to the need to avoid unpleasant scandal at the Congress, which was attended by a number of celebrated foreign writers, including Babel's good friend André Malraux.[13] The writers on display at the Congress were safe precisely because they were on display. The message, though, was clear: their continued "liberty" was predicated on their following the new socialist realist line. "He who is not for us is against us."

AND THEN IT WAS BABEL'S TURN TO SPEAK. As he stepped up to the microphone there was much expectation. He did not take himself as seriously as some of the other writers in the hall. He did not, for example, have the poetic aura of Boris Pasternak, with his intense gaze framed by high cheekbones. Babel was a little chubby and wore wire-rimmed spectacles; while he had only just turned forty, his hair was retreating far back from his forehead. He was garrulous and mischievous, known for his jokes. Yet, of those in the room, only Pasternak could have claimed to be Babel's rival in literary stature. The publication of *Red Cavalry* (1926), a collection of short stories drawing on his experiences riding with the Cossacks in the Civil War, made Babel the most famous writer in the Soviet Union. Whether it was composing a story about a brutal episode from the war, or about the Jewish criminal underground of Odessa, or about events from his childhood, Babel was a writer of uncompromising standards, whose every sentence was carefully worked, tested, and repeatedly polished. In this he was the product of his childhood immersion in French literature and his fascination with the work of Gustave Flaubert and Guy de Maupassant. It was not only the mot juste he was after, it was the perfect way of punctuating it, too. "No iron spike can pierce a human heart as icily as a period in the right place," he wrote in a piece about translating Maupassant.[14] His reputation spread beyond the Soviet Union, and *Red Cavalry* was translated into French in 1928 and into English in 1929, and earned the admiration of Ernest Hemingway among others.

Babel's talent was not the only reason there was so much expectation in the Hall of Columns, though. He was also in trouble. Just as he was being discovered by a generation of enthusiastic French, English, and American readers, parts of the Soviet literary establishment had already turned on him. In 1928, the critic Alexander Voronsky, an early champion of Babel's work, wrote an article publicly chastising the writer for his low productivity.[15] Babel had been on the defensive ever since and, six years later, was still without a major work to follow up *Red Cavalry*. Why was he not writing? Or, perhaps more to the point, why was he not being published?

In the build-up to the Congress, the implicit criticism of Babel's silence was made explicit. The American radical Max Eastman published a book earlier that year called *Artists in Uniform*, attacking the Soviet Union's cultural policies under Stalin. Eastman had been in the Soviet Union in the early 1920s and was responsible for smuggling Lenin's "Suppressed Testament" out of the country. When the document was published it caused a sensation, as it criticized Stalin and favored Trotsky's candidacy to be Lenin's successor. In the power struggle that followed Eastman became a firm ally of Trotsky. Unsurprisingly, Stalin loathed him.[16] There was a section in *Artists in Uniform* that Eastman called "The Literary Inquisition" in which he devoted a chapter to "The Silence of Isaac Babyel" [*sic*]. Eastman pointed out that of all Soviet writers, Babel had commanded the greatest respect abroad. "Why was this world-wide expectancy left hanging in the air?" wrote Eastman. "Why did Isaac Babyel turn his back on a fame already international, retire into the background and publish no word, save some recollections from childhood, for five years?"[17] Eastman's answer was that Babel was "an artist and not a recruiting sergeant" who refused "to surrender his incomparable pen into the hands of these new slave-drivers of creation, these brigadiers of the boy scouts of poetry, these professional vulgarians prostituting the idea of the liberation of all society by the proletariat to the task of enslaving all utterance and all creative life to an iron-ribbed bureaucratic machine."[18] Having Eastman fight in your corner was dangerous. With *Pravda* publishing transcripts of the major speeches for the wider public to read, Babel knew that he needed to defuse the issue of his silence.

Babel began conventionally enough, applauding the unity of the gathered writers before inveighing against "trite, vulgar, commonplace, contrived clichés." It is the job of writers, he said, "to help the triumph of the new Bolshevik taste in this country." A "new style" was needed and Babel knew just who writers should learn from. "Look at how Stalin hammers out his speeches," Babel said, "how his words are wrought of iron, how terse they are, how muscular, how much respect they show for the reader." The hall burst into applause. "I don't suggest here that we should all write like Stalin, but I do say that we must all work at our words as he does." More applause.

This was not wholly disingenuous. For one thing, Babel *had* been committed to the Bolshevik cause. As a child, he lived through the pogroms whipped up by the anti-Semitic rhetoric of Tsar Nicholas II and his government. As a young man, Babel had been denied entry to university because he was Jewish. He enlisted in the army to fight in the First World War, only for the front to disintegrate on his arrival with the news arriving of the revolution back home. Babel undertook a treacherous journey back to Petersburg, hiding for twelve days in a Kiev cellar while the Red Army fought for the city. Having secured passage to Petersburg, he was robbed on the train and thrown out barefoot into the snow. When he finally arrived in the city, he took a job for a few months as a translator with the Cheka. He then served as an embedded reporter with the Red Cavalry in Poland. He had certainly been on the "right" side during the revolution.

Invoking Stalin in his speech was transparently about self-preservation. Babel was a spinner of tall tales. At the Congress he told Malraux's wife, Clara, that he regularly went to the Kremlin with Gorky to meet with Stalin.[19] There were rumors in literary circles that at one of these meetings Stalin asked Babel to write a novel about him. "I'll think about it, Iossif Vissarionovich," was Babel's supposed reply.[20] The truth was that Babel avoided literary meetings at which Stalin was present. He was right to be cautious. Stalin certainly knew about Babel and did not view him favorably. This was down to General Semyon Budenny, the commander of the Red Cavalry and a close advisor of Stalin, who was infuriated by Babel's stories and publicly attacked him as "a literary degenerate."[21]

Babel led a complicated love life. His wife, Evgenia, had emigrated from the Soviet Union in 1925 because Babel was having an affair with a beautiful actress, Tamara Kashrina. Babel and Kashrina had a son, Mikhail, but Kashrina married another writer, Vsevolod Ivanov, soon after the boy was born. Ivanov adopted the boy and raised him as his own. When Babel had trouble securing a passport to visit his wife, Evgenia, and daughter, Nathalie, in Paris in 1932, he appealed to Gorky for help. Gorky pressured Lazar Kaganovich, Stalin's deputy, to take the issue up with his boss. While Babel was ultimately granted a passport, Stalin initially pronounced Babel "not worth spending foreign currency on."[22] In another letter to Kaganovich, Stalin praised the novelist Mikhail Sholokhov as having "great artistic talent . . . not like 'our' frivolous Babel, who keeps writing about things of which he knows nothing (for example, *The Cavalry*)."[23] It is not clear what was worse in Stalin's eyes: Babel writing about things of which he knew nothing, or Babel writing nothing at all.

In front of the expectant audience, Babel initially tried to make a joke of his lack of productivity. He described himself as the "past master" of the art of silence. The audience laughed. What followed was an implicit plea for more time. He pointed out that were he living in a capitalist country he "would have long since croaked from starvation" if he had not sacrificed his art to commercial demands. He applauded the consideration extended toward writers by the authorities in the Soviet Union. "They don't push you in the belly if you have something inside there and they don't insist too much on whether the baby will be a redhead, just light brown, or very dark, on what sort of things he'll have to say," he said. "I am not happy about my silence. Indeed, it saddens me. But perhaps this is one more proof of the attitude toward the writer in this country." It was a weak argument but an argument nonetheless: the tolerance of Babel's failures reflected well on the literary sophistication of the Soviet Union because, unlike the capitalist West, it understood that literature could not be produced to order. This, though, was the Soviet Union that had reformed itself through the Five-Year Plan. It was *productive*. How long would Stalin and his dangerous bureaucrats wait for Babel's next major work to gestate? How long would his silence be tolerated? Babel was no fool. He knew what happened to writers who fell too far from favor. But no one in the Hall of Columns that day, not even as perceptive a writer as Babel, anticipated the true horror of what was coming.

IT WAS LATE IN THE AFTERNOON on December 1, 1934, when Sergei Kirov arrived at the Smolny Institute in Leningrad. He had been working from home, preparing a report that he had to deliver that evening to the Leningrad Party. Having been recently elevated to the Secretariat of the Communist Party, he was a busy man with work on his mind, and perhaps that was why he did not notice the figure that turned away from him in the corridor, nor hear the footsteps as this same man began to follow him. As Kirov turned a corner, the man closed in, drew a Nagant M1895 revolver from his pocket, and shot Kirov in the back of the head. He died instantly.

The assassin was Leonid Nikolaev, the son of a cleaning lady and an alcoholic carpenter, a Communist who had failed at a number of jobs and was unemployed.[24] The murder caused a sensation. Was Nikolaev a lone gunman with a grievance? Had Kirov been sleeping with his wife? Was he part of a dissident political faction within the Soviet Union? In the pay of foreign agents? Or was the killing organized by the NKVD on the orders of Stalin? The latter theory gained much traction outside the Soviet Union in the years and decades that followed. It was rumored that Nikolaev had been arrested and freed on several previous occasions despite being found with a gun. In the aftermath of the killing, Kirov's bodyguard died in a car crash before he could give evidence. The NKVD officials responsible for protecting Kirov were given unusually light sentences. Yet no hard evidence emerged linking Stalin directly to the Kirov murder.[25]

What is indisputable, though, is that Stalin used the murder as a pretext to launch his brutal purges against his enemies on the right and left of the party. As the NKVD sought to unearth the conspiracy behind the murder, new measures were implemented to speed up political trials and for executions to immediately follow sentencing. The investigations led inevitably to Stalin's political opponents, who were supposedly being organized from exile by Leon Trotsky. The man Stalin placed in charge of purging these enemies was Nikolai Yezhov, who at just short of five foot was nicknamed "the bloodthirsty dwarf."[26] A ruthless bureaucrat, Yezhov rose quickly through the ranks, despite his heavy drinking, his sexual promiscuity, and his explosive temper. He took over the investigation into Kirov's murder when Stalin became impatient with the time it was taking to uncover the conspiracy he knew to be there. Yezhov was given the victim's job, replacing Kirov as secretary of the Central Committee. Two years later, in the autumn of 1936, Yezhov was put in charge of the NKVD. The man he replaced in that position, Genrikh Yagoda, would later "confess" to playing a role in the Kirov assassination. Under Yezhov, the purges gathered terrifying momentum.

IN SEPTEMBER 1936, with the Moscow evenings beginning to chill, Babel paced his study, winding a piece of twine repeatedly around his fingers like a rosary. Abruptly he stopped, paused, leaned over one of the pieces of paper arranged on the shelves around him, jotted something down. The pacing resumed. It had been a terrible year, filled with loss and fear, but Babel could not afford to stop working. He needed to write. He had begun longer projects, including a novella, *Kolya Topuz,* about a former Odessan gangster who struggles to adapt to life on a collective farm before trying his hand as a miner. There were the first chapters of a novel about a Jewish widow leaving the shtetl for Moscow. There were fragments of stories. There were translations of

Sholem Aleichem's Yiddish tales. He was writing, he was working, but he was not *finishing,* not *publishing.* There were, though,
mouths to feed: his wife and daughter in Paris, his sister and
mother in Brussels. What he earned he gave away to those he
felt needed it more. Antonina Pirozhkova, a thirty-year-old engineer who became his second wife after they met in 1932, described his kindness as "bordering on the catastrophic."[27] But
these were times in which kindness was needed, so Babel kept
pacing and winding.

The dangers of incurring official disapproval became more
acute after Kirov's assassination. The year began with a warning. Dmitri Shostakovich, the foremost composer in the Soviet
Union, saw his opera, *Lady Macbeth of Mtsensk,* attacked in an
editorial in *Pravda.* The editorial, without a byline, accused
Shostakovich of sacrificing good music that everyone can enjoy
"on the altar of petit-bourgeois formalism." A rumor circulated
that the article was authored by Stalin himself. What followed
was an official campaign against formalism—that is, any kind of
art that seemed abstract or pretentious or elitist. While many
writers panicked, Babel remained calm, toughened by his public
battles with General Budenny. Once again, the literary community leaned on Gorky for help. In March, Malraux visited Moscow, and Babel took him to meet Gorky. Malraux made it clear
that Western left-wing intellectuals were outraged at Shostakovich's treatment and the campaign that followed.[28] The meeting left a deep impression on Gorky, who wrote to Stalin telling
him that there needed to be a change in policy regarding Shostakovich. Gorky told Stalin he had been impressed with Malraux
and that Babel had vouched for his standing in European circles.
Malraux possessed, Gorky conceded, a weakness "typical of the
entire European intelligentsia—'the individual, his creative independence, the freedom of his inner growth' etc." The implication was that this weakness ought to be indulged for the sake of

strengthening the bonds of the Popular Front against fascism, or, as Gorky put it, "the broader unification of the European intelligentsia."[29] Gorky knew how to push the right buttons with Stalin, persuading him to reduce the temperature of the attack on artists.

Babel *did* complete one work, *Maria,* a play set during the Civil War, and gave public readings at Moscow theaters. He was optimistic of staging it in both Russian and Yiddish versions. That, though, was before Kirov was murdered. The play was canceled before its first performance, and when it was published in a theater journal in April 1935, it was accompanied by a critical review by an arts editor from *Pravda.*[30] Babel should not have been surprised: Gorky felt the play exhibited a "Baudelairean passion for rotten meat."[31] The only avenue to publishing left open to Babel was putting out new editions of his old stories—a new collected edition was coming out that very month. Otherwise, he made most of his income from the film industry, writing and editing scripts. The money was good, and he could work under the radar, as his name was easily left out of the credits.[32]

Throughout the summer and into the autumn, Babel's desperate attempts to work were frequently interrupted by visitors. Those whose family and friends had disappeared came to him for help, begging him to put in a good word. Babel could not refuse them and got dressed up and headed out to speak to anyone he thought had influence, former military contacts mostly.[33] This was courageous on Babel's part, for causing too much of a fuss could have made him a target. He missed his chance to escape when Malraux and André Gide had insisted both Babel and Pasternak attend the International Congress of Writers for the Defense of Culture in Paris the previous year (this was the precursor to the Congress attended by Spender in Spain). Perhaps Babel was too optimistic, thinking that with Gorky alive, the situation might improve.

Then, in June, Gorky died. He was laid out in the Hall of Columns, where he had presided at the Congress two years previously. Babel's grief was mingled with dread. "Now they are not going to let me live," he told Antonina.[34] Friends began to disappear, arrested in the night by the secret police. In August came the first of the Show Trials, in the same building that hosted the Writers' Congress and Gorky's lying in state. The most famous defendants were the Old Bolsheviks Grigory Zinoviev and Lev Kamenev, both accused of involvement in a Trotsky-inspired conspiracy to murder not just Kirov but also Stalin and a number of other prominent Communist politicians.[35] Among those charged as conspirators was Efim Dreitser, a friend of Babel's.[36] They were all found guilty and promptly executed. While the trial took place, Stalin's war on writers gathered momentum. A group of supposedly Trotskyist writers were denounced in *Literaturnaya Gazeta*.[37] Babel's name was not among them.[38] He was spared—for now at least—but it was clear that by the autumn of 1936, his situation was getting much worse. His friends in the West could not help him: Malraux was fighting with the Republicans in Spain and Gide, after his most recent visit, had been denounced for damning Stalinism in *Retour de l'URSS*.

FRIENDS AND WRITERS CONTINUED TO DISAPPEAR, but Babel was not taken. He had a new protector, although the protection she offered was laced with danger. She was his former lover, Yevgenia Feigenberg. Babel had sought a reconciliation with his wife in 1927 but, while stopping over in Berlin on his way to Paris, he met Yevgenia, an ambitious and charismatic young woman who was working as a typist at the Soviet Trade Mission.[39] Yevgenia was the daughter of a rabbi from the backwater town of Gomel, which she had escaped by marrying Lazar Khayutin, a journalist in Odessa. In that bustling port town, she immersed herself in the literary scene, where she first came across Babel. But Odessa was not big enough to contain Yevgenia, and so she ditched Khayutin for Alexander Gladun, a man with connections in publishing and the foreign ministry, whom she met while he was on a business trip in the city. He took her first to Moscow and then to London, where Gladun had a position at the Soviet Embassy. That went sour when MI5 uncovered an espionage network run in part by the Soviet Trade Delegation. Britain responded by cutting off diplomatic relations with the USSR. Gladun was forced to return to Moscow; Yevgenia went to work in Berlin. Although still married to Gladun, Yevgenia clearly wanted Babel, and when he met her in Berlin, he did little to resist. They took a drunken tour of the city in the back of a taxi before ending up in Babel's hotel room. He resumed the affair with her on his return to Moscow, where they met at a discreet apartment she kept just outside the city. When the affair ended, they remained friends and occasional collaborators: Yevgenia was an editor at an important journal, *USSR Under Construction*, and she relied on Babel's writing and editing skills to help her.[40]

When the purges escalated, Yevgenia protected Babel. That she could do this was down to a simple fact: Yevgenia was by then the wife of Yezhov, architect of the Great Terror and head of the NKVD.[41] When she first met him, in the resort town of Sochi, she immediately realized that despite his physical and intellectual vulgarity, his hard drinking, his promiscuity, and his sadism, he was a man rising rapidly in the party hierarchy. She was not wrong, and at the height of the purges she was chauffeured to parties in a gold-painted Chrysler Airflow sedan, wearing one of the hundred gowns she collected. The marriage was an open one: Yezhov held drunken orgies in which he slept with men and women; Yevgenia pursued affairs with writers and intellectuals through the literary salon she hosted.[42] Indeed, just the previous month, in August 1936, Babel had been a guest at the Yezhov dacha. Babel had been careful not to resume the affair, though, and he tended to avoid seeing Yevgenia when her husband was present as he detected a "hostile attitude on his part." Needless to say, Babel and Yezhov never talked politics.[43] With her husband in charge of the purges, perhaps she could keep her former lover safe. Babel kept pacing his room, winding the twine around his fingers, working, waiting.

EIGHT

McCarthy

NEW YORK CITY, 1936

ONLY IN RETROSPECT did Mary McCarthy realize the import of her answer. It was November 1936 and as a young reviewer making a name for herself in literary circles, McCarthy had secured an invitation to a Manhattan party in honor of the veteran cartoonist Art Young. It was a radical crowd: Young, now in his seventies, had twice been put on trial under the Espionage Act for his work with *The New Masses*. With the cocktails flowing, this should have been a celebration of left-wing solidarity. The Comintern had adopted the Popular Front policy the previous summer; the International Brigades were on their way to save Madrid; the Communist Party of the USA was backing President Roosevelt. But all was not well. "The whole room was under constraint," McCarthy felt.

The question came from James T. Farrell, a novelist whose depictions of working-class Chicago had earned him the reputation as one of the most influential left-wing writers in the United States: "Do you think Trotsky entitled to a hearing?" McCarthy was thrown. Farrell had become a good friend. He had been impressed by McCarthy's uncompromising attack on the state of literary criticism in a series of articles for *The Nation* the previous year. When she went on to deliver a rave review of *The Young Manhood of Studs Lonigan,* the second novel in his Lonigan series, Farrell sought her out.[1] They were both from the Midwest, of Irish descent, and loved baseball. McCarthy knew that the question was not an innocent one by the way Farrell asked it—this was clearly not idle Party chatter.

McCarthy asked what Trotsky had done. She heard the mutters of disbelief around her. *"Where has she been?"* She was told that Trotsky supposedly collaborated on a counterrevolutionary plot to murder Soviet leaders. McCarthy looked at Farrell helplessly. "What do you want me to say? I don't know anything about it." Farrell kept pressing. "Trotsky denies the charges," he said. "He declares it's a GPU fabrication. Do you think he's entitled to a hearing?" McCarthy felt her mind clear. "Why of course." She went on to agree that yes, Trotsky, did have the right to asylum as well as a hearing.

And that was that. Farrell moved on to another group, taking his loaded question with him. McCarthy did not think much more of it. She had other things on her mind. She was twenty-four and newly single. She had divorced her husband, Harold Johnsrud, in May and spent the summer out west, in Reno and Seattle, visiting family and doing some freelance writing. On her return she was supposed to join her handsome but feckless lover, John Porter, on a trip to Mexico but, bored of him, she had sent him on ahead with no intention of following. Instead she had moved into a small studio on Gay Street in Greenwich Village and thrown herself into the bohemian pleasures of the Manhattan literary scene.

Her timing was poor—the scene was beginning to sour. Four days after the party, McCarthy received a letter from an organization that called itself the Committee for the Defense of Leon Trotsky and was stunned to see her name above the letterhead. She was furious. "This was the kind of thing the Communists were always being accused of pulling," she later recalled. No matter her friendship with Farrell, she was determined to pull out as a matter of principle. Then the phone calls started.

The calls were "not precisely threatening" but "peculiar" and they kept coming, almost always after dark, often quite late. The voice on the line would exhort her in standardized phrases to abandon the Committee and then immediately hang up. "Behind these phone calls," she wrote, "there was a sense of the Party wheeling its forces into would-be disciplined formations, like a fleet or an army maneuvering." Many of those that Farrell and his Trotsky-supporting allies had cajoled into joining the Committee began to drop out.

F. W. Dupee, the literary editor of *The New Masses,* had been given a list of names and told to ask those on it to resign. His first call was to McCarthy. She simply laughed. If intimidation had forced some to back out, it had precisely the opposite effect on the stubborn recipient. "I had been saved from having to decide about the Committee; *I* did not decide it—the Communists with their pressure tactics took the matter out of my hands."[2] Again, she responded in the moment, doing what her gut told her was right. The simple decision to leave her name on that letterhead was "a pivotal decision, perhaps *the* pivotal decision of my life."[3] Battle lines were being drawn over Trotsky and the Moscow Trials and, while the New Yorkers did not know it at the time, the combatants were gearing up for a fight that would go deep into the Cold War—the fight for the future of the left and the role of literature in politics.

McCarthy thought of herself as a woman of the left, but she had always been skeptical of the Communist Party itself. As an undergraduate at Vassar she had had no interest in the "sloppily dressed Socialist girls at college who paraded for Norman Thomas" but in her senior year had suffered a "disturbing shock" when she read about the case of Sacco and Vanzetti, the anarchists who had been sent to the electric chair in 1927 for a crime they had clearly not committed.[4]

In June 1933, just one week after graduating, she had married

Johnsrud, a theater actor based in New York City.[5] By that point, the literary world was deeply enmeshed with the radical left. The Communist Party of the USA had only sixty-five thousand members, but among that group were large numbers of intellectuals, a generation that had been shaped by the Wall Street Crash and the Great Depression. McCarthy was skeptical of front organizations and never joined the Party, but like so many others in her milieu, she was an earnest fellow traveler. She attended the annual May Day parade and went to a debate about the purges that immediately followed the Kirov assassination, but she never shook off her distaste for the way Communists behaved. "The superiority I felt to the Communists I knew had, for me at any rate, good grounding; it was based on their lack of humor, their fanaticism, and the slow drip of cant that thickened their utterance like a nasal catarrh," she wrote. "*And yet* I was tremendously impressed by them. They made me feel petty and shallow; they had, shall I say, a daily ugliness in their life that made my pretty life tawdry." What she never reconciled was the Marxist approach to literature, which she found inflexible, even puritanical. She was not the kind of critic and writer to sacrifice aesthetics to politics—her lacerating reviews were testament to that. She was dedicated to the literary complexity of modernism in a way that she never could be to politics. In the summer of 1934, when Karl Radek ranted and raved about *Ulysses* at the Soviet Writers' Congress in Moscow, McCarthy devoured the newly published Random House edition of Joyce's novel in her Manhattan apartment.

Still, in the summer of 1936 she came very close to joining the Party. A Communist organizer almost convinced her that what was needed were critics like her operating from within. While out West she wrote a rapturous review in *The Nation* for Sylvia Townsend Warner's *Summer Will Show*, a historical novel set in the 1848 revolution in Paris. Warner, the Communist novelist who had so repulsed Spender when they met in Madrid, ended the novel with her embattled heroine uplifted by reading *The Communist Manifesto*. It made a mark on McCarthy. Like so many writers, she was roused by the fight against rising fascism and became obsessed with the Spanish Civil War. "I read the paper every morning with tears of exaltation in my eyes, and my sympathies rained equally on Communists, Socialists, Anarchists, and the brave Catholic Basques," she wrote. "My heart was tense and swollen with Popular Front solidarity. I applauded the Lincoln Battalion, protested non-intervention, hurried into Wanamaker's to look for cotton-lace stockings: I was boycotting silk on account of Japan in China. I was careful to smoke only union-made cigarettes; the white package with Sir Walter Raleigh's portrait came proudly out of my pocketbook to rebuke Chesterfields and Luckies."[6]

All the while she was, in her own words, "ignorant of the fissure that was opening," a fissure caused by the Moscow Trials.[7] "Nobody had told me of the trial of Zinoviev and Kamenev— the trial of the sixteen—or of the new trial that was being prepared in Moscow, the trial of Pyatakov and Radek."[8] The speed with which politicians and writers could fall from grace was startling: just two years after being given his platform at the Writers' Congress and Radek was in the dock. When those late-night phone calls started, McCarthy began asking awkward questions. Some fifty intellectuals signed an open letter, published in *The New Masses,* urging the board of the Trotsky Defense League to resign. These efforts to silence Trotsky's supporters only emboldened McCarthy. Curled up on her sofa in her Gay Street studio, McCarthy read transcripts of the second trial. She was the daughter and granddaughter of lawyers, and she made short work of the prosecution's case. It was full of "glaring discrepancies" and easily disprovable claims, the most obvious of which was that there had been a conspiratorial meeting between

Lev Sedov, Trotsky's son, and E. S. Holtzman at the Hotel Bristol in Copenhagen in 1936.[9] The Hotel Bristol had burned down in 1912. The more she read the more obvious it became: it was "a monstrous frame up."

This was no easy truth to tell in Manhattan. Stalinism was in intellectual fashion, and to be a Stalinist "was what smart, successful people in that New York world were."[10] To claim the trials were a sham was to commit not just a political heresy but a social one, too. "The Moscow trials were an historical fact and those of us who tried to undo them were uneasily felt to be crackpots, who were trying to turn the clock back," McCarthy wrote.[11] And it was not just the trials. If they were a lie, then what else? The scales began to fall from McCarthy's eyes. She began to preach with the zeal of a convert. Over lunch with Margaret Marshall, the books editor of *The Nation,* it emerged that her good friend Dwight Macdonald, who described himself as a "mild fellow traveler," had swallowed the Moscow line on the trials.[12] "[McCarthy and Marshall] took it for granted that the Moscow Trials—the second of which had just been concluded—were frame-ups," Macdonald recalled. "As usual, I was incredulous. I said it couldn't be and why did they confess and so on. And also, as usual, to my credit, I was somewhat shaken. Shaken enough to buy a few days later the transcript of the trial, which the comrades were foolish enough to sell at a cheap price. And when I read the record of the second Moscow trial I concluded that Mary had been right, that indeed it was a frame-up."[13]

It felt good to have a cause. McCarthy had become concerned about her bohemian lifestyle. "I realized one day that in twenty-four hours I had slept with three different men," she wrote.[14] She was living at an intense pitch, working as an editorial assistant for the publisher Covici-Friede during the day, writing reviews in spare moments, and attending meetings of the Trotsky committee and socializing with authors in the evenings. While she had been annoyed with Farrell for his presumption in signing her up to the Committee for the Defense of Leon Trotsky, her friendship with him survived in large part out of solidarity in the face of Stalinist hostility. A fixture in McCarthy's calendar were Farrell's Lexington Avenue parties, which became increasingly fractious as the trials divided former friends. "An orthodoxy was cracking, like ice floes on the Volga," McCarthy wrote.[15] Trotsky's supporters were organizing, with Farrell leading the charge. By this time Trotsky, found guilty in absentia in Moscow, was seeking asylum in Mexico and a decision was made to hold a countertrial in which he would be given the opportunity to defend himself against the accusations being made back in Moscow. The Party again mobilized its forces, and an open letter was published condemning these American Trotskyists, signed by Malcolm Cowley, Lillian Hellman, Theodore Dreiser, and other Soviet-sympathizing writers.

In April 1937, a commission of inquiry, chaired by the venerable American philosopher John Dewey, traveled down to Frida Kahlo and Diego Rivera's villa in Coyoacan, Mexico, and spent eight days examining the evidence against Trotsky. The villa was fortified, and armed guards patrolled the streets outside. The Soviet government and the Communist Party USA had been invited to send representatives but unsurprisingly declined. Just as unsurprisingly, the commission found that the Moscow Trials were indeed "frame-ups" and that Trotsky was not guilty. Farrell was in attendance and described it, somewhat breathlessly, as a "spectacle rare in history," like watching Robespierre or Cromwell defending themselves, although these two obviously lacked the "intellectual breadth" of Trotsky.[16] Farrell relished the drama of the moment; after the hearing, when Trotsky went for a holiday to Cuernavaca, Farrell "took over the guard of Trotsky's papers . . . sitting on a table with pistols in holsters, bullets strung across his shoulders and chest, and a machine gun in hand."[17]

BACK IN NEW YORK, McCarthy mixed sex and politics. At one of Farrell's parties she met Philip Rahv, whose intellectual intensity and thick Slavic accent made him a formidable proposition (the writer Delmore Schwartz called him "manic-impressive"). Knowing he spoke Russian, German, French, Yiddish, and Hebrew, and that he was living off the little he earned from the Federal Writers' Project, she commissioned him to read some foreign manuscripts for Covici-Friede. The professional soon turned personal. "My dear," she wrote one friend, "I have the most Levantine lover!"[18]

Rahv had been a true believer in the Communist cause but his faith was failing. As a child in Ukraine, he lived through the revolution, hiding in his parents' shop during the worst of the fighting. He emigrated to the United States and lived in poverty as a young man, sleeping on park benches and forced to wait in the breadline. He was a determined autodidact, however, and began writing poetry and reading up on radical politics. He was recruited to the Party and began working as a journalist for pro-Communist newspapers. In 1934 Rahv and William Phillips (whose Jewish parents had also immigrated from Ukraine) became the editors of *Partisan Review,* a magazine founded by the John Reed Club of New York. The John Reed Clubs were Communist organizations, and therefore *Partisan Review* was expected to follow the Party line from Moscow. Yet even in this early incarnation of the magazine, Rahv and Phillips expressed discomfort with "mechanically applied Marxism" and the "sloganized and inorganic writing" being championed in the Soviet Union.[19] While they made the case for politically engaged literature, they did not think that this should automatically invalidate the great modernist writers they loved, such as Eliot, Faulkner, Joyce, and Proust. These, surely, were writers who *attacked* bourgeois society, and their works could hardly be read as unthinking expressions of it. The Soviet Writers' Congress had made an enemy of modernism, however, and it was a position Rahv and Phillips found difficult to reconcile with their own thinking.

Partisan Review folded when the John Reed Clubs were dissolved because they were perceived as too hard-line and doctrinaire to fit with the Comintern's policy shift to the Popular Front. Adopting a friendlier, more tolerant approach to cultural policy, the Comintern organized the First Congress of American Writers at the Mecca Temple and the progressive New School for Social Research in 1935 to celebrate cultural solidarity in the face of the fascist threat. This was the first time leftist American writers had come together en masse to speak publicly, and the idea was clearly modeled on the Soviet Writers' Congress of the previous year. In the final session of the Congress, the League of American Writers was established, an organization that was open to fellow travelers as well as Party members.

To Rahv and Phillips, there was something cynical in the way the Party was changing positions, and the Moscow Trials deepened their suspicion. They were bolstered by Sidney Hook, Phillips's former philosophy professor, who had become the most prominent American Communist to turn publicly against the Party. In the late spring of 1937, McCarthy and Rahv moved into the apartment of one of their friends, on Beekman Place in midtown Manhattan. They read about the May Days fighting in Barcelona, in which Orwell was involved, and were appalled by the way the Communists were treating the POUM. McCarthy recalled a cocktail party at which she got into a furious row with the playwright Lillian Hellman about the murder of POUM leader Andrés Nin. (In her *Intellectual Memoirs* McCarthy admits her memory of this event is hazy and it might well have been an argument with another ardent Stalinist writer, Leane Zugsmith.)[20]

McCarthy and her friends knew that they had to keep up the momentum generated by the Trotsky countertrial in Coyoacan. The very day Farrell returned from Mexico, he met with McCarthy, Rahv, and their allies to plan for the Second Congress of American Writers, scheduled for June 1937. The Party, buoyed by the success of the First Congress, had ambitious plans for the sequel and saw in it an opportunity for high-level cultural propaganda. Writers from any background were welcome—the more famous the better—as long as they were anti-fascist. The organizers secured a significant coup in persuading Ernest Hemingway to speak at the opening-night event at Carnegie Hall; he was the most famous American writer around and came fresh from reporting on the front lines in Spain. McCarthy was determined that the Congress should not become an uncritical anti-fascist love-in, and the decision was made to get into the sessions and confront the Stalinists on their own turf.

The night of June 4, 1937, Carnegie Hall sold out all 3,500 seats (Farrell was among many who failed to get a ticket). To the consternation of the organizers, Hemingway did not show up on time, and when he finally arrived, he had clearly been drinking. He paced the wings muttering to himself: "Why the hell am I making this speech?" Despite his tough-guy persona, Hemingway suffered from dreadful stage fright—his only real previous public-speaking engagement had been the reading with Spender in Paris the previous month—and he was only persuaded into speaking at the Congress by his good friend Archibald MacLeish.[21]

If securing Hemingway's presence represented a triumph for the Congress's Communist organizers, the content of his speech, with its emphasis on the necessity of the individual writer to tell truth to power, would have made the more doctrinaire among them a little queasy. "A writer's problem does not change," Hemingway said. "He himself changes but his problem remains the same. It is always how to write truly and having found what is true, to protect it in such a way that it becomes a part of the experience of the person who reads it."

The remainder of the Congress took place at the New School, where 353 writer-delegates took part in closed sessions. On the Sunday morning, McCarthy, Rahv, Phillips, Macdonald, and Eleanor Clark attended a panel on criticism presided over by the Marxist literary critic Granville Hicks.[22] With McCarthy leading the charge, they stood up and attacked the factionalism of the Party and the narrow way in which it interpreted the purpose of literature.[23] The delegates did not take them all that seriously: Earl Browder, general secretary of the Communist Party of the USA, condescendingly dismissed them as "muddle headed," and Hicks accused them of "sentimentalism."

Just a week after the Congress a third trial took place in Moscow, although this one was conducted in secret. What the Kremlin called "The Case of the Trotskyist Anti-Soviet Military Organization" was a brutal purge of the Red Army, in which many high-ranking officers, including Marshal Mikhail Tukhachevsky, a brilliant strategist and hero of the Russian Civil War, were sentenced to death. Once news of the trial filtered out, McCarthy felt "on the one hand, grief and horror; on the other, exultation."[24] Painful as it might be, this small but growing band of left-wing dissenters was being proved right. Now they needed to be heard—they needed their own magazine.

Rahv and Phillips wanted to revive *Partisan Review* as a platform from which to champion both Marxism and literary modernism but struggled to find the money to operate independently. It was Macdonald who introduced them to George L. K. Morris, a wealthy abstract painter whom he knew from Yale. Morris agreed to put up the $3,000 a year needed to get *Parti-*

san Review operating again. Another Yale friend, Dupee, left *The New Masses* to join this new group of anti-Stalinists (both Rahv and Dupee were promptly kicked out of the Party). In December 1937, *Partisan Review* was relaunched with an editorial board of Rahv, Phillips, McCarthy, Macdonald, Dupee, and Morris.

The office was in Union Square, where, as McCarthy described it, "radical demonstrations were always held and which was surrounded by cheap dress shops, cafeterias, subway kiosks and run-down office buildings."[25] They were a provocative island of anti-Stalinism surrounded by Communist-sympathizing hostility, a group bonded by their experience of calling out the trials for the shams they were. The editorial statement of the first relaunched edition stressed that the new magazine was committed to independent literature: "Formerly associated with the Communist Party, *Partisan Review* strove from the first against its drive to equate the interests of literature with those of factional politics. Our reappearance on an independent basis signifies our conviction that the totalitarian trend is inherent in that movement and that it can no longer be combatted from within."[26] It was, according to McCarthy, their commitment to publishing modernist writers of little (or dubious) political commitment that was truly heretical. She wrote that "the daring of our attitude was summed up in the statement that we would print a poem by T. S. Eliot if we could get one (later we did)."[27] Eliot was a cultural elitist, a monarchist, and a Catholic convert—about as far from the ideal socialist realist writer as it was possible to get. In 1940, *Partisan Review* published "East Coker," one of his obscurely brilliant *Four Quartets*.

From the first issue, the magazine was saturated with prestige. It included an extract from Farrell's new novel and a short story by Delmore Schwartz that announced a formidable new talent. There was a strange prose poem by Pablo Picasso, accompanied by etchings depicting General Franco as Quixote, which the editors claimed was Picasso's first "politically-inspired art" (a bit of editorial exaggeration: he had painted *Guernica* the previous June).[28] There were poems by Wallace Stevens and James Agee, and book reviews by Sidney Hook and Lionel Trilling. Lionel Abel, the playwright, critic, and translator, wrote an admiring piece about the Italian anti-Communist novelist Ignazio Silone (who would be published in the magazine himself in the third issue). The masthead weighed in, too: Dupee wrote an essay on Kafka, Rahv wrote an essay on Hemingway, and McCarthy penned a "Theater Chronicle," the first of a regular column. Macdonald, in an essay that perfectly summed up the brash self-confidence of the relaunched magazine, wrote a piece that made fun of *The New Yorker* and its readership. Finally, there was an essay on Flaubert's politics by Edmund Wilson, arguably America's foremost literary critic.

For all their efforts to focus on the literary and eschew the political, the issue of the magazine's perceived Trotskyism was impossible to escape. In the months leading up to the publication of the first edition there were numerous attacks in the Communist press. The most evocative headline belonged to the *Daily Worker*: "A Literary Snake Sheds His Skin for Trotsky." In Austria and Germany, the Soviet Union and the Comintern had successfully crushed left-wing groups that did not toe the Party line; in Spain, despite the purported inclusivity of the Popular Front, members of non-Communist Marxist groups, including the POUM, had been imprisoned and murdered; in the Soviet Union anyone even tenuously associated with dissent from Stalin was for the gulag or the execution chamber. Now, in the United States, a new generation of anti-Communist leftists was rallying around *Partisan Review*. It was a development with far-reaching consequences for the cultural Cold War.

Looking back on this period McCarthy claimed that the Trotskyism of the group was "an exaggeration."[29] This might be a little too much revisionism. Certainly, that first editorial statement warned that the fights ahead would center on charges from the Communists that *Partisan Review* was little more than a vehicle for Trotsky and his ideas. The editors assumed—correctly—that they would be accused of fascism through the "convenient medium of Trotskyism" and that "every effort" would be made "to excommunicate the new generation."[30] And they *did* provide a platform, and not just for avowed Trotskyists, such as the American journalist Herbert Solow and Victor Serge, the Russian writer released in 1936 from Soviet prison; by the August–September 1938 edition, they had begun to publish the old man himself.[31] Trotsky's "Art and Politics" was a carefully chosen essay—it was Trotsky's cultural politics, and his belief that literature did not have to be dictated by a Party line, that appealed to those in the *Partisan Review* circle. Trotsky, it seemed, had found an important new platform for his ideas at the very moment at which the Soviet Union, through the Moscow Show Trials and, eventually, through the Nazi-Soviet pact, was losing credibility with the foreign intellectuals it had fought so hard to seduce.

The trials were not over, however. The accusations might have been elaborate fictions, but the sentences were real. The network of Old Bolsheviks and Red Army heroes who were "complicit" in the murder of Kirov and who had "conspired" with the British, Germans, and Japanese to murder Stalin was broken, all but one of its members executed. Only that one remained at large, and it was time for him to serve his sentence.

SYLVIA AGELHOFF WAS A DEVOTED STUDENT of Sidney Hook at New York University. Impressed by her mentor's work in helping organize the defense of Trotsky, she became a devoted Trotskyist herself. In September 1938, she arrived in Paris for the first

Congress of the Fourth International, a meeting of Trotsky's supporters, where she was to work as an interpreter. This was not without risk. Trotsky's son had died in Paris in February of "complications" after a suspicious appendectomy; "Etienne," an NKVD agent posing as a Trotskyist (real name Mark Zborowski), had checked Sedov into a private clinic and informed Moscow of his actions, with reliable results. In July, a corpse was found in the Seine.[32] The head and legs had been chopped off (the legs were subsequently found in a sack; the head was not found). It was Rudolf Klement, Trotsky's German translator and the man who should have been chairing the Congress.

At the Congress, "Etienne" introduced Agelhoff to a playboy by the name of Jacques Mornard, who claimed to have deserted from the Belgian army. Mornard seduced Agelhoff, buying her expensive gifts and taking her to sophisticated restaurants. Mornard was not really Mornard, though—he was Ramon Mercader, a highly trained NKVD agent. Mercader had been recruited at some point in 1936 by Leonid Eitingon, who ran the Barcelona NKVD station during the Spanish Civil War. Eitingon was the lover of Caridad Mercader, a radical Spanish leftist and Ramon's mother, and he arranged for her son, who then commanded a Republican army unit, to receive instruction in guerrilla warfare. Ramon was a keen student and helped train foreigners recruited by the NKVD—including, it is speculated, David Crook, the Englishman who spied on Orwell.[33] In the summer of 1937, Ramon traveled to Moscow, where he received further training.

With the Spanish-language skills he acquired in the war and his existing experience as an assassin, Eitingon was charged by Moscow with the mission to kill Trotsky (Operation UTKA, which translates as "duck"). He put his protégé, Mercader, into play. With Eitingon pulling the strings, in the autumn of 1939, Caridad and Ramon relocated to New York, where Mercader resumed his affair with Agelhoff after a six-month hiatus.[34] He also assumed a new identity, telling Agelhoff this was to avoid being drafted by the Belgian army. He was now Frank Jacson, a French-Canadian businessman with interests in, of all places, Mexico.

When Jacson-Mornard-Mercader traveled to Mexico City for work, Agelhoff came with him. Her sister, Ruth, had been Trotsky's secretary, and she was soon making herself useful at his villa. Mercader played a patient game, slowly inveigling his way into the trust of those around Trotsky.

Unbeknownst to Mercader, another assassination mission was being run in parallel. At 4 A.M. on May 24, a group disguised in police and military uniforms and led by the Mexican muralist David Siqueiros and the Soviet illegal Iosef Grigulevich (who'd led the team that captured, tortured, and murdered Andrés Nin), broke into Trotsky's compound and opened fire. They kept shooting until they were out of ammunition, then fled. Somehow, despite the seventy-three bullet holes the police later found in the walls, they failed to kill Trotsky, who had hidden on the floor of the bedroom. With one exception, nobody had been hurt; the body of the American bodyguard, Robert Sheldon Harte, who had let the assassins in (his complicity is disputed), was found in a well, covered in lime, a month later.[35] Grigulevich supposedly put the lack of success down to his team suffering from "fear and tequila."[36]

The failed raid should have made Mercader's job even harder. The security of the compound was drastically increased—more fortifications, more guards—but that was not a problem, as "Jacson" became a trusted part of the Trotsky circle. It was through the trust he built that he managed to get Trotsky alone in his office, ostensibly to read an article "Jacson" had composed about American Trotskyists. Despite the heat, he had a long raincoat draped over his arm, inside of which was $890, a fourteen-inch knife, a .45 Star automatic pistol, and a pick, its handle shortened for concealment.

Mercader struck Trotsky on the head with the pick. The plan had been to kill him with one blow and then to leave as quickly and quietly as possible. His mother and Eitingon were waiting around the corner in a getaway car. Mercader's courage failed him at the last moment and he closed his eyes as he swung. He smashed a hole into Trotsky's skull, but his target did not lose consciousness. Blood pouring from the wound, Trotsky let out a wail before jumping on Mercader and biting his hand. Joe Hansen, an American bodyguard, sounded the alarm and discovered the blood-drenched Trotsky stumbling out of his study. Another bodyguard, Harold Robins, beat the dazed Mercader to the floor, demanding he reveal his identity. Mercader denied he was working for the NKVD, even when Hansen broke his own hand punching him in the head. Trotsky was rushed to the hospital, operated on, and slipped into a coma. He died the following day, August 21, 1940.

To McCarthy and the *Partisan Review* circle it was further proof of Stalin's cynicism and ruthlessness. Many other writers and thinkers who had remained loyal to the Soviet Union during the trials had finally given up on Stalinism after the signing of the Molotov-Ribbentrop pact the previous year; in the elegant phrasing of a *Partisan Review* editorial, the Communist Party USA "molted almost its entire brilliant plumage of fellow travelers."[37] The following year, when Adolf Hitler launched Operation Barbarossa and invaded the Soviet Union, he precipitated an allegiance of convenience with the Allies. For a few crucial years, Uncle Joe was a friend of the Western powers. But the anti-Communist left, mourning the death of the last of the Old Bolsheviks and shaken by the reach of Stalin's hit men, was not about to forget his crimes.

NINE

Babel

MOSCOW, 1939

THEY CAME FOR BABEL BEFORE DAWN. Asleep in his dacha in Peredelkino, the writers' commune outside of Moscow, he was awakened by knocking at his bedroom door. "Who's there?" he asked. "Me," replied Antonina, his wife, with strain in her voice. Babel immediately knew something was not right; she was supposed to be at their apartment in Moscow. He dressed and opened the door. He barely had time to register the two men in military uniform standing behind Antonina before they pushed past her and ordered him to raise his hands. Babel stood, silent, as they searched his pockets for a concealed weapon. He was ordered to remain in the bedroom while they searched the dacha. Babel and Antonina sat huddled on the bed, barely speaking. They had waited for this for too long to be surprised, but it took time for the gravity of the situation to sink in. So many of their friends had disappeared like this, in the night, never to be heard from again. Antonina had had more time to process the situation: she was at the couple's Moscow apartment when the men pounded on the door at 5 A.M., claiming there was someone hiding in the attic. They said they needed to find Babel, as he had information about this suspect. The lies were half-hearted; Antonina knew Babel was their quarry but there was nothing she could do. Holding each other, the couple listened as the men went through Babel's desk and drawers. They piled up his man-

uscripts and tied them off into bundles. They gathered up notebooks and letters. Altogether they filled nine files with papers,
the work Babel had spent the last decade wrestling with.[1] These
were the only copies of the unfinished novels and stories he was
working on, and they now belonged to the NKVD. "They didn't
let me finish," was all Babel said.[2]

With the search complete, the officers ordered the couple
out to the waiting car. Things moved fast. In an undertone only
Antonina could hear, Babel told her to "inform André," that is,
to get a message out to Malraux in Paris. Perhaps his old friend
might intervene, make some noise, embarrass Stalin into clemency. The couple were bundled into the car, and as the sun came
up, they were driven to Moscow. On the drive, Babel began to
recover himself. He even ventured a joke. "So, I guess you don't
get much sleep, do you?" he said to the NKVD officer next to
him. When the car arrived at the infamous Lubyanka prison,
Babel got out, kissed Antonina, told her they would see each
other again, and walked through the gates. They both knew
few walked back out. The same day the NKVD sealed off his
Moscow study and cleared it of all written material. In the weeks
and months that followed copies of his books were withdrawn
from libraries. The man had been arrested; the writer was being
erased.

BABEL WAS ARRESTED on May 15, 1939, when the worst of the
Great Terror was over. At the peak of the purges in 1937 there
seemed no rhyme or reason for most of the arrests. Anything—
gossip, rumors, lies—could be used as pretext by the NKVD.
Sometimes there was no pretext at all, and people were simply
arrested by quota. So how had Babel survived so long? There was
certainly evidence to damn him in the eyes of the bloodthirsty
authorities. For all the care he took to avoid incurring official

displeasure with his speech at the 1934 Writers Congress, he was privately indiscreet about the event and was overheard by an NKVD informant. In an undated report, Babel was quoted saying: "We have to demonstrate to the world the unanimity of the Union's literary forces. But seeing as how all this is being done artificially, under the stick, the congress feels dead, like a tsarist parade. Let our press go ahead and overinflate the stupid fabrications about the delegates' colossal enthusiasm. After all, there are also correspondents from foreign newspapers who will shed true light on this literary requiem." In the context *tsarist* was a particularly dangerous choice of adjective and *requiem* an unwise choice of noun.

This, though, was nothing compared to what he was caught saying in the immediate aftermath of the first show trial in the summer of 1936. An NKVD report, which was submitted directly to Yezhov in September, detailed a conversation between Babel and the filmmaker Sergei Eisenstein in an Odessa hotel room. The room had presumably been bugged, as neither man would have dared speak like they did in front of someone they did not absolutely trust.[3] In reference to the purges, Babel was quoted as saying, "You cannot imagine or appreciate the scale on which people perished and what significance this has for history. This is a terrible business. You and I, of course, know nothing, whether or not there has been a struggle with the 'boss' due to personal attitudes of a number of people toward him. Who made the Revolution? Who was in the first Politburo?" At this point Babel took up a piece of paper and wrote down the names of all the Old Bolsheviks. Once done he crossed out those who had died, fled, or been executed. There was a lot of crossing out. Babel was careful to tear up the paper until it was illegible. Then came a further indiscretion. "But take Trotsky," Babel said. "You cannot imagine his charm and the strength of his influence on the people he met. Trotsky will indisputably continue the struggle and many will support him."[4] Babel was speaking from experience: he had discussed literature with Trotsky at a mutual friend's salon in 1924.

Very many people were being killed for far less; they, though, were not protected by Yezhov's wife. When the Babel-Eisenstein report landed on Yezhov's desk, the "bloodthirsty dwarf" was approaching the zenith of his power. On September 26, 1936, he was made People's Commissar of Internal Affairs and effectively became the second most powerful man in the USSR.[5] At forty-one, he was of a younger generation (a year younger than Babel, in fact) being favored by Stalin and he worked with the "boss" directly, almost every day. Records show that during the course of the terror he met with Stalin more than 1,100 times. Yezhov was an obsessive in his work, a bureaucrat with an eye for detail: during the height of the purges he apparently specified what types of bushes should be planted over the mass graves.

The organization of the show trials required meticulous planning, as each trial included the denunciations that enabled its successor. At the first show trial, of the "Trotsky-Zinoviev Center" in August 1936, the seeds were sown for the second trial, in January 1937, at which Karl Radek implicated the old Bolshevik Nikolai Bukharin, previously a rival to Stalin for the leadership of the Party, among many others. Radek escaped with ten years of hard labor as a reward for his work but was killed in the camps, reputedly by an NKVD operative. The third, and biggest, show trial, of the so-called "Right Trotskyites," resulted in the execution of Bukharin, Alexei Rykov, and several other prominent Soviet politicians. Yagoda, former head of the NKVD, was also executed.

Indeed, running parallel to the show trials was the more discreet, but no less ruthless, purge of the NKVD itself. At a speech to the Officer's Club in March 1937, Yezhov gleefully told the assembled secret policemen that their old boss, Yagoda, was a

German spy and had been so since 1907. Three thousand of their colleagues had been arrested and were to be executed. "I may be small in stature," he told them, "but my hands are strong—Stalin's hands." His zeal was palpable. "We are launching a major attack on the Enemy; let there be no resentment if we bump someone with an elbow. Better that ten innocent people should suffer than one spy get away. When you chop wood, chips fly."[6] Chips flew in the military, too. In the January trial, Radek implicated Marshal Tukhachevsky, the most powerful general in the Red Army. He and seven other high-ranking officers were executed after a secret trial in June. A devastating purge of military officers followed. Anyone who served in the Spanish Civil War—whether as officer, diplomat, spy, or journalist—was also in grave danger, as the denunciations and betrayals entangled almost everyone.[7]

The trials were just the public tip of the iceberg—beneath the waterline was carnage. The purges worked in two ways. The first was the liquidation of individuals identified by the NKVD and signed off by the Politburo. Many of these were people Yezhov knew personally, both old friends and former colleagues.[8] The second were the quotas for arrests and executions farmed out to the regions. These were targets that had to be met, and victims needed to be found. It is estimated 1,500,000 were arrested and 700,000 executed during the Great Terror.[9] Writers were ruthlessly targeted. As many as 2,000 were arrested, and 1,500 of these were either executed or died in the camps. Of the 700 delegates who attended that first Writers Congress in the summer of 1934, only 50 made it to the second Congress when it was held in 1954.[10]

Yet one literary salon was protected. While her husband showed up for morning meetings with blood spatter on his cuffs, his wife, Yevgenia, enjoyed the life of a Kremlin socialite. She was full of energy at official functions, capable of tempting even the stuffiest members of the Politburo into a foxtrot. When she was not living the high life with her husband's political friends, she hosted a salon of literary types, several of whom she had affairs with. Babel was her favorite but she also slept with Mikhail Koltsov, a leading Russian journalist who reported on the Spanish Civil War, and Vsevolod Meyerhold, the great theater director.[11] Her latest fling was Mikhail Sholokhov, author of *And Quiet Flows the Don,* a novel that Stalin particularly enjoyed. Indeed, Sholokhov's favor with Stalin was one of the reasons Yevgenia was attracted to him; with the purges gathering momentum she realized she would need all the help she could get.

In the first months of 1938, Yezhov overreached. He was exhausted from his nocturnal schedule of murder, yet he continued to arrest and execute with frenzied determination. He drank heavily and, when drunk, became boastful, claiming not even the most powerful members of the Politburo were safe from him. At one banquet he drank himself insensible.[12] The wind began to turn. When sober, Yezhov could read the signs as well as anyone. Some of his deputies were arrested, and members of the Politburo began complaining to Stalin about Yezhov's excesses. In August, Stalin informed Yezhov that he would be getting a new deputy: Lavrentiy Beria. Where Yezhov was frantic, Beria was controlled. Yezhov watched the torture of prisoners; Beria took part. As Yezhov had consumed Yagoda, so Beria was to consume Yezhov. Yezhov started executing anyone he feared might incriminate him in any way, but the noose continued to tighten. He drunkenly raged against Beria and even claimed, in one boozy bout, that Stalin should be killed.[13]

Then came humiliation. Yezhov found out about Yevgenia's affair with Sholokhov and used his NKVD resources to bug the hotel room in which they met. After reading the transcript of their sex session, Yezhov slapped his wife in front of friends. Sholokhov realized there was something fishy going on. When he discovered he was being followed, Sholokhov complained straight to Stalin. After Gorky's death, he became the only writer who could confront Stalin in this way. Yezhov was promptly summoned to the Politburo, where he was forced to apologize to the man who was sleeping with his wife.

Yezhov wriggled on the hook. He discovered Beria was going to use Yevgenia to trap him; she had worked in London in the late 1920s and it was decided she was an English spy. Stalin previously suggested Yezhov divorce Yevgenia, and now he went through with it.[14] After he had her diplomat ex-husband— Gladun—shot, another ex-lover, the publisher Simon Uritsky, began to talk. Uritsky told the NKVD about Yevgenia's affair with Babel. Amid all this Yevgenia had a breakdown and was taken first to a sanatorium in the Crimea, then transferred to the Vorovsky Nerve Clinic outside Moscow, from where she wrote a pleading letter to Stalin. He ignored it. Yevgenia managed to get a letter out to Yezhov and offered to commit suicide. Perhaps she realized that her death would increase the chances of their adopted nine-year-old daughter, Natasha, surviving. Yezhov sent Yevgenia sleeping pills concealed in a bouquet of flowers, and on November 19 she took an overdose, dying two days later. "Stalin can't understand her death," Babel told Antonina days later. "His own nerves are made of steel so he just cannot understand how, in other people, they give out."[15]

Yezhov resigned from the NKVD on November 23. The monster he fed turned on him. He was isolated, shunned, and consoled himself with "drunken bisexual orgies in his Kremlin apartment."[16] As the purges slowed down, Stalin and his circle blamed Yezhov for the murderous excesses of the previous years and began to call it the Yezhovshchina, the times of Yezhov. He was allowed to linger on in the Politburo and the Central Committee until April 10, 1939, when he was arrested by Beria and locked up in Sukhanov prison.[17] He confessed to having spied for England, Japan, *and* Poland. And, whether it was a conscious act of revenge, or whether he just cracked under torture, he also denounced his wife's former lovers, among them Meyerhold, Koltsov, and, of course, Babel. All three were arrested on the same day.

ON BEING PROCESSED INTO LUBYANKA, Babel was subjected to the usual degrading rituals. They took his passport, the keys to his flat and his dacha, his toothpaste, his shaving cream, a sponge, and finally his garters and braces, the latter to prevent him attempting suicide. Then he was stripped and searched, photographed, and fingerprinted. He had a better sense of the NKVD than many other writers who fell into their hands, given his three-week stint as a translator for the Cheka in December 1917. He remained fascinated by the secret police, and it was rumored he had tried to write a novel about the Cheka. While staying with Gorky, Babel once found himself alone with Yagoda, Yezhov's predecessor as head of the NKVD. "Genrikh Grigorevich, tell me, how should someone act if he falls into your men's paws?" Babel asked. Yagoda replied, "Deny everything, whatever the charges, just say *no* and keep on saying *no*. If one denies everything, we are powerless."[18] Perhaps this was going through Babel's mind as the guards led him through the Lubyanka courtyard to the Inner Prison, the six-story yellow building where he was to be locked up. Babel might also, though, have recalled that Yagoda ultimately confessed to having murdered Kirov, to having ordered the poisoning of Maxim Gorky and his son, to having been part of a coup, and to having attempted to kill Yezhov by spraying mercury on the curtains of his office.[19] Even Yagoda was clearly unable to deny everything.

On May 29, the guards hauled Babel out of his cell and took him to the investigators' office, where he was cross-examined by two NKVD interrogators, whose names are given in the file as Kuleshov and Schwartzmann. We have only their account of what transpired so, as Babel taught his readers, it is essential to read between the lines, to be sensitive to what is not there.

Q: You have been arrested for treacherous anti-Soviet activities. Do you acknowledge your guilt?
A: No, I do not.

Q: How can you reconcile that declaration of innocence with the fact of your arrest?
A: I consider my arrest the result of a fateful coincidence and of my own inability to write. During the last few years I have not published a single major work and this might be considered sabotage and an unwillingness to write under Soviet conditions.

Q: You wish to say you have been arrested as a writer? Does that not strike you as an excessively naïve explanation of your arrest?[20]

Babel was prepared to confess but only to the "wrong" crime: he was guilty of failing to write literature that conformed to the edicts of socialist realism, and he was guilty of failing to write. This confession was never going to satisfy Kuleshov and Schwartzmann, though—they were not interested in literature.[21] They pushed Babel on his trips abroad, on his contacts with Trotskyists. Babel was instructed to write down his life story and document all his encounters with "suspicious elements." He told them about the literary salon he had attended in 1924 at Alexander Voronksy's, at which Radek had introduced Trotsky as a surprise guest. Kuleshov and Schwartzmann were getting somewhere.

For three days Babel held out but after that the resistance he offered began to crumble. His interrogators led him to construct a narrative by which his literary silence was explained by his participation in a conspiracy. "Undoubtedly constant contact with Trotskyists had a fatal effect on my writing," he said. "For a long while it concealed from me the true visage of our Soviet land, and was the cause of the spiritual and literary crisis that I suffered for many years."[22] Babel began to denounce his own work, especially *Red Cavalry*. He confessed to grooming a younger generation of writers: "my reputation for literary 'independence' and as a 'fighter for quality' attracted those who were inclined towards formalism."[23] He admitted mocking the Writers' Union and telling these young writers that Soviet literature was in a state of decline. He admitted talking with intellectuals inimical to the Soviet Union when he lived in Paris and that he succumbed to the "Westernizing tendencies" of his friend and fellow writer Ilya Ehrenburg, a champion of experimental modernist writing. Babel "confessed" that it was Ehrenburg who had encouraged him to read Hemingway and Céline. The interrogators were not interested in this "literary talk," these "anti-Soviet conversations"; they wanted to know about "directly hostile activities." Babel had already incriminated himself, but the interrogators wanted more. And they got it.

"In 1933, during my second visit to Paris," Babel said, "I was recruited by the writer André Malraux to spy for France."[24] He was previously willing to confess to being an insubordinate writer, to exaggerate his Trotskyist connections. This, though, was a departure into the absurd. Why would Babel confess to taking part in international espionage? Antonina later remembered a conversation she had with Babel at the height of the trials, in which they struggled to understand why the accused were confessing to such outlandish conspiracies. The idea that the prisoners were being tortured was unthinkable, Antonina recalled.[25] It is hard to think Babel was not more skeptical; he had seen the workings of political violence with his own eyes during the Civil War.

The NKVD used torture as a matter of course during the Great Terror. It even had a cozy euphemism: "French wrestling." Interrogators went to work with the *zhguti,* a kind of club, or the *dubinka,* a truncheon.[26] There is no record of how they tortured Babel but Meyerhold, the theater director arrested on the same day as Babel, wrote a letter to Stalin's confidant Vyacheslav Molotov in the hope of his intervening. In the letter Meyerhold described eighteen-hour interrogations during which he was forced to lie down on the floor to be beaten on the feet and spine with a rubber strap. He was given an hour's respite before the interrogation recommenced with the interrogators now beating the bruised areas of his body, which Meyerhold described as feeling like "boiling water" was being poured on them. "I howled and wept from the pain," he wrote.

Babel would have made a lousy spy. He told the interrogators that he helped Malraux with research for a book the Frenchman was planning on the USSR. Babel said he told Malraux about the failures of collectivization. Groping around he must have remembered that Malraux was a pilot and told the interrogators he had given information about the growth of the Soviet air force—all of which was common knowledge, as Babel had no access to confidential information (he told them what he had read in the newspapers). The interrogators pressed him on Ehrenburg's role in all of this. Was he spying for France too? Babel told them Ehrenburg asked about the purges and Yezhov's role in them and that he told his fellow writer what he knew.

This was when the interrogation took its second surprising turn. With the mention of Yezhov's name the interrogators picked up a new scent. "The investigators are aware of your intimate ties and spying connections with the English intelligence agent Yevgenia Khayutina-Yezhova," they told him. "Do not try to hide the facts from us."[27] Babel told them about his affair with Yevgenia, about the drunken fling in Paris, and their subsequent affair in Moscow. But in the first interrogation he said he knew nothing of any "spying connections." He described her as a "typical little 'featherhead,' who parroted others' words and spouted all the usual Trotskyist terminology."[28] During the second interrogation, Babel was asked ever more absurd questions in relation to Yevgenia. His resistance was gone. Had she not confided in him her plot to murder Stalin and his trusted advisor Kliment Voroshilov? Did she not ask Babel to be her recruiting agent, to help her find the assassins? Babel gave names of his co-conspirators and even admitted knowing of an anti-Stalin conspiracy being orchestrated by Yezhov himself. The interrogators squeezed the names they wanted out of Babel. Long broken, he implicated his friends—Sergei Eisenstein, Solomon Mikhoels, Yuri Olesha, Boris Pasternak, many others—just as he had been implicated by others before him (people had been informing on Babel since 1934).[29]

During the course of the summer of 1939 the interrogations ceased. Babel suffered from respiratory difficulties even in the best of conditions, and in prison he contracted chronic bronchitis. He did not know what was going to happen next—there was no trial scheduled—and he had no contact with the outside world. Nevertheless, on September 11, the day that the interrogations resumed, Babel wrote a letter to Beria, the reptilian head of the NKVD, in which he said prison was his "salvation" and that he was a reformed man. "With horrifying clarity," he wrote, "the mistakes and crimes of my life rose before me, the decay and foulness of the circles I moved in, which, for the most part, were Trotskyist." He denounced the way he had lived with a "swaggering bravado and a promiscuous private life . . . In my solitude I could see the Soviet land with new eyes as she is in reality, indescribably beautiful." The second half of the letter explained why he went to such lengths to display his penitence: Babel was asking to have his manuscripts back, to be given the chance to put them in order for publication. He even wanted to write a new novel "where in fictional form I would tell the story, in many ways quite typical, of what led to my fall and my crimes against the socialist motherland."[30] Needless to say, his request was not granted.

By October he was back in the interrogation room but, having had time to reflect and think rationally about his situation, his manner had changed. He fought back.

Q: Accused Babel, do you have anything to add to your previous testimony?

A: I can add nothing, since I have said everything about my counter-revolutionary activities and work as a spy. However, I would like the investigators to note that while I was giving my preliminary testimony I committed a crime, even while in prison.

Q: What crime?

A: I slandered certain people and gave false testimony about my terrorist activities.

Q: Are you trying to create difficulties for the investigators?

A: No, that was not my intention since I am nothing as far as the NKVD is concerned. I lied to the investigators by reason of my own faint-heartedness.

Q: Tell us whom you slandered and when you were lying.

A: The testimony I gave about my counter-revolutionary ties with Yezhov's wife (Gladun-Khayutina) was false. It is untrue that I carried out terrorist activities under the direction of

Yezhov. I also know nothing about the anti-Soviet activities
of those surrounding Yevgenia Yezhova. I fabricated my
testimony about S. M. Eisenstein and S. M. Mikhoels.[31]

It was one last courageous effort to save his friends. He did
not try to save himself, continuing to admit to spying, but did
his best to spare those he had implicated. He knew it was almost
certainly futile—and the investigators duly ignored it—but he
persisted.

As far as the NKVD were concerned, the investigation was
complete and Babel's file was handed to the Procurator General's
office. On November 5, Babel persuaded the prison director
to forward a note to the Procurator to ask to be cross-examined
in person. When that was ignored, he wrote again, on November
21, this time explaining his purpose. "There are incorrect
and fictitious assertions in my testimony attributing anti-Soviet
activities to persons who are working honestly for the good of
the U.S.S.R. and without any thought for themselves," he wrote.
"The idea that my words might not only fail to help the investigators
but be of direct harm to my motherland is causing me
indescribable suffering. I consider it my first duty to remove this
terrible stain from my conscience."[32] Ignored again and refusing
to give up, he wrote again, on January 2. By then he had been
moved from the Lubyanka to Butyrki prison. On January 25 he
was given his indictment and told that his trial would be the next
day. He wrote back immediately asking that he be given the opportunity
to make a statement about the way he had "slandered a
number of quite innocent people." He asked for an attorney and
to see the case file. He even tried to call defense witnesses, including
Ehrenburg, Eisenstein, and Mikhoels, all friends whom
he feared he had implicated.

The following morning the guards took Babel to an office in
the prison for his trial. It was, fittingly enough, the office that

Beria used when he was on site. As Babel entered the room he was confronted by the Military Tribunal, chaired by Vasily Ulrikh, a fat little man with a pompous moustache. Ulrikh asked if Babel had read the indictment. Yes. Did he object to any of the judges? No. Babel asked again if he might read his case file, summon witnesses, and be defended by a lawyer. The judges conferred briefly and declined his request. So far everything had gone as expected. But Babel had one last act of defiance in him.

"Do you admit your guilt?"
"I do not consider myself guilty. All the testimony I gave
    during the investigation is false."

As the judges read excerpts from his testimony back to him, he denied it all, systematically and deliberately, everything he had been pressured into "confessing."

"I was friendly with Malraux but he did not recruit me as a
    spy, we talked about literature and the Soviet Union . . ."
"But you yourself testified that you worked as a spy with
    Malraux."
"That's not true. The Communist Vaillant-Couturier
    introduced me to Malraux. Malraux is a friend of the
    Soviet Union and was very helpful with translations into
    French. What could I tell him about our aviation? Only
    what I knew from reading Pravda, and he did not ask
    about anything else. I categorically deny that I was linked
    with French intelligence."[33]

Now came the most fantastical allegations: ·

"Did you have any ties with Yezhov?"
"I never had any conversations about terror with Yezhov."

"You testified under investigation that the assassination of
    Comrade Stalin was being prepared in the Caucasus."
"I heard talk of that kind in the Writers' Union . . ."
"Then what about the preparations of the Kosarev-Yezhova
    band to kill Stalin and Voroshilov?"
"That is also an invention."

What about his close relations with Yevgenia Yezhova? Did he
deny those, too?

"I visited Yezhova's flat and met with friends at her home but
    there were no anti-Soviet conversations there."
"Do you wish to add anything to the present record?"
"No, I have nothing to add."

In a parody of court procedure, Babel made a final statement,
by now under intense emotional duress.

"In 1916, when I had written my first story I took it to
Gorky . . . Then I participated in the Civil War. In 1921 I began
writing again. Recently I have been very occupied with a
work of which I completed the first draft by the end of 1938.
I am totally innocent, I have not been a spy and I have never
committed any acts against the Soviet Union. In my testimony
during the investigation I libelled myself. I have only one
request, that I be allowed to complete my last work . . ."

The judges' deliberations were brief. Babel was found guilty
of being a Trotskyist agent, a French spy, and part of a terrorist
conspiracy. He was sentenced to death. At 1:30 the following
morning, January 27, 1940, in some miserable blood-spattered
room, an executioner shot Babel. He died with his future masterpieces locked inside him.

A week later, on February 3, a weeping and screaming Yezhov was dragged by the hands into an execution chamber he had ordered built himself, a deadly annex to the Lubyanka prison.[34] The busy bureaucrat of the Great Terror had displayed his usual ruthless efficiency in the design. The back wall was made of logs to absorb the bullets, the floor was sloped so the blood could run off, and there were hoses to help the process. Yezhov had watched many people die in that room. He thrashed and whined before the bullet silenced him. Yezhov's body was, like Babel's, taken to the Donskoi Monastery, where their remains were incinerated in the crematorium. The ashes of the writer and the executioner were dumped in the same mass grave.

Part Three

WAR

TEN

Philby

CORDOBA, CAMBRIDGE, VIENNA & LONDON, 1934–1942

KIM PHILBY WOKE to the hammering on his Cordoba hotel room door. When he got groggily out of bed and let them in, the Civil Guards, carrying rifles, ordered him to pack his bag. He was to be taken to the city's fascist headquarters for questioning. Philby nervously complied. He was an accredited journalist with a British passport. His cover was rock solid. But in the ticket-pocket of his trousers were instructions on how to write coded messages to his handler in case of emergencies. Ironically this was just such an emergency because if Franco's forces discovered he was a Soviet spy he would be tortured and shot. "I was conscious that something might have to be done about the tell-tale paper tucked away in my trousers," he wrote. "But how to get rid of it?" His plan to throw it away during the walk to headquarters was stymied by a watchful guard. It was still on him when he was led into a brightly lit room for his interrogation.[1]

This was April 1937: Orwell had just returned from the front to find Barcelona in a state of high tension; Koestler was languishing in a Seville prison; Spender had returned to London to agitate for Hyndman's release from the International Brigades. Philby was on the other side of the trenches. While professing to be a reporter for a British news agency covering the Nationalist campaign, he was secretly reporting everything he could about Franco's forces to the NKVD.

Philby had made an elementary mistake. He wanted to see a bullfight and left Seville for Cordoba without a pass, having been assured by a Nationalist officer that he would not need one. The authorities in Cordoba disagreed. A major in the Civil Guard interrogated him and was skeptical of his bullfight story. "I became aware, with growing unease, that my interrogator was a confirmed anglophobe," Philby wrote. The men who had arrested him put on gloves and began searching his suitcase. They measured it inside and out, and tapped every part of it, looking for hidden compartments. Finding nothing, the major turned to Philby and ordered him to empty his pockets. Thinking fast, Philby reached for his back pocket and took out his wallet. Instead of placing it on the table in front of him he threw it to the far end. "As I had hoped," he wrote, "all three men made a dive at it, spreadeagling themselves across the table." Philby deftly took out the code sheet, put it in his mouth, and "with a crunch and a swallow it was gone."[2] The Civil Guards, finding nothing incriminating, ordered him to leave town the following morning. Philby walked back out into the sunny Cordoba morning. He could have been forgiven for doing so with a skip. Unwittingly, the Civil Guards had released a Soviet spy who in the following weeks would be given the mission to assassinate Franco and, in the years that followed, became the most successful penetration agent in the history of Soviet intelligence.

HAROLD ADRIAN RUSSELL PHILBY was born in 1912 in Punjab, where his father, St. John Philby, worked for the Indian Civil Service. St. John was an overbearing, confrontational man with high expectations of his eldest son. He also immersed himself in the local culture in a way that few other colonial officials did, and it was his son's facility with Punjabi as a small boy that earned him the nickname "Kim," after the Rudyard Kipling character, an Irish orphan who grew up a beggar on the streets of Lahore. That the fictional Kim ends up becoming a spy in the Great Game of espionage between Britain and Russia is an extraordinary example of nominative determinism.

Following in the footsteps of his father, Philby was educated at Westminster School and Cambridge University. With unemployment rising at home and fascism rising abroad, Philby, like so many young British intellectuals, became interested in left-wing politics and a committed socialist. It was only in his last days at university that he resolved to join the Communist Party, and he approached Maurice Dobb, a Marxist economist and outspoken Party member at Pembroke College. Philby wanted to go to Austria, and Dobb put him in touch with a group in Paris that served as a front for the Comintern, who in turn connected him with the Communist underground in Vienna.

Philby arrived just before the uprising of February 1934, in which groups of socialists skirmished with the Home Guard, deployed by the fascistic Chancellor Englebert Dollfuss (Spender wrote about these clashes in his celebrated long poem *Vienna*). Philby, who had been working as a courier between radical left groups in Vienna, Budapest, and Prague, threw himself into action. When Dollfuss's forces began using artillery on public housing, strongholds of the socialist movement, Philby helped treat those who were wounded and smuggled fugitives out of the city, hiding them in the Vienna sewer system to evade detection. Not long after arriving in Austria he had begun a relationship with Litzi Friedmann, a Communist who had been previously arrested for her activism. When they discovered the police were on to her, he married her to help get her safely out of the country. He was only twenty-two.

Back in London he became a Soviet spy. The photographer Edith Suschitsky, an Austrian Communist he had met in Vienna, invited him to meet with a person of interest.[3] Suschitsky led him on an elaborate journey around London, embarking and disembarking the tube at the last moment and, once she was certain they were not being followed, emerging at Regent's Park, where they made their way to a man sitting alone on a bench. He introduced himself to Philby as "Hallan." His real name was Arnold Deutsch. (He would later use the cryptonym "Otto.") "He was a marvelous man," Philby remembered. "Simply marvelous. I felt that immediately."[4]

Deutsch was Austrian and Jewish and an ideologically committed Communist. He had a Ph.D. in chemistry from the University of Vienna and had become a follower of the psychiatrist and sexologist Wilhelm Reich (in Vienna he was monitored by the police unit responsible for vice and pornography). He moved to England to pursue his studies at University College London and, despite developing the alias of "Stefan Lange" during his training in Moscow, used his own name, probably because he could then use his cousin, Oscar Deutsch, owner of Odeon Cinemas, as a reference. Deutsch lived in the Lawn Road Flats in Hampstead, where his neighbor was Agatha Christie.

Initially, Deutsch sought to temper Philby's eagerness, convincing him that as an activist his impact could only be limited. If he disguised his Communist beliefs, though, a man with his credentials could work his way into the heart of the British establishment, where he could prove a far more effective agent of change. Philby was persuaded. He felt his future "looked romantic."[5] Deutsch reported his success to Ignati Reif ("Marr"), who as an illegal resident in London was operating under deep nonofficial cover. Philby was given the code name "Söhnchen."[6]

Reif did not last long as resident; in early 1935, he was called in by a suspicious Home Office for an interview and left the country soon after. He was eventually replaced as illegal resident by Teodor Maly ("Paul," "Theo," or "Man") but in the interim

Alexander Orlov ("Swede" or "Big Bill") arrived to take direct control of the agents in case Deutsch was compromised. Orlov pretended to be an American refrigerator salesman but had to leave when recognized by an old friend on the streets of London. Philby built a strong relationship with all his handlers, Deutsch and Maly especially. Moscow Center eagerly sought information about Philby, about his planned career, his contacts, and his relationship with his father.

St. John Philby was of special interest to the NKVD because they believed him to be an agent of British intelligence. After leaving the Indian Civil Service he became a close advisor of Ibn Saud, the founder of modern Saudi Arabia, and worked as a representative of Standard Oil. It seemed to the Soviets inconceivable that he was not connected to British intelligence (in fact, he was opposed to imperialism and an outspoken critic of British foreign policy). One of Philby's first assignments was to spy on his own father, photographing any documents he thought relevant. His father had always been aggressive and demanding while Philby had been comparatively mild and suffered from a stutter, and St. John made no secret of the fact that he disapproved of his son's politics and disliked his wife. Perhaps it felt good to get one over the old man, even if Philby found nothing of substance for Moscow to work with.

More productive was the assignment given to Philby to identify further recruits at Cambridge. He produced a list of seven names for Deutsch, and at the top was Donald Maclean, the son of a former Cabinet minister, whose intellectual brilliance had opened a career in the Foreign Office. Philby made the initial approach and by December 1934 Maclean was an agent of Soviet intelligence.

Orlov wanted another name off the list: Guy Burgess. While Burgess was a staunch Communist and had even traveled to the

Soviet Union, Philby had misgivings, worrying that his friend's debauched lifestyle made him unreliable.[7] Burgess was charismatic, gay, and hard drinking, and he loved to shock. It was hard to imagine him maintaining cover. Deutsch shared Philby's skepticism. Yet Burgess forced their hand. When Maclean, like Philby, began to break with his left-wing friends, Burgess realized something was up and began to publicly tease him about being a member of the Comintern. He jeopardized the whole operation, and Philby was left with no choice but to recruit him, too, figuring that if he was brought in, he might be counted on to exercise some discretion. It was a decision with far-reaching consequences.

Philby did not just break with the left; he reinvented himself as a fascist sympathizer. He got a job editing an Anglo-German trade magazine and joined the Nazi-sympathizing Anglo-German Fellowship. He made several trips to Berlin and became personally acquainted with Nazi Foreign Minister Joachim von Ribbentrop. His old friends were horrified, and Philby later admitted he found the work "profoundly repulsive."[8]

Philby's involvement with the magazine and fellowship group provided his handlers with valuable information about British attitudes to an increasingly belligerent Germany, and they were disappointed when the trade magazine folded. To Philby's surprise, for his next mission the NKVD decided to send him to Spain. He went as a freelance journalist, but rather than travel to Republican Madrid or Barcelona like his left-wing contemporaries, Philby went to cover Franco's insurgency. He made a deal with a British news agency and sailed for Lisbon in February 1937. He made his way to Seville and was in the city at the same time as Koestler. They were both clandestine Communist agents, Philby for the NKVD, Koestler for the Comintern— the big difference, of course, was that Koestler was locked up in prison.

This was a dramatic escalation for Philby. If he were discovered in Britain, he faced prison; if Franco's forces discovered him, he would be executed. As he tried to get as much information about troop numbers and materiel as possible, Philby got to know Franco's press attachés, including Luís Bolín, the man who had arrested Koestler. (Bolín later remembered Philby as a "decent chap.")[9] Yet Philby might well have ended up in the cells with Koestler were it not for his quick thinking in swallowing his code sheet. As a consequence, he needed replacement codes, and he sent a letter to his Paris contact to that effect. He recognized the handwriting of the reply: Burgess. They arranged to meet at a hotel in Gibraltar, where Burgess delivered the updated codes. He also gave Philby a new mission, one that had come from Yezhov and, by implication, Stalin: the assassination of Franco.[10]

The idea of killing Franco was one that Philby had discussed with his handlers before leaving but it is doubtful that he expected to be the assassin. He later denied that he had been assigned the mission and did not include it in his memoir, perhaps because he failed so abjectly. On his return to London in May, Maly reported to Moscow Center that Söhnchen was "in a very depressed state" because of his failure. Maly wrote that "even if he had been able to get to Salamanca and even if he had been able to get close to F [Franco], which is a separate matter, because only two or three journalists have been able to do that so far, then he, despite his willingness, would not be able to do what was expected of him. For all his loyalty and willingness to sacrifice himself, he does not have the physical courage and other qualities necessary."[11]

The perversity of the situation was that the second time Philby went out to Spain he had no problem at all getting close to Franco. Thanks to the quality of his freelance work, and to the intervention of his father with the assistant editor, Philby was taken on as a correspondent with the *Times*. The work remained dangerous; on assignment in the eastern part of the country a car carrying Philby and three other journalists was hit by a shell. The three others were killed; Philby suffered a small head wound. He acquitted himself admirably in the immediate aftermath of the explosion, ordering soldiers to get his colleagues out of the car. The story made its way to the Nationalist upper echelons, and Philby was informed that Franco wanted to reward him for his bravery with the Red Cross of Military Merit. In March 1938 Philby traveled to headquarters in Burgos, where Franco personally pinned the cross onto Philby's lapel. The story was widely reported in Spain and Britain. The man he had previously been instructed to assassinate had provided him with ironclad cover as a right-wing journalist.

Philby had no problem with access to the information he and his handlers wanted after that. He interviewed Franco four times for the *Times*, visited battlefields, diligently filed his copy to his editors, and diligently posted his letters to his contact in Paris (these were disguised as love letters; the real message was written in liquid developer on the back).[12] He also met his handlers in person. An agent from Paris (Ozolin-Haskin, codename "Pierre") traveled down to the border with Spain, where he was briefed by Philby before going to meet Orlov in Republican territory. This procedure was too time-consuming, though, so Philby began to meet with Orlov himself, in Narbonne.

Everything was going smoothly until the purges wiped out most of Philby's handlers. Reif was the first to be executed, back in the Soviet Union. Maly was recalled and knew why but went anyway; he was shot as a German spy. Ozolin-Haskin was also executed. Orlov made a run for it, escaping to the United States, where he defected. Deutsch was spared but only because another NKVD agent, Ignace Poretsky, defected in Switzerland and betrayed him. By the strange logic of the time, Deutsch, having been accused by a traitor, was now a victim of the Trotskyist conspiracy rather than a collaborator in it. Poretsky was killed by an NKVD assassin, machine-gunned on a side road in Lausanne. In the Netherlands, another NKVD agent fleeing the purges, William Krivitsky, defected. When debriefed by MI5 agent Jane Archer in 1940, Krivitsky said that Soviet intelligence had an English journalist in Spain who had been instructed to assassinate Franco. Fortunately for Philby, the defector did not know his name. Krivitsky was later found shot in an American hotel room.

Philby's contacts had all disappeared, his identity had almost been betrayed, and to compound it all, the Soviet Union made a deal with the devil, signing the Molotov-Ribbentrop Pact in August 1939. After returning from Spain, the *Times* sent Philby to Arras, France, to report on the British Expeditionary Force. He reported what he found to the NKVD, too, but not without qualms. Where was his information going? He was giving the Soviet Union troop numbers and positions behind the Maginot Line. Did the Soviets really need this information? Or were they passing it on to their new allies, the Nazis? Was Philby, the antifascist spy, now indirectly working for Hitler?

Moscow Center was also having its doubts. With such huge turnover, the NKVD was in chaos, and new agents took over the running of Philby. Tainted by his association with the executed conspirators, he was the object of suspicion, and reports were commissioned on his work and character. Philby later maintained that his loyalty to the Soviet Union never wavered, but the NKVD files show that he began missing meetings and became difficult to deal with. In February 1940 there was a complete break in communication. A report of April 1, 1940, documented how Philby had begun to "experience a certain disillusionment with us."[13] In June he reached out through Maclean, claiming to have important information, but for reasons not disclosed in his file, the Center rejected the approach. Philby was in the cold for almost a year.

It is not hard to understand why Moscow changed their minds and decided to reconnect with Philby in December 1940: Söhnchen was now working for the Secret Intelligence Service (SIS), also known as MI6, which was responsible for spying outside of British territory (MI5 was responsible for intelligence operations on British soil, including in colonial territory). Philby had dropped hints about his interest in working for one of the intelligence agencies for some time, and his name made it into a pool of potential recruits.[14] While it is unclear who first proposed him as a candidate for the service, at some point Burgess heard that Philby was being considered and agitated on behalf of his friend.

Burgess, like Philby, had broken with his left-wing university friends, although he did so in inimitable style, becoming an assistant to Jack McNamara, a gay Conservative MP and member of the Anglo-German Fellowship. (Burgess had been the one who recommended Philby to its members.) McNamara and Burgess went on research assignments to Nazi Germany, where, by Burgess's account, they had lots of sex with young men in the Hitlerjugend.[15]

Burgess, who took a job with the BBC, mixed with the great and the good, counting politicians and writers among his friends (in 1938 he spent one memorable afternoon as a guest of Winston Churchill). It was in this period that he got to know W. H. Auden, Louis MacNeice, and Christopher Isherwood. He was also good at recruiting friends as spies. To Deutsch, he recommended Anthony Blunt, his friend from Trinity College. Burgess had liberated Blunt sexually and converted him to left-wing politics, and in return Blunt had helped Burgess get into the Apostles, a "secret" society at Cambridge that included E. M. Forster and John Maynard Keynes. Blunt in turn recommended to Deutsch the intellectually formidable John Cairncross, the final member of what became known as the Cambridge Five.[16]

Despite some difficult times—he was hospitalized with syphilis, arrested for soliciting in a Paddington station toilet, and had a nervous breakdown—Burgess managed to secure a job in British intelligence. He was first approached by Major Valentine Vivian of SIS with the idea of infiltrating groups of clandestine communists at Oxbridge and the BBC, but both he and his SIS handlers realized he lacked the temperament and had burned too many bridges at his alma mater.[17] Instead he joined Section D, which was responsible for sabotage and subversion. To his new SIS bosses, he recommended Philby. After two interviews with Majorie Maxse, a journalist and an SIS recruiter, at St. Ermin's Hotel (Burgess was present at the second meeting), Philby signed up as an employee of SIS. As per standard procedure, the service consulted his MI5 file but it was clean; his interest in radical left-wing causes was understood to have been a youthful flirtation.

Philby was also assigned to Section D. Burgess had come up with the idea of establishing a training school for agents, teaching them underground work, and it was Philby's job to implement this plan. Burgess, with characteristic flair, suggested it be called Guy Fawkes College. Station 17 was soon established at a site near Hertford, but it did not last long. Section D was soon hived off from SIS and Philby was transferred to its replacement, the Special Operations Executive, housed on Baker Street in London. At the same time, Burgess left SIS for the Ministry of Information. With the SOE, Philby was responsible for training foreign agents in propaganda and subversion at a new training school in Beaulieu, Hampshire. It was while he was lecturing new recruits in June 1941 that the Nazis launched Operation Barbarossa and invaded the Soviet Union. Both of Philby's employers were now on the same side. The NKVD retained their suspicions, however, fearing he was a plant—they could simply not rationalize how easily he had secured himself a position at SIS and how amateurish the organization appeared to be.

In September 1941, Philby resigned from the SOE and took a position at the heart of SIS, assigned to Section V (counter-espionage), which was run by Felix Cowgill, a pipe-smoking former officer in the Indian Police. The job of Section V was to get hold of information about foreign espionage through illegal means and relay this information to MI5, who were responsible for the security of all British territory. Moscow Center referred to Section V as "the Hotel." Philby was responsible for running the Iberian subsection, drawing on the knowledge of Spain he had acquired while reporting on the war.

It was while running Section V that Philby read some reports that amused and intrigued him. One of the section's responsibilities was running agents operating in Northwest Africa and, of all the reports that came across his desk, Philby's eye was caught by those written by the service's agent in Freetown, in the British colony of Sierra Leone. The author was someone with whom Philby would enter into a strange kind of friendship, one that would somehow survive his betrayals. The agent with the literary gift was Graham Greene, and he was about to become entangled in Philby's big play.

ELEVEN

Greene

FREETOWN, ST. ALBANS & LONDON, 1941–1944

GRAHAM GREENE HAD A GREAT IDEA for Kim Philby: a spy brothel. Greene had already identified "an admirable Madame" to run the place, which was to be set up in Bissau in Portuguese Guinea, where French Vichy officers stationed in Dakar "were apt to take holidays," and Greene "felt that valuable information could be obtained from many of her visitors."[1] Of particular interest was the seaworthiness of the French battleship *Richelieu*, which had been damaged in holding off an Allied assault on Dakar in September 1940, and, if ready for combat, could do serious harm to British supply lines. Philby was amused by Agent 59200's imaginative scheme. "For kicks, I put the plan to my superiors," he wrote, "and we discussed it seriously before rejecting it as unlikely to be what is now called cost-effective."[2]

Greene was, of course, no stranger to inventing plots. At thirty-seven, he was a successful author, having published thrillers such as *Stamboul Train* (1932) and *A Gun for Sale* (1936), as well as more ambitious novels like *Brighton Rock* (1938) and *The Power and the Glory* (1940). He was also no stranger to brothels—in fact, he became something of an expert—and while he later referred to his scheme as "a rather wild plan," he was disappointed when it was rejected. It was, he felt, one of his better proposals.

Freetown was not a frontline posting, but Greene's clandestine work was consequential. Freetown was an important port on the route from southern Africa to Europe, and one of Greene's most important responsibilities was to uncover illegal diamond smuggling coming through Angola, a colony of neutral Portugal (the Nazis needed diamonds, which were used in precision tooling, so stopping the supply was imperative).[3] As such, he needed to keep an eye on suspected German agents in West African ports. There was also the prospect of a Vichy invasion from French Guinea, and Greene needed "to have agents near the border on the lookout for any possible movements by the French."[4] It was not exactly the stuff of James Bond—he did not have a gun and drove a second-hand Morris—but it was real intelligence work.

SPYING WAS IN THE FAMILY. Greene's uncle, Sir William Graham Greene, had been Permanent Secretary to the Board of the Admiralty and had been instrumental in setting up the Naval Intelligence department. Greene's eldest brother, Herbert, was a less patriotic operator, having provided naval intelligence to the Japanese in the 1930s before working for another, mysterious benefactor during the Spanish Civil War. His youngest sister, Elisabeth, had joined SIS in 1938, working as secretary to Captain Cuthbert Bowlby, head of the Middle East Section. When Bowlby went out to run the Cairo station, Elisabeth went with him, meeting another SIS agent, Rodney Dennys, whom she would later marry. Dennys later became a script advisor for the Bond film *On Her Majesty's Secret Service*.[5] Elisabeth made the case for her brother to join the service, but despite her advocacy they wanted to vet him thoroughly, possibly because of his brief flirtation with the Communist Party back in 1925, or because of Herbert's dubious activities.[6] He was invited to a series of boozy parties hosted by a man called "Smith" at which SIS agents could get the measure of their potential recruit. He passed muster.

The service represented an exciting way for Greene to avoid enlisting while earning good money; in a letter to the poet John Betjeman he said he feared the prospect of the Pioneer Corps, "the haunt of middle-aged professional men like myself."[7] He had a family to support and fretted about how the war affected his income. In the months before the war began, he had rented a studio in Bloomsbury where, aided by Benzedrine tablets, he crashed out a commercial thriller, *The Confidential Agent*, in the morning, while working on the ambitious *The Power and the Glory* in the afternoons. He sent his wife, Vivien, and the two children to stay with his parents in Crowborough, East Sussex, where he hoped they would be safe from German bombs. This also cleared the way for him to continue an affair he was having with Dorothy Glover, his Bloomsbury landlord. He tried working for the Ministry of Information but found the work pettily bureaucratic, so he quit and became an air raid warden at night and the literary editor of the *Spectator* by day. The pressures of war demanded a greater contribution, though, and Greene knew he would not make much of a frontline soldier.

In August 1941, Greene wrote to his mother to tell her that he was going to Africa with the Colonial Service. Over the following months, he received training on a demanding course for Intelligence Corps officers at Oriel College, Oxford. He was not cut out for the rough-and-tumble stuff—the instructor gave up on teaching him how to ride a motorbike when he damaged two—but Greene was a keen student of his tradecraft, making copious notes in shorthand on how to recruit agents, how to intercept letters, and how best to maintain cover and avoid surveillance.[8]

On December 9, he boarded a cargo ship in Liverpool with twelve other passengers and, after being drilled in watching for U-boats and using the fixed machine guns, they set out for Lagos, Nigeria. The journey was horrible. He was seasick, it was freezing cold on deck, and the prospect of a submarine attack filled him with dread; he wrote in his diary that "even a bird can look like a periscope."[9] His fears deepened when he found out that, along with depth charges used to deter sub attacks, the boat was carrying TNT in its cargo hold. To deal with it all he drank—heavily. On Christmas day, he awoke with such a terrible hangover that he promptly downed a bottle of champagne to help deal with it.

After four weeks at sea they docked in Freetown. To Greene it was a return; he had arrived in the same port on a previous trip to Liberia in 1935.[10] "It felt odd & poetic & encouraging coming back after so many years," he wrote in his journal. "Like seeing a place you've dreamed of. Even the sweet hot smell from the land—is it the starved greenery and the red soil, the smoke from the huts in Kru town, or the fires in the bush clearing the ground for planting?—was oddly familiar."[11] Greene always maintained a deep affection for West Africa but it was, by his own admission, a "sentimental" love, and one tainted by an almost Victorian sense of imperial entitlement. He was highly critical of many aspects of British colonialism, but he also held patronizing and often racist attitudes toward the "Africans."

Greene's arrival, by his later recollection, was an anticlimax. Staying with the secretary of agriculture, he had no "cover" and no idea who his contact should be: "I knew my number, and that was all (it was not 007)."[12] Eventually, "a major with a large moustache" came for drinks and asked Greene to go for a walk, leading him to a house whose owner was away and, in the shade of the garden, gave him his "cover": he was to be an inspector for the Department of Trade.[13] The situation became needlessly complicated when the department refused to go along and Greene had to find another cover story, eventually joining the Criminal Investigating Department (CID) as a plainclothes police officer.

Greene's accounts of his time in Freetown should be treated with a degree of skepticism. While the problems with his cover were real, his biographer, Norman Sherry, pointed out that the major with the moustache is in all likelihood a fabrication, as Dr. John Martyn, his initial host in Freetown, was the MI5 representative there. This was Martyn's turf—MI5 was responsible for security in British colonies—and he did not take kindly to an interloper. Nicknamed "Filthy Freddie" for his relentless vulgarity, Martyn was described by Philby as a "tropical boozer with sub-homicidal tendencies."[14] Greene soon escaped Filthy Freddie's crude jokes when he flew to Lagos for more training in coding and decoding. He seemed to have enjoyed himself with the hard-drinking colonial set; one night, as he walked home, he fell six feet into an open sewer.

Once his training was complete, he returned to Freetown via Accra and an American base in Liberia. He did not make an auspicious start to his work as a spy. Back in Freetown he announced his safe arrival "by means of a book code (I had chosen a novel of T. F. Powys from which I could detach sufficiently lubricious phrases for my own amusement), and a large safe came in the next convoy with a leaflet of instruction and my codes."[15] He later claimed that he misread the instructions and accidentally set up a new combination without knowing what it was. He reached for the Powys again and sent another coded message to London; the safe had to be broken open with a blowtorch.

In a letter to his mother—"Dearest Mumma"—he described how he moved into a "dingy little Creole villa about two miles out of town," located on the Brookfield flats below the hill that served as the European quarter.[16] On one side was "a transport camp in process of erection with two steam shovels going all day" and on the other shrub land that was used as a toilet by locals living in the nearby slum. The result was a "plague of houseflies" and vultures perched on his roof. At night, the cockroaches came out, and rats "would swing on my bedroom curtains."[17] If that wasn't enough to keep him awake, stray dogs barked and howled at the moon. It was brutally hot and there was a shortage of water until the rains came, and when they did the ground around his villa turned to swamp and the insect population exploded. Someone broke in and stole his glasses and a favorite fountain pen, and he had to install wire mesh on the windows. His cook, whose food he loved, went mad and his steward went to prison. "It's lucky," he wrote, "I have a masochistic trend and a feeling for squalor."[18] Nevertheless, it was while stationed in Freetown that he started going gray.

THE SPY BROTHEL was not Greene's only scheme. Another was a proposed "rescue by bogus Communist agents of a left-wing agitator who was under house arrest."[19] This African intellectual (whose identity remains a mystery) was apparently a friend of Victor Gollancz, the publisher of Koestler's *Spanish Testament* and Orwell's *Road to Wigan Pier*, although how Greene had learned of the intellectual's plight is not clear. The idea was to whisk him off to the port city of Conakry, then under Vichy control, where he would give information to his "Soviet" handlers, who would eventually be revealed as British agents. He would then be threatened with exposure to the French unless he cooperated more fully. Greene had meticulously thought through the plan and appeared to have been intercepting letters to and from the "agitator."[20] Again, this plan was killed by London; Greene was told they feared it could cause a scandal if something went wrong.

The failure of a third plan contributed to Greene leaving his posting. Again, the premise was something out of his fiction: he wanted to get American Episcopalian monks to spy for him. The monks were willing, but the problem was the Holy Cross mission was based in Liberia and Greene had severely criticized the Liberian government in his travelogue, *Journey Without Maps*. He feared he might be arrested if he returned. Instead he arranged for the monks to travel to Kailahun, just over the Sierra Leone border, so he could give them radio-transmitting equipment. Greene suggested as cover they pretend to be collecting a delivery of food from Fortnum & Mason, the luxury grocer known for preparing hampers for the royal family. His boss in Lagos ordered him to cancel the operation, however, as a boat was due to dock from Angola and needed to be searched for diamonds.[21] Greene reluctantly complied but then gave a full account to London about what had happened and offered his resignation. It was refused.

Aside from concocting these schemes, Greene found much of the work dull. Every other morning, he went to the police station to collect encoded telegrams that he then had to laboriously decode. Occasionally a bag arrived for him by boat. He did not trust many of the agents he inherited and doubted much of the information they gave him. He did not like searching or interrogating passengers—"the squalor and intimacy of a man's suitcase"—on ships that docked in Freetown, and it is hard to ascertain what tangible impact he made as a spy.[22] It seems he was, at least in part, responsible for the arrest of three Portuguese agents working for German intelligence.[23] Certainly both Philby and Dennys felt he was a good agent wasted in Freetown.[24] He later recalled whiling away many hours in the bar of the City Hotel wondering what he was doing in West Africa at all.

The posting also presented an unexpected challenge to his writing. He had plenty of time to work and, by September 1942, had a new novel, *The Ministry of Fear,* ready for publication. The difficulty lay in getting the manuscript to his agent, as he had only one copy and worried—justifiably—that if he sent it by ship it would end up on the bottom of the ocean. His solution was to slowly type out a copy that he then sent in several parts, so that if one part was lost it would not mean all his work was lost. While *The Ministry of Fear* was a well-constructed thriller that was kindly received, there was a more important book brewing. Throughout his time in Freetown, Greene kept a journal, storing away sensory details and quirks of character. Even though he disguised his entries with shorthand and fragments, this was a direct violation of SIS rules. These journal entries were the raw material from which he drew for *The Heart of the Matter,* the novel that, when it was published in 1948, brought him more acclaim and controversy than any other, sold handsomely, and made him a literary celebrity along the way.[25]

In November 1942, his father died, and so erratic was the mail at this stage that Greene learned of his falling ill only after the death. He missed his wife, Vivien, and his children, and he also missed Dorothy, his lover. His relationship with his superior in Lagos had completely broken down, and following Operation Torch, the Allied invasion of French North Africa, London's priorities in the region were changing. Greene's time in the field was over; he burned his files and his codebooks and set sail for home. He returned to Britain on March 1, 1943, to work for the Iberian subsection at SIS headquarters in St. Albans: from sub-Sahara to the suburbs. He was to have much better relations with his new boss, Kim Philby.

BRITISH INTELLIGENCE had two major, interrelated successes during the Second World War. The first occurred in the summer of 1941, when Dilly Knox and his Bletchley Park team (including Alan Turing) cracked the German codes encrypted by the Enigma machine. The information obtained from cracking the codes, designated "Ultra," gave Britain a huge strategic advantage over the Germans. The second success was the double-cross system, the complete penetration of the Abwehr (German military intelligence) to the point where every single German spy on British soil was working for British intelligence. The two successes were interrelated because Ultra material could be used to cross-check the effectiveness of the double agents.

Even before the war began, MI5 was running double agents in the Abwehr. With the fall of France in June 1940, Britain became isolated and, perversely enough, this created the perfect environment to run a counterespionage operation of unprecedented ambition. With Portugal and Sweden (both neutral) the only two countries by which foreign agents could try to gain entry to Britain, the intelligence services were able to monitor the comings and goings of agents much more easily. The double agents were run by a secret subsection within MI5, but because the information they fed to the Germans had to come from a variety of sources (Army, Navy, Air Force, Foreign Office), they needed a body that could make decisions about what could be leaked and what carried too great a risk. In January 1941, the Twenty ("XX," or double-cross) Committee was established to make those decisions and to coordinate the operation.

The Twenty Committee was chaired by J. C. Masterman, an Oxford history don who was the author of popular detective novels. His interest in intrigue was well served at "the club," as the Twenty Committee was known to its members: their entire purpose was to concoct an elaborate plausible fiction. Masterman, a first-class cricketer, loved to use the sport's terminology—"wickets," "net practice," "no balls," "stumpings"—as metaphors for his agents' work, and likened his agents to star bowlers and batsmen.[26] His biggest star was Agent Garbo.

As early as the winter of 1941 codebreakers at Bletchley Park were intercepting messages delivered from an agent code-named "Arabel" to the Abwehr, in which the agent reported information gleaned from a network of informers all over Britain. The messages, though, were odd. They referred to orgies in Liverpool amusement centers, naval maneuvers on Lake Windermere, and Glaswegians drinking liters of wine instead of pints of beer. The mystery was solved by Philby's Section V agents in Lisbon who realized that Arabel was in fact Juan Pujol, a Catalan pacifist and failed chicken farmer, who tried several times to get recruited by the British. Realizing that Pujol, using tourist guides, newspapers, and a fertile imagination, had thoroughly deceived the Abwehr, he was spirited to London to continue his work, his network of thirty imaginary subagents coming with him. His handler in London was Tomás Harris, a close friend of Philby's from his days on Section D.

Lisbon during the war was, in Masterman's description, "a busy ant-heap of spies and agents."[27] António Salazar, the fascist ruler of Portugal, was sympathetic to the Axis, and the Portuguese police turned a blind eye to Abwehr operations. That was why, when he was stranded in Lisbon after fleeing Vichy France, Koestler was so scared he was going to be turned over to the Nazis (he was, in fact, being monitored by the Portuguese secret police). As Britain developed its double-cross system, Lisbon became the key battleground in the espionage war. And Lisbon was Greene and Philby's turf.

IN MARCH 1943, Greene was assigned to Philby's Iberian team. There were only six of them in the subsection, working out of a drawing room of Glenalmond, a country house on the Earl of Verulam's estate in St. Albans. Philby marshaled his group of dedicated amateurs in their counterintelligence work, their long, intense shifts punctuated by trips to the King Harry pub for a boozy lunch. "No one could have been a better chief than Kim Philby when he was in charge of the Iberian section of V,"

Greene wrote. "He worked harder than anyone and never gave the impression of labour."[28]

Philby had reason to work hard. He was determined to climb the SIS hierarchy, and in order to do so he needed to make his subsection the best in Section V. His work as a Soviet agent placed him at an advantage, as he was already schooled in intrigue and tradecraft in a way many of his colleagues were not. Picking a careful path through the factional battles both within SIS and between the service and MI5, Philby marked himself out as the best operator in the counterespionage section. His brief began to expand as Cowgill gave him responsibility for North Africa, then Italy. When Cowgill went to the United States, Philby was left in charge of Section V's intelligence operations.

At the same time, he tried to learn as much about the service as possible without attracting undue attention. On top of his regular work he volunteered for night shifts at the service's Broadway Street headquarters in London, where he could monitor incoming messages from all over the world. He became a drinking partner of the chief archivist and managed to copy the whole of the Russian source book, which gave details of all agents who had operated in the Soviet Union and all operations that had taken place on Soviet soil.

In order to protect himself, Philby had to avoid friendship with his colleagues. Greene was something of an exception, and he later recalled that of all those with whom he worked in SIS, Greene was the one man with whom he had "human contact."[29] When Greene first arrived, before being shipped to Freetown, Philby had a long conversation with him during which they clearly hit it off. Philby remembered his return to headquarters as "wholly delightful" and that Greene "added to the gaiety of the service," particularly enjoying the "terse, sometimes devastating marginalia" he added to incoming reports.[30]

This chumminess did not prevent Philby having certain expectations of his recruit. One secretary later recalled Greene trembling with rage after receiving a "caning from the headmaster."[31] These canings were infrequent, however, as Greene made a much better desk man than field agent. He was assigned to the Portuguese desk, and Philby soon promoted him to running it. Greene took over from Charles de Salis, a poet and linguist who had become friends with Federico García Lorca as a young man in Spain. In August 1943, Salis was dispatched to Lisbon to provide support for agents in the field. Greene took over. Despite his restlessness and his impatience with bureaucracy, Greene was good at the job. His friend Malcolm Muggeridge, a fellow writer who had also been recommended to SIS by Elisabeth Greene, was the field agent in Lourenço Marques, Mozambique, and therefore under Greene's jurisdiction. Muggeridge felt that Greene had been "too nice" for the field but that he was "tremendously good at dealing with agents."[32] He became known for his loyalty to his men. According to Tim Milne, another agent in the Iberian subsection, Greene "bombarded everyone for weeks with pleas and arguments on behalf of a former SIS agent who had ended up in a Lisbon jail."[33]

Some of the most important work Greene did was the least glamorous; he was placed in charge of producing a "Purple Primer" on Portugal, trawling the vast card catalogue held by SIS and documenting all agents, contacts, and enemy intelligence agents in the country. When it was complete, Philby wrote the introduction.[34] This dossier was used by the Allies to demonstrate to Salazar just how much they knew about Portuguese collaboration and, sensing which way the wind was blowing, he had all German agents expelled and any Portuguese working for the Germans arrested.

With the combination of the Ultra material and the network of double agents, the Abwehr never stood a chance in Lisbon.

The British sent "Klop" Ustinov, a Russian who had worked at the German Embassy in London, to the city in the spring of 1944 to try to "turn" those who were identified as vulnerable. Ustinov, father of the actor, was good at his work; Greene later remembered that "those Abwehr who were not working for us, we knew were working with completely imaginary agents and receiving pay to give to their agents who did *not* exist. The Abwehr were wiped out in a sense."[35]

The novelist in him was taking notice. The double agents and their case officers were essentially storytellers, composing plausible fictions to deliver back to their German spymasters, telling them what they wanted to hear. For many it was an easy, if risky, way to double their pay. Even more intriguing were cases like that of Pujol, who began making stuff up all by himself. Another case cropped up in Lisbon while Greene was on the Portugal desk: a Nazi agent code-named "Ostro," who was in fact Paul Fidrmuc, a Czech businessman. It was quickly established that Ostro was either exaggerating half-baked gossip or making up much of the information he was giving the Abwehr. So wild were his reports, in fact, that MI5 considered assassinating him because his misinformation would clash so wildly with that of their carefully coordinated double agent network.[36]

The absurdity of the situation in Lisbon, with agents selling fictional information to credulous spy agencies, stuck with Greene, and he kicked around ideas for how to transform the stories of "creative" agents like Garbo and Ostro into fiction. Shortly after the war Alberto Cavalcanti, a Brazilian film director, asked Greene to write the script for a spy comedy. Greene had the idea of a British agent in Tallinn in 1938 selling made-up information to meet the financial demands of his extravagant wife. The film never got made—wringing humor from the idea of selling information to the Nazis did not wash—but Greene repurposed the setup for his blackly comic 1958 novel, *Our Man in Havana,* in which James Wormold, an expat vacuum cleaner salesman in Cuba, ends up selling increasingly implausible information to the SIS.[37]

IN THE SUMMER OF 1943 Section V moved from the quiet suburbs of St. Albans to 7 Ryder Street in the center of London, between Piccadilly Circus and Green Park, close to SIS headquarters at 54 Broadway. In the new building, Greene got his own office and, aside from going for drinks at the King's Arms on St. James's Street, spent less time with Philby. His friend was busy and his hard work was not going unnoticed. Philby had played a key part in the defection in Istanbul of the German Abwehr agent Erich Vermehren, a coup that caused so much damage to the German cause that the Abwehr was disbanded. Vermehren was debriefed by Philby and Nicholas Elliott, the agent on the ground in Turkey, at Philby's mother's flat in Kensington. Among the valuable information Vermehren gave up was a list of Catholic anti-Nazis in Germany who could be relied upon to oppose the Communists after the war. Philby passed that list on to Moscow, most likely with fatal consequences to every name on it.

With Philby's stock rising, he was responsible for helping train a whole new set of spies: the Americans. After negotiations between SIS and "Wild Bill" Donovan, the head of the new Office of Strategic Services, an American counterespionage department known as X-2 moved into the Ryder Street building. The idea was that these callow Americans would learn their craft firsthand from Section V. Norman Holmes Pearson, a professor of literature at Yale, was placed in charge because it was thought his literary sophistication would appeal to British intelligence officers.[38] He had studied at Oxford, was a friend of the poet

Hilda "H. D." Doolittle, and would go on to collaborate with Auden on popular poetry anthologies.[39]

The first batch of Americans to arrive were, in Philby's words, a "notably bewildered group."[40] Muggeridge, now working a desk job in the French subsection, was more evocative. "Ah, those first OSS arrivals in London!" Muggeridge wrote. "How well I remember them arriving like *jeunes filles en fleur* straight from a finishing school, all fresh and innocent, to start work in our frowsty old intelligence brothel. All too soon they were ravished and corrupted, becoming indistinguishable from seasoned pros who had been in the game for a quarter of a century or more." Much fun was had at the Americans' expense. One story Greene later told is that he noticed one of the OSS filing cabinets did not lock properly and, knowing that because of the threat of bombing, papers left out on desks incurred an immediate fine, he snuck in after work and placed some documents on a random desk. When Pearson was on the verge of discovering the ruse, Greene told Philby about it over a pint and it was quietly dropped.[41]

Such was the flow of information from Bletchley Park decrypts and reports from agents in the field that the added manpower was welcome. Less welcome were OSS agents trying to make their mark in Lisbon. Philby recalled one running around with bags of money generally getting in the way and another who managed to "recruit" a known double agent of the Abwehr. There was among the Americans one officer who stood out: James Jesus Angleton, who impressed even Philby. Angleton's father was a soldier and met his mother, of Mexican and Apache descent, while campaigning against Pancho Villa. As a child, he lived in Italy but was sent to Malvern College, an elite boarding school in England, for his education. As an undergraduate at Yale he wrote poetry and published *Furioso,* a poetry magazine with some distinguished contributors, including E. E. Cummings and William Carlos Williams. When, after Pearl Harbor, he decided to volunteer, Pearson decided his star student would make an excellent spy: deciphering modernist poetry was, to Pearson's mind, the best preparation for a career as a spy. In one sense, Pearson's reasoning seemed sound: Angleton rose rapidly through the ranks in the OSS and later the CIA. But Pearson's theory was flawed. The obscure and complex poetry of modernism invited the sensitive reader to find meaning everywhere, to distinguish between fine distinctions of ambiguity; one could end up misreading the plain meanings of reality in this way, and that could lead one down the dark paths toward paranoia. And Philby would prove a most unwelcome guide.

Angleton was only twenty-four when he arrived to run the Italian desk of X-2, but he had the gravitas of a much older man. He left the Ryder Street office to lunch with his prestigious literary friends, including William Empson, I. A. Richards, and T. S. Eliot.[42] Under Philby's guidance, Angleton swiftly learned the rules of the game. "Once I met Philby, the world of intelligence that had once interested me consumed me," Angleton said. The pair became close, recognizing each other's talent. It was to prove a consequential relationship for espionage in the Cold War.

In May 1944, Greene quit SIS. The timing was surprising. Operation Overlord was only a month away, and the intelligence services were busily planning for the Allied invasion. They knew they would be playing a hugely important role in ensuring the Germans were misinformed and confused as the troops landed on the beaches of Normandy. It is strange that amid these preparations and with invasion imminent, Greene should quit, especially as it represented a culmination of all the hard work Section V had put in over the preceding months and years to build up a network of agents. Why did he leave so suddenly? Something about Philby spooked him.

In May 1943, Sir Stewart Menzies, who as "C" was head of SIS, created a new section to deal specifically with the Communist threat: Section IX. With the Allies winning the war, it was clear that attention would soon shift back to the old enemy: the Soviet Union. An experienced MI5 officer was drafted in to get Section IX going, but it was understood that once the corner was turned against the Nazis, an SIS officer would take over. Moscow Center instructed Agent Söhnchen to get the job at any cost. The problem was his boss, Cowgill, wanted Sections V and IX to merge after the war with him in charge.

Philby got to work. It was essential that he remain concealed as he pulled the strings, and in Colonel Valentine Vivian he found the right puppet. In Philby's description he was a "reedy figure" with "carefully dressed crinkles in his hair, and wet eyes."[43] Cowgill was a brusque operator and unsparing in his criticisms of Vivian, sometimes reducing the older man to tears. Philby had provided Vivian with a shoulder to cry on; now he started whispering in his ear. Cowgill had left a trail of resentment in his wake, and Philby directed Vivian toward these injured parties, especially those who had influence over "C." Representatives from MI5, Naval intelligence, and the Foreign Office were soon in alignment: Cowgill was too abrasive for the job. With Cowgill out of the way, Philby emerged as the most credible candidate. "C" gave him the job in September 1944; Cowgill resigned in a huff. The much-vaunted Secret Intelligence Service had placed a Soviet spy in charge of anti-Communist espionage.

What Greene knew and when he knew it remains a mystery. Philby wanted Greene to take over the Iberian section when he moved up, but Greene declined the promotion. He later claimed he disliked Philby's cold ambition and did not want to become a "tiny cog in the machinery of [Philby's] intrigue" and that there was a more deserving candidate anyway. According to Tim Milne, who also worked in the Iberian section, Greene took him and Philby out to persuade them *not* to promote him.[44] What is odd is the time discrepancy. Did Philby attempt to involve Greene, who resigned four months before Philby's ascent, in his scheme? If he did, then Greene's resignation risked exposing the scheme to Cowgill.

Or was Greene spooked by something else? It was around this time that Angleton was told by "C" that the Soviets had penetrated British intelligence. Did this rumor reach Greene? If so, did he begin to suspect his drinking partner? Philby was an accomplished performer who used his stutter to buy himself time to think, and held his drink impeccably. Did Greene, a novelist who intently observed those around him for details of their characters, penetrate this facade? Did he recognize another composer of elaborate fiction? He was once asked what he would have done if he had known Philby was a spy. He said he would have given him twenty-four hours as a friend and then reported him. For now, as colleagues in the SIS they were through. But it was not the last they saw of each other: the Cold War found a way of bringing them back together.

TWELVE
Hemingway

RAMBOUILLET & PARIS, 1944–1945

THE GERMAN ANTITANK SHELL EXPLODED close enough to hurl Ernest Hemingway from the sidecar of the motorbike.[1] He landed facedown in the mud, stunned by the force of the explosion. Another shell went off nearby. As he raised his head to try to get his bearings a volley of machine-gun fire sent mud spattering in his face. He decided to lie still. The ringing in his ears was punctuated by snatched fragments of German carried on the wind and the occasional burst of fire from a light tank up ahead. The seconds turned into minutes, the minutes into hours. The ringing in his ears was not getting quieter. In London, a few weeks before, he had been in a car wreck that left him with fifty stitches in his scalp and a bad concussion.[2] That concussion was back with a vengeance.

The guns went silent and the only shooting Hemingway heard was that of Robert Capa's camera (the photographer had also been thrown from the sidecar). Convincing himself that Capa thought he was dead and was photographing the fresh corpse of the most famous writer in America, his anger built. As it got dark, and with American gunfire driving the Germans off, Hemingway got stiffly to his feet and started tearing into a bemused Capa for what he believed was morbid opportunism. But his rage blew itself out quickly; Hemingway was having too much fun to bear much of a grudge.

Racing round the country roads of Normandy, Hemingway was in his element. The change was remarkable. In the preceding months in Cuba he had drunk heavily, sinking frequently into black moods. His marriage to Martha Gellhorn was falling apart. He had stopped washing and his beard grew tangled and thick. War revitalized him. He shaved off his beard, preserving only a clipped military moustache. In London, he socialized furiously and sought opportunities that would take him to the front lines, so that he could write his dispatches for *Collier's*, a weekly magazine that had a circulation in excess of 2,500,000 by the end of the war. He spent D-Day amid the blood, vomit, and brine of a landing craft making for Fox Green beach; after returning to London, he flew in a bomber targeting V-1 rocket launch sites near Drancourt. He was in a de Havilland Mosquito when a V-1 exploded close by, and, according to the pilot, the plane "danced around like a leaf in a whirlwind."[3] Hemingway, taking ever greater risks, relished the danger.

After the Normandy landings, he managed to get himself attached as a reporter to General George Patton's tank corps, then to General Omar Bradley's First Army, before ending up with the Twenty-Second Infantry Regiment. Colonel "Buck" Lanham did not care what Hemingway got up to, which suited Hemingway perfectly. He was given a jeep and a driver, an Army private named Archie "Red" Pelkey, who, in Hemingway's description, had "bright red hair, six years of regular Army, four words of French, a missing front tooth."[4] The pair loaded the jeep up with a box full of maps and any rifles and grenades he could scrounge. Hemingway was not one to let an opportunity pass and, on his adventures, he "liberated" whatever he could lay his hands on, including the motorbike-with-sidecar and the wine cellar of a chateau.

In the fields and villages of Normandy, Hemingway blurred

the lines between reportage, reconnaissance, and combat. Just two days before he was thrown from his motorbike near St. Pois, Reuters reported that Hemingway and Pelkey took six German prisoners by throwing grenades into a farmhouse in which they were holed up. He seemed to carry little regard for his own safety and was lucky to not be worse hurt when he was sent flying from the motorbike. The concussion demanded rest, so Hemingway had Pelkey drive him to Mont Saint-Michel to regroup. A small island off the Normandy coast, connected to the mainland by a thin causeway, Mont Saint-Michel had been the site of a monastery since the eighth century. Hemingway installed himself at one of the island's finest hotels, La Mère Poulard, and, assisted by a group of other war correspondents, launched himself on a campaign of fine dining and serious drinking. John Ford, the film director celebrated for his Westerns, shot footage of Hemingway and Capa enjoying themselves.

Ford was working as a propagandist for the Office of Strategic Services. In the following days Hemingway managed to get himself a role as a liaison between the OSS and the French resistance. How exactly this happened is, even by the standards of Hemingway's notoriously slippery and contradictory biography, hard to pin down. According to one account he met with an OSS officer at Mont Saint-Michel and was given a brassard of the Free French Interior.[5] In another telling, Hemingway went rogue after leaving the island, recruiting a band of French Communist irregulars to become his private army; having made himself useful, the OSS decided to use him. Another version has Hemingway fighting with the resistance at the liberation of Chartres on August 18. What is for certain is that on August 20, David Bruce, head of OSS operations in Europe, met Hemingway in Chartres, and together they ran their own intelligence operation on the eve of the liberation of Paris.[6] It is a story that became inscribed in Hemingway mythology but it is also a story about the birth of the Central Intelligence Agency.

THE FOUNDING OF THE OSS was the result of British intervention. In June 1940 Churchill sent William Stephenson, a wealthy Canadian businessman, to Washington, DC, to establish the British Security Coordination (BSC). The goals of this clandestine outfit, based on the thirty-sixth floor of the Rockefeller Center, were to expose Axis activity in the United States, share intelligence, and shift American public opinion toward a pro-British position. As part of his work Stephenson lobbied President Roosevelt to create an American intelligence organization that could coordinate with the British agencies. Stephenson even identified the man he thought should run it: William Donovan, a hero of the First World War, who received the Medal of Honor for refusing to leave the command of his troops despite being shot in the knee. Such was his courage in the face of fire that his men gave him the nickname "Wild Bill." Roosevelt trusted Donovan and, unhappy with the reports he was getting through diplomatic channels about Britain's capacity to resist German invasion, sent him on a fact-finding mission to London in the summer of 1940. Unlike Joseph Kennedy, the defeatist American ambassador in London, Donovan believed that Britain could hold out if they received material support from the United States. As a result, he found British favor, including with Sir Stewart Menzies, head of SIS.

Back in Washington, Donovan drew up a plan for his spy agency with the help of an officer from British Naval Intelligence, Ian Fleming. Despite the opposition of J. Edgar Hoover's FBI, Roosevelt issued an executive order on July 11, 1940, establishing the Office of the Coordinator of Information, the bland name of which disguised its significance. "Wild Bill" and the future creator of James Bond successfully devised the first itera-tion of what became the CIA.

Hoover persisted in trying to kill the new agency, but Roos-evelt backed it, giving it a bigger budget and a larger scope when, in June 1942, it was rebranded the Office of Strategic Services. As a lawyer and a politician, Donovan was well connected, and he staffed his agency with the American elite: members of the DuPont, Mellon, Vanderbilt, and Whitney families worked for the OSS. J. P. Morgan's sons were both agents. Little wonder OSS soon acquired the nickname "Oh So Social."[7] Academics and literary figures were also employed. The playwright Robert Sherwood helped devise propaganda strategy. From his posi-tion as Librarian of Congress, the poet Archibald MacLeish (a good friend of Hemingway) helped set up the Research and Analysis branch (among the analysts were the historian Arthur Schlesinger Jr. and the German American philosopher Herbert Marcuse).

The man Donovan valued most, though, was Bruce. The forty-four-year-old lawyer and politician from a wealthy Virginia family had married Ailsa Mellon, daughter of Andrew Mellon, one of the richest men in America. But Bruce was not merely another well-heeled dilettante. He was good at his job. Donovan first made him head of Secret Intelligence and then sent him to London to run all operations in the European theater. Bruce's diary from the time documents a dizzying number of social en-gagements at Claridge's and the Ritz, as he mixed with English aristocracy and spymasters. He dined several times with "C," and even went to visit Felix Cowgill's Section V. In his diary, he noted that on that occasion he met Philby.[8]

By D-Day, Bruce had 2,900 people working for his London station. (There were 11,000 OSS officers and agents overall.)[9] Ahead of the Normandy invasion he helped organize a joint operation with the British (code-named "Sussex") by which two-man OSS and SIS teams were dropped behind enemy lines to gather intelligence. Bruce established a commando training facility in the countryside, and eighty-five OSS commandos parachuted into France to work with the resistance on sabotage projects. After the invasion, a further 276 OSS, British, and French commandos, known as the "Jedburghs," were dropped in.[10]

These were the kind of daring actions that appealed to Donovan and Bruce. They both subscribed to a code of courage and honor straight out of the Hemingway playbook. Knowing Wild Bill's predilection for frontline action, Generals George Marshall and Dwight Eisenhower forbade him from participating in the Normandy landings. He ignored the order and, taking Bruce with him, managed to wangle his way onto the USS *Tuscaloosa*. Furthermore, Donovan then finagled his way onto Utah Beach, cutting his chin when Bruce crashed into him trying to evade the guns of a strafing Messerschmitt. Making their way inland, the pair came under machine-gun fire and dove behind a hedgerow. It was only then that the two highest ranking spies in the OSS realized they had forgotten their suicide pills. Donovan informed Bruce that if they were to be captured, he would shoot Bruce first and then himself. Bruce, one imagines, was delighted when his boss decided to call it a day and return to the boat. Still, it was not long before Bruce was back on the front lines with a recklessly brave egomaniac.

THE OSS HAD INITIALLY REJECTED HEMINGWAY. And before he was rejected by them, he was recruited by the NKVD. Hemingway became fascinated by spies and guerrilla warfare while reporting on the Spanish Civil War. In September 1937, Hemingway was introduced to Alexander Orlov at the Gaylord Hotel in Madrid. Hemingway wanted to learn more about the NKVD's covert operations, and Orlov offered him a tour of one of their training camps at Benimàmet. The tour was given by Leonid Eitingon, who, three years later, organized the assassination of Trotsky. Afterward, Hemingway and Orlov drank Polish vodka and shot at one of the camp's rifle ranges.[11] Orlov thought the writer a good shot. Hemingway's newfound fascination with counterespionage and sabotage was expressed in his terrible play *The Fifth Column* and his brilliant novel *For Whom the Bell Tolls*.

The NKVD had already taken note of Hemingway's ardent anti-fascism, and his NKVD file records that they were particularly impressed by his speech at the American Writers Congress of June 1937.[12] In the autumn of 1940 they sought to recruit him. Jacob Golos, who ran a network of Soviet spies in the United States (including, later, members of the OSS), had a series of meetings that culminated in Hemingway giving him stamps that were to serve as a material password for future contact. He was to trust only those NKVD agents who had these stamps. Moscow Center gave him the codename ARGO. How seriously Hemingway took this is not known. He was sympathetic toward the Soviets for their having intervened on the side of the Republicans in Spain, a sympathy that was heightened by his anger at the British and Americans for failing to do so. He was a staunch anti-fascist. But it is hard to imagine his having the discipline for espionage, especially given the NKVD's strict rules for its agents in the field. He flew to China later that year to report on the war with Japan, and plans were made to make contact with an NKVD agent there. The meeting did not take place.[13] At the end of that trip, while in Manila, he debriefed American Military Intelligence (G-2) about his meetings with leaders of the two rival factions fighting the Japanese, Chiang Kai-shek (Kuomintang) and Zhou En-lai (the Communists). On his return to the United States, he reported what he had learned to Henry Morgenthau, Roosevelt's secretary of the Treasury. He clearly was no Communist ideologue.

His enthusiasm for espionage found new outlets. Back in Cuba, after Pearl Harbor and America's entrance into the war, Hemingway set up a private network of spies to root out possible Axis agents in Havana, all done with the approval of the American Embassy. Hemingway used his wide network of contacts, from card players and bartenders to aristocrats and priests, to deliver him information about anything suspicious. He then reported to Robert Joyce at the embassy. He called the network the Crook Factory; they did not uncover any Nazi spies. Hemingway's next scheme, again given the ambassador's blessing, was to equip his fishing boat, the *Pilar,* with bazookas, machine guns, and grenades, and go hunting U-boats off the Cuban coast. Appearing harmless, the "fishermen" hoped to get close enough to a German sub to throw grenades down the hatch or pierce the hull with a bazooka. Hemingway spent over a year on Operation Friendless, as he called it, but sighted only one German submarine, which got away before Hemingway and his crew could get close enough to attack.[14]

Gellhorn wanted to be closer to the action and left to report on the war from Europe. Despite their marital difficulties, she wanted Hemingway to join her and, on encountering Joyce in Italy, came up with a plan to do so. Joyce had recently left the embassy in Havana and was now working for the OSS. At Gellhorn's prompting, he cabled Whitney Shepardson, head of Secret Intelligence, recommending they offer Hemingway work. Internal reports reveal that the OSS was skeptical of Hemingway's politics (too red) and of his capacity for following orders (too unpredictable). After his candidacy bounced around different departments, Shepardson replied to Joyce in April 1944 with a rejection. "We may be wrong," he wrote, "but feel that although he has conspicuous ability for this type of work, he would be too much of an individualist to work under military supervision."[15]

Gellhorn tried another route. She was a good friend of Eleanor Roosevelt and at a White House dinner, she met a very tall, very handsome young Norwegian-British air attaché named Roald Dahl. The future children's author was in fact clandestinely working for Stephenson's BSC, keeping a close watch on Vice President Henry Wallace, with whom he played tennis and whose Communist sympathies made him suspect. Dahl also used his personal charms to sleep with important women, including Clare Boothe Luce, seeking to stir pro-British sentiment or pick up relevant high society gossip. When Gellhorn appealed to him on Hemingway's behalf, Dahl was only too keen to help his literary hero. A meeting was arranged, and the pair sparred at a New York boxing ring before retreating to the Gladstone Hotel for champagne and caviar, which they ate out of a two-kilo tin.[16] Dahl secured Hemingway passage to London as a correspondent of the RAF. Hemingway was about to get his chance to be a secret service agent after all.

WHILE OUT DOING HIS OWN RECONNAISSANCE in the fields of Normandy, Hemingway ran into two car-loads of French resistance fighters. They were affiliated with the Francs-Tireurs et Partisans, the Communist branch of the resistance, and while poorly armed and dressed in tattered clothes, they were ready for a fight. They took a liking to the hulking American, and he got them organized, liberating clothing and weapons from the American military. He stationed his band at the Hotel Grand Veneur in Rambouillet, a small town twenty-five miles southwest of Paris. This town was a strategically important location, as it was on the route the Allied armies were planning to take as they marched on Paris. The Germans had abandoned Rambouillet, but there were concerns that with no opposing troops present, they might retake it and then set up ambushes and lay minefields. On August 18, Hemingway and his men went in to hold the town and recce the surrounding area.

When Bruce met Hemingway in nearby Chartres a couple of days later, he decided to join him in Rambouillet despite the fact that Donovan was due in town that day. In his diary, Bruce wrote that he was "enchanted" by his new friend. It is not hard to understand the appeal. In the 1920s, as a young veteran of the First World War, Bruce lived for a time in Paris, admiring the American artists and writers of the cultural avant-garde. He had been a good friend of F. Scott Fitzgerald (they'd met at Princeton) but did not know Hemingway, only his work.[17] As a teenager Bruce had harbored literary ambitions, translating French poetry and plays; during the war he read Shakespeare on the long flights between Washington and London. Hemingway offered something special to someone like Bruce. With the hypermasculine code he distilled in the early Nick Adams stories and *The Sun Also Rises* and *A Farewell to Arms*, Hemingway created literature that was neither "effete" nor "foreign." Nor was he simply trying to be European: Hemingway was cosmopolitan, but he was also distinctly American. Hemingway's idea of what constituted a hero was hugely influential over a certain class of American reader. Little wonder that the cultivated machismo he curated in his fiction pervaded the culture of the OSS. In turn, for a few days in August 1944, the OSS gave Hemingway the opportunity to develop another aspect of his legend.

Bruce was amazed by Hemingway's setup at the Grand Veneur. His team occupied eight rooms, with Hemingway's functioning as headquarters. Maps were tacked to the wall, and there was a constant stream of men coming in to deliver reports of sightings of German forces. "Carbines stood in each corner," Bruce wrote, "revolvers of every nationality were heaped carelessly on the bed, the bathtub was filled with hand grenades, and the basin with brandy bottles, while under the bed was a cache of Army rations and whisky."[18] Hemingway ruled the roost, dispensing discipline with his fists.

By Hemingway's estimate there were some 150 German troops just north of Rambouillet, and one of his patrols had watched them laying land mines. Bruce raced off to deliver this information to the American army at Maintenon, returning with two crates of hand grenades and a promise of reinforcements from the local resistance. Bruce described the hotel that night as "bedlam," as agents and reporters came and went, with rumors circulating that the town was going to be a staging point for the invasion of Paris. By Bruce's estimate there were thirty Americans, including two drunken AWOL paratroopers, at the hotel that night, plus ten French Communists, fourteen gendarmes, a Free French secret service operative code-named "Mouthard" (real name Michel Pasteau), and Airey Neave, a British former POW who had escaped from Colditz and was now with military intelligence. The numerous eyewitness accounts of that night in Rambouillet cheerfully contradict each other, but on one thing they are consistent: there was considerable drinking.

The following day the party dispersed. The reporters followed fresh rumors that the American forces were going to march on Paris using a different route. Hemingway and Bruce were left with a handful of OSS agents and the French Communists to hold Rambouillet. Hemingway and Mouthard continued to interrogate anyone coming from the direction of Paris, getting information about minefields and troop movements. Bruce carried with him a radio and transmitter, and he relayed any important information gathered to OSS headquarters. Bruce was informed that there would be an airdrop that night, and he and Hemingway took a jeep out into the dark to pick up a crate of bazookas and grenades.

The spoils of liberation were mixed with violent retribution. In his diary, Bruce recorded himself and Hemingway lending Mouthard a revolver to execute a suspected collaborator—only, in the same entry, to marvel at the "hunting alleys" of the local chateau (which Bruce had promptly requisitioned). Accounts of interrogations in the Hotel Veneur were followed by details of dining on "a Paté de Foie Gras stuffed abundantly with truffles."[19] Bruce had seen mutilated corpses left behind by the SS, with eyes gouged out and genitals torn off, but he also enjoyed some fine filet mignon. Surrounded by death, the agent and the writer were determined to remain bon viveurs. In this Bruce had been seduced by Hemingway's modus operandi: to live in a way that could be fashioned into future fiction, whether in the pages of his stories or while sitting at the bar.

On the rainy morning of August 24, after six days of holding Rambouillet, Hemingway and his gang joined the Allied forces as they marched on Paris. Leading the column was General Philippe Leclerc's Second French Armored Division. The previous evening Hemingway and Bruce briefed Leclerc's intelligence officer about what lay ahead (Leclerc himself had dismissed the pair with an expletive).[20] Most of the German forces had withdrawn, but there were still pockets of Nazi resistance. Some nine kilometers outside of Versailles, the column came to a crossroads, and Hemingway knew the ambush was coming. "Past the aerodrome toward Buc they had 88s that commanded all that stretch of road," he wrote. "As we came closer to where the tanks were operating around Trappes I became increasingly apprehensive."[21]

Sure enough, the shells whistled in. "I hit the deck as an 88 shell burst alongside the road," Hemingway wrote. A cacophony of gunfire erupted as the French forces and German tanks began exchanging fire. Hemingway's private army had done its job, though. They had given the French the location of the German 88s ahead of time and the artillery, in Hemingway's phrase, "slammed into them."[22] Soon enough the column was back on the march.

This incident is exemplary of the way stories about Hemingway took on a life of their own. In Hemingway's account, published in *Collier's* on October 7, he wrote that he "had never been a great lover of contact" and that his men spent the battle using rubble to fill potholes in the road. Yet Bruce, having breakfast at a local farm during the "contact," was somehow led to believe that Hemingway and his band had been involved in the fighting. In his diary, he wrote that "Hemingway and the Private Army . . . had been engaged in a battle between French tanks and two Boche 88 guns."[23] Did he fight, or did he hide? The problem is exacerbated by the fact that as an accredited reporter Hemingway was forbidden from fighting and could incriminate himself by writing about it. Out of these kinds of discrepancies, the Hemingway myth was generated.

As the column neared Paris, Hemingway recalled the French tanks "smashing round like so many drunken elephants in a native village."[24] He temporarily lost Pelkey, who mistook the explosions of a burning munitions dump for a battle and rushed off to join it. When they were reunited, Pelkey started asking Hemingway about Paris. In an article for *Collier's* he rendered the conversation in his typically laconic style.

PELKEY: "They say this Paris is quite a town, Papa. You ever been into it?"

HEMINGWAY: "Yeah."

PELKEY: "They're a good outfit. Best outfit I ever been with. No discipline. Got to admit that. Drinking all the time. Got to admit that. But plenty fighting outfit. Nobody gives a damn if they get killed or not. *Compris?*"

HEMINGWAY: "Yeah."

In fact, Hemingway's spare responses were the result of his trying to contain his emotions. "I had a funny choke in my throat," he wrote, "and I had to clean my glasses because there now, below us, gray and always beautiful, was spread the city that I love best in all the world."[25]

FROM THE MOMENT HEMINGWAY and his band got to the banks of the Seine on the outskirts of Paris, they were greeted by people lining the streets, draping flags from their windows, and breaking out the booze in celebration. "In the course of the afternoon," Bruce wrote, "we had beer, cider, white and red Bordeaux, white and red Burgundy, champagne, rum, whiskey, cognac, armagnac, and Calvados."[26] It was, he said, "enough to wreck one's constitution." Nevertheless, they survived and stopped overnight a mile short of the Pont de Sèvres.

The following day they entered Paris. Amid the frantic celebrations there was still danger. At a large square near the Bois de Boulogne, Hemingway and Bruce dived for the cover of a shop-front doorway on hearing the crack of sniper fire. A tank's cannon destroyed the sniper and his vantage. The surging crowds brought the liberating army almost to a halt. Hemingway and Bruce decided to peel off and make their own way into the center of the city. Using back streets—Hemingway knew the city intimately—they made their way to the Avenue Foch. At the base of the Arc de Triomphe they found six veterans standing guard over the tomb of the unknown soldier. A French captain invited them to ascend.

From the top of the Arc de Triomphe, the writer and the spy surveyed the liberation of Paris. "The view was breathtaking," Bruce wrote. "One saw the golden dome of the Invalides, the green roof of the Madeleine, Sacré-Coeur, and other familiar landmarks. Tanks were firing in various streets. Part of the Arc was under fire from snipers. A shell from a German 88 nicked one of its sides."[27] The Majestic Hotel, which the Germans used as military headquarters, was on fire, and firefights were crackling all over the city. Still, Parisians packed every square, making it almost impossible to get anywhere. Hemingway noticed that the Champs-Élysées was temporarily clear of people, possibly because of snipers. They got back in their jeep and sped down the avenue at full speed. They went first to the Traveller's, a private members' club where Bruce and Hemingway drank champagne before once again getting caught up in the celebrating crowd, this time at the Place de l'Opéra. They eventually retreated to the Ritz Hotel, which they found deserted except for the manager, Claude Auzello. This seemed as good a place as any for Hemingway and his band to set up shop. "Ausiello [sic] asked what he could immediately do for us," Bruce wrote, "and we answered that we would like fifty martini cocktails" (less well known is Bruce's verdict that, without a barman, the martinis weren't very good).[28]

Hemingway established himself in room 31 at the Ritz and the next morning took his band with him to see Sylvia Beach, the owner of the famous Shakespeare & Company bookshop, which had been closed during the occupation (Beach spent six months in an internment camp).[29] Beach was a champion of modernist literature: she had published *Ulysses* in 1922 and had promoted Hemingway's first book, *Three Stories and Ten Poems,* the following year. Her bookshop remained a hub for Paris's cultured expats.

Hemingway threw himself back into the romance of Paris. Mary Welsh, an American reporter with whom he had begun an affair in London, joined him in the city, and they visited those old friends of his who were still there. He even found Picasso painting in his old studio. His friend Marlene Dietrich also took a suite at the Ritz, using it as a base between assignments singing for the troops.[30]

The liberation of the Ritz became part of Hemingway folklore.

With each retelling the tales got taller. In one account, he and his men plotted to enter the city before Leclerc's army but were foiled when General Patton got wind of their scheme and had them surrounded. Another version, that Hemingway favored later in his life, was that he and his men were the first into Paris and that they had watched Leclerc's arrival from the Ritz. It is one of the many ironies of this episode that Hemingway spent the days before the liberation of Paris scrupulously gathering verifiable intelligence while simultaneously burnishing the fiction of his biography.

RECKLESS ADVENTURISM might have burnished the Hemingway brand, but it was Donovan's undoing. The maverick quality of the OSS did not sit well with many in the American military and political establishment, and Donovan knew he faced an uphill struggle to establish his agency on a permanent footing. His most powerful enemy was J. Edgar Hoover, who did not want an intelligence agency to rival his FBI; Donovan suspected him of leaking confidential documents proposing a postwar intelligence service to the press. In February 1945, the newspapers accused Donovan and Roosevelt of planning a "super spy system" and a series of articles in the *Washington Times-Herald* warned that this agency would use secret funds for "bribery and luxury living," comparing the proposed agency to the novels of thriller writer E. Phillips Oppenheim.[31] The negative publicity meant plans for a peacetime OSS were shelved.

Roosevelt had not given up on Donovan's proposal, however, and commissioned an informal review of the OSS, assigning one of his trusted aides, Colonel Richard Park, to the job. Park's report was devastating for Donovan: it characterized the OSS as a dangerously incompetent old boys' network run by an unstable maverick. While Park grudgingly acknowledged some of the OSS's successes, his report focused on the numerous operational failures and excessive spending. Donovan's personality was part of the problem, Park argued, especially his enthusiasm for wild schemes. It was a point hard to dispute. "Woe to the officer," Bruce recalled, "who turned down a project because, on its face, it seemed ridiculous, or at least unusual."[32] Examples of these dubious schemes were numerous, including a plan to drop pornography on German positions as a means of distracting and dispiriting their forces and another to inject female hormones into the vegetables Hitler ate in order that his voice might raise an octave and his hair, including his moustache, fall out. In the final months of the war, Donovan enthused over a scheme to daub foxes with glow-in-the-dark paint and release them in Japan, where fox spirits were considered ominous omens. He also seriously considered the idea of strapping incendiary bombs to bats and releasing them on Tokyo.[33] While none of these outlandish plans were implemented, they reeked of amateurism. Park also expressed serious—and well-founded—concerns that the OSS had been penetrated by British and Soviet intelligence services.[34] Yet while it was incompetent and porous, the OSS, Park argued, also somehow managed to display "all the earmarks of a gestapo system." It was clear that his report was designed to kill the OSS from a variety of angles.

Any last hopes Donovan had of saving the OSS evaporated on the morning of April 13, 1945, almost a year after Bruce and Hemingway had participated in the liberation of Paris. Donovan was shaving in the bathroom of his suite ahead of breakfast with William J. Casey, one of his best and most trusted OSS officers, when he was informed that President Roosevelt had died the previous night. According to Casey, Donovan sat on his bed for three hours, mourning Roosevelt. He was also mourning his agency.

When Harry Truman read the Park report, the OSS was finished.[35] In October 1945 the new president disbanded the OSS, giving Donovan ten days to shut it down. Parts of the agency were hived off and preserved, however. The Research and Analysis team moved into the State Department, while Bruce's Secret Intelligence operations and X-2, the counterespionage team that worked with Philby, Greene, and the SIS, went to the War Department.

That was far from the end of the matter, however. No sooner had the Second World War ended than the United States entered a different kind of conflict, one in which a global intelligence agency suddenly seemed more necessary than ever. The Soviet Union boasted a highly sophisticated network of agents all over the world and had penetrated the intelligence services of most of its rivals. In almost every department—espionage, counterespionage, propaganda, covert actions—they were ahead of the Americans. Donovan's methods might have been flawed, but his basic idea was correct: the United States needed a permanent intelligence agency to fight the cold war that followed the hot one.

When the Central Intelligence Agency was created in 1947, it traced its lineage directly back to the OSS. Allen Dulles and Lawrence Houston, both former OSS officers, were instrumental in writing up the legislation that created the new agency. Some OSS officers operating abroad, including Richard Helms in Germany and James Jesus Angleton in Italy, were retained after the OSS was disbanded and integrated into the new agency. Ultimately, four OSS officers (Dulles, William Colby, Casey, and Helms) became CIA directors.

The CIA inherited more than just personnel from the OSS: it also retained in its DNA some of Donovan's adventurism. This was enabled by its structure: the CIA became an agency that both gathered intelligence and launched special operations. In this regard it was different from the SIS, which was responsible only for overseas intelligence (the Special Operations Executive was responsible for special operations). What this meant was that the CIA was responsible for both espionage and commando missions. This was to prove of enormous consequence in the coming decades. OSS agents had learned from resistance groups in Europe about guerrilla warfare and sabotage and, in turn, strategies for suppressing insurgent fighters, knowledge that they were soon putting to use in their proxy wars with the Soviet Union. While Donovan's eccentricities were gone, the obsession with bold, even reckless "actions" remained, resulting in some of the most controversial operations of the Cold War, typified by the failed invasion of Cuba at the Bay of Pigs in 1961.

The CIA also inherited the cultural politics of the OSS. Donovan's agency was one of cosmopolitan interventionists like Bruce, much more progressive and cultivated than the reactionaries in J. Edgar Hoover's FBI, who harassed and spied on a whole generation of American writers.[36] If in the aftermath of the Second World War there were to be a Pax Americana, these representatives of the American elite believed strongly that it should be based not just on economic and military power but also on strong cultural foundations. It would be necessary, by their way of thinking, to prove to the world that American democratic capitalism produced more than just cheap consumer goods; in fact, it would be necessary to demonstrate that it was a political and economic system in which sophisticated culture would flourish. This meant that while the CIA was gathering intelligence, destabilizing regimes, and conducting covert actions, it was also invested in promoting art and literature that it perceived as being in the American interest. The United States might be known for Coca-Cola and the Ford motor car, but it should also be known for the books of William Faulkner and Ernest Hemingway. It was important, though, that such cultural propaganda be kept secret if it were to prove effective; the former officers of the OSS prepared to use their new agency to open a literary front in the Cold War.

THIRTEEN

Orwell & Koestler

LONDON, 1944–1945

WHEN GEORGE ORWELL ARRIVED IN PARIS, he went look-ing for a gun. Wearing the uniform of a war correspondent, he stashed his suitcase and typewriter at the Hotel Scribe, where the other foreign reporters were based. Back on the streets he was alert and wary. How hard would it be for the NKVD to kill him? His experiences in Spain taught him how ruthless Soviet agents were in eliminating their enemies, and Trotsky's assass-ination was evidence of the range of Stalin's reach. Perhaps he was overrating his reputation with the Soviets, perhaps he was being paranoid. Nevertheless, Orwell wanted a gun and he knew just the writer to get one from: Ernest Hemingway.

This was March 1945 and the war in Europe was nearing its end. The Allies had crossed the Rhine and the Red Army was closing on Berlin. After his adventures during the liberation of Paris, Hemingway went on to cover the war in Germany. Paris, though, remained his base, and when he was in town, usually staying at the Ritz, the great and the good came to call. Jean-Paul Sartre and Simone de Beauvoir were recent guests, finding Papa in high spirits; Hemingway drank Sartre into the worst hang-over of his life.

Relying on these stories of Hemingway's conviviality, and

their mutual friendship of Cyril Connolly, Orwell made his way to the Ritz, looked up the famous writer in the register, and went up to room 117. He knocked on the door, Hemingway opened it. The burly American faced a tall, reed-thin Englishman with a clipped moustache. "Who are you?" he asked. "Eric Blair," Orwell replied. "Well, what the fucking hell do you want?" asked Hemingway. "I'm George Orwell," the visitor clarified. "Why the fucking hell didn't you say so?" said Hemingway, reaching for the scotch. "Have a drink. Have a double. Straight or with water, there's no soda."[1]

Hemingway thought Orwell looked "very gaunt . . . in bad shape" and invited him to stay and eat. Orwell declined but asked if Hemingway might have a gun he could borrow. All Hemingway had that Orwell could conceal on his person was a .32 Colt with a short barrel. Hemingway warned his guest that if he shot someone with it "they would probably die eventually, but that there might be a long interval." Hemingway then offered Orwell "a couple of people" to watch over him "if 'They' were after him." Orwell declined, saying the gun was all he needed. Hemingway had Orwell tailed to make sure he was not being followed (his men assured him that Orwell was not being watched). So, according to Hemingway, went the only meeting between these two writers.

Once again, however, Hemingway's memory tended to serve his personal mythology above the truth. Certainly it is strange that for such a dramatic meeting, Orwell never wrote a word about it, even in the letters he was sending home from France.[2] It does look like the two writers met briefly in Paris (although whether at the Ritz or the Scribe is contested). They were both in the city in the early spring of 1945. Three years later, in a letter to Orwell's friend Cyril Connolly, Hemingway wrote, "If you ever see Orwell, remember me to him, will you? I like him very much and it was a moment when I had no time when I met him."[3] A hurried meeting, a missed opportunity: this seems plausible enough.

Four years later, in 1952, Hemingway wrote, in a letter to Harvey Breit, that Orwell feared being "knocked off by the communists and he asked me to loan him a pistol." Hemingway then wrote for a third time about this meeting with Orwell. In *True at First Light,* the "fictional memoir" published posthumously in 1999, Hemingway claimed that Orwell had come to room 117 of the Ritz "where there was still a small arsenal" from the weapons he and his partisans had collected the previous year.[4] In this version, Hemingway added the detail of having Orwell followed to make sure he was safe.

Was Hemingway making this up? What complicates this theory is that there is another version of the meeting, which comes from Paul Potts, a poet Orwell met and befriended in London in 1944. Potts claimed Orwell told him of meeting Hemingway, including the detail of his initially introducing himself as Eric Blair. But in the Potts account there is no mention of a gun. What really happened that day in the Ritz (or the Scribe) is impossible to know. Hemingway's retellings, however, do explain something about Orwell's change in status. In 1945 Orwell was a distinguished writer and Hemingway, with his interest in the Spanish Civil War, may well have read *Homage to Catalonia.* He might also have recognized Orwell's byline from the columns he wrote for *Partisan Review,* or, while in London before D-Day, from his reviews and essays in the British press. He was not, though, in the same league as Hemingway, who was about as famous a writer could get. That was soon to change. After the war, Hemingway's stock declined as his work soured. Orwell, in contrast, became the iconic writer of a generation, grappling with a refigured world order divided between Western capitalism and Soviet communism. In his drink-addled braggadocio,

Hemingway appears to have seduced himself into the idea that he helped out Orwell more than he may have actually done.

Yet amid the embellishment there also emerges a kernel of important truth. Orwell *was* afraid of the NKVD and he *did* want a gun. Later that year, back in London, Orwell bought a Luger from Rodney Phillips, so it is certainly credible that he was looking for a gun in Paris.[5] He would soon become convinced that Communists were spying on him and going through his mail. While much of this had no basis in fact—there was no Soviet hit squad hunting him through the streets of Paris—the NKVD had only a few months previously sought to sabotage his work. As Orwell had learned in Spain, just because he was paranoid did not mean they weren't after him.

When the Second World War began, Orwell had wanted to fight. He was back in his element, energized by the conflict as he had been by the war in Spain; Connolly described him slipping into the war "as into an old tweed jacket."[6] Some on the left quailed at the idea of supporting the war, but Orwell, a critic of empire and jingoism, was clear-sighted about the threat of fascism. "The intellectuals who are at present pointing out that democracy and fascism are the same thing, depress me horribly," he wrote to Victor Gollancz in January 1940.[7] He had himself subscribed to a similar argument against intervention until the bombs started to fall. It was living in London during the Blitz that roused his inner patriot, and he sought to resolve the conflict between his patriotism and his socialism in print, firing off a volley of important essays, including "My Country Right or Left" and "The Lion and the Unicorn," the latter published as part of a series he edited (with Tosco Fyvel, a German-born Jewish journalist who worked for British intelligence later in the war) called Searchlight Books. In these essays he made the argument that Britain needed to defeat fascism and that in order to do so, Britain needed to undergo radical political change, to cast off the nineteenth-century vestiges of imperialism and laissez-faire capitalism and embrace socialism. A united Britain could then emerge victorious from the war as a model of a socialist society that did not resort to the totalitarian methods deployed by the Soviet Union. This was a future worth fighting for.

The British Army would not let him fight, however. In the early years of the war the military were suspicious of those who had served in Spain, but in Orwell's case there was a much more straightforward reason for rejecting him: his lungs. Orwell suffered from bronchitis as an infant and had contracted pneumonia multiple times. In 1938, he was admitted to Preston Hall sanatorium and was initially diagnosed with bronchiectasis and subsequently found to have tuberculosis. During the war, Orwell's health improved, and a Harley Street pulmonologist told him he had nothing worse than chronic bronchiectasis.[8] Still, it was not enough to get him past the Medical Board, who declared him unfit for service. Instead he enlisted as a sergeant in the Home Guard, in which he served with his publisher, Fred Warburg. He took this work seriously, drawing on his experiences in Spain to instruct his men in street-fighting, field fortifications, and the use of mortars.

In the summer of 1941 he began serving his country as a propagandist. The BBC Eastern Service made him a talks assistant with a responsibility of broadcasting material to India. He summarized news reports on the progress of the war and organized cultural programs. He secured a prestigious list of contributors, including Mulk Raj Anand, Cyril Connolly, T. S. Eliot, E. M. Forster, Stephen Spender, and Dylan Thomas, who all read from their own work. William Empson, who worked next door to Orwell at the BBC and was in charge of broadcasting to China, also contributed. This was a sociable time, despite, or perhaps because of, the bombing of London. Orwell had regular lunches with Connolly and Spender, and developed new friendships with Anthony Powell and Malcolm Muggeridge, meeting at the Bodega off the Strand. Later in the war, through a mutual friend, he got to know Graham Greene, whose writing he admired, and the two dined regularly in Soho restaurants.[9]

In the ferment of wartime London, Orwell's reputation continued to grow, thanks to the reviews and essays he published in *Horizon* from 1940 and the regular column he wrote for *Partisan Review* from 1941. As an influential voice on the non-Communist left he came into the social orbit of reformist politicians and left-leaning publishers and journalists. Edward Hulton and Gerald Barry founded an informal dining club that met every Tuesday at the Shanghai restaurant in Soho, and they invited prominent intellectuals and politicians to meet and discuss the way the country should be reformed after the war. Orwell was invited to join by David Astor, who was busy shaking up his father's paper, the *Observer*. William Beveridge, whose 1942 report laid the foundations of the British welfare state, was in the club, as was Stafford Cripps, the Labour politician and former ambassador to the Soviet Union who had joined Churchill's War Cabinet on his return from Moscow in 1942. That June, when Cripps handpicked some writers to meet with him and discuss Britain's political future, Orwell was among them.

Drawn inevitably to these networks of influence were Soviet spies. Among the most notorious meetings of the Shanghai dining club was a furious row between Guy Burgess and the Polish journalist Isaac Deutscher (who later became famous for his biographies of Trotsky and Stalin).[10] When Orwell recorded in his diary going to meet Cripps, he also noted that Burgess was in attendance; he already knew Burgess as they frequently collaborated in their work at the BBC.[11] It was, though, another figure from the Shanghai dining club whom Orwell needed to watch

out for. At some point that year—the date is not clear—Orwell
went for lunch with Astor, Deutscher, and Peter Smollett, a high-
ranking official in the Ministry of Information, running the
Russian section. Before the war, Smollett was a well-connected
journalist who had made his reputation by writing about the Soviet Union. He was close to Churchill's trusted advisor, Brendan Bracken, and it is perhaps through this connection that he
had secured the Ministry of Information position. He promoted
Anglo-Soviet relations by organizing a series of high-profile
events, including a choral performance at the Royal Albert Hall
to celebrate the twenty-fifth anniversary of the founding of the
Red Army, complete with readings by Laurence Olivier and
John Gielgud. He also organized for the film *USSR at War* to be
screened at factories around the country, with a total estimated
audience of 1.25 million. He was good at his job, and Astor
wanted him to be editor at the *Observer*.[12] He also wanted Orwell to work for the newspaper. Perhaps that had been the reason
for their meeting. It seems to have gone off well, and years later
Smollett recalled the lunch fondly to Astor.[13] Orwell would have
reason to regret coming into Smollett's orbit.

IN THE SOCIAL SCENE OF WARTIME LONDON, Orwell's most
important new friendship was the one he forged with Arthur
Koestler. Both men admired each other's work and, thanks to
the match-making of Fred Warburg, they first met in February 1941,
a month after Orwell had positively reviewed *Darkness at Noon*.
Koestler had been released from Pentonville prison the previous
December, and after writing *Scum of the Earth*, his memoir of his
imprisonment in France during the Nazi occupation, had been
assigned to the Aliens' Pioneer Corps, a depository for foreigners
who could not be trusted to fight. He endured basic training and
was stationed in Cheltenham, spending his days digging tank

traps and fake craters to deceive German bombers. He managed to evade some of this back-breaking work by giving lectures to the Army Educational Corps, but when his commanding officer—the dour Major McKay—clamped down on this, Koestler collapsed and was taken to hospital. He claimed he had had a nervous breakdown, but the medical corporal suspected he had deliberately overdosed on codeine pills.[14] As Koestler convalesced he was declared unfit for service and offered a job in either military intelligence or the Ministry of Information—he chose the latter.

Free from military duty, Koestler plunged into the social life of literary London. He moved in with Connolly, who threw a big party for him, at which he met Spender, Louis MacNeice, Philip Toynbee, and John Lehmann. Another night he got drunk with Dylan Thomas, Michael Foot, and Joe Alsop. The author of *Spanish Testament* and *Darkness at Noon* was a big draw, and he always put on a performance. He was confrontational, arguing lucidly despite his thick accent, he drank heavily, and he chased women. "Like everyone who talks of ethics all day long," Connolly later said, "one could not trust him half an hour with one's wife, one's best friend, one's manuscripts or one's wine merchant—he'd lose them all. He burns with the envious paranoiac hunger of the Central European ant-heap, he despises everybody and can't conceal the fact when he's drunk, yet I believe he is probably one of the most powerful forces for good in the country."[15]

By day he was, like Orwell, a propagandist. Koestler spent the spring of 1942 writing anti-Nazi broadcasts for the Home Service of the BBC. He was motivated by a sense of personal urgency, and one of his priorities was to raise awareness of what was happening in the Nazi concentration camps, where he feared many family and friends were interned. He also worked on "black" propaganda for Richard Crossman in the War Office.[16] While

Orwell swiftly became disenchanted by propaganda work, finding it almost pointless, Koestler embraced it, drawing on his time
in the Comintern for different strategies. Sensing this aptitude,
Crossman invited Koestler to meet Dick White, head of MI5.
This being British intelligence, it took place over a game of cro-
quet. Also invited were Victor Rothschild, by then a senior MI5
officer, and the legal philosopher Herbert Hart. White wanted
them to band together and come up with new propaganda ideas
"to make Goebbels sit up."[17] Nothing came of this proposal, but
Koestler became increasingly expert in cultural propaganda.

As a further sign of Koestler's social ascent, he and Daphne
Hardy were invited to move into the Kensington mansion of
George Strauss, the wealthy backer of *Tribune* (where Orwell
was literary editor). The house, close to Hyde Park, was a social
hub of the Labour Party, and Aneurin Bevan, Michael Foot,
John Strachey, and Crossman were frequent guests. Despite
working closely with Strauss, Orwell was a relatively infrequent
visitor—his ascetic lifestyle was at odds with the opulence of the
dinners—but on one occasion at which he was present Koestler,
who had a weakness for the metaphysical, somehow persuaded
him to take part in a levitation experiment. Orwell remained
steadfastly on the ground. Koestler later admitted to finding
Orwell intimidating, like a "real Burmah [*sic*] police sergeant,"
so at least he had the courage to ask.[18] Nevertheless, despite his
friend's capacity for excess, Orwell valued Koestler and asked
him to contribute to Searchlight Books.

After years of turmoil and time spent in Spanish, French, and
British prisons, Koestler should have been having the time of his
life. Instead he suffered a breakdown. One of the catalysts was a
meeting with the Polish resistance fighter Jan Karski, who had
seen firsthand what was happening in the Belsen concentration
camp. Koestler feared his mother was in Auschwitz, and many
of his friends were unaccounted for, presumably in the camps.

His horror at hearing the details of the slaughter was followed by outrage at the continued skepticism with which these accounts were treated by many in Britain. The suffering of those he loved left him repulsed at his own hedonism. His drinking and promiscuity were followed by self-lacerating hangovers, and his relationship with Daphne fell apart.

In the midst of what he called his "neurosis," Koestler became fascinated by Mamaine Paget, whom he nicknamed "Mermaid." He was not alone in his fascination. While Paget was a debutante who had been presented at court, she worked for the Ministry of Economic Warfare and preferred to mix with intellectuals and writers than high society types. Edmund Wilson, in London for *The New Yorker*, was smitten by her and, despite being married to Mary McCarthy, wrote a poem about her beauty that he published in *The New Yorker*. Wilson proposed to Paget on a subsequent visit.

Paget and her twin sister, Celia, owned the house Connolly rented, and it was through this connection that Koestler first met her in January 1944. But Koestler's fascination with Paget turned violent. Despite his feelings for her, Koestler took Celia out to dinner and tried to sleep with her. She rejected him. The following night, Koestler took Paget out and, afterward, raped her.

"I know that I behaved in a rather swinish way," he subsequently wrote to her. "I got you to allow me to make love to you by the usual old tricks and cunning—but I still believe that is permissible if the result is enjoyed by both. Without an element of initial rape there is no delight."[19] Despite Koestler's horrific assault that night and his egregious attempt to rationalize it, he and Paget began an intense relationship. Koestler was locked into self-destructive behavior. When Hemingway arrived in London ahead of the D-Day landings, Connolly decided to throw a party for him. Hemingway was late and by the time he arrived, with his head in a bandage after his car accident, Koestler was already

well oiled on Connolly's potent punch. Paget sat next to Hemingway over dinner but, embarrassed by her lover's boorishness,
tried to leave early, prompting what she called "violent protests"
from Koestler. By the end of the party he had managed to insult
everybody in the room.[20]

Unsurprisingly, given his state of mind, Koestler suffered
from writer's block. His doctor prescribed him drugs (possibly
some form of amphetamine) to help him get past it, but he was
nevertheless forced to abandon the novel he was working on.
And while he was heartened by the success of Allied landings
on D-Day, he grew increasingly concerned about the placatory
rhetoric directed toward the Soviet Union. For his propaganda
work he had been preoccupied with attacking the Nazis from
every conceivable angle, but with the tide of war having turned,
he feared the Allies were complacent about the threat posed by
Stalin in a postwar world. It was during this period that he received a package of dog-eared manuscript pages from Orwell.
Koestler read *Animal Farm* with enraptured rapidity. "Envious
congratulations," Koestler wrote to Orwell. "This is a glorious
and heart-breaking allegory; it has the poesy of a fairytale and
the precision of a chess problem. Reviewers will say that it ranks
with Swift, and I shall agree with them."[21]

ORWELL WROTE *ANIMAL FARM* in just over three months, beginning in November 1943 and finishing in February 1944. The
book had been brewing ever since he returned from Spain with
the idea of "exposing the Soviet myth in a story that could be
easily understood by almost anyone and which could be easily translated into other languages."[22] The outbreak of war distracted him from those plans, but by the summer of 1942 he was
back thinking about Spain again. Alex Comfort, an anarchist
and pacifist (and future author of *The Joy of Sex*), approached

Orwell to write an essay for *New Road,* a magazine he was editing. Over the following months, Orwell wrote the excoriating "Looking Back on the Spanish War," which eventually came out, albeit with certain sections cut, in *New Road* in June 1943.[23]

Writing about Spain again stirred up dormant emotions and, after leaving the BBC in November and taking the position of literary editor at *Tribune,* he found he had time to go back to a story about the "Soviet myth." "You will be glad to hear that I *am* writing a book again at last," Orwell wrote to his literary agent, Leonard Moore. "While with the BBC I hardly had time to set pen to paper, but in this job with the Tribune I think I can so organise my time as to get 2 spare days a week for my own work. The thing I am doing is quite short, so if nothing intervenes it should be done in 3 or 4 months."[24] Orwell was clearly excited by the prospect of writing a new novel and told Philip Rahv, his editor at *Partisan Review,* about it in a letter a few days later.

Orwell's idea was to take a genre and subvert it. He chose to tell his story of the Russian Revolution and the subsequent slide into Stalinism as a fairy tale. Animated by the philosophy of an old pig named Old Major (a fusion of Marx and Lenin), the animals of Manor Farm, angered by their treatment at the hands of their owner, Mr. Jones (Tsar Nicholas II), decide to rebel. The revolution is successfully led by the pigs Snowball (Trotsky) and Napoleon (Stalin), who subsequently defeat the farmer when he seeks to retake the farm in the Battle of the Cowshed (the Russian Civil War). For a brief period, the animals rejoice in their victory, and agree to live under the seven commandments of "Animalism," which include vows not to drink, walk on two legs, sleep in beds, or kill other animals. The final commandment declares that "All Animals are Equal."[25]

With Jones defeated, the pigs (the Bolsheviks) begin to consolidate their power, appropriating milk and apples for their own consumption (loosely analogous to the Kronstadt Rebellion) while the other animals are expected to do the work, with Boxer the horse (the proletariat) working hardest of all. A power struggle erupts between Snowball and Napoleon, which the latter wins, forcing Snowball into exile. (Napoleon was "especially successful with the sheep.")[26] Despite having earlier dismissed the idea, Napoleon now demands the animals build a windmill (the Five-Year Plan), and when it is destroyed in a storm, he blames Snowball for sabotaging the project: "The animals were shocked beyond measure to learn that even Snowball could be guilty of such an action."[27] Napoleon also seeks to change the methods of food production (collectivization), only for its failure to drive the animals to the brink of starvation. Nevertheless, the animals are forced to work even harder to rebuild the windmill with walls twice as thick.

The novel takes a sinister and violent turn as a group of pigs (Old Bolsheviks like Bukharin and Zinoviev) who had previously spoken up against Napoleon's methods "confess" to being in league with Snowball and are executed (the Moscow Show Trials).[28] They have their throats ripped out by a group of violent dogs (the NKVD) that Napoleon had secretly reared from pups. Other animals confess to similar crimes and are killed (the Yezhov Purges). The history of the animal rebellion is rewritten to eliminate Snowball's role and aggrandize Napoleon's heroics.

Through his chief propagandist, Squealer, Napoleon warns the animals that conflict with Mr. Pilkington (the United States and the United Kingdom), a neighboring farmer, is inevitable. As such, he tells the animals he plans to sell a pile of valuable timber to a rival farmer, Mr. Frederick (Nazi Germany). This alliance (the Molotov-Ribbentrop Pact) is shattered when Napoleon discovers Frederick has paid in counterfeit currency and attacks Animal Farm (Operation Barbarossa). Frederick's men blow up the windmill but are eventually repelled, although only at a great cost. The wounded Boxer is secretly sold to a knacker's yard and, while the windmill is rebuilt, the animals see none of the benefits—such as modern stalls, plentiful food, shorter working days—that Snowball had promised them after the rebellion.

The pigs start walking on their hind legs, carrying whips and drinking whisky. The seven commandments are replaced by just one daubed on the wall of the barn: "All animals are equal, but some animals are more equal than others."[29] Napoleon decides to enter into a new alliance with his rival farmers. The novel famously ends with a dinner party where the pigs eat, drink, and play cards with humans (the Tehran Conference) and the watching animals are unable to distinguish between them: "The creatures outside looked from pig to man, and from man to pig, and from pig to man again: but already it was impossible to say which was which."[30]

The fable-like quality of the book and its subsequent status as a classic often obscure the fact that Orwell was writing about a contemporary crisis. The betrayal of Napoleon by Frederick, that is, Stalin's betrayal by Hitler, had taken place only two years before he began the book, and the events on which Orwell had based the final scene of the novel had taken place as he was writing. The satire was biting and fresh and all the more effective for it.

As early as January 1944, Orwell told Moore that "we may have some difficulties about finding a publisher."[31] He was certain Gollancz would not take it and suspected Warburg would not, either. He asked Moore to look into which publishers had supplies of paper (which was being rationed). Orwell knew he would have to at least offer it to Gollancz, as he had first refusal on his fiction. Orwell described it as a "little fairy story, about 30,000 words, with a political meaning" but warned Gollancz that it was "completely unacceptable politically from your point of view (it is anti-Stalin)."[32] Gollancz could not contain his annoyance at being called a Stalinist stooge; in 1941, he had edited *Betrayal of the Left*, a collection of essays attacking Communist policy in the wake of the Molotov-Ribbentrop pact, a collection to which Orwell had contributed two essays. Orwell was not being entirely straight with Gollancz, however, as *Animal Farm* was more than merely an attack on Stalin—it was a root-and-branch critique of the Bolshevik revolution and the Communist society that had been constructed as a result. Once Gollancz had read the manuscript, he grudgingly acknowledged that Orwell was right: the satire of the book was too much for him and he could not publish "a general attack of this nature."[33]

Orwell moved on quickly, giving the manuscript to André Deutsch, who recommended it to Nicholson & Watson. To Deutsch's embarrassment they, too, rejected it. Orwell then took it to Jonathan Cape. One of the publisher's readers, Veronica Wedgwood, had asked for Orwell's work in the past, and Orwell thought they might go for *Animal Farm*. The signs were auspicious as Daniel George, the chief reader of fiction, recommended publication. In May, Orwell met with Cape, who agreed to publish. Contract negotiations began and Orwell was happy with the terms, only asking that publication happen as quickly as possible.[34] He wanted his book out there before the war ended, to cut through the pro-Soviet sentiment of official propaganda.

On June 19, though, Cape wrote to Moore to tell him he was not going to publish after all. There had been some wrangling with Gollancz about the rights to Orwell's future novels but the real reason for the rejection was more sinister. During negotiations, Cape told Moore that he wanted, "as a matter of policy" to consult a "senior official" at the Ministry of Information. At this meeting, the unnamed official discouraged publication. What is remarkable is that this official then followed up with a letter in which he told Cape that publishing *Animal Farm* would damage relations with the Soviet Union and therefore undermine the war effort. The pressure applied by the official caused Cape to crack. "I must confess that this expression of opinion has given me seriously to think," Cape wrote to Moore. "I can see now that it might be regarded as something which it was highly ill-advised to publish at the present time."[35] Cape expressed particular concern that the leaders of the farmyard revolution were depicted as pigs. "I think the choice of pigs as the ruling caste will no doubt give offence to many people, and particularly to anyone who is a bit touchy, as undoubtedly the Russians are," he wrote. When Orwell received a copy of the letter, he appended a pithy annotation in the margin: "balls."

Orwell was furious. He used his regular column in *Tribune* to attack the practice of what he called "veiled censorship" by the Ministry of Information, although did not mention Cape by name. Wedgwood, one of the Cape readers who had recommended publication, left shortly afterward and offered to serialize *Animal Farm* in *Time and Tide,* but Orwell felt the magazine was too right-wing a venue and would lead to his novel being dismissed as reactionary anti-communism. *Animal Farm* was also rejected by Faber. T. S. Eliot wrote a long letter in which he explained that there was "no conviction . . . that this is the right point of view from which to criticise the political situation at the present time."[36] Orwell became disheartened. He suspected that Gollancz and the Ministry of Information were poisoning the well with mainstream firms, and he began to look seriously into self-publishing.

What Orwell did not know at the time, but came to later suspect, was that there was more going on than weak-willed capitulation to political censorship. The Ministry official who warned Cape against publication was Orwell's old acquaintance from the Shanghai dining club, Peter Smollett—or, to give his real name, Hans Peter Smolka. Later awarded an OBE for his war work, Smolka was a slippery figure, and contradictory stories are told about his past. What is agreed is that he was a naturalized British citizen, originally from Austria, who had first arrived in the country in 1933 as a correspondent of *Neue Freie Presse*. Before that, he had been active in Vienna's Communist underground. He was a friend of Litzi Friedmann, who, during the resistance to Dollfuss, introduced Smolka to her English lover, Kim Philby.

It is disputed when Smolka first began working for Soviet intelligence. According to one account he was recruited by the NKVD's Teodor Maly, before he arrived in Britain and used his journalism as cover.[37] Philby, on the other hand, claimed he was responsible for Smolka's recruitment in 1939. "We used to run into each other at receptions and cocktail parties, and we had many friends in common," Philby recalled. "He often came to me with news items, and sometimes in the form of ordinary routine gossip he brought me very valuable information. And, you know, he would wink as he did it."[38] Philby, in a break with his training, formalized the relationship (the winking was replaced by a system of offering each other cigarettes) but kept it secret from the NKVD's London resident, Anatoly Gorsky. When Philby left town, he asked Burgess to discreetly liaise with Smolka in his stead, but the garrulous Burgess ended up revealing what was going on to Gorsky. As a result, a black mark was placed in Philby's file and he suffered "several extremely unpleasant hours" as his handler reminded him of the importance of following the rules.[39] A wary Moscow Center told Philby to drop relations with Smolka, who was given the code name "Abo" and passed on to Gorsky. They would have cause to thank Philby, however, when, two years later, Smolka secured his position at the Ministry of Information. Agent Abo's intervention did not kill *Animal Farm* but delayed its publication, and subsequent impact, by as much as a year.

Orwell believed that Warburg, who had published *Homage to Catalonia*, might also find *Animal Farm* politically unpalatable, although that might have masked a desire on Orwell's part to go with a publisher with a larger audience. Warburg's firm was still relatively small-scale, had developed a reputation as a "Trotskyist" house, and their limitations were exacerbated by the paper shortage. Warburg gave every indication of wanting to publish *Animal Farm*, but Orwell did not show him the crumpled manuscript until late in July 1944. By the end of August, the deal was agreed (£100 advance) with a projected publication date of March 1945. As Orwell feared, however, paper rationing did result in the book being delayed until August, by which time the war in Europe was over.

Despite the difficulty in finding a publisher and the delays in production, *Animal Farm* was an immediate hit. All 4,500 copies of the first edition sold out, and Warburg had to start looking for more paper so that he could meet the demand of a second print run (a further ten thousand were printed in November). One story that Orwell later told Dwight Macdonald was that when the Queen Mother asked for a copy, Secker & Warburg had to apologize for being completely sold out, and the Royal Messenger had to go out in full regalia aboard his carriage to the anarchist bookshop on Red Lion Street for a copy.[40]

Frank Morley, an editor who had moved from Faber to Harcourt Brace in New York City, spent a day in Bowes & Bowes, a Cambridge bookshop, in an effort to find out what the British public was reading. Customers kept coming to ask for *Animal Farm*, which had sold out. Morley managed to get hold of a copy from the postal order department, read it, and decided his firm had to have it. It was published in the United States in August 1946, with a first edition of 50,000 copies. *Animal Farm* was then selected for the Book of the Month Club, which guaranteed it a huge readership: there were two Book of the Month Club printings, the first of 430,000 copies and the second of 110,000 copies.[41]

With *Animal Farm,* Orwell would far exceed the expectations he had of his novel finding a large readership; during his lifetime, the novel was translated into Danish, Dutch, Estonian, Farsi, French, German, Icelandic, Italian, Japanese, Korean, Norwegian, Polish, Portuguese, Russian, Spanish, Swedish, Telugu, and Ukrainian. He refused payment for translations made for editions distributed to refugees, students, and working-class organizations.[42]

Orwell's urgency in getting *Animal Farm* out was well-founded. After six years of isolation and bombing, Britain was on its knees and there was a strong left-wing impetus toward social change. In June 1945, Clement Attlee's Labour Party, which included many friends of Orwell's, won the general election in a landslide. He saw for himself the devastation of France and Germany when he traveled there as a war correspondent for the *Observer* in the spring of 1945 and feared what would rise from the ashes. The huge losses suffered by the Soviet Union and the courage of the Red Army had provoked a revisionist assessment of Stalin and his rule. Communist groups had been some of the bravest resistance fighters all over Europe, and as the dust settled they began to mobilize politically. *Animal Farm* was Orwell's way of warning of the risks of giving ground (both figuratively and literally) to Stalinism. He felt the British, especially, did not grasp the full horror of totalitarianism.

This was not a recent epiphany. Back in September 1944, he had written an essay about Koestler's work in which he warned of the consequences of the fact that "there is almost no English writer to whom it has happened to see totalitarianism from the inside." Orwell made himself at least a partial exception to this, having witnessed the purges of Spain. "The special world created by secret police forces, censorship of opinion, torture, and frame-up trials is, of course, known about and to some extent disapproved of," Orwell wrote, "but it has made very little emotional impact. One result of this is there exists in England almost no literature of disillusionment with the Soviet Union."[43] The left was facing a postwar reckoning without the common enemy of fascism. "The sin of nearly all left-wingers from 1933 onwards," Orwell wrote, "is that they have wanted to be anti-Fascist without being anti-totalitarian."[44]

READING *ANIMAL FARM* unlocked something in Koestler. He started to write with an emetic abandon. He began an essay on the Soviet Union and Stalinism that grew into three essays: "Anatomy of Myth," "Soviet Myth and Reality," and "The End of an Illusion." This triptych drew deeply on his own experiences to point out the radical disjunction between what the Soviet Union purported to be and what the reality was on the ground. He recalled seeing from a train the starving peasants of Ukraine during the great famine of 1932–33, a catastrophe that did not officially exist in the Soviet Union. The power of these essays was drawn from the fact that as an ardent Communist Koestler had allowed himself to be deceived. He had denied the famine despite seeing those starving peasants with his own eyes. "My bones ache from writing 12 hours per day, can't sleep," he wrote in his diary. "Got diarrhoea, and this is happiness."[45]

In May 1945, Koestler published these essays in *The Yogi and the Commissar*, a collection put out, ironically enough, by Jonathan Cape. This latest success was further evidence that, as one reviewer remarked, Koestler was becoming a cult figure: "Mr Koestler has raised ex-communism to the status of a glamorous and almost Byronic career, and I find Koestlerian young men talking of their entirely mythical communist past merely to seem more interesting."[46] After a visit to a febrile Palestine, Koestler returned to Britain buzzing with plans. He was determined that he would be involved in the cultural and intellectual reconstruction of Europe and, to that end, he invited Orwell to spend Christmas with him to discuss what lay ahead.

The invitation was not entirely about business. The previous year, while in hospital in Cologne with a bronchial illness, not long after his purported meeting with Hemingway, Orwell received a wire from the *Observer* that his wife, Eileen, had died. Her health had been precarious in the preceding months; she was pale, fatigued, losing weight, and suffering from persistent bleeding. With doctors concerned about a cancerous growth, she had undergone a hysterectomy at a hospital in Newcastle and died of cardiac arrest while under general anesthetic.[47] There are conflicting accounts of how Orwell responded. Close friends said he grieved bitterly, but those who knew him less well found him unnervingly stoic. He went back out to Europe after the funeral to finish his reporting stint. The couple had adopted a son, Richard, in the summer of 1944 and Orwell, typically pragmatic, decided that the boy needed a mother. On his return, he began proposing to women he knew. Knowing this, Koestler and Paget decided to play matchmaker, setting up Orwell with her twin sister, Celia Kirwan, who was recently separated and seeking a divorce. Koestler and Paget were living in Bwlch Ocyn, a remote seventeenth-century farmhouse in North Wales. Orwell, carrying Richard in one hand and his suitcase in the other, met Kirwan on the platform in London. On the train ride to Llandudno she found him compelling, and it was the beginning of an important friendship. Kirwan gently rejected his eventual proposal.

The visit did not begin auspiciously. Koestler had written a play, *Twilight Bar*, which Orwell had (rightly) trashed in the December issue of *Tribune*. Orwell did not think this sort of criticism should be taken personally; Koestler had an ungodly temper. When Koestler picked up Orwell and Kirwan in Llandudno, there was an awkward silence in the car. "That was a bloody awful review you wrote, wasn't it?" Koestler said, no longer able to contain himself. "Yes," replied Orwell. "And it's a bloody awful play, isn't it."

The frostiness did not last, however, and on long walks in the hills around his home, Koestler told Orwell of the need to form a new intellectual group to take the lead in debates about the postwar world. Too many of the existing organizations, he argued, were Soviet fronts or weak at the knees. His plan was to establish the League for the Dignity and Rights of Man to fight against totalitarianism, and he persuaded Orwell to write the manifesto. Orwell composed it inside a week and Koestler sent it to Bertrand Russell, who was living across the valley. The philosopher agreed to join so long as there was greater emphasis placed on opposing atomic weapons. Koestler pushed the idea of "psychological disarmament," by which he meant he wanted free circulation of texts and ideas, unrestricted travel, and an end to censorship. He knew it was a policy the Soviet Union could not stomach.

The proposed League fell apart, however, under rather sordid circumstances. Koestler verbally attacked Russell's wife, Patricia, who was representing him in discussions while Russell was in Cambridge. As a result, Russell withdrew. As it turned out, Russell was having an affair in Cambridge, which Patricia knew about, and as revenge she might (or might not) have slept with Koestler while Paget was in London. There were conflicting allegations, and the relationship between Koestler and Russell soured. Whatever happened, there was more going on than a dispute about manifesto rhetoric. To complete the circle, Paget recorded in her diary that Russell made a pass at her.

As the League fizzled out, Orwell and Koestler started to

head in different directions. They disagreed about the most effective way to take on the Soviet Union and totalitarianism more generally. Koestler was increasingly vested in confrontational cultural warfare. He wanted collective action, to rally writers to the cause, and deploy some of the tactics he had learned from the Comintern against the enemy. In the coming years, the early phases of the Cold War, he became one of the most vocal agitators on the front line against Soviet Communism. Orwell, his health increasingly fragile, felt the urgency to work, believing that his writing was a far more formidable weapon against totalitarianism. That had to take priority. When Koestler tried to persuade him to head up the British branch of PEN, the international writers' advocacy group, Orwell declined, saying it was "just throwing one's time and abilities down the drain."[48] In order to protect his time and his writing, Orwell retreated. While Koestler was embarked on a journey that would take him to New York, Paris, and Berlin and involve him in the clandestine work of the CIA, Orwell used the earnings from *Animal Farm* to buy a farmhouse on the Scottish island of Jura, where he wrote his most important, and final, book: *Nineteen Eighty-Four*.

Part Four

DIVISION

FOURTEEN

Orwell

JURA, 1948

OVERCOME WITH ANOTHER VIOLENT COUGHING FIT, George Orwell stopped typing and collapsed back onto his bed. He fought to get air into his damaged lungs, his skeletal body racked with pain, waiting for the fit to pass. The work was exhausting; he was a bad typist and his manuscript had been revised with Biro and pencil markings to the point of illegibility. The paraffin heater keeping the room warm did not help. Nor did his heavy smoking. As the coughing abated, Orwell was so weak he could do little but listen to the wind whipping outside the remote cottage he now called home. Fewer than 250 people lived on the island of Jura. Barnhill, the abandoned farmhouse Orwell had moved into with his son, Richard, and his sister, Avril, was twenty-five miles of rutted track away from Craighouse, the main settlement on the island. That meant Orwell was hours of difficult travel from Jura's only doctor. He knew he should not be taking risks with his health; he had spent seven months of the previous year in a Glasgow hospital. He had been treated with streptomycin, then an experimental drug, which had helped with the tuberculosis but caused Orwell to suffer awful side effects: his body was covered in a rash, his throat and mouth blistered, his nails disintegrated, and his hair came out in clumps. When he slept his lips bled to such a degree that when he woke, he had to wash off the dried blood to be able to open his mouth. Nevertheless, he kept writing. When his right arm had to be put in a cast (possibly as a way to reduce pressure on his lung), he forced himself to write with his left.[1] Back on Jura, he continued to suffer from night sweats and lost alarming amounts of weight. He wrote to friends trying to hire a stenographer but, with the long trip to Barnhill hardly enticing, nothing had come off. He was stuck. If he decided to relocate to London or Glasgow, where he could find a typist much more easily, the journey would almost certainly put him back in the hospital. If he waited, who knew how long the book might take to come out? Orwell felt the urgent need to get his novel read, so he decided to do the typing himself. *Nineteen Eighty-Four* was important enough for Orwell to gamble with his life.

Once he recovered from his coughing fits, he propped himself up and resumed the laborious single-finger tapping of the keys, transforming the mess of ink and pencil into a clean final copy, bringing into focus a vision of the future that was to become indelibly stamped on the cultural imagination. From his bedroom in Barnhill in 1948, Orwell transported to the bedroom of Winston Smith, in the dingy, bleak London of 1984, a future in which a revolution and a nuclear war had left Britain, renamed Airstrip One, in the grip of the Party, a totalitarian cabal ruled by the omniscient Big Brother:

> The telescreen was giving forth an ear-splitting whistle which continued on the same note for thirty seconds. It was nought seven fifteen, getting-up time for office workers. Winston wrenched his body out of bed—naked, for a member of the Outer Party received only three thousand clothing coupons annually, and a suit of pyjamas was six hundred—and seized a dingy singlet and a pair of shorts that were lying across a chair. The Physical Jerks would begin in three minutes. The next moment he was doubled up

by a violent coughing fit which nearly always attacked him soon after waking up. It emptied his lungs so completely that he could only begin breathing again by lying on his back and taking a series of deep gasps.[2]

Winston was not as sick as his creator, though; he managed to get through the compulsory routine of stretches and exercises. It was not his health that placed him in peril. Winston had begun to keep a diary in which he had recorded rebellious and heretical thoughts:

Whether he went on with the diary, or whether he did not go on with it, made no difference. The Thought Police would get him just the same. He had committed— would still have committed, even if he had never set pen to paper—the essential crime that contained all others in itself. Thoughtcrime, they called it. Thoughtcrime was not a thing that could be concealed for ever. You might dodge successfully for a while, even for years, but sooner or later they were bound to get you.[3]

To be arrested by the Thought Police did not result in mere imprisonment and execution. The consequence of committing a thoughtcrime was total erasure: "Your name was removed from the registers, every record of everything you had ever done was wiped out, your one-time existence was denied and then forgotten. You were abolished, annihilated: *vaporized* was the usual word."[4]

Winston Smith was horrified by the way the Party manipulated the past. He knew how this worked from the inside because his job at the Ministry of Truth was to rewrite old newspaper articles so that recorded history fit with what the Party wanted in the present. His diary was an attempt to leave a record outside of this official archive. He was writing so that the future would have some "truthful" account of its past. George Orwell was writing for different reasons: he was inventing a future in order to speak urgently to the present. If writing his diary meant Winston Smith was ensuring his own annihilation, Orwell's novel was an effort to make such annihilations less possible. And both writers were running out of time. Winston Smith knew he would not be able to hide from the Thought Police for long. And his creator was also being stalked by death. The cloth he used to try to stifle his coughs was stained with blood.

THE URGENCY ORWELL FELT to get his book published was also down to the speed with which the world was changing after the end of the Second World War. Orwell completed the first twelve pages at the end of June 1945, the month after the Allies had secured victory in Europe. Due to his poor health, other work commitments, and the move from London to Jura, Orwell had completed only fifty pages of *Nineteen Eighty-Four* by September 1946. It took him a further year to complete the first draft and then another to revise it. By the time the novel was ready to be typed up, it had taken longer than three years to write (*Animal Farm* took three months). This period brought a radical reorganization of the world map in ways that Orwell's novel both anticipated and reflected.

In *Nineteen Eighty-Four*, the world is divided between three vast super-states: Oceania, Eurasia, and Eastasia. Oceania was formed by the absorption of the British Empire into the United States; Eurasia by the Soviet Union's takeover of continental Europe; Eastasia by the fusion of China, Japan, and much of Southeast Asia. These super-states are so large as to make it impossible for them to destroy each other but they are nevertheless in a constant state of war. While these states subject each other's populations to terror through the use of rocket bombs—some twenty or thirty a week fall on London—the real fighting occurs in the territory that the three powers do not occupy: equatorial Africa, the Middle East, southern India, and Indonesia. These conquered territories are exploited for slave labor to fuel the perpetual war economy, which in turn allows the governments of the super-states to keep their populace under authoritarian control. Two states will often gang up on the other if it gets too powerful, but these allegiances shift at the first opportunity for betrayal. Through this "the balance of power always remains roughly even, and the territory which forms the heartland of each super-state always remains inviolate."[5]

As Orwell was inventing this dystopian future, the postwar world was being divided between two superpowers: the United States and the Soviet Union. He had seen it coming. When asked about the origins of *Nineteen Eighty-Four*, Orwell later wrote that it came from reading news reports about the Tehran Conference of November 1943, the first of the Big Three summits in which Churchill, Stalin, and Roosevelt began planning for how the world was to be carved up after the war. At the time of the meeting, Orwell had just begun working on *Animal Farm* and it became the culminating scene of his allegory: the meeting of the farmers and the pigs. This scene is described through the eyes of the other farm animals who, looking in to the farmhouse from the outside, witness the pigs and the men, over booze and cards, coming to a self-interested accommodation. To the watching animals, man and pig become indistinguishable. At Tehran, Stalin sat down with his capitalist and imperialist wartime allies and began dividing territory as part of a projected settlement. What was often ignored in the ending of *Animal Farm* was that this carve-up did not presage future peace and stability; the animals are sent rushing back to the window on hearing an "uproar of voices" and, returning, find a "violent quarrel was in process." It

turned out that both Mr. Pilkington and Napoleon had simultaneously played the ace of spades. Amid the tumult of war, Tehran had allowed Orwell a glimpse of what was to come. It was a
result of the conference that Orwell began thinking about the
implications of a world divided into "zones of influence."[6]

If for Orwell the economic and military power of the USA
and the USSR made a postwar vision of competing super-states
credible, then the advent of the nuclear bomb made it inevitable.
On August 6, 1945, the American bomber *Enola Gay* dropped a
nuclear bomb on Hiroshima, with eighty thousand people killed
by either the blast or the resulting firestorm. Three days later the
Americans dropped a second bomb, this time on Nagasaki, killing a further forty thousand. Two months later Orwell published
an article in *Tribune* about how the power of this weapon would
reshape the world order. "From various symptoms one can in-
fer that the Russians do not yet possess the secret of making the
atomic bomb," he wrote, "on the other hand, the consensus of
opinion seems to be that they will possess it within a few years.
So we have before us the prospect of two or three monstrous
super-states, each possessed of a weapon by which millions of
people can be wiped out in a few seconds, dividing the world
between them."[7] The result, as far as Orwell was concerned,
would be the end of "large-scale wars at the cost of prolonging
indefinitely a 'peace that is no peace.'" It was a vision of postwar purgatory and Orwell felt that "few people have considered
its ideological implications—that is, the kind of world-view, the
kind of beliefs, and the kind of social structure that would probably prevail in a State which was at once *unconquerable* and in a
permanent state of 'cold war' with its neighbours."[8] This was the
first time this phrase had been used: Orwell, who was planning
his novel about the "ideological implications" of this new world
order, had given the Cold War its name.

Even before Germans had been defeated, it was clear to the

British Foreign Office that the Soviet Union was intent on "buttressing up her security system" in the Balkans, Central Europe, and Eastern Europe "as a first line of defense."[9] Sure enough, with the war won, Stalin showed no sign of relinquishing control of the territory left unrecognizable by the Nazis' "transformative violence."[10] These were nations in which political and intellectual elites had been wiped out and the demographic makeup of their population had been fundamentally altered through the Holocaust, ethnic cleansing, and forced displacement. Communist takeovers began before the war was even over. In May 1944, Enver Hoxha's communist National Liberation Movement deposed King Zog of Albania. In Poland, despite the efforts of Britain and the United States on behalf of the Polish government-in-exile, the Communist Party exerted increasing control from the moment the Soviet Union recognized the Lublin Committee of the Polish Workers Party as the provisional government in the winter of 1944. In Yugoslavia, the Popular Front won elections by a huge margin in November 1945 and established Communist one-party rule, although its leader, Josef Broz Tito, proved too independent and unpredictable for Stalin's liking. In 1946, both Bulgaria and Romania came under Communist control. In Hungary, the power grab was deliberately deferred until the Allied Control Commission had left in 1947.

In September 1947, Communist Party leaders from around the world met in Warsaw for the formation of the Communist Information Bureau (Cominform), a successor institution to the Comintern, designed to coordinate international Communism. When Yugoslavia was ejected from the Cominform the following year, there followed a wave of purges of Communist Parties across Europe, rooting out supposed American spies and ideological deviants. The Communist Parties of Central and Eastern Europe had been successfully Stalinized.

On March 5, 1946, Winston Churchill gave a speech in Fulton, Missouri, that brought the increasing hostility between the Soviet Union and the West into the open. Having lost the general election to Clement Attlee's Labour Party the previous year, Churchill was liberated from political expediency. To an audience at Westminster College, with President Truman present, Churchill said:

> From Stettin in the Baltic to Trieste in the Adriatic, an iron curtain has descended across the Continent. Behind that line lie all the capitals of the ancient states of Central and Eastern Europe. Warsaw, Berlin, Prague, Vienna, Budapest, Belgrade, Bucharest, and Sofia, all these famous cities and the populations around them lie in what I must call the Soviet sphere, and all are subject in one form or another, not only to Soviet influence but to a very high and, in many cases, increasing measure of control from Moscow.[11]

Churchill went on to argue that while the Soviet Union did not desire fresh fighting, they wanted the "fruits of war and the indefinite expansion of their power and doctrines" and only if "Western Democracies stand together" could they be stopped.

Truman knew of Churchill's speech ahead of time. He was more suspicious of Stalin and his motivations than Roosevelt had been and was preparing his response to Soviet ambition. The previous month George Kennan, the *chargé d'affaires* in the U.S. Embassy in Moscow, had sent his "Long Telegram," an analysis of Soviet motives and ambitions that proved foundational for American Cold War policy. In it Kennan warned that the Soviet Union would seek to "undermine general political and strategic potential of major Western powers," to "set Western powers against each other," and "to weaken power and influence of Western powers over colonial, backward and dependent peoples."[12] Kennan argued, though, that the United States did not need to go to war with the USSR and that it could be effectively contained through the adoption of policies that would negate the spread of Soviet influence.

The result was the Truman Doctrine, which was first deployed in dealing with the crisis in Greece. Since the German evacuation of the country, the Communists and the Royalists had been competing for political control. The British occupation had initially secured a period of calm before the victory of the Royalists in 1946 elections—which the Communists boycotted—resulted in the outbreak of civil war. At first Britain backed the Royalists but by 1947 was in such financial difficulty that they could no longer afford to support them. The United States stepped in and, in March, Truman made a speech that, while addressing the particular issues confronting Greece, also opened into a statement of wider foreign policy: "I believe that it must be the policy of the United States to support free peoples who are resisting attempted subjugation by armed minorities or by outside pressures. I believe that we must assist free peoples to work out their own destinies their own way."[13] This support was, at this stage at least, mostly economic.

The ideas outlined in the Truman Doctrine were formalized in June of that year when Secretary of State George Marshall launched the European Recovery Program (better known as the Marshall Plan) at his speech for Harvard University's commencement. Marshall insisted that "our policy is directed not against any country or doctrine, but against hunger, poverty, desperation, and chaos." In the very next sentence, however, he said that its purpose "should be the revival of a working economy in the world so as to permit the emergence of political and social conditions in which free institutions can exist."[14] The rhetoric might not have been fiery, but the implication was clear.

The Marshall Plan was supposed to cover *all* of Europe, but at a Paris meeting about the plan, the Soviet delegation walked out, and as a consequence those nations under Soviet sway refused to participate. In a speech to the United Nations General Assembly in September, deputy foreign minister Andrei Vyshinsky claimed the Truman Doctrine and the Marshall Plan were an attempt by the United States "to impose its will on other independent states, while at the same time obviously using the economic resources distributed as relief to individual needy nations as an instrument of political pressure."[15]

Tension increased across Europe. In February 1948, Communists seized control of Czechoslovakia through a Soviet-backed coup. Finland and Norway, both of which shared borders with the Soviet Union, looked on nervously. In Germany relations between the occupying powers worsened. At the Potsdam Summit of 1945 Germany had been divided into four zones: American, British, French, and Soviet. Berlin, which was now located in Soviet territory, was also divided into four zones controlled by the Allied Powers (the western part of the city was under American, British, and French control, the eastern under Soviet). No agreement could be reached on reparations or reconstruction. The Soviet Union did not want Germany to be able to rearm itself, but the United States feared a weak and impoverished Germany would fall prey to Communism. In June 1948, when the Western powers implemented currency reform—introducing the new Deutsche Mark—despite Soviet opposition, Stalin ordered the closing of the border between the Western and Soviet zones and, more important, all land and water routes in and out of Berlin. The flight paths remained open, however, and, rather than capitulate to Soviet pressure, or escalate with military action, the Americans, British, and French coordinated an ambitious plan to supply West Berlin by air. The blockade was eventually lifted in May 1949. The following September, the hopes of finding an agreement for a unified Germany ended as the Federal Republic of Germany was founded in the west and the German Democratic Republic in the east.

Therefore, by the time Orwell finished *Nineteen Eighty-Four* in November 1948, the book's vision of a world divided between super-states already seemed to have been realized. While he was revising the final pages of the novel in his bed in Jura, the Policy Planning Staff of the State Department, headed by Kennan, was finalizing plans for a "North Atlantic Security Pact" that, when it was launched as NATO in May the following year, formalized the military relationship of the United States and its West European allies.[16] In August 1949, the Soviet Union, already buffered behind its satellite states, finally achieved military-technological parity when it successfully tested its first nuclear bomb in Semipalatinsk, Kazakhstan. Oceania and Eurasia were locked into the "Cold War" Orwell had predicted.

AFTER HE FINISHED TYPING the final draft of *Nineteen Eighty-Four*, Orwell sent it off and collapsed. His work had brought him to the brink of death. He spent all of December in bed and when he had gathered enough strength, left Jura and moved to Cranham, a private sanatorium in the Cotswold hills. As he had been with his other books, Orwell was downbeat about his new novel. He told Anthony Powell that it was "a good idea ruined" and told Julian Symons that he had "ballsed it up rather, partly owing to being so ill while I was writing it."[17] Fred Warburg, his publisher, knew differently and rushed it into production. *Nineteen Eighty-Four* was published on June 8, 1949, and sold 49,917 copies in its first year in the UK. In the United States, Harcourt Brace sold 170,000 copies, with a further 190,000 via a Book of the Month Club edition.[18] The novel won high praise from the cultural mandarins in both Britain and the United States, even when their interpretation differed. To V. S. Pritchett it offered a bleak prognosis of the future and he wrote that he had "never read a novel more frightening and depressing," while for Philip Rahv the novel was part of the cure, as he put it, "the best antidote to the totalitarian disease." Either way, Lionel Trilling summed up many critical responses in regarding it as "a momentous book."

And so it proved—it was almost immediately recognized that *Nineteen Eighty-Four* was a seriously powerful—indeed the *most* powerful—weapon yet deployed in the cultural Cold War. *Nineteen Eighty-Four* was not just a novel about the emergent Cold War, it was a part of it. Here was a taste of what it would be to live under a totalitarian regime more total than previously conceived. And while Orwell created his dystopia in a future Britain, the novel was packed with references to the contemporary USSR, designed to be picked up by his readers. In the world of *Nineteen Eighty-Four,* the Party came to power through a revolution and is presided over by the absolute power of a mustachioed leader, Big Brother. Everybody calls each other comrade, but some comrades are more equal than others. The Inner Party live in luxurious flats with their white-jacketed servants and have access to the finest food and tobacco. Enemies of the party are hunted down by the Thought Police who always come at night and who execute their prisoners in the cellar of the Ministry of Love with a bullet to the back of the neck, all hallmarks of the NKVD. Allusion is made to the "great purges" of the 1950s—a thinly disguised reference to the Moscow Trials of the 1930s. In the final part of the novel, the genetic relationship of Stalinism and Ingsoc is made explicit. O'Brien explains to Winston, whom he is interrogating and torturing, that the regime differs from its historical precedents in its refusal to allow the existence of martyrs. The only regime to have come close in this regard was the Soviet Union:

The Russians persecuted heresy more cruelly than the Inquisition had done. And they imagined that they had learned from the mistakes of the past; they knew, at any rate, that one must not make martyrs. Before they exposed their victims to public trial, they deliberately set themselves to destroy their dignity. They wore them down by torture and solitude until they were despicable, cringing wretches, confessing whatever was put into their mouths, covering themselves with abuse, accusing and sheltering behind one another, whimpering for mercy.[19]

It is not just the suppression of dissent that preoccupied Orwell when writing the novel. What he called the Sacred Principles of Ingsoc—"Newspeak, doublethink, the mutability of the past"—were Orwell's way of satirizing the way Stalinist totalitarianism attacked the very idea of objective reality.[20] Winston's job at the Ministry of Truth is to rewrite old newspapers so that the archive—the raw material of history—reflects the current policies of the Party. This was a logical extension of the Stalinist policy of doctoring documents and photographs to erase individuals who had fallen out of favor. In the pseudoscience of Trofim Lysenko (which fascinated Orwell), the carefully falsified economic statistics, the exaggerations of Stalin's role in the revolution and the Russian Civil War, Orwell saw a totalitarian attack on verifiable fact.[21] This is something that had haunted him since Spain, when he had read with incredulous anger distorted accounts of events he had witnessed firsthand. The clarity of style in *Homage to Catalonia* was born out of a desire to speak directly to the truth of his experience without embellishment.

As in Stalin's Soviet Union, the Party of *Nineteen Eighty-Four* requires an internal enemy, a Judas. Emmanuel Goldstein is the necessary "Enemy of the People," one of the founders of the Party who has since "engaged in counter-revolutionary activities, had been condemned to death and had mysteriously escaped and disappeared." Broadcasts of his speeches are the subject of the

Two Minutes Hate, in which Party members vent their fury at the screen. If this is not enough to have readers thinking of Trotsky, Goldstein is made to resemble him, too: he has a "lean Jewish face, with a great fuzzy aureole of white hair and a small goatee beard—a clever face, and yet somehow inherently despicable, with a kind of senile silliness in the long thin nose near the end of which a pair of spectacles was perched." Like Trotsky, he is the useful bogeyman of the regime, the arch-conspirator organizing his plots to undermine every aspect of Party life. He brings subversive elements into his clandestine network through the circulation of something known only as "the book," a heretical text that, once read, ushers you into his resistance, "the Brotherhood."

In this way, Orwell directly connects dissent with reading and writing. Indeed, one of Winston's first crimes is to start keeping his diary in a notebook the likes of which are no longer manufactured. Since the revolution the Party had "hunted down and destroyed" books so effectively that it was "very unlikely that there existed anywhere in Oceania a copy of a book printed earlier than 1960."[22] Novels continue to be produced but only ones that fall in line with Ingsoc ideology. There is a Planning Committee that issues a general directive on the content of novels, which are then written by machine in the Fiction Department of the Ministry of Truth. Any subsequent changes are dealt with by the Rewrite Squad. In this system, books "were just a commodity to be produced, like jam or bootlaces."[23] Some of the classics still circulate in Oceania but only in redacted editions, in which the original English ("Oldspeak") is gradually being replaced with the simplified "Newspeak": "By 2050—earlier probably—all real knowledge of Oldspeak will have disappeared. The whole literature of the past will have been destroyed. Chaucer, Shakespeare, Milton, Byron—they'll exist only in Newspeak versions, not merely changed into something different, but actually changed into something contradictory of what they used to be."[24]

Literature was proscribed by Stalinism, too, of course, and the conception of *Nineteen Eighty-Four* is bound up with this. In February 1944, while finishing *Animal Farm*, Orwell wrote to Gleb Struve, a Russian émigré and literary scholar, to thank him for sending a book about Soviet Russian literature, which had "roused my interest in Zamyatin's 'We,' which I had not heard of before. I am interested in that kind of book, and even keep making notes for one myself that may get written sooner or later."[25] Zamyatin's novel was a dystopic vision of a future ruled entirely by the extreme rationality of One State, in which identity is reduced to a number and surveillance is continuous. The book was banned by the Soviet censor in 1921 and Zamyatin's reputation never recovered. Only thanks to the intercession of Maxim Gorky was he allowed to go into exile in 1931, going to Paris, where he died in poverty; had he stayed in Russia he would surely have faced the same fate as Babel. Yet despite the best efforts of the Soviet censors to kill the book, *We* had survived in exile and helped inspire Orwell to write his own take on an authoritarian dystopia.

In *Nineteen Eighty-Four* the regime is always one step ahead of Winston. The harder he rebels, the further he entangles himself. When he is finally arrested and interrogated, O'Brien tells Winston that *he,* not Goldstein, is the author of "the book," which Winston had begun to read before his arrest. The implications of this leave Winston in despair. Does Goldstein even exist? Does Big Brother? The totalitarian nightmare Orwell created in *Nineteen Eighty-Four* was one from which you did not awake. Winston is duly broken and, in the final line of the novel, realizes that "he loved Big Brother." The bleakness of this ending was too much for some readers, who felt it an expression of a dying and disenchanted writer's extreme pessimism. But the verdict that Orwell had succumbed to defeatism failed to account for the fact of his writing the book in the first place. As the novel made clear, imaginative fiction was a weapon that provoked disproportionate fear in totalitarian governments. Orwell used it.

ORWELL WANTED HIS BOOKS to undermine Stalinism and took efforts to maximize their chances of doing so. Indeed, an important rationale when writing *Animal Farm* as a short fable was to enable easy translation. He took practical steps to ensure his books reached readers in countries under Soviet control. In 1947 he wrote a preface for the Ukrainian edition of *Animal Farm*, in which he said that, "for the past ten years I have been convinced that the destruction of the Soviet myth was essential if we wanted a revival of the Socialist movement."[26] The Ukrainian edition was published in a periodical distributed in a displaced persons camp in the American zone of Germany. To Orwell's frustration a large number of copies were seized and handed over to the Soviets by the American military government, although some two thousand still made it through.[27] Orwell was committed to trying to get banned books into the Soviet Union. He wrote to Koestler in September 1947, urging him to have his work translated into Ukrainian and distributed for free. "I am sure we ought to help these people all we can," he wrote, "and I have been saying ever since 1945 that the DPs were a godsent opportunity for breaking down the wall between Russia and the west. If our government won't see this, one must do what one can privately."[28]

The following year, in a letter to his agent, Leonard Moore, he emphasized that he "did not want any fee for *Animal Farm* from Poles or any other Slavs."[29] A Russian edition of *Animal Farm* was put out by Possev, an émigré publisher based in London and Frankfurt, in 1949, which also circulated in displaced person camps.[30] Possev then came up with a more ambitious plan. "They want to issue a booklet and say, what is no doubt true, that it would be quite easy for them to get a few thousand copies of it through the Iron Curtain, I suppose via Berlin or Vienna," Orwell wrote to Moore. "Of course I am willing enough for them to do this, but it will cost money, i.e. for the printing and binding."[31] It appears Orwell used earnings from the German publication of *Nineteen Eighty-Four* to subsidize this project: Possev published the book version in 1950.

There was never any ambiguity about what Orwell was writing *against*. What was less clear to many of his readers was what he was writing *for*. This was an old issue with Orwell. In Spain, for example, he had gone out determined to fight against the fascists but arrived not sure whether he would do so for the anarchists, the communists, or the socialists. When Orwell had written *Animal Farm*, William Empson had sent him a letter warning him that he "must expect to be 'misunderstood' on a large scale about this book."[32] The warning proved prescient, as right-wing intellectuals and commentators, in the United States especially, took the attack on Soviet communism to be a defense of liberal democracy and the free market. Orwell complained to Spender that he "had not written a book against Stalin in order to provide propaganda for capitalists."[33] Orwell addressed the issue of his politics in a 1946 essay, "Why I Write." "Every line of serious work that I have written since 1936," he wrote, "has been written, directly or indirectly, *against* totalitarianism and *for* democratic socialism, as I understand it."[34]

In the case of *Nineteen Eighty-Four* some reviewers felt the novel was an attack *on* socialism. *Life* described it as being an indictment of a "regimented left-wing police state" and the New York *Daily News* interpreted it as directed against the Labour Party. These were the first signs of the novel's future as a bible of hard-right libertarians in which "Orwellian" became a descriptor for the surveillance state; the John Birch Society not only sold copies of *Nineteen Eighty-Four* but also changed the last four digits of their phone number to 1984.[35]

Orwell *was* critical of the Labour Party but only for not going far enough; he wanted to see the House of Lords and titles abolished, and an end to the elite public schools.[36] Orwell was so upset by the early reviews that he composed a clarifying press release which he had Fred Warburg issue, and followed it up with a statement in which he wrote, "My recent novel is *not* intended as an attack on socialism or on the British Labour Party (of which I am a supporter) but as a show up of the perversions to which a centralized economy is liable and which have already been partly realized in communism and fascism. . . ."[37]

Were these reviews simply a reflection of the editorial politics of their respective publications? It seems others were also convinced of this position. When Warburg first received the manuscript, he wrote a summary of the novel for in-house use (Orwell never read it). "The political system which prevails is Ingsoc = English Socialism," Warburg wrote. "This I take to be a deliberate and sadistic attack on socialism and socialist parties generally. It seems to indicate a final breach between Orwell and Socialism."[38] This was a big deal, Warburg felt, and he believed the novel was worth "a cool million votes to the conservative party." He even hoped to get Winston Churchill to write the introduction.

Some of the trouble can be explained by the term "Ingsoc." Why did he name this totalitarian political philosophy in a way that invited readers to interpret it as a condensation of "English socialism"? He had written about his fear that unless the people retained strong democratic control over a centralized government, socialism could be too easily subverted and breed a new power-motivated oligarchy, and he believed it was necessary to argue that this could happen in England as easily as anywhere else, that there was no innate superiority to the British political system.[39] The Ingsoc of *Nineteen Eighty-Four* was a deliberate perversion of the idea of socialism—as he understood it—much as the German National Socialists had deployed it.[40] But had he done enough to make that clear to the reader? In "the book," there is a passage in which socialism is described as "a theory which appeared in the early nineteenth century and was the last link in a chain of thought stretching back to the slave rebellions of antiquity." Yet this socialism is "infected by the Utopianism of past ages" and "from about 1900 onwards the aim of establishing liberty and equality was more and more openly abandoned."[41] It is not hard to understand how readers became confused. The picture was further complicated by the way the Britain of the novel is a mere colony of the United States, renamed "Airstrip One," with dollars as currency, and it is not clear how this state of affairs could be interpreted as a defense of capitalism. Yet the fact that Orwell felt the need to publicly clarify his intentions points to an ambiguity in the novel that could be misinterpreted or even exploited.

Did this add up to Orwell being complicit in Cold War propaganda, as reviewers with Communist-sympathizing publications suggested? Ultimately Orwell wanted to reach as many readers as possible, and this sometimes involved making compromises that did not fit with his politics. He knew this. In correspondence with his agent about the serialization of the novel by a "reactionary" Dutch newspaper, Orwell wrote: "I don't know if we can help that. Obviously a book of that type is liable to be made use of by Conservatives, Catholics, etc."[42] When the *Evening Standard* gave the novel a rave review, an excerpt— "the most important book published since the war"—was used on the jacket, despite the fact that it came from a Beaverbrook publication that Orwell despised (the review had suggested the novel be "required reading" for Labour MPs).[43]

Nineteen Eighty-Four was also "made use of" by publications that were part of a deliberate propaganda strategy. In May 1949,

Orwell received a letter from Melvin Lasky, editor of the German magazine *Der Monat,* asking Orwell for a contribution. Orwell replied, saying he was not able to do so but suggested Lasky serialize his forthcoming novel instead.[44] During the war Lasky was an information officer attached to the Seventh Army, and he stayed on in Berlin after VE Day, working as a freelance journalist for *Partisan Review.* Concerned by the way the Soviet Union appeared to be winning over the German intelligentsia, he proposed to the American Office of the Military Government that a publication to counter Communist propaganda be established. *Der Monat* was that publication. Its first issue came out in October 1948, in time for copies to be airlifted into blockaded Berlin.[45] Both Koestler and Spender contributed to the first issue, and Orwell was listed as *Der Monat's* London correspondent. The magazine serialized *Nineteen Eighty-Four* between November 1949 and March 1950. Orwell knew that it was "an American army magazine" and this did not deter him.[46]

The desire to fight totalitarianism was so strongly felt by writers like Orwell that it could be used to make them complicit, witting or not, in state propaganda. *Nineteen Eighty-Four* was a novel that knew something about complicity, too. One of the ways that O'Brien breaks Winston is by showing how far he had compromised his own ethics in his desire to destroy Big Brother. During his interrogation, O'Brien asks Winston if he feels "morally superior" to the Party. Winston is convinced he is. But then O'Brien plays back a secret recording of the night he had posed as an agent of Goldstein, during which Winston was asked to what lengths he would go in service of the Brotherhood: "He heard himself promising to lie, to steal, to forge, to murder, to encourage drug-taking and prostitution, to disseminate venereal diseases, to throw vitriol in a child's face."[47] In seeking to rebel against the regime, Winston displays just how infected he has become by its hatred and violence.

Orwell was not naive. In the Second World War he had worked as a propagandist for the BBC's Indian Service on the understanding that whatever helped defeat fascism was the lesser evil. The threat of Stalinism was just as potent to Orwell. Records released in 1996 show that Orwell had an informal relationship with the Information Research Department, established in January 1948 by the Foreign Office to counter Soviet propaganda and infiltration.[48] The IRD sought to circulate existing anti-Soviet publications and commissioned new ones. Orwell's liaison at the IRD was Celia Kirwan, whom he had met when Koestler tried to play matchmaker at Christmas in North Wales in 1945. In March 1949, she visited Orwell and in her report of the meeting said she "discussed some aspects of our work with him in great confidence, and he was delighted to learn of them, and expressed his wholehearted and enthusiastic approval of our aims."[49] Orwell asked the IRD to help subsidize the Possev edition of *Animal Farm,* but it came to nothing. They did, though, ensure the publication of Burmese, Chinese, and Arabic editions of the novel and even produced a graphic novel version for distribution in Latin America, the Middle East, and East Asia. (Hugh Wilford points out that Old Major was given a Lenin-style beard and Napoleon was given a Stalin-style moustache to reinforce "the allegorical elements of the tale.")[50] He was too ill to do anything directly for the IRD other than recommend writers and publishers for them to work with, but on May 2, 1949, the month before *Nineteen Eighty-Four* was published, he sent Kirwan a letter:

I enclose a list with about 35 names. It isn't very sensational and I don't suppose it will tell your friends anything they don't know. At the same time it isn't a bad idea to have the people who are probably unreliable listed. If it had been done earlier it would have stopped people like Peter

Smollett worming their way into important propaganda jobs where they were probably able to do us a lot of harm. Even as it stands I imagine this list is very libellous, or slanderous, or whatever the term is, so will you please see that it is returned to me without fail.[51]

It is true that the inclusion of many of the names was hardly sensational and most of those listed were accused of little more than being "stupid" or "silly." The inclusion of Smollett, the Ministry of Information official who had persuaded Jonathan Cape to ditch *Animal Farm*, was more serious. Next to Smollett's name, Orwell wrote: "[a]lmost certainly agent of some kind. Said to be careerist. Very dishonest."[52] He was right—Smollett, whose real name was Smolka, was working for the NKVD.

Amid the names of those he had publicly derided for their fellow traveling, there was one striking betrayal: Stephen Spender, with the annotation, "Sentimental sympathizer, & very unreliable. Easily influenced. Tendency toward homosexuality."[53] Spender had become a friend, despite the way Orwell had initially attacked his politics and sexuality, and when Orwell was in the hospital, he came to visit. And as Orwell knew, Spender had irrevocably broken with Communism—with which he had merely flirted in the first place—after coming back from Spain. His inclusion in the list bespeaks either a callousness on Orwell's part, or, perhaps more plausibly, a growing paranoia about the true reach of Stalinism. He sent his letter shortly after the end of the Berlin Airlift, with tensions high. He and Koestler had repeatedly tried to get the British press to attend to the way Eastern Europeans had been treated by the Soviet Union (particularly acute was raising awareness about Katyn, the camp where the Soviet Union had massacred fifteen thousand Poles). They both felt Soviet sympathizers (and in some cases agents) were obstructing or suppressing the truth. On top of his experiences in Spain, this might help explain why Orwell was so closely monitoring his fellow writers and intellectuals.[54] Furthermore, the list was, at least in part, something of a game he played with his friend Richard Rees. Yet, even when it is taken in context, the fact remains that Orwell shared this list with a secretive government department, not knowing what might be done with the names on it. For the author of *Nineteen Eighty-Four*, this was a surprising act of complicity.

ON OCTOBER 13, 1949, Orwell, propped up in bed, wearing a red corduroy jacket, married Sonia Brownell in a ceremony conducted by Reverend W. H. Braine. One of the witnesses recalled him "beaming with pleasure" throughout.[55] David Astor, the best man, led the wedding party out for a lunch at the Ritz. Orwell remained in bed, too sick to move. Brownell had been an assistant of Cyril Connolly's at *Horizon* when Orwell had got to know her at the beginning of the war. She had risen to become an important editor on the magazine, forceful in her opinions. After Eileen's death, before Orwell moved to Jura, Sonia grew closer to Orwell, occasionally helping him out by babysitting Richard. At some stage they slept together.[56] When Orwell proposed marriage in the winter of 1945, she gently rejected him.[57] While he was on his Scottish island writing *Nineteen Eighty-Four*, she spent her time between London and Paris. She mixed with Left Bank intellectuals and had an intense affair with the philosopher Maurice Merleau-Ponty (she confessed to him that she had had a one-night stand with Koestler during the war, as a result of which she had an abortion).[58] Merleau-Ponty was married with a child and did not want to break up his family, so he ended the relationship in early 1949.[59]

Orwell remained in touch and urged her to visit him on Jura. Some have speculated that the character of Julia in *Nineteen*

Eighty-Four was modeled on Brownell. When Orwell proposed to her in the summer of 1949, she accepted. There was, predictably, much skepticism; Malcolm Muggeridge who, along with Anthony Powell, had helped procure Orwell's jacket for the ceremony, found the whole thing "slightly macabre and incomprehensible."[60] Connolly was outraged. There was no pretense by either Orwell or Sonia that this was a romantic union. Orwell wanted some solace in what he hoped were the final years of his life, and someone to whom he could entrust his literary legacy (Richard was to remain in Avril's care). Brownell appears to have believed she could nurse him back to health. Those who visited him the months after the marriage certainly noticed an upturn in his spirits. Arrangements were made to go to a sanatorium in the Swiss Alps. Orwell was planning another novel. On January 21, 1950, an artery burst in his lungs and he died.

After hearing the news, Koestler set about writing an obituary for his friend, mentor, and rival. Under the headline "A Rebel's Progress," Koestler extolled Orwell's authenticity. "George Orwell looked and behaved exactly as the reader of his books expected him to look and behave," he wrote. This, as Koestler conceded, did not always make him an easy person to get along with, and his intellectual honesty was such that "it made him appear almost inhuman at times." However, this unity of work and character made him, in Koestler's estimation, "the only writer of genius among the *littérateurs* of social revolt between the two wars." "His life," he went on, "was one consistent series of rebellions both against the condition of society in general and his own particular predicament: against humanity's drift towards 1984 and his own drift towards the final breakdown." His fight against tuberculosis had ended in defeat and one that might well have been accelerated by the intensity with which he rebelled. The battle between his work and totalitarianism was another matter.

FIFTEEN
McCarthy

NEW YORK CITY, 1949

ON A RAINY FRIDAY, MARCH 25, 1949, Mary McCarthy walked
up Park Avenue toward the art deco grandeur of the Waldorf-
Astoria Hotel, exhilarated by the impending conflict. As she approached the entrance, she was forced to pick her way through
a crowd: large groups of picketers with their homemade signs,
cops trying to prevent fights breaking out, reporters hoping they
would. She presented her ticket and entered the lobby. She was
where she wanted to be: enemy territory.

Over the course of the weekend, the Waldorf hosted the Scientific and Cultural Conference for World Peace, the brainchild
of the freshly established Communist Information Bureau. The
World Congress of Intellectuals in Defense of Peace had been
hosted in Wroclaw, Poland, the previous year and now the Cominform wanted to replicate it on American soil, using the National Council for the Arts, Sciences and Professions, one of its
American front organizations, to provide funding and logistics.
This maneuvering was not lost on the host nation—a report
prepared by the House Un-American Activities Committee
(HUAC) the following April described it as a "supermobiliza-
tion of the inveterate wheelhorses and supporters of the Communist Party and its auxiliaries." (The Soviet Union did not have
a monopoly on absurd rhetoric.)[1]

The United States' anti-Communism extended far beyond

the picketers on Park Avenue. In Hollywood, the blacklist was in force and the so-called Hollywood Ten had been convicted of contempt of Congress in April 1948 for refusing to testify in front of the HUAC. The following August, in front of the same committee, Whittaker Chambers, a former Communist turned journalist, would accuse Alger Hiss, a senior U.S. government official, of being a Soviet spy. Since January, eleven members of the American Communist Party had been on trial for violating the Smith Act, accused of advocating the violent overthrow of the government.

It is therefore not hard to understand why McCarthy had to pick her way through so many protesters on that rainy March day. Veterans, religious groups, and Russian and East European émigrés picketed all three days of the conference and the police claimed as many as two thousand protesters gathered around the hotel by the end of the first night. Some of it got quite intense: members of the Committee for Freedom of Religion apparently threatened delegates (one woman carried a sign reading "Exterminate the Red Rats" and tried to shoot attendees with a water gun).[2]

Despite this fevered atmosphere, the organizers of the conference had done an excellent job of securing some 650 intellectual and scholarly "sponsors," among them Leonard Bernstein, Marlon Brando, Aaron Copland, Albert Einstein, and Frank Lloyd Wright. Prestigious African American intellectuals, including W. E. B. DuBois, Langston Hughes, and Paul Robeson, were also sponsors, as were several writers who had stood by the Soviet Union through the trials and purges, including Howard Fast, Clifford Odets, and the celebrity Stalinist couple Dashiell Hammett and Lillian Hellman.

McCarthy had a bone to pick with the latter. In the spring of 1948, McCarthy had taught for a semester at Sarah Lawrence College in Westchester County and was invited to dinner with the president, along with several students, Stephen Spender, who was also a visiting teacher, and Hellman. According to McCarthy, she arrived at the party to find Hellman trashing the reputation of John Dos Passos, who had, Hellman claimed, "turned against the Spanish Loyalists" because "he was disappointed by the food in Madrid." McCarthy (who believed Hellman initially mistook her for a student or junior faculty) immediately came to the defense of her old friend, assuring the students that Dos Passos turned against the Communists only because they "were running the show and murdering Trotskyists, POUMists and Anarchists."[3] She said the murder of Andrés Nin in particular had been the cause for Dos Passos's disillusion. Hellman's multitude of bracelets apparently began to jangle as she trembled in "fury and surprise."[4] Spender, wryly amused, remembered that the room "divided at once into two little groups" and that McCarthy and Hellman "hurled insults at each other." It was a foreshadowing of conflicts to come.

At the Waldorf, Hellman and her allies were mobilizing under the banner of "peace." The Soviet line was this: the world, still ravaged by the legacy of the Second World War, was threatened by American imperialism backed by the appalling power of the atomic bomb. Unless American aggression was curbed and the atomic threat curtailed, another war was inevitable. Evidence of this militaristic character, according to this narrative of Western imperialism, was the impending formation of NATO, negotiations about which were already under way. This account conveniently ignored Stalin's own land grab in Eastern and Central Europe. Instead, Soviet propaganda sought to keep the focus on the awful power of the American atom bomb, seeking to turn its strategic vulnerability to its advantage by claiming they were the true agents of global peace. Never mind that the network of spies around the Manhattan Project had ensured that Soviet scientists were catching up fast, but for now it was important to paint the United States as an ambitious and aggressive power possessed of an unconscionable weapon.

To McCarthy, the hypocrisy of the conference was too much to take. Here the Soviet Union was clandestinely arranging for a grand gathering of intellectuals in New York City while back in the Soviet Union a whole generation of authors had "disappeared" or been silenced. Direct action was needed and, just as they had done with the Congress of American Writers in 1937, McCarthy and Dwight Macdonald decided to infiltrate the conference and confront the speakers from the floor. On the day, they were joined by the poet Robert Lowell and the composer Nicolas Nabokov. They bought tickets for $3 each and arrived with an umbrella to rap against the floor if they were denied the chance to speak. After a decade on the periphery, McCarthy relished being back on the front lines of the old fight.

HER ENTRANCE BACK INTO THIS ARENA was a long time coming. Even before the first issue of *Partisan Review* came out in December 1937, events had been set in motion that took McCarthy out of the political fray. That October, McCarthy had showed up to the *Partisan Review* office in Union Square to find Edmund Wilson there. She had watched him deliver a lecture at Vassar during her senior year and they were both on the Trotsky Defense Committee, but this was the first time she had properly met him. Rahv and Phillips were eager to secure his services as a contributor and invited him for a lunch meeting. McCarthy felt overdressed in a black silk dress and a fox stole, and Wilson ignored her for much of the lunch, with the exception of complimenting her on the articles she and Margaret Marshall had written about the poor state of American literary criticism.[5] Two weeks later Wilson phoned Marshall to ask both women to lunch. McCarthy got thoroughly drunk and woke up in bed next to Marshall in a room in the Chelsea Hotel. The third time the trio met, when McCarthy and Marshall were invited for dinner at Wilson's home in Stamford, Connecticut, McCarthy slept with him. He was forty-two, she was twenty-five. By February they were married.

They lived first in Stamford and then in Wellfleet on Cape Cod. It was far from an idyllic marriage. Wilson was frequently abusive. After one drunken beating, McCarthy, then three months pregnant, began weeping uncontrollably and could not stop. Wilson had her committed to the Payne Whitney Clinic in New York for psychiatric observation. Fortunately, the fetus was unharmed, and Reuel was born the following Christmas day.

Wilson was a spoiled, demanding alcoholic. McCarthy's nickname for him was "the Minotaur," and he was determined to keep her trapped in his maze; he controlled their finances and refused to let her have a car. When sober he could be supportive, and he set up a spare room with a typewriter for her to work on her fiction. Looking back on these days, McCarthy was convinced that without this impetus she would never have become a novelist. While Wilson wrestled with the history of Marxism, Communism, and revolution in *To the Finland Station,* McCarthy threw herself into writing short stories, stories that would become her first novel, *The Company She Keeps.*

The interlinked stories were heavily autobiographical. Meg Sergent, McCarthy's fictional alter ego, dumps a husband for a lover ("Cruel and Barbarous Treatment"), has sex with a married man she meets on a train ("The Man in the Brooks Brothers Shirt"), and works for an antiques con man ("Rogue's Gallery"). All of this drew on McCarthy's experiences living in New York City. Her sexual frankness was married to biting satire of the intellectual milieu of the 1930s. In "The Genial Host," Sergent attacks the smug Stalinism of the guests at a Manhattan dinner, while in "Portrait of the Intellectual as a Yale Man" she depicts the disenchantment of an optimistic young Marxist. Jim Barnett, the intellectual in question, begins as an editor at the Communist-sympathizing *Liberal* but resigns when Sergent is fired from the same magazine for her vocal defense of Trotsky. Barnett has an affair with Sergent and becomes enmeshed in the Trotsky Defense Committee before finally leaving it all behind for a cushy corporate journalism job at *Destiny,* a magazine modeled on Henry Luce's *Time.*

The publication of one of these stories, "The Man in the Brooks Brothers Shirt," in *Partisan Review* in the summer of 1941 announced McCarthy as a major new fiction writer. The following year *The Company She Keeps* was reviewed by Malcolm Cowley in *The New Republic,* Christopher Isherwood in *The Nation,* and Clifton Fadiman in *The New Yorker.* The caliber of the reviewers was an indication of the seriousness with which her work was being treated, as were the mixed verdicts; her talent unnerved reviewers, many of whom had been left rattled by her critiques of the general state of literary criticism. Wilson, unable to avoid being patronizing even in a compliment, thought she might make a "female Stendhal."[6] With a true assessment of her work's worth occluded by the poisonous politics of New York literary culture, perhaps the most accurate barometer was the opinion of Vladimir Nabokov, who privately praised McCarthy's novel to Wilson; Nabokov was not a writer who gave up praise easily.[7]

The final story in *The Company She Keeps* is the remarkable "Ghostly Father, I Confess," in which Sergent is now married to Frederick, an oppressive and stifling husband. Here was the irony of McCarthy's marriage to Wilson: it made her profoundly unhappy, but it also made her into the writer she wanted to be. Living on Cape Cod she had felt isolated, detached from the vibrant literary milieu of the city. The only relief was visits from friends, like the Macdonalds or the Nabokovs, or dinner with Katy and John Dos Passos in Provincetown. In the early days of the marriage, even Wilson's old friend Scott Fitzgerald came up, but he got drunk and McCarthy found his visit depressing.

The end of the marriage was ugly. In an official deposition, McCarthy accused Wilson of domestic abuse; in his response Wilson claimed McCarthy suffered "hysterical delusions."[8] In January 1945, McCarthy took Reuel and left, filing for divorce on grounds of "extreme cruelty." They formally separated in February 1945 and divorced in December 1946.[9] Decades later it emerged that amid all this she had been having an affair with the art critic Clement Greenberg, whose own reputation was made by "Avant-Garde and Kitsch," an essay published in *Partisan Review* in 1939. McCarthy had been drawn back to that world.

IF McCARTHY AND THE *PARTISAN REVIEW* CROWD were right about the Moscow Show Trials, they were wrong about the Second World War. In November 1940, McCarthy wrote a short piece for *The New Republic* about the way the war was being covered by American reporters (conclusion: badly). It is not, however, her critique of the press that is most striking, it is the glibness of tone. She wrote that "for most of us, the war has been a rather ghastly kind of entertainment, more heartrending—yes, and more exciting, more dangerous—than the Lindbergh baby or the Johnstown flood. Why else do we listen to three, four, five, and six broadcasts of stale news in a day and, on a particularly ferocious day, buy two and three newspapers? And how impatient we get if the news is dull!" Later in the piece she asked a series of rhetorical questions, those that, apparently, "we are all asking": "Can Hitler survive victory? Will satisfied fascism retain the same character as hungry fascism? What is the new world-state that Hitler is planning? Is there sabotage? Is there resistance? Is there anything left of the socialist movement? Is there any hope for revolution if Hitler is stalemated? And what if he is not?"[10]

The questions, bizarrely misjudged as they seem now, are revealing in themselves, for McCarthy still believed that the only way to defeat fascism was through revolution, not through supporting the imperialist British. In the autumn of 1939, a *Partisan Review* editorial opined that the best that could result from a British victory was a "new Versailles, followed by the same round of political convulsions as ended up in the triumph of fascism." The editors argued that "fascism is produced by the internal development of monopoly capitalism" and "if fascism turned to aggression as a matter of principle, spreading the true faith with fire and sword in Islamic fashion, one would expect to find Italy and Germany fighting together in this war. Actually, of course, the economic and geographical differences between the two nations have proved to be decisive, and Italy is not only neutral but may well repeat her performance of the last war and join the Allies." It is an editorial to which history has not been kind.

At the end of the same issue of the magazine was a letter from the League for Cultural Freedom and Socialism that called upon "all American artists, writers and professional workers to join us in this statement of implacable opposition to this dance of war in which Wall Street joins with the Roosevelt administration."[11] The letter was signed by the editors of *Partisan Review*—Rahv, Phillips, Dupee, and Macdonald—as well as by many other future Cold Warriors, including James Laughlin, Melvin Lasky, and James Burnham.

Wilson was also an isolationist, although he was in no small part motivated by his acute Anglophobia. Looking back at the war from 1959, McCarthy said that the "psychology of the 1930s spilled over into the 1940s. You were supposed to be wised up about the War and not let yourself be a victim of propaganda . . . We were in terror of being 'soft.'"[12] When Rahv did go "soft" in a 1941 editorial ("this is our war") it divided this new generation of American intellectuals. When the United States finally entered the war after the attack on Pearl Harbor in December 1941, *Partisan Review* declared its support. Macdonald resigned in protest and McCarthy said it was not until the war was effectively over, with the full extent of the Holocaust revealed, that she could admit to herself that American intervention was justified. At a gathering of friends, among them Macdonald, Dupee, and the Italian anarchist Nicola Chiaromonte, in August 1945 she suddenly said that she had "supported the war all along; we all did." She felt a tremendous sense of relief.[13]

Chiaromonte was among a number of European refugee writers who came to New York during or immediately after the war, invigorating intellectual life in the city. As a result, *Partisan Review* acquired an even more cosmopolitan, transatlantic tenor and developed a close relationship with the British magazine *Horizon,* edited by Cyril Connolly. The summer of 1944 edition featured pieces, one after the other, by Koestler, Orwell, and Spender, the anti-Stalinist veterans of Spain. Of the many intellectual emigres, McCarthy became particularly close to Hannah Arendt, a brilliant student of Martin Heidegger's, who had been held in a Vichy internment camp before fleeing to the United States.

Liberated from Wilson, McCarthy threw herself into life, writing for a larger audience in *The New Yorker,* taking a teaching job at Bard, and working on a new novel (*The Oasis*). She became involved with Bowden Broadwater, a researcher and writer for *The New Yorker,* a bitchy, boyish man in a fine suit, eight years her junior, who ended up becoming a production editor at *Partisan Review.* They married in December 1946.

If the Wilson years had been a hiatus from political engagement, McCarthy was back with a vengeance. She plunged once more into the argumentative medium of the New York intellectual scene.

Early in 1948, McCarthy set up the Europe-America Groups,

an organization to foster greater intellectual bonds between the United States and a recovering Europe. Funds were raised and used to ship periodicals and books (including *Darkness at Noon* and *The Partisan Reader,* a compilation of essays from *Partisan Review)* to Europe. Chiaromonte was the man on the ground, dispensing money to struggling writers as he saw fit.[14] The *Partisan Review* boys were in (admittedly tepid) support, as were old allies like Hook and Macdonald. Albert Camus ran a sister organization in France. The emphasis was on internationalism and a third way between American capitalism and Soviet Communism, both of which, it was declared, constituted a threat to high culture. However, the Europe-America Groups was dissolved when the first tranche of money ran out.

McCarthy had envisioned developing the organization into a political movement that would escalate its criticism of American militarization in Europe. This would have necessitated a split with the *Partisan Review* crowd and Hook, whose anti-Communism was hardening. The anti-Communist left was becoming increasingly fractious and it was hard enough keeping the peace *within* the *Partisan Review* editorial offices let alone between the different groups and interests outside of it. With the Stalinists on their doorstep, the Scientific and Cultural Conference for World Peace should have been an opportunity for solidarity between these different factions, but in the run-up to the event McCarthy and Hook ended up in a dispute about the best way to protest.

Hook, whom McCarthy credited with educating her about Marxism in the late '30s, was a domineering figure. He was short, bespectacled, and wore a clipped moustache, yet despite this almost comical appearance, gave his ideological opponents the terrors because of his formidable intellect and ruthless methods of argumentation. He thought McCarthy's idea of infiltrating the conference hopelessly naive. "That just shows how little you know about politics," he told her in a phone call.[15] The situation was complicated by the fact that McCarthy's satirical novel, *The Oasis*, had just been published in the British magazine *Horizon*, much to the displeasure of many in the New York crowd who recognized their unflattering portraits.

Hook's plan was to create a counterconference. He was a persuasive organizer and had played a key role in assembling the Trotsky Defense Committee. Some of his old allies from that fight, including John Dewey, rallied to his side. The weekend before the conference at the Waldorf began, Hook announced to the press that the newly formed Americans for Intellectual Freedom would be holding its own gathering at Freedom House on West Fortieth Street. The group, which had first congregated in Macdonald's apartment and included Farrell and Phillips, had secured a bridal suite at the Waldorf to be their headquarters. In imitation of their Communist-backed rivals, they secured prestigious sponsors, among them Benedetto Croce, T. S. Eliot, Karl Jaspers, André Malraux, Bertrand Russell, and Igor Stravinsky.[16] The plan was to get as much press coverage as possible.

While the methods of these two groups—McCarthy's and Hook's—differed, their goal was the same: to expose what they saw as the hypocrisy of intellectuals speaking freely at a convention in New York City while so many of their number were being silenced on the other side of the Iron Curtain. Their actions were motivated, in large part, by a defense of literature, and of literary writers, in the face of persecution by the totalitarian state. In doing so, they were laying the bedrock for Western cultural warfare on the Soviet Union.

THE COVER OF THE JANUARY 1949 ISSUE of *Partisan Review* had announced its usual stellar cast of contributors. McCarthy was there, writing about Laurence Olivier's *Hamlet* (her final theater column). Orwell had an essay about Mohandas Gandhi, who had been murdered by a Hindu nationalist assassin the previous January, while Spender included the third excerpt from a chapter of his forthcoming memoir *World Within World*. Also flagged on the cover was a newly translated short story by a Russian writer who, in the notes on contributors, the editors described as "one of the best known Russian writers of the nineteen-twenties who disappeared during the purge of the nineteen-thirties."[17] The story, translated by Mirra Ginsburg, was titled "The Sin of Jesus" and its author was Isaac Babel.[18]

Publishing a brilliant modernist short story was par for the course at *Partisan Review* but publishing a brilliant modernist short story by a Russian writer who was a victim of the Stalinist Terror gave the effort the character of a preemptive strike against the Scientific and Cultural Conference for World Peace. To McCarthy and her group of infiltrators, stories like Babel's were the key issue. They wanted to confront the Soviet sympathizers with the names of those who had "disappeared." At an anti-fascist conference arranged by André Malraux in Paris in 1936, Babel had been among the star speakers. Nothing had been heard from him in the West since. Where had he gone?

Despite—or in some ways because of—the anti-Communist tenor of the moment, the conference was packed. "Peace" was not a hard sell in 1949, amid war exhaustion and nuclear anxiety. As well as the two thousand who attended the opening banquet at the hotel, the conference sold out an event at Carnegie Hall on the second day. In a final flourish, the closing session took place at Madison Square Garden, where a crowd of eighteen thousand watched from almost total darkness as a series of speakers were picked out in dramatic spotlights, culminating just before midnight in Dmitri Shostakovich playing the second movement of his Fifth Symphony. The *New York Times* reported that Shostakovich's closing performance received a "tremendous ovation."[19]

Shostakovich, undoubtedly the biggest draw among the delegates, had not wanted to even attend the conference, but was "asked" personally by Stalin to go. During the purges, Shostakovich had fallen into official disgrace when his opera, *Lady Macbeth of Mtsensk,* was excoriated for "petit-bourgeois formalism" in an unsigned *Pravda* editorial reputedly authored by Stalin himself. This trip was part of his rehabilitation. At a press conference held before the proceedings opened, Alexander Fadeyev, the general secretary of the Union of Soviet Writers, inveighed against the "North Atlantic Pact" and the U.S. atomic weapons program. While Fadeyev ranted, Nicolas Nabokov watched Shostakovich's reaction from just a few feet away. Nabokov felt he gave the impression of being "a trapped man . . . disturbed, hurt and terribly shy."[20] It was an accurate assessment: the great composer had nowhere to turn.

At the opening banquet in the Grand Ballroom of the Waldorf, the organizers had to deal with their first deviation—not from the infiltrators, but from one of their own delegates. There was commotion at the high table when a panicked Harlow Shapley, the toastmaster, rushed over to Lillian Hellman, who was chain-smoking, drinking, and chatting to Shostakovich. Shapley had Norman Cousins's speech clutched in his hand and, as she read it, Hellman realized why Shapley was shaken. Cousins, the editor of the *Saturday Review of Literature,* had been presumably invited to speak because of his staunch opposition to the atomic bomb. In his speech, Cousins told the foreign delegates to "tell the folks at home that it is a lie to say that any single group controls the United States—not excluding Wall Street or the American Communist Party. Tell the folks at home that Americans are anti-Communist but not anti-humanitarian, and that being anti-Communist does not automatically mean that they are pro-war."[21] When they realized what Cousins was doing, the audience booed and hissed. Hellman, scenting sabotage, sought to put Cousins in his place when it was her turn to speak. "I would recommend, Mr. Cousins, that when you are invited out to dinner, you wait until you get home before you talk about your hosts," she told those gathered in the ballroom. The headline on the front page of the *New York Times* the following morning read "Our Way Defended to 2,000 Opening 'Culture' Meeting."

Hook and his group tried to take advantage of the media's willingness to print anti-Communist stories. At their Waldorf headquarters they composed and printed press releases and statements; when Nicolas Nabokov arrived at the bridal suite he described it as looking "like a vacated bordello taken over by a printer or a publisher gone berserk."[22] A mimeograph machine churned out pamphlets that were stored in one bathroom, while the other was used for private meetings. Hook was in his rambunctious element, and he even confronted Shapley in his hotel room, demanding to know why he had been denied the opportunity to speak at the conference. According to Phillips, the group "employed questionable tactics, such as intercepting mail and messages and issuing misleading statements in the name of the conference—tactics that upset all but the most hardened veterans of Communist and anti-Communist organizational fights."[23] The group also initiated a telephone campaign urging non-Communist sponsors to withdraw.[24]

The counterconference was a success. The venue at Freedom House was packed to its 450-person capacity. Thanks to some quick organizational thinking, a space was roped off in Bryant Park for the overflow, with five hundred more listening to speeches by the likes of Hook, Max Eastman, and Arthur Schlesinger Jr. relayed through loudspeakers. Back at the Waldorf, McCarthy and her allies assembled: Macdonald, Nabokov, Elizabeth Hardwick, and Robert Lowell. "They'll start hazing you the minute you try to open your mouth," Hook told them. "What you must do is go in there with chains or ropes or something to tie yourself to your chair so they can't remove you." This was far too melodramatic for McCarthy; they left the ropes and chains at home. Not that they were wholly unequipped. "[W]e took the precaution of bringing umbrellas," McCarthy recalled, "in order to make a demonstration and possibly as a weapon if we had to."[25] As soon as proceedings began at the Writing and Publishing panel, which took place in the eight-hundred-capacity Starlight Roof, McCarthy and her team banged their umbrellas on the floor. Louis Untermeyer, the chairman, told the room that everyone would get two minutes to ask a question but only if the noisy protest ceased.

Norman Mailer, who was among the speakers, recalled seeing McCarthy issuing instructions to her friends in the audience: "Mary was the play caller for the group—the quarterback. She'd turn or point or nod to one or the other of them, signaling them to speak."[26] McCarthy directed her question to Harvard's F. O. Matthiessen, asking him how two of the authors whose work he championed, Emerson and Thoreau, would fare in the Soviet Union. Matthiessen fudged an answer. Lowell asked Shostakovich how the criticism of the government helped his own work. A nervous Shostakovich—Macdonald described him as physically shaking—offered only some vague clichés about the importance of criticism. This was in stark contrast to the rhetoric of his speech the following day at the same venue, in which he "told 800 cheering persons [. . .] that 'a small clique of hatemongers' was preparing world public opinion for the transition from cold war to 'outright aggression'" (although, for all its fiery rhetoric, the speech was read by a translator, not by Shostakovich).[27]

The most striking confrontation was between Macdonald and Fadeyev, both of whom relished a fight. Macdonald described Fadeyev as "a big, bulky, square-shouldered man, with a ruddy, fleshy, big-jawed face and iron-grey hair; his expression was cold and wooden; he looked more like a plain-clothes detective than a writer."[28] In his own account, Macdonald did not pull any punches, telling the room that Fadeyev "represents precisely that exploitation of culture by the war-making State which it is the alleged purpose of this conference to protest against." Having put Fadeyev in his place, Macdonald then asked three questions. One was about Fadeyev's previous attacks on American culture; another was about how he had responded to his own novel, *Young Guard,* meeting with official disfavor. The third question was the most pointed, however. Macdonald listed six writers—Boris Pasternak, Ivan Katayev, Anna Akhmatova, Mikhail Zoshchenko, Boris Pilnyak, and Isaac Babel—and demanded to know what had happened to them: "Are they alive? Are they free or in prison?" In response, Fadeyev simply stated that Pasternak had the dacha next door to his and that Zoshchenko had published a novel in 1947.

There was one more surprise in store. Securing Mailer was a coup for the conference, just like Hemingway was for the Second Congress of American Writers back in 1937. Mailer was one of the most exciting young American novelists on the scene, still high on the success of *The Naked and the Dead,* published the previous year. "They gave him the floor and he embarked on a masterly sort of Ciceronian speech," McCarthy recalled. Macdonald said that Mailer spoke with such intensity he began to sweat. He called himself a "Trojan Horse" and attacked both the United States and the Soviet Union for "moving toward state capitalism" and argued that both were "caught in a mechanism which is steadily grinding on to produce war."[29]

At the end of the session McCarthy and Howard Fast began arguing vociferously. To his credit, Fast invited McCarthy and her friends to a reception for the foreign delegates at the Hotel Sutton, where scotch was served in a dingy, smoky room. Macdonald came away from the evening struck by how much common ground there was between the two groups: they read the same books, watched the same films, and, for the most part, supported the same left-wing causes. He also came away thinking that "these Stalinoids are much less dangerous and effective than I had expected."[30] He was right.

The conference at the Waldorf was the end of a certain type of Soviet cultural propaganda, the type that had been so successfully masterminded by Willi Münzenberg and the Comintern in the 1930s. Large-scale congresses were too messy, too easily sabotaged, and support among Western intellectuals was waning, particularly in the United States. Selling the idea of "peace" also became more challenging when the Russians tested their first atomic bomb. Yet if it was the death of one form of cultural propaganda, it played an important role in the birth of another: the idea of attacking intellectual freedom in the Soviet Union was to become the focus of an ambitious new phase in the way America waged the cultural Cold War. Sitting among the delegates at the Freedom House counterconference was an Estonian émigré named Michael Josselson, there at the behest of his boss, Frank Wisner, who ran the innocuous-sounding Office of Policy Coordination at the freshly minted Central Intelligence Agency.[31] Through David Dubinsky, the head of the Ladies' Garment Workers Union, the CIA clandestinely funneled funds to the Americans for Intellectual Freedom, allowing Hook and his allies to rent the Waldorf suite. The money appeared to have been well spent: what the conference showed was that if attacks on Soviet suppression of free expression came from the left, they were much more credible than coming from the reactionary right. If the Soviets tried to bring the intellectuals of the world together through the concept of "peace," then the Americans could try to do the same with the concept of "freedom." Behind the scenes, cogs were beginning to turn.

The key figure in this new American strategy was the dissident writer, denied the freedom to write and publish behind the Iron Curtain. Yet, as Macdonald's question to Fadeyev had made clear, it was very difficult to know what had befallen those writers who had fallen into political disfavor. What had befallen those whose pens had long been silent? Where they alive? In prison? The emerging Cold War, it turned out, placed all but the most obedient of authors in grave danger. The Stalinist war on writers had entered a perilous new phase.

SIXTEEN

Akhmatova

LENINGRAD, 1945–1953

IN NOVEMBER 1945, Joseph Stalin addressed the Politburo, warning that while the Great Patriotic War had been won, the struggle was far from over. The Allies had accepted the unconditional surrender of German forces just seven months previously, but already tensions were growing between the Soviet Union and the Western powers. Stalin told the assembled Soviet leadership that they were now engaged in a "tooth and nail struggle against servility before foreign figures."[1] This struggle was unlikely to take the shape of an open conflict—at least not in the immediate future. While the military might of the United States, equipped as it was with the atom bomb, was an evident concern, the Red Army occupied vast swaths of Europe and far outnumbered the Western forces. And everybody was exhausted; there was no appetite for more fighting. What Stalin feared was a more insidious threat: an ideological attack that could undermine a Soviet Union crippled by the war.

In the 1930s, the ideological threat of democratic capitalism had appeared limited. The economy of the United States had been ravaged by the Great Depression and improved only after the leftward tilt of Roosevelt's New Deal. In Europe, the failures of capitalism had helped usher in the rise of fascism. The postwar picture was very different, however. The United States was resurgent, its economy entering what would later be known as the long boom. Furthermore, Stalin feared—rightly, it transpired—that the Americans were prepared to use their wealth to stimulate the recovery of its European allies and, in so doing, shape the political future of the continent. To Stalin this was a form of imperialism, an American attempt to spread its version of democratic capitalism around the world. Furthermore, he suspected the Western powers had deliberately delayed opening a second front during the war in order to ensure the Soviet Union emerged weakened from the conflict. And there was no question that a Soviet populace struggling with poverty, disease, and starvation might look to Western prosperity and start asking difficult questions. The war had brought the country together, but victory had come at a tremendous cost, with some 27 million dead and more than 1,700 cities in ruins.[2] The Soviet Union was faced with a vast rebuilding operation, and there was little prospect for improvement in living conditions in the immediate future.

Stalin responded to this sense of vulnerability in typically paranoid style: he geared up for a new ideological crackdown, and this time the focus would be anyone who had come in contact with Western values. Just as they had done during the period of the Popular Front and the Spanish Civil War, during the Second World War the Politburo had sought alliances across the political spectrum in the fight with fascism, and many citizens hoped the postwar Soviet Union would become a more politically open society than it had been in the authoritarian 1930s. They were mistaken; a campaign of persecution began that was ruthless in its logic. Volunteers who had fought in the Spanish Civil War, Red Army soldiers who had been in German POW camps, and anyone who had fought or worked in Western territory during the war became a candidate for the gulag.

The new anti-Western policy was to be entrusted to Andrei Zhdanov, a Soviet official who had wormed his way up the Party hierarchy to earn his position as Stalin's most trusted advisor. He was a canny political operator, and he knew that his new responsibility would make him vulnerable—Kirov's fate was testament to that. Perhaps his biggest problem was that since the assassination of Kirov, he had been in charge of the Communist Party in Leningrad, a city that in its very founding by Peter the Great had been conceived as a window on the West and remained a city more cosmopolitan than the rest of the country. Now the Kremlin wanted the city's intellectuals silenced—all that was needed was a symbolic sacrifice. The new Cold War purge would begin with a poet of St. Petersburg.

ON THE NIGHT OF AUGUST 7, 1946, Anna Akhmatova stood on the stage of Leningrad's Bolshoi Drama Theater and recited her poems. Her voice was deep, strange, almost otherworldly, and the audience listened in reverential silence. The city had always lionized its poets, from Pushkin to Blok and, having emerged from a harrowing war, the people of the city were again gathering to be consoled and exhilarated by the declaiming of verses. Akhmatova was an emissary from a past that over the last two decades had been suppressed: a poet forged in the experimental decades that preceded the revolution; a poet who carried herself in a manner that was aloof, mysterious, even aristocratic; a poet who spoke of sadness, suffering, and the desires of both flesh and spirit. She brought out an almost cultlike devotion in her readers, who learned her poems by heart. When Akhmatova finished her reading there was a beat of silence before the applause crashed over her like a flood. She bathed in the adulation, the fervor of the audience leaving her flushed and proud. "They were mainly young men," said one eyewitness, "they stand, applaud, grow wild, roar."[3] The audience had experienced something extraordinary in Stalin's Soviet Union and they knew it.

That this kind of poetry could command such adulation was not acceptable to the Kremlin—it smacked of heresy. Since the mid-1920s, Akhmatova's poetry had gone unpublished, and for years at a time she had disappeared from public life. Her problems with the Kremlin went right back to the aftermath of the revolution; she was tainted by association with her ex-husband, Nikolai Gumilev, a poet whose monarchist politics incurred the displeasure of the Bolsheviks. Lenin's secret police, the Cheka, soon closed in on him; he was implicated in a "conspiracy" of military officers and other conservative figures to supposedly overthrow the regime. They executed him on August 25, 1921. Akhmatova and Gumilev had divorced in 1918, but she was nevertheless marked by the authorities and sentenced to what she called "civic death."[4] Her work stopped being published in the Soviet Union in 1925. (Gumilev, as we have seen, remained a target of the regime long after his death and was denounced at the 1934 First Congress of the Union of Soviet Writers.)

Unlike so many of her fellow writers, Akhmatova survived the Great Terror of the thirties, but she did so only at a terrible cost. In 1935 the NKVD had arrested both Akhmatova's twenty-three-year-old son, Lev Gumilev, and Nikolai Punin, the art critic with whom she was in a relationship. Akhmatova traveled from Leningrad to Moscow to appeal directly to Stalin for clemency, hand-delivering a letter to the Kremlin. Stalin ordered both men released; Punin returned to his life with Akhmatova, Lev returned to his studies. In March 1938, however, Lev was rearrested and sentenced to ten years in the gulag, forced to work on the construction of the White Sea Canal. For six months the authorities would not let Akhmatova see her son. He was eventually deported to Norilsk, in the Arctic Circle. Lev was effectively held hostage, a guarantee of his mother's silence.

The advent of war dramatically changed the mood of the

country, however, and previously proscribed writers, including Akhmatova and Boris Pasternak, were allowed to publish their poems in the newspapers and read their work in public again, a reflection of a spirit of wartime solidarity that had replaced the paranoia and dread of the thirties.[5] The readings proved immensely popular, with crowds flocking to hear publicly declaimed the poems that until recently they only dared read in furtive secrecy.[6] The Central Committee of the Communist Party emphasized the need for a popular patriotism, and writers who were prepared to provide rhetorical uplift were encouraged to do so.

For all that she had suffered at the hands of the government, Akhmatova was determined to play her part in the war effort. She was in Moscow when she learned that the Germans were advancing rapidly on Leningrad, but she returned to her home city nonetheless and, at the request of the authorities, broadcast a message of defiance over the radio. As the city prepared for the siege, handwritten copies of her poems, including some that had never been officially published, circulated among the populace—some even made it to the front lines. Akhmatova pitched in as best she could, working as a fire monitor and stitching sandbags, but as the siege tightened, she was airlifted out of the city and, along with other famous writers, moved to Tashkent for her safety.[7]

Despite the German bombardment and the desperate lack of food and medicine, Leningrad held out for 872 days before the Red Army relieved it in January 1944. Akhmatova returned to her hometown the following June in a state of mental and physical fragility. Never healthy, she had contracted scarlet fever and typhus while in Tashkent, and she was full of anxiety for Lev, who had persuaded the authorities to release him from his Arctic exile to let him fight on the front lines as the Red Army marched on Berlin. She feared her son would be assigned to a penal regiment made up of the soldiers considered most expendable.

Akhmatova's return elicited a new disappointment. While in Central Asia, Vladimir Garshin had written to her and proposed marriage. Garshin was a doctor who had met Akhmatova in the late thirties, when she was a patient in his hospital. He had helped her through the arrest of her son and the collapse of her relationship with Punin, and she was excited for their future together. Yet she found him much changed on her return to the city. Akhmatova later claimed he had lost his mind during the siege, although other accounts suggest that while he had suffered a great deal he had just changed his mind about the prospective marriage. The siege had certainly left deep psychological scars on everyone who had suffered through it. Some six hundred thousand people had died in the city, many of disease, starvation, or the extreme cold. Bodies were hauled off in carts as the bombs rained down. There were rumors of cannibalism. As a doctor, Garshin had seen many horrors. His wife, from whom he was estranged, died freezing and starving on the street, and Garshin had to identify her from her clothes because the rats had eaten her face.[8]

After the war was won and the country began to gather itself and gradually rebuild, there was hope that such suffering and the solidarity of the war years would prevent a return to brutal Stalinist authoritarianism.[9] Akhmatova's reentering public life was symbolic of this hope. To her delight she had been permitted to sign a contract for a new edition of her poems in March 1946.[10] Those that gathered to listen to her read at the Bolshoi Drama Theater the following August were therefore not just groping nostalgically for a lost past but were also invested in the possibility of a better, more open future. Amid the rapturous applause it might just have seemed plausible.

Not everyone left the theater happy, however. In the audience was a functionary of the Agitprop Department of the Central Committee who immediately sent an angry memo to his boss, Georgi Alexandrov, declaring that all Akhmatova had spoken about was sex and God. Alexandrov took the memo up the Politburo food chain until it reached the top. Hearing of the reception Akhmatova had received, Stalin's response was ominous. "Who organized this?" he said.[11] Just like that, the poet's success had given Stalin and Zhdanov the pretext they needed to begin their next purge. Akhmatova was tainted by the West, a modernist poet who typified the cosmopolitanism of her home city. If there was to be a cultural war with the West and its corrupting values, then sacrificial victims were needed. Akhmatova's stage was also an altar.

TWO WEEKS AFTER she had delivered her bravura reading at the Bolshoi Drama Theater, Akhmatova went to the Leningrad Union of Writers, where she had recently been elected to the board, another signal that she was no longer a pariah. It became immediately apparent that something was wrong, however. Everybody she encountered seemed to avoid making eye contact, shrinking from her in silence as she walked through the corridors. Akhmatova would soon know why: she had been denounced.

The morning edition of *Pravda* carried a resolution of the Central Committee condemning two journals, *Leningrad* and *Star*, both of which were damned for their having published Akhmatova and fellow writer Mikhail Zoshchenko. "I knew absolutely nothing about it," she later recalled. "I had not looked at the morning papers and had not turned on the radio, and apparently no one thought of calling me."[12] The author of the resolution was Zhdanov. He was well known to Russia's writers for his presiding role at the 1934 Writers Conference, at which he had announced the mandate for socialist realism, a doctrine that Akhmatova was now being accused of violating. "The strength of Soviet literature, the most advanced literature in the world," Zhdanov wrote, "consists in the fact that it is a literature that does not and cannot have other interests besides the interests of the people, the interests of the state."[13] Akhmatova's work was in violation of these interests. "Akhmatova is a typical representative of the empty, unprincipled poetry alien to our people," Zhdanov wrote. "Her poems, permeated with a spirit of pessimism and decadence, 'art for art's sake,' are reluctant to walk in step with their people and cannot be countenanced in Soviet literature."[14] By publishing her work, *Leningrad* and *Star* were responsible for causing "ideological disarray" and fostering a culture that groveled "before the modern bourgeois culture of the West." These words were carefully chosen; they closely echoed Stalin's warnings to the Politburo.

Zhdanov delivered the next blow in person. On the evening of September 4, he addressed the Leningrad Union of Soviet Writers, to announce the expulsion of Akhmatova and Zoshchenko from their ranks. He arrived onstage to mild applause. One writer present, Innokenty Basalayev, remembered the "strange and weird silence" that fell over the room when Zhdanov started speaking, with the audience "mute, frozen, turned to ice."[15] A member of the audience, feeling nauseous, staggered back through the rows of chairs to the exit but was not allowed to leave. Zhdanov continued to denounce the two writers until one in the morning. "Not a word, not a whisper was heard from the steps of the grand formal entrance," Basalayev wrote. "Several hundred people left the building slowly and silently. Just as silently they passed along the straight *allée* to the empty square and silently went off to the late trolleys and buses. Everything was unexpected and incomprehensible."[16]

Any hopes of a more open future were dashed—the state had

tightened its ideological grip on culture. The only thing that seemed to have changed was that the Central Committee was now making public its rationale.[17] Stalin was deeply invested in this crackdown on the Leningrad intelligentsia and personally interrogated the editors of *Leningrad* and *Star*. He enjoyed Zhdanov's "superb" report, congratulated him on the action he had taken in Leningrad, and even made some editorial emendations to the report before demanding it be published as a pamphlet.[18] The Zhdanov resolution was a signal of things to come.

Even as she was giving her readings, in Moscow and Leningrad, Akhmatova knew she was taking a risk. She had been submerged in obscurity for so long that when she broke the surface, she could do nothing but gasp for breath, some part of her knowing that the hand of the state, the hand of Stalin, would soon push her back under. She knew they were watching her carefully. It was not just her "bourgeois" poetry that they held against her—she had also had clandestine meetings with a representative of the West.

IT BEGAN WITH A CHANCE ENCOUNTER in the Writers' Bookshop on Nevsky Prospect. Isaiah Berlin was visiting Leningrad from Moscow, where he was assigned to the British Embassy as First Secretary, on the hunt for books from the prerevolutionary era. Invited to the back room of the shop, which functioned as an informal writers' club, he struck up a conversation with the literary critic Vladimir Orlov. Berlin asked about the city's famous writers and what had happened to them during the siege. When Orlov offered to set up a meeting with Akhmatova, Berlin was shaken; she seemed a figure from the remote past.

Berlin's own past lay in this city. He had been born in Riga, the son of a Jewish timber merchant, but his family had relocated to Petrograd, as it was then known, in 1916. He was only seven when the October Revolution swept the Bolsheviks to power; the fear of Lenin's Cheka and persistent anti-Semitism prompted them to emigrate to Britain in 1921. A precocious student, Berlin went to Oxford, where he eventually became a distinguished historian of ideas, a champion of liberalism, and a fellow of All Souls College. In 1940, frustrated that his foreign birth precluded him from joining the war effort, Berlin became embroiled in a scheme of one of his less dependable friends— Guy Burgess.

Burgess told Berlin he was heading to Moscow for MI5 and invited him to come along as a press officer to the embassy there. The pair flew to New York, from where they were supposed to travel to Moscow, but Berlin's visa had not come through and Burgess was suddenly recalled to London. Deciding to stay in the United States, Berlin got a job with the British Press Service and the Ministry of Information before ending up at the Foreign Office in Washington, writing reports on the American political scene that found favor with Churchill. He made contacts in the American political establishment, including some, like Arthur Schlesinger Jr., George Kennan, and Chip Bohlen, who went on to play influential roles in the Cold War.

In 1945, with the war in Europe won, Berlin was invited by the British ambassador in Moscow, Archibald Clark Kerr, to write a report on British-Soviet relations and spend six months in Moscow, with the idea that his fluency in the language and knowledge of Russia's history and culture would allow him to take the political temperature of the Soviet Union. He arrived in September and soon immersed himself in the city's cultural elite, dining with the film director Sergei Eisenstein and travelling to Peredelkino to meet Boris Pasternak at his dacha.[19] At one of these meetings, Pasternak gave him the first few chapters of the novel he was working on, asking that he deliver them to his sisters in Oxford. At the time, Berlin had no idea that the work in his custody represented the first iteration of *Doctor Zhivago,* which would become one of the most explosive literary works of the Cold War. Berlin was aware, however, that wherever he went he was being followed, and the maid in the embassy apartment made unsubtle attempts to entrap him by asking loaded questions about Trotsky.[20] In order to visit the family he still had in the city Berlin would first attend a ballet performance, leaving partway through in order to throw off surveillance.

Knowing that he could bring unwanted official attention through his mere presence, Berlin tried to be discreet when visiting Akhmatova. Orlov phoned ahead and he and Berlin went to her apartment in the Sheremetev Palace that afternoon, making their way down the snow-lined streets, the buildings still pitted by damage from bombs and shells. "A stately, grey-haired lady, a white shawl draped about her shoulders, slowly rose to greet us," Berlin wrote. "[She] was immensely dignified, with unhurried gestures, a noble head, beautiful, somewhat severe features, and an expression of immense sadness. I bowed. It seemed appropriate, for she looked and moved like a tragic queen."[21] The room she lived in was bare, with little furniture and few books, but was distinguished by a portrait of her hung on the wall, sketched by Modigliani in Paris in 1911.[22]

The conversation had barely begun when Berlin thought he was having an auditory hallucination, hearing his own name being shouted outside. It turned out that Randolph Churchill, son of Winston, was outside bellowing "Isaiah" over and again. Churchill was in Russia as a journalist and was staying in the same hotel as Berlin, whom he knew from their days as undergraduates at Oxford. Churchill had been having trouble communicating to the hotel staff that he needed an ice box for his caviar; learning from a mutual acquaintance that Berlin was at the Sheremetev Palace, he went to find his Russian-speaking chum to help resolve this impasse. Not knowing which apartment

Berlin was visiting, Churchill made do with bellowing his name in the courtyard. Berlin hurried out to help resolve Churchill's crisis before he drew any more unwanted attention to his host. He phoned Akhmatova later to apologize for his hasty exit and, to his relief, she suggested they meet again that evening.

The meeting that followed has become the subject of much fascination.[23] Berlin arrived at nine o'clock and while Akhmatova initially had another guest, once they were alone the conversation became intimate and intense. At 3 A.M. Akhmatova's son, Lev, arrived, and they ate boiled potatoes, Akhmatova embarrassed by the modesty of her hospitality. The pair carried on talking after Lev went to bed, speaking into the dawn about her life, her work, and Russian literature more generally. Berlin told her about the writers he knew who had emigrated to the West, and she told him about those who had disappeared in the purges. Their conversation was laced with nostalgia, grief, but also desire. It was later rumored that they had slept together but, while clearly drawn to each other, the relationship was not consummated. Akhmatova at fifty-six had lived a life full of passionate affairs with both men and women and, from what she later told others about their meeting, she seems to have mistaken Berlin for being far more self-possessed than he really was. Berlin was thirty-six, balding and bespectacled, and sexually inexperienced. He spent a good part of the evening desperate for the toilet.[24]

At some point Akhmatova began to recite her own poetry. Berlin knew her stature within Russian letters but did not know her work well. He was exhilarated by what he heard. She recited the long poem she was working on, *Poem Without a Hero*, which Berlin realized was to be the defining work of her oeuvre, the "final memorial of her life as a poet." There were aspects of the poem that Berlin did not understand—complex images and personal references—but he knew it was a work of profound importance.

"I realised even then," Berlin later wrote, "that I was listening to a work of genius."[25] He asked her if he could transcribe it, but she refused. What Berlin did not realize as he stumbled out into the snowy Leningrad morning was that *Poem Without a Hero* was still a work in progress—and that his meeting with Akhmatova would become part of the poem.

Soon after his departure, Akhmatova began to rework *Poem Without a Hero,* as she would continue to do until she finished it in 1962, encoding Berlin into its lines as a "Guest from the Future."[26] This was a statement of optimism on Akhmatova's part: in Berlin she had found a representative of what she hoped were her future readers. Throughout the 1930s she dared only read her poems to her most trusted friends and then immediately burned the manuscripts in her ashtray. Here was someone who gave her hope that her work might find future readers beyond these private rituals. He gave her hope that her work might one day emerge from the Stalinist night.

BERLIN WAS PROFOUNDLY AFFECTED, TOO. The following month, he delivered the report that the British Foreign Office had commissioned. The meeting with Akhmatova had given him a new resolve. Instead of a strategic document about the potential for future Anglo-Soviet relations, the memorandum he wrote was about Russian literature and what had happened to it under Communism. He documented the various ways the Kremlin's cultural policy had changed since 1917 and gave a clear and well-informed account of what had happened during the purges, showing great skepticism over reports that some of the writers who had disappeared might still be alive. (On Berlin's list of victims were Babel and Mandelstam, who, after serving a period in exile, had been arrested a second time in May 1938 and sent to a labor camp, where he died, officially of illness.)

Two months later, Berlin's friend from Washington, George Kennan, sent his famous "Long Telegram" from the American embassy in Moscow in which he warned that Stalin's foreign policy was "impervious to the logic of reason" but was "highly sensitive to logic of force."[27] It was a document that was foundational in shaping U.S. policy toward the Soviet Union. Berlin's memorandum had nowhere near the impact of Kennan's telegram, but it did make an important argument about how culture might play an important role in any future conflict with the Soviet Union. Berlin emphasized, over and again, quite how potent literature was in Soviet life. Even works of transparent propaganda sold out and "there probably exists no country today where poetry old and new, good and indifferent, is sold in such quantities and read so avidly as it is in the Soviet Union."[28] As such, writers had political potential of which the state was fearful. "Writers are generally considered as persons who need a good deal of watching, since they deal in the dangerous commodity of ideas, and are therefore fended off from private, individual contact with foreigners," he wrote.[29] Helping that dangerous commodity of ideas to circulate would seem to be in the interests of those looking to undermine the Soviet Union.

Akhmatova was of course being watched herself and, following her meeting with Berlin, was to be watched ever more closely in the future.[30] Berlin learned that as a result of Churchill's brash interruption, wild rumors had begun to circulate that a British delegation had been sent to persuade Akhmatova to abandon Russia and that Winston Churchill was personally arranging for her to be flown to Britain. Wary of putting her in even more danger, Berlin did not write about his meeting with Akhmatova at the time (he eventually published an account of it in 1980). The damage, though, was done. Years later Akhmatova told Berlin that Stalin, on hearing of their meeting, said: "This means our nun is now receiving visits from foreign spies."[31]

The pair next met on January 6, 1946, just before Berlin returned to Britain. That the secret police were aware of the visit became apparent when the following day uniformed officers appeared at the foot of the staircase to her apartment and, in case that did not send a clear enough message, a microphone was unsubtly installed in the ceiling from the apartment above.[32] Nadezhda Mandelstam, the widow of the poet Osip, later wrote in her masterful memoir *Hope Against Hope* about how obvious the surveillance was when she visited Akhmatova's apartment: the plainclothes officers assigned to the gate of the palace changed their shifts regularly and once, while they were out walking together Mandelstam noticed a flashbulb going off.

Aside from this surveillance, there seemed to be no further consequences. Lev finally returned from Berlin, unscathed by the fighting, and resumed his studies at the university. Akhmatova was giving readings again, including at Moscow's Hall of Columns alongside Pasternak, and in March she signed a contract for her new book of poems. It was a period of optimism that lasted until that moment when Akhmatova walked down the halls of the Leningrad Writers Union and found nobody would meet her eyes.

BORIS PASTERNAK DESCRIBED hearing about the Zhdanov resolution as like experiencing an earthquake, with the cultural world of the Soviet Union shaken to its foundations.[33] This was about more than the ostracizing of two famous writers; the aftershocks grew in intensity and began to spread. In the terms outlined by Zhdanov, there were two "camps": the "imperialist," led by the United States and its allies in Western Europe; and the "democratic," which was the camp of the Soviet Union and its Communist satellites. The attacks on Western-sympathizing Akhmatova and Zoshchenko were followed by ideological crackdowns on music, cinema, scholarship, and the sciences. The same summer that Akhmatova's poetry was condemned, foreign books and periodicals were banned, as well as any unofficial contacts with foreigners.[34] The State Museum of Modern Western Art was closed, and scholars who claimed Western influence on Russian culture were condemned. Scientific researchers who shared their work with Westerners were publicly condemned, and in order to put deviant, unpatriotic officials on trial, "honor courts" were established.[35]

For Akhmatova, the author of "bourgeois" verse, the consequences of her inevitable expulsion from the Writers' Union were disastrous as it made it nigh on impossible to make money through her pen. The first print run of the new collection of poems in which she had invested so much hope was pulped. Other writers began to cross the street to avoid speaking with her and she began to take to her bed, refusing to face the outside world. Even buying basic groceries became a problem—she had effectively been made a noncitizen and was therefore ineligible for a ration card.

A wave of panic swept through the intellectual community, many of whom were haunted by the Yezhov purges. An orgy of denunciation began and the novelist Alexander Fadeyev, the ideologically accommodating new head of the Union of Writers, led from the front, insisting that Akhmatova's work was decadent and anti-Soviet and those who had previously praised her were grievously mistaken. Those who refused to participate in these rituals of ideological purification were punished; Pasternak, who holed himself up in his dacha at Peredelkino, was kicked off the board of the Union of Writers. Some speculated that he was in fact being punished for helping Akhmatova financially.[36] He, too, had a collection of poems in the works that was destroyed before it could reach readers.[37] Akhmatova became a symbolic pariah to a whole new generation of young Russians as the Zhdanov resolution was incorporated into school textbooks.[38] The Soviet citizen was being steeled for cultural combat in the emerging Cold War.

The crackdown was not confined to the Soviet Union. What began as an attack on Akhmatova and Zoshchenko in Leningrad soon reverberated in Bucharest, Budapest, Prague, Sofia, and Warsaw. In the aftermath of the war, the Kremlin claimed that it supported free elections in the East and Central European countries occupied by the Red Army as a means of placating Western governments who suspected the plan was to impose Communist rule. The facade that these "people's democracies" would retain political autonomy soon began to crumble; in early 1947 the Politburo prepared for the forcible imposition of the Soviet model of governance and with it a purge of Western influence. Stalin believed this move vindicated when the Marshall Plan was launched in April 1948, which confirmed his suspicion that the United States had its eyes on Eastern Europe and was seeking to wrest control from the Soviet Union by economic means. It was nothing less than a "Trojan Horse attack."[39] In order to ensure that the fortifications would hold, Stalin demanded absolute control. Each of these nations was to be ruled by a Communist Party that was obedient to Moscow, each was to reform its economy along Stalinist lines, and each was to ensure the obedience of its citizenship by granting power to the secret police.

As part of this consolidation of power, Stalin ordered a meeting in Poland in September 1947 at which the Cominform was created, an organization to coordinate Communist activity around the world and an heir to the Comintern. During the war, the Comintern had been dissolved, in part to demonstrate to the United States that the Soviet Union did not intend to foment revolution. A consequence of this was that Communist Parties in different countries began to act with increasing independence from Moscow. Many Communists across Europe had played heroic roles in the defeat of fascism—the ragtag band of French Communists who fought with Hemingway, for example, or Tito's Partisans in Yugoslavia—and as a result felt they had earned the right to make their own decisions about their political future. These deviant branches of Communism had to be pared back, and any wartime legacy of cooperation with other political parties and movements crushed. At the meeting in Poland, those whom Stalin wanted to discipline were shamed as "right-wing deviationists."[40] The Cominform would help get them on the correct track by exporting Zhdanov's "two camps" mentality. Eastern Europe was to be a buffer zone not only against military invasions but also the invasion of dangerous ideas.

In Czechoslovakia, where the Communists had been making electoral gains and hoped to attain power democratically, the Soviets helped engineer a coup in February 1948, by which the Communist Party seized control. In Hungary the Communist Party made improbable electoral gains, eventually taking complete control of government after winning a claimed 95.6 percent of the vote in May 1949.[41] In Poland, the Communist Party, which had previously been a relatively small player on the political scene, made huge gains through rigged elections, while in Romania and Bulgaria, where the Communists were even more unpopular, political power was seized by "subversion and violence."[42]

This was a catastrophic development for Bulgarian, Czechoslovak, Hungarian, Polish, and Romanian intellectuals, artists, and writers who, like Akhmatova, were perceived as being "servile before the West." The early years of the Cold War were marked by a series of show trials and purges in these countries, all designed to enforce Stalinist discipline on societies that had traditionally enjoyed close relations with countries on their western borders. Politicians of all stripes, including members of the Communist leadership, were put on trial and executed.[43] It was all a bleak restaging of the Stalinist 1930s, complete with the brutal collectivizing of agriculture. As the historian Tony Judt put it, "the second Stalinist Ice Age was beginning."[44]

There is no question that Stalin had always been anti-Semitic (something inextricably connected to his hatred of Trotsky) but in the immediate aftermath of the war it appeared there might be a brighter future for Russia's Jews, not least because Moscow supported the creation of a Jewish state in the Middle East (although that enthusiasm swiftly waned when it became clear that Israel was not going to be an ally of the Soviet Union). This optimism did not last long. Stalin's behavior was increasingly marked by paranoia when it came to the Soviet Union's Jewish population (many of the Communist politicians persecuted in Eastern Europe were Jewish). The authorities went after the Jewish Anti-Fascist Committee, despite the role it had played garnering support for the Soviet Union from Western countries during the war. Its leader, Solomon Mikhoels, an actor and a theater director, was killed in a car accident staged by the security services, and its other members were arrested. In strategically placed articles, Jews were referred to as "rootless cosmopolitans," the euphemism chosen to emphasize their exclusion from the nationalist project and to suggest they constituted a fifth column.[45] Yiddish newspapers, schools, and theaters were closed. In August 1952, thirteen prominent members of the Jewish Anti-Fascist Committee, including the poets Peretz Markish, Itzik Feffer, David Hofstein, Leib Kvitko, and the novelist David Bergelson, were found guilty of espionage and treason, among other charges, and executed in the basement of the Lubyanka in what was later known as the "Night of the Murdered Poets." In one night, the rich Russian-Yiddish literary tradition was wiped out.

In this fearful climate of paranoia and fear, with every night bringing the threat of new arrests, Akhmatova refused to break. "Misfortunes crashed down on her like avalanches," wrote Ilya Ehrenburg; "it needed more than common fortitude to preserve such dignity, composure, and pride."[46] While other intellectuals repented of their "crimes" and sought to regain official favor, Akhmatova remained aloof. In September 1949, Punin, her partner in the 1920s and '30s, was arrested along with many of his university colleagues. He was sent to Vorkuta in the far north, where he eventually died in the camps. Still, Akhmatova held strong. Then they did the one thing she could not tolerate; they came back for her son.

SEVENTEEN

Koestler

BERLIN, 1950

ARTHUR KOESTLER RECOGNIZED this was his moment. As he approached the lectern, he looked out over the crowd, some fifteen thousand strong, knowing that they were eagerly anticipating what he had to say. He was the undoubted star of the Congress for Cultural Freedom and he knew it. Over the four-day meeting of anti-Communist intellectuals in West Berlin, Koestler had inveighed against the Soviet Union and its intellectual apologists. On the closing day, June 29, he was scheduled to speak last, and he clutched in his hands the "Freedom Manifesto," a document he had worked on long into the boozy nights after the previous days' proceedings were finished. He was frayed, exhausted, but the adrenaline was doing its work. The Sommergarten, framed by its ring of poplars, was bathed in sunshine. Looming over Koestler and his audience was the Funkturm, the distinctive radio tower designed in imitation of the Eiffel Tower. It was a fitting backdrop for Koestler to communicate a message he hoped would resonate beyond this park and city and, with intensity and rhetorical flourish, he began to read the Freedom Manifesto.

The speech immediately made clear his allegiance, drawing as it did from the Declaration of Independence: "We hold it to be self-evident that intellectual freedom is one of the inalienable rights of man," Koestler declared. He read through each of the fourteen points of the manifesto, building momentum. Once he had finished, he paused, with self-conscious theatricality, before switching to German and shouting into the microphone: *"Freunde, die Freiheit had die Offensive ergriffen!"* (Friends, freedom has seized the initiative!)[1] Until Koestler took the stand, the speeches had been sedate. Now the surprised crowd roared its appreciation, people leaping to their feet to applaud. To the beleaguered citizens of West Berlin, a frontier town in a Cold War that was heating up fast, this was an uplifting rallying cry.

West Berlin was, in British delegate Hugh Trevor-Roper's words, "a forlorn island in the Russian sea," a democratic enclave some one hundred miles behind the Iron Curtain.[2] The Berlin Airlift might have ended the previous year but the city's status remained precarious; it would be the first place to fall if relations between the United States and the Soviet Union worsened.[3] And fears that another global conflict was looming had escalated dramatically on the first day of the Congress. On June 25 the Korean People's Army, backed by the Soviet Union and China, crossed into South Korea. At the end of the Second World War, Korea had been divided along the Thirty-Eighth Parallel between the Soviet-liberated north and the American-liberated south, and the invasion was the moment the Cold War erupted into open conflict. Two days later, with the South Korean forces routed and the government having abandoned Seoul, the United Nations Security Council passed a resolution recommending its members provide the south with military assistance. Denouncing the resolution as illegitimate, the Soviets abstained from the council. For the citizens of West Berlin, living in a city and a country that was also divided along ideological lines, this was a frightening escalation.

Koestler described the arrival of the one hundred delegates of the Congress for Cultural Freedom as an "intellectual airlift." The French police had given Koestler a bodyguard as he set off,

for fear of his being assassinated by Communist agents. On arrival in Frankfurt, Koestler and his colleagues boarded C-47
military transport planes for the flight into Berlin. The bulk of
the conference took place at the Titania-Palast, a luxurious cinema built in in the 1920s. After a call for a minute's silence (for
Korea and for victims of totalitarianism) the Congress opened
with a rousing rendition of Beethoven's *Egmont Overture*. The
program announced no fewer than five honorary presidents, all
of whom were prestigious philosophers from different countries:
Benedetto Croce (Italy), John Dewey (United States), Karl Jaspers (Germany/Switzerland), Jacques Maritain (France), and
Bertrand Russell (United Kingdom).[4] There were messages of
support from André Gide, John Dos Passos, and Eleanor Roosevelt. The organizers could not be accused of failing to take themselves seriously.

On the first day, the Titania-Palast was surrounded by a police cordon, but what clashes there were took place inside. It
emerged that there were two very different ways to fight for freedom. The British, French, and Italian delegates wanted to celebrate the achievements of social democracy and find ways for
intellectuals to avoid being drawn into simplistic antinomies of
capitalism versus communism, West versus East. To a fired-up
Koestler, this was little short of appeasement. Determined to
intervene in this debate, he declared that the Soviet Union had
to be confronted and condemned. There cannot be "neutrality
towards the bubonic plague," he said.[5] The choice European
intellectuals faced, Koestler argued, was between "total tyranny
versus relative freedom." According to one observer he spoke
"with skillful demagogic artistry"; according to another, he sent
his opponents into a fury by "grinning like a Cheshire cat" after
finishing.[6] Whatever his fellow delegates thought, the audience
in Titania-Palast liked what it heard and gave Koestler the loud-
est ovation of the conference.[7]

To Koestler, the Korean invasion was another example of how the Soviet Union would exploit perceived weakness. Before Mao Zedong's Communist Party won the Chinese Civil War in October 1949, Stalin had been hesitant to sanction an invasion of Korea. However, the United States' failure to intervene in China made Stalin think they would be unlikely do so in Korea, especially after withdrawing their occupying forces. As a result, he now gave Kim Il-sung, the North Korean leader, permission to attack, and he also used economic incentives to get Mao to promise to support the invasion with men and materiel. Since acquiring the atomic bomb the previous summer, the Soviet Union was free to pursue a more robust foreign policy, and Koestler believed that unless this Soviet aggression was met with force, it would only get worse. He knew Communists; Berlin was the city in which he had been recruited into the Comintern. In his mind there was no more room for neutralism, for third-way socialism, or any argument that made an equivalence between Soviet totalitarianism and American imperialism, and he was disgusted by those who claimed the witch hunt of Communists by Senator Joe McCarthy, or the work of the House Un-American Activities Committee, was in some way comparable to the Moscow purges. As he put it in the eleventh point of the Freedom Manifesto: "the theory and practice of the totalitarian state are the greatest challenge which man has been called on to meet in the course of civilized history." In the twelfth point he followed with the declaration that "indifference or neutrality in the face of such a challenge amounts to a betrayal of mankind and to the abdication of a free mind."[8]

From the first day of the Congress, Koestler had taken on those delegates he suspected of the crime of "neutralism." Relentlessly confrontational, he liked to make conflict personal— he needed a personal enemy. In Berlin, this meant Ignazio Silone, author of the classic anti-fascist novel *Fontamara*. Like

Koestler, Silone was a former Communist; both men had authored essays in *The God That Failed,* published the previous year, yet Koestler thought him weak. The softly spoken Silone felt they should be celebrating the achievements of European social democracy and was skeptical of American motives. During one of Silone's speeches, Koestler scribbled a note that read: "I always wondered whether basically Silone is honest or not. Now I know he is not."[9]

Yet Silone was not Koestler's real target; he was simply the best available substitute for the intellectual with whom he most wanted to grapple. Koestler's absent antagonist was Jean-Paul Sartre, who had refused to participate in the Berlin Congress. Koestler believed firmly that the future of France—a nation polarized between those who supported the Communist Party and those who sided with Charles De Gaulle, whose political philosophy was tinged with the authoritarian—would decide the future of continental Europe. The novel Koestler had completed earlier in 1950, *The Age of Longing,* imagined a France that had succumbed to Soviet takeover; he felt it a real threat. In the years after the Second World War, Sartre had attacked the Soviet Union for its cultural policies and argued for a socialism that was not subject to the Party line. For this, he was subject to attacks in the Communist press, with *L'Humanité* even referring to him as "Koestler's double."[10] However, by 1950 Sartre was coming around. He did not join the French Communist Party but, even when critical of specific Soviet policies, became openly sympathetic to the USSR and expressed antipathy to the United States.[11] To Koestler's mind, this kind of fellow traveling constituted a grave danger in a country that gave such credence to its intellectuals. It was an issue beyond France, too. Sartre and his allies among the French existentialists had become the dominant voice on the postwar intellectual scene, and one of the reasons Koestler was going to Berlin was to take them on. It had therefore felt like the workings of fate when, on boarding the night train to Frankfurt at Gare de l'Est in Paris, Koestler found that Sartre was in the next cabin to his. They had not spoken since their most recent falling-out eighteen months before, but they conversed politely over food and wine. For a short while they headed in the same direction even if they both knew they were traveling to very different destinations.

THE TWO MEN had met several years earlier, when Koestler returned to Paris in October 1946 as a literary star. He had fled the city six years earlier with a warrant out for his arrest as an "enemy alien" and the German army closing in, but now he had gone from being hunted to being celebrated. The novel he had been scrambling to finish back then had become a huge best seller. *Le Zéro et l'Infini,* the French translation of *Darkness at Noon,* sold seven thousand copies in the first month, and so desperate were readers to get their own copy that people were selling it secondhand for seven or eight times the cover price. When new editions went to press, lines formed outside the offices of the publisher, Calmann-Lévy. By the time Koestler arrived, three hundred thousand copies had been sold, and by the end of the first two years of its publication, that figure grew to more than a half million.[12]

It was a literary sensation that had a direct political impact. In October 1945, elections had been held to form a Constituent Assembly that would be charged with drafting a constitution for the Fourth French Republic. The French Communists had won more votes than any other party in that election, as just over 5 million French people backed a party whose popularity was buoyed by the wartime heroics of Communist resistance groups. De Gaulle, who was in charge of the Provisional Government, resigned after a dispute with Communist ministers in January

1946. But when the new constitution, drawn up by the Communists and socialists, went to a referendum, it was rejected. François Mauriac contended that this turn against the Communist Party was due to *Le Zéro et l'infini*. While that might have overstated the case, Koestler's novel had reignited the debate about Stalinism, the Moscow Show Trials, and the purges, and he was soon being denounced in the Communist press. Apocryphal stories circulated that the Communists sought to have the book pulped and, when that failed, to buy copies and burn them.[13]

Soon after arriving, Koestler sought out Albert Camus and they were soon drinking together at the Café de Flore. The following day he introduced himself to Sartre and Simone de Beauvoir in the bar of the Hôtel Pont-Royal. He was, for the moment, part of the existentialist set, and, perhaps energized by the appetites of their new friend, the group enjoyed some spectacular debauches. Sartre and Beauvoir had an open relationship, and she was initially attracted to Koestler, despite his belligerence and vanity. They had a one-night stand after which their friendship soured. Meanwhile, Mamaine Paget, still with Koestler despite his earlier assault, arrived in Paris to join Koestler, but was soon having an intense affair with Camus. (They first kissed on the dance floor of the Scheherazade night club while Koestler was busy drunkenly arguing with a thoroughly intoxicated Sartre, likely about Communism.)

Riding the momentum of his newfound fame and with his contacts growing, Koestler sought to revive the idea of a cultural collective. Despite the help of Orwell, the League for the Dignity and Rights of Man had foundered, but perhaps the French, with their greater commitment to political engagement, might be more receptive to the idea? He persuaded André Malraux to host a meeting of writers of the independent left at his Boulogne-Sur-Seine apartment. Malraux, whom Koestler knew since their anti-fascist activist days back in the 1930s, was now minister of information in the French government. Koestler's idea was to launch a volume of essays from all the writers present. While Camus was broadly favorable, Sartre was against it because he felt it was anti-Soviet in intent. Surprisingly, Malraux was also skeptical, so once again Koestler was frustrated and returned to Britain disappointed.

Subsequently, Koestler became more vociferous in his attacks on the French Communist Party, describing it as a "Trojan horse" for the USSR, at the very moment that *Scum of the Earth* and *The Yogi and the Commissar* came out in French translations.[14] Both books were almost guaranteed to cause a stir in France—the former attacked the French for their collaboration with the Nazis; the latter included essays that were an unambiguous assault on Communism—and they certainly provoked a response from the French left. Merleau-Ponty hit back in a series of essays, and Koestler was vilified as an agent of American imperialism. The French left was splitting into factions, and even the friendship of Camus and Sartre was beginning to fall apart.

At issue between Koestler and Sartre was the United States. Sartre was staunchly anti-American and agreed with Merleau-Ponty's description of the Marshall Plan as the "generosity of an ogre."[15] Beauvoir put it around that Koestler's anti-Communism was causing him to "team up with the worst reactionaries."[16] When Koestler returned to Paris in January 1948, the tension between the political and the personal broke on another drunken night out. After numerous shots of vodka at a Russian bar, Sartre propositioned Paget, prompting a furious Koestler to hurl a glass at Sartre's head. It missed and shattered on the wall behind him—but Koestler was not done. When he tried to hit Sartre, Camus intervened. Koestler punched him instead, giving him a black eye, and then disappeared into the night. (Paget had told Koestler about her affair with Camus, so there was doubtless an element of revenge in his blow.) While Koestler apologized to the group for his behavior, the Communist coup in Czechoslovakia in February 1948 only pulled them further apart, with Koestler seeing it as a grim confirmation of Soviet ambition. He was done with the existentialists (not all of whom were as pro-Communist as he claimed) and the existentialists were done with him.

It turned out Beauvoir was not wrong: Koestler *did* let himself get mixed up with conservative reactionaries. With his books selling well in the United States and having taken over the London Letter column in *Partisan Review* from Orwell, Koestler decided it was time to cross the Atlantic. He was invited by the International Rescue and Relief Committee, which did valuable work resettling East European refugees, to give a lecture tour taking in New York City, Washington, Los Angeles, San Francisco, Chicago, and Boston. It was only when he was a good way into this tour that he realized the IRRC, despite its admirable work, was supported by deeply conservative anti-Communists and that his lecture tour had been conceived as a bolster to McCarthyism. (Ironically, he almost had to cancel after being denied a visa, because an FBI agent had read *Darkness at Noon* and somehow thought it pro-Communist. Only the intervention of Chip Bohlen, a State Department official, got him off the visa blacklist, and even then only with the personal approval of J. Edgar Hoover.)[17]

Koestler's reception in the United States, a whirlwind of media appearances and social engagements, was even more rapturous than in France two years before. He was most excited to meet the *Partisan Review* crowd. He hit it off with Philip Rahv, William Phillips, and James Burnham, but over dinner Sidney Hook and Koestler had a ferocious row about the best methods for fighting Stalinism—something of an anti-Communist cockfight to try to impress McCarthy. She made a strong impression on Koestler, and he invited her to see him in his hotel room a few days later; she agreed but on the condition that he did not try anything. When she arrived Koestler "made a pass" but McCarthy resisted, and Koestler, she later wrote, pinned her down like a "garage mechanic." McCarthy struggled free—other women were not so fortunate with Koestler—but she was shaken by this attempted rape.[18] As he had shown in so many other instances, Koestler's courage in Spain, and in his escape from Vichy France to London, was considerable; his sexual aggression toward women was cowardly and despicable.

Between dinners and cocktail parties Koestler met Max Eastman, Lionel Trilling, Hannah Arendt, Dwight Macdonald, John Dos Passos, and Edmund Wilson, who remained a great admirer of Koestler's partner, Paget. He also caught up with W. H. Auden and Stephen Spender, who were in town, and later met Arthur Schlesinger Jr. at Harvard. Koestler gave a much-anticipated speech at Carnegie Hall in which he was beginning to propound the ideas that he would refine by the time of the Congress in Berlin. Entitled the "Radical's Dilemma," the speech developed out of an article he wrote for *Partisan Review*—it was the kind of thing to send shivers down Sartre's spine. "I feel the enormous burden which is falling on your shoulders," he said. "For there will either be a *Pax Americana* in the world or there will be no pax."[19]

While Koestler enjoyed liberal New York, he was less enamored by Los Angeles. At an event host by the IRRC in Hollywood, he was introduced to Ronald Reagan, Gary Cooper, and Robert Montgomery, all of whom had very recently been cooperating witnesses for the HUAC. These people made Koestler uncomfortable but, as a tonic, he met with Langston Hughes, his old friend from their days traveling in the USSR in the 1930s. Back in New York, before his return to Britain, he managed to squeeze in a night clubbing in Harlem with Marlene Dietrich and Erich Maria Remarque.

Koestler was simultaneously drawn to and repelled by the United States. After a tumultuous, and disenchanting, trip to a newly independent Israel he decided to settle in France. He bought a house named Verte Rive on the banks of the Seine, opposite the forest of Fontainebleau, just south of Paris. This new venture began well enough, but soon he was struggling with his writing. His book on the origins of human creativity, *Insight and Outlook,* had taken a critical kicking and, shaken, he found himself unable to continue work on his novel-in-progress. He continued to try to work, defeating his hangovers with cold showers and Benzedrine, but the only thing that flowed was the autobiographical essay he wrote for *The God That Failed.* This collection of essays had been conceived by Koestler and Richard Crossman during an argument that was becoming familiar. Koestler had worked for Crossman in the German section of the Political Warfare Executive during the war, but he felt his friend, now a Labour MP, and British socialists more generally, did not comprehend the true menace of the Soviet Union and that only ex-Communists really understood it. "You hate our Cassandra cries and resent us as allies," Koestler said, "but, when all is said, we ex-Communists are the only people on your side who know what it's all about."[20] Crossman commissioned essays from Franz Borkenau, André Gide, Louis Fischer, Ignazio Silone, Stephen Spender, and Richard Wright, all of whom told their stories of Communist conversion and eventual apostasy. *The God That Failed* became a surprise best seller, a companion text to the Berlin Congress.

As Koestler entered one of his more self-destructive phases, his relationship with Paget began to fall apart. He continued to cheat on her relentlessly, including with his new secretary, twenty-two-year-old Cynthia Jeffries (who eventually became his third wife). Paget had periods of serious illness—she suffered badly from asthma—and in these times Koestler was apparently caring and patient. But when she was well, they fought frequently. Paget wrote to her sister, Celia, after one argument turned violent and Koestler hit her. It was, she wrote, the third time he had done so. Koestler's drinking intensified. After one particularly heavy session he drove home only to black out at the wheel. He woke up in prison with two black eyes and, when he was not immediately allowed to make a phone call, punched one of the officers. This was Christmas Eve 1949, and he was supposed to be hosting a party at Verte Rive that day. Fortunately for Koestler, one of his influential guests had the contacts to get him out.[21]

Paget was trapped between her continued love for Koestler and her knowledge that their relationship was a disaster. In an effort to change things for the better, they decided to get married. There was a basic ceremony at the British Embassy with plans for the couple and the guests to reconvene at the Café de Flore later that evening. Paget went for a nap and when she arrived for the reception, Koestler was already steaming drunk. He went on to offend most of the guests, forced everyone to go to a nightclub, and then abandoned Paget, driving off into the night. Fortunately, Stephen Spender, who had been dining with a friend at the Café de Flore when the Koestler party arrived, and who had subsequently been on the receiving end of some of Koestler's vitriol, stepped in and took Paget back to the flat he was borrowing from a friend. "I've always wanted to spend a night with you," Spender joked. "It's too bad it was your wedding night."[22]

What kept Koestler going amid this chaos was his anti-Communist crusading. As Stalinist purges swept through Eastern Europe, Koestler learned of Hungarian friends who had fallen victim. He helped anti-Communist authors like Ruth Fischer find publishers for their work, and then promoted the books once they were out. Perhaps his most important intervention, though, was in the Kravchenko affair. Viktor Kravchenko was a Soviet defector, an engineer from Ukraine who had served as a captain in the Red Army during the war. In his memoir, *I Chose Freedom,* Kravchenko revealed some of the scale of the famine that had been caused by collectivization in Ukraine in 1932–33, and described the vast network of penal labor camps used by the regime. It was a book that had had a similar impact in France as *Darkness at Noon,* selling in vast numbers even as it was derided by the Communist Party and its allies. *Les Lettres Françaises* accused Kravchenko's book of being an invention of the American secret services. Kravchenko sued them for libel, and the case became the focal point of furious intellectual debate—dubbed, rather hysterically, "the trial of the century." Koestler helped arrange for Grete Buber-Neumann to fly over from the United States to be a witness for Kravchenko; she was a former Communist who had been interned in both Nazi and Soviet camps. Kravchenko won the case but was awarded only symbolic damages.[23] However, the publicity generated for the book, and for the allegations it contained, was of huge value to the anti-Communist cause.

To Koestler's immense frustration, though, the Communist propaganda machine was beginning to crank back into action. The "Peace" conferences in Wroclaw, New York, and Paris were evidence that the Comintern strategies pioneered by his old mentor Willi Münzenberg were being deployed again. Münzenberg had sought to carefully detach himself from the Communist Party in the late 1930s, but the Party sensed his disenchantment, and he was expelled in 1938. He escaped from a French camp during the war and disappeared—his decayed corpse was found months later by French hunters deep inside the woods near Saint Marcelin. The cause of death was listed as suicide, but there was no note, and the coroner gave no medical evidence that he had died from hanging, the stated cause of expiration. Both the NKVD and the Gestapo were suspected of garroting him.[24] Münzenberg's methods survived, however, and Koestler was infuriated to see so many intellectuals gulled by Cominform front organizations, their true purpose thinly veiled by rhetoric about world peace. (The emblem of the Paris conference, attended by some thirty thousand people at the Buffalo Stadium in April 1949, was Picasso's famous Dove of Peace.) The anti-Communist left did themselves few favors. All of the attention garnered by Sidney Hook's counterconference in New York inspired a similar event being staged in Paris, this time organized by the French socialist David Rousset. The International Day of Resistance to Dictatorship and War, despite its catchy title, was an incoherent mess. Sartre attended only to denounce American imperialism and resign. Koestler was not even invited to participate, probably because he was thought too confrontational.

Still, the idea of hosting another rival gathering of liberal, socialist, and other anti-Communist intellectuals and writers was floated (Hook, Ruth Fischer, and Lasky, the editor of *Der Monat*, which had serialized *Nineteen Eighty-Four*, would all later claim credit). In the fall of 1949, James Burnham wrote to Koestler about "important changes" that had bearing on "Chateau Conservation projects."[25] Fond of espionage, the well-connected Burnham was using coded language to tell Koestler that there was American support for a cultural counteroffensive. Soon after a delegation including Borkenau, Hook, Lasky, and Manès Sperber came to visit Koestler and talk strategy. Meetings like this later prompted the Communist weekly *l'Action* to print a map of Fontaine-le-Port with an arrow pointing out Verte Rive, accompanied by the caption: "This is the headquarters of the

Cold War. This is where Chip Bohlen, the American Ambassador, trains his para-military, fascist militia."[26]

The plan for the Berlin Congress in motion, Burnham traveled to Paris to discuss strategy and potential delegates with Koestler. The vision Koestler had shared with Orwell as they tramped the Welsh hills over Christmas 1945 was finally being realized. To an excited Koestler, the only downside was that the "Old Burma Sergeant" was no longer around to take the fight to Berlin with him.

THE UNITED STATES began the Cold War with a much more powerful economy than the Soviet Union and the crucial strategic advantage of nuclear weapons, but in terms of espionage and propaganda, they lagged far behind. At the end of the Second World War, American intelligence agencies knew almost nothing of the inner workings of the USSR, and, as they struggled to track the movements of the Red Army behind the Iron Curtain, they feared this ignorance could lead to the kind of vulnerability that resulted in the surprise attack at Pearl Harbor. All the while, Soviet spies had infiltrated the State Department, the OSS, and, most important, the Manhattan Project. That the USSR was able to achieve atomic parity so quickly was down to the work of a network that had penetrated deep into Los Alamos. It was only when the Signal Intelligence Service (later the NSA) began the Venona Project, decrypting messages sent by Soviet intelligence agencies during the war, that the scale of Soviet spying was revealed. Most notably, in January 1950, Klaus Fuchs, a German physicist, confessed to MI5 interrogators (who were tipped off by the Americans) that he had given information to the NKVD while working at Los Alamos. In June of that year, Julius and Ethel Rosenberg were arrested and charged with espionage for passing over nuclear secrets. Despite a high-profile campaign to save them, both would be executed in 1953.

The need to combat the Soviet Union's espionage and propaganda networks was signaled as a priority by Kennan, who had returned to Moscow in 1944 as deputy chief of mission (he had previously worked at the embassy in the 1930s). Kennan had studied the Great Terror, giving him an insight into Stalin's ruthlessness. He believed any effort at cooperation was futile. In his "Long Telegram," he warned that the Soviet Union had "an elaborate and far-flung apparatus for exertion of its influence in other countries, an apparatus of amazing flexibility and versatility, managed by people whose experience and skill in underground methods are presumably without parallel in history."[27] The Americans needed to find a way to counter this sinister apparatus. Kennan was recalled to Washington to help make it happen.

In the Georgetown district of Washington, an influential group of diplomats and intelligence officers met for regular dinner parties, at which they drank heavily while debating the next steps in the Cold War. These dinners were often hosted by a former OSS officer, Frank Wisner, and attended by Kennan, Dean Acheson (future secretary of state), Chip Bohlen (Special Adviser to Secretary of State George Marshall and future ambassador to the Soviet Union), and David Bruce, the OSS officer who fought with Hemingway before the liberation of Paris (future ambassador to France, Germany, and Britain). The consensus was that the United States needed a powerful overseas intelligence service.[28] In April 1947, Secretary of State George Marshall asked Kennan to set up a team to devise Cold War strategy. Two months later, Kennan authored an essay in the journal *Foreign Affairs,* hiding his identity behind the pseudonym "X," in which he outlined the idea of "containment," by which the United States would seek to prevent Communist expansion across the globe. The idea of containment found overt expression in the Truman Doctrine and the Marshall Plan. The third component of Kennan's Cold War strategy, which was charged with implementing containment covertly, was the Central Intelligence Agency.

The CIA was founded on July 26, 1947, ostensibly as an espionage organization. Kennan and his allies, though, wanted it to take on covert action, too. Exploiting some loose rhetoric in the National Security Act, and without congressional or legal mandate, the CIA promptly set out to defeat the Communists in the Italian election, scheduled for April 1948. A $200 million fund, made up in large part of "captured Axis loot," was raided to fund the operation, which was coordinated on the ground by Rome station chief James Jesus Angleton, the former modernist poet who, working for OSS during the war, had become close to Kim Philby.[29] Suitcases stuffed with money were used to bribe Italian politicians in the Hotel Hassler at the top of the Spanish Steps. Funds were channeled to the political arm of the Vatican, and CIA fronts distributed propaganda. The Christian Democrats duly won the election by a wide margin.

The month after the Italian elections, the CIA formalized its clandestine operations. National Security Council directive 10/2, drafted by Kennan, came into effect in June 1948. Its first clause read:

> The National Security Council, taking cognizance of the vicious covert activities of the USSR, its satellite countries and Communist groups to discredit and defeat the aims and activities of the United States and other Western powers, has determined that, in the interests of world peace and US national security, the overt foreign activities of the US Government must be supplemented by covert operations.[30]

The Office of Policy Coordination, given a deliberately bland name, was set up to take on this covert work, skimming hundreds of millions off the Marshall Plan for funds.[31] Wisner, a corporate lawyer from a wealthy Mississippi family, was placed in charge. Working in a "controlled frenzy, twelve hours or more a day, six days a week," Wisner's OPC grew rapidly from a few men in rodent-infested temporary offices in Washington (dubbed the Rat Palace) into an organization "bigger than the rest of the agency combined."[32] Wisner launched a range of operations, including counterfeiting money and market manipulation, bribery, creating secret stockpiles of weapons and explosives in enemy territory, and the training of paramilitary groups to be sent into Soviet-controlled territory. Within the first three years he opened forty-seven stations in foreign cities. Amid all this frenzied activity, Wisner and his team conceived a plan for cultural warfare with the Soviet Union, to win "the battle for Picasso's mind."[33] Operation QKOPERA was born.[34]

It had been in the autumn of 1948, prompted by the Berlin blockade, that the OPC had hired Michael Josselson to become its first Berlin agent.[35] The Estonian had lived in Berlin and Paris before moving to the United States and becoming a citizen. Thanks to his language skills he became an intelligence officer during the war, working as an interrogator for the Intelligence Section of the Psychological Warfare Division, interviewing German prisoners. After the war, he stayed in Berlin with the American military government, working on de-Nazification. He became good friends with Lasky, and together they began to take an interest in cultural warfare, with Josselson attending the Scientific and Cultural Conference for World Peace held at the Waldorf-Astoria in New York in March 1949. The OPC used a front to fund Sidney Hook's counterconference at Freedom House and paid for the suite they used as a base at the Waldorf-Astoria Hotel itself. Josselson thought the counterconference a success, and the OPC decided to fund a similar setup for the Paris Peace Conference. Wisner cabled Averell Harriman, of the European Cooperation Administration (which ran the Marshall Plan), to ask for $16,000 for a counterdemonstration in Paris. An OPC agent, working with Irving Brown, a trade unionist with the American Federation of Labor, channeled the money to the French socialist organizers. They also used various front organizations to disguise the fact that they paid for the travel of the American, German, and Italian delegation. Like many of the intellectuals who participated, these secret backers were disappointed with the results, especially the rampant anti-Americanism of the French delegates. Wisner liked the idea of running a Deminform to rival the Cominform but worried that with the wrong people involved it would degenerate into "a nuts folly of miscellaneous goats and monkeys whose antics would completely discredit the work and statements of the serious and responsible liberals."[36]

While Wisner and the OPC pondered its next move, Borkenau, Ruth Fischer, and Lasky met in a Frankfurt hotel to discuss plans for an ambitious anti-Communist conference in West Berlin, with the goal, in Fischer's words, of giving "the Politburo hell right at the gates of their own hell."[37] Fischer, a brilliant former Communist organizer in Germany and Austria, was secretly working for "the Pond," an American intelligence outfit created during the Second World War and which operated separately from the OSS. Through these channels, her proposal for a Berlin conference found its way through the State Department to the OPC. Josselson, now on the OPC payroll, wrote a January 1950 memorandum, with the help of Lasky, outlining how the Congress would work. Wisner approved of the plan and gave Josselson a budget of $50,000 to put it into action. There was a catch, though: Wisner did not want Lasky involved, as his connections to the U.S. military would lead people to suspect that it was an American propaganda exercise, rather than a meeting of independent intellectuals. By then, though, it was too late: Lasky had announced that he was general secretary of the forthcoming conference and had even invited Ernst Reuter, the mayor of West Berlin, to chair the event.

In the days before the conference, Lasky hosted a meeting of the Congress's star chamber, which included Brown, Burnham, Hook, Koestler, and Silone. This group, with no little in-fighting, steered the course of the conference. Josselson stayed in the background, watching the dynamics play out, concerned by the way Koestler's hard-line approach was alienating influential delegates. The British, led by Trevor-Roper, were increasingly uncomfortable and demanded that Koestler strike out a line in the Freedom Manifesto that declared that "totalitarian ideologies which deny spiritual freedom, do not enjoy the right to citizenship in the free republic of the spirit."[38] This seemed to the British transparently McCarthyist. By the time Trevor-Roper returned to Britain his discomfort had blossomed into animosity. An historian of Nazism, he claimed in an article in the *Guardian* that the uncompromising ex-Communists had ended up appealing to latent German nationalism and was appalled by the "hysterical German applause that greeted" a speech by Borkenau. It carried with it, Trevor-Roper claimed, an "echo of Nuremberg."[39] If there was to be an alliance of liberal intellectuals, Trevor-Roper wrote, it must come from "those who have never swallowed, and therefore never needed to re-vomit, that obscurantist doctrinal rubbish whose residue can never be fully discharged from the system." In Britain, Trevor-Roper's article left the reputation of the Congress in tatters. Russell resigned as chairman and was only persuaded to reverse his position by a personal visit from Koestler. There was no appetite among many intellectuals, British or otherwise, for the hard-line approach taken by Burnham, who delivered the most frightening speech of the Congress.

Speaking with what one reporter described as the "deliberately un-emphatic smoothness of a YMCA preacher," Burnham told the assembled delegates that there were "good" and "bad" atom bombs. Even Koestler described Burnham privately as a "dangerous lunatic."[40] There was clearly more to Burnham than met the eye.

Despite some of the negative publicity, Wisner and the OPC were delighted with the way the Berlin Congress had come off, and, on Josselson's advice, set about making it a permanent institution. The only issue as far as Wisner was concerned was the continued presence of Lasky. There was something personal in Wisner's disdain—he did not like the cut of Lasky's jib—but more important, Communist propaganda fixated on Lasky being in the pay of the American secret services. This was dangerous territory. It was essential to Wisner that the source of the Congress's funding be kept secret, and while he was not troubled by rumors of American backing, he did not want it traced to the CIA and the OPC specifically. It was not so much Soviet counterpropaganda that Wisner feared, but the reaction of Republican members of Congress on discovering that he was spending millions of dollars on ex-Communists. Against the wishes of his friend Josselson, Lasky was eased out by Wisner. Still, keeping the source of funding secret was easier said than done with delegates like Koestler, who had experience working for Comintern front organizations and knew how these things worked. Even before the Congress began, Koestler was mixing with people from the American and British intelligence world. In February 1949, he had met with the newly founded Information Research Department to advise them on anti-Communist propaganda.[41] When Koestler was on his lecture tour in the United States, Burnham introduced Koestler to some of his political and intelligence contacts, including "Wild Bill" Donovan. Koestler met the former head of the OSS at his New York town house, recording in his diary that they discussed the need for "psychological warfare" with the USSR.[42] After the Berlin Congress, with Burnham's help, Koestler plunged deeper into the web of intrigue that lay behind it, even finding his way to one of Wisner's famous Georgetown dinner parties. Then, when he seemed destined for a leading role in the coming Kulturkampf, Burnham betrayed him.

KOESTLER WAS RIDING a dangerous high at the end of the Berlin Congress, relishing the challenge of forming a permanent organization, which was to be set up in Paris. As a member of the five-man executive committee, he got straight down to practical business, writing a prospectus for the Congress for Cultural Freedom and even setting up accounting and card-filing systems for the new office on Avenue Montaigne. He was bursting with ideas, proposing a radio station to broadcast across the Iron Curtain (this in the days before Radio Liberty and Radio Free Europe began broadcasting), the establishment of an anti-Communist mass movement across small-town France (called *Les Amis de la Liberté*), and also the creation of a monthly magazine, a kind of European *Partisan Review*, to take on the perceived anti-Americanism of Sartre's *Les Temps Modernes*. These ambitious projects were rejected by other members of the executive committee, Silone and François Bondy, a Swiss journalist whom Koestler grew to despise. In the long run, many of them were adopted (including the idea of a magazine, which was launched as *Preuves*, with Bondy as editor) but, at the time, Koestler was furious and felt he, the star of Berlin, was being undermined.

According to Paget, Koestler was "in a great state about the Congress ever since Berlin."[43] The Communists redoubled their attacks on what they called Koestler's Kultur Kongress (an allusion to the Ku Klux Klan). A pamphlet circulated, written by novelist Jean Kanapa, that claimed Koestler had been "turned" by Franco's fascists while he was in prison and now worked for British intelligence. He was used to these kinds of slurs from the Communists but struggled to cope with the idea that he was being outmaneuvered by the moderates in the fight for the future of the CCF. In August 1950, he went to Paris for a CCF meeting and suffered a spectacular breakdown. Raymond Aron, the French intellectual, discovered Koestler outside his apartment "in a state of nervous collapse."[44] What precipitated it is unclear. Certainly there had been trouble: Koestler had been in some sort of altercation with an unnamed member of the CCF, got drunk, made a pass at a friend's daughter, crashed his car, and collapsed, all in one day. Paget thought he was suffering from delirium tremens because he was hallucinating, and while the drink certainly seemed a powerful factor, so too was his Benzedrine habit. Koestler resolved to clean up (not for the first time) and resigned from the executive committee of the CCF.

Down but not out, Koestler traveled to New York City in the fall of 1950. While he had promised Paget a return to London, he instead resolved to settle in the United States, using his American royalties to buy an island in the Delaware River in Bucks County, Pennsylvania. He was incapable of rest and soon had a new scheme in motion, this time to start a Fund for Intellectual Freedom for refugee writers, to which successful Western writers would contribute by giving a percentage of their royalties. He secured an unlikely collaborator in this project: Graham Greene agreed to donate 10 percent of his continental European royalties. He also persuaded John Dos Passos, James Farrell, and Aldous Huxley to participate, but the scheme ended up a failure.

Koestler was also incapable of avoiding controversy. In a series of articles, he attacked European socialism and called for the foundation of a European army. This rightward shift did not go down well with American liberals. The legacy of Roosevelt was coming under sustained attack from Republicans who claimed that the New Deal had been but the first stage in a slide via socialism to communism. These forces secured a great victory with the conviction of Alger Hiss for perjury at the beginning of the year. Hiss had been a high-ranking and well-connected State Department official under Roosevelt who was part of the United States delegation at the Yalta Conference with Churchill and Stalin in 1945. Ever since he had been denounced by Whittaker Chambers, Hiss had been a target of Republicans who, led by Congressman Richard Nixon, made political capital from connecting the New Deal to the idea of Communist infiltration. Hiss was handsome and distinguished, and the great and the good of the Washington establishment testified to his character. Chambers was duplicitous and sleazy, but he was right. Koestler, unlike most on the liberal left, could see this and wrote an article in January 1951 about how the two had been miscast—they were playing each other's roles. To compound his betrayal of the liberal elite, Koestler then visited Chambers at his Maryland farm. In person, Chambers was too much for Koestler, who concluded he was "sincere but fanatical."[45] The following year, Chambers published *Witness,* a memoir in which he attacked not only Communism but also liberalism. It was a huge best seller.

Despite what happened in the aftermath of the Berlin Congress, Koestler had not given up on the CCF, even with the continued successes of the moderates. At the second international meeting of the Congress, held in Brussels in November, Nicolas Nabokov was chosen as general secretary. Koestler, absent because he was trying to secure permanent residency in the United States, felt slighted as he had backed the more pugnacious Louis Fischer for the job. The next Congress was to take place in Paris and, under Nabokov's guidance, would be a gigantic arts festival. Koestler threatened to resign when he discovered that they wanted to invite Beauvoir and Sartre to participate.[46]

All the while, Koestler was getting clued up about where the money was coming from. When he arrived in the United States in the autumn of 1950, Burnham told Koestler that his resignation from the executive committee after his breakdown had meant the "symbolic liquidation of the Congress" and vowed to put it right. He invited Koestler to come to Washington to meet "some serious persons who have specific interests that intersect our own—and I am not referring to the editors of the *Partisan Review*."[47] It was not wildly difficult to guess the identity of these serious persons. Koestler picked up on what he called a "disarming phrase" in a CCF financial report, which revealed that "the budget for the next six months had been submitted to Mr. Irving Brown and approved by him." The Comintern agent in him saw how this kind of admission might be exploited; they were, he warned, handing their enemies arguments "on a silver platter." Koestler wrote to Burnham to demand a cull of the moderates or he was out. Burnham urged him to be patient and come to Washington. The serious persons were still waiting.

In April 1951, Koestler and Paget traveled down to the capital, where they were dinner guests of Wisner's. Koestler tried to lure his host into talking about the CIA's involvement in the CCF, but Wisner remained noncommittal. At the dinner was another CIA operative, Robert Joyce, who had tried to recruit Hemingway into the OSS during the war. From his conversations with Joyce, it became clear to Koestler how deeply the CIA was implicated in the Congress. Koestler was not queasy about the secret funding of cultural propaganda—this was how things worked, as he knew from his time having been a cultural propagandist for both the Soviet Union and the British government. Indeed, far from pulling back, in his conversations with Donovan and others Koestler had agitated for a more robust approach to psychological warfare. What annoyed Koestler, who had not betrayed his status as a Comintern agent while imprisoned by Franco's fascists, was the ease with which he had found out what was going on behind the scenes.[48]

What he knew about Burnham is another matter. Burnham was more than just a liaison between the CIA and intellectuals; since the autumn of 1949 he had been working for the CIA as a "consultant" with the OPC, as part of the Political and Psychological Group (which was packed with Yale alumni and former OSS operatives, including E. Howard Hunt, spy novelist and future Nixon "plumber").[49] He played a central role in helping the OPC plan the Berlin Congress. Wisner told Burnham to avoid being too prominent, and as cover he took his wife to Berlin, to make it look like he was traveling as a private citizen.

It was little surprise that someone who had written an admiring book about Machiavelli in 1943 threw himself into the power politics of running the CCF. Back in 1946, Orwell had reviewed Burnham's work and detected in him a "fascinated admiration" for Stalin's power. He seemed to relish the apocalyptic fantasies he conjured up about the future. Burnham was credited with anticipating the superpower standoff of the Cold War but, as Orwell pointed out, almost all his subsequent predictions (Germany will win the war, Russia and Japan will ally to destroy the United States, Russia will take over all of Europe) were wrong. In 1950, he published *The Coming Defeat of Communism*, in which he argued that a strategy of containment was as good as appeasement and that the USSR needed to be destroyed by a war in Eastern Europe. He was fanatical in his anti-Communism and a relentless intriguer. He hired Louis Gibarti, who had been one of Münzenberg's most experienced and ruthless Comintern operatives, to be his eyes and ears in the Congress's Paris office, and he had no compunction about sidelining those who got in his way.

Burnham had already played a role in pushing Koestler aside, writing a memorandum to the OPC in November 1950 warning of his potential "domination of the Congress."[50] Yet Burnham had played the most important role in mollifying Koestler when he threatened to quit altogether, perhaps seeing value in him as an attack dog to be used against his moderate opponents. In May 1951, however, Burnham wrote a memo to the OPC in which he said that "[t]here can be little doubt that Arthur Koestler's personality is neurotic in the strict pathological sense. Observations over a number of months shows a manic depressive cycle. There is also an aggressive compensatory defense mechanism, and at least one specific obsession. This obsession might be described as a fixation on 'conspiracy.'" Burnham went on to say that Koestler was determined to unearth "American networks and clandestine activities" and should be refused security clearance and denied any role in "organizational matters."[51] These last two words were underlined. What prompted this knife in the back is not clear. Perhaps Burnham was seeking to protect himself, having been responsible for introducing the unstable Koestler to Wisner and the OPC. Perhaps, as was always possible with Koestler, it was the consequence of a row. Or perhaps Burnham really had come to think Koestler a liability. Either way Burnham was soon sidelined himself, as the arrival of Walter Bedell Smith and Allen Dulles at the CIA prompted a reorganization of the agency and a clipping of the OPC's wings.

Koestler resigned from the CCF in July 1951. His time as a Cold Warrior was drawing to a close. He slipped into another period of turmoil, self-doubt, and destructive behavior. After years of unhappiness, he and Paget finally split. Her health was still fragile. In 1954, back home in London, she had an asthma attack and died in the same hospital as Orwell. Koestler was in Italy at the time and flew back immediately for the funeral. He sat up the night before, beside her open coffin, and wrote about the experience in a letter to Camus, with whom Paget had had such an intense affair. At the funeral, the Paget family ignored

Koestler: it was clear they blamed him for her death.[52] Koestler was in crisis and contemplated giving up writing altogether. He thought about converting to Catholicism. He consciously decided to stop writing fiction and became interested in parapsychology. Over the next decades, he became much less politically active, aside from his campaign to end the death penalty in Britain. After being diagnosed with leukemia, he committed suicide, along with Cynthia, his third wife, through an overdose of barbiturates washed down with alcohol, in 1983.

Koestler wanted to fight the Cold War the way that he fought fascists for the Comintern, and as such his speeches and organizing carried with it an edge of zealotry. To the hard-liner, this made him charismatic; to the moderate, he was repellent. Koestler was as responsible as anybody for the existence of the Congress for Cultural Freedom. In Berlin, his strategy of direct and aggressive confrontation with the Soviet Union had won out. Little did he realize, as those fifteen thousand Berliners cheered his closing address, that he had won the battle but lost the war. In the United States, McCarthy, the HUAC, and the FBI were pursuing anyone with even the slightest association with the Communist Party, so it was ironic that what ultimately cost Koestler was his excess of anti-Communism. The CIA wanted the world to see the intellectuals of Western democracy celebrating the Western democratic way of life. They did not want demagogues whipping up conflict, making ultimatums. Koestler fought the Cold War too hard.

EIGHTEEN

Fast

NEW YORK, 1949–1957

THE SMALL CITY OF PEEKSKILL, an hour's drive north of New York City in affluent Westchester County, might have seemed an unlikely venue for a riot, but, late in the summer of 1949 it was the site of a violent confrontation between American Communists and anti-Communist protesters as the picturesque countryside of the Hudson Valley erupted into a Cold War battleground. The cause of the violence was the staging of a benefit concert for the Civil Rights Congress at which Paul Robeson was the star attraction. Earlier in the year, Robeson attended the World Congress for Peace in Paris, a Communist-backed gathering of sympathetic figures from around the world. While in Paris, Robeson was quoted as saying that it "was unthinkable that American Negroes would go to war on behalf of those who have oppressed us for generations against a country which in one generation has raised our people to the full dignity of mankind."[1] The remark, which was at best a misquote and at worst a fabrication, was reported by many American newspapers and received with outrage.

Despite threats and fears of protests, Robeson was determined to sing, along with Woody Guthrie and Pete Seeger, at the scheduled concert in Peekskill. The MC for the event was the novelist Howard Fast, after Robeson the most famous American champion of the Communist cause. Fast, thirty-four, was the son of Jewish immigrants from Ukraine and Britain, and had grown up in poverty in New York City. He was outspoken in his radical politics, and his historical novels always carried a leftist message. In 1943 he joined the Communist Party of the USA.[2] His books were huge best sellers; *Freedom Road,* his 1944 novel about a group of formerly enslaved people in reconstruction America, sold 30 million copies in ten years and was translated into eighty-two languages.[3] Earlier in the year, Fast had been one of the organizers of the Scientific and Cultural Conference for World Peace in New York City, where he was confronted by Mary McCarthy and her anti-Stalinist allies. Fast was facing prison for contempt of Congress after refusing to name names at a House Un-American Activities Committee hearing in April 1946, but if anything, this had intensified his activism.

On arrival at the concert venue, the Lakeland Acres picnic grounds, Robeson, Fast, and their allies found three hundred protesters, many of them veterans, waiting for them. The road was blocked, preventing the concert from going ahead, and, as the day wore on, the anti-Communists made a bonfire, throwing in pamphlets and books that were to be sold at the concert. When the protesters started throwing rocks, fighting broke out that went on for at least two hours. At a subsequent fund-raiser in Harlem, Fast told his audience that despite their overwhelming superiority in numbers the protesters "were not very brave hand-to-hand in the dark." One witness said she saw Fast fighting with a Coke bottle in each hand.[4]

Undeterred, Fast and Robeson went ahead with a second attempt to stage the concert in September. This time they bused in thousands of supporters, some of them armed with baseball bats, to form a barrier around the venue. In *Peekskill, USA,* the book he wrote about the riot, Fast claimed the head of security for the concert found two men with high-powered rifles in the woods near the venue. Fearing Robeson was to be shot, Fast wanted to call off the gig, but a group of volunteers instead formed a human shield around the singer when he performed. The concert went off without disturbance, but as the performers and concert-goers left, they were ambushed. The anti-Communist mob came out of the woods clutching rocks to hurl at the passing cars, and there were accusations that the police, placing their vehicles in the road, had deliberately slowed down the vehicles to make them easier targets. Some 145 people were injured, three of them seriously, and buses and cars were badly damaged. Robeson's car had its windows smashed but the singer was unhurt. While anti-Communist veterans were blamed, it was clear that other groups—Fast accused the Ku Klux Klan and the American Legion being among them—had joined the protests. Concertgoers told the *New York Times* that they had been corralled by police for more than an hour on a local golf course, with many "singled out for a 'working over.'"[5]

In his account of the riot, Fast announced that what he had witnessed that day had changed him. "I am not just a writer anymore," he said, "and this is something writers who read this must understand, that from here on, we must make our writing a sword that will cut this monster of fascism to pieces or we will make no more literature."[6] In a 1950 tract, *Literature and Reality,* he claimed American culture was like "a foul fistula, overloaded with pus," which "exploded" when the fascist-supporting Ezra Pound was given the Bollingen Award for poetry in 1949.[7] He attacked aesthetes like T. S. Eliot and turncoats like Richard Wright, who, Fast argued, was betraying both African Americans and the Communist cause. John Steinbeck, once valiant, had allowed his art to "rot." Orwell was nothing but the author of "childish and wicked little opium dreams" that bear the label "Made in Wall Street."[8] Fast held antipathy especially for Franz Kafka, who, he said, sat near the top of the "cultural dung heap of reaction."[9] Where were great writers who could live up to the

legacy of Mark Twain, Jack London, and the young Upton Sinclair? The implication was that there was only one writer fit for
the purpose of fighting rising American fascism and "the promulgation of World War III"—Fast himself.[10] The American political
establishment had other ideas.

While Fast was, as should be evident, rather given to exaggeration, the Peekskill riots *were* a violent expression of an increasingly rabid anti-Communism gripping American society. There
had been a powerful strain of anti-Communism in American
politics before the Second World War that was contained by the
alliance with the Soviet Union during the conflict. The advent
of the Cold War, however, caused it to erupt with renewed force.
The Communist Party of the USA reached its peak membership
in 1947, with more than seventy-five thousand registered, but
while the Party wielded influence in trade unions and through
their front organizations, it hardly constituted a serious threat
to the United States. While the government, the Manhattan
Project, and Office of Strategic Services had all been penetrated
by Soviet spies, some of whom were American citizens, the idea
of widespread infiltration of American institutions by Communists grew into a conspiracy theory used as expedient political
capital in the Cold War.[11] It was a stick with which to beat the
progressive Democrats who, under Roosevelt, were perceived as
having indulged the radical left. Those who had supported progressive causes in the 1930s, or even just sided with the Republicans in the Spanish Civil War, came under suspicion. Even New
Deal liberals felt the heat.

The House Un-American Activities Committee, created in
1938, had been made permanent in 1945. During the war, it had
gone after Japanese Americans, but as tensions increased with
the Soviet Union it returned to its pre-war pursuit of communists. Fast himself had faced the HUAC in April 1946 and had
been cited for contempt of Congress as a result. He was on the

board of the Joint Anti-Fascist Refugee Committee, which had helped set up a hospital in Toulouse for wounded Republicans fleeing across the border during and after the Spanish Civil War. The HUAC demanded to see the donor records of the committee, believing it to be a communist front, but Fast, along with other members of the board, refused to hand over documents or name their donors. Despite pleading the First and Fifth Amendments, Fast was cited for contempt. At his court case the following year he was found guilty, sentenced to three months in jail, and ordered to pay a $500 fine.

Due to his large readership, Fast was a particular target of the American authorities, and his FBI file would eventually grow to over one thousand pages. He was constantly harassed by the FBI, who read his mail and tailed him around New York. They made obvious efforts to entrap him; he was approached by an undercover agent who said he knew a spy who could provide Fast with the plans of an American battleship. He saw straight through the ploy and called the police.[12] When Fast saw the same agent tailing him at the conference at the Waldorf, he confronted him. "I knew his mission was to get me—to kill me, and I let everyone know," Fast wrote. "I accused him to his face."[13] The threat Fast perceived to his life was typical of his rhetorical excess. For example, in letters to friends abroad he wrote about how fascism was now "cloaked in The Star Spangled Banner" and claimed that "secret arrests are a daily occurrence."[14] There was substance to his fears, though. His daughter recalled the family looking on in silent alarm as Fast fished a bug out of a chandelier in their house. The babysitter, it turned out, was an FBI informant and had presumably planted it there.[15]

Fast's work was also targeted. In April 1947, the Truman administration, under pressure from a Republican-controlled Congress for supposedly being soft on Communism, instituted a loyalty program for federal employees (by 1952 the FBI "had checked out two million employees and conducted 20,000 full-field investigations").[16] Included among questions asked at loyalty hearings was: "Do you read Howard Fast?"[17] The New York City Board of Education banned his historical novel *Citizen Tom Paine,* and ordered copies to be taken out of school and public libraries. The notoriety this generated actually resulted in sales for the book surging, both in the United States and abroad, but other doors were closing on Fast at every turn. He was no longer interviewed in the mainstream press and no longer invited to appear on radio shows. Columbia Pictures dropped the idea of doing a film of *The Last Frontier,* for which they had paid $35,000.[18] In 1947 he was banned from speaking at campuses in New York City, including City College, Brooklyn College, and Hunter College, with universities nervous about the HUAC coming after them.

In the summer of 1948 HUAC, using evidence gathered by the FBI, went after Hollywood, and nineteen suspected Communists were issued subpoenas.[19] Initially the accused group retained the support of the industry with stars like Lauren Bacall, Humphrey Bogart, Judy Garland, Gene Kelly, and Burt Lancaster defending them in public.[20] "The Nineteen" sought to make it an issue of freedom of speech, but at the hearings it swiftly became about their membership in the Communist Party. After hearing evidence from "friendly" witnesses, like actors Ronald Reagan and Gary Cooper, and producer Walt Disney, about Communist infiltration of Hollywood, the "unfriendly" witnesses were denied the chance to read from prepared statements. After bad-tempered exchanges, several were confronted with evidence of their Party membership. The hearings devolved into the shouting of accusations, and some of the accused were forcibly removed from the stand. Ten of these "unfriendly" witnesses were, just like Fast and the members of the JAFRC, indicted for contempt. In the aftermath, many of those Hollywood celebrities who had rallied behind them withdrew their support, claiming they supported free speech but not Communism. The studios announced the firing of the Hollywood Ten and said they would no longer employ Communists, creating a blacklist.[21]

All of this happened before the man who gave this anti-Communist crusade its name came to the fore. The following year, on February 9, 1950, Wisconsin Senator Joseph McCarthy gave a speech to a dinner at the Ohio County Women's Republican Club in Wheeling, West Virginia, in which he claimed to hold in his hand a list of 205 Communists working in the State Department. It was an incendiary allegation, coming just a month after the Hiss conviction. Days later, Dean Acheson, the secretary of state, declared that he would not "turn my back on Alger Hiss," and prominent Republicans were soon baying for Acheson's dismissal.

The timing and specificity of McCarthy's allegations captured the public's attention, even if he changed the number of supposed Communists on the list each time he was asked. The Truman administration called his bluff, asking him to submit his list of names. As a result, McCarthy went on the hunt for evidence to support his allegation, with a reckless self-promoting abandon that created its own momentum.

ON JUNE 7, 1950, a year after the Peekskill Riots, Fast traveled down from New York to Washington to surrender to the police. His appeal to have his conviction for contempt of Congress overturned had failed. After delivering an impassioned attack on the Truman administration to reporters outside the courthouse, in which he claimed he and his colleagues on the Jewish Anti-Fascist Refugee Committee were victims of the United States seeking a Cold War alliance with Franco's Spain, Fast was sentenced to three months in prison, with the judge throwing out last-minute requests for probation or suspended sentences.[22] He was taken down to the holding cell—the "bullpen" in the basement of the courthouse—and then on to the DC district prison. Fast was surprised by how imposing it was with its "red brick walls, armed guards, and towering cell blocks." The new prisoners were driven through a series of electric gates, unloaded, and led down a long corridor, at the end of which Fast was confronted by a sight that stuck with him. "There on long benches sat about a hundred men, black men and white men, all of them naked," he wrote. "They sat despondently, hunched over, heads bent, evoking pictures of the extermination camps of World War Two."[23] Fast, too, was made to strip. The naked men were fingerprinted, questioned, and then made to a shower with antiseptic soap and walk through an antiseptic footbath before being issued with a blue prison uniform.

To Fast, the prison felt like the ones he had seen in old Hollywood films. In his memoir, *Being Red,* he wrote fondly about his first cellmate, a "poor frightened kid of eighteen who had first been caught when he was 12 and had already spent years of his young life in prisons and reformatories." As Fast got to know him, the reason for his fear became apparent: he told Fast that he had been raped "at least a hundred times" in prisons over the years. Fast was outraged to discover that this boy had been inside for fifty-eight days without indictment. At night, he was kept awake by the howls and entreaties of the prisoners two rows beneath, who had been sentenced to death.[24]

Fortunately for Fast, he was there for just nine days before being transferred to Mill Point, a model prison deep in rural West Virginia with only three hundred inmates. Surrounded by the Monongahela National Forest, the prison was minimum security, with boundaries of the facility marked by signpost rather than walls. While Fast was disgusted to find the prison segregated and while he suffered from cluster headaches during his three months there, Mill Point was a relatively benign institution. Prisoners were expected to work, and Fast was placed in the education department, where he helped design and edit the prison newsletter. He initially volunteered to teach fellow prisoners to read and write in Mill Point's night school, but a federal edict soon banned Communists from holding educational roles in its prisons. Later in the summer, when the Hollywood Ten were sentenced to one year in jail, the screenwriter Albert Maltz, with whom Fast had a tumultuous friendship, joined him at Mill Point.

By bribing an infirmary guard with candy, Fast managed to secure the only toilet with a seat so that he could preserve his morning ritual of reading the newspaper on the john. It was not particularly happy reading; the Korean War broke out in July and the same month Julius Rosenberg was arrested for espionage. Toward the end of Fast's sentence, Nevada Senator Pat McCarran introduced the Internal Security Act to the Senate, which would give the government sweeping powers to fight back against the Soviet Union's plans to "establish a Communist totalitarian dictatorship in the countries throughout the world."[25] As well as giving the government power to detain perceived subversives without trial in times of national emergency and demanding Communist organizations register with the attorney general, the act also prevented anyone who had belonged to a "totalitarian" organization from entering the United States (Koestler and Greene were denied visas under the act).[26] Both Fast and Robeson were designated security risks and, under the provision of the act, refused passports.[27]

Amid the renewed intensity of these crackdowns, Fast's incarceration was a rallying point for Communists and fellow traveling writers. Soon after he was sentenced, a delegation of Soviet authors published an open letter in the *Literaturnaya Gazeta* that claimed the United States was now operating a regime of "total terror" and likened the persecution of Fast to the "Spanish Inquisition."[28] Novelists, poets, and journalists from around the world wrote in solidarity, and Pablo Neruda sent him a poem entitled "Ode to Howard Fast." This hardly helped moderate Fast's ego; he told correspondents that he had been sent to such a remote location to reduce the possibility of protests and vigils outside the prison.

The rise of McCarthyism and the treatment of writers like Fast was a particular challenge to the intellectuals of the anti-Communist left. The moderates associated with the Paris-based Congress for Cultural Freedom retained their belief that Communism could be defeated only from the liberal left, and they recoiled at the excesses of McCarthy's red-baiting. The Congress's New York–based sister organization, confusingly known as the Committee for Cultural Freedom, was much more hard-line in believing Communism had to be crushed.

In 1952 the Committee would decide to host a conference to debate the issue of McCarthyism, which had opened such division on the non-Communist left. Mary McCarthy, who in her recently published novel *Groves of Academe* had attacked McCarthyism's invasion of the American campus, was invited by the New York–based Committee to speak on a panel entitled "Who Threatens Cultural Freedom in America Today?" She warned that "what we will do . . . if we persist in our demands for loyalty, a positive citizenship, testimonials, confessions of error, in the investigative efforts of McCarthy and McCarran, will be to create new underground men behind the facade of conformity, new lies, new evasions . . ."[29] The reference to the Underground Man was a deliberate allusion to Fyodor Dostoevsky: America was in danger of forcing its own writers underground, just as Russia had done, under both Tsarist and Communist rule. But Max Eastman, the former Trotskyist who in the 1930s had spoken out about the persecution of Babel and other suppressed writers, had no truck with McCarthy's position. "The real threat to cultural freedom," he declared, "is the worldwide communist conspiracy."[30] When the committee's board met the following month, Dwight Macdonald suggested they publicly condemn Joseph McCarthy and his methods. His proposal was voted down.[31] The committee seemed only interested in cultural freedom within the Soviet Union.[32]

It was not just writers on the non-Communist left who were conflicted about speaking up against the Red Scare. While Fast embraced the role of martyr to McCarthyism, he was also sensitive to those who did not speak up on his behalf. Why were Hemingway and Steinbeck silent about his imprisonment? In the atmosphere of the time it took courage to speak up, as any writer perceived as apologizing for Communism was publicly shamed. In April 1950, for example, the *Chicago Daily Tribune* published an article in which it named twenty writers who were "pushing their pens" on behalf of the Soviet Union. Fast was top of a list that included Dashiell Hammett, Lillian Hellman, Langston Hughes, Dorothy Parker, and, incongruously, Orson Welles. These, the article claimed, were just the tip of the iceberg, and in support of this claim quoted J. B. Mathews, a former HUAC investigator, who asserted that "60 percent of all the professional writers in the country are leftist."[33]

AFTER HIS RELEASE ON AUGUST 29 (nine days early for good behavior), Fast fought back against McCarthyism in the way he knew best: by writing a novel. Fast later claimed that he began mentally composing *Spartacus* "during the hours of hard labor as a political prisoner."[34] This made for a good origin story, though he wasn't exactly breaking rocks at Mill Point. His letters home had spoken of the pride he took in helping build a fountain or laying a path (the lack of alcohol also resulted in Fast coming out much fitter than he went in). In fact, he could have started writing while inside had he wanted—the prison authorities gave him access to paper and a typewriter, but he used it only to write letters.

Fast did, though, spend the long hours in his cell developing his idea for a novel about the life of a slave and gladiator who led a rebellion against Imperial Rome. He had already done some research into the Roman Empire as part of a planned book about the life of Jesus (who, he wanted to argue, was essentially a socialist). While reading about Rosa Luxemburg in a book he found in the prison library, he became interested in why the German Communists had named their group the Spartacus League (Spartakusbund). He proceeded to read "every scrap and thread of information that I could find in that small prison library."[35] After his release he immersed himself in books about Rome and even planned a research trip to Italy before once again being denied a passport. Undeterred, he took a crash course in Latin and, in between protests against the Korean War and against the Franco government in Spain, campaigns on behalf of persecuted fellow leftists, and immersion in the Rosenberg trial, Fast wrote *Spartacus*.

In Fast's telling, the story of Spartacus is one of class struggle but it comes served with lashings of sex and violence. Rome is depicted—not without relish—as decadent and cruel, with the Roman nobility overfed and oversexed. In the first fifty pages alone, we get a member of the Roman nobility trying to seduce a houseguest by taking her to watch his stud horse at work, the nobleman's wife trying to seduce her nephew, and that nephew having a gay romp with a distinguished general. It is that general, Crassus, who helped put down the slave rebellion, who begins to tell the story of Spartacus.

Compared to these Romans, Spartacus is ascetic and macho,

Lenin in sword and sandals, inspiring loyalty in his fellow slaves, whether it be in the gold mines of Nubia or Lentulus Batiatus's gladiator school in Capua. In the latter, the seeds of the rebellion are sown: a Jewish gladiator refuses to finish off a Thracian rival; a black fighter is killed as he attempts to rush the Roman spectators rather than take on Spartacus. The symbolism was not especially subtle: if there were to be a working-class rebellion in contemporary America, it had to spring from ethnic and racial solidarity. Spartacus's rebellion is suppressed but, in the closing pages of the novel, Fast assured the reader that his hero had ignited a flame "which burned high and low but never went out—and the name of Spartacus did not perish." The gladiator was a martyr to a future victory, when the Roman Empire would be torn down, "not by the slaves alone, but by slaves and serfs and peasants and by free barbarians who joined with them."[36] It was not hard to see the appeal of this kind of martyr hero to the newly liberated author.

Fast's ability to build tension marked him out as an excellent storyteller, and in *Spartacus* he deployed an ambitious flashback structure, but the novel slipped too easily into overripe prose and melodrama to be considered a work of serious literary merit. It was Fast's gift as an author to be able to write in a way that carried a broad appeal even if that appeal did not last more than one reading. Nevertheless, he was convinced *Spartacus* was a major novel. In March 1951, as he was finishing it up, he said it was "shaping up more excitingly than anything I have done in years, and I am really enchanted by the project."[37] Once he finished writing in June he felt he had created something "enduring" and submitted the 550-page manuscript to Little, Brown, who had published his two most recent books. His enthusiasm was well-founded, as *Spartacus* had all the trappings of a best seller: sex, violence, and a romping plot. Fast had a huge global readership despite (and sometimes because of) the controversies swirling around him, and some of his previous books, including *Citizen Tom Paine* and *Freedom Road*, sold millions of copies. Yet forces were already maneuvering against Fast and his book. The idea of a best-selling novel written by an American Communist at the height of McCarthy's purges was about as welcome as a slave rebellion in Imperial Rome.

Rumors reached Fast that the HUAC were going to open a new investigation into him, and he knew the FBI were doing their best to disrupt his ability to travel and work. Angus Cameron, the editor-in-chief at Little, Brown, encouraged him to think about using a pseudonym as means of heading off potential problems but Fast was not the kind of writer to be cowed. He believed his track record would see him through, having published ten books in the last twelve years, all with major publishing houses. The backing of Cameron was also important. He was a star of the American publishing scene who had just finished editing J. D. Salinger's *The Catcher in the Rye*. Cameron championed the novel's cause, telling the Little, Brown board it was both "an entertaining and meaningful novel."[38] He knew it had huge potential to become a best seller even though he also knew Fast's name was politically toxic.

Little did Cameron realize he was a target, too. In 1947, he had been involved in a public fight with Arthur Schlesinger Jr., the Harvard historian and liberal anti-Communist, who accused Cameron of rejecting Orwell's *Nineteen Eighty-Four* for political reasons. In the summer of 1951, he found himself being accused of running a Communist conspiracy at Little, Brown. Louis Budenz, a former editor of the *Daily Worker* turned anti-Communist crusader, told the Senate Internal Security Subcommittee that Cameron was a member of the CPUSA. Nine days later, *Counterattack*, a hard-line anti-Communist newsletter, devoted all of its six pages to Little, Brown and Cameron, claiming that the publishing house had become little more than a Communist front organization. It included a list of all the subversives that Little, Brown had published, including Fast.[39] Cameron called a company board meeting but could not make it, trapped in Maine by bad weather. In his absence, the board decided he would in the future have to get their approval before engaging in any political activities. As a consequence, Cameron resigned.

Fast believed Cameron had been forced out because of his support for *Spartacus* and even claimed J. Edgar Hoover had sent an agent to Little, Brown's offices in Boston to tell the company to no longer publish his novels. Cameron later maintained that he had resigned because of the restrictions the board were placing on him, and that *Spartacus* was only one aspect of that. Cameron was blacklisted (he formed his own publishing house, Cameron and Associates, in 1952) and Fast needed to find a new publisher.

Every house he approached rejected the novel. First Viking, then Scribner, then Harper & Brothers all came up with reasons of varying plausibility for not wanting it. Alfred Knopf returned it unopened with a note saying he would not dirty his hands with a manuscript sent to him by Fast. "I do not know whether he sent a carbon copy of the letter to J. Edgar Hoover," Fast wrote.[40] Simon & Schuster returned it without a note and Doubleday rejected it but said they would place it in bookstores if he published it himself. It was an idea that caught Fast's imagination. There was an element of financial risk in self-publishing, but it would allow him to circumvent what appeared to be a concerted effort to prevent him getting his book out with a mainstream house. Enclosing Cameron's effusive reader's report, he sent letters to various left-leaning institutions asking for their financial backing. At one fund-raiser, he claimed the book had met with near universal praise from every publisher he had sent it to, but that they were forced to reject it by the FBI. This was typical of Fast's penchant for exaggeration, but he was right that substantial indirect pressure was being applied. It is worth noting that even that particular fund-raiser—a privately hosted one—was infiltrated by an FBI informant.[41]

To raise the money, Fast sold specially bound and autographed editions on subscription for $5 ahead of publication, with a regular edition retailing at $3.[42] When it became evident that something remarkable was happening, he took a risk and paid for a full-page advertisement in the *New York Times Book Review*. Within three months he sold forty-eight thousand copies of *Spartacus*, through direct mail and in collaboration with a small left-wing publisher called Citadel. After publication, he put together an even cheaper paperback, which he sold to members of trade unions for $1 a copy.[43] Fast became a one-man marketing machine, pushing the book on libraries, Jewish institutions, and friends. Meanwhile he hired a copy editor and designer and turned his basement on the Upper West Side into a warehouse.[44] By April 1952, Fast had reissued his novel seven times, and he formed Blue Heron Press as a venue for other radical writers.

In the Soviet Union, literary repression forced writers underground, with their work circulating in illegal editions from hand to hand, a risky proposition but the only option for readers in a country where all routes to publication were ultimately controlled by the state. The situation was different in the United States, as Fast proved. The irony was that his strategy to circumvent censorship and repression was to adopt the free market thinking so dear to many of his critics. Fast the Communist became a capitalist entrepreneur. And his success in the context of the historical moment was incredible. Amid the convulsions of McCarthyism, Fast self-published a novel that became a massive best seller.[45]

NINETEEN

Spender &
Philby

ON THE EVENING OF MAY 24, 1951, the phone rang in the Spender household. Stephen and Natasha Spender, who were married in 1941, had moved into the house on Loudon Road, in elegant St. John's Wood, in 1945, and it had become a social hub for a cultured London set, where Stephen's literary cohort mixed with Natasha's friends from her work as a concert pianist. Natasha picked up the phone. It was Guy Burgess, asking for W. H. Auden, who was visiting from New York and staying with the Spenders before his annual holiday in Italy. Auden was not there, she told Burgess, but he might catch him at their other house, on Blenheim Place, where Stephen kept his study. Burgess rang off in a hurry.

When Spender picked up the phone in Blenheim Place, he was more than a little surprised to find Burgess on the end of the line. Their paths had crossed frequently in the 1930s and he had attended the Spenders' wedding, but they had not seen much of him since. "I'm so glad you answered," Burgess told Spender, "because I want to tell you how much I agreed with everything you wrote about communism in your autobiography. It expresses the dilemma of a generation."[1] Spender's memoir, *World Within World,* had been published earlier that year to great critical acclaim and commercial success, and Burgess sounded to

Spender sincere in his praise. Burgess asked Spender to pass on the message that he wanted to meet with Auden. Back in New York, Auden had apparently invited Burgess to stay with him in Italy for part of the summer, and it seemed like the call was related to that offer.[2] Burgess never got hold of Auden, though, and the following day he and his Foreign Office colleague Donald Maclean disappeared.

Two weeks later, on June 7, the Foreign Office revealed that Burgess and Maclean were missing, sparking a frenzy of speculation about their whereabouts. Publicly at least, it was circulated that while both men were privy to "Anglo-American state secrets," neither man was suspected of defecting.[3] Maclean's father-in-law, Francis Marling, a Chicago oil executive, told the press that his son's disappearance was simply "a recurrence of a breakdown he suffered a year ago."[4] As journalists learned more about Burgess and Maclean's boozing, it was thought they might be on a bender. "On Binge in Paris?" asked the *Globe and Mail* on June 9. Both men were known to be "high strung, erratic" and could therefore be "on a tremendous spree."[5] This was not without precedent: Burgess had almost been fired by the diplomatic service in 1949 for going on the rampage in Gibraltar and Tangier, where he failed to pay his bills, sang about having sex with young boys, and drunkenly revealed the identity of SIS officers.[6] Having subsequently been posted to Washington, his outrageous behavior there earned him the displeasure of the Virginia State Police, the State Department, and the British ambassador, and he was sent home.

It soon became clear that it was more serious than a drunken binge. Despite "an exhaustive search of every avenue on this side of the Iron Curtain," the pair remained at large.[7] It was reported the car they had rented had been found in Southampton, where they had boarded a ferry to St. Malo. Their luggage had been left on board but offered up "no helpful clues."[8] Maclean's heavily pregnant wife, Melinda, received a telegram sent from Paris, the content of which seemed to come from Maclean, but when the police recovered the original handwritten message that had been submitted for transcription, it was not in his handwriting. Burgess's mother also received a telegram, again with the source message handwritten by someone other than the purported author, this time from Rome, in which he told her he was "embarking on a long Mediterranean holiday."[9]

How much Spender followed the manhunt is not clear; he had relocated to Italy for the summer and was staying with his family in a wing of an old hotel in the fishing village of Torri del Benaco on Lake Garda (he got cheap rates because André Gide, whom Spender knew, had stayed there).[10] On June 9, a Reuters reporter reached him on the phone. Spender told the reporter about the phone conversation he had had with Burgess and that it did not "fit in with the theory that he had gone over to the Communists." Spender pointed out that Burgess had "warmly congratulated" him on *World Within World,* and as this book was "very strongly anti-Communist, it seems rather strange that he should say this if he was just about to leave for Russia." The same report carried quotes from Auden, who said it was "preposterous" that Burgess might have defected. "His whole temperament would be against it," Auden said.

The following day, June 10, the Italian police swarmed the town of Forio on the volcanic island of Ischia, in the Bay of Naples, where a student had spotted somebody matching the description of Burgess. This was also the village where Auden had his villa. Things were about to get complicated for the poet. As well as reporting on the fruitless searches of Forio, the Reuters correspondent interviewed Auden, who said he had last met with Burgess in New York in March and had heard nothing from him since. Spender, though, had told the reporter about Burgess's telephone call. This discrepancy made it look like Auden might be covering for Burgess.[11]

Donald Seaman, a journalist with the *Daily Express,* read the Reuters dispatch and, sensing a big story, left for Italy. In his interview with Seaman, Auden clarified that Burgess had tried to get hold of him before disappearing but that he had been unsuccessful in doing so. However, Auden revealed that Burgess had been a Communist in the 1930s, that he retained Communist sympathies, and that they had discussed the atom spies Klaus Fuchs and Alan Nunn May.

Seaman's story was published on June 13, and not only did he report what Auden had said about Burgess's past, but he also added some sensational—and inaccurate—details of his own. The journalist claimed Auden had known Burgess from their undergraduate days at Cambridge—Auden had in fact gone to Oxford—and that he had been friends with Maclean at Gresham's School—impossible, as Auden was six years older than him. Auden had inadvertently become an important lead in one of the major espionage crises of the Cold War.

On June 14, Auden wrote to Spender. "The combination of that phone call [from Burgess to Spender] and some lady who thought she saw La B in the train on his way to Ischia, has turned this place into a madhouse," Auden wrote. "The house watched night and day by plain-clothes men, etc etc. The climax has been the interview with me published in the *Daily Express* which I dare say you've seen." Auden said he had tried to straighten things out in an interview with Reuters but that the "whole business makes me sick to my stomach." He was beginning to have doubts about Burgess. "I still believe Guy to be a victim," he wrote, "but the horrible thing about our age is that one cannot be certain."[12]

At this point Spender received a disturbing letter from the

poet and editor John Lehmann, a friend since 1930. Lehmann, having seen Spender's quotes in the papers, sent him a warning, telling him that "someone whom you know very well" was "absolutely sure" Burgess was a spy.[13] This "someone" was Rosamond, Lehmann's sister, a novelist whom Spender had known since his undergraduate days. Back in 1938, Rosamond's lover, Goronwy Rees, had told her in absolute confidence that Burgess tried to recruit him. Rees, a Marxist intellectual and a Fellow of All Souls College, Oxford, told her how, over a bottle of whisky, Burgess dramatically announced that he was "a Comintern agent and have been ever since I came down from Cambridge."[14] What is not clear is whether Burgess was successful in his recruitment. Rees later denied working for the NKVD but, while he seems to have done little if any spying, Moscow Center considered him their man, giving him the cryptonyms "Gross" and "Fleet." Rees broke with Communism over the Molotov-Ribbentrop Pact, sending Burgess into a panic. Fearing betrayal, he sent a message to the NKVD demanding Rees be assassinated. When Moscow refused, Burgess told Rees that he too had given up his work for "the Comintern" over the alliance with Nazi Germany.[15]

That the letter sent Spender into a panic is still not enough to explain what he did next. When Seaman came to interview him, Spender showed the reporter Lehmann's letter and allowed him to take it away, ostensibly so that he could report the contents to his office.[16] This was a sensational scoop: evidence, albeit secondhand, that Burgess was in fact a spy. The *Daily Express* published the letter on its front page, naming Lehmann as its author. The same day, Lehmann dashed off a furious letter to Spender. "I don't think I can find words to describe to you what I feel about your conduct—or what anyone else feels who's in any way connected with it, or us," he wrote. "It would never have occurred to me that a friend could calmly, without asking permission, give a private letter to the press [and it is] without parallel in the dealings of gentlemen. . . . You can't expect me to want to have anything more to do with someone who has been guilty of so gross a breach of trust."[17]

The "trouble" Lehmann spoke of involved MI5, who immediately interviewed him to find out what he knew about Burgess. By then MI5 and SIS were already working on the Auden-Burgess-Spender connection. Alerted by the news stories about Burgess's mysterious telephone call, SIS sent a telegram to MI5 on June 11, asking them to check whether Burgess had called Auden in Ischia on May 24 (they were clearly confused at this stage, as the call had taken place between two numbers in London).[18] An SIS agent then met with Auden directly to ask about the significance of the call, but Auden said that Burgess was probably just trying to finalize his holiday plans. Back in Britain, Auden's and Spender's names kept coming up as MI5 interviewed Burgess's friends and lovers.[19]

On June 20 SIS received a signal from its Rome station about the affair. Spender, the SIS agent reported, insisted he had passed on Burgess's message. Auden insisted he never received it. One of them was lying. A week later, the SIS agent confronted a drunk Auden about the discrepancy, and the poet "reluctantly admitted Spender was probably right."[20] Many years later, Spender claimed that not only had he and Natasha told Auden about the call but that he even remembered Auden's response: "Do I HAVE to see him? He's always drunk!"[21] Why did Auden lie? The same day that he claimed to the SIS agent that he had not received Burgess's message, he wrote another letter to Spender about "the B+M business." "Whatever the real facts are they are unintelligible; even the word betrayal has become meaningless," he wrote. "I still refuse to say, however, one can trust no-one." If it is true, he argued, "that they were already under suspicion by MI5, then why did the Foreign Office a) do nothing for days after they went missing b) insist on a totally preposterous story about the love that dare not tell its name?"

From Auden's MI5 file it is not entirely clear what this "preposterous story" was, but what is clear is that investigators attached particular significance to Burgess's homosexuality. MI5 interviewed as many of his former lovers as they could find.[22] The FBI pushed the connection to the point of absurdity. They interviewed Christopher Isherwood in Santa Monica in June and got him to admit that Burgess was "very likely a homosexual." (Hardly a secret.)[23] An FBI report sent to MI5 made much of the fact that Auden, Isherwood, and Spender knew Burgess, claiming their source to be "London newspaper circles." As the MI5 officer who received this report disdainfully noted, this "source" appeared to be the *Daily Express*. The FBI report also had information, from a source "of unknown reliability," that Auden, Isherwood, Erika Mann, and Klaus Mann were part of a "group of persons engaged in sexual perversions." (Auden had married Erika Mann to help her escape Nazi Germany.)[24] What relevance did this have to the disappearance of Burgess and Maclean? To the FBI and MI5, it was enough that Auden was gay, as, in their eyes, that made it likely he was part of Burgess's "circle." His sexuality alone placed him under suspicion.

In Britain, homosexuality was illegal, and the intelligence services assumed that this made gay men susceptible to blackmail, particularly those in positions of influence. In the United States, the previous year had brought a purge of gay employees in government jobs. In February 1950, John Peurifoy, deputy undersecretary of state for administration, announced that ninety-one homosexuals had been forced out of the State Department as "security risks," the beginning of a "Lavender Scare" that cost hundreds of government employees their jobs in the following years.[25] Guy George Gabrielson, the Republican National

Committee chairman, claimed that "sexual perverts who have infiltrated our government" were "perhaps as dangerous as the actual Communists."[26] Auden had played an unwitting part in generating this paranoia; in the 1930s, his circle had jokingly coined the term "Homintern" to refer to a global homosexual community, an idea that appeared a dangerous reality to reactionary anti-Communists in the United States.[27] Since 1946, Auden had been a U.S. citizen (he had moved to the country in 1939 to make a fresh start), and so self-preservation was an understandable motive for trying to put distance between himself and Burgess, and the prurient imagination of the FBI. The problem was that in doing so, he only succeeded in entangling himself further in the scandal, as investigators on both sides of the Atlantic clutched desperately at any clues they could find.

In his second letter to Spender, Auden had made another point: why, if Burgess and Maclean were already under suspicion, did the authorities "do nothing for days after they went missing?" It was a question being asked by many, as Maclean *was* suspected of being a spy and subject to surveillance by MI5 at the time of his disappearance. His identity had been discovered by American cryptanalyst Meredith Gardner, who was working on the VENONA project. Gardner's decrypt proved Maclean was a Soviet agent code-named "Homer," but because the Americans wanted to keep VENONA secret (it did not become public knowledge until the late 1980s), MI5 was instructed to watch Maclean and try to catch him meeting his Soviet case officer. The stakes were high as Maclean, the man in charge of the American desk at the Foreign Office, was presumed to be party to a lot of damaging information about the United States. That he managed to disappear was partly due to the ineptitude of an underresourced MI5, but it was no coincidence that the Russians exfiltrated him just as MI5 were closing in. Maclean had clearly been warned. Who was responsible? Who was the mole?

IT WAS WITH UNDERSTANDABLE ALARM that Kim Philby realized the Americans were on to Maclean. In 1949, Philby had been sent to Washington as liaison between SIS and the CIA and FBI, a position that gave him access to highly sensitive information on both sides of the Atlantic. This included the VENONA decrypts. Even before he left for the United States, Philby had been briefed that there were suspicions about a leak in the British Embassy in Washington during the final year of the war, and Philby soon realized the source of these leaks was Maclean. This situation caused him "deep anxiety" because if Maclean were picked up, he might well give up Philby. Maclean's heavy drinking and increasingly erratic behavior were hardly reassuring.

On first arriving in the United States, Philby found the focus was not on the embassy leak but on Klaus Fuchs. It was Fuchs's confession, to MI5 interrogator William "Jim" Skardon, that set off the chain reaction of arrests and confessions that led to the Rosenbergs. The focus on the atom spies allowed Philby to get on with his job (well, both of them) while keeping an eye out for developments about Maclean. Moscow Center wanted to keep their man in place for as long as possible but, they assured Philby, would get Maclean out "before the net closed in."[28]

In Washington, Philby resumed his friendship with James Jesus Angleton, the OSS agent he knew in London during the war, now a rising star in counterespionage. Over lobster and wine at their weekly lunch at a local restaurant, Angleton sought to strengthen the fledgling CIA's position with SIS, and Philby played along. It was a friendship that would haunt Angleton long into his career as an intelligence officer, one in which he became increasingly paranoid and prone to outlandish conspiracy.[29] Philby also met regularly with the head of the Office of Policy Coordination, Frank Wisner, whom he described as "a youngish man for so responsible a job, balding and running self-importantly to fat."[30] Wisner's team would go on to fund the Berlin Congress and other cultural warfare schemes, but Philby worked with the OPC most closely on a more ambitious project: an attempt, in Philby's description, "to detach an East European country from the Socialist bloc."[31]

That country was Albania. The plan was for a group of dissidents, which the SIS code-named the "Pixies," to be dropped into the country, from where they would connect with anti-Communist forces and launch an insurgency. The Pixies were given intelligence training on Malta before being dropped secretly on the Albanian coast in October 1949. They were promptly ambushed, and those who were not killed fled to Greece. It was a disaster; the Albanian security forces seemed to have known they were coming.[32]

In the summer of 1950 Philby discovered that Burgess was being sent to Washington and, despite the risks involved, took him in as a lodger in his neoclassical house on Nebraska Avenue. This was partly motivated by wanting to keep an eye on Burgess, with his tendency to get into "personal scrapes of a spectacular nature."[33] It also allowed Burgess to act as courier between Philby and his case officer, Valeri Makayev, an illegal resident in New York.[34] Not long after Burgess arrived, Philby told him that Maclean was about to be discovered. According to Philby, Burgess then deliberately got himself sent home by behaving badly (he earned three speeding tickets in one day, he had his lover in the car, and, by the third ticket, had been drinking).[35] Before he returned to London, Burgess met Philby at a Chinese restaurant and they discussed a plan by which Burgess would tip off both Maclean and the London residency if Maclean was compromised. Philby recalled driving Burgess to the station the next morning and telling him ("only half-jocularly"): "Don't you go too."

On May 7, 1951, Burgess arranged for Anthony Blunt to speak with Yuri Modin, the London resident, to tell him that it was time to get Maclean out, insisting that Maclean was in no shape to resist interrogation. Two days later Moscow Center ordered Maclean's exfiltration. There was a twist, however. Modin explained to Burgess that Maclean needed an escort at least part of the way. In fact Moscow had decided Burgess was a liability and had to go. "The Center had concluded that we had not one but two burnt-out agents on our hands," Modin later recalled.[36]

By then MI5 agents were watching Maclean. On May 25 he was seen leaving the Foreign Office carrying a cardboard box. He went to Victoria Station, had a drink, and boarded a 6:10 P.M. train. All seemed normal—which was exactly how Maclean wanted it to appear: Soviet agents had figured out that Maclean was not being observed during evenings and over the weekend (due, apparently, to a lack of resources). As a result, he would not be noticed as missing until Monday, May 28. And while the Soviet London residency believed he was going to be arrested on the Monday, MI5 were in fact not planning to do so until between June 18 and 25 as they continued to gather intelligence on their target.[37]

Wild rumors later circulated about the runaway diplomats having been picked up by a Soviet submarine, but Burgess and Maclean took a far more conventional, if convoluted, path to Moscow. They boarded the pleasure boat *Falaise* at midnight on May 25 and disembarked at St. Malo the next day. From there they traveled by train to Paris via Rennes, and then on to Switzerland, picking up fake passports from the Soviet embassy in

Berne. They booked flights from Zurich to Stockholm via a stopover in Prague (which was their real destination). In Prague's
airport they were picked up by Soviet intelligence officers.

Philby learned that Burgess had gone only when he was called
into the British Embassy in Washington, where he was informed
by Geoffrey Paterson, the MI5 representative in the city, that
"the bird had flown." Philby did his best to "register dawning
horror." When Paterson told him Burgess had gone, too, Philby's
consternation was "no pretence."[38] After enduring a meeting
in which Paterson delivered the news to the FBI, Philby went
home and, after stashing a trowel and the camera he used to
photograph documents in his briefcase, drove out to the Great
Falls National Park and, after digging a hole with the trowel,
buried his equipment in a secluded patch on the banks of the Potomac. By Philby's calculation there was a lot of circumstantial
evidence that could be used against him (his youthful Communist sympathies, his recruitment to the intelligence services by
Burgess, the failure of operations he had been involved with, his
knowledge of the Maclean case) but nothing concrete. He could
have activated his escape plan there and then but, after assessing
his options, decided to stay where he was and fight it out.

He didn't stay there for long. Philby was summoned back to
London to discuss the disappearance of his former friends with
MI5. The night before his flight, he had one last dinner with an
unsuspecting Angleton. The Anglo-American relationship was
about to get a lot less cordial. The CIA were already looking into
Philby, and two conflicting memos were written. One, authored
by Bill Harvey, concluded that he was most likely a Soviet spy;
another, written by Angleton, claimed that Philby mostly likely
did not know what Burgess was up to and warned the agency
against making hasty accusations.[39]

Divisions were opening up in British intelligence, too. Many
in MI5 suspected Philby but MI6 was standing by their man.

They agreed to let Philby meet with Dick White, head of MI5 counterintelligence, but only on the understanding that he was helping them in their inquiries about Burgess and Maclean. The conversation, over tea and cigarettes, was cordial, but White was left dissatisfied by some of Philby's answers. The CIA, meanwhile, sent over Harvey's memo and informed British intelligence that Philby would not be allowed to return to Washington and that the British needed to clean house. White summoned Philby for another interview, and, after more aggressive questioning, caught him lying, first about having never spoken to Burgess about Maclean, and then about how he had funded himself as a freelance reporter in the Spanish Civil War (when the NKVD had been paying him).[40]

While MI6 continued to defend Philby (his friend Nicholas Elliott his biggest champion), the combined pressure of the CIA and MI5 meant that "C" had no choice but to fire him. Even if he were innocent, his long-standing friendship with Burgess compromised him. He was told to resign and was offered £4,000 in lieu of a pension, an offer he accepted.[41]

For several months nothing happened with the investigation until "C" again got in touch in November and invited him up to London. Philby was informed that there was a judicial inquiry into the disappearance of Burgess and Maclean and he was to be questioned again. Philby was driven across a wintry St. James's Park to MI5 headquarters at Leconfield House, where he was ushered up to the fifth floor and into the alarming presence of a former MI5 agent named Helenus "Buster" Milmo; Philby knew the service used the experienced barrister when they went in "for the kill."[42] After four hours of confrontational interrogation, during which Milmo shouted himself hoarse, they reached a stalemate. Philby was asked to turn over his passport as he left. "I find myself unable to avoid the conclusion that Philby is and has been for many years a Soviet agent," Milmo reported. "There's no hope of confession but he's guilty as hell."[43] Still, there was no hard evidence, so MI5 sent Skardon, the man who had induced Fuchs to confess, to conduct a series of interviews with Philby at his home. Fuchs, though, was a physicist, not a high-ranking intelligence agent, and Philby was careful to avoid the "little traps" that Skardon laid for him. After a series of interviews, the last of which took place in January 1952, Skardon felt the case against Philby was "unproven."[44]

Philby spent the next years in internal exile, and after months spent fruitlessly looking for a job, he was taken on by an ex-MI6 colleague in his import-export business. Without the evidence to convict, there was no motivation to make any official suspicions public. Aware that they were being watched, Philby and Modin did not communicate with each other for three years. As an institution, SIS never wanted to believe that their prized operator could be the "Third Man" who had warned Burgess and Maclean. Meanwhile, the new "C," John Sinclair (Menzies had retired), demanded White and MI5 lay off Philby, claiming that the case appeared to be a miscarriage of justice. Anxious that their agent not be left destitute, the Soviets arranged to deliver $5,000 in cash to Philby via Anthony Blunt.

Philby was called back in for interrogation in early October 1955 at an MI6 safe house near Sloane Square, with his questioners concluding that he was innocent after all. When White, now head of MI5, read the transcript, he was furious with MI6 for giving their man an easy ride. Across the Atlantic, news of Philby's potential rehabilitation did not go down well. FBI director J. Edgar Hoover, convinced of his guilt, leaked it to the New York *Daily News* that Philby was suspected of being the Third Man (Carol Reed's superb film of that name, scripted by Graham Greene, had been released in 1949); he was duly named in the October 23 edition of the paper. Libel law prevented Philby from being named in Britain, however, but that did not stop the press descending en masse to his home in Crowborough (the same East Sussex town in which Graham Greene's parents lived).

In seeking to expose him, however, his enemies inadvertently gave him an out. Philby finally became known to the British public when the Labour Party MP Marcus Lipton used parliamentary privilege to name him in the House of Commons. Philby locked himself in his mother's flat in London, disconnected the doorbell, and buried the phone under a pile of cushions. If Lipton had evidence, Philby was finished. But what evidence could an MP have that MI5 did not? On November 7, trapped between Lipton's legally problematic assertion and deadlock between MI5 and MI6 over Philby's guilt, Harold Macmillan, then Foreign Secretary, was forced to announce to the Commons that he had "no reason to conclude that Mr. Philby has at any time betrayed the interests of his country, or to identify him with the so-called third man, if there even was one." Philby, the master spy, was exonerated.

IT IS A MARKER of just how seriously Auden's potential role in the defection was taken that as late as June 25, a full month after Burgess and Maclean first disappeared, the FBI and the CIA were demanding MI5 share the "results of Auden and Philby interviews."[45] What complicated matters for Auden, although without his knowledge, was that in Italy he fell under SIS's jurisdiction; unlike MI5 they were reluctant to show their hand and favored playing a waiting game. It was also becoming apparent that Auden had most probably been used by Burgess as a diversion, hoping to confuse the investigators.[46] Still, MI5 wanted to interview Auden and they clearly did not trust him. A. M. Martin, leading the investigation for MI5, told SIS that the "value of the interview may well lie as much in what Auden fails to say as in what he volunteers." It is not a testament to the rigors of

SIS procedure that Auden somehow managed to elude them in his travels around Italy. By the time he returned to the United States, he was no longer of active interest but was still placed on the Traffic Index, whereby an alert would be triggered every time he traveled in or out of Britain.

Spender, whose London houses were subject to surveillance, was also subject to a failed follow-up. Back in England, he attended the rather disastrous premiere of his verse play *To the Island* in Oxford. Hot in pursuit was MI5's Skardon. The famous interrogator somehow failed to track down Spender, though, despite knowing what hotel he was staying at and the location of the playhouse. While Spender appeared only to have played the role of messenger between Burgess and Auden, his MI5 file complicated the picture. That had been opened in 1934, when Spender began to associate with Communists MI5 had been keeping tabs on. They knew about his failed "espionage" mission in the Spanish Civil War, when he had gone in search of information about the crew of the *Komsomol,* a Soviet ship that had been sunk by the Italians. A defense security officer in Gibraltar had asked headquarters for additional information on Spender upon finding out he was in the pay of the Soviet embassy. MI5 shared this information with SIS, saying they felt it would be prudent "to keep a sharper eye on him in the future."[47] This involved intercepting some of his communications with Harry Pollitt, and placing him on a list of suspect characters. Special Branch ordered customs agents to search his baggage every time he came in and out of the country.[48] This involvement with Communism, however fleeting, did not look good in hindsight, even if later entries in his file showed that MI5 changed their mind about him after his public disavowal.[49] With evidence mounting against Philby and resources directed to investigating his past, interest in Spender waned. Still, like Auden, he was placed on the Traffic Index as a precautionary measure. What is ironic about Spender's case is that soon after being investigated by MI5 and the FBI, he was cultivated, without his knowledge, by the SIS and the CIA.

BOTH THE AMERICAN AND BRITISH intelligence services had come up with the idea of setting up an intellectual magazine to not only win over those British intellectuals who remained skeptical of, if not hostile to, American influence but also to reach readers in present and former British colonies, where both the United States and Britain feared infiltration by Communists. The CIA had already been involved in setting up the Congress for Cultural Freedom, which oversaw the production of intellectual anti-Communist magazines in German (*Der Monat*) and France (*Preuves*).[50] The new English magazine would be known as *Encounter*. On the CIA side, this was a project run by Wisner's Office of Policy Coordination. Early in 1951, Wisner's team had traveled to London from Washington to discuss the "need for camouflaging the source of secret funds supplied to apparently respectable bodies in which we were interested" (they were accompanied by the SIS representative in Washington, who was, of course, Kim Philby). At a meeting with the SIS and the Foreign Office, Wisner said it was "essential to secure the cooperation of people with conspicuous access to wealth in their own right." The CIA found their useful rich person in Julius Fleischmann, heir to an American yeast fortune, whose Farfield Foundation would become the principal vehicle through which the CIA funded the Congress for Cultural Freedom, under the jurisdiction of which the new magazine was to be launched.

On the British side, the key figure was Monty Woodhouse. A brilliant scholar of Classics at Oxford, where he had been taught by Isaiah Berlin, Woodhouse signed up with the Special Operations Executive during the Second World War, parachuting into occupied Greece to conduct sabotage operations. After the war he worked, ostensibly at least, as a diplomat in Greece before returning to London and joining SIS. In 1951 he became station chief in Tehran—a tricky appointment, as Prime Minister Clement Attlee had arranged for an economic boycott of Iran after they decided to nationalize their oil industry, including the Anglo-Persian Oil Company. When Churchill was reelected prime minister in 1951, he made the decision to find a more radical solution to the problem, and SIS began looking at ways to oust the democratically elected Prime Minister Mohammad Mosaddegh and replace him the more pliable Mohammad Reza Pahlavi. Woodhouse was a key player in the planning of what the SIS called Operation Boot, and once the British had persuaded the Americans to intervene (fearing Iran coming under Soviet influence), he worked with the CIA on initial plans for the coup. Two years later, with Woodhouse long since having returned to Britain, Mossadegh was forced out and Pahlavi installed as Shah.

Early in 1952, Woodhouse took up a position in the Information Research Department (responsible for anti-Communist propaganda) and was given his own "semi-autonomous team" that operated out of an SIS office near St. James's Park underground station.[51] In meetings with the CIA's Michael Josselson and Lawrence de Neufville at the Royal Automobile Club on Pall Mall, Woodhouse made the case for British intelligence partly funding the new magazine. The idea was for *Encounter* to have one British and one American editor, and it was agreed that the salary of the British editor and his secretary were to be paid indirectly by the IRD. Woodhouse would arrange for the Foreign Office to buy up copies of the magazine to be distributed through the British Council in India and East Asia. The British also secured rich individuals to serve as plausible benefactors for the magazine. Malcolm Muggeridge, who had worked with

Graham Greene at SIS during the war and was heavily involved in plans for *Encounter*, persuaded Victor Rothschild and Alexander Korda to allow SIS to channel money through their bank accounts.[52] The IRD also arranged for one of its employees, Margot Walmsley, to be the *Encounter* office manager. While the initial needs of the magazine were to be met through envelopes of cash delivered by courier from the IRD, eventually a system would be established by which money was paid to Secker & Warburg, then moved to the British Society for Cultural Freedom before being transferred to *Encounter*. Josselson would consult Woodhouse on important matters relating to the magazine.[53]

In a journal entry of March 12, 1953, Spender recorded a "request from the Paris Committee of the Congress for Cultural Freedom, that I should edit, together with Irving Kristol, a magazine."[54] The idea of a stable job was very appealing to Spender. Despite his reputation, freelance writing did not pay the bills. Since the war he had taken various positions that, while they paid well, meant he had to travel extensively, forcing him to be apart for long stretches from Natasha and his two young children. He had worked first as a cultural ambassador for UNESCO and then become increasingly involved in the Congress for Cultural Freedom, giving lectures all over the globe, and helping Nabokov with his Masterpieces of the Twentieth Century festival, a cultural extravaganza that took place in Paris in the summer of 1952.[55] It featured, among much else, paintings by Picasso, Stravinsky's music, and a drunken cameo from William Faulkner. The patron of the festival was Julius Fleischmann, who sat on the Board of the Metropolitan Opera, was a Fellow of the Royal Society of Arts, and the director of the Ballet Russes in Monte Carlo. Spender had been lobbying for the creation of a new literary journal along the lines of *Horizon*. Spender was told that Fleischmann was giving his backing to the new magazine and, coincidentally enough, he was based in Cincinnati, where Spender was spending the semester as an invited professor.

A couple of days after Spender made the entry in his journal, Kristol, his future coeditor, came to talk through plans for the magazine, the prospect of which became even more appealing when it was decided to set up the editorial office in London, rather than at the Congress for Cultural Freedom headquarters on the Boulevard Haussmann in Paris.[56] Spender warned that distance from CCF's headquarters had to be editorial, too, telling the executive committee that no one of consequence would write for the magazine if it were perceived to have been created "for the purpose of putting across the American version of the Cold War."[57] (This had been the reason, Spender believed, for the failure of *Perspectives USA,* a cultural publication funded by the Ford Foundation and aimed at the European market.)[58]

Furthering the recruitment effort, Spender met with Fleischmann, and on April 30, he received a letter detailing his salary and responsibilities from Fredric Warburg, Orwell's publisher, whose house was going to help with the production of the new magazine. By September, he and Kristol were installed in their office on the Haymarket just off Piccadilly Circus, putting together the first issue of *Encounter.* The entire ten-thousand-copy print run of the first issue sold out.

There were two reasons for this instant success. One was that there was a significant gap in the market. Several potential rival magazines had folded, not least of them Cyril Connolly's *Horizon* (where Spender had been an unofficial editor), and the only one making a success of itself was the weekly *New Statesman.* Edited by Orwell's old nemesis Kingsley Martin, the *New Statesman* was perceived as being soft on Communism, and there was a hunger for a left-leaning intellectual magazine that was critical of the Soviet Union. The second reason the magazine sold so well was the controversy created by one specific article. Spender secured some good contributions for the first issue, including excerpts from Virginia Woolf's diary and new fiction by his old friend Christopher Isherwood. There were contributions from Albert Camus and John Kenneth Galbraith, and poetry by Edith Sitwell and Cecil Day-Lewis. But the piece that got everybody talking was an essay by American literary scholar Leslie Fiedler on the Rosenbergs.

Fiedler's essay argued that the Rosenbergs had been tried twice. At the first trial, which took place in a New York federal court in March 1951, they were found guilty of treason for passing atomic secrets to the Soviet Union. The evidence for their guilt was, in Fiedler's argument, overwhelming. In the second trial, which took place in the court of global public opinion, the Rosenbergs were found innocent by a significant number of prominent European intellectuals. Jean-Paul Sartre, who described the execution as a "legal lynching," had led the protests in France, where rallies were held demanding clemency. Fiedler attacked what he perceived as the hypocrisies of these fellow-traveling bien-pensants who made themselves the dupes of Communist propaganda by defending "flagrantly guilty" spies. More than that, Fiedler argued that Communists actually relished the suffering of the Rosenbergs, exploiting them as martyrs, and he summarily dismissed those who, while accepting they might be guilty, argued against the severity of the sentence. As a former member of the Young Communist League, Fiedler, like Koestler, had the zeal of the apostate; it was a piece thin on specifics and rich in anti-Communist rhetoric. There were even flourishes of outright provocation. "There is no political act," he declared, "that is not marred these days by the obsessive envy and anguish of many Europeans in regard to America." Yet ultimately it was not Fiedler's shaky logic, or the Euro-baiting, that riled *Encounter*'s first readers, but his lapse in taste: he delivered a callous analysis of a letter Ethel Rosenberg sent to Eisenhower as a plea for clemency ("embarrassing . . . in its deliberate and transparent craftiness") and followed that by claiming that in their letters to each other while in prison the Rosenbergs had "exploited their final intimacies to strike a blow in the cold war."[59] But to many readers it was Fiedler who was striking a blow in the cultural Cold War, and a low blow at that.

Spender was furious about the article, which he thought should not have run, and his anger was echoed in the correspondence he received in response. E. M. Forster told Spender that he had been offended by the "contempt and severity with which [Fiedler] treats Ethel Rosenberg's last days," Czeslaw Milosz, the Polish dissident author of *The Captive Mind,* told Spender he disliked it, and T. S. Eliot turned down an invitation to write for *Encounter* as it was so obviously published under "American auspices."[60] Even a staunch anti-Communist like Sidney Hook felt that piece lacked tact when he read it in proofs. In the short editorial that opened the first edition, Spender and Kristol had declared that they sought "to promote no 'line'," but an article like Fiedler's undermined their effort to appear independent, a position already difficult to maintain with sponsorship from the Congress for Cultural Freedom.[61] In fact the Paris office had sought to tone down the anti-Communism of the first issue, pushing for articles by Koestler and Aron to be postponed until later editions. Kristol conceded to these requests but insisted on the Fiedler piece. Spender wrote to Josselson at the CCF to complain. "As far as my own personal position is concerned," he wrote, "the implied criticism that I am putting in articles which serve American purposes is naturally very painful to me."[62] The irony, of course, was that he was making this complaint to Josselson, an undercover CIA agent.

Josselson shared Spender's concerns, but for different reasons. Spender, having spent extended periods of time teaching in the United States, had come to believe that the way forward for European culture was in collaboration with America against Soviet totalitarianism, a position he had expounded in a series of articles for the *New York Times* in the late 1940s and early 1950s. These articles, along with his contribution to *The God That Failed,* were a big part of why he had been appointed editor in the first place; he seemed an ideal candidate to head an Anglo-American magazine of the non-Communist left. But Josselson did not want *Encounter* to appear a vehicle for American Cold War propaganda, because that would defeat the purpose of launching it in the first place. A lot of effort had gone into disguising the fact that the magazine was funded by American interests, so to run a piece as bluntly anti-Communist as Fiedler's was self-defeating.

In the years that followed, Spender insisted he never knew where the money for *Encounter* came from, and his correspondence from the time appears to back this up. He was certainly capable of being naive and was certainly pliable. And his anger at being thought a tool of American propaganda in the fallout from the Rosenberg article was genuine. Yet pleading ignorance can only explain so much. Spender later claimed he did inquire about the sources of funding but was repeatedly reassured that there was nothing sinister going on. Spender's biographer, John Sutherland, insists he knew nothing while others who have studied the period, including Frances Stonor Saunders and James Smith, find that improbable. In the later stages of the Second World War, Spender had worked for the Political Warfare Executive, the German branch of which was run by Richard Crossman, who was later Spender's editor on *The God That Failed.* Spender had many other friends who worked in intelligence, including Muggeridge, A. J. Ayer, and Stuart Hampshire. He certainly knew people he could ask, people who might find answers to difficult questions. How could he have been ignorant? There is another explanation.

Decades later Spender wrote an entry into his journal after reading a book about the Cambridge Spies. "The career of Burgess seems incredible," he wrote, "that a person who could scarcely have been let into, say Leonard and Virginia's [Woolf's] should have had the run of the Foreign Office, the BBC, etc., and ended up, when he was considered too outrageous for anywhere else, at the British Embassy in Washington."[63] Spender might well have added the SOE, SIS, and IRD to his list of Burgess's haunts. How could these organizations have been ignorant of so flamboyant and unpredictable a spy in their very midst? A similar question might be asked about why, despite the evidence, many SIS agents continued to believe in the innocence of Philby in the years after Burgess and Maclean defected. Perhaps the answer was that they did not want to know the truth. The same case can be made for Spender. The editorship of *Encounter* was a good job at a good time for him. It eased his financial worries and allowed him to spend time with his family. It also placed him back at the heart of literary London. Perhaps he knew enough not to want to know more.

Part Five

ESCALATION

TWENTY
Greene

MALAYA & VIETNAM, 1950–1955

DEEP IN THE JUNGLE OF PAHANG IN MALAYA, the Gurkha unit halted, waiting for their famous guest to finish retching. Graham Greene felt bad enough as it was, but now his vomiting placed the patrol's life in danger: so much for the quiet Englishman. When hunting insurgents in the jungle, the Gurkhas operated under "security silence," knowing that any noise might give away their position and put them at risk of ambush.[1] And as Greene was discovering, it was very difficult to be sick *silently*. After pulling himself together, he discovered a bloated leech feasting on his neck. No sooner had the Gurkhas resumed their patrol through the jungle than Greene began retching again and, as they ascended a particularly steep hill, Greene, slipping in the rain, had to be relieved of his pack. At one point, he became so exhausted that he passed out.[2] It was misery of his own making: one thing Greene was determined to do in Malaya in the winter of 1950 was go on jungle patrol.

Major McGregor Cheers, the officer in charge of this fourteen-strong Gurkha unit, had agreed to take Greene on a short mission through territory controlled by the Communist insurgents. The mission was to cross nine miles of jungle between the base and a main road, looking for enemy camps. The problem for Greene was that the Gurkha patrols did things differently from other British army units. Instead of following established trails, they drew a direct line between themselves and their objective and cut straight through the jungle, no matter how dense. As captured enemy intelligence reports made clear, this kind of dedication and discipline made the Gurkhas the insurgents' most feared opponent among the British forces in Malaya. This reputation was also the reason Greene wanted to trek with them.

He was given plenty of cause to regret his decision. The march was punishing, cutting through thick undergrowth and climbing and descending steep hills in the pouring rain. Within the first hour of the trek his body was covered in scratches from the trees, and by the end of the first day he was beaten. Greene was a heavy drinker, and his spirits were briefly lifted by tea and rum during the first halt. At night, he slept back-to-back with Major Cheers on a bed of logs and leaves, kept awake by the torrential rain and tormented by the idea that he was holding up the patrol. In the early hours, having managed to drift off, he awoke with the Major's arms around his throat, with the officer in the throes of a nightmare about being ambushed. On the second night, Greene pulled a fat leech off his backside, and with his body racked by nausea, slept fitfully while dreaming he was at the Ritz. "Visibility was sometimes twenty feet," he wrote. "Almost every day water poured down upon it, making the steep, slippery slopes of the innumerable hills a cruel effort to climb. One was never dry and at night one was never in quiet—the ugly din of insects came between the newcomer and sleep."[3]

Pushing himself to the limit was the reason Greene was in Malaya. He found himself in the grip of a depression that only danger appeared to lift. From his schoolboy days, when he claimed to have played Russian roulette, he had deliberately placed himself in perilous situations. He sometimes wondered if he had ever been happier than when he was living in London during the German bombardment, an experience that had found its way into the novel he had just finished writing, *The End*

of the Affair. Did he have a death wish? It seemed more the imminent threat of death that he desired, helping as it did to beat
back the crushing ennui that beset him. "I hadn't the courage for
suicide," he later wrote, "but it became a habit with me to visit
troubled places, not to seek material for novels but to regain the
sense of insecurity which I had enjoyed during the three Blitzes
on London."[4] The publication of *The Heart of the Matter* two
years earlier had made Greene famous, thanks as much to the
scandal surrounding the book as to its quality. Drawing heavily
on his wartime posting in Freetown, Greene's novel featured an
imperial policeman, Henry Scobie, who tries to live with integrity despite the bribery and corruption around him. Yet when he
begins an adulterous affair with a young woman who survived
a shipwreck, he becomes subject to blackmail and believes the
only way he can extricate himself from the situation, and protect
his wife's reputation, is to kill himself by gradually poisoning
himself, hoping to make his death look like a heart attack. Scobie is a Catholic, and the passages in which he seeks to rationalize
his suicide were what caused outrage among devout readers. The
book was banned in Ireland, and Greene was threatened with
excommunication by the Vatican.

The success of the book, and the scandal surrounding it, established him as a major novelist; after the publication of *The
End of the Affair,* his new status was reflected in his appearance
on the cover of *Time,* which announced Greene as "The Next
Dostoevsky." He hated this kind of attention, much preferring to
be in places in which he could go largely unrecognized, such as
on a recent, revivifying trip back to Sierra Leone.

It wasn't just fame he was fleeing in the Malaya jungle: as ever,
Greene's romantic life was a mess. In 1946, he had begun an affair with Catherine Walston, an American married to a wealthy
English farmer. At the time, he was living in Bloomsbury with
his other mistress, Dorothy, while still married to Vivien. Vivien

finally split with him in 1947, when she discovered a letter intended for Catherine, but she refused to grant him a divorce and Catherine refused to leave her husband. While Catherine's husband knew of Greene's affair with his wife, he did not publicly acknowledge it and was horrified when he discovered his private life reinvented as the premise of *The End of the Affair*. It was a sorry mess, mostly of Greene's own making. His need for escape combined with his need for danger found an outlet in the emerging conflicts of the global Cold War, in which nationalist movements, Communist insurgencies, and fading empires competed for control.

Greene was determined to thrust himself into the front lines of these conflicts. In 1948, he twice visited Vienna, a city pitted by bomb craters and divided between the Soviets and the Western powers, to work on his screenplay for *The Third Man*. He worked his contacts to take a nighttime tour of the city's rat-infested sewers, which were used to cross illegally between the city's different sectors. He also spent several nights drinking with Peter Smollett, the *Times* correspondent in the city, whom Orwell had included in his suspect list (Smollett is credited with telling Greene about Vienna's penicillin racket, which became central to the plot of *The Third Man*).[5] It is not known whether Greene and Smollett made the connection that they both knew Kim Philby (Philby had recruited Smollett to the NKVD in London). When Greene heard that the Communists were taking over in Prague (by revolution or coup d'etat, depending on your perspective), he took the train there to witness it. Instead of finding himself amid crowds and violence, he ended up getting drunk at an impromptu party in the basement of a hotel. In August 1950, before traveling to Malaya, he contemplated going to India to visit the contested Portuguese colonial territory of Goa, where tensions were escalating. Another potential destination was Korea, where the South Korean and UN forces appeared to be losing to the invading North Koreans.

Greene decided on Malaya. Asia was in the grip of radical political change in the years after the Second World War. The Japanese had defeated the European colonial powers in the region, often with embarrassing ease, but after the dropping of nuclear weapons on Hiroshima and Nagasaki, the ensuing Japanese surrender created a power vacuum. In some places, such as Indonesia, a former Dutch colony, nationalist movements filled that void, declaring independence. In others, such as Malaya and Vietnam, nationalist forces came into direct conflict with returning British and French colonists seeking to reassert control. What complicated this picture was that, as had been the case in Europe, many of the most effective fighters to have resisted the Japanese were Communists. This placed the Americans in a difficult position. Under FDR they had loudly championed a postwar future of self-determination, but under Truman the emphasis was placed on the containment of the spread of communism. The latter priority won out, and as a result the process of decolonization was shaped by the dynamics of the unfolding Cold War.

The decision to travel to Malaya was made easier when in September Greene's brother, Hugh, was seconded from the BBC to Kuala Lumpur as head of Emergency Information Services, responsible for running psychological warfare against the Communist insurgency. The British had declared a state of emergency in Malaya in June 1948 in response to two separate fatal attacks on rubber planters by fighters of the Malayan Communist Party.[6] The MCP, led by Chin Peng, a Maoist who had fought in the resistance to Japanese occupation during the war, found shelter in the jungle, from where it launched attacks on rubber plantations and tin mines and other manifestations of British colonial influence, as well as against Malaysians perceived to be collaborating with the British. Their guerrilla campaign against the British was known as the War of the Running Dogs.

The insurgents relied on an extensive underground network of Communists and sympathizers, known as the Min Yuen, to help supply them with food, equipment, and information (Greene soon learned to avoid talking about his movements over the telephone or in front of hotel staff).[7] The MCP used ambushes, assassinations, and sabotage as part of a terror campaign, often mutilating victims to send a message. The British used counterterror strategies that were to become grimly familiar during the later prosecution of the Cold War around the world: they dropped herbicides and defoliants (including Agent Orange) to try to expose enemy camps, used aerial bombardment indiscriminately, deployed helicopters for lightning raids, and, when the enemy proved elusive, took out their frustration on those they held responsible for supporting them. The Chinese "squatter communities" came in for especially harsh treatment as villages were burned, torture used in interrogations, and unarmed civilians massacred.[8] Eventually these communities were forcibly relocated to "fortified villages" as part of a strategy of starving the insurgents out of the jungle. This, as Greene noted, was the "most important weapon" in the British armory, as "no one could subsist on the jungle."[9] Chin Peng and his forces grew weaker and eventually retreated into Thailand.

Greene arrived in November 1950 and, thanks to his connections and his press accreditation, traveled extensively through the country, including visiting planters who lived in constant fear of being attacked. Everywhere he went he saw the evidence of war but no actual fighting. "The war was like a mist," he wrote, "it pervaded everything; it sapped the spirits; it wouldn't clear."[10] He recorded in his diary some of the more harrowing evidence ("Disembowelling by bandits of trussed victims—in one case

3 children").[11] Even his brutal jungle trek with the Gurkhas resulted only in the discovery of two abandoned enemy camps.

In his dispatches Greene argued that with the world's attention focused on Korea, Malaya had become the forgotten war. Britain certainly tried to sell the Malayan Emergency to its allies, especially the Americans, as another front in the Cold War, but it was hard to shake off the impression that this was a grubby colonial conflict, motivated by Britain's desperate economic need: Malaysia was a rich source of both rubber and tin, the price of which had shot up as a result of the Korean War. Greene later wrote that a "cloud of moral disapprobation hung over Malaya in 1951," a year that was the most violent of the conflict, in which more than a thousand civilians and members of the security forces were killed, including the British High Commissioner, Sir Henry Gurney.[12] And Greene was soon ready to forget it himself. He found the war depressing and the cities boring, and his experiences failed to live up to his expectation of frontline excitement. His march through the jungle summed it up: what had seemed like the kind of adventure he had been craving turned out to be a grueling trial. His relief on getting out of the jungle was palpable; now he sought a way out of Malaya, too.

One incident stuck with him: the violent murder of a Malay police constable after an ambush at a tin mine. "The scowl & open mouth of death," he wrote in his journal. "Beaten about the mouth, stabbed through the heart. Like a new joint at the butcher's. Feeling off meals & off colour afterwards . . . Restless night with bad dreams."[13] Greene would give this ugly memory to one of his future characters, the cynical British journalist Thomas Fowler, the narrator of *The Quiet American,* who at one point in the novel flips through his memories as if he is going through "pictures in an album" until he comes to "the body of a bayoneted Malay which a Gurkha patrol had brought at the back of a lorry into a mining camp in Pahang, and the Chinese coolies stood by and giggled with nerves, while a brother Malay put a cushion under the dead head."[14] For Greene, as for Fowler, Malaya was the backstory to the real war: the battle for Indochina, the battle for Vietnam. It was a conflict that, in all its complex manifestations, in its cruelty and futility, would become one of the foundational conflicts of the Cold War.

THERE IS A REMARKABLE PASSAGE early in *The Quiet American* in which Fowler gives Alden Pyle, a callow American ostensibly working for the Economic Aid Mission in Saigon but really an operative of the CIA, the lowdown on the war. It's a spiel Fowler has delivered before and he feels like "a record always turned on for the benefit of newcomers." Fowler, though, knows that what he tells Pyle is just "arid bones of background," and that the American would need experience to flesh it out:

> He would have to learn for himself the real background that held you as a smell does: the gold of the rice fields under a flat late sun: the fishers' fragile cranes hovering over the fields like mosquitoes: the cups of tea on an old abbot's platform, with his bed and his commercial calendars, his buckets and broken cups and the junk of a lifetime washed up around his chair: the mollusc hats of the girls repairing the road where a mine had burst: the gold and the young green and the bright dresses of the south, and in the north the deep browns and the black clothes and the circle of enemy mountains and the drone of planes.[15]

The understated lyricism of the passage captures something of Fowler's—and Greene's—infatuation with the country, with its light and color, but in each clause the aesthetic is entwined with menace: the sun is setting, the mosquitoes hover, the cups are broken, the mine has burst, and the planes drone overhead. Vietnam provoked in Greene a genuine response even as he embraced the more sordid clichés of Orientalist fantasy in the brothels and opium dens of Cholon. But that genuine response was conditioned by the "exhilaration that a measure of danger brings to the visitor with a return ticket."[16] He loved the cafes on the Rue Catinat *because* of the grenade netting, not despite it.

Greene arrived in Saigon for the first time on January 25, 1951. The previous month Jean de Lattre de Tassigny had been appointed Commander in Chief of the French Expeditionary Corps and High Commissioner for Indochina. It was an appointment that changed the course of the war.[17] De Lattre was vain, bad-tempered, and a bully, yet he was a brilliant military leader who had served with distinction in both world wars. The novelist was impressed by the general—"a terrific soldier"—and when Greene arrived, De Lattre hosted him as an honored guest in Hanoi, where he presented him with "a shoulder flash of the First French Army, which he commanded at the fall of Strasbourg."[18]

The French and their Vietnamese allies desperately needed a charismatic leader to inspire their deflated troops. The enemy had just such a figure in Ho Chi Minh, who commanded profound loyalty from his followers. In 1941, Ho had formed the Viet Minh, a united front among nationalist independence movements. His credentials as leader were impeccable: he had campaigned for Vietnamese independence since before the Great War and spent thirty years abroad seeking to organize a political movement strong enough to force out the colonial French. While living in Paris in 1921, he had mixed in left-wing circles and became a communist. He traveled to the Soviet Union, where he got frostbite while waiting in line to pay his respect to Lenin's corpse. Having spent much of the 1930s eluding the French security services, he finally returned to Vietnam during the Second World War.[19] Ho fought alongside the OSS against the Japanese believing that, with Roosevelt's stated commitment to postwar decolonization, the Americans would support Vietnamese independence, and he was dismayed when they failed to oppose the return of the French to Saigon after the Japanese were defeated. From Hanoi in the north, Ho declared Vietnamese independence, and the Indochina War began.

Unlike in Malaya, where there were deep divisions between the largely ethnic Chinese insurgents and the larger Malay population, the Vietnamese Communists offered a unifying nationalist narrative, their position strengthening by the day. The triumph of Mao's Communists in the Chinese Civil War meant Ho's forces could be supplied by their ally across the northern border. Their superior motivation and tactics resulted in a series of victories over the French Expeditionary Corps in the north of the country, with the French forced back to the Red River Delta, where they held on precariously to Hanoi. The war was unpopular in France, but withdrawal was not considered an option, so the decision was made to change strategy via the establishment of a Vietnamese army, an increased reliance on American materiel, and the appointment of De Lattre.

The urgent priority for De Lattre was to prevent the fall of Hanoi. Led by General Vo Nguyen Giap, the forces of the Viet Minh staged a full-blooded assault on the Red River Delta in January 1951, just before Greene arrived in the country. The key battle was fought at Vinh Yen, northwest of Hanoi. De Lattre took personal command of the battle, flying into Vinh Yen on his spotter plane, and, drawing on all the resources he could muster, pulled off a renowned if bloody victory.[20] What proved decisive was his deployment of the heaviest aerial bombardment of the whole war and, specifically, the use of American-supplied napalm. Some 6,000 Viet Minh troops were killed and 8,000 wounded. Giap attacked again, in March, on the coast and was again repelled by the French using napalm. A third assault came from the south, in the area around Phat Diem, in May, and this time Giap gambled too recklessly, with a further 9,000 Viet Minh killed and 1,000 captured. These losses, combined with the psychological damage inflicted by the horrific new weapon that dropped fire from the sky, forced Giap to return to guerrilla tactics.[21]

Even before the victory at Vinh Yen, De Lattre knew that if the French were to avoid defeat, let alone win the war, they would need more help from the United States. To make the war more palatable to the Americans, the French framed it as a war of Cold War containment. De Lattre told one American journalist, Robert Shaplen, that he was there to save Vietnam "from Peking and Moscow" and warned that Tonkin (the colonial name for the Red River Delta region) was the "keystone of the defense of Southeast Asia." "If Tonkin falls," he said, "Siam falls with Burma, and Malaya is dangerously compromised. Without Tonkin the rest of Indochina is soon lost."[22] This domino theory proved persuasive in Washington, not for the last time.

GREENE ARRIVED IN PHAT DIEM on a landing craft early on a December morning, having used the cover of night to creep up the river from Nam Dinh. The enemy had the town surrounded so instead of docking at the naval station, the craft pulled in by the marketplace, which was on fire. Disembarking, Greene was shocked by the destruction of a town he had visited on his first trip to Vietnam ten months earlier. He had been particularly attracted to Phat Diem because it was a staunchly Catholic enclave, run by Bishop Le Huu Tu, who commanded a two-thousand-strong private army. It even had its own cathedral. Back in January, Greene had persuaded himself that these men were all the more powerful for being soldiers of faith and that he "would have felt more confidence fighting in their ranks than in the ranks of the 1,000,000 armed Malay police."[23] On hearing reports of how valiantly the Catholic militia had fought in repelling the assault on Phat Diem in the spring, Greene had felt vindicated and told his brother he was dismayed not to have been there to see it. He had not anticipated, on his eventual return, to find the town in ruins. A regrouped Viet Minh was back on the front foot. They had infiltrated Phat Diem on the day of a religious festival, rising up in the night, striking at key targets, and wresting control of the city. The following day French forces had swept in to try to retake the city, dropping parachutists and managing to push the Viet Minh some six hundred yards out of the town.

De Lattre had helped Greene get into Phat Diem back in January, but now the general was ill disposed toward the bishop and his forces. While their anti-Communism was beyond doubt, they were also ardently nationalistic and considered the French colonial interlopers. De Lattre believed the bishop had deliberately withheld information from him about Viet Minh troop movements that had resulted in a number of ambushes and defeats for his men. In one of these attacks his son, Bernard, who was leading a platoon of Vietnamese troops, was killed.

When Greene had returned to the country in October he found the increasingly paranoid De Lattre far less welcoming. The Sûreté Fédérales, the French colonial police, had warned De Lattre that Greene was working for British intelligence, in league with Arthur Trevor-Wilson, the British consul in Saigon. It was an assumption with some grounding. The pair had been colleagues in Kim Philby's Section V of MI6 during the war, and Trevor-Wilson continued to work for the service under diplomatic cover. And as both Englishmen were Catholics and had traveled to Phat Diem together back in January, De Lattre suspected they were intriguing with the bishop. As a result he had Trevor-Wilson kicked out of the country and got the police to follow Greene. In later years, Greene would make a joke out of it— imagine tailing a middle-aged novelist?—but it is most likely that he was still providing MI6 with information, even if only in an informal arrangement. De Lattre might have been wrong about the details, but he was right to regard Greene with suspicion.

Greene immediately went looking for frontline action in Phat Diem. He picked his way through the rubble-strewn streets (which reminded him of the London Blitz) and persuaded a group of French parachutists making their way to a village on the outskirts, in which the enemy were supposedly gathering for an attack, to take him on patrol. They snaked warily along in single file until they came to a canal that could be crossed only one at a time via a plank. Greene was initially confused as to why the soldiers were avoiding looking at the canal in front of them. He later shared his realization with Fowler in *The Quiet American*:

> The canal was full of bodies: I am reminded now of an Irish stew containing too much meat. The bodies overlapped: one head, seal-grey, and anonymous as a convict with a shaven scalp, stuck up out of the water like a buoy. There was no blood: I suppose it had flowed away a long time ago. I have no idea how many there were[.][24]

The plank at the crossing was too flimsy to take their weight, but a soldier found a punt and they were able to push their way through the bodies to the other side. They found the farm buildings where the enemy were supposed to be hiding abandoned, but then Greene heard two shots from the front of the patrol. In the novel, Fowler presumes they have been ambushed: "I awaited, with exhilaration, the permanent thing." But the shots had come from the French and no fire was returned. A mother and her child had broken cover and run, only to be gunned down:

> They were very clearly dead: a small neat clot of blood on the woman's forehead, and the child might have been

sleeping. He was about six years old and he lay like an embryo in the womb with his little bony knees drawn up. "*Mal chance*" the lieutenant said. He bent down and turned the child over. He was wearing a holy medal round his neck, and I said to myself, "The juju doesn't work." There was a gnawed piece of loaf under his body. I thought, "I hate war."[25]

Fowler is not Greene, of course. For one thing, Greene *did* believe in the "juju" while Fowler is an atheist. But Greene did share with his creation a need to bear witness. As he did with the stabbed and beaten corpse of the Malayan policeman, or with those bodies floating in the canal, Greene forced his attention, and, later, that of his reader, onto the violence done to the body by these wars. To many of his readers, the conflicts of the Cold War were fought between unfamiliar belligerents at a great distance. It was too easy for their complicity in that violence to be understood only in the abstract.

The Quiet American, though, shows that one did not have to be on the other side of the world to fail to understand the suffering being created by these proxy wars. Pyle, the American agent, cannot see the literal consequences of violence even when they are right before his eyes; he does not see mutilated bodies, only intellectual abstractions and political puzzle pieces. He does not believe the French can preside over a unified Vietnam, because they are tainted by their colonial past while the nationalism espoused by the Communists is, he thinks, just a front for the influence of the Soviet Union and China. He argues that only a Third Force can save Vietnam and is secretly charged with finding the right candidate to lead such a force and then to supply them with what weapons they need.

This was no fictionalized premise; Greene knew that the concept of a Third Force was one circulating among American officials at the time. The French, this argument went, were only interested in perpetuating their own influence, which was why they propped up a weak and unpopular leader like Emperor Bao Dai. Without a strong nationalist leader in the south to rival Ho's popularity in the north, it was argued, there was no way to win the war. When visiting Ben Tre, southwest of Saigon, Greene stayed with one such American official, Leo Hochstetter, public affairs director of the Economic Aid Mission and a champion of the Third Force theory.[26] It was, to Greene's mind, a strategy naive in conception and dangerous in execution, for there were ban-dits and mercenaries only too happy to tell the Americans what they wanted to hear in order to part them from their guns and money. A Third Force solution was a fantasy, not least because of its remote chances of gaining popular support, especially if it was obvious that it was backed by another Western power. In fact, to Greene's mind, by arming factions, whose motives they did not understand, the Americans actually threatened to complicate the conflict further and put more innocent Vietnamese in the firing line. And perhaps what angered Greene the most was that Americans like Pyle had convinced themselves they were doing noble work.

AT 11 A.M. ON JANUARY 9, 1952, two car bombs exploded within moments of one another in the center of Saigon, one outside the City Hall, the other on the Place de Théâtre. The immediate aftermath of the latter explosion was captured in a photograph published in *Life* magazine.[27] In the picture, the figure with his back to the viewer appears seated, propping himself up on his right arm; it is only on closer inspection that you see the pool of blood around him and realize his legs have been blown out from beneath him by the explosion. Cars, burning and smoking, clut-ter the foreground, while the tree-lined boulevard stretches into the background. It was an iconic image of the war: revolutionary violence framed by the colonial project that provoked it. Or so it seemed. Early reports claimed this attack was a brutal escalation in Viet Minh terror tactics, but it was soon claimed by General Thé, the leader of an independent band of fighters who opposed both the French occupiers and the Viet Minh. The previous June, Thé and 2,500 followers, who were part of the Caodaist religious sect, seized weapons and disappeared over the border into Cambodia, from where they launched their attacks (Caodaism was a monotheistic religion established in Vietnam in the 1920s that quickly attracted large numbers of believers).

Greene saw the photo and made these attacks the fulcrum of the novel he was writing. In *The Quiet American*, the fictional Pyle identifies the real-life Thé as the leader of a Third Force that could reclaim the nationalist agenda from Ho Chi Minh. As the novel unfolds, the reader discovers clues to Pyle's clandestine activities: when a diplomatic bag addressed to Pyle is accidentally opened it is found to contain plastic for explosives; in Thé's Cao Dao stronghold, Pyle becomes evasive when Fowler surprises him deep in discussion with an agent of the general. On the day of the explosion, Pyle warns his lover Phuong to avoid the square at a specific time. (Pyle thinks the plan is to kill French officers, whom he considers expendable, but the result is the horrific death of innocent Vietnamese civilians.)

Greene's belief that the Americans were culpable for the car bombs verged on conspiracy theory. He believed Americans had been warned to avoid the area of the explosion (in the novel Fowler overhears embassy workers saying they have been told to do just that). He heard one story of an American consul being arrested with explosives on the road to Thé's hideout and another of two American women found dead on a plantation in the Tay Ninh region, whose presence there was never explained. He was even suspicious of the photograph in *Life* magazine, suggesting that only somebody who had been tipped off could have been on the scene and able to capture the immediate aftermath of the blast.[28]

There were a number of holes in Greene's theory. The photographer, for example, was no agency plant but simply an enterprising Vietnamese freelancer. Furthermore, what would be the point in trying to blame Ho Chi Minh for the attacks and squeeze propaganda value out of such a graphic and disturbing image if Thé was only too willing to publicly claim the attack as his own? It seemed insufficient evidence of an American conspiracy. Perhaps Greene knew information he could not disclose. British intelligence certainly believed there to be secret American support for Thé, and the French security services were apparently wary of attacking the rebel bandit because of his involvement with American elements. There is, though, no hard evidence of American complicity with Thé at this time.

WHEN GREENE LEFT VIETNAM IN MARCH 1952, the French were becoming increasingly dependent on American support. De Lattre had returned to Paris at the beginning of the year, dying shortly thereafter of cancer. Giap kept up the pressure with his guerrilla attacks, and by the end of the year the United States bore a third of the cost of the war.[29] By early 1954, the Americans were responsible for up to 80 percent of the cost. Even with some five hundred thousand troops under French command, there seemed little hope of making any tangible gains; the best the French could hope for was to perpetuate an expensive stalemate. The war was becoming more and more unpopular in France, and the idea of a negotiated settlement, as had ended the Korean War, held wide appeal.

A bullish Dwight Eisenhower exhorted the French to keep fighting and even pondered direct intervention, but with the military still exhausted from the Korean War, there was little

appetite for sending American troops into another Asian theater.[30] The Chinese, with 250,000 troops stationed on its border
with Vietnam as a precautionary measure, were also eager to
avoid being sucked into another costly war, as they had been in
Korea, and the Soviet Union was in the process of seeking more
constructive relations with the West. Talks were scheduled in
Geneva for May.

In an attempt to secure a stronger negotiating position, the
French and the Viet Minh sought a convincing victory in the
field. In the northwest, near the border with Laos, French forces
sought to lure Giap into a large-scale confrontation at Dien
Bien Phu. The French thought they had the superior firepower
but Giap outwitted them, using a huge labor force of 250,000
to drag heavy artillery into the surrounding mountains. Using these powerful guns, the Viet Minh destroyed the French
airstrip, denying them the ability to resupply. With the eyes of
the world on them, the French struggled to withstand the siege.
After fifty-five days of bombardment and a final massed assault,
they surrendered. The French were left to negotiate a settlement
with a weaker hand.

The Geneva Accords divided Vietnam in two along the Seventeenth Parallel, with the promise of elections that would unify
the country in 1956. The hard-liners in the Viet Minh wanted
greater concessions, but China warned their allies of the possibility of American intervention if they pushed harder. Ho Chi
Minh was persuaded to play the long game; he would doubtless
win any nationwide election if it were held. Realizing this, the
Americans refused to sign the agreement, fearing that it simply delayed the fall of the country to Communism. Setting out
to bolster South Vietnam, they finally found their Third Force
leader in Ngo Dinh Diem, who, despite French concerns, was appointed prime minister by Emperor Bao Dai in June 1954. Diem
was fervently opposed to Communism and colonialism, and de-

spite his authoritarian methods and unabashed nepotism, the Americans helped him take control of the country. In 1955, he got rid of Bao Dai by transforming South Vietnam into a republic with himself as president.[31] Diem brought the bandits, rebels, and religious sects into line, reorganized the army, and defeated the criminal gang that controlled Saigon (although this was far from the end of corruption in the city). When the French failed to convince the Americans to get rid of Diem, they withdrew their forces.

The French had lost their colonial war, but the American war on Communism in Vietnam was only just beginning. Having attained power, Diem had no intention of jeopardizing it by agreeing to the elections supposedly mandated by the Geneva Accords. Nor did his backers seem interested in acquiescence.

Greene finished writing *The Quiet American* in June 1955 and it was published in the United States the following March. The publication of a novel that depicted American intervention in Vietnam as dangerously myopic at the very moment when the United States was becoming more heavily involved in the country was met with inevitable hostility. *Newsweek* launched a preemptive strike in January, accusing Greene of being anti-American and motivated in his vendetta against the United States by his being denied a visa under the McCarran Act (for his brief membership in the Communist Party). *Newsweek* later followed up this review with an article about how *The Quiet American* had received glowing reviews in the Soviet Union, perhaps failing to grasp that their own hostility to the novel was a motivating factor in its popularity in official Communist circles. Offense was not taken exclusively by McCarthyites and hard-line anti-Communists. In *The New Yorker*, A. J. Liebling wrote a review that began bitchily dismissive and ended by lashing out at "Mr. Greene's nasty little plastic bomb" of a book. "There is a difference, after all," Liebling wrote, "between calling your over-successful off-shoot a silly ass and accusing him of murder."[32]

Greene might have been guilty of a certain amount of conspiratorial thinking, but American policy soon made his ideas flesh. A real-life Pyle emerged as a key player in Vietnam at the same time as the novel was published: Edward Lansdale, a former OSS officer, waged a large-scale secret campaign against North Vietnam and did as much as anyone to take the United States into war. Even before Diem was established as a leader sympathetic to U.S. interests, the CIA set up a special unit, the Saigon Military Mission, which was separate to their Saigon station, and was run by Lansdale.[33] In direct violation of the Geneva Accords, the Mission sent secret squads into North Vietnam to conduct sabotage, to circulate propaganda, and to contaminate fuel supplies (many of these fighters were captured, some even defected). When Diem came to power, Lansdale was one of his closest advisors. So similar was Lansdale to Pyle that it was frequently assumed that Greene must have based his character on him. Like Pyle, Lansdale was a staunch believer in American exceptionalism and was willing to use clandestine methods to achieve his aims. Like Pyle, he even had a pet dog that followed him everywhere. Perhaps most uncanny was the fact that Lansdale at one stage even sought to cultivate General Thé as part of his plan to build a Third Force in Indochina.

As American involvement increased year by year, so the reputation of Greene's novel grew. It was not just that it had so accurately diagnosed the problems the French faced in Indochina, but it was eerily prescient in the way it predicted United States involvement. To a generation of American reporters, following Fowler's beat a decade later, the book was an essential item in their luggage. As David Halberstam later remembered, the correspondents sent out to cover the Vietnam War had whole chunks of *The Quiet American* committed to memory. "It was our Bible," he said.[34]

TWENTY-ONE

Akhmatova, Fast & Solzhenitsyn

LENINGRAD, NEW YORK & EKIBASTUZ, 1952–1956

IN AUGUST 1950, Aleksandr Solzhenitsyn arrived in the middle of the night at the Ekibastuz camp complex in the remote steppes of Kazakhstan. The camps were lit up by bright floodlights, allowing the prisoners—known as *zeks*—to see the lengths to which the authorities had gone to keep them in this place. Solzhenitsyn and his cohort were assigned to the camp for political prisoners—considered much more dangerous by the regime than ordinary criminals—which was secured by two fences, between which dogs prowled. All around the perimeter was a strip of freshly plowed land, the idea being that any prisoner who somehow managed to get over the fences would leave footprints behind. Inside the camp, the barracks where the prisoners slept had bars on the windows and doors secured by heavy padlocks.[1]

The journey to Ekibastuz had been arduous. Solzhenitsyn had been arrested in February 1945 while serving on the Prussian Front for writing letters to a friend in which he made jokes at the expense of Stalin. Despite being a decorated artillery officer, he was accused of creating anti-Soviet propaganda and imprisoned in the Lubyanka, where the Special Board of the NKVD sentenced him to eight years in the camps. The first months of his sentence had involved a peripatetic journey through the prisons of Moscow and its surroundings: first Butyrki jail, then the Krasnaya Presnya transit prison, then the "New Jerusalem," a work camp thirty miles west of Moscow, then Kaluga Gate, before returning to Butyrki.[2]

It was in the latter that he discovered that thanks to his undergraduate degree in mathematics and physics, he was to be assigned to a prison institute, known as a *sharashka,* where inmates did scientific research for the various arms of the state. (It was also a way of exploiting the talents of the large number of technical experts who had been purged in the preceding decade.) In these institutes the work was less arduous, the conditions more sanitary, and the rations better, and Solzhenitsyn, who had harbored literary ambitions since his youth, began writing poems. Despite this upturn in his fortunes, Solzhenitsyn was deeply troubled by the fact that he and his fellow inmates were putting their specialist knowledge at the service of Stalin's postwar industrialization program. He was particularly impressed when Dmitri Panin, with whom he had become friends, invented a mechanical coding device, but destroyed the technical drawings before they fell into the hands of the NKVD.

Gradually, Solzhenitsyn's behavior became more insubordinate, and, along with Panin he was transferred out of the relative comfort of the *sharashka.* The long journey east began with crossing vast swathes of the country in a "Stolypin car," a train carriage that had no windows, and cells instead of compartments. Solzhenitsyn was eventually held in the old, damp prison of Omsk (where Dostoevsky had been imprisoned) before being taken across the Kazakhstan desert in the back of a truck crammed full of other prisoners. On arrival in Ekibastuz, he had his head shaved and was issued with patches to be sewn onto his camp clothes, onto which would be painted the number by which he would henceforth be known to the prison authorities. The sense of isolation was profound; stretching around them for hundreds of miles was nothing but the flat steppe, the vultures circling high above often the only other living creature in sight. Once a month they could receive a parcel, but only two times a year were the prisoners permitted to send a letter back to the outside world.

The discipline in these camps was severe. Guards trained machine guns on the *zeks* when they moved from the barracks to roll call, from roll call to the canteen, and from canteen to the worksite. Most of the jobs inside the camp were administered by regular criminals, who were incentivized to punish the "politicals." Solzhenitsyn was fortunate in one sense in that he fell in with a brigade that was assigned to bricklaying, which was less punishing than some of the other jobs in the camp. He would later write about the strange sense of satisfaction he derived from being good at his work, about the feeling of solidarity among the brigade as they made sure they met their daily quota. But then Solzhenitsyn would come to himself and remember they were building the walls to their own prison.

In Ekibastuz he was permitted the use of a pencil and paper, on the condition that everything was submitted to the wardens for inspection.[3] Every opportunity he got, he would write out the poems he was composing in his head, but because writing anything about the camps, or anything that was critical of the regime, was risky as it could land the author with a spell in the hole, or worse, he would commit his lines to memory and destroy the fragments of paper in the barracks stove. Solzhenitsyn's main literary project was a long autobiographical poem, which he called "The Way," and which he committed to memory using a rosary of his own construction. He estimated that during his time in the gulag he memorized some twelve thousand lines in this way.[4]

Solzhenitsyn was not alone—many other *zeks* turned to literature in the camp. For many it was a way of keeping themselves sane in inhuman conditions. Some of the camps had theater troupes, and while the content was censored by the authorities, their performances were a rare source of joy to many inmates. Others recited poems from memory to their fellow prisoners, who would often donate part of their rations in gratitude. Solzhenitsyn was very careful and only recited sections from "The Way" to his most trusted friends. He knew that if he wanted to find a larger audience, he would need to be patient, to wait until he could find himself in circumstances in which he could safely transcribe all the lines of poetry he had locked away. And for that to happen he needed to survive, starting with the winter.

In *One Day in the Life of Ivan Denisovich*, a novel for which he drew on his first winter in Ekibastuz, Solzhenitsyn has the eponymous Ivan, an uneducated but cunning *zek*, ask an almost existential question: "How can you expect a man who's warm to understand a man who's cold?"[5] In one sense, the novel, not published until 1962, is itself an attempt to answer that question, an attempt, in two hundred compressed pages, to give the reader a sense of the misery of the gulag winter. After an apparently mild autumn, the seasonal change was marked by a chilling wind, which blew across thousands of miles of steppe without interruption. The next development was the drop in temperature, down to a near-unimaginable thirty or forty degrees below zero, conditions in which the smallest error in judgment could result in death. Solzhenitsyn would wake to find ice two inches thick on the windows of the barracks, but no matter the cold, the brigade would still have to assemble for roll call and head off to meet its work quota for the day, even if the mortar was freezing in the buckets. What *One Day in the Life of Ivan Denisovich* makes clear is the importance of ensuring one's camp clothing was well maintained and that any other protective layers of any sort were invaluable. As a bricklayer, Solzhenitsyn had to be especially attentive to his mittens, ensuring that any holes were immediately fixed, because if you touched the brick with your bare skin it would immediately stick to it and you would have to tear your hand away, leaving lumps of skin behind.[6]

What made things worse was the feeling that these conditions would never end. While many prisoners had been sentenced to a certain number of years in jail, this often became irrelevant as the authorities would arbitrarily extend their incarceration; the camp commander at Ekibastuz apparently boasted that he had only ever allowed the release of one prisoner. There were escape attempts, but even the most successful of these resulted in the prisoners—confined by geography as much as by fences—being rounded up a few weeks later. With little or no hope of release, the *zeks* had little incentive beyond—the considerable—fear of punishment to obey the rules and meet work quotas. At Ekibastuz there were mutinies that resulted in the prisoners winning some concessions but often at the cost of severe retribution by the authorities.[7]

Stalin had no incentive to release the prisoners, either. For a state that was seeking to recover after the Second World War, to industrialize as quickly as possible, and to keep pace in an arms race with the United States, the gulag was a source of valuable slave labor. In the 1930s, the prison camps had been integrated into the Soviet economy, with prisoners exploited to mine metals and cut timber, and when war broke out, factories had been built adjacent to the camps to produce ammunition, weapons, and vehicles for the Red Army. In the early 1950s, the gulag population reached its peak, with 2.4 million prisoners in total.[8]

In 1952, to try to motivate the prisoners, a system was introduced by which they were paid a cut of what the camp earned, although that was then "taxed" (to pay the guards and for the upkeep of the prison) and the remainder, about 13 percent of their original earnings, divided in two with half to be spent in

vouchers on additional foodstuffs (including sweets and con-
densed milk) and the other half to be paid out to them on their
eventual release.

It did not take much insight to realize that this new system,
while making life more comfortable in the camps, did not increase the prospect of release. Solzhenitsyn was entering the last
year of his sentence, but half expected new charges at any time.
To make matters worse, in January 1952, his second winter in
Ekibastuz, he was admitted to the camp hospital with a worrying lump in his groin. He was diagnosed with cancer and operated upon, the surgeons cutting out the tumor, leaving sandbags
resting on the wound to stanch the bleeding.[9] He made a good
recovery but feared the disease's return. Like so many of those
he had known in the gulag, he feared he would die out in this
camp on the Kazakhstan steppe.

IN LENINGRAD, Akhmatova held out little hope for Stalin's renewed war on literature abating. On November 6, 1949, Lev
Gumilev had come home on his lunch break from his work as a
researcher at the Museum of Ethnography as usual, checking up
on his mother, who had been running a fever and suffering from
chest pains and a violent cough. This time, though, the secret
police were waiting for him. He was forced to quickly gather
up what possessions he needed and was taken away. Akhmatova
was so distressed by the shock of the arrest that she lost consciousness. For the following days she was bedbound and feverish, desperate for news of her son.[10]

Lev's arrest brought back all the trauma of the Great Terror.
One of the poems Akhmatova had read to Isaiah Berlin was *Requiem*, composed after Lev had been arrested and sent to the
camps in 1938. Partway through her recitation she had broken

off to tell him about the circumstances of the arrest and, in the months following, how she had been tormented by the refusal of the authorities to let her know what had become of him. She had spent day after day in the lines outside the walls of the Kresty prison waiting to hear any news of him. In a story that she later used as a preface to *Requiem,* she recounted how one day someone in the prison line recognized her and, as a result, the woman standing behind her, through "lips blue with cold," asked Akhmatova: "And could you describe *this?*" *Requiem* had been her response to that challenge.

One of the cruelties of life under Stalinism was that if a loved one was taken away in the middle of the night, one dare not kick up too much of a fuss for fear of further retribution being enacted on one's family. It was almost impossible to get any kind of official acknowledgment or explanation; people simply disappeared. By writing a poem that described her own suffering after the disappearance of her son and her ignorance of what had become of him, Akhmatova hoped to give voice to all those thousands who had suffered a similar fate, caught between dwindling hope and uncertain bereavement. If the Stalinist state was deaf to their grief, then at least Akhmatova could allow them to speak to posterity.[11]

Lev's new arrest threatened even that, however. One of the reasons she told Berlin not to transcribe *Requiem* was that she believed it would soon be published. Now it was among the evidence she needed to destroy. Methodically and ruthlessly, she went through her notebooks and manuscripts and burned anything that might be used against her and, in turn, her son. It was first and foremost an act of self-preservation but, in a perverse way, it was also an act of faith in her poems. Some of them, at least, she believed would survive their cremation, whether because they had been scrawled clandestinely on scraps of paper by listeners at private readings, or preserved in Akhmatova's memory, waiting for a time when their transcription might not threaten her life or that of Lev. That, at least, was the hope.

Once Akhmatova had recovered enough to get out of bed, she resolved to track down her son. She discovered that he had been transferred to Lefortovo Prison in Moscow and left for the capital immediately, taking with her whatever money she had to give to him. Staying with friends in Moscow, she tried to find out what he was being charged with, whether he was healthy, when he would be sentenced. She was permitted to hand over one hundred rubles a month, delivered through a small window by the prison entrance (that this money was accepted was one of the only ways of knowing if the recipient was alive). In September 1950 Lev was sentenced to ten years of hard labor in the gulag in Kazakhstan. The rules of the camp meant he would be allowed only very limited correspondence; Akhmatova could send him one parcel per month.[12]

Having for so long refused to "repent," Akhmatova had no qualms about using her poetry to try to save her son. With the help of Alexander Fadeyev, she published a short cycle of poems, "In Praise of Peace," in the magazine *Ogonyok*. In a clunky style that seemed almost a pastiche of socialist realism, these poems lauded Stalin for rebuilding the country after the war. If Stalin noticed Akhmatova's act of abasement, he gave no sign. Her situation was desperate. Lev was being held first in a camp near Karaganda, some three hundred kilometers south of Ekibastuz in Kazakhstan, before being transferred to the Kemerovo region of Siberia. With only a small income from translation work, she struggled to get the money together to send the parcels and relied increasingly on friends. In May 1951, under severe stress, she suffered a heart attack. There appeared little hope as the country tilted back toward the terror of the 1930s. Stalin, ill of health, bad of temper, and seeing enemies everywhere, was preparing to consolidate his power in the way he knew best.

In 1952 Stalin accused a group of doctors, almost all of whom were Jewish, of plotting to kill him and other prominent Soviet leaders (Zhdanov's death, in 1948, was supposedly a result of this scheme). As had happened with the Kirov assassination, the plot itself seemed to be a convenient vehicle by which Stalin could expose a larger conspiracy and, by implicating them in it, ensure the removal of anyone seeking to dilute his power. Hundreds of doctors were arrested in September 1952 as the investigation began to expand at a dramatic rate.

Meanwhile, Stalin announced that for the first time in thirteen years there would be a Party Congress. In the lead-up to the meeting, which took place in October 1952, Stalin published a twenty-five-thousand-word essay entitled "The Economic Problems of Socialism in the USSR," of which more than 20 million copies were printed. The essay set the tone for the Congress, promoting an uncompromising stance in both domestic economic policy and international relations.[13] Stalin was hardening Moscow's position, speaking ominously of "capitalist encirclement."[14] At the Congress the speeches warned of traitors and fifth columnists while Stalin, with rumors of his deteriorating health abounding, put any potential successors on notice by expanding the nine-man Politburo into a twenty-five-strong Presidium. At a closed meeting of the Central Committee he denounced his previously trusted aides Vyacheslav Molotov, Anastas Mikoyan, and Kliment Voroshilov. During the Great Terror, he had killed off all remaining members of Lenin's first Politburo; now it appeared he was looking to eliminate his own.

The stage was set for another round of show trials and mass purges that would allow Stalin to eliminate his perceived enemies. In January 1953, the nine architects of the Doctors' Plot,

belonging to a supposed "Zionist spy organization," were denounced on the front page of Pravda, part of a "tsunami of an-
tisemitic propaganda."[15] In hospitals some patients refused to
take medicine they believed to be poisoned. There were rumors
of mass deportations planned for Soviet Jews. With their leader
growing ever more paranoid and unpredictable, even the most
powerful politicians in the Presidium feared they might be next
to disappear.

ON MARCH 1, 1953, having spent the day fearful of disturbing
Stalin in his quarters, at 10 P.M., the guards at his dacha in Kunt-
sevo decided to send in a maid with some mail that needed his
attention. Stalin had been up drinking with his inner circle until 6 A.M. the previous night and it was not uncommon for him
to sleep late, but as the night drew in, his staff became nervous.
The maid found him sprawled on the floor, his pajamas soaked
in urine. He had suffered a severe stroke, could barely move, and
could not talk.[16] The news of his collapse was not made public
until three days later, on March 4, when it was announced on
Radio Moscow. The following day he began to vomit blood, his
blood pressure dropped, and he struggled to breathe. He died
that night.

In the ensuing power struggle, Nikita Khrushchev emerged
as Stalin's heir, despite Georgy Malenkov having been favored
for the role. Another candidate for the leadership, Lavrentiy
Beria, the head of the secret police, was outmaneuvered by
Khrushchev and his allies, arrested, taken to a secret facility under military escort (including twenty tanks), and, the following
December, executed by a shot to the back of the head, a procedure with which he was intimately familiar. The irony was that
Beria had been instrumental in proposing liberal reforms in the
aftermath of Stalin's death, although he did so not out of any

conviction but out of political calculation. With Beria gone, the secret police were once again reorganized, taking on a new acronym: the KGB.

Khrushchev soon began pushing through reforms, and under his guidance the Stalinist excesses of the postwar period came to an end. A prisoner amnesty was declared, food prices were lowered, and the Doctors' Plot disavowed. The change in atmosphere within the Soviet Union was reflected in less aggressive posturing in its foreign policy, too. Stalin had been demanding his allies continue to tie up American forces in the Korean War, but by June the new Kremlin leadership softened this position sufficiently for an armistice to be agreed, effectively ending the conflict.[17] In the months that followed Stalin's death, there were signs that it might prompt more radical change. There were revolts in the Siberian camps of Kengir, Norilsk, and Vorkuta, and in East Germany a construction workers' strike developed into widespread unrest.[18] In both cases, the military was used to restore order—the Kremlin wanted reform on its terms, not rebellion.

Akhmatova knew that the country faced a reckoning. The crimes that had been committed under Stalin had affected almost everyone in the country, whether victims or perpetrators:

Shakespeare's dramas—all these effective villainies, passions, duels—are trifles, child's play, in comparison with what we had to live through. I won't even dare speak about what those punished or sent to the camps endured. This cannot be expressed in words. But each of our wonderful lives is a Shakespearean drama raised to the thousandth degree. Mute separations, mute black, bloody events in every family. Invisible mourning worn by mothers and wives. Now the arrested are returning, and two Russias stare at each other in the eyes: the ones that put them in prison and the ones who were put in prison. A new epoch has begun.[19]

Yet if Akhmatova was relieved no longer to be living in Stalin's "torture chamber" she also believed that there was no "glue" with which to repair all the damage done. And while prisoners were coming home, Lev was not among them.

As Akhmatova continued to seek her son's release, the situation for her and her fellow writers gradually improved. She was allowed to work on translations and even offered a dacha in a writers' colony outside Leningrad.[20] The prospect of being rehabilitated was now far less remote. The period of cultural liberation that followed Stalin's death became known as "the Thaw," taking its name from Ilya Ehrenburg's 1954 novella, in which he dared to mention the taboo subject of the Yezhov purges. That same year, the work of Isaac Babel returned to bookshops and libraries. The poetry of Marina Tsvetaeva and the strange novels of Yuri Olesha were also rehabilitated, as were those books of Dostoevsky that had previously been considered subversive.[21] In 1956, Vladimir Dudintsev published the novel *Not by Bread Alone*, a huge popular success, and one openly critical of economic stagnation and excessive bureaucracy.

In February 1956, Khrushchev made a speech to a closed session of the Twentieth Party Congress of the Communist Party of the Soviet Union, in which he took the bold step of attacking Stalin and his legacy directly.[22] To a stunned audience, the First Secretary said the country had been in thrall to a "cult of the individual," and that it "is impermissible and foreign to the spirit of Marxism-Leninism to elevate one person, to transform him into a superman possessing supernatural characteristics, akin to those of a god. Such a man supposedly knows everything, sees everything, thinks for everyone, can do anything, is infallible in his behavior." He accused Stalin of vain self-aggrandizement, including the claims he made about his leadership during the Second World War. But most important, Khrushchev focused his speech on his predecessor's deployment of "administrative violence, mass repressions, and terror" on the population of the Soviet Union. Using materials drawn from the NKVD archives he pointed out the suspicious circumstances surrounding the Kirov assassination, the event that had triggered the Great Terror of the 1930s. He said the files showed evidence of hundreds of thousands of false accusations, wrongful imprisonments and executions, and invented conspiracies, including the Doctors' Plot.

There was no doubt that Khrushchev's motives in making the speech were in part self-serving—he had, after all, been part of Stalin's Politburo and a participant in the purges—but the break with Stalinism was complete. While he had been speaking to a closed session, word of his stunning address was soon speeding around the country and across the world. The process of de-Stalinization, which had begun surreptitiously in the years after his death, now became formalized Kremlin policy, as the Soviet Union began to open up in all manner of ways. They joined the International Labour Organization, the World Health Organization, the Red Cross, the International Olympic Committee, and the United Nations Educational, Scientific, and Cultural Organization. Between 1956 and 1958, 2 million Soviet citizens traveled abroad and there were 1.5 million foreign visitors to the country.[23] Writers and artists suddenly found new possibilities open to them and twenty thousand were sent abroad on cultural exchanges between 1955 and 1958.[24] Initially at least, Khrushchev de-escalated Cold War tensions: he removed troops from Austria and Finland, relinquished Soviet territorial claims against Turkey, and reconciled with Tito's Yugoslavia. The Kremlin even began the process of ending the gulag system of forced labor.

The month after the "Secret Speech," Fadeyev wrote to the Chief Military Prosecutor on Akhmatova's behalf, explaining Lev's case, hoping the changed atmosphere might finally secure his release. Fadeyev pointed out that not only was Lev a "serious scholar" who might have been subject to false accusations by "careerists," but also that his mother, after being condemned by Zhdanov, had shown herself to be a "true Soviet patriot." The propagandist poetry she had published had not been in vain, after all. Akhmatova and her son were reunited in May.[25]

LIKE SO MANY COMMUNISTS who had remained loyal to the Party through the Show Trials and the Nazi-Soviet pact, Howard Fast was devastated when he learned of the death of Stalin. While some of his Party friends expressed relief that he was gone, Fast had always been a loyalist. He had even gone so far as to defend Stalin against accusations of anti-Semitism during the Doctors' Plot, claiming that he saw no reasons to disbelieve the Kremlin's claims of Zionist conspiracy. He asked to be shown evidence of "any single act of antisemitism which has occurred in any of the socialist nations."[26] For Fast the Cold War had become a zero-sum game, by which any criticism of the Soviet Union would only play into the hands of his enemies. And at the time of Stalin's death, that meant Joseph McCarthy.

On February 13, 1953, Fast had made a combative appearance in front of the Senate Subcommittee on Investigations, which had been entrusted to McCarthy by the Eisenhower administration. The committee had traditionally been used to investigate corruption in the executive branch, but McCarthy exploited its flexible mandate to continue his pursuit of perceived Communists, hiring Roy Cohn, a twenty-six-year-old lawyer who had helped prosecute the Rosenbergs, as chief counsel (Fast was one of the Rosenbergs' most vocal champions). To send a message to the outspoken novelist, the subpoena had been issued in the middle of the night.

Fast had not been the target of this investigation; rather, he was being used as evidence against his former government employers. McCarthy's first target was the Voice of America, the State Department's foreign radio operation, which was used to combat Soviet propaganda. McCarthy believed the VOA had been infiltrated by Communists during the Second World War, when it was part of the Office of War Information. Fast worked for the OWI in 1942 and 1943, which seemed proof enough.

In an executive session (held behind closed doors) on February 13, 1953, Fast jumped through many of the same hoops as at his HUAC hearing. Cohn repeatedly asked if he had been a member of the Communist Party, and Fast responded each time by pleading the First and the Fifth Amendments. Cohn and McCarthy then got down to business, asking Fast about how he got the job in the OWI and which government department had brought out editions of his books. Fast ducked and weaved, trying to be evasive and claiming to have forgotten names. At one stage McCarthy said that he was not a reader of Fast's books. "You missed something good," quipped Benedict Wolf, Fast's lawyer. "If you are interested in the history of the United States," Fast added, "it might be important to read them." McCarthy was unimpressed and demanded that Fast produce his records. Before leaving, Fast made a statement condemning "the gestapo methods" employed in his being issued with a subpoena, with people banging on his door in the middle of the night. "Would you say they were the GPU type tactics or NKVD type tactics also?" McCarthy responded. Fast stuck by his choice of description.

Fast had to return five days later to face McCarthy a second time, this time in a public session, with a packed audience and with the TV cameras rolling. Once again there was the back-and-forth about Fast's membership in the Communist Party, only this time Fast, perhaps aware of the larger audience, could not resist taunting the committee. He began to explain why he was not answering, giving the history of the Fifth Amendment, but he was repeatedly shut down. McCarthy said he was not about to let the hearing turn into a "transmission belt for the communist party."[27] Fast then got into a shouting match with Senator Charles Potter, who lost both legs in World War Two. Potter asked him if he would serve his country in Korea if he were drafted. Fast retorted angrily he had been serving his country his whole life. Potter demanded he answer the question. Fast said he would serve if drafted but refused to answer whether he would fight against a Communist enemy. According to one report this brought a "murmur of obvious disapproval" from the audience.[28]

McCarthy went after Fast's books next, making a target of the United States Information Service's Overseas Library program. Cohn and David Schine, a McCarthy staffer, had been dispatched to Europe to ferret out anti-American books in these libraries. A directive went out banning books written by "any controversial persons, Communists, fellow travellers, et cetera" and while the phrase "any controversial persons" was withdrawn the following day, the libraries were soon being cleared of anything remotely controversial. Needless to say, Fast's novels were some of the first to go. In a moment that became symbolic of the excesses of McCarthyism, some libraries, without a place to store them, burned the banned books.

While Fast's books were being banned and destroyed, the Soviet Union decided to celebrate them by awarding him the Stalin Prize that December. He was pictured, with the other winners, on the front cover of *Pravda*. The prize was awarded by the International Committee, headed by Louis Aragon, and as well as a medal Fast received $25,000. (Without a passport, Fast received the prize at a ceremony in New York.) He later claimed that, while welcome, it represented only a small fraction of the royalties he was due for sales in the Soviet Union. He had a point. Fast was a hugely popular author in Russia, and between 1948 and 1957, "over 2,500,000 copies of his work were printed in the 12 languages of the U.S.S.R."[29] All his works were translated and his novels, especially *The Last Frontier* and *Freedom Road*, were required reading in schools and universities. Suffice it to say that being on the front cover of *Pravda* did not help Fast when it came to defending himself from accusations of being a Communist stooge back home.

Going into 1954, things began to look better for Fast and the radical left in the United States. The landmark case *Brown v. Board of Education* ruled segregation in public schools illegal, and civil rights and labor groups were organizing more and more effectively. The Red Scare was diminishing as McCarthy, increasingly reckless and drinking heavily, began to overreach. He expanded his investigation to the U.S. Army and began calling out the Eisenhower administration for failing to be tough enough on Communism. In March of that year, somebody had leaked records of McCarthy's efforts to secure special treatment for Schine, who had been drafted into the army in November 1953 while working on McCarthy's staff. His boss, along with Cohn, had sought to prevent Schine being called up and, when those efforts failed, both men had used their influence—and the threat of investigation—to ensure Schine got an easy posting with weekend passes. Cohn's motivation for trying to protect Schine was his intimate—if not sexual—relationship with the staffer. McCarthy accused the army of seeking to smear him as a response to his investigation of Communist infiltration in their ranks. As a result, the Senate convened a hearing of its Subcommittee on Investigations, chaired by the Republican senator

Karl Mundt (South Dakota), to get to the bottom of the matter. The Army-McCarthy hearings, as they were known, were broadcast on TV, and McCarthy's boorish behavior turned public opinion against him. Sensing weakness, the politicians who previously feared him cut him down. "America is beginning to shake loose of the nightmare of this past decade," Fast said.

Then his world was turned upside down by Khrushchev's Secret Speech, which he described as a "shattering and terrible analysis of Stalin and his crimes." The effect of reading it was "bone-chilling" and little wonder, for not only had he been lied to all these years, but he had been complicit in amplifying those lies.[30] In the causes of racial justice and workers' rights, he had also served the ends of a criminally totalitarian regime. It was the kind of revelation to break one's faith.

Fast later claimed he had nursed private doubts for years, particularly around Stalin's anti-Semitic policies of the late 1940s and early 1950s. He had even aired his concerns at a secret meeting with Fadeyev in a basement room of the Salle Pleyel in Paris, where much of the 1950 Peace Congress took place. The two had corresponded since meeting at the Scientific and Cultural Conference for World Peace at the Waldorf the previous year, and while Fast's later claims that he brought formal charges of anti-Semitism against the Soviet Central Committee were a self-aggrandizing fantasy, he did raise a number of issues.[31] Foremost was the fate of the Yiddish writers who had been arrested the previous year. The authors David Bergelson, Itzik Feffer, Peretz Markish, and Leib Kvitko had all disappeared, and the actor and theater director Solomon Mikhoels had been conveniently killed in a car accident. In response to Fast's concerns, Fadeyev simply said: "There is no antisemitism in the Soviet Union." It was a phrase Fadeyev repeated like a mantra until, when Fast pushed him too far, he disgorged a ludicrous conspiracy theory in which Itzik Feffer had been recruited as a radical Zionist agent on a 1943 visit to the United States and was engaged in a conspiracy to establish an anti-Communist Jewish state in Crimea. By this theory, when Mikhoels found out, Feffer had him killed—and the other writers were in on the conspiracy.[32] This was the cover story for the overnight destruction of Yiddish culture in Russia. Fast knew this was nonsense but maintained Party discipline, just as he would do with the Doctors' Plot.

After Khrushchev's speech, Fast prepared to break with the Party, further convinced of his decision by the brutality with which the Soviet Union repressed the uprising in Hungary in October of that year. He left the CPUSA shortly thereafter. In January 1957, the story of Fast's defection broke and was considered momentous enough to earn its place on the front page of the *New York Times*.[33] By the end of the year he published *The Naked God*, an account of his time in the Party, in which he declared Communism to be a "prison of man's best and boldest dreams."

While his defection was greeted with outrage and smears in the Soviet Union, Fast soon worked his way back into the cultural mainstream in the United States. In 1958, he sold the film rights of *Spartacus* to Kirk Douglas, who had Fast write a first draft of the script. When that proved unusable, Douglas asked veteran screenwriter Dalton Trumbo to fix it. Trumbo was one of the Hollywood Ten, who had been blacklisted after their appearance before HUAC, so the film had a former Communist scriptwriter helping adapt a novel written by a former Communist author, both of whom had been sent to prison for contempt in HUAC hearings.

In *Spartacus*, Fast created a climactic scene in which the Roman general Crassus demands the slave army give up Spartacus in exchange for leniency. In response, every soldier declares, "I am Spartacus." In adapting this scene for the screen, Trumbo said it was a way of celebrating the solidarity among radical intellectuals who refused to name names at the HUAC and

McCarthy hearings. Alas, the same solidarity did not pertain to the Hollywood studio. Fast claimed he was "directly responsible for half the finished script," but the credit went to Trumbo.[34] Fast also described working with "obstinate and arrogant" Douglas as a "nightmare" and was irked that Stanley Kubrick, the director, and actors Laurence Olivier and Peter Ustinov had also re-written parts of the script. Fast was mollified by the vast earnings he made not just from the film's success but from the sales of a paperback reprint of his novel. Later on, Fast and his family disputed Douglas's claim that it was he who had heroically ended the persecution of Communist writers in the American film industry by employing Trumbo to adapt Fast's novels.[35] Other directors and producers had employed blacklisted writers before, it was true, but in the mythology of Hollywood, the making of *Spartacus* became the symbolic moment when the blacklist was broken and the specter of McCarthyism was finally exorcised.

SOLZHENITSYN DID NOT KNOW IT AT THE TIME, but Stalin died on the first night the former *zek* spent without an armed guard in eight years. To his surprise, Solzhenitsyn had been released from Ekibastuz at the end of his sentence. As a political prisoner there was no question of him returning to normal society; instead he had been sent into internal exile in Kok Terek, a small town in the far east of Kazakhstan, just over two hundred kilometers from the border with China. It had taken eighteen days to get there. Despite having only his jacket for a bed in the mud hut that was his temporary new home, Solzhenitsyn slept soundly that night, enjoying the novelty of being alone. The next morning, he was woken by his landlady urging him to go into town and listen to what was being piped over the loudspeakers in the central square (she had been too frightened to tell him herself).[36] When he made out what was being broadcast, he had to control the urge to celebrate. It had been making a joke at Stalin's expense that had caused him to be plunged into the gulag in the first place, and he knew better than to show his true feelings, so he made his way back to his hut wearing a mask of solemnity.

As an exile, Solzhenitsyn had to conform to many restrictions: he had to carry a special identity card and was forbidden to leave Kok Terek unless he secured special permission from the Ministry of Internal Affairs. He also had to report to local officials twice a month. But he could get a job, he could live where he wanted within the town, and, most important of all, he had the privacy that would give him the freedom to write. The very day of Stalin's death, he returned to his room and wrote a poem to commemorate it. And now he was writing not just to console himself, he was writing to bear witness.

Over the following three years, the gulag ejected some five million prisoners.[37] Among them were writers who were determined to tell their countrymen—and the wider world—what had happened. Varlam Shalamov was also released in 1953, and he spent the next two decades composing his blackly funny short stories about camp life, collected as *Kolyma Tales*.[38] Two years later, Yevgenia Ginzburg was released from Kolyma (her second spell in the gulag), after which she began writing her masterful memoir, *Journey into the Whirlwind*.

Akhmatova claimed that "not a single piece of literature" had been printed under Stalin's rule.[39] His ruthlessness had meant any act of dissent resulted in often lethal consequences; those few who dared to mock him, like Akhmatova's friend Osip Mandelstam, wound up dead. In his 1945 memorandum about Russian literature under Stalin, Isaiah Berlin wrote that there was a "defeatist acceptance of the present situation among most of the intellectuals" and that there was "little fight left even in the most rebellious and individualistic."[40]

Berlin had underestimated Russia's writers, however. In his

dacha at Peredelkino, Boris Pasternak, an admirer and ally of Akhmatova, heard about Stalin's death as he was finishing the first draft of a novel whose explosive capacity not even he could fully understand. In Moscow, a young literary scholar, Andrei Sinyavsky, whose faith in Communism had been broken by the suppression of Akhmatova and Pasternak, wandered the streets of the city, packed with mourners, and pondered his future, the seeds of his dissent already sown. And way out in Kok Terek, Solzhenitsyn continued to write as he rebuilt his life. He knew very well that the written word was a potent weapon in the Soviet Union—it was what had landed him in the gulag in the first place. Now he prepared to turn that weapon back on the regime. Russia's writers not only had plenty of fight left in them, they were about to start the kind of fights that would change the course of the Cold War.

TWENTY-TWO

Wright

PARIS, ACCRA & BANDUNG, 1952–1956

IN JANUARY 1955, Richard Wright was home alone in his Paris apartment. His wife, Ellen, had taken his two daughters out to allow him to focus on his latest project. He had recently returned from a trip to Spain and was working on a book about the country under Franco's dictatorship. He began distractedly reading the newspaper when a story caught his attention. "I bent forward and read the item a second time," he wrote. "*Twenty-nine free and independent nations of Asia and Africa are meeting in Bandung, Indonesia, to discuss 'racialism and colonialism'* . . . what is this? I scanned the list of nations involved: China, India, Indonesia, Japan, Burma, Egypt, Turkey, the Philippines, Ethiopia, Gold Coast, etc. My God! I began a rapid calculation of the populations of the nations listed and, when my total topped the billion mark, I stopped, pulled off my glasses and tried to think. . . ."

Wright got up, paced the room, and tried to organize his whirling thoughts. The potential consequences of such a meeting seemed huge; in the Cold War the nations of Africa and Asia were viewed as sites of contestation, to be protected from the ideological spread of rival influence. This conference suggested to Wright that these nations, many of them newly independent, were not going to be passive pawns in the global contest between the United States and the Soviet Union, but that they envisioned themselves as a third, independent force, some 1.5 billion strong.

"This smacked of something new," he thought, "something beyond Left and Right."[1]

The idea of the Bandung Conference resonated with Wright on a profoundly personal level. He was a black American who had grown up in a Jim Crow South that denied his very humanity; having escaped north to Chicago, he had sought solace from the terror of his childhood in the solidarity of Communism. Yet the apparent racial equality of the Communist Party concealed different kinds of restrictions on Wright's freedom, particularly when it came to his writing. Where was he to turn? The Party seemed only to want to exploit him for their own political ends, while the United States government trumpeted the cause of freedom to the world as it persecuted and oppressed its black citizens at home. Even as his first novel, *Native Son*, published in 1940, made him the most celebrated and successful African American novelist in the United States, Wright suffered daily abuse and humiliation (refusals of service, whispered slurs) in supposedly liberal New York City. That his wife, Ellen, was white, seemed only to compound the hostility.

This was the reason he was living in Paris in the first place. He had left the United States for France in May 1946 on the SS *Brazil,* and after the old cargo ship had sailed past the Statue of Liberty, he wrote in a letter to his friend Ralph Ellison that, "[a]lready the harsh race lines of America are fading."[2] He was not the first black writer to have sought solace in Paris: the Harlem Renaissance poets Countee Cullen and Langston Hughes had both lived there in the 1920s.

Arriving on the Continent, Wright and his family sailed into the port city of Le Havre past the wrecks of boats sunk during the war and then headed toward the capital. Despite the problems with the supply of heat and electricity, and the rationing of food and clothing, Wright felt liberated in Paris. For all these privations there remained the legacy of literary glamor; the Lost

Generation of Fitzgerald and Hemingway might be long gone, but Gertrude Stein was still there hosting literary salons. Indeed, accompanied by two limos from the American embassy, she had met Wright on his arrival in Paris and helped him get established in the city.[3]

Wright had not come to Paris to hang out with expat Americans, though, and he was soon part of the Left Bank café scene. He had met Simone de Beauvoir, Albert Camus, and Jean-Paul Sartre when they visited the United States at the end of the war, and when Sartre and Beauvoir launched *Les Temps Modernes* in October 1945, it included Wright's story "Fire and Cloud."[4] At the Café de Flore and Les Deux Magots, he found allies who shared his discomfort at being trapped in the ideological vise of the Cold War. They were repulsed by American racism and saw the postwar Americanization of Europe as a threat to French culture, but they were also wary of Soviet Communism and its capacity for foreign aggression and domestic suppression. When Sartre formed the Rassemblement Démocratique Révolutionnaire, a group that briefly championed a third way out of the bilateral conflict of the Cold War, Wright gladly joined.

Wright had not planned to settle in France, but after returning to the United States in 1947 he decided to make the move permanent. He found his homeland swept up in triumphalist "Americanism," and he was worried by the easy way people spoke of impending war with the Soviet Union. The Red Scare was entering its stride, and the predatory HUAC was sweeping through American cultural institutions. "Russia has her cultural purges and so do we; only in Russia it is official, and with us it is the force and so-called moral power of the community," he wrote. "But the results in the end are the same, that is, the suppression of the individual."[5]

The country had, to his mind, taken a hard turn to the right, away from Roosevelt's New Deal liberalism toward nationalism and anti-Communist intolerance; there was no sign, he thought, that winning a war against a fascist, racist enemy had done much to change attitudes back home. In the South, returning African American GIs were being lynched, while in Chicago there was a race riot designed to prevent black veterans from returning to state housing. Walking through Manhattan, Wright overheard passersby muttering the N-word just loud enough for him to hear. Beauvoir, who stayed with the Wrights in New York at the time, could not believe what she saw and heard. Feeling strangled by the "petty humiliations, daily insults," he returned to Paris for good.[6]

France, however, had its own problems. The political situation was unstable; the country veered from one end of the political spectrum to another as it sought to find the path to recovery from the war and reckon (or not) with its Vichy past. The conservatism of Charles de Gaulle offered one answer, the Communist Party of France another. The prestige of the nation had been badly damaged by the war, and many felt uncomfortable having to take money from the Americans, via the Marshall Plan, in order to get back on their feet. Such insecurity was one of the reasons that France was determined not to give up control of its colonies in Africa and Asia.

In the preceding month, Wright had been reading stories in the French newspapers of a growing insurrection in Algeria, led by the Front de Libération Nationale (FLN); for the preceding year, he had been reading about the defeat of the French colonial forces in their war with the Viet Minh in Indochina. Now the proposed meeting at Bandung seemed to herald a change in the world order. "The despised, the insulted, the hurt, the dispossessed—in short, the underdogs of the human race were meeting," he wrote.[7] Wright felt he was as well positioned as anyone to write about this meeting. "I'm an American Negro," he told Ellen that day, "as such, I have had a burden of race consciousness. So have these people. I worked in my youth as a common laborer and I have a class consciousness. So have these people." Her response was simple: "If you feel that way, you have to go."⁸

WRIGHT CERTAINLY UNDERSTOOD what it meant to be an outsider. His childhood, evoked so vividly in his memoir *Black Boy,* was one scarred by suffering. He was born near Natchez, Mississippi, the grandchild of slaves on both maternal and paternal sides. His father, a sharecropper, deserted the family when Wright was six years old, and his mother, unable to feed Richard and his younger brother, put them into an orphanage for a spell. The family moved to Jackson to stay with Wright's maternal grandmother and then out to his aunt and uncle's in Elaine, Arkansas, until they were forced to flee when his uncle, a saloon owner, was murdered by a local white man who wanted his business. The rest of the family fled under cover of night hearing that a lynch mob was coming for them. They continued a peripatetic existence, complicated by Wright's mother suffering a series of strokes. He was almost always hungry. He did not complete a year of formal schooling until he was twelve. Even though he was an excellent student, he had to drop out after just a few weeks of high school to earn money.

The family joined the Great Migration north to Chicago, trying to escape the terror of the Jim Crow South. Wright took what work he could find. He sat for the exams to be a postal clerk and, in the meantime, worked menial jobs, reading Dostoevsky, Proust, and Stein in the evenings. He began writing and joined an African American literary group on the South Side. With the onset of the Great Depression, Wright was sucked into radical politics. "Some mornings I found leaflets on my steps telling of China, Russia, and Germany," he wrote in *Black Boy,* "on some days I witnessed as many as five thousand jobless Negroes, led by Communists, surging through the streets."[9] He was skeptical but curious, and he began to frequent the South Side's Washington Park to listen to the Communist speakers. "I felt that Communists could not possibly have a sincere interest in Negroes," he wrote. "I was cynical and I would rather have heard a white man say that he hated Negroes, which I could have readily believed, than to have heard him say that he respected Negroes, which would have made me doubt him."[10]

Nevertheless, Abe Aaron, a Jewish friend from the post office and fellow aspiring writer, persuaded Wright to come to a meeting of the John Reed Club, chapters of which were established across the major cities of the United States to support left-wing writers. He took home magazines from his first meeting, read them through the night and, at dawn, in a fever of inspiration wrote "a wild, crude poem in free verse, coining images of black hands playing, working, holding bayonets, stiffening finally in death . . ."[11] The John Reed Club and the Communist Party made Wright feel welcome, and they encouraged him to write; for the first time in his life, he felt he belonged somewhere.

The problem Wright ran into was that he was a writer of ambition and talent. While he felt valued by the politics of Communism, when it came to literature it was not socialist realism but the modernist writing of Eliot, Joyce, and Stein that really spoke to him. Comrades questioned why he was reading "bourgeois" books and told him they would only "confuse" him.[12] At this time, he began doing research for a book about black Communists (he wanted to call it *Heroes, Red and Black*), but local Party officials suspected he might be spying—the paranoia and purges of the 1930s were not confined to Russia.[13] "I dismissed the warning about the Soviet Union's trouble with intellectuals," he wrote. "I felt that it simply did not apply to me."[14] He was mistaken. When Harry Hayward, a senior Party official depicted

George Orwell in Barcelona, leaving the Lenin barracks for the front in the Spanish Civil War. Orwell can be seen toward the back towering over his fellow POUM fighters, 1937. *UCL Library Services, Special Collections, Orwell Archive*

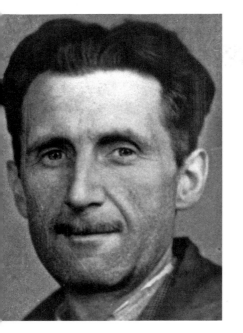

George Orwell's accreditation photograph for membership in the National Union of Journalists, 1943. *Branch National Union of Journalists*

Stephen Spender, whose combination of poetic talent and good looks made him a star of the 1930s literary scene, 1934. *World History Archive/Alamy*

Andrei Zhdanov (*left*) and Maxim Gorky (*right*) presiding over the 1934 First Congress of the Union of Soviet Writers. *Süddeutsche Zeitung Photo/Alamy*

Kliment Voroshilov, Vyacheslav Molotov, Joseph Stalin, and Nikolai Yezhov (*left to right*) on the banks of the Moscow-Volga Canal, 1937.

Isaac Babel's mug shot, taken after his arrest by the NKVD, 1939.

Ernest Hemingway (*center*) and OSS officer David Bruce (*left*) share a drink on the march to Paris, 1944. *Ernest Hemingway Photographs Collection, John F. Kennedy Presidential Library and Museum, Boston*

His reputation made by his novel *Native Son*, Richard Wright, pictured here in 1943, made his break with Communism public the following year.
Gordon Parks, U.S. Farm Security Administration/ Office of War Information Collection, Library of Congress, Washington, D.C.

Richard Wright attending an intellectual study club while visiting Indonesia for the Bandung Conference, 1955.
Richard Wright Papers, James Weldon Johnson Collection of Negro Arts and Letters, Beinecke Rare Book and Manuscript Library, Yale University

Arthur Koestler addresses the Congress for Cultural Freedom in West Berlin, 1950. *Copyright UPI/Süddeutsche Zeitung Photo*

Simone de Beauvoir and Jean-Paul Sartre—with whom Arthur Koestler fell out over their support of Communism—meeting with Che Guevara, 1960. *UtCon Collection/Alamy*

The great poets Anna Akhmatova and Boris Pasternak survived Stalin's purges only to become targets of the Kremlin during the Cold War, 1946. *Sputnik/Alamy*

Sputnik-1 being displayed beneath a statue of Lenin at the Soviet pavilion of Expo 58 in Brussels, where the CIA were secretly distributing copies of Boris Pasternak's *Doctor Zhivago*, 1958. *Wouter Hagens*

Howard Fast receiving the Stalin Prize in New York City at a ceremony attended by Eslanda Robeson (*left*); W. E. B. DuBois (*seated*); and Fast's wife, Bette, and daughter, Rachel (*both at right*). Photograph by Julian Lazarus. By permission of the Special Collections and University Archives, Rutgers University Libraries.

Mary McCarthy—who faced off against Howard Fast at the 1949 Scientific and Cultural Conference for World Peace—in the year that her novel *The Group* became a bestseller, 1963. Dick DeMarsico/Library of Congress

Stephen Spender, editor of *Encounter,* at the height of his influence in the late 1950s, long before the CIA's secret funding of the magazine became public. *Chronicle/Alamy*

Kim Philby giving a press conference in his mother's London flat, having been cleared of being a Communist spy by Foreign Secretary Harold Macmillan, 1955. *Trinity Mirror/Mirrorpix/Alamy*

A commemorative stamp issued by the Soviet Union in honor of Kim Philby, 1990.

Graham Greene receiving a shoe shine on the film set of *Our Man in Havana* in Cuba, 1959. *Copyright Peter Stackpole/LIFE Picture Collection/Getty*

John le Carré reads a copy of Graham Greene's espionage comedy, *Our Man in Havana*, 1960s. *Copyright Interfoto/Alamy*

Andrei Sinyavsky and
Yulii Daniel carrying
the coffin lid at Boris
Pasternak's funeral, 1960.
Copyright Sovfoto

Andrei Sinyavsky and
Yulii Daniel in the dock
at their trial, 1966.
Copyright TASS/Sovfoto

Mary McCarthy meets Pham Van Dong, prime minister of North Vietnam, 1968. *Archives and Special Collections, Vassar College Library*

Mary McCarthy visits a bomb site in Hanoi, 1968. *Archives and Special Collections, Vassar College Library*

Aleksandr Solzhenitsyn addresses the world's press outside Heinrich Böll's house in West Germany after been deported from the Soviet Union, 1974. *Bert Verhoeff/Anefo/Dutch National Archives, The Hague*

Portrait of Nicaraguan poet and former Sandinista revolutionary Gioconda Belli, taken in Germany in 2001. *Süddeutsche Zeitung Photo/Alamy*

Václav Havel waving to a crowd of demonstrators in Wenceslas Square in Prague, 1989. *CTK/Alamy*

as the obnoxious Buddy Nealson in *Black Boy,* came to Chicago to purge "Trotskyist elements," Wright was firmly in his sights. Privately Hayward referred to Wright as a "smuggler of reaction" and a "bastard intellectual."[15]

In order to display his loyalty, Wright was asked to travel to Switzerland and the Soviet Union on Party duties. He refused, saying he had writing commitments. At the next meeting, he asked to leave the Party. When, some weeks later, a group of his former comrades implored him to attend another meeting, it turned out to be the show trial of his friend David Poindexter, who was charged with acting against the Party's interests. After three hours of attacks, Poindexter pleaded guilty. Little wonder Wright wanted to get out of Chicago and move to New York City.

Wright had published some stories and poems in Chicago newspapers and magazines. Having worked at the Illinois Writers Workshop and the Federal Theater Project, which were funded by Roosevelt's Works Progress Administration, he hoped to find a similar position in New York. When that took longer than expected, he ended up working for the U.S. Communist Party's paper, the *Daily Worker.* War in Spain and the rise of fascism in Germany and Italy caused him to set aside his concerns about the way the Party was being run in the United States and offer his public support. He attended the second meeting of the Communist-backed League of American Writers, at which Hemingway gave his famous anti-fascist speech. There Wright signed a declaration in support of Stalin over the Moscow Show Trials.[16] Even the Molotov-Ribbentrop Pact, which prompted an exodus from the League of American Writers, could not dissuade him: he called it a "great step toward peace."[17]

After years of struggling with rejections, Wright got his big break. At the age of twenty-nine he won a competition held by the prestigious magazine *Story,* the first prize of which was $500 and a publishing deal with Harper & Brothers. His entry was picked ahead of 500 others and announced in February 1938. His collection of stories, *Uncle Tom's Children,* received rave reviews and praise from the First Lady, Eleanor Roosevelt. In Britain, Orwell's publisher, Victor Gollancz, bought the book and asked Paul Robeson to write the introduction. It was swiftly translated into Russian and received high praise from *Pravda.*[18]

His next book was even more explosive. Having earned a place in the creative program of the New York Writers' Workshop, he was free to focus entirely on his work. Every day he took a legal pad and fountain pen to his favorite bench in Fort Greene Park in Brooklyn and wrote *Native Son.*[19] He drew on his experience helping out at the South Side Boys Club in Chicago, where he listened to stories of boys who had got into trouble with the law, to create Bigger Thomas, the angry antihero who makes every page of the novel so compelling. *Native Son* was considered for publication for the Book of the Month Club, which would guarantee terrific sales, but publication would happen only if Wright agreed to tone down certain aspects of his novel. This put him in a very difficult position but, as his biographer Hazel Rowley puts it, he ultimately "gave in to white pressure."[20] It was the beginning of a complicated relationship with the publishing industry, as Wright sought to balance his integrity with the demands of being a professional writer in the American midcentury. He cut explicit references to masturbation but also suppressed passages that showed the desire of Mary Dalton, a white woman, for Thomas.[21] The changes were accepted, and the book was published by the Book of the Month Club in March 1940. The first print run of 170,000 sold out in only a few days.[22]

The final breakdown of Wright's relationship with the Communist Party came during the war. He and Ellen, a Communist Party organizer from Brooklyn, were married in 1941 and she was five months pregnant with their first daughter, Julia, when the Japanese attacked Pearl Harbor.[23] Wright thought the United

States should stay out of the war, doggedly following the Party line that the British and the French were imperialists and should not be helped. Furthermore, why should black Americans fight for freedom abroad when they did not have it at home? "They are asking us to die for a freedom we never had!" Wright wrote.[24] He did everything he could to avoid the draft, asking contacts to intercede on his behalf, hoping he might get a position at the Office of War Information; he was understandably terrified by the prospect of serving as a private in a segregated army. The family even contemplated moving to Canada.

When the Germans launched Operation Barbarossa and invaded Soviet territory, Communist policy once again turned 180 degrees overnight. No longer was this a war fought between European imperialists, it was now an existential fight with the forces of fascism in which the Soviet Union and the United States must stand shoulder to shoulder. Wright was disgusted by this cynicism. After a period in which he ceased to perform Party activities, he made a public break with the Communist Party in an article titled "I Tried to Be a Communist," published in two installments in *The Atlantic Monthly* in 1944. A version of this essay, itself excerpted from *Black Boy*, was published, alongside essays by Gide, Koestler, and Spender, in *The God That Failed* in 1949.[25]

Wright was stuck between a rock and a hard place. To the Soviet Union and the Communist Party of the USA he was now a "renegade" and a "reactionary."[26] However, the publication of his memoir, *Black Boy*, in 1945, was clear evidence that his opposition to Soviet Communism did not mean his position on American racism was softening. The book was a visceral rendering of the horror of growing up in the Jim Crow South, and Senator Theodore Bilbo of Mississippi made sure it was banned in his state, demanding that the ban should cover the whole country. The FBI had had him under surveillance since 1942, when a complaint about *12 Million Black Voices*, a collection of photographs of African Americans drawn from the Security Farm Administration files annotated by Wright, landed on J. Edgar Hoover's desk. He sent a memo ordering Wright's work to be investigated. Little wonder Wright started taking French lessons.

IN PARISIAN EXILE, Wright witnessed the emergence of a whole new set of global relations. The European colonial powers that had dominated the world were on their knees and prevented from total collapse only by American loans. Even then, their empires were beginning to fray and unravel as the populations of Britain and France demanded that the rebuilding of their own countries take precedence over the need to sustain colonies. Exploiting this weakness was a new generation of highly motivated nationalist leaders pushing for independence, such as Sukarno, who declared Indonesian independence from the Netherlands in 1945; Ho Chi Minh, who declared Vietnamese independence two weeks later; and Jawaharlal Nehru, who led India to independence from Britain in 1947.

The Cold War was inextricably bound up with decolonization as it became an increasingly global conflict. In theory, both superpowers were opposed to colonialism; Lenin had famously declared imperialism to be "the highest stage of capitalism" and the Soviet Union supported independence movements around the world; under the leadership of Roosevelt, the United States, itself a nation freed from colonial rule, championed the right of nations to freedom and self-determination. But while the Soviet Union sought to encourage independence, it did so insisting that any new regime follow the Moscow line. And while the United States was opposed to colonialism, this was undercut by the racist belief that Africans and Asians were incapable of governing themselves, and that this made them vulnerable to the malign influence of Moscow. For this reason the United States supported the British in Malaya and deployed their own armed forces in the Philippines, which had gained its independence from the United States in 1946, to help suppress a Communist guerrilla uprising. As was the case in Vietnam, the Europeans were wise to this game and often presented their own struggle for colonial control as a fight to keep out Communists, even when they knew it was not true. For example, Britain falsely claimed Jomo Kenyatta of Kenya was a Communist; the French did the same with Sékou Touré of Guinea.[27]

Furthermore, the United States' desire for certain resources meant turning a blind eye to some of the worst colonial abuses. In an example that particularly riled Wright, the Americans entered into a close relationship with Belgium in order to secure access to uranium mined in the Belgian Congo (they also bought uranium from apartheid South Africa).[28] There was also the American and British involvement in the coup that replaced the democratically elected Mohammad Mossadegh with Shah Reza Pahlavi in oil-rich Iran in August 1953. Around the world, the United States set up military bases to protect trade routes and guard access to raw materials; the Soviet Union responded by fomenting disruption and rebellion in ways that would damage American interests.

Such neocolonial assertion was clearly perceived as a threat to those African and Asian nations caught in the Cold War crossfire, and leaders like Gamal Abdel Nasser of Egypt, Nehru, and Sukarno resolved to do something about it. The result was the "Third World" movement—a term popularized by the Martinique intellectual Frantz Fanon, adapted from the period of the French Revolution, when the clergy was defined as the First Estate, the Second Estate was the nobility, and the Third Estate the common people.[29] Fanon's expression, with its connotation of revolution and power in numbers, put the First World (the

United States and Western Europe) and the Second World (the Soviet Union and its allies) on notice. Leaders of nations that had shaken off colonial rule wanted full economic and political sovereignty and sought to achieve it through alliances with each other. That was why they planned to meet at Bandung.

In Paris, Wright became involved in black solidarity movements. He was invited to join the editorial board of a new magazine, *Présence Africaine*, which was edited by the Senegalese writer Alioune Diop. The magazine was designed to celebrate black culture, embracing the concept of *négritude*, which rejected European ideas of assimilation and embraced African culture and tradition. Aimé Césaire, a poet from Martinique, who helped coin the concept of *négritude*, was on the editorial board with Wright while Camus, Gide, and Sartre served as patrons.[30] While Wright viewed himself as Western, and believed in racial assimilation, he was determined to be an ally in any fight against racism and colonialism.

He was also disturbed by the way American racism was creeping into Paris. Thanks to the strength of the dollar, American tourists were flocking to Paris, and Wright heard rumors that American visitors were persuading French hotels not to rent rooms to black guests.[31] In October 1950 he decided to fight back and form an organization called the Franco-American Fellowship to represent black Americans in Paris. He suspected he, like many other black intellectuals, was being watched, so at the first meeting of the group he encouraged members to arrive at the workers' bistro where it was hosted in ones and twos.[32] Wright was right to be suspicious: the State Department suspected the Fellowship to be a Communist Front, sending informers to infiltrate the group and report back to the embassy about what was being said and planned. U.S. Army intelligence also had an informer placed inside it ("a Negro musician from Philadelphia" who had previously informed on Paul Robeson).[33] After running the Franco-American Fellowship for just over a year, Wright resigned, and it fell apart (by then he knew that some members were informing).

The situation for black leftists was worsening in the United States as the authorities cracked down on critics of U.S. race policies, claiming these played into the hands of Soviet propaganda. Wright's onetime friend and colleague Ben Davis was jailed under the Smith Act, W. E. B. DuBois was arrested because of his association with the World Peace Council, and Paul Robeson had his passport revoked. The spread of American power brought the agents of the Red Scare to Wright's Parisian doorstep; David Schine, who worked for Senator Joseph McCarthy, came to Paris to question Wright about his past. (Wright's books were among those that Roy Cohn and Schine were having removed from the libraries of the United States Information Service.) When Wright refused to play ball, Schine told the writer that he and Cohn had recently summoned Langston Hughes to appear before HUAC. The threat was clear.

While he had broken with the Communist Party, he was disgusted with the witch hunt of those on the left. ("There is more freedom in one square block of Paris than there is in the entire United States of America," he wrote.)[34] Having become more interested in ideas of black political solidarity, Wright decided to see what that looked like on the ground. While on a self-imposed writing retreat in London, not far from Greenwich Park (he was working on his existential novel, *The Outsider*), Wright frequently visited with George Padmore, the Trinidadian novelist and influential figure in anti-colonial liberation movements. Padmore was a confidant of Kwame Nkrumah, the prime minister of Gold Coast (present-day Ghana) who was seeking to secure independence from Britain; Padmore encouraged Wright to go and see his friend in action. Wright, who had briefly met Nkrumah in New York years before, had long desired to visit Africa and this seemed the perfect opportunity.

In June 1953 Wright sailed from Liverpool to Takoradi before taking a bus into Accra. Looking out the window at the people, the landscape, and the climate left him disoriented. "There was nothing here that I could predict, anticipate or rely upon," he wrote.[35] While he spent time with Nkrumah as he campaigned for support of a white paper on constitutional reform that was perceived as the final step before a declaration of independence, the leader was totally consumed by his efforts to unite the disparate elements of the country and remained enigmatic to Wright's eyes. He had been given a $3,000 advance to write a book about his experience in Gold Coast—what became *Black Power*—but he struggled for material, felt depressed, and began to seek an early passage home.[36]

Despite his personal travails, Wright was aware that he was witness to a defining moment in history. On July 10, having published his white paper, Nkrumah delivered his call for independence in a rousing speech that became popularly known as the "Motion of Destiny." In it, Nkrumah made clear that there was more than just the future of an independent Ghana at stake. "The eyes and ears of the world are upon you," he told the assembled parliament in Accra, "yea, our oppressed brothers throughout this vast continent of Africa and the New World are looking to you with desperate hope, as an inspiration to continue their grim fight against cruelties which we in this corner of Africa have never known—cruelties which are a disgrace to humanity, and to the civilization which the white man has set himself to teach us."[37] Wright congratulated Nkrumah personally and then wrote to Padmore to tell him about the "moving and eloquent words he had just heard."[38]

By the time he left Gold Coast, Wright was less enthused. He had not found the solidarity he expected and was taken aback by how easily he was identified as an outsider. "I was black and they were black but my blackness did not help me," he wrote. Tribal ritual and religious mysticism left him cold: he was rational, secular, and, as he noted, "western to the bone."[39] This led him to some dubious generalizations about the people he met; he told Nkrumah there was a "kind of sodden vagueness" in the "African mentality" and concluded that the only way he would succeed in ruling the country after independence was through "militarism."[40]

What he did not disclose in *Black Power* was how deeply skeptical he was of Nkrumah himself. Wright's enthusiasm for black solidarity was certainly genuine, as was his fervent opposition to colonialism, but he was also haunted by the familiar specter of Communism. He believed one of the reasons that Nkrumah had kept his distance from him is that he feared that Wright would be able to identify the Communist methods he was using to organize his party.[41] So strongly did he feel that, he took the extraordinary step of volunteering a four-page memorandum to the American consulate. Wright told them that while he did not believe there was any "direct relation" between Nkrumah's party and any foreign Communist organization, "it is a Communist minded political party, borrowing Marxist concepts and applying them with a great deal of flexibility to local African social and economic conditions."[42] He pointed out that Nkrumah slept with a portrait of Lenin in his bedroom—not an encouraging sign to those who feared he might be privately sympathetic to Moscow.

The difficulty of disentangling decolonization from the Cold War that Wright confronted in the Gold Coast was one of the reasons Bandung excited him so much: could such a power bloc help these newly independent nations navigate a third way? If an Iron Curtain had fallen across Europe, could the prospect of a "color curtain" dividing Africa and Asia from the rest of the world reshape the balance of power? His experience with Nkrumah left him with more questions than ever. He hoped to find some answers in Indonesia.

WRIGHT'S JOURNEY TO BANDUNG was a fitting prelude to the conference, a whirlwind tour of North Africa, South Asia, and Southeast Asia. He flew from Madrid to Rome, and from there, as they crossed the Mediterranean, he saw the "far flung lake of shimmering lights" of Cairo. In Egypt the plane picked up its first load of delegates, "red-fezzed North Africans from Morocco, Algeria and Tunisia."[43] As the plane headed east to Baghdad, Wright was shown pictures of emaciated Palestinian refugees and was told their plight would be brought up at the conference. Wright struck up a conversation with an Indonesian student returning from his time at the University of Leiden. "You an American?" the student asked. "Yes." "Negro?" "Yes." The student relaxed. "I was to get to know that reaction very well," Wright wrote.[44] As a victim of racism, he was on the inside at Bandung.

In Karachi, Sikhs boarded—"they had bushy black beards, Oxford accents and they sat together in a knot"—and in Calcutta, Hindus—"they wore Western clothes and seemed urbanized."[45] He took a sleeping pill and awoke to Japanese and American reporters boarding the plane in Bangkok. "High over the jungles of Malaya and political discussions raged," Wright wrote.[46] As people shouted to make themselves heard over the noise of the engines, those discussions kept coming back to the same subject: what role China was going to play at the conference.

The decision to invite Communist China had prompted much skepticism in the West about whether this was a genuinely neutral meeting in the context of the Cold War. Nehru, who was understood to be the driving force behind the conference, had visited China as a guest of Mao the previous November, and that Chinese Premier Zhou En-lai was now coming to Bandung appeared to be evidence of Communist conspiracy, even though the Indian leader was not a Communist himself. "A group of American newspapermen had made a list of all the delegates going to Bandung and had checked them all off according to their political leanings and had come to the conclusion that the West would emerge victorious from its clash with China's evil genius Chou En-lai [sic]," Wright wrote. "I was baffled. Were we going to a football game?"[47] Wright believed the approach of Western governments and the Western press betrayed their fear of what was happening. Claims that the conference, by excluding white nations, was itself racist showed how defensive the Europeans and the Americans were. "There's gonna be a hot time in old Bandung," Wright thought.[48]

The fear that the Cold War was also about to turn hot was real. In the American press, stories circulated that the Chinese were preparing an operation to launch an attack to take the islands of Quemoy (Kinmen) and Matsu in the Taiwanese Strait, an act of aggression against U.S.-supported Taiwan (then still known as Formosa). In the American press, there was bullish talk of the use of nuclear weapons. It was precisely this kind of aggressive posturing on the part of the United States, Wright believed, that brought about Bandung in the first place. Ever since the onset of the Cold War, the United States had "launched a campaign, the intensity of which it did not appreciate, to frighten the men of the Kremlin, and month after month that campaign kept up, flooding the world on all levels of communication. And it was successful, too successful; it not only scared and deterred Russian Communists but it also frightened the living daylights out of the human race. It was a campaign so fierce, so deadly, so unrelenting that it created precisely what it sought to defeat, that is, an organization of Asia and Africa around a Communist cell on a global scale: BANDUNG."[49] The gathering in Indonesia prompted anxiety in the Imperial West, for whom, Wright argued, "the conference loomed like a long-buried ghost rising from a muddy grave."[50]

On landing in Jakarta on April 12, Wright found the airport decorated with the flags of the twenty-nine participating nations. Just as in the Gold Coast, the climate took him by surprise. "The heat was like a Turkish bath; the humidity was higher than in the African jungle," he wrote. Jakarta was like Accra, he found: hectic, squalid, and overwhelming. There was everywhere a "naked and immediate" preoccupation with making money, although few people seemed to actually have any. The marks of colonialism and poverty were evident: he saw a man squatting over the edge of one of the Dutch-built canals "defecating in broad daylight into the canal's muddy, swirling water; I saw another, then another"; farther down he saw women washing their clothes, children bathing, and one child brushing their teeth, all in the same water.[51]

Mochtar Lubis, an Indonesian novelist, provided the new arrival with a tour of the city. Wright gave talks to writers' groups, the local chapter of PEN, and met members of the local elite but found himself in disagreement with them over the future of the country.[52] He argued that they needed to industrialize to free themselves from their dependency on the West; they claimed that this was too Western a perspective and that they needed to focus more on preserving their own values. Wright the secular materialist found this attitude frustrating. Just as in the Gold Coast, his verdict was harsher in his journal. "The Negro problem is as nothing compared to this boiling cauldron of racial hatred," he wrote.[53]

They set off for Bandung and the conference itself. "My friend

Lubis was behind the wheel of the car," Wright wrote, "and the temperature dropped as we climbed into the mountains where the volcanic craters could be seen crowned by haloes of white, fluffy clouds."[54] They rolled into the city, which was decorated with "a forest of banners proclaiming Asian and African solidarity."[55] There were high-security measures at the conference, with guards armed with machine guns and grenades lining the streets and checkpoints set up at regular intervals. Crowds were already gathered in the street, and wherever Wright went he was badgered for an autograph.

On April 18 the conference began. "I'd no sooner climbed into the press gallery and looked down upon the vast assembly of delegates, many of them clad in their exotic national costumes, than I could sense an important juncture of history in the making."[56] Wright took diligent notes as the luminaries of the emergent Third World movement took their turns at the podium: Jawaharlal Nehru, Gamal Abdel Nasser, U Nu (Burma), John Kotelawala (Sri Lanka), Muhammad Ali Jinnah (Pakistan), and Sukarno and Ali Sastroamidjojo (Indonesia). What struck Wright was the emotional intensity with which almost all of these speakers addressed the damage of colonialism, even those leaders who were notionally sympathetic to the West.

In his opening address, Sukarno argued that this experience of colonialism gave the assembled countries a moral authority. The perspective of the two superpowers was distorted by their conflict with each other, and so it was up to those who had been exploited and ignored to take responsibility for the "well-being of mankind."[57] Above all, this meant avoiding atomic war, and as a result denuclearization was one of the key themes of the conference. But nonalignment itself was deemed essential to securing peace. Nehru, in a closed session, said, "If all the world were to be divided up between these two big blocs, what would be the result? The inevitable result would be war. Therefore, every step that takes place in reducing that area in the world which may be called the 'unaligned area' is a dangerous step and leads to war."[58]

There were some specific areas of agreement: the meeting called on France to recognize the right to independence of Algeria, Morocco, and Tunisia, on South Africa to end its policy of apartheid, and on the United Nations to implement its resolutions on Palestine. Otherwise, the final communiqué, with its ten basic principles, stressed more general economic and cultural cooperation, as well as respect for human rights, opposition to racism, and nonintervention in the affairs of other countries.

After the conference ended, Wright spent an hour in a private meeting with Nehru, who expressed his frustration as to why the United States had been so afraid that Communists would infiltrate the conference. Nehru's daughter, Indira Gandhi, a future ruler of India, asked Wright why the Americans did not realize that attacking her father might well end up bringing about the very thing they feared. "Do they know what they are doing? Don't they know that if they destroy my father, they will be opening the gates to anarchy, to Communism even?" she said.[59]

But Wright believed the Communist threat to be real, just that it was not as immediate as the American State Department and media made out. "Russia had no defenders at Bandung," he wrote. China, however, was another matter. In Zhou En-lai he saw someone playing his cards close to his chest. The premier did not seek to gain support from the other delegates in China's conflict with the United States over Taiwan, and he did not make the ideological case for Maoism. "He knew that the time for that was not ripe," Wright wrote, "that the distance that separated Red China from the religious nations of Asia and Africa was great indeed."[60] Zhou instead positioned China as a country that had suffered at the hands of colonial powers and that saw the value of future Third World solidarity.

His suspicions about Zhou's true motivations, however, could not detract from the historic nature of the conference for Wright.[61] In *The Color Curtain*, the book he wrote about Bandung, he reached for hyperbolic language when trying to communicate the importance of what he had seen:

> Bandung was no simple exercise in Left and Right politics; it was no mere minor episode in the Cold War; it was no Communist Front meeting. The seizure of power was not on the agenda; Bandung was not concerned with how to take power. ALL THE MEN THERE REPRESENTED GOVERNMENTS THAT HAD ALREADY SEIZED POWER AND THEY DID NOT KNOW WHAT TO DO WITH IT. Bandung was a decisive moment in the consciousness of 65 percent of the human race, and that moment meant: HOW SHALL THE HUMAN RACE BE ORGANIZED? The decisions or lack of them flowing from Bandung will condition the totality of human life on earth.[62]

In terms of the way forward, Wright was more candid in his journal than he was in *The Color Curtain*. He privately dismissed the way some nativist speakers stressed the need to revive religious practices and traditions as "pathetic exultations of past and dead cultures."[63] In *The Color Curtain*, he phrased this more diplomatically, insisting that the only way forward for these nations was to adopt the "rational and secular" approach of the Western-educated elite. For that to happen, the West must also "meet the challenge of the miraculous unity of Bandung openly and selflessly." Otherwise, Wright warned, the people of Africa and Asia might see their only passage to freedom being lit by the Communist lamp of Zhou En-Lai.[64]

THE BANDUNG CONFERENCE took place at a felicitous moment for the Third World movement. India was independent, Ghana was soon to follow, and in Indochina, Ho Chi-Minh's forces had defeated the French. Algeria was in revolt. As historian Odd Arne Westad puts it, the conference "caught the moment of greatest hope and expectation in the anti-colonial struggle."[65] The following year, Nasser and Nehru broadened the scope of their movement by meeting with Yugoslav leader Tito on an is- land in the Adriatic (Yugoslavia was Communist but had broken with Moscow). In 1961, Algeria, Egypt, Ghana, India, Indone- sia, and Yugoslavia met in Belgrade to form the Non-Aligned Movement.[66]

If Nehru's goal at Bandung was to prevent the world being divided into two power blocs by the United States and the Soviet Union, it enjoyed a measure of success and, while its leadership changed, the Non-Aligned Movement remained influential un- til, decades later, the Soviet invasion of Afghanistan fractured relationships beyond repair. Long before then, the pan-Asian solidarity of Bandung disintegrated as India fought border wars with both China (in the Himalayas) and Pakistan (in Kashmir) in the early sixties. Ultimately, the movement could not prevent the Cold War coming to Africa and Asia, as it did to Vietnam, Cambodia, Laos, Angola, Congo, Ethiopia, and Eritrea, to name but a few.[67]

There were also systemic problems that the conference had avoided confronting. For all the talk of economic cooperation, in reality it was almost impossible for Third World nations to com- pete in a global system that was designed to benefit the West.[68]

When these countries hit what became known as the "development barrier," some leaders turned to authoritarian methods as means to accelerate reform but also to shore up their own power. Heroes of independence, like Nkrumah and Sukarno, started to look more and more like dictators as their policies took an autocratic turn. At Bandung the issue of political rights and democracy went unspoken, largely because Nehru placed a priority on achieving solidarity ahead of raising issues that could alienate those leaders whose political legitimacy was, by democratic standards, questionable. It was, Westad argues, "a move that would return to haunt the non-aligned movement throughout its existence."[69]

For Wright, back in Paris, any optimism he had felt in Indonesia soon soured. Being opposed to both sides in the Cold War came at a cost, and he felt more of an outsider than ever. In 1956 he found himself opposing both the Franco-British-Israeli invasion of Suez and the Soviet invasion of Hungary at the same time, refusing to sign petitions condemning the latter unless signatories also condemned the former. The atmosphere in Paris, with the Algerian War raging, was becoming increasingly tense. With the city a hub for Communist-sympathizing intellectuals, anti-colonial activists, and African American exiles, informers and spies were everywhere. One of the hubs of expat intellectual life in the city was *The Paris Review,* a magazine that was, as William Styron explained in an editorial in the first issue, supposed to be a haven for "non-drumbeaters and non-axe-grinders."[70] Yet one of the founders of the magazine, Peter Matthiessen, was in fact a CIA agent using *The Paris Review* as cover. The magazine was partially funded by some of the same CIA fronts as the CCF.[71] Nothing was as it seemed, and Wright felt nobody could be trusted. Personal suspicions and political tensions opened fissures in the black expat community. In *Island of Hallucination,* a novel Wright wrote in the years after Bandung (and which remains unpublished), the protagonist says of Paris: "Goddam! This town crawls with serpents."[72]

Increasingly, the rattles of those serpents were audible. Publicly, his critics accused him of having "poisoned the mind of Europe" on the United States because of the way he spoke about American racism, and covertly, the intelligence agencies were keeping a close eye on him. According to his biographer, Addison Gayle, the surveillance of Wright amounted to "a pattern of harassment" on the part of U.S. intelligence agencies that at times resembled "a personal vendetta," and it left him stressed and paranoid.[73] His FBI file was novel-length, having begun in 1935 and tracking his associations with the Communist Party until 1942.[74] Since Wright had moved to France, the Bureau believed him to be serving Communist interests through his work, even if he had broken with them publicly; the Franco-American Fellowship aroused particular concerns. Sources and informants accused him of being a secret Communist, and he was listed as a "possible subversive among US personnel in France."[75] According to his FBI file, Wright was also spied on by Navy intelligence, the U.S. Information Service, and the Foreign Liaison service.

The story became even more complicated after Bandung, however. On his return he learned that his colleagues on *Présence Africaine* were planning a follow-up conference to be held in Paris in September (Les Congrès des Ecrivains et Artistes Noirs), to feature prominent black leaders and intellectuals from around the world. Wright was on the executive committee and given responsibility for helping shape the American delegation. He was concerned, however, that the Communists were looking to infiltrate and dominate the conference, and he went to the American Embassy to raise the issue. In a report sent back to the State Department in Washington, the embassy said Wright had warned them that "there was a distinct danger that the Communists might exploit the Congress to their own ends."[76] Wright asked for assistance in ensuring African American delegates who were less sympathetic to Moscow, such as Ralph Ellison, Chester Himes, and Langston Hughes, were invited ahead of Soviet apologists, who would be denied visas. It was the first of several visits to the embassy about the conference. He also called on the help of Michael Josselson, of the Congress for Cultural Freedom, to support his position. What was Wright's motivation? Undoubtedly, he genuinely disliked the idea of Communist infiltration of a cause he valued highly, but with the potential withdrawal of his passport held over him, self-preservation was another possible impetus. How successful Wright's intervention was is hard to judge; none of the three writers he suggested attended and the two African American delegates who were denied visas—W. E. B. DuBois and Paul Robeson—had long been on the State Department's radar.

At the conference itself, hosted at the Sorbonne's Amphitheatre Descartes, Wright was torn between the American and African delegations, feeling allegiances to both (this manifested in the delegates debating whether *Black Boy* was fundamentally an American or African memoir). It had started well enough, with Diop, in his opening remarks, reminding the delegates that they were meeting in solidarity, and that the conference was a kind of second Bandung. James Baldwin, who was in attendance and would write up his experiences for *Encounter,* recalled that while Diop's speech was roundly applauded, the "atmosphere was strange." "Everyone was tense with the question of which direction the conference would take," Baldwin wrote. "Hanging in the air . . . were the great specters of America and Russia, of the battle going on between them for the domination of the world."[77]

Wright, sitting at the top table, was disconcerted when a speech by DuBois was read out in the opening session, in which he stated that the United States had blocked him from being there "because I am a socialist and because I believe in peace

with Communist States like the Soviet Union."[78] To make matters worse, DuBois went on to say that "any Negro-American
who travels abroad today must either not discuss race conditions
in the United States or say the sort of thing which our State
Department wishes the world to believe."[79] The French audience cheered; the American delegates, Wright, included, felt
outflanked.[80] In his own speech, Wright reiterated his secular,
Western values, alienating those delegates that championed
black nationalism and *négritude*. He even made the argument
that colonialism had had the beneficial effect of destroying old
myths and traditions. It was not a popular opinion; Baldwin
called it a "tactless way of expressing a debatable idea."[81]

   After the conference, to Wright's horror, the American novelist Kay Boyle wrote to him to tell him that a rumor was going around that he was working with the State Department or
the FBI in order to be able to keep his passport.[82] That someone
from the embassy was clearly talking about him only deepened
Wright's paranoia; he was sure that American intelligence was
trying to smear him. When *Time* magazine attributed a quotation to him in which he claimed that "the Negro problem in the
United States has not changed in 300 years," he believed that
the CIA had planted it to undermine him.[83]

   By then, though, it was too late: the CIA *had* undermined
him—but in a manner he had not anticipated. Somehow, six
years before it became public, Wright discovered that the Congress for Cultural Freedom was being funded by the CIA.[84] Not
only had the magazines belonging to the CCF, including *Encounter, Preuves,* and *Cuadernos,* published excerpts from *Black
Power* and *The Color Curtain* but, worst of all, the CCF had paid
his passage to Bandung, including $500 for expenses.[85] It is not
clear whether Wright also knew that another organization with
which he was involved, the American Society for African Culture, and through which he had sought stronger connections

with French-speaking black nationalists, was also a CIA front.[86] Wright had been used, and it was not hard to figure out why. As James Baldwin put it when he discovered who was behind the CCF years later, "I'd have been a fool to think they were subsidizing me—they were not doing *that*; they were proving to themselves how liberal they were."[87]

Wright had suspected the CCF were associated in some way with the State Department and had sought assurances of his authorial independence before traveling to Indonesia, but the involvement of the CIA was a different order of complicity. It was a devastating revelation.[88] When Richard Crossman, the British politician, asked if he wanted to write something for the forthcoming ten-year anniversary reissue of *The God That Failed*, Wright responded furiously, claiming that with what he now knew, he could see it for the Cold War propaganda it was.[89] Wright could not win; as the CIA sought to exploit his status for their cultural propaganda, the FBI was intensifying its surveillance of him and other influential black figures. In 1956, the year after Bandung, Hoover launched COINTELPRO, a covert program targeting American political organizations that were seen as counter to the government interest. Given Hoover's racism, civil rights and black nationalist parties were high on that list. Martin Luther King Jr., who visited Wright in Paris, was a particular target.

THE YEARS THAT FOLLOWED the Bandung Conference were not happy ones for Wright, as he suffered a number of professional and personal setbacks. In June 1959, he fell ill with amoebic dysentery and was treated with bismuth, which was legal at the time but later banned because of the disastrous side effects of heavy metal poisoning. As his condition got worse, Wright got increasingly paranoid and warned friends of plots against him.[90]

He claimed to have received a letter from Sartre attacking him, only to later explain that the letter—never found—was a forgery.[91] On November 26, 1960, he was admitted to the Eugene Gibez clinic in Paris. Two days later, he was found dead. The doctor recorded the cause as a heart attack. He was fifty-two.

Wright's premature death immediately became the subject of conjecture. Who was the mystery woman who had apparently visited him the day of his death? Why was Wright convinced the FBI and CIA, along with French intelligence, were out to get him? Some, like his friend the political cartoonist Ollie Harrington, were convinced he was murdered.[92] Wright's daughter, Julia, felt the CIA had deliberately sought to isolate him "in order to make him more vulnerable."[93] Other friends pointed the finger at his Russian doctor, Vladimir Schwarzmann, for prescribing too many drugs (in addition to bismuth: emetine, penicillin, sulpha, tranquilizers, and small doses of arsenic).[94] Wright's body was cremated without an autopsy, however, so there was no proof that he had been poisoned, nor has any documentary evidence emerged to prove that he was killed by any agency. His death became another insoluble mystery in the intrigue of the Cold War.

TWENTY-THREE

Pasternak

MOSCOW, 1956–1960

IN THE EARLY AFTERNOON OF May 13, 1956, Alexander Fadeyev, agitated and drunk at his dacha, stripped naked and, with a Nagant revolver, shot himself through the heart. His body was found by his eleven-year-old son, Mischa. On the nightstand was a suicide note, in which Fadeyev raged about the treatment of literature by "the self-confident, ignorant leadership of the Party." The best writers, he wrote, had been "physically exterminated" and literature had been "debased, persecuted and destroyed." He lashed out at the "ignoramuses" in the Khrushchev regime, from whom he expected "worse than from the satrap Stalin." "My life as a writer loses all meaning, and I leave this life with great joy, seeing it as a deliverance from this foul existence where meanness, lies and slander rain down on you," he wrote.[1] The KGB were soon on the scene and sealed off the office. The suicide note was filed away, its contents kept secret, and the official reasons given for his death was the combination of a nervous disorder and alcohol.

The KGB had good reason for suppressing Fadeyev's jeremiad. Of all the Soviet Union's writers, he was the most fervent Party loyalist. For the previous two decades he had been the figurehead of Soviet literature, the general secretary of the Writers' Union, who had headed the delegations at the conference at the Waldorf in New York in 1949 and the Paris Peace Congress the following year. He never wavered from the Party line. When Dwight Macdonald asked him about the disappearance of writers at the Waldorf, he claimed they were alive and well, when he knew they were not. When Howard Fast asked him about anti-Semitism in the Soviet Union, he claimed there was no such thing, despite having personally provided lists of Jewish writers to the authorities. Domestically, while he did try to protect some writers he was more than happy to crack the ideological whip, often with devastating consequences for those receiving the lash.[2] During the purges he signed letters that led to the arrest of his fellow writers, knowing they would be sent to the gulag or worse.[3] He sold his soul to Stalin—and it came at a price.

The preceding February, Fadeyev had been shaken to the core by Nikita Khrushchev's Secret Speech at the Twentieth Party Congress. For Fadeyev, the condemnation of Stalinism was a disaster. He had been faithful, but he had not been blind. He knew what had happened under Stalin. He had blood on his hands. He soon found himself being pushed to the margins under the new regime and began to drink heavily and behave erratically. It is not clear whether it was guilt or fear that prompted him to pull the trigger.

Fadeyev's body was laid out in the Hall of Columns, just as Stalin's had been. Among the guard of honor was Boris Pasternak, a poet who had steadfastly refused to make the same bargain as Fadeyev. Even at the height of the purges, Pasternak had refused to inform on friends and did what he could to protect his fellow writers. It was perhaps only his international reputation that spared him from being sent to the camps or executed. On many occasions Fadeyev had publicly upbraided and bullied Pasternak, deriding his "political neutrality," his "individualism," and his "formalist tricks."[4] But in private Fadeyev revered Pasternak's poetry and he even made efforts to try to protect him. They had neighboring dachas at the writers' community at Peredelkino and had retained a strange kind of friendship. Looking at Fadeyev's corpse, Pasternak said that, in taking his own life, "Alexander Alexandrovich had rehabilitated himself."[5]

It was a time for rehabilitation in Russia. The postwar purges— led by Second Secretary Andrei Zhdanov—had swiftly crushed any expectation that the end of the war would bring a new era of cultural liberalization. That had to wait until the old man was dead. Pasternak had not been denounced by Zhdanov but being well-known and admired in the West, and having spent much of the war translating Shakespeare, he knew he would be a target, too. Despite his secret passion for Pasternak's work, Fadeyev subjected him to public harangues, and a new edition of his poetry was banned in 1947. The publisher eventually had to destroy the entire run.[6] In the autumn of 1949 the secret police did to Pasternak what they had done to Akhmatova: they took a hostage. Pasternak's lover, Olga Ivinskaya, was arrested and interrogated. She was told that Pasternak, whose parents had moved to Oxford at the end of their lives, was an English spy. Less fantastically, they asked questions about Pasternak's new literary project, a novel he was working on.[7] The MGB, as the security services were known between 1946 and 1953, were interested in Doctor Zhivago from its earliest drafts. Ivinskaya was then sent to a camp and not released until Stalin's death in 1953.

UNDER KHRUSHCHEV, Soviet culture underwent the period of reform and cultural liberalization known as the Thaw, but Pasternak was skeptical about how much had substantively changed. He believed Khrushchev looked like a pig and behaved like one, too. In the summer of 1956 he wrote a poem—which he recited only among trusted friends—in which he claimed Stalin's cult of personality had been replaced by "nothing but porcine snouts" and that people were driven to "shoot themselves from drunkenness because they cannot stand it anymore."[8] Khrushchev was, to the poet's mind, a vulgarian who cared for culture only when it could be politically exploited. Pasternak's judgment was borne out years later when, sensing that the ideological tide was turning, Khrushchev derided modern art displayed at the Manege Gallery in Moscow. He asked one artist if he was "a pederast or a normal person" and told another that he deserved to have his trousers taken down and be dumped in a pile of nettles. The art itself he pronounced to be "dog shit."

Art and literature that attacked Stalin was seen as politically expedient by Khrushchev and his allies and, as a result, they permitted the circulation of work that would have been unthinkable in previous decades. But there remained limits on work that criticized the current regime, or Communism more generally. There was a new line drawn, and *Doctor Zhivago* was on the wrong side of it.

By the time of Khrushchev's speech, Pasternak had privately circulated excerpts of the manuscript of his novel and conducted readings for his friends at his dacha. In April 1954, the journal *Znama* had published some poems that were to be part of the last section of *Doctor Zhivago,* and these were accompanied by a note about the plot of the forthcoming novel. Still, Pasternak did not believe the government would allow him to publish it when it was done. "You mark my words," he told Ivinskaya, "they will not publish this novel for anything in the world. I don't believe they will ever publish it. I have come to the conclusion that I should pass it around to be read by all and sundry."[9]

Pasternak was right. *Novy Mir,* the most liberal of the literary journals in Moscow, repeatedly rejected his efforts to publish parts of the novel. After all, *Doctor Zhivago* did not just criticize Stalinism, it appeared to undermine the whole revolutionary project. It was a grand, sweeping novel, redolent of the great works of nineteenth-century Russian literature. The hero, Yuri

Zhivago, is a doctor and poet who is torn between his love for two women and between his duty to society and his duty to his art. While Zhivago is initially enthused by the possibilities of the revolution, he becomes disenchanted with the way Communism strips out the spiritual and the poetical from life. He seeks a retreat from society that will allow him the privacy to write what he wants. What made this premise even more intolerable for the authorities was that the novel ends before the Stalinist purges begin—that is, before the period when criticism of official policy was accepted. *Doctor Zhivago* was a work of heresy and Pasternak knew it.

In May 1956, Pasternak gave the manuscript of *Doctor Zhivago* to Sergio D'Angelo, a young Italian, who had taken the train out to Peredelkino hoping to bump into the poet. D'Angelo's primary job was in the Italian section of Radio Moscow, the Soviet Union's official international broadcaster, but he had a sideline as a literary scout for the Italian Communist publisher Giangiacomo Feltrinelli. It had taken little more than a few hours of conversation with D'Angelo for Pasternak to hand over a book he knew might land him in jail or worse. "You are now invited to attend my execution," he told the Italian as he left.[10] He had made his decision on what seemed like the spur of the moment, but he knew it was a choice that would carry serious consequences. He could not have anticipated how seismic those consequences would be.

THE KGB KNEW that *Doctor Zhivago* was a problem. They had informers who had attended some of Pasternak's private readings and it was clear this novel was not going to follow the Party line. The bad news for the secret police was that D'Angelo had made it out of the Soviet Union without being searched and had passed the manuscript to Feltrinelli in Berlin. Feltrinelli had then used a trusted courier to get a contract directly into the hands of Pasternak. The good news, though, was that Feltrinelli was a Communist and so in theory could be leaned upon by the Soviet authorities.

In August, KGB chairman Ivan Serov delivered a report to the Politburo in which he revealed that Pasternak had given permission for Feltrinelli to make publishing deals with firms in Britain and France. Serov also quoted from letters that the KGB had intercepted, in which Pasternak said he would be torn "limb from limb" for sending his book into the West. It was clear that he was not as naive as some of his defenders claimed. He knew he was in trouble and was determined to face it down.[11]

One option for the Soviet authorities was to publish the book in the Soviet Union before it was published in the West, but a report by the Central Committee's cultural department effectively killed off that idea. The book, the report claimed, was impossible to publish because of the way it undermined the revolution. Instead, the Committee determined that Feltrinelli should be squeezed and that they should try to persuade Pasternak to change course. The head of the culture department, Dmitri Polikarpov, told Ivinskaya that the novel could be published in the Soviet Union but only once it had been thoroughly edited. Pasternak was unimpressed by this proposition. Anticipating what was coming, he asked a French friend, Hélène Peltier, to smuggle out a note for Feltrinelli, which read: "If ever you receive a letter other than in French, you must absolutely not do what is requested of you—the only valid letters shall be those written in French."[12]

The Kremlin ordered the Italian Communist Party to get the manuscript back, and Feltrinelli agreed to put his publication plans on hold.[13] Yet just as they appeared to have contained the problem, new complications arose. In October, students marched on the parliament in Budapest, protesting the political repression of the Soviet-backed Communist government. Demonstrators pulled down a statue of Stalin and tried to gain access to the Radio Budapest building to broadcast their demands to the nation. Agents of the Hungarian secret police opened fire on the crowd. The situation swiftly escalated, and soon the whole country was gripped by revolt. The Hungarian rebels hoped for protection from the Western powers, but when the Russian tanks rolled in at the beginning of November, nobody came to their aid. Tens of thousands of Hungarians were thrown in jail and hundreds were executed. Feltrinelli, like many European Communists, was horrified at the brutality with which the Soviet Union cracked down on the revolution, and as a result was determined not to be pushed around and to publish *Doctor Zhivago*.

On the other end, Pasternak was pressured into writing telegrams to Feltrinelli asking that he return the manuscript but as they were in Italian and Russian, the publisher knew they did not reflect the author's true intentions. (Pasternak, meanwhile, used trusted intermediaries to transmit his true wishes.) Alexei Surkov, a poet and Party loyalist, traveled to Milan to confront Feltrinelli, brandishing one of these telegrams. When that got him nowhere, he gave a press conference in which he lamented that *Doctor Zhivago* would become the first work of Russian literature to be initially published abroad since Boris Pilnyak's *Mahogany* in Germany in 1929. The analogy masked a threat: Pilnyak had been a neighbor of Pasternak's at Peredelkino in the 1930s, when the fallout from the foreign publication of *Mahogany* had made him a target for the regime. Pasternak had been visiting with Pilnyak when he was arrested in 1937. Found guilty of being a Japanese spy and of plotting to assassinate Stalin, he was executed with a bullet to the back of the neck.[14]

But the KGB's efforts were in vain. The book was launched at the Hotel Continental in Milan on November 22, 1957. The first edition of six thousand copies sold out on the first day, and there were multiple reprints. In June it was published in France, in September in the United States and the United Kingdom, and in October in Germany. In the United States it topped the best seller list from November 1958 to May 1959. It seemed like the only country in which this Russian masterpiece was not being read was Russia. The CIA decided to do something about that.

A SOVIET TOURIST visiting the 1958 World's Fair in Brussels might have decided that *The Thinker*, Auguste Rodin's famous sculpture, was enough of a temptation to lure them into the Vatican pavilion, that opium den for the spiritually needy masses. While taking in Rodin's masterpiece, which was on loan from the Louvre, the Soviet visitor might have heard an unexpected Russian voice. This was Irina Posnova, a Ukrainian exile and the daughter of an Orthodox theologian, who invited visitors behind a curtain into a concealed library. There Posnova, possibly accompanied by a Russian priest going by the name of Father Pierre, revealed her illegal stash: Russian editions of religious texts either banned or difficult to get hold of in the Soviet Union. The hope was that the recipient of this gift might take the word of God back into the atheist darkness of the Soviet Union.

Such was the case for the first eight months of the fair's run. For those who arrived in September, though, there was something more tantalizing on offer in the Vatican's secret library: a Russian edition of *Doctor Zhivago*. Of those visitors who accepted the gift, some tore off the blue covers and dumped them in the trash to better secrete the pages in their luggage for their return home. Thanks to a combination of the CIA, the Dutch intelligence services, and the hospitality of the pope, Pasternak's novel was returning to Russia.

The distribution of *Doctor Zhivago* was a propaganda coup for the United States. Expo 58 was the first World's Fair hosted in the Cold War era and therefore an opportunity to make a powerful ideological statement. The Soviet Union had seized the opportunity by spending more than $50 million to construct a vast pavilion to exhibit their technological prowess. Displayed before the imposing gaze of a giant statue of Lenin was a replica of Sputnik-1, which the previous year had become the first satellite to be launched into Earth's orbit. This unexpected success had precipitated a crisis in the United States, with fears that beyond the launching pad the Soviet Union was leaving the West behind. A year before the launch of Sputnik-1, Khrushchev had declared, "Whether you like it or not, history is on our side. We will bury you." With Sputnik, that prediction had suddenly seemed much less far-fetched. And if the Soviet Union could develop the technology to get into space quicker than the United States, did that mean they were also making military advances? Lyndon Johnson, the Democratic majority leader, declared it a worse defeat than Pearl Harbor. This was not just political point scoring; the rocket that delivered Sputnik was an ICBM and the implication was that if the Soviets could launch a rocket into space, they would have little trouble launching one at the United States.[15] Anxieties about a "missile gap" prompted renewed investment in education, research, and the military even if President Eisenhower knew that Soviet missile capacity was not what official Soviet sources claimed. Secret overflights of high-altitude U-2 aircraft, equipped with powerful cameras, showed that when it came to missile numbers, Khrushchev was bluffing. Nevertheless, in launching Sputnik, the Soviet Union had secured an important Cold War victory. To rub it in, at the fair the Soviets also displayed a replica of Sputnik-2, the second satellite to make it into orbit and the first to carry a living creature (Laika the dog).

Anything that could be done to undermine Soviet triumphalism in Brussels was seized upon by the CIA. They had long been using books as weapons in a variety of countries, but the *Zhivago* operation, code-named AEDINOSAUR, was their most ambitious yet. Over the previous decade the CIA had funded a number of different schemes for getting printed matter beyond the Iron Curtain. From 1952 to 1957, millions of balloons were launched from three sites in West Germany, carrying propaganda leaflets into Czechoslovakia, Hungary, and Poland (the Czechoslovak air force was ordered to shoot these balloons down). By 1956 the strategy shifted to direct mailing of pamphlets and books to strategically selected addresses in Warsaw Pact countries. This assumption that books had the capacity to change people in ways that other methods could not was unsurprising in this generation of college-educated Americans: it underpinned the liberal arts ethos that was fundamental to the way they had been educated. Books were inspirational, revelatory, and as such, the CIA found them "the most important weapon of strategic (long-range) propaganda."[16] As a result, the CIA also secretly subsidized publishers who brought out banned books in their original languages, presuming some of these would find their way into the Eastern bloc. One such publisher, Bedford Publishing Company, had a budget that grew from an initial $10,000 in 1956 to more than $1 million by the late sixties.[17] The goal of the program was to institute Western values through "psychology, literature, the theater and the visual arts" rather than "directly antagonizing materials."[18] As such, the type of books sent across the Iron Curtain were not just politically charged, like Orwell's *Nineteen Eighty-Four* and Koestler's *Darkness at Noon,* but also seemingly apolitical works, like Joyce's *Portrait of the Artist as a Young Man* and Nabokov's memoir *Speak, Memory.*

It is not clear where and when it happened, but at some point, a British spy managed to laboriously photograph, page by page, the Russian manuscript of *Doctor Zhivago* and send it to CIA headquarters at Langley in January 1958. The agency realized it had something special. John Maury, the head of the Soviet Russia division, wrote to Frank Wisner, describing the novel as "the most heretical literary work by a Soviet author since Stalin's death."[19] Maury was an astute reader; the novel did not call for an uprising against the Kremlin, or enumerate the historical crimes of the Soviet Union, but it did ignore pretty much every single edict issued by the Communist Party as to the purpose of literature and how it should be made.

Wisner and the CIA were invested in the idea that literature that did not look like propaganda was much more effective at winning hearts and minds than polemical material—this had been their whole rationale for backing the non-Communist left and magazines like *Encounter*. It was easy for the Soviet authorities to dismiss a novel by someone like Koestler as propaganda. But Pasternak was different. He was prepared to criticize the regime, but his criticism was difficult to dismiss because it grew out of a self-evident love for both Russia and literature. *Doctor Zhivago* was not written as propaganda or out of ideological fervor, but nevertheless it was banned by Moscow, and this suited the CIA's needs perfectly. The lead character, Zhivago, a doctor and a poet, refuses to engage with politics and it was this, Maury argued, that was "fundamental." "This book has great propaganda value," read a CIA memo, "not only for its thought-provoking nature, but also for the circumstances of its publication: we have the opportunity to make Soviet citizens wonder what is wrong with their government, when a fine literary work by the man acknowledged to be the greatest living Russian writer is not even available in his own country in his own language for his own people to read."[20]

The CIA developed a two-pronged plan of attack. First, they would do everything they could to promote *Doctor Zhivago* in the West and, from the beginning, this involved a plan to get the attention of the Nobel Prize committee in Sweden.[21] The second prong was getting Russian-language copies of the novel into the Soviet Union. The CIA explored different ways of getting the book published in the States but changed plan when they heard that an anti-Communist Dutch publisher, Mouton, was in negotiations with Feltrinelli over a Russian-language edition. The CIA asked for Dutch intelligence to figure out if Mouton might be able to produce an early run for their exclusive use, but on the condition that their role in it remain secret. Dutch agents used an intermediary, a retired army officer, to approach Mouton with a deal: he needed one thousand copies by early September, he could provide page proofs, and the whole process had to be handled with the utmost discretion. In return they would be paid handsomely and in cash. (One of the Mouton editors later claimed the army officer told them that if they did not do the deal, he would offer the proofs to a rival publisher).[22] Mouton agreed and, once this advance run was complete, the one thousand copies were distributed to CIA stations around Europe, with the largest package being sent to Brussels for the Expo.[23] From there, copies of the novel found their way back into the Soviet Union. One even made it into the hands of Pasternak himself, who was disappointed to find it full of errors, based as it was on an earlier typescript. However, he soon had more pressing problems to worry about.

IN THE LATE SUMMER OF 1958 rumors began to circulate that Pasternak was the favorite to win the Nobel Prize. The Soviet Union had long pressed the case of Mikhail Sholokhov, whose *And Quiet Flows the Don* was considered the greatest Russian novel since the revolution, but, to their dismay, he did not even make the shortlist. Pasternak's inclusion on that list (along with Karen Blixen and Alberto Moravia) caused the Kremlin to consider its response should he win. Once again, the suggestion that an adapted version of the novel should be published was rejected. The Soviet Embassy in Stockholm was ordered to communicate to the Swedish intellectual community that selecting Pasternak would constitute "an unfriendly act."[24]

On the afternoon of October 23, Pasternak took his usual walk in the surrounding countryside, only to be confronted by foreign journalists seeking his reaction to winning the Nobel Prize (the Moscow correspondents of the major American and European outlets had rushed off to Peredelkino as soon as they heard the news of his win). He had little to say but was obviously delighted and returned to his dacha to celebrate. The following day, the novelist Konstantin Fedin was instructed to visit Pasternak and urge him to reject the prize. Pasternak refused. There were two days of official silence on the matter before the backlash began.[25]

Pasternak was vilified in the press for his "shameful, unpatriotic attitude."[26] The rejection letter he had received from *Novy Mir* after seeking to publish an excerpt of *Doctor Zhivago* with them was published in a prominent literary journal. He was expelled from the Union of Soviet Writers, which meant the denial of various benefits, including a pension. The KGB placed him under ostentatious surveillance.

Reeling, Pasternak contemplated suicide and suggested that Ivinskaya join him in taking an overdose of Nembutal.[27] She managed to talk him out of it. With the ferocity of the attacks on him intensifying, Pasternak drove into Moscow and sent a telegram to the Swedish Academy renouncing the prize. If he hoped this would defuse the crisis, he could not have been more wrong, as his change of mind was transparently due to the pressure to which he had been subjected by the Kremlin. Not only had the Soviet Union refused to publish *Doctor Zhivago;* now it was forcing its author to reject the highest literary honor. Newspapers around the world carried protests by writers and intellectuals at

Pasternak's treatment. Ernest Hemingway offered him a place to stay. Nehru interceded directly with Khrushchev. Pasternak's rejection of the prize did nothing to abate the campaign against him—if anything, it intensified it. One polemic insisted Pasternak should be kicked out of the country. Fearing exile, he agreed to write a letter appealing directly to Khrushchev. He also put his name to an open letter, published in *Pravda*, in which he claimed he had rejected the Nobel Prize because of the way it was being politically exploited in the West.

The *Zhivago* affair had, of course, been exploited in the West, but the heavy-handed approach of the Soviet authorities had made such exploitation easier. Khrushchev had sought to convince the world that he was more politically and culturally liberal, that the age of Stalinist repression was an aberration. The treatment of Pasternak, though, coming hard on the heels of the suppression of the Hungarian uprising, was a scandal that carried ugly echoes of the 1930s and the suppression of many of the best writers of Pasternak's generation. The toll it took on Pasternak was considerable, and while the international scandal offered him protection from imprisonment, he was effectively placed in internal exile. He continued to write and receive visitors in his dacha but, suffering from lung cancer, he became weaker by the day. One of his correspondents at this time was Stephen Spender, the two poets exchanging letters about the poetry they admired.[28] Pasternak died on the evening of May 30, 1960, surrounded by his family.

IT BEGAN WITH A SMALL HANDWRITTEN NOTE stuck up by the ticket counter at Moscow's Kiev station. "At four o'clock on the afternoon of Thursday, June 2," it read, "the last leave-taking of Boris Leonidovich Pasternak, the greatest poet of present day Russia, will be held."[29] The location was carefully chosen: trains for Peredelkino departed from Kiev station. Pasternak's death on May 30, 1960, had been met with calculated silence by the official organs of the government and the Communist Party. Only *Literatura i Zhizn* (Literature and Life) carried a perfunctory announcement from the board of the Literary Fund on June 1, which was reprinted by the more prestigious *Literaturnaya Gazeta* (Literary Gazette) the following day—that of the funeral—and only then at the very bottom of the back page.

Earlier in May, Khrushchev had succeeded in publicly embarrassing Eisenhower, signaling the end of a period of détente between the two superpowers. On May 1, an American U-2 spy plane, photographing Russian missile launch sites from high altitude, had been shot down over the Soviet Union. The CIA had assured Eisenhower that a self-destruct device would have obliterated any evidence of spy-camera equipment and that the pilot, Francis Gary Powers, had no chance of surviving a crash from such high altitude. As a consequence, Eisenhower agreed to the use of a CIA-concocted cover story: NASA released a statement saying one of their weather research planes had gone missing over northern Turkey. Khrushchev set his trap, claiming that this was no weather research plane but actually one used for spying. He withheld one crucial bit of information: Powers was alive. When the Americans stuck to their story, assuming the Russians had no proof, Khrushchev played his hand, disclosing that not only had Powers survived but that he had confessed to the true purpose of his mission. Incriminating photographic equipment had also survived the crash. Outmaneuvered, Eisenhower privately considered resigning. The Americans were due to meet with the Russians, British, and French at the Four Powers Summit on May 15, a meeting planned as a steppingstone toward ending the Cold War. Now it promised to be stage for Soviet crowing. Khrushchev did not disappoint: he demanded an apology from Eisenhower and when it did not come, the meeting collapsed and with it hopes of a truce in the Cold War.

The U-2 incident had been a victory for the hard-liners in the Kremlin. They had exposed the American president lying about an illegal spying program not only to his own people but to the rest of the world, too. Such was the geopolitical climate when Pasternak died. The last thing the Kremlin needed was an event like Pasternak's funeral turning into a rallying point for internal dissent and a new round of international condemnation. For that reason, the news of Pasternak's death was deliberately suppressed, with all the major newspapers ignoring it. The strategy might have worked, too, had Pasternak not meant so much to so many.

Moscow's network of writers, intellectuals, and students sprang into action, and more notices like the one posted at Kiev station began to appear around the city, replaced as soon as the police tore them down. Taking another approach, the Kremlin used their informants in Moscow cultural circles to put it about that the secret police would be present at the funeral and that they would photograph all mourners. Members of the Union of Soviet Writers were given unofficial warnings that the funeral should be avoided. As a result, Konstantin Fedin, the newly appointed chairman of the union, who had been a good friend and neighbor to Pasternak, claimed to be ill and did not attend. But still, the mourners came, and by the hundreds.

Among them was Priscilla Johnson, a journalist for the North American Newspaper Alliance, a large newspaper syndicate.[30] "From the moment I set foot on the suburban platform of Moscow's Kiev Station just after one o'clock on the afternoon of June 2, I sensed that there were people around me who were determined to be present at his funeral," she wrote. "The first mourners I saw were an elderly man and two elderly women who huddled together and stared up at a blackboard where arrivals and departures of the suburban trains were scrawled in chalk. I knew them by their black clothes and by the sprigs of lilac and tulip they held in their hands." Aboard the train Johnson spotted familiar venerable faces from Moscow's cultural scene as well as students and young poets coming to pay their respects to the master.

On arrival, the crowd made their way through the countryside to Pasternak's dacha. Branches of pine trees had been cut and arranged on the lawn to protect the grass from the crowd. Waiting patiently under the blooming lilac trees, the mourners took their turn to enter the house and pay their respects. According to Alexander Gladkov, who wrote a memoir about his friendship with Pasternak, it was not hard to spot "the alien element" in the midst of this group: the secret policemen went about their work, logging names, taking pictures, listening in on conversations.[31] Inside the dacha, the great pianist Sviatoslav Richter played on Pasternak's old upright, signaling the beginning of the funeral procession with Chopin's "Marche Funèbre." The officials present wanted Pasternak's body placed in a blue van parked out front so they could drive it up the hill to the burial plot. But while their instructions were to get the whole thing over and done with as quickly as possible, the pallbearers, and the crowd around them, had other ideas. "As the pallbearers set a fast pace down the roadway and the crowd of about a thousand struggled to keep up, a cloud of dust swirled over the open coffin and a broiling, late afternoon sun beat down," Johnson wrote. "At moments, in the crowd, I glimpsed Pasternak's body in profile; the rest of the time, only a lock of white hair was visible."[32]

Graveside, Pasternak's old friend Valentin Asmus, a short, white-haired philosophy professor, gave a speech. Then, despite the best efforts of the literary fund officials to wrap things up, a young actor from the Moscow Art Theater started to recite Pasternak's "Hamlet." This was a banned poem, appearing as it did among the collection of poems gathered at the end of *Doctor Zhivago,* yet, according to Johnson "a thousand pairs of lips moved in silent unison."[33] The lid was placed on the coffin and it was lowered into the grave. The crowd was encouraged to disperse, but around fifty mourners remained graveside, taking turns to recite poems. The secret policemen took notes but did not break up the group.

PASTERNAK'S FUNERAL HAD BECOME THE FOCUS of a modest kind of defiance, a civilized but determined protest. Even attending the funeral had demanded courage, but there was clearly resolution to honor Pasternak, even if it meant personal risk. "Anxious to have a complete story of Pasternak's burial reach the outside world, yet not daring to speak more than a few words to a Western journalist," Johnson wrote, "Russians of all ages appeared again and again at my side to whisper the name of a speaker, the title of a poem being recited, or a bit of information about the man who was being buried."[34]

Among this crowd of mourners was one devotee who had a more ambitious plan of defiance. He had already taken the first steps in following Pasternak's example, by having his work smuggled out to be published abroad, disguising his identity by using the pseudonym Abram Tertz. The KGB were already on the case and their agents, mingled with the crowd, were on the alert for any rumors about the identity of this mysterious new writer. Yet Tertz was hiding in plain sight: he was the bearded man solemnly carrying Pasternak's coffin lid. It was a symbolic gesture that almost everyone there that day could only appreciate in retrospect. Andrei Sinyavsky, for that was his name, was ready to take up Pasternak's mantle.

Part Six

CRISIS

TWENTY-FOUR

Greene

HAVANA, 1957–1963

GRAHAM GREENE CAME TO CUBA in November 1957 to write a comic novel about spying. The idea for the book was taken from his wartime experience with SIS and the case of Agent Garbo, a spy based in Lisbon who sold the Nazis reports from a supposed network of agents all over Britain. When British intelligence intercepted these reports, they realized they were nonsense. It turned out Garbo was Juan Pujol Garcia, who had developed a hatred of fascism during the Spanish Civil War and was writing reports out of a combination of British newspapers, guidebooks, and his own imagination. So impressed were SIS by the work of this amateur that they subsequently put him on the payroll.

Stationed in Sierra Leone, Greene had seen how easy it would be to game the system himself, to make up agents, charge fictional expenses, and secure an easy living making up plausible reports using largely publicly available information. For the novel he was planning, he wanted to create a British Garbo, an agent who deceives the secret service with fictitious reports not because of any ideological purpose but because he needs the money. Greene's initial plan, when he had first thought of the story as a movie treatment, had been to set the novel in Estonia in the build-up to the Second World War. He realized, however, that an English agent inadvertently conspiring with Nazism was too dark for the kind of comic tone he had in mind. The corruption, sleaze, and glamor of Havana was a much better fit for what he wanted. He also decided to bring the action into the contemporary moment. He decided that having his novel set "in fantastic Havana, among the absurdities of the Cold War" was "allowably comic."[1] As Greene soon learned, however, there was much more to Cuba than the decadence of Havana, and the Cold War was about to come to the country in a way that was anything but comic.

GREENE BEGAN TO VISIT HAVANA in the early 1950s, "for the sake of the Floridita restaurant (famous for daiquiris and Morro crabs), for the brothel life, the roulette in every hotel, the fruit machines spilling out jackpots of silver dollars, the Shanghai Theatre, where for one dollar and twenty-five cents one could see a nude cabaret of extreme obscenity with the bluest of blue films in the interval."[2] This was a city that allowed Greene to freely indulge his appetite for booze, sex, and drugs (cocaine in Cuba, opium in Vietnam, Benzedrine back in London) with a bit of gambling on the side. The seediness and squalor, the ostentatious wealth, the cosmopolitan crowd—it all seemed perfect for a spy thriller. On those early trips, he later maintained, he had been oblivious to the "sad political background of arbitrary imprisonment and torture." By 1957, though, the country was in the grip of an insurrection and it was impossible to avoid the increasingly dictatorial methods Fulgencio Batista's corrupt regime used in their bid to cling to power. As he had done in Malaysia and Vietnam, Greene wanted to get closer to the combat zone and decided to travel to Santiago.

Greene chose Santiago because, as the capital of Oriente province, it was the closest city to the Sierra Maestra mountain range, the base of a band of guerrilla fighters growing in numbers and influence. Led by Fidel Castro, the 26th of July Movement took its name from a failed attack on the Moncado army barracks in 1953. Castro, a twenty-six-year-old with political ambitions, had organized the attack in the hope of triggering a revolution against Batista, who had taken control of Cuba in a military coup the previous year. The attack was a failure, many of the rebels were killed, and Castro was thrown in prison. On his release he went into exile in Mexico, from where he reorganized his band. A group of guerrillas sailed back to Cuba in 1955 on an American yacht called the *Granma* and, despite taking heavy casualties, set up a base in the Sierra Maestra, from where they launched attacks against Batista's forces and recruited supporters across the country. As the 26th of July Movement grew in influence, it became a rallying point for the other dissident groups fighting the Batista regime.

Before flying to Santiago, an intermediary arranged for Greene to meet with members of the *lucha clandestina* (the Castro-supporting underground) at a restaurant called El Chico on the outskirts of Havana. Greene wanted to find a way to interview Castro; his supporters saw the value in having a prestigious novelist sympathetic to their cause. At the dinner, Greene met Nydia Sarabia, a courier for the 26th of July Movement, who was taking the same plane as him to Santiago the following morning. Greene was persuaded to take a suitcase of warm clothes destined for the rebels in the mountains on the flight, as it would look less suspicious to the authorities for a foreigner to be carrying woolen jumpers and socks.[3]

To Greene's surprise, and suspicion, a journalist with *Time* magazine insisted on accompanying him to Santiago. It seemed fishy, so Greene had his driver warn Sarabia when she arrived at the airport that he had company. She instructed him to behave like they had never met. She would call him at his hotel the following morning.

The atmosphere on arrival in Santiago was conducive to

paranoia. "The night was hot and humid," Greene wrote, "it was nearly the hour of the unofficial curfew, and the hotel clerk made no pretense of welcoming strangers. The taxis soon packed up and went, the square cleared of people, a squad of soldiers went by, a man in a dirty white drill suit rocked himself backwards and forwards in a chair in the hall, making a small draft in the mosquitoey evening. [. . .] The smell of a police station lay over the city."[4]

The next morning the *Time* reporter came to Greene's room with a man in a gabardine suit professing to be Castro's public relations manager in Santiago. Greene immediately sussed him for a spy, but before he could get rid of him, his phone started ringing. The man in the suit looked concerned as Greene ushered him out of the room. It was Sarabia on the line, giving Greene an address—on the Calle San Francisco—at which to meet. When the man in the suit returned to the room, he accused Greene of speaking with Batista's agents and demanded to know what he had told them. Greene refused, accused the man in the suit of being a spy himself, and left the hotel in a fluster. No sooner had he got into a taxi than someone ducked in uninvited claiming to speak "British" and offering to show Greene the sights. Having lost the man in the suit, Greene now needed to lose his tour guide, surely a Batista informer. He asked to be taken to a church on the Calle San Francisco and then hid in the cool of the cloisters, supervised by a suspicious priest, until he was sure the guide was bored of waiting for him and left. Then, as Greene marched up the road in the midday heat looking for the Castro organization's safe house, the man in the suit pulled up with the *Time* journalist and told Greene to get in. There had been a misunderstanding—they were all on the same side after all.

The way he later described this farcical chain of events was in keeping with the tone of the novel he was writing, with Greene playing the role of the hapless Englishman plunged into a world of espionage he fails to understand. In *Our Man in Havana,* Greene has Jim Wormold, a struggling vacuum cleaner salesman, approached by the British secret service to do work for them. Paid on commission, abandoned by his wife, and with a daughter who has expensive tastes, Wormold begins to invent agents and deliver invented reports to London as a way to increase his income. Such is the credulity of the Secret Service that the more outrageous Wormold's lies, the more believable they seem. Greene classified the novel as an "entertainment."

His trip to Santiago, like his novel, ended on a much darker note. In the Santiago safe house, he met Armando Hart, one of the founding members of Castro's movement and an influential leader in the urban underground. Hart had been arrested in a government crackdown that followed a failed assassination attempt on Batista during which rebel forces staged a frontal assault on the presidential palace; Greene met him shortly after he had managed to escape from prison. Also present was Haydée Santamaría, who had been part of the original band that attacked the Moncado barracks. She had been captured but refused to talk, even after being shown the castrated and blinded bodies of her fiancé and her brother. Santamaría had subsequently married Hart, and the pair played important roles in the government after the revolution.

Greene finished writing *Our Man in Havana* in the summer of 1958, with a more sinister undercurrent to the story than originally planned. He might not have realized it when he first chose it as his location, but Cuba was the perfect Cold War location. The "unpleasant doings" that had previously taken place out of sight of the tourists are, in the world of the novel, becoming more prominent as the regime is "creaking dangerously towards its end."[5] Wormold has to try to outmaneuver Captain Segura, the Cuban secret police chief nicknamed "the Red Vulture," who is a "specialist in torture and mutilation" and has a cigarette case made of the skin of one of his victims to prove it.[6] Greene modeled Segura on Esteban Ventura, who was known for his white linen suit and being, in Greene's words, the "chief torturer" in Batista's police force. (Greene noted with satisfaction that when Batista fled the country on New Year's Eve 1958, Ventura had to force his way onto the plane out of Havana at gunpoint. The attack dog turned on its master.)[7]

Bearing in mind the very tangible threat presented by Ventura and his service, why did the 26th of July Movement take the risk of meeting with Greene? Hart and Santamaría, both intellectuals, certainly saw the value in having a prestigious ally like Greene on the global stage, but they also had tangible goals that they hoped to achieve by meeting him. They told him that the British were supplying weapons to the Batista regime, and asked him to do what he could to make this public. In October 1958, Greene, now back in Britain, wrote to Hugh Delargy, the Labour MP for Thurrock, asking if he might raise the issue of the arms sales (the United States had imposed an embargo on sales to Batista the previous March). When Delargy asked questions to this end in the Commons, the government, flustered, denied that there had been export licenses granted (although they later admitted there had been). It was a public relations victory for the Cuban rebels.

When Castro and his forces took control of the country in January 1959, Greene waded into the political fray himself, writing a letter to the editor of the *Times* attacking the dangerous ignorance with which Britain had behaved toward Cuba. He zeroed in on the claims made by Selwyn Lloyd, the Foreign Secretary, that Britain was unaware of any civil war in Cuba when the weapons had been sold. Greene speculated as to how the Foreign Office was getting its information: it had been obvious enough to him on his last visit that the country was at war. The implication was that either British intelligence (and the Foreign Office) were being deceived by the Batista regime about the true state of affairs, or that the government knew what was going on and chose to turn a blind eye in order to make arms sales. In the context of the Cold War, that these sales might help contain a left-wing insurrection made such a calculated obscurity even more desirable.

What remains a mystery is Greene's motivation in intervening on behalf of Cuba. Certainly, his politics were drifting leftward, and he admired the fact that Castro's radicalism—at this stage the Cuban leader did not classify himself as a Marxist-Leninist—did not preclude a respect for Greene's beloved Catholicism. And Greene's distaste for the United States and its foreign policy, sharpened in Indochina, had been intensified by his being denied a visa under the McCarran Act. Batista's regime was effectively propped up by the United States and, throughout Cuba, Greene had seen American self-interest coming at the cost of the exploitation and repression of ordinary Cubans. Indeed, while in Saigon he saw the dangers presented by American idealism and naiveté, in Havana he saw only American greed and corruption.

What is harder to understand is Greene's criticisms of his own government or his writing a novel that ridiculed its intelligence agencies. While his SIS file remains classified, Greene's biographers have assembled evidence that he was still working informally for his old employer, providing them with information (as part of this relationship, it is claimed, SIS also picked up the tab on his considerable expenses). His Castro contacts might have been less sympathetic if they had known he was passing on information to the British secret service. Perhaps Greene was using his outspoken politics as cover for gaining exactly this kind of information.[8] Perhaps British intelligence did not oppose the publication of *Our Man in Havana* for similar reasons.[9] Or perhaps the explanation is more straightforward: that Greene was capable of living with the apparent contradiction of supporting the Cuban Revolution while at the same time passing on information to SIS. He was someone who seemed to switch between different modes without seeming to care that they often contradicted each other. He felt acute pity for the downtrodden and the abused but was capable of being cold, even cruel, in his personal relations. He was serious about his Catholic faith but sinned with the best of them. He criticized authority in its many guises, including the British government and the empire, but furthered its ends in his work for the intelligence services. The contradictions were even present in his work, where he oscillated between writing "entertainments" and works of self-conscious literary ambition.

IN *THE EIGHTEENTH BRUMAIRE OF LOUIS BONAPARTE*, Karl Marx wrote that "all great world-historic facts and personages appear, so to speak, twice . . . the first time as tragedy, the second time as farce."[10] In *Our Man in Havana*, Greene inadvertently reversed this formula. His novel was a farcical rehearsal for the Cuban Missile Crisis.

From its opening pages, the novel riffs on the absurdity of life under threat of atomic extinction. Wormold's chief professional anxiety is that nobody wants to buy his company's latest model—the Atomic Pile Suction Cleaner—because of the associations of its name, and as he is paid on commission this is only deepening his financial worries. His eccentric German friend, Dr. Hasselbacher, tells him not to worry too much about his long-term future. "We live in an atomic age, Mr Wormold," he says. "Push a button—piff bang—where are we? Another scotch, please."[11] To Wormold, though, the Cold War is unreal, certainly not possessed of the immediacy of his personal anxieties: the bully who persecuted him at school exists for him in a way that Khrushchev or "the scientists who tested the new H-bomb on Christmas Island" do not.[12]

If the enormity of nuclear war makes it impossible to reconcile with life as lived, then the clandestine way the war is being fought between intelligence agencies appears absurd in a different way. Hawthorne, the secret service agent who recruits Wormold, and his superiors are shown to be playing a game of make-believe in which they cling to their jargon and protocols as a means of convincing themselves of their utility. When trying to recruit his man, Hawthorne ushers Wormold into a hotel bathroom and runs the tap to counter possible bugs. He starts talking about how previous operations have failed for a lack of precautions and a confused Wormold says that it sounds like he is talking about the secret service. "It *is* the Secret Service, old man, or so the novelists call it," Hawthorne replies.[13] Having got Wormold on board, Hawthorne returns to London and briefs the Chief on his new asset. Greene included details, such as the light outside the chief's office that turns green when it is safe to enter, that were taken directly from his time at SIS. The Chief, however, is shown to be even more of a fantasist than Hawthorne, taking the snippets of information he gets about Wormold and, through the filter of his "literary imagination," persuading himself, in quite some detail, that this rather feckless vacuum cleaner salesman is in fact a "merchant adventurer" prepared to embrace his patriotic duty.

When Wormold begins inventing his agents it is not that he is a particularly brilliant liar, it is that he is now operating in a world in which fiction is ready currency. In Sierra Leone, Greene had noticed that the service was always eager to add more cards to its files, irrespective of whether the information contained therein was useful or true; each card added another small part to a vast, unreadable story. The problem for Wormold is that he gets caught up in telling his tale, and his story starts to become the most exciting one in town. When things begin to unravel, and real people start being confused for Wormold's fictional agents, he tells his friend Hasselbacher that his agents are no more real than characters in novels. "Are they always invented?" Hasselbacher asks. "I don't know how a novelist works, Mr. Wormold. I have never known one before you."[14]

INITIALLY, IT HAD SEEMED there might be a path to peaceful coexistence between America and Cuba. In 1959, Castro had visited the United States and met with Vice President Richard Nixon as both parties explored the possibility of a reconfigured relationship but the new leader soon grew impatient with American criticism of his radical reformist agenda and was angered by Cuban emigres being allowed to fly missions designed to undermine his government into Cuban airspace from bases in Florida.[15] The situation soon spiraled into outright hostility. Early in 1960 Castro nationalized the sugar plantations, hurting American owners and investors. The United States responded by lowering the sugar quota imported from Cuba. Castro's government in turn struck a deal with the Soviet Union, by which they would take sugar exports in exchange for cheap oil. When local American-owned refineries refused to process the Soviet crude, Castro nationalized them, too. In October 1960, the U.S. imposed a trade embargo, and Castro nationalized all remaining American property on the island.

The following month John F. Kennedy was elected. On the campaign trail he attacked his predecessor, Eisenhower, for having been weak on Cuba and, once in office, accused the previous administration of allowing "a hostile and militant communist satellite" to be established just 90 miles from the U.S. coast. The Kennedy administration decided it was going to take out Castro and install a government much more amenable to U.S. interests.

Just a few months after taking office, in April 1961, the president authorized the invasion of Cuba by Brigade 2506, a paramilitary unit made up mostly of Cuban exiles recruited and trained by the CIA. Launching from Guatemala, some 1,300 counterrevolutionaries tried to invade at the Bahia los Cochinos—the Bay of Pigs—but were met with well-organized Cuban resistance.[16] Kennedy refused to countenance the use of full-blown U.S. air support, as he did not want the operation to be perceived as an American-led invasion, and the majority of the Brigade were captured. The whole operation was a disaster, ill conceived and poorly executed, and Kennedy was angry at the CIA and at his own naivete. For Castro, the attempted invasion was evidence he could advertise to the world that the United States was bent on toppling his revolutionary government. To Khrushchev it was an invitation to challenge the mettle of a seemingly weak and inexperienced opponent, first in Berlin, and later back in Cuba.

Badly bruised, Kennedy and his advisors had to rethink their options. In March 1960, Eisenhower had commissioned the CIA to look into clandestine operations against Cuba. In November 1961, Kennedy authorized what became known as Operation Mongoose, with the goal of trying to undermine the Castro regime and, if possible, to assassinate Castro himself. The Church Committee, a 1975 Senate select committee looking into the conduct of the intelligence services, including the CIA, revealed there were at least eight attempts to kill Castro between 1960 and 1965, but those were but a portion of the outlandish operations pursued by the Americans.[17] The Operation Mongoose team was led by Edward Lansdale, whom Greene knew from Vietnam. With Cuba, Lansdale had to be more creative in his approach than he had been when running covert operations into North Vietnam, especially after the debacle at the Bay of Pigs. The demand for action came straight from the top, with Robert Kennedy, the attorney general, leading meetings and demanding tangible results. Proposed actions included the blowing up of a railroad bridge in the Pinar del Rio province, staging a grenade attack on the Chinese embassy in Havana, mining Cuban ports, setting alight a tanker in the waters off Havana, and attacking key oil refineries. The State Department drew up plans for damaging the Cuban economy, and the CIA infiltrated Cuban exiles back into the country to set up weapons caches.[18] As well as working with the exiles, the CIA exploited the fact that the Mafia had lost lucrative business in the revolution to try to get them to assassinate Castro. The Operation Mongoose team proposed bizarre schemes for discrediting Castro, such as drugging him with hallucinogens before he gave one of his speeches or getting chemicals into his clothing that would cause his hair— and, most important, his beard—to fall out. According to the Church Committee, the CIA planned to get him to smoke cigars spiked with highly toxic botulinum, to inject him with poison through a syringe secreted inside a pen, or, knowing he liked diving, to hide an explosive inside a large seashell.

Having seen the limitations of using exile paramilitaries at the Bay of Pigs, the Pentagon, under direction from the Kennedys, began to think of ways they could stage a provocation that could be used to justify a full-scale military invasion of Cuba. One plan was to stage a terror campaign, including bombings, in Miami and Washington, which could be blamed on Castro. Another proposal was to blow up a U.S. vessel outside the Guantanamo naval base, which remained under American control, and blame the Cubans. Other options included attacking another Caribbean nation but making it look like Cuban troops were responsible and even simulating the downing of a civilian plane and blaming it on the Cuban air force.

Even though Greene intended Wormold's deceptions to be primarily comic, he had clearly tapped into something fundamental about the way the Cold War was being fought. The Soviet Union's propensity for self-serving fantasy—the inflated harvests, the invented statistics, the implausible conspiracies— had been much attacked in the West, perhaps most memorably in *Animal Farm*. But as the stakes grew higher, the agents of the United States also drifted into the make-believe. It was not just that espionage blurred the lines between fact and fiction, it was that spies were creating alternate realities. They were weaponizing storytelling, and the deeper they sunk into this imaginary world, the less believable their stories got. Take one of Lansdale's more outlandish schemes: he wanted to spread rumors in Cuba that Castro was the Antichrist and then, on All Souls' Day, to launch star shells (also known as "lightballs") from a U.S. submarine to light up the night and presage the Second Coming of Christ.[19] This was Wormold on acid.

IN *OUR MAN IN HAVANA*, Wormold soon learns that he needs one massive lie to help bind together all his smaller ones. After a visit to Santiago, he files a report about rumors of "big military installations under construction" in the mountains. One of his "agents" has spied "a large concrete platform too extensive for any building" and reports that there is "strange machinery in transport."[20] Wormold promises to send over his agent's sketches of this machinery. He disassembles one of his vacuum cleaners and makes "a series of careful drawings" of the various parts.[21] He then adds a man in a bowler hat for scale, so that each piece appears huge. The cleaner he uses is, of course, the "Atomic Pile."

Wormold's reports cause a stir back at London headquarters, where the service assumes the constructions "have a Communist origin."[22] They demand Wormold use his agents to get photographs of these potential launch sites, and there is much handwringing about how much information should be shared with the Americans. "Of course we are only a small country," Captain

Segura tells Wormold, "but we lie very close to the American coast. And we point at your own Jamaica base. If a country is surrounded, as Russia is, it will try to punch a hole through from inside."[23] Wormold's invented launch site exposed a clear American vulnerability: the proximity of Cuba to the United States.

Again, Greene was ahead of the curve. After the Bay of Pigs, the anti-Castro hawks in the Kennedy administration were primed for any provocation that could allow them to initiate military action. On the morning of Tuesday, October 16, 1962, they got more provocation than they would ever have wanted. Photographs from a U-2 spy plane revealed that missile launch sites had been constructed in several locations that would place much of the eastern seaboard of the U.S. within range of surface-to-surface missiles. The photographs also captured images of the missiles themselves. It was clear that this was beyond the capacities of the Cuban military at the time—this was the work of the Soviet Union.

The previous April, Khrushchev had suggested to Castro that installing missiles would be the best guarantee of deterring an American invasion. By July, the first Soviet personnel arrived in Cuba to begin their work; by September the first missiles arrived. There had been rumors circulating among Cuban exiles and CIA agents that missiles were being moved and launch sites being constructed, but it was only when the U-2 photographs came through that the seriousness of the situation became clear. Kennedy, weakened by the defeat at the Bay of Pigs, knew that he had to respond to Khrushchev's provocation. To Kennedy it seemed he had only three options: force Khrushchev to back down; buy Khrushchev's cooperation through concessions; or bomb the missile sites and invade Cuba.

The problem with the first option was that Kennedy did not have much leverage. The United States already had surface-to-surface missiles pointed at the Soviet Union in Turkey, so they could not raise the stakes without pointing out their own hypocrisy. The second option was more plausible, but might come at a heavy price for Kennedy, both in terms of his political reputation at home, where he would be accused of weakness in the fight against Communism, and on the world stage. If Kennedy rolled over in Cuba, would not the Soviet Union begin exerting pressure all over the globe? The third option was certainly a way of showing strength but, while his military advisors were convinced the invasion could be successfully carried off, the chances of the U.S. being hit by a nuclear weapon were high. It was also likely that military action against Cuba would swiftly escalate into global nuclear conflict. Kennedy decided to give the first two options a chance to work.

On October 22, Kennedy delivered a televised address to the nation in which he announced that the Soviet Union had installed nuclear missiles in Cuba. He called on Khrushchev to back down and, as a means of buying time, set up a naval blockade of Cuba to prevent Soviet ships bringing further missiles to the island. Both sides began a massive mobilization of their armed forces at strategic locations around the world.

With tensions escalating, Castro wrote to Khrushchev that he feared an American attack was coming "within the next 24 to 72 hours." He fully expected airstrikes and felt a full invasion was possible. In the event of the latter, he urged the Soviet Union to launch a nuclear strike on the United States. "However harsh and terrible the solution, there would be no other," Castro wrote. The same day, however, Khrushchev sent a rather long, rambling letter to Kennedy in which he appeared to offer to withdraw the missiles in exchange for a pledge not to invade Cuba and an end to the blockade.

Having seemingly made a breakthrough the previous evening, the tension ratcheted back up the following day when a U-2 spy plane was shot down over Cuba by a Soviet surface-to-air missile. Kennedy was urged to bomb the relevant launch site in retaliation but resisted the demands of his generals. Meanwhile, a second letter arrived from Moscow demanding much tougher terms than the previous day's missive, including that the United States agree to remove its missiles from Turkey. Kennedy and his Executive Committee decided to ignore this second letter and agree to the terms of the first. Robert Kennedy met with Anatoly Dobrynin, the Soviet ambassador in Washington, to confirm the agreement—part of which was in fact a secret understanding that the U.S. would remove its missiles from Turkey at a later date (they did so in April 1963). The crisis was at an end.

GREENE RETURNED TO CUBA IN 1963 to see how the revolution was faring after the missile crisis. For Castro, the resolution of the crisis had proved a humiliation. The Americans and the Soviets had communicated through back channels and left him in the cold. Cuba had been used as a pawn in the Cold War, and his relationship with the Russians was never the same again. Castro was hardly the kind of character to be coopted by anyone, and from that moment forth he was more resolved to do things his own way. This did not mean breaking with the Soviet Union— with the U.S. seeking to isolate Cuba, it would have been suicide for his regime—but it did mean an alliance in which he no longer fully trusted Moscow. So, while the Soviet Union continued to subsidize the Cuban economy, Castro was determined to pursue his own course in terms of foreign policy. Through his trusted ambassador, the charismatic Che Guevara, contacts were made with left-wing independence movements around the world, particularly in Latin America and sub-Saharan Africa.

Greene watched Castro deliver one of his long, discursive speeches and concluded that the people had lost none of their faith in the leader of the revolution. Traveling the country, Greene was impressed with the improvements that had been made in terms of infrastructure and education, especially in the countryside. In Havana he found a vibrant cultural scene, all the healthier for having rejected dogmatism, noting that "socialist realism is a joke and not a threat."[24] Greene was not totally taken in, however. He was under no illusion as to what happened to those who opposed the Castro regime. Speaking to some of his old contacts, he learned of the persecution of homosexuals, who were sent to labor camps for "re-education." He disliked the "puritan" streak in Communism and feared that Cuba, for so long a site of hedonism, was going to succumb to it. Still, Greene believed these excesses would be overcome as the regime matured and was confident that in Castro "there is a new voice in the communist world."[25]

TWENTY-FIVE
Le Carré

BERLIN, 1961

WITH THE LIGHTS BLAZING in the windows of the British Embassy in Bonn in the early hours of a Sunday morning, Second Secretary David Cornwell realized something serious must have happened. He was returning from a campaign rally for Willy Brandt of the Social Democratic Party in Nuremberg, where rumors circulated of some sort of impending change in Berlin. Back in Bonn, Cornwell soon discovered what it was: the East German government, with startling speed, was closing the border.

Under the supervision of the security secretary Erich Honecker, a small team holed up in a police station near the Alexanderplatz coordinated Operation Rose, the surprise sealing off of all routes to West Berlin both from East Berlin and from East Germany on the outer edges of the city. For manpower the operation drew on the police, the East German army, local militias, and even the Red Army. The East German secret police, the Stasi, run by Erich Mielke, were responsible for ensuring that the closure did not result in any kind of uprising. Mielke, a former NKVD agent trained in Moscow who had worked for Alexander Orlov during the Spanish Civil War, was exactly the kind of cold-blooded operator to guarantee there was no repeat of the unrest of 1953, when disastrous Stalinist economic policies resulted in roughly one million East German workers rising up in protest. Those demonstrations had been suppressed only through violence, with the German Democratic Republic deploying tanks on the streets, and it was crucial to the regime that there was no repeat. In advance of the operation, Honecker and his team amassed, as discreetly as possible, 18,200 concrete posts, 150 tons of barbed wire, five tons of binding wire, and two tons of staples.[1] In the early hours of August 13—chosen because it was a Sunday—the East German and Soviet forces sprang into action, sealing off 193 streets with barbed wire and concrete bolsters. Tank traps were installed on wider thoroughfares. In some roads the streetlights were switched off to conceal what was happening. At the Brandenburg Gate, under searchlights, crews of workers used hydraulic drills to tear up the road and render it impassable to vehicles. Train stations were closed, and the sewer system patrolled. By dawn, the border was locked down. The American, British, and French diplomatic and intelligence services were caught by surprise.[2]

Cornwell was not just the Second Secretary. And he was not just Cornwell. Just two months previously he had arrived in Bonn after completing his training as an agent of the Secret Intelligence Service (SIS or, as it is also known, MI6), although his status as such was concealed from all but a few highly placed officials. Ostensibly, he was in West Germany agitating for Britain's entry into the European Common Market (the EEC) but this was cover for his real work in the SIS section housed within the embassy. But Cornwell had another secret, too. A week after arriving in Germany, his first novel, *Call for the Dead*, was published by Victor Gollancz, with the author's identity concealed behind the pseudonym John le Carré.

"BERLIN IS THE TESTICLES OF THE WEST," Khrushchev liked to say. "Every time I want to make the West scream, I squeeze on

Berlin."[3] Now Khrushchev was squeezing. The situation had been heading toward crisis since the end of the Second World War, as East Germans flooded across the border to the West, with disastrous economic consequences for the East. It was not only the sheer number of people leaving, but that among those seeking a better life in the West were a disproportionately high number of the most skilled and educated East Germans. The ruling Socialist Unity Party (SED) sought to quell the exodus by closing the Inner German Border, which ran from the Baltic Sea to Czechoslovakia, in 1952. But the border between East and West Berlin remained porous, with large numbers of emigrants funneling into the Western sectors of the city. By the summer of 1961, almost twenty thousand emigrants per month were exiting the East via Berlin. It appeared inevitable that if this flood did not abate, East Germany would collapse. Something had to give.

That same summer, Khrushchev was sizing up a new, young adversary in John F. Kennedy, elected the previous year, and he was keen to see how far he could push him in Europe, especially after the Bay of Pigs fiasco. In November 1958, Khrushchev had issued an ultimatum, demanding that NATO forces leave West Berlin or else he would hand over access to East Berlin to the SED, whose First Secretary, Walter Ulbricht, long coveted the sealing of the border within the city. Eisenhower held firm in the face of these threats, but with every East German that crossed to the West, the pressure mounted. Kennedy had spoken of Berlin as "the great testing place of Western courage and will," and with NATO troops vastly outnumbered, he vowed to increase American military presence in West Germany and Berlin.[4] Khrushchev responded by collaring the British ambassador to Moscow, Frank Roberts, at the Bolshoi Ballet and telling him that "six hydrogen bombs would do for Britain, and nine for France."[5] The escalation of threats culminated in the closing of the border and nobody, on either side, knew exactly what was going to happen next. Any kind of military engagement could swiftly spiral into thermonuclear war.[6]

What was clear was that SIS needed all the help it could get, and Cornwell was sent, in his words, to "flesh out our station in Berlin."[7] No sooner had he landed than he went to see for himself the "barbed wire entanglements" springing up on the border. "I went with a colleague from the Embassy and as we stared back at the weasel faces of the brainwashed little thugs who guarded the Kremlin's latest battlement, he told me to wipe the grin off my face," Cornwell later recalled. "I was not aware I had been grinning, so it must have been one of those soupy grins that comes over me at dreadfully serious moments. There was certainly nothing to grin at in what I saw, and inside myself I felt nothing but disgust and terror, which was exactly what I was supposed to feel: the Wall was perfect theater as well as a perfect symbol of the monstrosity of ideology gone mad."[8]

There was panic in the immediate aftermath of the border closing, with many desperately seeking to flee to the West; Cornwell saw people "jumping out of windows" and heard shooting. It felt like the Cold War was about to ignite on the streets of Berlin. "For three or four nights I hardly slept, and I got into that extraordinary vortex, which you can get into at that age, of sleeplessness and crisis—you forget to eat and you forget to go to bed and you forget to shave," he wrote. "You are crazy-bright and capable of anything."[9] There was a pressing need to gather information. The closure of the border obviously had dramatic ramifications for those agents being run by SIS in the GDR. "Somewhere beyond the Wall, networks of British and American and French and West German secret agents had been caught napping," Cornwell wrote. "None, to my knowledge, had forecast the event, and now they would have to live with their lack of success. Many of them probably had other allegiances anyway. Others would become what are called stay-behind agents, who would henceforth have to communicate by means of hidden radios and prearranged methods of secret writing, set up just for this eventuality."[10]

Over the next weeks and months, Cornwell, traveling back and forth between Bonn and Berlin, watched firsthand the "progress from barbed wire to breeze block." Windows and doorways of houses on the border were cemented up, and a wall was built across Potsdamer Platz, a taste of what was to come. On August 24, the first East German was killed attempting to cross the border, shot while swimming across a canal; less than a week later a second victim was shot. Still, this did not deter people from trying to cross, and ever more formidable barriers were put in place. From October, construction began on a permanent fortification running through the middle of the city.

While Cornwell the spy was at work, so was le Carré the writer. A novel was beginning to take shape, one with the Wall running through it. He later recalled having "this notion of a story about this beat-up agent runner trying to get his agents out of the East." As with *Call for the Dead,* he knew that SIS would have to vet his book and hoped, because he did not run agents in East Germany himself, that he might get it past his employers. Yet his own espionage work—and more specifically his disillusionment with his work—*did* make it into the book. If the Wall was a metaphor for the way monstrous means were being deployed in pursuit of fugitive ends, then it also made Cornwell reflect on the ethical compromises being made by the West in its secret conflict with Communism. It was the living product of an unhinged war, the fighting of which Cornwell had begun to question. As he later put it, "a disgusting gesture of history coincided with some desperate mechanism inside myself, and in six weeks gave me the book that altered my life."[11] It did more than that: it altered the way people thought about the Cold War.

"I WATCHED THE RAMPARTS of the cold war going up on the still-warm ashes of the hot one," le Carré (as he was by then known to the world; he remained David Cornwell only to his family and close friends) later wrote about his time in Berlin in the early 1960s.[12] He was familiar with those ashes. Cornwell had first visited Berlin in 1949, at the end of a year spent studying at the University of Bern—a year that changed the trajectory of his life. He had been a promising schoolboy at Sherborne, an elite private school, but quit before his final term began, desperate to get away from the malign influence of his father, Ronnie Cornwell, a charismatic, manipulative con man.[13] A few days shy of his seventeenth birthday, he moved to Switzerland, choosing it because he spoke German and had previously skied at St. Moritz. Having managed to get himself enrolled at the University of Bern, he studied German literature, wrote poems and stories, and became romantically entangled. Then came "the Great Call." Attending the English church in Kirchenfeld, he was approached by "a thirty-something mumsy lady named Wendy from the British embassy's visa section," who asked him if he wanted to serve his country.[14] He signed documents pledging him to secrecy and began going to left-wing gatherings, reporting on who attended and what they said. Not yet eighteen and he was working as an agent for MI6.

Toward the end of his first year in Bern, he traveled in Germany, a trip that had a profound effect on him. This was the country of Goethe, Schiller, and Büchner, of Mann and Hesse, the writers he adored, but it was also a country of craters and camps. He passed through "the flattened cities of the Ruhr" and visited "the concentration camps of Dachau and Bergen-Belsen while the stench still lingered in the huts."[15] He obtained a visa to visit West Berlin not long after the end of the blockade of the city. While in the city he contracted mumps, and after a period "sick as a dog on an old Wehrmacht mattress in a makeshift German field hospital in the Berlin Underground" he returned to England to recuperate. On turning eighteen he was required to enlist for his National Service and, after basic training, he was selected for Officer Cadet School, where, presumably because of his work for SIS, he was assigned to the Intelligence Corps. At the culmination of his training, he was posted to Austria—a much safer destination than either Korea or Malaya, where many of his fellow officers were sent. As a field security officer in Graz, Cornwell's main job was to interrogate people who had crossed illegally into the West, screening refugees and trying to weed out potential spies. One day his commanding officer showed him two photographs. If he saw either man, he was to report it immediately and, if no commanding officer was available, arrest them himself. The photographs were of Burgess and Maclean.

The pair's defection played a significant role in Cornwell's intelligence career. If he actually wanted a career in espionage, he needed to get a degree first, and was told as much by one "Major Smith," who, on a visit to Graz from Vienna, assured Cornwell he was under consideration for the Secret Service.[16] Despite the lateness of his application, Cornwell managed to secure a place at Oxford, to study French and German. While he went about his studies, Cornwell would also work for MI5. In 1953, as a response to the Maclean and Burgess defection, Dick White, the new head of the security service, ordered a reorganization in which he charged a whole department (F Branch) with responsibility for domestic countersubversion, an important part of which involved trying to infiltrate left-wing student groups.

Cornwell was recruited to do this work by George Leggett, an MI5 analyst who had previously served as an interpreter at the Potsdam Conference. Just as Philby, Maclean, and Burgess had been told to embrace right-wing political groups by their Soviet handlers, Cornwell was told to embrace the left. The idea was that he would report on the activities of suspected Communists while also hoping that he might himself get recruited by Soviet intelligence (known in espionage jargon as "a dangle"). Despite his best efforts, attending numerous Anglo-Soviet Friendship meetings at the Soviet Embassy, he was never approached by the KGB. This, he suspected, was because of how thoroughly British intelligence was penetrated at the time or, equally as plausible, that he "just didn't smell right."

Leggett and Cornwell met for lunches in Woodstock, a pictur-esque market town outside Oxford, to discuss any information Cornwell had gathered. At one meeting, Leggett introduced Cornwell to Maxwell Knight, an MI5 agent with a brilliant rep-utation for agent running.[17] One of his best agents, Olga Gray, had not only infiltrated the British Communist Party by be-coming secretary to its general secretary, Harry Pollitt, but had also played the key role in securing the 1938 arrests of members of a Soviet spy ring operating at the Woolwich Arsenal. Knight was eccentric and charismatic; Ian Fleming used aspects of Knight's personality for "M," James Bond's boss. In the 1950s he became known as a BBC presenter of natural history shows, running a broadcast career in parallel to his espionage work. The young, patriotic Cornwell was excited to be working for men like Knight, even if that meant betraying those who trusted him. The two men remained close in the years to come, with Cornwell, a gifted artist, illustrating some of Knight's books on natural history. And perhaps of special interest to the literary-minded Cornwell was that Knight was also an author, publish-ing a number of detective stories.

Despite being summoned to London for interviews and being vetted by SIS, Cornwell did not directly become a spy after university, as he initially sought the stability and financial security of a job in teaching. The problem of his father's criminality had resurfaced. A check he wrote for Cornwell's university fees had bounced, and Ronnie's businesses came under police investigation. (Cornwell even had to appear at the Royal Courts of Justice to answer questions about his father raised by the Receiver in Bankruptcy.) Even if money could be found to pay his final year's fees, he faced an additional problem: he and his girlfriend, Ann, had become engaged, and under university rules, he would not be able to marry and continue his studies without special permission. He decided instead to take a year off teaching at a private school in Somerset. Afterward, he duly returned to Oxford, having secured the necessary permission from the rector. On graduating, he took a job teaching at Eton College. For a moment, a career in education, rather than espionage, beckoned. But Cornwell soon became impatient with life as a teacher and wrote to Dick Thistlethwaite, an MI5 officer with whom he had remained in touch, to say that he wanted to "come inside." It was, he later remembered, "as if all my life had been preparing me for this moment."[18]

IF THERE WAS ONE RECURRING THEME in Cornwell's experiences as a spy it was betrayal. When he joined MI5 in the spring of 1958, he found it "riven with suspicion and rumor." Located in wealthy Mayfair, the Leconfield House headquarters, a seven-story building with no windows on the ground floor and bomb-proof basement, was surprisingly shabby. Cornwell arrived an idealistic, motivated twenty-six-year-old who was rapidly disenchanted by the ineptitude he saw around him in the overcrowded offices, separated only by ad hoc partitions. A large number of his fellow officers were, in his words, "former colonial coppers and pink-cheeked chaps on loan from the armed services" wallowing in nostalgia for the war or the empire. They appeared to have little understanding of the country they were supposed to be protecting.[19] The other officers "looked like what we were: former lawyers, journalists, dons, schoolmasters, missionaries—former everything, with Burton suits and mortgages and armpits, and a shared but unspoken conviction that the real secret service must be somewhere else. A few of us were clever, a few seriously stupid, and a handful, as ever in a business where charlatans are listened to respectfully, cogently mad."[20]

The madness could take many forms, but the most powerful was the paranoia that infected the service, a legacy of the deep penetration of Burgess and Maclean into the British establishment and intelligence services. The MI5 hierarchy were also convinced of Philby's guilt, even if they had not been able to prove it. There were fears of more agents embedded in the service, fears exacerbated by the CIA. "It was witch hunt time," Cornwell wrote. "It was the time of James Jesus Angleton of the CIA who kept telling us we were being controlled by the Kremlin. Some of us ended up believing him. Not me [. . .] Angleton, let it never be forgotten, had the distinction of being trained in the art of running double agents by none other than Kim Philby. The humiliation of this, we now know, had unhinged him and he saw the KGB's hand in everything—particularly everything British. And the Brits, desperate to preserve a special relationship that was special to no one but themselves, were bending over backwards to feed his frenzy."[21] The net of suspicion was cast increasingly wide: Roger Hollis, who in 1956 succeeded White as director-general of MI5, was forced to defend himself from allegations of spying, while another group of agents in the service suspected Prime Minister Howard Wilson of Soviet connections.

After only ten days of immersive training, most of which was spent deciphering the process of calling up files, Cornwell was ready to get to work. The head of D Branch, which dealt with counterespionage, gave a talk on Soviet illegals, the KGB agents who were not attached to the embassy and were often in the country under deep cover. The new recruits were told not to worry about these illegals, however, as there were none operating in Britain that were not already known to the service. This seemed an act of astonishing complacency on the part of an agency that had unwittingly let illegals run agents in the heart of the British establishment for the best part of a decade.[22] All the more frustrating then, that Cornwell's work in F2 Branch focused on vetting civil servants based on their files, seeking to sniff out suspect connections to Communist causes. He would then interview those who were suspected, drawing on his experience interrogating suspected spies in Austria while with the intelligence corps.[23] When Cornwell transferred to F4 Branch, which was responsible for running countersubversion agents, he began working with the service's network of undercover operators informing on the inner workings of the British Communist Party. Cornwell was always loyal to his agents, whom he described as "heroic, underpaid, and remarkably successful," but his heart was not in the work. "Spying on a decaying British Communist Party twenty-five thousand strong that had to be held together by MI5 informants did not meet my aspirations," he wrote.[24] The danger was clearly elsewhere.

If working for MI5 was disappointing and tedious, it at the very least forced him to return to writing. "I began writing because I was going mad with boredom," he wrote. "Not the apathetic, listless kind of boredom that doesn't want to get out of bed in the morning, but the screaming, frenetic sort that races around in circles looking for real work and finding none."[25] His inspiration, in more than one way, was his office-mate,

John Bingham, "a kindly, gracious, astute man, ex-journalist, ex–Control Commission [which ran the defeated Axis countries after the Second World War], intelligence professional to his fingertips."[26] Bingham wrote thrillers with titles like *The Paton Street Case* and *The Double Agent,* some of which were televised for *The Alfred Hitchcock Hour.* Cornwell often saw him writing on his lunch break and decided he needed to do the same. With his "bumbly manners, shrewd eye and shrewder ear," Bingham became one of the models for George Smiley (the other was Cornwell's friend and mentor, the Reverend Vivian Green, who had been one of his schoolteachers and was history tutor and chaplain at Lincoln College). Cornwell even lifted the way Bingham wiped his glasses with the end of his tie. Cornwell abandoned the book about a public school that he'd begun while at Eton (this later became *A Murder of Quality)* and started to write a thriller in which Smiley seeks to expose an East German spy ring. The plot turns on the seeming suicide of Samuel Fennan, a Foreign Office official, after he has been subjected to a standard screening interview by Smiley, the kind of interview that Cornwell had conducted while at F2 Branch, yet the brilliance of *Call for the Dead* was not just in its tightly wound plot, but that he began to populate a world with characters he would develop in his subsequent fictions, an approach he self-consciously took from the French novelist Balzac.[27] The idea was that some characters would play the lead role in some stories and then become background figures in others. At the end of *Call for the Dead* he deliberately let the East German agent Hans-Dieter Mundt escape, as he was already planning his involvement in a second novel. Bingham read the manuscript and secured Cornwell a literary agent.[28] Cornwell cleared the novel with Bernard Hill, MI5's lawyer.

At the same time, Cornwell applied for a transfer to SIS. He sat for his Foreign Office exams, was interviewed by the selection board, and joined in June 1960. This was not a popular move within MI5, who hated their snobbish sister organization, whom they referred to as "those shits across the park." To Cornwell, though, SIS represented more glamour and excitement than the largely deskbound work of MI5. The headquarters were in Broadway Buildings, by St. James' Park underground station, with the dubious cover provided by a plaque claiming it was the home of the Minimax Fire Extinguisher Company.

Cornwell's training began in London and then moved to Fort Monckton, in Gosport on the south coast. In the capital he learned about psychology, how to "read" agents and double agents, how to "forge papers, make skeleton keys, pick locks and operate secret electronic equipment."[29] He was also taught how to use hidden cameras and to develop film. Training then moved on into the use of "safe houses, dead letter-boxes, surveillance techniques, ciphers (coding and decoding) and clandestine wireless communication."[30] On the south coast, things got more action packed; Cornwell shot at pop-up targets with a 9 mm automatic pistol, received unarmed combat training, and was instructed in knife fighting by a veteran of the Shanghai police force. He learned how to handle and detonate explosives and how to land and extract agents from a hostile coastline at night. There were missions in which trainees had to evade guards and make their way through barbed wire fences to reach an objective. In a culminating exercise, Cornwell had to live undercover in Brighton, posing as a German tourist. He was arrested by local police—on MI6 orders—and subjected to interrogation in which he had to maintain his cover.[31] While Cornwell the spy claimed never to have made much use of this training, le Carré the writer was clearly paying close attention.

While undergoing training, a call came through from Cornwell's literary agent to tell him that Victor Gollancz, Orwell's old publisher, had bought Call for the Dead. As an active intelligence agent, Cornwell needed to publish under a pseudonym and, despite resistance from the publisher who wanted something more Anglo-Saxon, he chose John le Carré. (In some interviews he says he saw the name on a shop, in others he says he simply can't remember why he chose it.) His debut was published while he was on his first SIS posting, in West Germany, on the front lines of the Cold War. He then returned to his public school murder mystery, in which Smiley played the role of detective, and finished it quickly; *A Murder of Quality* was published the following year. With two short but cleverly constructed novels under his belt, Cornwell was laying the foundations for a second career as a writer. His next book would make le Carré famous.

IN THE OPENING PAGES of *The Spy Who Came In from the Cold*, Alec Leamas, an officer of the "Circus" (le Carré's fictional version of the secret service, which takes its name from the location of its headquarters on London's Cambridge Circus), waits tired and anxious at a checkpoint in the Berlin Wall. One of his agents, Karl, has been blown and he's on the run from Hans-Dieter Mundt, the vicious head of the East German "Abteilung" (the fictional version of the Stasi). Leamas has been waiting all day and, at dusk, a car arrives at the checkpoint. This might be his man. He watches, tense, as the car passes through the document check and then the customs inspection. He rushes outside into the cold October evening to find the car is being driven by Elvira, Karl's lover, and she is alone. She tells him Karl made a run for it when the secret police came for him, that he will try to cross over this same checkpoint on his bicycle when it is dark. Leamas returns to his post behind the sandbags, winning over the West German border guards by producing some scotch to pour in their coffee.

There was only one light in the checkpoint, a reading lamp with a green shade, but the glow of the arclights, like artificial moonlight, filled the cabin. Darkness had fallen, and with it silence. They spoke as if they were afraid of being overheard. Leamas went to the window and waited, in front of him the road and to either side the Wall, a dirty ugly thing of breeze blocks and strands of barbed wire, lit with cheap yellow light, like the backdrop for a concentration camp. East and west of the Wall lay the unrestored part of Berlin, a half-world of ruin, drawn in two dimensions, crags of war.[32]

One of the sentries spots a man with a bicycle. Through his binoculars, Leamas identifies him as Karl. He makes it through the document check and then through customs. There is only one officer of the Volkspolizei left between the agent and the white line that marks West Berlin. Something spooks Karl and he starts to pedal, fast, leaning over the handlebars. Suddenly searchlights come on and pick him out in bright light. A siren wails.

The East German sentry fired, quite carefully, away from them, into his own sector. The first shot seemed to thrust Karl forward, the second to pull him back. Somehow he was still moving, still on the bicycle, passing the sentry, and the sentry was still shooting at him. Then he sagged, rolled to the ground, and they heard quite clearly the clatter of the bike as it fell. Leamas hoped to God he was dead.

This opening chapter was a concentration of everything that was best about le Carré's writing in his first two books: the spare prose, the escalation of tension, and the lack of sentimentality. But there was something else, too. Anger.

The Wall was the catalyst. Cornwell later recalled that "[s]taring at the Wall was like staring at frustration itself, and it touched an anger in me that found its way into the book." It had sent him into what he called a forty-eight-hour "fugue state," and when he came out of it, he wrote the book in just five weeks, early in the morning, scribbling away on the ferry as he commuted across the Rhine from his home in Königswinter to work in Bonn, and late at night in the embassy.[33] Some of his frustration was personal as his relationship with his wife, Ann, was beginning to deteriorate. But he was also becoming professionally disillusioned as he started to seriously question the ethics of espionage. George Smiley, the protagonist in his first two novels, was not given to anger and frustration; Leamas was something different, however. Cornwell created him after a chance encounter at a bar in a London airport, when a "rough-edged, kind of Trevor Howard figure, walked in and sat himself at the bar beside me. He fished in his pocket, put down a great handful of change in heavens-knows-which currencies and denominations, and then said, 'A large scotch.'" Cornwell recalled him having a "slight Irish accent" and a "deadness in the face"; he looked like he'd had "the hell posted out of him . . . It was the embodiment, suddenly, of somebody I'd been looking for. It was he, and I never spoke to him, but he was my guy, Alec Leamas, and I knew he was going to die at the Berlin Wall."[34] Here was a vessel for his rage.

Cornwell always claimed that the novel was "sheer fiction from start to finish, uninformed by personal experience," and while this might be true on a strictly literal level—he never ran agents in East Germany, for example—he drew deeply on his experiences with SIS in Germany in the writing of it. The setup of the novel, with the Circus scrambling to save a network of blown agents, had its precursor in reality. On the day that Cornwell was formally initiated into the service, he was informed that SIS agent George Blake had confessed to being a Soviet spy.

"The scale of Blake's betrayal remains, even by the standards of the period, monumental," Cornwell wrote, "literally hundreds of British agents—Blake himself could no longer calculate how many—betrayed; covert audio operations deemed vital to the national security, such as, but not exclusively, the Berlin audio tunnel, blown before they were launched; and the entire break-down of MI6's [SIS's] personnel, safe houses, order of battle and outstations across the globe."[35] Blake, born George Behar to a Dutch mother and a naturalized British father (originally of Egyptian-Jewish background), fought for the Dutch resistance in the Second World War before fleeing to England, where he served first in the navy before being recruited by SIS.[36] He was captured by Communist forces during the Korean War and was turned during his three years in captivity.[37]

Blake was stationed in Beirut when his duplicity was discovered, but he had inflicted the greatest damage while stationed in Berlin. Cornwell's posting to the embassy in Bonn was put on hold while SIS regrouped; at least his cover, as a new recruit, had not been blown. But his Head of Station in Bonn, Peter Lunn, had worked closely with Blake in Berlin. At night, after Lunn had left the station, Blake had copied his boss's index cards list-ing all of SIS's agents in Germany, which resulted, according to KGB archives, in the elimination of the entire network in East Germany between 1953 and 1955.[38] It is estimated Blake be-trayed four hundred agents, many of whom were imprisoned or killed.[39] Blake was discovered when a high-ranking Polish intel-ligence officer, Michael Goleniewski, defected in Berlin, bringing with him SIS documents that could have come only from a lim-ited number of British officers. At his trial, in May 1961, Blake pleaded guilty to five counts of offenses relating to the Official Secrets Act and was sentenced to forty-two years in prison, at the time the longest prison sentence handed out by a British court.[40]

The following November, with Cornwell established in Bonn, there came revelations of another betrayal. Heinz Felfe, head of Soviet counterespionage in the West German intelligence service (the BND), was arrested. Felfe had worked for SIS after the war but was dropped when the service suspected he might be working for the Soviets. The Americans had long harbored suspicions about him, yet, working for the BND, he had access to troves of top secret information and had effectively sabotaged numerous operations against the KGB. After being found guilty of spying, he was traded for West German agents being held by the Soviets.

Felfe was an example of the kind of ethical compromise being made in the Cold War.[41] In what would become a recurring theme all over the world, the Americans and the British aligned themselves with politically repugnant groups because they believed it the most effective way to fight encroaching Communism. In Germany that meant collaborating with former Nazis (many of whom still believed in their cause and sought to gain influence and power in the new Germany), and Felfe was undoubtedly one of this despicable lot. Raised in Dresden, he had joined the SS at the age of seventeen and moved into its intelligence branch, the SD, during the war. He had been captured by Canadian troops in the Netherlands and confessed under British interrogation to being an ardent devotee of Hitler.[42] Nevertheless, after the war, SIS had recruited him and dispatched him to Cologne to spy on the Communist Party. After he was ditched by the suspicious British, he worked his way into the Gehlen Organization, the precursor to the BND.[43] Reinhard Gehlen had been a Wehrmacht general and head of military intelligence on the Eastern Front who, on realizing the war was lost, cut a deal with the Americans. He recruited former Abwehr, SS, and Gestapo officers to form the "Org," a semiofficial German intelligence agency, based at Pullach outside Munich.[44] One of those agents was Hans Clemens, a former SS captain, who in turn recruited Felfe.

"In arbitrarily deciding that former or present Nazis were loyal by definition to the anti-communist flag, Dulles [of the CIA] and his Western allies had of course deluded themselves on a grand scale," Cornwell wrote. "As every schoolchild knows, anyone with a murky past is a sitting duck for blackmail. Add now the smouldering resentment of military defeat, the loss of pride, unspoken outrage at the Allied mass bombing of your beloved hometown—Dresden, for instance—and you have as potent a recipe for recruitment as the KGB or Stasi could possibly wish for."[45] Moscow Center invented a network of agents for Felfe, then drip-fed German intelligence a mixture of fact and fiction that helped Felfe rise up the organization until, like Philby in SIS, he was charged with running Soviet counterespionage.

Cornwell remains reticent about his work for SIS in Germany, but his biographer, Adam Sisman, using other sources, claims he was charged with uncovering Nazi cells and recruiting agents to penetrate them. While he was hunting for fascists, his employers, and their American allies, were happily collaborating with proven Nazis like Gehlen. Decades later, le Carré reflected on how these ethical compromises were connected to *The Spy Who Came In from the Cold.* "Few secret operations into East Germany could take place without the connivance of the BND," he wrote. "And did Leamas, on his regular visits, perhaps come across the *Herr Doktor's* [Gehlen's] valued chief of counterintelligence, Heinz Felfe, formerly of the SS and the Sicherheitsdienst? He must have done. Felfe was a legendary operator. Had he not single-handedly unmasked a raft of Soviet spies?"[46]

In *The Spy Who Came In from the Cold,* it is Mundt, the East German spy chief, who embodies the bad conscience of the Cold

War. Mundt is a sadistic former Nazi, and Leamas, posing as a retired agent going rapidly to seed, gets himself recruited by the East Germans with the plan, he thinks, of framing Mundt. But it turns out Leamas was being played by his own side and that his role is to protect Mundt, who is covertly working for the Circus, from his rival, the diligent ideologue Josef Fiedler. That Fiedler is Jewish makes Mundt relish the destruction of his rival even more. Both East and West accommodate this monster, Mundt, in the hope that he will help them further the destruction of each other, yet in doing so, they compromise the very causes they supposedly stand for. It was a sordid vision of the ethics of the secret war being fought on both sides of the Iron Curtain.

And what made this all the harder to swallow was that these shabby compromises did not prevent the West from losing the espionage war. If the building of the Wall represented an admission of defeat on the part of the Communists in the battle for the world's hearts and minds, then the defections of Maclean and Burgess and the revelations of the duplicity of Blake and Felfe were signs that in the battles between rival intelligence services, the Communists were routing their opponents. As Cornwell put it years later, "If the cold war had indeed been fought by the spies, the Soviet Union would have won hands down." Both MI5 and SIS "were penetrated to the gills, and found out about it far too late."[47] But the biggest betrayal was yet to come.

IN JANUARY 1963, Kim Philby received a request that did not feel right. His Head of Station in Beirut, Peter Lunn, not long arrived from his previous posting in Bonn, requested a meeting at his secretary's apartment in the Christian quarter of the city. It seemed a location chosen for discretion, far from Beirut's expat bars and fancy hotels. For the last year Philby had been expecting something like this. Anatoly Golitsyn, a major in the KGB, had defected to the CIA in Helsinki in December 1961, sending a convulsion of panic through Moscow Center and its stations around the world. Yuri Modin, Philby's handler in the years before the Burgess-Maclean defection, was sufficiently alarmed to travel, via Pakistan, to Beirut to inform Philby of the danger in person. With his nerves shredded, Philby began drinking even more heavily, and the day he set off for the meeting with Lunn he still had a bandage on his head from a drunken fall after a party.

Philby was not surprised when it was not Lunn who answered the door. Instead, it was Nicholas Elliott, the brilliant SIS agent with whom he had had a close friendship since the days of the war. "I rather thought it would be you," Philby said.[48]

Elliott was a grandee of SIS. One of his recent operations had involved luring Blake back to the United Kingdom from Beirut so that he could be arrested. Elliott sat on the selection board that had interviewed Cornwell, who described him as "the most charming, witty, elegant, courteous, compulsively entertaining spy I ever met [. . .] He was thin as a wand, and seemed always to hover slightly above the ground at a jaunty angle, a quiet smile on his face, and one elbow cocked for the martini glass or cigarette."[49] He was a bon vivant and a raconteur, but there was nothing jovial about the way he greeted Philby. With the windows open and the sounds of busy Beirut street life drifting in, Elliott rather formally asked after Philby's health and invited him to take some tea. Elliott sat down and began rolling his fountain pen back and forth under his palm. "Sorry for getting right on with it," Elliott said. "Kim, I don't have time to postpone this. And we've known each other for ever, so, if you don't mind, I'll get right to the point. Unfortunately it's not very pleasant. I came to tell you that your past has caught up with you." The interrogation had begun.

Philby reacted as he had done after the Burgess-Maclean defections, denying everything, blaming a paranoid MI5 witch hunt. But he knew this time it was different for no other reason than it was Elliott who had come for him. When he had first been accused of being the third man, none of his colleagues had stood by him as resolutely as Elliott. And it was Elliott who had brought him back in from the cold when, in the summer of 1956, he persuaded David Astor to take on Philby as a stringer for the *Observer* (as part of the deal Philby also wrote for the *Economist*). He then managed to persuade the hierarchy at SIS to take him on as an agent based in Lebanon, using his reporting as a cover. This was no easy task as Dick White, then recently appointed Chief at MI6, had been convinced of Philby's guilt when he worked at MI5 (although surveillance of Philby between 1951 and 1955 uncovered only that he was cruel to his wife). Still, the agency needed as many eyes and ears as possible in the Middle East, with Nasser playing the Soviets and the Americans against each other while on the path to confrontation with Britain (which duly arrived in the Suez Crisis later that year). Shortly after arriving in Beirut, Philby was approached by a KGB officer and, making a mockery of the trust placed in him by Elliot, resumed his work for the Soviet Union.

During his debriefing by British intelligence in the spring of 1962, Golitsyn revealed the existence of a spy network dubbed "the Ring of Five," which revived the hunt for those who were complicit with Burgess and Maclean.[50] This time, evidence against Philby emerged from deep in his past. Back in 1935, he had sought to recruit Flora Solomon, a Russian-Jewish friend who later introduced him to his wife, Aileen. Solomon was very much a woman of the left in the 1930s—she had been hired to improve working conditions at Marks & Spencer after complaining directly to one of the owners—but rejected Philby's offer to work clandestinely for the communists. After the war, she'd become an ardent Zionist, and it was at a function at the Weizmann Institute of Science in Rehovot, Israel, in August 1962, that she told Victor Rothschild, a distinguished scientist and wartime MI5 officer, of Philby's approach. Her motivations were twofold: she was angered by what she perceived as anti-Israel bias in Philby's reporting on the Middle East for the *Observer,* and also at the way Philby had first abused then neglected his wife, Aileen, who had been found dead in their house in Crowborough in December 1957. Aileen had suffered from psychological problems for much of her life and, in her last years, drank heavily before dying from heart failure. Solomon blamed Philby, who had bullied his wife when they were together, then washed his hands of her when he was posted to Beirut. When Rothschild reported his conversation with Solomon, MI5 officers interviewed her, delighted to finally get something tangible on Philby.

Philby did not know these details, but he knew they must have something substantive on him to persuade Elliott of his guilt. As he had not been "sandbagged" and taken back to the UK, he figured out there must be other options on the table than a long prison term. Having seen the severity of the sentence handed out to Blake, he knew that if found guilty he would be locked up for the rest of his life. And Elliott did have an offer. If Philby confessed to having spied for the Soviet Union until 1949, and revealed everything he had told the KGB, as well as disclosed who else was working for them, he was to be granted immunity. The specific year was important, as it was when Philby moved to Washington—if it was discovered he had spied there, the Americans would doubtless seek to have him extradited. He was given twenty-four hours to make his decision.

Philby returned to the apartment at the appointed time the next day and produced two sheets of paper on which he had typed a very partial confession: he had been a spy between 1936 and 1946, he had written, but not thereafter, although he did admit to warning Maclean that the net was closing in 1951, but only out of friendship. While this document was short on detail, it appeared that Philby had painted himself into a corner. It was enough to send him to jail, giving Elliott the leverage needed to extract more from his mark. Philby invited Elliott to dinner that night with his third wife, Eleanor, but, on arrival, Philby was passed out drunk. The next day, Elliott reciprocated, inviting them to dinner at Chez Temporal, one of Beirut's finest restaurants. In the bathroom, Philby handed over more pages, with more details. There was another interrogation session at the apartment the following day, in which Elliott came with a list of names. He asked that Philby identify those who were working with the Soviets (Philby offered up only deliberate misinformation). Then came a surprise. Elliott, who was running the Africa desk at SIS, said he was leaving Beirut for the Congo, a fiercely contested Cold War battleground. Lunn would take over the interrogation.[51]

Philby later maintained that he had been stringing Elliott along with his partial or misleading confessions, playing for time. He seized his moment, sending an emergency signal to his KGB case officer by standing on the balcony of his apartment holding a book. After meeting with his Soviet handler at an Armenian restaurant, he set about stalling Lunn. On January 23, the KGB made their move, spiriting Philby to the docks in a car with diplomatic plates. In torrential rain, Philby boarded a freighter, the *Dolmatova,* and disappeared out to sea and behind the Iron Curtain.

The sensational news spread rapidly through the intelligence agencies of the West. In Bonn, Cornwell remembered the word being broken. "Summoning me to his office late one evening," he wrote, "my Head of Station informed me, strictly for my own information, of what every Englishman would be reading in his newspaper the next day: that Kim Philby, MI6's brilliant former head of counter-intelligence, once tipped to become Chief of the Service, was also a Russian spy and, as we were only gradually allowed to know, had been since 1937."[52] Those in MI5 who had long wanted Philby's scalp were stunned. J. Edgar Hoover, at the FBI, was furious and only further convinced of the ineptitude of British intelligence. Hardest hit was James Jesus Angleton, head of counterintelligence at the CIA, Philby's former protégé during his days as a maverick officer in the OSS. SIS had deliberately kept the CIA out of the loop on the operation in Beirut, so Angleton learned of Philby's guilt at the same time as he learned of his defection. It was a revelation that sent an already paranoid man deeper into what he called, quoting T. S. Eliot's poem *Gerontion*, the "wilderness of mirrors."[53] On March 3, 1963, the *Observer* announced that Philby, its Middle East correspondent, was missing but it was not until July 1 that the British government publicly confirmed that he was a Soviet spy; on July 3, the Soviet newspaper *Izvestia* announced that Philby had been granted Soviet citizenship. The master spy had evaded his would-be captors once again.

Or so it seemed. Elliott later claimed that it had never occurred to him that Philby would flee, which seems extraordinary in such an experienced operator. And it is not like Elliott was working alone. He collaborated closely with Lunn throughout the operation—in fact, Lunn was in the same building when Philby came to meet Elliott, listening to what they discussed through the bugs that had been installed in the apartment. Both men were also in regular contact with Dick White. Did all three of them decide not to bother having Philby watched? When Elliott left for the Congo, he told Philby that Lunn was heading off on a skiing trip. It was almost as if he were telling him the coast was clear. This is what Philby himself later came to suspect, especially as he had a trip back to London planned for later in the year, where any operation would have been under British jurisdiction and therefore the responsibility of MI5. "My view, and that of my superiors here in Moscow," he said, "is that the whole thing was deliberately staged so as to push me into escaping, because the last thing the British government wanted at that time was me in London, a security scandal and a sensational trial."[54]

IN OCTOBER 1962, a few months before Philby's defection, the London Pavilion on Shaftesbury Avenue hosted the premiere of *Dr. No*, the first James Bond movie adaptation. It was a suitably glamorous affair, with Sean Connery and other stars in attendance. Ian Fleming, Bond's creator and a former Naval Intelligence officer, invited Somerset Maugham, another celebrated author-spy, to be his special guest. Fleming's novels had become a sensation in Britain in 1957, when *From Russia with Love* was serialized in the *Daily Express*, and in March 1961 Fleming had received the best endorsement he could get in the United States when John F. Kennedy, freshly elected president, told *Life* magazine that *From Russia with Love* was, alongside works by Churchill and Stendhal, one of his ten favorite books.[55] The same article revealed that such was Kennedy's admiration for Fleming that Allen Dulles, the CIA director, had arranged for the novelist to come over for dinner with the president.

Bond offered a consoling fantasy of Cold War espionage, in which the gentleman spy wins no matter the odds. Philby's defection painted a rather more sordid picture in which the charismatic gentleman was actually working for the enemy. For that matter Kennedy's enthusiasm for actual clandestine adventurism had foundered at the Bay of Pigs.[56]

The Spy Who Came In from the Cold was published on September 13, 1963. Such was the demand that it had to be reprinted three times before publication. Gollancz marketed it as a serious, literary spy story that, above all, was realistic. Cornwell's ongoing use of a pseudonym and the seeming precision of the technical language of espionage gave the novel a sense of authenticity. This frustrated Cornwell, who knew he would not have gotten the book past SIS had it disclosed anything resembling real operations. "The proof that the novel was *not* 'authentic'— how many times did I have to repeat this?—had been delivered by the fact that it was published," he said.[57] In fact, much of the jargon was invented from scratch by le Carré, only to be later adopted by British spies who devoured his books, the fiction becoming the reality, which later validated the novels' veracity. But while that circularity was yet to come, *The Spy Who Came In from the Cold* did offer a bitter authenticity. The novel confronted the cynicism of the secret war in a manner whose only real precedent was Graham Greene's *The Quiet American,* and Greene himself called it "the best spy story I have ever read."[58] It did not go down so well with the CIA, however. Richard Helms, the Deputy Director for Intelligence and Plans who in 1966 would take over as director of the agency, detested it, claiming le Carré's novel, with its bleak cynicism, was guilty of "undermining the very bedrock of intelligence."[59] Frank Wisner, who had retired from the CIA in 1962, called le Carré and Greene "dupes" and "ill-wishing and grudge-bearing types."[60]

For the first time in his life, Cornwell had money, not only from his book deals but also from selling the film rights to Paramount. After publication, he met with his accountant to find out if he had enough in the bank to resign from SIS. He rather feared he was to be forced out anyway. There was speculation about his real identity; Greene wrote to Gollancz and asked if he could tell him the name of his author, joking that Blake must have taken up writing while in prison.[61]

It was when Cornwell was given a new posting in Hamburg that le Carré finally caught up with him. Early in 1964 he received a call from the *Sunday Times* and was told he was going to be outed as le Carré. He admitted to being the man behind the pseudonym, but denied that he worked for SIS. His denial was not taken very seriously. At a meeting with White back in London, Cornwell was told that he could no longer work under diplomatic cover but was apparently offered the opportunity to continue spying while working as a journalist. Cornwell declined. White would later complain that *The Spy Who Came In from the Cold* presented the world with "a service without trust or loyalty, where agents are sacrificed and deceived without compunction."[62] Cornwell did in fact believe that SIS was "in a state of corporate rot."[63] And Philby was the worm that had gnawed its way through this decayed apple. Now that he had left the service, le Carré dedicated himself to his writing full time. The seed of his next great novel, *Tinker, Tailor, Soldier, Spy,* had been planted. When he returned to the rot at the heart of British intelligence, it would, in his phrase, be "Philby's murky lamp" that lit his path."[64]

Part Seven

RECKONING

TWENTY-SIX

Sinyavsky

MOSCOW, 1964–1966

AFTER FIVE YEARS OF FRUSTRATION in their hunt for the most wanted writer in Russia, the KGB finally caught a break.[1] Since 1959, a dissident novelist had been publishing his work in the West under the pseudonym Abram Tertz. Even that name was a provocation, inspired as it was by Abrashka Tertz, a legendary Jewish bandit who was celebrated in Odessan folk songs. This writer, whoever it was, appeared to be reveling in their status as a literary outlaw. Anti-Communist magazines and journals in the United States and Western Europe gloatingly published every new Tertz manuscript that was smuggled out from behind the Iron Curtain. Stephen Spender's *Encounter* published the first English translation of Tertz's debut novel, *The Trial Begins,* in its entirety in 1960, announcing Tertz as a major new Russian writer. The Congress for Cultural Freedom's other magazines, including *Tempo Presente* in Italy, *Preuves* in France, and *Der Monat* in West Germany, also published *The Trial Begins.*[2] And to make matters worse, Tertz was inspiring others. Calling himself Nikolai Arzhak, another writer began publishing his work in the same places that had published Tertz.[3] And then another, using the pseudonym Ivan Ivanovich Ivanov, did the same. Coming on the heels of the Pasternak scandal, these breaches were an embarrassment and gave ammunition to the critics who claimed

the Soviet Union was an oppressive society where true writers
dare not publish their work.

Soviet intelligence had successfully infiltrated the Manhattan
Project, the U.S. State Department, the British Foreign Office,
and the top echelons of SIS yet, despite their best efforts, had
been repeatedly defied by the writer behind the pseudonym.
From its inception, the KGB operation had been a confused mess:
they initially could not work out whether Tertz was a genuine
dissident *within* the Soviet Union, or an enterprising émigré
posing as such from a safe berth in the West. Their own experts
had hampered the pursuit. The KGB had commissioned their
agents and cooperative literary critics to analyze *The Trial Begins*
and Tertz's heretical literary essay, "On Socialist Realism," and
while some insisted Tertz must be living in Moscow, others
concluded that because of perceived mistakes about life in the
city, this was almost certainly the work of someone outside the
Soviet Union.[4] Other KGB reports supported this interpretation,
claiming Tertz must be living in the West. This contradicted another report from the KGB's Paris residency, which asserted that
the manuscript for *The Trial Begins* had been smuggled out of
Moscow to France. The matter was further confused by the KGB
focusing almost exclusively on Jewish writers. *The Trial Begins*
took as its subject Stalin's anti-Semitic Doctors' Plot and that,
combined with the choice of a "Jewish" pseudonym, threw off
the KGB agents. For years, numerous writers were placed under
surveillance with no results. The investigators soon ran out of
options.

Early in 1964, the KGB picked up the trail. One of their agents,
working under the codename "Yefimov," had embedded himself
in the Moscow literary community and informed his handlers
that a relatively obscure writer, Yulii Daniel, was in possession
of "anti-Soviet material." The son of a Yiddish playwright, Daniel was known as a translator of foreign poetry, but this report

suggested he might be involved in subversive activities. A second report came in to Moscow Center, this time from an agent in Yalta, claiming that Daniel was in possession of a manuscript that "deserved 15 years imprisonment." Was Daniel the man behind Tertz? He did not seem to fit, but perhaps he could lead the KGB to other dissident writers, perhaps even to Tertz. The hunt was on.

The KGB started to monitor all of Daniel's activities, observing his routines, his interactions with his colleagues at the Gorky Institute of World Literature, and the people with whom he socialized. They became convinced that he was not Tertz but the other writer who used the pen name Nikolai Arzhak. They also began to formulate suspicions about a well-known literary critic who worked alongside Daniel at the Gorky Institute. Ironically enough, their suspect was someone they had tried to recruit in his student days. Could this man, with his scruffy Dostoyevsky beard and pronounced case of strabismus, be Tertz?

Daniel had unknowingly led the KGB to Andrei Sinyavsky. To all appearances, he was a respected, if liberal, scholar and literary critic. During the Thaw, Sinyavsky had worked to rehabilitate the reputations of writers suppressed under Stalin, especially that of Pasternak, whom he had befriended not long before the poet's death. This had given him problems with the authorities when *Doctor Zhivago* was published in 1958, but Sinyavsky managed to negotiate those skillfully enough that the KGB did not suspect him of anything more than trying to rehabilitate a controversial poet.[5]

In fact, Sinyavsky had turned away from Communism as a student, during the period of Zhdanov's cultural purge at the end of the Second World War. His hostility to the Kremlin hardened when, in 1951, his father, a member of the nobility who had given up everything to join the revolution, was arrested as an American spy. The charges against him were obviously falsified—his "crime" had been dispensing U.S.-made supplies during a charitable drive back in the 1920s—but he was sentenced to nine months in prison and then placed into internal exile.[6] He had emerged from prison tormented by paranoia, telling his son he felt the authorities had developed a way of electronically monitoring his thoughts, before passing away in 1956. If the Zhdanov purge had eroded Sinyavsky's faith in Soviet Communism, the treatment of his father demonstrated the arbitrary brutality upon which Stalin had constructed his rule. Beneath the respectable surface there now lurked a dissident seething with resentment.

FINDING SINYAVSKY WAS PROGRESS, but the KGB could not act without proof. In May 1964, under the direction of Vladimir Semichastny, the agency launched Operation Epigoni. It was imperative that neither writer realized he was being watched: if they were spooked, they might stop sending their work out, and the KGB would lose their chance to uncover the smuggling network. Using one of their embedded agents, they arranged for Sinyavsky to be called away from Moscow on official Gorky Institute business. In his absence, KGB officers broke into his apartment, searched his papers, and planted bugs. Getting uninterrupted access to Daniel's apartment proved trickier as members of his extended family also lived there. It never seemed to be unoccupied and, to complicate matters further, the family owned a dog. Eventually an agent, pretending to be a relative of a neighbor, managed to get wax impressions of the keys, allowing the KGB to get in and out quickly in the small windows of time they were afforded.

Operation Epigoni lasted a year, as the KGB slowly built up a picture of Sinyavsky's and Daniel's clandestine behavior. They needed to be patient as Sinyavsky, especially, was discreet and treated new acquaintances with suspicion. The key to the KGB's success was finding the conduit between the writers and the West. They suspected—correctly—that it was Hélène Peltier. There was some irony in this: the KGB had previously sought to entrap Peltier using Sinyavsky's help when they were both students at Moscow State University. Her father was the French naval attaché in Moscow, and the KGB wanted Sinyavsky to exploit his friendship with her to get information about the father's work. Instead, he devised a way to warn her of what was going on without the secret police realizing, creating a bond of trust between them.

Peltier, who after graduating in Moscow became a scholar of Slavic literature at the University of Toulouse, had remained on the KGB's radar. In 1956 she had visited the Russian capital and met with Boris Pasternak, who had given her a copy of the *Doctor Zhivago* manuscript to smuggle out to George Katkov, a Russian émigré historian at the University of Oxford. Peltier subsequently became one of the French translators of the novel and visited with Pasternak over the Christmas holidays of 1957.[7] The KGB were sure Peltier was helping Sinyavsky and Daniel in the same way she had helped Pasternak and, by this time, they were sure Sinyavsky was Tertz, and Daniel was Arzhak. The problem was that even after a year of surveillance, they did not have any hard evidence.

In the summer of 1965, Tertz struck again, as the anti-Communist *New Leader,* edited by Russian émigré Sol Levitas, devoted half its July edition to *Thought Unaware,* a collection of aphorisms and reflections that had been smuggled to the magazine on "93 separate slips of paper." The agents working on Epigoni intercepted a letter to Sinyavsky from someone called "Alfreda" requesting a meeting at the Hotel Bucharest. The lack of return address aroused further suspicions. Could this be Peltier? The KGB immediately placed Sinyavsky under twenty-four-hour surveillance, sure that, finally, the net was closing.

"Alfreda" was not Peltier, though, but a close friend of hers, Alfreda Aucouturier, whose husband had worked with Peltier on the French translation of *Zhivago*. Using hidden cameras, agents managed to film a meeting between Sinyavsky and Aucouturier at a metro station, but to their great frustration there was no evidence that any material had exchanged hands.

The agents running the operation faced a dilemma. They could either continue to monitor both writers and hope one of them slipped up, or they could arrest Aucouturier and hope she had incriminating manuscripts on her. If she did not—and they had not witnessed any exchange of papers—then their surveillance operation would be blown, and the writers would know the KGB were on to them. The agents working on Epigoni decided to gamble. They ordered the search of Aucouturier's luggage as she left via the Polish border on September 8. To their frustration they found nothing. KGB officers interrogated Aucouturier but, by the direction of the questioning, she swiftly realized that they had little solid evidence against her, or against Sinyavsky and Daniel. The KGB were faced with only one course of action: they allowed Aucouturier to leave the country and arranged to have Sinyavsky and Daniel arrested. On September 13 they took them in.

In his brilliant autobiographical novel, *Goodnight!*, Sinyavsky recalled the moment his pursuers finally caught up with him:

> They grabbed me near Nikitsky Gate. Late for my lecture at a Moscow Art Theatre workshop, I was waiting at a bus stop, keeping an eye out for my bus, when suddenly from behind me came a voice that sounded familiar asking "Andrei Donatovich?!" As if he doubted it was really me but still was delighted by the off chance that it might be. Having turned obligingly around and, to my surprise, seeing no one who would have called me by name so distinctly

and so fondly, I continued to swivel on my heel and lost my balance. Then I was propelled by a gentle yet precise movement into the open door of a car that sped away, as if on command, the instant I was shoved inside. No one on the street caught so much as a glimpse of what had happened.[8]

IN THE INTERROGATION ROOMS of Moscow's Lefortovo Prison, both Sinyavsky and Daniel confessed to smuggling their work out for publication in the West but denied that their intentions had been anti-Soviet. Both writers refused to implicate Peltier as their collaborator. This limited admission of guilt was not what the KGB was after, so they tried an old tactic. An agent code-named "Mikhailov" was bundled into Sinyavsky's cell with a credible cover story and told to glean as much as possible from his mark. It seems incredible that Sinyavsky did not cotton on to this ploy, but perhaps he was thrown by the fact that "Mikhailov" was an illegal, an agent who had worked in deep cover in the West and therefore might have appeared a genuine foreigner. It seems likely that the agent was Geli Fyodorovich Vasilyev, who had assumed the name Rudolf Steiner for his work in Austria and Latin America, and his knowledge and experience of the Western world might well have blinded Sinyavsky to the fact that he was a stool pigeon. When the plant was "released," Sinyavsky entrusted him with passwords and codes to pass on to his wife. The trap was set. All Sinyavsky's communications with Maria were duly monitored and, according to the KGB file, "invaluable information" was gathered about Sinyavsky's network of contacts.

The key figure in this dissident network was Andrei Remizov, the third man working behind the pseudonym Ivan Ivanovich Ivanov. Remizov was the head librarian at the Moscow Library of Foreign Literature, a privileged position through which he traveled abroad and had access to banned books. He had smuggled out an essay about the oppressive state of the Soviet literary scene, which was published in the June 1964 issue of *Encounter*. It did not take Remizov long to crack. He admitted smuggling out some of Sinyavsky's manuscripts when he went abroad on official business. He also confessed to passing manuscripts on to Peltier.

Following these admissions, the initial plan was to put Remizov on trial with the others. However, his mental state rapidly deteriorated and he became suicidal. The decision was made to use him as the star prosecution witness instead. In order to ensure the success of this plan, the KGB needed to protect him from contact with the wives of Sinyavsky and Daniel, Maria Rozanova and Larisa Bogoraz, who were doing everything they could to help their husbands' cases. To do so, the KGB fabricated some Ministry of Culture business and had Remizov sent out to Kursk and Tula. Complicating their scheme, Remizov was a mess, and they soon realized they also needed to protect him from himself: he was kept on round-the-clock suicide watch.

The KGB had one last operation up their sleeve. Bogoraz, Daniel's wife, had been carefully preparing a dossier containing details of their arrest and detention for publication in the West, which she wanted to make public before the trial. Once a surveillance team had uncovered the existence of the dossier, another illegal was put into play. Posing as a sympathetic Western businessman prepared to smuggle the information out to the Western press, Bogoraz entrusted the KGB agent with the dossier, who delivered it straight to his handlers at Moscow Center.

Still, despite the KGB's effort at containing the situation, the news of the writers' detention leaked. Their arrest on September 13 sent shock waves through the Moscow literary world. Leonid Brezhnev had become general secretary in 1964 after participating in a plot to oust Khrushchev, and the hard-liners in the party wanted to punish those who had taken advantage of the former leader's indulgence. Here was an opportunity to adamantly counter the claims, made by Western propaganda, that the Soviet Union was growing weaker and that internal dissent was growing stronger. Many Russian intellectuals felt that the liberalization of Soviet culture—a slow, hard-earned process—was now in jeopardy and that a crackdown would follow.

One of the biggest breakthroughs for the liberals had been the granting of official permission for a group of Soviet writers to attend a conference of the European Community of Writers (ECW) in Rome that year. The ECW, founded in Naples in 1958, was sympathetic to the Soviet Union and had held its 1963 conference in Leningrad. Alexander Tvardovsky, the editor of *Novy Mir,* had been responsible for brokering the deal, which allowed genuine writers, not just state functionaries, to travel and talk about their work. For example, Vasily Aksyonov, who had made his name writing about the Soviet counterculture and its obsession with rock music, jazz, and Western fashion, was part of the group that went to Rome.

By the time the conference opened on October 9, rumors had filtered out about the arrests of Sinyavsky and Daniel. Giancarlo Vigorelli, the secretary general of the ECW, challenged the Soviet delegates, telling them what he had heard. The Russians representatives stuck to the official line, but the story of the arrests was picked up by various news agencies, and the Moscow correspondents of the Western newspapers started sniffing around. On October 18, the *New York Times* confirmed that Sinyavsky had been arrested and was accused of pursuing "anti-Soviet propaganda" under the guise of Tertz. The following day, the same paper reported the arrest of a writer by the name of "Daniello."

Western journalists started following the paper trail. Representatives of the American publisher Pantheon, which had released both "On Socialist Realism" and *The Trial Begins* as books in 1960, said that they had received the manuscripts from *Kultura,* a dissident Polish journal based in Paris. The editor of *Kultura* was Jerzy Giedroyc, who had been raised in Russia and fought for the London-based Polish government-in-exile during the war. *Kultura* was by then funded by the Free Europe Committee, which had been set up with financial assistance from the CIA in May 1949 (initially as the National Committee for Free Europe), and Giedroyc had been one of the delegates at the Congress for Cultural Freedom in West Berlin in 1950.[9] Giedroyc, a hard drinker who always sported an aristocratic neckerchief, was not easily pushed around, and he decided to bluff. He denied that Sinyavsky was Tertz, instead claiming that it was a "well-known figure" in Russian literary circles, but not one based in Moscow. His attempt at misdirection was pointless by this stage, as both writers had already confessed to their pseudonyms. By early November Giedroyc retracted his earlier claims and admitted the KGB had got the right writers. In a triumphant Paris press conference, Alexei Surkov, secretary of the Union of Soviet Writers, officially confirmed Sinyavsky and Daniel had been arrested.

Some of the facts now established, the story began to gather momentum and it became an intellectual cause célèbre. At the beginning of December, a group of prominent American writers sent an open letter to Soviet Premier Alexei Kosygin:

> If these prosecutions are carried out, they will blight not only the new growth of your own culture in the freer atmosphere of the post-Stalin decade, but also that East-West dialogue, which is being created by the steadily increasing contacts between Soviet and Eastern intellectuals. We therefore ask you to review the Sinyavsky-Daniel case in a broader context than it seems to have been considered up to now.[10]

On December 10, Mikhail Sholokhov, still the Soviet Union's most celebrated "official" writer, was due to receive his Nobel Prize in Stockholm, presenting another opportunity to intercede on behalf of Sinyavsky and Daniel. Mark Bonham Carter, who had published Tertz in Britain with his firm, Collins, tried rather naively to appeal directly to Sholokhov—a Soviet hardliner if ever there was one—in the hope that he would show solidarity with his fellow writers. Bonham Carter discovered which room Sholokhov was staying in at his Stockholm hotel, and after four unanswered phone calls went to knock on the door. Sholokhov stonewalled him.

The protests from Western writers and intellectuals put pressure on the Soviet authorities, but it was events in Russia that proved most seriously consequential. For months the Soviet press had been gleefully reporting the civic unrest that was spreading through the campuses and towns of the United States. The protests in support of civil rights and against the Vietnam War, and the way some of them had been violently suppressed, were taken as evidence of American hypocrisy and weakness. Within the Soviet Union, this kind of public dissent was unheard-of and, until now, unthinkable. The arrests of Sinyavsky and Daniel would open a crack in the granite facade.

It is hard to overestimate the importance of what happened on Pushkin Square on December 5, 1965. The date and location of the protest were carefully chosen: December 5 was Constitution Day, when the ratification of the 1936 Soviet Constitution (often known as the "Stalin Constitution") was celebrated. The protesters had chosen it because, ostensibly at least, the constitution claimed to offer protections of freedom of speech, and that the incarceration of the writers was in violation of these laws. The protesters also demanded that, in line with Soviet law, the accused be given a public trial. The location was also symbolic. A fifty-strong group of protesters, led by Alexander Esenin-Volpin, and including some of Sinyavsky's students at the Gorky Institute, gathered under the statue of Pushkin, the national poet, defender of artistic freedom, and teller of truth to power. Another two hundred came along to watch. The group managed to unfurl three of their four banners before the police stepped in and broke things up. One protester scrambled up onto the pediment of the Pushkin statue to make a speech but was unceremoniously dragged down. Later reports in the West would claim that twenty protesters had been arrested.

Esenin-Volpin was among those taken in and interrogated. He was the son of Sergei Esenin, a poet famous for having been briefly married to American dancer Isadora Duncan and for writing his last poem in his own blood before hanging himself in 1925. Esenin-Volpin was an eccentric, a brilliant mathematician who suffered from a stutter and was utterly fearless. He had twice been consigned to mental institutions—an increasingly common tactic deployed by the authorities for silencing dissent—but continued to make a nuisance of himself. After two and a half hours of questioning he was released and assured there would be a public trial for Sinyavsky and Daniel.

There were severe repercussions for many of the protesters: some forty students were expelled from their universities; the poet Leonid Gubanov and Yulia Vishnevskaya, a high school student, were held in psychiatric wards for a month. The writer Vladimir Bykovsky, arrested three days before the protest in which he planned to participate, spent eight months in a mental institution. Despite the speed with which it had been broken up, word of the protest leaked out and was reported in the Western press. The news was given serious play in Western newspapers before being repackaged and—a gift to anti-Soviet propaganda agencies—broadcast back into the Soviet Union through Radio Liberty. It might have been a modest crowd, it might have been swiftly broken up, but something important had taken place:

public dissent on the streets of the Soviet Union. From that point on, groups of dissidents would gather every year on December 5 to register their protest against the regime. It was the beginning of something previously unthinkable: a human rights movement in the Soviet Union.[11]

SINYAVSKY'S WORK was not only illegal for having been smuggled to the West but also heretical in content. His manifesto-essay, "On Socialist Realism," began with a rhetorical flourish:

> What is socialist realism? What is the meaning of this strange and jarring phrase? Can there be a socialist, capitalist, Christian or Mohammedan realism? Does this irrational concept have a natural existence? Perhaps it does not exist at all, perhaps it is only the nightmare of a terrified intellectual during the dark and magical night of Stalin's dictatorship? Perhaps a crude propaganda trick of Zhdanov or a senile fancy of Gorky? Is it fiction, myth or propaganda?
>
> Such questions, we are told, are often asked in the West. They are hotly debated in Poland. They are also current among us, where they arouse eager minds, tempting them into the heresies of doubt and criticism.[12]

With irreverent energy Sinyavsky went about attacking the officially prescribed literary aesthetic. The KGB would have taken careful note of that "us": who was this group to which Tertz was referring? A literary underground?

Communism, Tertz argued, had been blinded by the utopian ideal it pursued and had been thoroughly perverted as a result:

> So that prisons should vanish forever, we built new prisons.
> So that all frontiers should fall, we surrounded ourselves

with a Chinese wall. So that work should become a rest
and a pleasure, we introduced forced labor. So that not one
drop of blood be shed any more, we killed and killed and
killed.

In the name of the Purpose we turned to the means that
our enemies used: we glorified Imperial Russia, we wrote
lies in *Pravda* [Truth], we set a new Tsar on the now empty
throne, we introduced officers' epaulettes and tortures. . . .
Sometimes we felt that only one final sacrifice was needed
for the triumph of Communism—the renunciation of
Communism.

O Lord, O Lord—pardon us our sins![13]

These words could have come directly out of the mouth of the
disenchanted Bolshevik Rubashov in Arthur Koestler's *Darkness
at Noon*. There was no question that the author of these heresies
would be heavily punished if his identity were discovered. Under Stalin he would have been executed.

In place of socialist realism, Sinyavsky called for a radical new
approach, calling for a "phantasmagoric art" in which "the gro-
tesque will replace realistic descriptions of ordinary life."[14] It was
a manifesto for a new Russian literature. *Doctor Zhivago* was the
last stand of traditional nineteenth-century realism; Tertz was
calling for a literature of the present. With *The Trial Begins*, he
answered his own call. If "On Socialist Realism" was the theory,
the novel was the practice. *The Trial Begins* is set in 1952–53, in
the last months leading up to Stalin's death, a time of paranoia
and anti-Semitism that culminated in the Doctors' Plot.

The novel opens with the narrator of the story in his high-
rise apartment as it is searched by plainclothes secret policemen. "Are you arresting me?" asks the narrator. "You are being
trusted," comes the reply.[15] At that moment one of the walls of
his room becomes transparent and he sees the city spread before

him. As he looks out over Moscow, the narrator is granted a fantastical vision of "the Master":

Above the clouds, amid the ragged clouds crimsoned by the rising sun, I saw a hand. Such was the invincible strength of the bloodshot fingers clenched into a fist and motionless above the earth, that I shivered in delight. Closing my eyes, I fell upon my knees and heard the Master speak. His voice came straight from heaven, at moments thundering like an artillery barrage, at others purring gently like an airplane.[16]

The Master (Stalin recast as God) has a task for the narrator: he is to tell the story of Vladimir Globov, a public prosecutor, and the Master's "beloved and faithful servant." Globov is due to prosecute a Jewish doctor by the name of Rabinovich for performing an illegal abortion (a clear allusion to the Doctors' Plot). The twist is that Rabinovich performed the abortion on Globov's wife, Marina, a self-obsessed siren who does not want to "tarnish" her beautiful body with pregnancy. To compound Globov's problems, his son, Seryozha, is arrested for writing a manifesto demanding the purification of Communism and an end to the murderous corruption of the Master's regime. Seryozha believes that a noble end demands a noble means, and for this heresy he is sent to a labor camp. At the novel's end, Rabinovich is sent to the same camp, as is the narrator of the story itself.

Reviewing *The Trial Begins* in the *Guardian*, English playwright Michael Frayn described it as "a flash of lightning no less illuminating in its way than Pasternak's *Zhivago*."[17] In *Time* magazine, it was celebrated as "perhaps the most remarkable novel to have come out of the Soviet Union since the Revolution 43 years ago."[18] Russian literature had withered and all but died in Stalin's cultural winter, and the legacy of Pushkin, Tolstoy, and Dostoevsky was imperiled. Pasternak's *Doctor Zhivago*, a novel that was decidedly nineteenth century in cast, had been a reminder of that lost lyricism. Tertz, though, was announcing himself as something new, a writer from inside the Soviet Union who had developed a brash and bizarre style that gleefully desecrated the utopian pieties of socialist realism (famously characterized as "boy meets girl meets tractor"). But now he was in the hands of the KGB.

THE SOVIET UNION put Sinyavsky and Daniel on public trial to send a message. Earlier in the sixties, writers who caused problems were arrested and sent to psychiatric wards. The poet Joseph Brodsky had been sent to a prison camp in 1964 after twice being locked up in mental institutions.[19] Valery Tarsis, a writer outspoken in his criticism of the regime, and Esenin-Volpin, the poet involved in the Pushkin Square protests, had also been imprisoned in psychiatric wards.[20] Writers too famous to imprison and too dangerous to publish, like Akhmatova and Pasternak, were effectively quarantined and their families threatened. Certainly, compared to the restrictions on writers under Stalin, there had been some progress toward liberalization. But the Kremlin was no longer interested in a soft touch. A big show trial would indicate that the winds had changed and deter anyone else seeking to publish in *tamizdat* (that is, sending their work for illegal publication abroad; *samizdat* was the illegal publication of texts within the Soviet Union).[21] "Our trial was supposed to be a present to the party from the KGB on the occasion of the 23rd Party Congress," Sinyavsky wrote in *Goodnight!* "A model trial served up with an eye on the West on a crisp snow-white napkin."

If the original intention was to have a big triumphant production, the authorities evidently got cold feet: in early 1966 the trial was moved from the Moscow Supreme Court to a much less conspicuous venue, the Moscow Oblast court. The reasons for changing their mind were self-evident: the trial was becoming an international scandal and a domestic irritant, instead of an opportunity to crack the ideological whip, a focus of protests from every direction. Once again, the issue of freedom of speech for writers was giving the West an easy propaganda victory when it most needed one. America was being criticized both at home and abroad for the belligerence of its foreign policy. In March 1965, Lyndon Johnson had ordered the beginning of Operation Rolling Thunder, a massive bombing campaign in North Vietnam; the following month, American marines invaded the Dominican Republic as part of a mission to "stabilize" the country and suppress the increasingly influential Communists. The case of Sinyavsky and Daniel proved a felicitous way of focusing international attention back onto the Soviet Union.

THAT THE STATE was determined to make an example of the two defendants became clear when *Izvestia*, the official paper of the Soviet government (*Pravda* was the paper of the Party), published an aggressive editorial on January 13, 1966, under the byline of Dmitri Eremin, a reactionary critic from the Union of Soviet Writers. Under the headline "Turncoats," Eremin accused Sinyavsky and Daniel of "treason" for the "dirty lampoons" they had written about their own country. Hiding behind their pseudonyms, they were "werewolves," shape-shifters who used their literary masks to "spatter on to paper everything that is most vile and filthy." This was the kind of hysterical rhetoric that had preceded the show trials of the 1930s; Eremin warned that foreign pleading would have no effect on the severity of the sentence. Sinyavsky and Daniel had insulted Chekhov and, worse, Lenin: "Into what bottomless bog of abomination must a so-called man of letters sink to cast a slur with his hooligan pen on the

name we hold sacred!" The attack ended with a dramatic escalation. "They are not just moral perverts," Eremin wrote, "but
active helpers of those who are stoking up the furnace of international tension, who would like to turn the cold war into a hot
war, and who have still not relinquished their delirious dream of
raising their hand against the Soviet Union."[22] This was the first
time any work by Tertz or Arzhak had been officially discussed
in the Soviet Union.

A follow-up attack was published in *Literaturnaya Gazeta*, the
official publication of the Union of Soviet Writers. Written by
Zoya Kedrina, a former colleague of Sinyavsky and Daniel at
the Gorky Institute, the piece began by quoting from foreign
reviews of Tertz's work and then set about refuting this praise.
It was a strange way to go about a takedown, as almost none of
Kedrina's readers would have read either Tertz's works or the
Western reviews of them. Still, despite the unusual setup, the
main function of the article was to further smear both the accused. The headline declared them "Heirs to Smerdyakov," a
reference to the illegitimate son in Dostoevsky's *Brothers Kara-
mazov*, who eventually murders his father and ends up killing
himself (he is also distinguished by torturing and killing stray
cats). "[I]f Dostoevsky had not created Smerdyakov," Kedrina
wrote, "putting into his image the whole force of his hatred for
corruptors of human souls, but Smerdyakov himself had written
novels, generalizing the phenomena of life from his Smerdyako-
vian position, we could easily establish Tertz's kinship with such
a 'tradition.' For there is no abyss of moral decay and corruption
that would intimidate the worthy heirs of Smerdyakov in their
striving to defile and persecute everything human in the Soviet
person: friendship, love, motherhood, the family."[23] It was not
an essay overflowing with subtlety but Kedrina made her point.

The publication of these two smears—their populist tone an
old tactic designed to foster public support in the persecution

of intellectuals and artists—provoked more urgent responses in the West. A *New York Times* editorial condemned the attacks as "Soviet McCarthyism," while forty-nine writers from five countries sent another open letter to Kosygin seeking clemency for Sinyavsky and Daniel.[24] To the West it was a clear and familiar signal that there would be no clemency and that the various appeals were being ignored. But this time there was a difference. Similar Kremlin-sanctioned smears had been published after Pasternak published *Zhivago,* and again when he won the Nobel. Now, however, the writers would be allowed to answer back. For the first time in the history of the Soviet Union, writers were to go on public trial for what they had written. Sinyavsky and Daniel would be given the opportunity to defend themselves and their work in a way that would have been unheard-of under Stalin. Much effort was put into the management of the trial itself— its openness was largely illusory—but the authorities were now committed to letting both Sinyavsky and Daniel take the stand. The challenge was to crush dissent without making it seem authoritarian. The world was watching.

THE TRIAL BEGAN AT 10 A.M. on February 10, 1966. Despite the brutal cold, a small group of supporters, mostly Sinyavsky's students, gathered on the side street by the entrance to the courthouse. It was immediately apparent that the authorities had a very limited definition of an "open" trial. Police officers and court attendants swarmed around the yellow five-story building, making sure that nobody got in who had not been authorized. Foreign journalists were refused entrance and remained on the streets with the sympathizers—and the plainclothes police. Invitation cards had been sent out to Soviet officials to ensure the audience was reliable, with each invite color-coded for each court session. These cards were checked twice, at the entrance to the building and at the foot of the stairwell leading to the courtroom. Inside the courtroom it was stifling, the heat cranked up and the 150-person-capacity room packed. The shades were drawn, and fluorescent lights beat down from the ceiling. Everything in the room—walls, furniture, shades—was painted yellow, making it uncompromisingly bright. Sitting in the dock were the two accused writers. In the transcript, Sinyavsky is described as "thin, short with a reddish unkempt beard. He wears a snow-white nylon shirt under a black woolen sweater with a round collar. He looks like a gnome, or rather like a good-natured goblin." Daniel, sitting in the dock beside him, is "tall, dark-haired, but growing bald, with a large strong mouth, nervous lips, dressed in a cowboy shirt and a worn jacket."[25]

The presiding judge, Lev Nikolayevich Smirnov, entered the room, a burly man who had prosecuted Nazi war criminals at the Nuremberg trials. The writers were to be prosecuted under Section 1 of Article 70 of the Russian Criminal Code, accused of "anti-Soviet agitation and propaganda." The prosecutor, Oleg Tyomushkin, was to lead the questioning. Sinyavsky and Daniel would also face two "public accusers" from the writers' union. Kedrina, the author of the recently published smear in *Literaturnaya Gazeta*, was selected for one of these roles, and the other went to a relatively obscure writer, Arkady Vasilyev. A court clerk proceeded to read the eighteen-page indictment, detailing what Sinyavsky and Daniel had written and how they had smuggled these writings out of the country, and asserted that the anti-Soviet character of these works had led to their exploitation as "bourgeois propaganda." When the clerk described the contents of Daniel's novella *This Is Moscow Speaking*, in which one day a year is declared a "Public Murder Day," there was a surge of indignation from the gallery. If Sinyavsky and Daniel had hoped for any sympathy in the courtroom, it swiftly became clear they were not going to get it.

The indictment made a distinction between the two writers: Sinyavsky refused to accept that his work was anti-Soviet, even though Remizov had testified that his former friend privately held such views; Daniel also denied that his work was anti-Soviet in character but, according to the indictment, conceded that "he had caused a certain amount of harm to the Soviet regime." The two writers had admitted their guilt under interrogation, and witnesses, especially Remizov, were ready to further damn the accused. From the point of view of the KGB, everything was primed. Then something remarkable happened, something that did not follow the show trial script: when Smirnov asked the two writers how they pleaded, they both responded, "Not guilty."

Daniel was the first to be cross-examined, and he gave a robust defense of his position. He went back on his previous testimony, insisting it was "muddled." It emerged that the prosecution's main strategy involved quoting passages from Daniel's stories out of context and then attributing the opinions expressed in these fragments to Daniel himself. (Prosecutor Tyomushkin was evidently not familiar with the intentional fallacy.) By pursuing this track, the trial soon began to resemble an undergraduate debate about literary criticism. Daniel dealt with all this nimbly. When asked to define the "ideological orientation of *This Is Moscow Calling*," he replied that "there is a difference between content and ideological orientation." When asked why he had expressed so much hatred for the Soviet people in that story, he asked, "to whom are you talking? To me or to my hero, or to someone else?" "No single character represents the author," he went on. "Maybe it's bad literature, but it is literature, and it doesn't put everything in terms of black and white."

There was an element of farce about the proceedings. At one stage there was a power failure and the lights went out. At another, the prosecutor mixed up the names of the accused. Eventually, Judge Smirnov lost patience, declaring, "This is not a literary debate, and we don't need digressions into the history of literature," after Daniel made the uncomfortable point that Sholokhov, the presiding luminary of Soviet literature, had himself been "assessed as anti-Soviet" at one stage.

Daniel's defense counsel did not appear to have much of a strategy beyond drawing the court's attention to Daniel's war record (he had gone from school straight to the front lines). Daniel himself questioned the whole premise that literature could be used as a weapon in the Cold War. "As regards the harm done to our state," he said, "I do not think a couple of books by us, or even a score of books, could inflict any considerable damage on it."

Then it was Sinyavsky's turn to be cross-examined. He responded with patience and dignity throughout, insisting that literature should not be read as an indication of the author's politics.

PROSECUTOR: Do these three works [*The Trial Begins,* "On Socialist Realism," and *Lyubimov*] reflect your political views?

SINYAVSKY: I am not a political writer. No writer expresses his political views through his literary work. An artistic work does not express political views. You wouldn't ask Pushkin or Gogol about their politics [indignation in the courtroom]. My works reflect my attitudes about the world, not politics.

At this stage the prosecution read passages from *The Trial Begins* in which two secret policemen talk about a device for reading people's thoughts and a system of filters in the sewers that would allow them to recover and piece back together manuscripts that have been torn up and flushed down the toilet. The prosecution also questioned Sinyavsky about the epilogue, which describes how the author ended up in a labor camp.

SINYAVSKY: I'll explain the scene in the camp. The actual
historical events in the story are strictly limited to
[the] end of 1952 and the beginning of 1953, from the
"Doctors' Plot" to the death of Stalin. But a number
of scenes only ostensibly refer to real events. This is
a literary work, not a political document [laughter in
the courtroom]. Please allow me to speak. One of my
characters is a madman—

JUDGE SMIRNOV [interrupting]: We are interested in
another aspect of your work. You write about thought-
readers and filters under toilets. In other words, someone
made a decision about the installation of such devices.
That's the sort of thing covered by Article 70—slander.
Doesn't this malign our people, our society, our system?

SINYAVSKY: No. These events refer to a specific period, on
the eve of Stalin's death. The characters in question are
police agents. This is the time of the Doctors' Plot, when
there were many arrests and an atmosphere of suspicion.
The epilogue, written in the first person as though coming
from the author, is dated 1956, the year when the story
was completed. The "I" in the story is neither Sinyavsky
nor Tertz: he is the fictitious author, whose mood is a
mixture of fear and exaltation. Kolyma [site of the labor
camp] would be the logical end of the road for him. This is
not reality, but something that appears to the author in his
nightmares. There is no attempt here to depict historical
reality of the year 1956 [laughter in the courtroom].
This is a literary device, the setting up of an imaginary
situation.

After being extensively cross-examined about *Lyubimov* the
interrogation turned to "On Socialist Realism":

PROSECUTOR: Here you write: "In the name of the ultimate goal, we resorted to the methods used by our enemies . . . We introduced tortures . . . we placed a new czar on the vacant throne . . . It seemed at times as if for the sake of a complete victory of Communism, all we had to do was to give up the idea of Communism itself." How are we to understand this?

SINYAVSKY: We glorified the old Russia, we put a new czar, Stalin, on the throne. As I said before, you must bear in mind that I was referring to the Stalinist era.

PROSECUTOR: And here is how you compare the West with us: "How can a believer possibly wish freedom from his God?" What are we to make of this?

SINYAVSKY: Western democracy is based on "freedom of the individual," "freedom of competition," etc. In the West they talk about freedom of choice. I am being ironical about this. The Lord God is not a parliament. For a religious person, the question of freedom does not arise. For a theologically minded person there can only be no "freedom of choice." I say all this with reference to Soviet writers, for whom there is no question of any freedom of choice. Either you believe or, if not [looking at the prisoner's dock], you go to jail.

These exchanges continued hour after hour for three days. Witnesses were called. Remizov, who had broken under interrogation and was now testifying for the prosecution, was clearly in a state of considerable agitation. During his testimony a cry came out from the gallery: "The witness has a noose around his neck!"[26] It was clear that Remizov was betraying his former friends and conspirators to save his own skin. Only one defense witness came forward to defend Sinyavsky. Professor Viktor

Duvakin of Moscow State University began giving his opinions on Sinyavsky's merits as a literary critic when he was abruptly cut short by the judge. For this act of considerable courage Duvakin was subsequently stripped of the right to teach.

The last act, before Smirnov delivered his sentence, was the final plea granted to both writers. This was their opportunity to speak without being badgered and interrupted. If by now they knew they were sure to be found guilty, this at least was a platform from which they could speak to posterity. In his peroration, Sinyavsky decided to emphasize once more the prosecution's philistine inability to understand that literature was invention, not reality:

> I am not going to try to explain the literary purposes of our works, or deliver a lecture, or beat my head against the wall, trying to prove something—that would be futile. All I want to do is to repeat a few elementary arguments about the nature of literature. The most rudimentary thing about literature—it is here that one's study of it begins—is that words are not deeds and that words and literary images are conventions: authors are not identical with the characters they create. This is an elementary truth and we tried to talk about it. But the prosecution stubbornly rejected the idea as an invention, a means of evasion and deceit [. . .] I feel deeply that juridical standards cannot be applied to literature. The nature of an artistic image is complex, and even the author himself cannot always explain it. I think that if Shakespeare (I am not comparing myself with Shakespeare, nobody can imagine that) had been asked: what is the meaning of *Hamlet,* or what is the meaning of *Macbeth,* is there some insidious meaning in them? I think that Shakespeare himself would not have been able to give an answer to such questions.

Daniel also went down fighting, the target of his ire Vasilyev, who had served as public accuser for the prosecution.

The public accuser, the writer Vasilyev, said that he was ac-cusing us both in the name of the living and in the name of those who fell in the war and whose names are engraved in gold on marble in the Writers' Club. I know these lists engraved in marble, I know the names of these people who fell in the war. I knew some of them personally, and their memory is sacred to me. But why does Vasilyev, quoting from Sinyavsky's article—". . . so that not one drop of blood should be shed, we killed and killed and killed . . ."—why, in quoting these words, did not Vasilyev remind us of cer-tain other names, or are they unknown to him? I mean the names of Babel, Mandelstam, Bruno Jasienski, Ivan Kata-yev, Koltsov, Tretyakov, Kvitko, Markish.

In collaborating with the state, Vasilyev might have enhanced his career as a bureaucrat, but he betrayed his calling as a writer. Indeed, Daniel's roll call of writers murdered by the regime was both an accusation and a declaration of allegiance. Sinyavsky and Daniel were joining those who had become martyrs to the creation of their art. And martyrs they were.

After the way the trial was conducted there could have been little doubt about the verdict. What was not expected was the scale of the punishment. Smirnov handed down extremely harsh sentences: Daniel got five years in a hard labor camp; Sinyavsky got seven years. After the verdict, outside the courthouse the foreign press tried to speak to the writers' wives as they left, but found their way barred by members of the Soviet Youth League. Maria Rozanova and Lisa Bogoraz embraced and walked off in opposite directions. The prisoners were taken off in a wagon in the driving snow.

THE SENTENCING OF SINYAVSKY AND DANIEL was greeted with outrage around the world. The PEN club sent a telegram to Kosygin describing the sentences as "savage and inhuman." Hannah Arendt, the German American theorist of totalitarianism, described it as "an ugly reminder of something one had hoped had passed into history." The American novelist William Styron said the trial had revealed that "there is still a dreadful totalitarian atmosphere" in Soviet Russia. Graham Greene, hardly a typical anti-Communist reactionary, demanded that the royalties from his novels published in the Soviet Union be given to Bogoraz and Rozanova. Auden rather helplessly described the sentences as a "very shocking thing."

What *was* truly shocking, certainly to the hard-liners in the Kremlin, was the response of the European communist parties. *L'Unita,* the official newspaper of the Italian Communist Party, carried an open letter demanding the release of Sinyavsky and Daniel, the first time the Italian Communist Party had publicly criticized the Soviet Union. Remarkably the letter was signed by Eugenio Montale and Ignazio Silone, established anti-Communists, and Alberto Moravia and Elsa Morante, who were sympathetic fellow travelers. The manifest unfairness of the trial had trumped ideological divisions. The Communist Parties of Britain and France followed suit. "Justice should not only be done but should be seen to be done," wrote John Gollan, general secretary of the British Communist Party, in the *Daily Worker.* "Unfortunately, this cannot be said in the case of this trial." An editorial in *L'Humanité,* signed by Louis Aragon, demanded a retrial. Previously sympathetic intellectuals were vocal in their condemnation. William Gibson, the American playwright, publicly rejected an invitation by the Institute of Soviet American Relations to come to Moscow, where two of his plays were being performed: "Like Sinyavsky and Daniel, I am a writer that abhors the lies which grease the machinery of every state [. . .]

I cannot honor my promise to visit your country while it so dishonors men like me." A delegation of Czechoslovak writers traveled to Moscow to demand an explanation, while the Communist Parties of Denmark, Norway, Sweden, and Austria also issued protests. In the United States, the *Worker,* the organ of the U.S. Communist Party, asked for clemency. For the Western Cold Warriors it was an astonishing and unexpected coup: a high-profile breakdown in international Communist solidarity. The erosion of Party discipline—the refusal to meekly accept the Party line coming from Moscow—was a crack in the foundation of the whole Soviet Empire.

Back in the Soviet Union, the authorities struggled to contain the fallout. The censors were forced to withhold Western Communist newspapers because of their criticism of the trial. What was not known in the West, certainly not until *Kultura* published it the following November, was that in a petition drafted in March, shortly after Sinyavsky and Daniel had been sent to the camps, sixty-three *Soviet* writers had asked the Presidium for their release, and offered themselves as surety. Such venerable figures as Kornei Chukovsky and Ilya Ehrenburg were among the signatories. The cracks were spreading.

The Kremlin stuck to its guns. On February 22 Sinyavsky was officially expelled from the Union of Soviet Writers, and three days later *Izvestia* published an article celebrating Zhdanov, the architect of Stalin's postwar cultural purges. The message was clear. But placing articles in *Izvestia* was straightforward—the Kremlin's problem was finding intellectuals who would publicly support the punishment meted out to the two writers. In the end *Literaturnaya Gazeta* published a condemnatory letter signed by eighteen members of the Moscow University philology department (not exactly a major-league response). It took until the Twenty-Third Congress of the Soviet Communist Party, on April 1, 1966, before a proper counterattack was organized.

Sholokhov was again mobilized, attacking the West for trying to elicit his sympathy and expressing disappointment that the two writers had not been subject to the "revolutionary justice" of the 1920s. Brezhnev, who had consolidated his hold on power, denounced the writers in his own speech. The Soviet Union was undergoing ideological retrenchment and, by refusing to budge on the Sinyavsky-Daniel issue, Brezhnev was letting the West know about it.

The Kremlin could not keep a lid on the problem, however. On April 17, the *New York Times* devoted fourteen pages to the publication of an unofficial transcript of the trial, in a translation by Max Hayward. The transcript was then published by Harper & Row as a book. The KGB ordered two of its illegals to investigate how this could have happened. The husband-and-wife team of Anatoli Andreyevich Tonkonog (code name "Tanov") and Yelena Timofeyevna Fyodorova (code name "Tanova") discovered, no doubt to much fury back at Moscow Center, that the sale of the trial transcript to unnamed Western buyers had been organized by one Nikolai Vasilyevich Dyakonov, who, while ostensibly a journalist with the Novosti Press Agency, was also a KGB agent (as a sideline, Dyakonov sold foreign currency, Russian abstract art, and banned literary works on the black market). There was no question of putting a rogue agent on trial, as it would reflect badly on their organization (it is not clear what other repercussions he faced), so the KGB went after others involved in smuggling the transcript out to the West. In January 1968, Alexander Ginzburg, Yuri Galanskov, Alexei Dobrovolsky, and Vera Lashkova were prosecuted for assembling and smuggling out the transcript and other documents, known as *The White Book*, to Possev Publishers, an anti-Communist émigré organization based in Germany. Ginzburg and Galanskov, who were editors of samizdat journals, were given five and seven years respectively.

In the months after Sinyavsky and Daniel were shipped off to prison camp, intellectuals kept up the pressure on the Soviet Union. Academics from nineteen different universities took out a quarter-page advertisement in the *New York Times* to protest the imprisonment. The spring issue of *Partisan Review* carried an open letter from 122 American intellectuals who appealed to the Soviet Union on behalf of the "international community of letters." The signatories were not simply the New York intellectual anti-Communists who were most closely associated with *Partisan Review*, but also included communist-sympathizers like Lillian Hellman, and champions of the counterculture in Allen Ginsberg and Thomas Pynchon. It was even signed by as apolitical a figure as Andy Warhol.

THE COVERAGE OF THE SINYAVSKY-DANIEL TRIAL was the last great propaganda victory for the anti-Communist cultural network secretly established by the CIA in the late 1940s and early 1950s. Leading the charge was *Encounter*, which, in its April 1966 issue, carried a photograph of Sinyavsky on its front page and announced "a new Tertz story" ("Pkhentz") and the first English translation of Sinyavsky's essay on Pasternak. It also carried a report on the trial.[27] In one sense, at least, the prosecutors had been right: Sinyavsky and Daniel had been accused of being part of a "Soviet literary underground" whose works had "been widely distributed in the United States, Britain and other capitalist countries to discredit the Soviet people, our Government, the Communist Party of the U.S.S.R. and its policies. Slanderous works of underground writers are being passed off by hostile propaganda as truthful accounts about the Soviet Union." In the prosecutor's overheated summation of his case, he declared that "[t]he social danger of their work, of what they have done, is particularly acute at this time, when ideological warfare is being stepped up, when an entire propaganda machine of international reaction, connected as it is with the intelligence services, is being brought into play to contaminate our youth with the poison of nihilism, to get its tentacles into our intellectual circles by hook or by crook."[28] In sentencing the accused, Smirnov said that the work of Sinyavsky and Daniel "attracted the attention of bourgeois propaganda organs by their anti-Soviet content and were exploited in the ideological struggle against the Soviet Union."[29]

During the trial, much had been made of the fact that the CIA-funded Radio Liberty had broadcast readings of *The Trial Begins* and *Lyubimov* into the Soviet Union. Sinyavsky responded to the allegations that he had fostered propaganda in his final plea to the court:

The question arises: what is propaganda, and what is literature? The viewpoint of the prosecution is that literature is a form of propaganda, and that there are only two kinds of propaganda: pro-Soviet or anti-Soviet. If literature is simply un-Soviet, it means that it is anti-Soviet. It is a poor business if writers are judged and categorized by such standards.

Sinyavsky was insistent both during and after the trial that he had told Peltier to find him a publisher that was not "anti-Soviet." Yet if his goal had been to keep his books out of the literary Cold War, he categorically failed—almost every word he smuggled abroad had appeared in journals funded by the Congress for Cultural Freedom. There is no reason to doubt Sinyavsky's good faith, but he was naive to believe he could send his work out into the West and avoid it being exploited as Cold War propaganda. What many better-informed writers in the West did not realize was just quite how deeply the CIA had infiltrated the cultural field with their front organizations, secret funding operations, and covert agents. The prosecution got a lot wrong, but there was no question that Sinyavsky's and Daniel's work had been exploited by the propaganda fronts established by American intelligence. The "propaganda machine of international reaction" might not have had tentacles, but it certainly existed. And amid the fallout from the Sinyavsky-Daniel trial, the rest of the world was about to find out.

TWENTY-SEVEN

Spender

LONDON, PARIS & PRAGUE, 1965–1968

BY THE MIDSIXTIES Stephen Spender was a doyen of the literary establishment on both sides of the Atlantic. Universities competed to offer him visiting professorships, he was elected an honorary member of the American Academy of Arts and Letters, and, in 1965, he became the first foreigner appointed the Consultant in Poetry at the Library of Congress, a position that demanded he take a step back from his work for *Encounter*. The distinguished critic Frank Kermode took over as literary editor, with Spender remaining on board as a contributing editor. He left *Encounter* in good shape, having developed relationships with many of the great writers of the era and having helped establish the magazine as one of the foremost intellectual forums of the preceding decade. His work had been canonized in a collected edition in 1955, and while he now wrote fewer poems, he had become a respected public intellectual and literary critic. At fifty-six, he still worked and traveled frenetically, straining to find time for his wife, Natasha, and his two children (Matthew was an undergraduate at Oxford, Lizzie was still at school). With his shock of white hair, he cut a distinguished figure: the handsome rebel-poet of the 1930s had become a doyen of the literary establishment. Then it all fell apart.

Without his realizing it, by the time he took his prestigious position at the Library of Congress, the wheels were already in motion. The coming scandal would expose the elaborate machinery the CIA had secretly constructed to wage the cultural Cold War, and Spender would get caught up in the gears. The previous year, Wright Patman, a Democratic congressman from Texas, led an investigation into the tax-exempt status of several foundations that revealed a number of them were in fact little more than CIA fronts. (The investigation began because the IRS had demanded foundations have their tax-exempt status revoked for engaging in stock speculation and other activities.) While this revelation caused some nervousness at Langley, there was little immediate follow-up. One publication did, however, begin to connect the dots as far as *Encounter* was concerned. In a September editorial, *The Nation* raised some pointed questions. "Should the CIA be permitted," the editors asked, "to channel funds to magazines—in London and New York—which pose as 'magazines of opinion' and are in competition with independent journals of opinion?"[1] The identity of the magazine in London was not hard to guess.

By this stage there were already rumors in intellectual circles in New York and London about the true source of funding behind the Congress for Cultural Freedom. Jason Epstein, a celebrated book editor at Random House and cofounder in 1963 (along with his wife, Barbara, and Bob Silvers) of *The New York Review of Books,* would later write that it seemed obvious at the time that with "no visible government agency" funding all these conferences and publications around the world, the presumption was that "there had to be an invisible one," and there was only one credible candidate.[2] Epstein told Spender of his suspicions, as did Mary McCarthy, but when Spender passed on his concerns to people at the CCF or the Farfield Foundation, he was reassured.[3] Julius Fleischmann even told him personally, while they were aboard his yacht in the Aegean, that there was nothing fishy about the funding.[4]

In April 1966, the situation became more serious. Spender was in Evanston, Illinois, preparing some lectures on American poetry for Northwestern University, when the *New York Times* published the results of a long-term investigation into the CIA's funding of a whole host of organizations and institutions. The reports documented the way the CIA moved money through different foundations as a means of camouflaging its origins, allowing it to pour funds into organizations it secretly supported, among them the CCF.

The U.S. government had fought hard to prevent the *New York Times* from going ahead with publication. The CIA's Angleton, Chip Bohlen, U.S. ambassador to France, and Dean Rusk, secretary of state, all tried to persuade the paper not to run the story because of the damage it would do to public confidence in the way America was waging the Cold War.[5] But the *Times* knew it had something sensational on its hands, and there was no way it was going to bow to establishment pressure.

The revelations gave critics of the CCF the ammunition they had been seeking, foremost among them the Irish historian Conor Cruise O'Brien, who seized on the fact that a number of luminaries, including J. K. Galbraith, George Kennan, Robert Oppenheimer, and Arthur Schlesinger Jr., had written a letter to the *New York Times* rebutting the idea that the CCF "had been used by the Central Intelligence Agency" and insisting upon its independence.[6] As more details emerged about how the CCF was funded, defending this position became untenable. In a televised debate, O'Brien asked Schlesinger if he had known that the CIA paid for the Congress when he signed the letter. Schlesinger paused before answering: "I *did* know about it while I was in government."[7]

Spender was rattled: the *New York Times* claimed that while *Encounter* was no longer in receipt of CIA funds it had been for a long time previously. (The CCF had secured a large grant

from the Ford Foundation in 1964 that cut ties with the Farfield Foundation and other CIA fronts.)[8] On May 10, Spender
coauthored a letter with fellow editor Melvin Lasky, saying they
knew nothing of "indirect benefactions" and that they were "part
of nobody's propaganda"[9] (Lasky, though, knew far more than he
was letting on). Spender wrote to Michael Josselson, who ran the
CCF, and Fleischmann, seeking assurances that Encounter had
not been in receipt of CIA money. Josselson responded by saying he had lawyers combing the financial records to make sure
they were clean. Fleischmann did not respond until September,
but when the letter finally came, he also assured Spender that
there was nothing untoward. Yet there had been no clear statement issued in response to the New York Times story, no retrac-
tion, and no legal action taken.

In May 1966, the month after the revelations, O'Brien struck
again. In a lecture to alumni of New York University, he accused
Encounter of working in the service of "the power structure in
Washington" and of tricking writers of integrity into unwittingly
collaborating with their project.[10] Excerpts of this lecture were
printed in Book Week, which was circulated at the PEN writers
conference in New York in July.

In response, Encounter ran a hit piece on O'Brien. In the magazine's anonymous "R." column (in fact authored by Goronwy
Rees), hints were dropped about O'Brien's conduct when a UN
diplomat in the Congo, and it was claimed that he was a crack-
pot, unhealthily obsessed with Encounter. He was accused of
making reckless allegations in the manner of Joe McCarthy
and ridiculed for "hunting for CIA agents beneath the beds of
Stephen Spender, Irving Kristol, Melvin Lasky, and Frank Kermode."[11] O'Brien's lawyers told him the article was libelous and
he filed suit in a Dublin court.

According to Mary McCarthy, at some point Spender, back in
London, was riding in a taxi with Nicolas Nabokov, the secre-

tary general of the CCF, when Nabokov apparently blurted out the truth that the CIA *was* behind the Congress and *Encounter,* and then he jumped out of the cab and ran off. This might well be an apocryphal tale—although not necessarily out of character for Nabokov—but Spender was certainly hearing enough to make him seriously concerned. Towards the end of 1966, Josselson and Lasky took Kermode and Spender out for lunch at the Garrick, a gentlemen's club in the West End of London, and again assured them they had nothing to fear.[12] The story refused to die, however. Animosity was building against the CIA for its part in the Vietnam War, and in intellectual circles, any kind of association with it was a stigma. And *Encounter*'s problems were mounting. Having still failed to offer any kind of legal response to the *New York Times* allegations, their lawyers now offered no defense in the O'Brien case in Dublin. They claimed that it was pointless to do so as they had no Irish property to defend but that did not stop it from looking deeply suspect. When O'Brien later threatened to take his case to a British court, *Encounter* apologized and offered to make a significant payment to a charity of his choice.

In February 1967, while Spender was at the Center for Advanced Studies at Wesleyan University in Connecticut, he received a call from a journalist at *Ramparts,* a California-based magazine that had been conducting its own long-term investigation into the CIA, focusing on its infiltration and secret subsidizing of student movements and labor unions.[13] Spender later wrote in his journal that the journalist told him *Ramparts* had proof that the CCF was funded by the CIA and that many of the foundations associated with it were also funded by the agency.[14] Presented with this new evidence, Spender was finally convinced of the truth.

As with the *New York Times* investigation, the CIA tried desperately to stop *Ramparts* from going to press with the story.

They had known about the investigation since early 1966 and, in collaboration with the FBI, set about smearing *Ramparts* and its journalists, claiming they were under the sway of the Soviets.[15] *Ramparts* remained undeterred, and their reports provided irrefutable evidence of the CIA exerting clandestine influence on American citizens. With Vietnam protests spilling from the campuses into the streets, the atmosphere in the United States was feverish. For Spender it was not difficult to see the consequences of being thought complicit with the CIA.

The efforts by Josselson and the CIA to keep obfuscating were over, and at a mid-March meeting of the directors of the CCF he admitted the allegations were true. The dam had burst. Kermode telephoned Spender to let him know that at a meeting at his house in Gloucestershire, Lasky had admitted to knowing about the CIA's role since 1963. The news sent Spender into a rage—he had never liked Lasky, and now he discovered that he had been duped by his fellow editor. He wrote a letter to the *New York Times* in which he said that he had been deceived over CIA funding and asked whether or not there should be a law that protects people like him from being deceived in the future.[16] Josselson wrote to Isaiah Berlin, asking him to intercede, saying that Spender was "pouring oil on the flames" with his actions.[17]

Spender next sought a showdown, demanding a meeting of the *Encounter* trustees in London. His wife, Natasha, worried about the ramifications and arranged for legal counsel. On April 20, Spender flew in from the United States and headed straight for his home in St. John's Wood. After freshening up, he and Kermode had a meeting with their lawyer and prepared formal statements. The trustees' meeting took place at a restaurant in Picadilly. While the minutes have not survived, what is beyond dispute is that Spender was subject to a further humiliation at the hands of Lasky. With tempers flaring, Lasky launched a personal attack on Spender, telling him to get off his high horse.

After all, he said, Spender's salary had, from the beginning, been secretly paid by the Foreign Office.

This was a devastating blow to Spender because it meant that the number of people deceiving him was far greater than he previously imagined. He left the meeting in a state of distress and, according to Kermode, went straight to the National Gallery on Trafalgar Square, calming himself down by looking at some paintings.[18] That night he telephoned Malcolm Muggeridge, who had been heavily involved in establishing *Encounter*. Spender confronted him: had Muggeridge not assured him that his salary came from contributions by Alexander Korda, Victor Rothschild, and the *Daily Telegraph*? "So I did, dear boy," Muggeridge replied, "but I wouldn't bet your bottom dollar that's where it *really* came from."[19]

The result of the meeting with the trustees was, in Spender's words, a "rather bitter and loathsome compromise," whereby *Encounter* would make a clean break with the CCF and limp on until June, when it would be relaunched on a fully independent footing with Spender at the helm.[20] Yet Lasky, who had promised to resign, changed his mind two days later and started maneuvering behind the scenes. At a second trustees meeting, at which Spender was not present, it was agreed that Lasky would stay on. "We've been shopped," Kermode told Natasha Spender afterward.[21] Spender and Kermode finally handed in their resignations, and graciously allowed the CCF time to put together a statement to save face.

Then came the third and final bombshell. A reporter from the *New York Times* called Spender and told him that Thomas Braden, a former OSS and CIA agent, had written an article defending the CIA's conduct but that in doing so, Braden had revealed many new details.[22] And Braden knew what he was talking about: he had been head of the CIA's International Organizations Division, responsible for anti-Communist psychological warfare.[23] Among them was his claim that one of the *Encounter* editors was a CIA agent. The journalist told Spender he had spoken to Lasky, who had accused Spender of being the agent. It is not clear whether the journalist had in fact done this, or whether they were bluffing—either way, they certainly got a reaction from Spender. He denied being a CIA agent and doubted whether anyone who knew him could believe such a fanciful claim. He said Kermode was clearly not an agent and said there was no way Irving Kristol was, either.[24] Even if he did not name Lasky explicitly, this left only one candidate. Spender also revealed that, while it had not been made public, he had already resigned from *Encounter*. The story announcing his resignation was carried on the front page of the *New York Times*.[25]

The exposure of the CCF's secret funding had serious consequences beyond *Encounter*. The CCF had established magazines or taken over the funding of magazines around the world, and those who had edited or contributed to them received blow-back.[26] *Mundo Nuevo*, which had helped popularize the writers of the Latin American boom, including Mario Vargas Llosa and Gabriel García Márquez, lost its credibility and its editor, Emir Rodríguez Monegal, resigned.[27] In India, the reputation of *Quest* was irreparably damaged by the revelations and it "ambled lamely" on until it folded in the 1970s.[28] *Hiwar*, which was based in Lebanon, was banned in Egypt (it had already been banned in Iraq) and collapsed in 1967.[29] In Uganda, *Transition* magazine, which had published important work by Chinua Achebe and Ngugi wa Thiong'o, came under intense attack. The magazine had long been a critic of the government in Kampala, and the revelations about the CCF was all the excuse the authorities needed to imprison its editor, Rajat Neogy (he was released the following year but only after a media campaign on his behalf).[30] In Japan, Hoki Ishihara, the editor of *Jiyu*, which was also revealed to have received CIA funding, claimed he needed police protection after his house was firebombed.[31] By comparison, Spender had it easy. He was, though, subjected to attacks by Lasky and the trustees of *Encounter* for airing his grievances about the funding scandal and the way Lasky and others had covered it up. One trustee, the Chicago sociologist Edward Shils, called Spender a "coward and a brute" and implied that his hostility toward Lasky—Shils called it a "pogrom"—was anti-Semitic.[32] When Natasha Spender went to the *Encounter* offices to retrieve her husband's paperwork, she discovered his locked filing cabinet had been broken into and rifled. She was told there had been a burglary. Spender donated a sum equivalent to his *Encounter* salary from March 1966, the date of the first *New York Times* revelations, to various charities. He never spoke to Lasky again and never read another word that was published in *Encounter*.

THE REVELATIONS about the CIA's clandestine support of writers and artists were part of a larger Cold War reckoning in the United States. The intellectuals themselves either tried their best to distance themselves from any suggestion of complicity or, in the case of those who had not taken the CCF's money, gleefully attacked those who had. Norman Mailer, in *Armies of the Night*, his account of the march on the Pentagon in protest of the Vietnam War, put it in typically pugnacious terms, describing the CCF as having been so thoroughly infested by the CIA that it called up the image of "cockroaches in a slum sink."[33] In the Summer 1967 issue of *Partisan Review*, editors Philip Rahv and William Phillips included "A Statement on the CIA," in which a disparate group of intellectuals, including Hannah Arendt, Lillian Hellman, Dwight Macdonald, and Norman Mailer, expressed their opposition to CIA funding and demanded that those magazines implicated do more to exorcise their association with the agency.[34] There was irony in this gesture: *Partisan Review* had itself been in receipt of funds sourced from the CIA.[35]

Others explored the larger ramifications for American culture. In the pages of *The New York Review of Books,* Epstein argued that "the fault of the CIA was not that it corrupted the innocent but it tried, in collusion with a group of insiders, to corner a free market." The system had been rigged to favor anti-Communist intellectuals, and the result was "an underground gravy train whose first-class compartments were not always occupied by first-class passengers."[36] The problem, Epstein pointed out, was not just the loss of earnings and influence of those who were not allowed to board that train, it was how this rigged system incentivized anti-Communism above all else. To Epstein, the failures of McCarthyism and the failures of the Vietnam War were the result of an anti-Communism that blinded American intellectuals to self-criticism. "The hysteria of the early Fifties and the killing that goes on today are not isolated and discrete symptoms but aspects of a larger sickness," he wrote, pointing out that in focusing on Soviet oppression of Eastern Europe, magazines like *Encounter* failed to address adequately "Latin American dictatorships supported by the United States, or about the Negro problem, or the protests throughout the world over our war in Vietnam."[37]

In an article for *The Nation* in September 1967, the historian Christopher Lasch echoed Epstein in arguing that the problems faced by American intellectuals "derived from the bankruptcy of social and political thought during the fifties" in which the Cold War was defined "as a struggle for cultural freedom." If the Johnson administration was suffering from a "credibility gap" in its statements about the Vietnam War, "what about the credibility of our most eminent intellectuals?" The damage done was substantive, Lasch argued, because in prosecuting the cultural Cold War, the Americans chose to "fight fire with fire," a strategy that was "self-defeating because the means corrupt the end."[38] The very cause that they were supposedly fighting for—cultural freedom—was undermined by the means of combat. This served as a larger analogy of the way the United States, and the CIA in particular, were fighting the Cold War: in seeking to spread freedom and American values, they had, among other things, propped up dictators in Cuba, Guatemala, and South Vietnam, and helped depose an elected ruler in Iran.

In Lasch's estimation, Spender at least "had the wit . . . to recognize the situation for what it was," quoting him as saying that he and his fellow writers and editors were "being used for concealed government propaganda" and that this made a "mockery" of intellectual freedom. At the same time, it was evident to anyone who had read *Encounter* that it was not simply pushing American propaganda: there was too much variety of content in each issue for that to appear credible. How much influence had the CIA exerted over editorial decisions? It was something that Spender worried over. As recently as September 1966, Josselson had told Spender that the "proudest achievement" of the Congress was "to have given a number of gifted people the means to publish intellectual magazines of the highest standing without any interference or any strings attached."[39]

Spender believed he had been making autonomous editorial decisions, and in the early days, he and Kristol had successfully prevented the CCF from imposing on the magazine a column about the Congress's activities. In the aftermath of the revelations, Spender's son, Matthew, asked him if he could remember specific pieces that had been suspiciously spiked and he recalled one, a laudatory piece about Castro's Cuba.[40] Frances Stonor Saunders has demonstrated that a 1958 piece by Dwight Macdonald, which Spender had initially accepted, was rejected under CCF pressure.[41] (However, that it was later published in another CCF journal, *Tempo Presente*, suggests that any such editorial interference was not particularly well organized.) Saunders also found evidence that a 1954 article by Emily Hahn on U.S. policy in China was spiked under CIA pressure.[42] And of course influence could take more subtle forms than banning the publication of stories. "It would be untrue to write that the Congress never tried to influence the editorial policy of *Encounter,*" Spender later recalled, "although the influence it attempted to exercise was by no means always political: simply, the people in Paris had bright ideas about the kind of articles we should put in."[43]

The question for Spender was how he could rebuild his reputation. He knew that, for some, he had been "indelibly branded" and that he was always going to face skepticism about his role with *Encounter* and what he knew when.[44] Even if he had not been aware of what had gone on—and the evidence from his papers suggests that he must have kept up an elaborate deception with many people for many years if he *did* know—he had certainly been credulous. Spender later said that, "It was as with the people who come and tell you that your wife is unfaithful to you. Then you ask her yourself, and if she denies it, you are satisfied with it."[45] Amid the anger and shame of betrayal, Spender decided that he had to do something. If his credibility, and the credibility of much of his generation had been tarnished, then what about the new generation that was challenging the old order? Around the world, radical movements were gaining momentum on university campuses. Just a year shy of his sixtieth birthday, Spender set an itinerary for New York, Paris, Berlin, and Prague, to get a taste of the spirit of '68 and the revolution against the establishment.

IN MAY 1968, Spender went to Paris to visit the occupied Sorbonne. His friend Mary McCarthy, recently returned to Paris aftter reporting in Hanoi, wrote to Hannah Arendt to say that he was there "expiating the CIA."[46] He certainly threw himself into the action. In the Latin Quarter he witnessed some of the street battles that took place between the protesters and the police. He gazed, fascinated, as the students constructed barricades by ripping up paving stones, felling trees across the Boulevard Saint-Germain, and dragging parked cars into the streets. He watched the students arm themselves with dustbin lids and improvised spears as they faced off against the ranks of the police, who slowly began marching down the street "like a thick wedge of mercury up a glass tube."[47] The students set fire to anything flammable lodged in the barricades as the police launched tear gas into their midst.

Spender was reminded of his own youth when his generation rose up to fight fascism and volunteered for action in the Spanish Civil War. Yet he was also struck by differences that he found harder to reconcile. The New Left was in many ways libertarian, distrusting the "system" at every turn and breaking social taboos on sex and drugs. In France, it defined itself in opposition to De Gaulle and the traditional values he espoused. Instead of the rigorous structures of the Old Left, which carried the taint of hierarchy, the New Left embraced spontaneity and direct democracy. Rather than focus exclusively on class, the new generation also stressed the importance of gender, race, and the Third World. Mostly students, these were middle-class rebels who felt alienated from consumer culture and angered by the failures of liberal democracy. They protested against nuclear weapons and the Vietnam War and saw in America a new imperial power wrapping its tendrils around the globe. Their intellectual idol was the German emigre philosopher Herbert Marcuse, and their political hero was the Cuban revolutionary Ernesto "Che" Guevara.

As Spender discovered in Paris, the opposition to American

capitalism did not translate into a support of Soviet Communism. On entering the courtyard of the Sorbonne, surrounded by what he described as "cliffs of buff-coloured stucco walls," Spender discovered tables piled high with revolutionary literature— none of it would have gone down well at the Kremlin.[48] "The brands of revolution offered by the students are Maoist, Castroite, Trotskyist," he wrote. Emblematic of this new movement's dissatisfaction with the Cold War dichotomy was the German student leader Rudi Dutschke, who had fled the totalitarian regime in East Germany, only to find himself disenchanted by the inequities of the West (the previous month he had survived being shot in the head by a young anti-Communist).

In New York the previous month, Spender had climbed an improvised ladder into the occupied dean's office at Columbia University to try to understand what motivated the students in their rebellion. He found them to be naive and directionless and that rather than setting an agenda, they were simply reacting to the demands of the moment. Spender could not see how this was going to get them anywhere. He was much more impressed with the African American protesters he met on the Columbia campus, as they seemed to have a much clearer sense of purpose. In Paris he came up against the same issue. The students did not want to think of themselves in the context of previous revolutions, nor did they want to learn from the failures of their predecessors. When it was pointed out, in an editorial in the *Times*, that the rebels had clearly not read *Animal Farm*, Spender realized "they would not want to read it and if they did read it could find there nothing which they thought applied in their case." Spender found them to be "unself-critical" and that they were quick to "take refuge in the idea theirs was an unprecedented generation."[49]

On May 20, Spender attended what was called the "grand spectacular of the writers" at the Grand Amphitheatre of the

Sorbonne. He arrived early—at 7:20 P.M.—and while Jean-Paul Sartre, the star attraction, was not scheduled to appear until 10 P.M., the room was already packed. When McCarthy arrived and took a seat in the area reserved for the press, at the back of the stage, Spender picked his way through the crowd to join her. Sitting on stage, and clearly too old to be students, the pair became a target of the crowd, who demanded their removal. Spender found it an unnerving experience as "looking at that immense shouting, moving, gesticulating mass was like looking into a cavernous mouth full of raging teeth."[50] McCarthy and Spender took up new berths to the side of the main platform. The room continued to fill until students began climbing up into the niches of the walls to get a view of the stage. When Sartre finally arrived, Spender had a ringside seat.

It was one of the paradoxes of the movement that while the students rejected the idea of authority, they were drawn to the charismatic leadership of Sartre, whose hostility to all bourgeois values was central to their approach. He had spoken up on behalf of the students and condemned the violent manner in which the police had attacked protesters. That morning his interview with one of the public faces of the movement, Daniel Cohn-Bendit, had been published in *Nouvelle Observateur*. There was much mutual admiration. Spender thought it remarkable that Sartre managed to negotiate the crowd to take his place on the stage, blinking at the audience from behind "lenses as thick as portholes." The questions started to pour in from the students. Spender felt there was something clinical about Sartre as, "computer-like," he "produced small neat packaged answers in his crackling voice."[51] Hundreds more listened outside, as Sartre's replies were broadcast through loudspeakers. "You must reinvent your tradition," Sartre said at one point, "a tradition worthy of this cultural revolution."[52]

As much as he was taken with the romantic aspects of this

youthful revolt, Spender's concern was that in the interests of creating a new tradition, the rebels were prepared to throw out what was valuable in the old. Attacking the hierarchies in society was one thing, but tearing down the university was another. In *The Young Rebels*, the book he wrote about his time among the students, he pointed out that Karl Marx would not have gotten very far without the British Museum. There was, he concluded, something alarming and nihilistic in this desire to destroy the very institution that had armed them with their rebellious ideas in the first place. More generally, he was disheartened by their wholesale rejection of anyone or anything old, for that meant Spender himself.

IF IN PARIS SPENDER FELT LEFT BEHIND, in Prague he rediscovered purpose. There he found himself confronted by the issue that had prompted his involvement in the cultural Cold War in the first place: freedom of literary expression. He arrived in the city in July and set about meeting with students and writers who had participated in the protests leading up to what became known as "the Prague Spring." After the cultural suffocation under the uncompromising rule of Antonin Novotny, a committed Stalinist, the energy and enthusiasm he found in Czechoslovakia delighted Spender. The efforts of the country's new leader Alexander Dubcek to create "socialism with a human face" was a project that appealed to the old radical in Spender, whose left-wing politics always accommodated the need for individual freedom.

Some of the Czechoslovak writers that Spender met traced the stirrings of rebellion back to a 1963 conference on the work of Franz Kafka. Since Kafka wrote in German, many of these writers had not previously been familiar with his strange stories, even though he had lived much of his life in Prague. As good Marxists, they had been taught that alienation was something that happens under capitalism, but in Kafka's depiction of an arbitrary and hostile bureaucratic state, many of them had recognized the alienation they felt under Communism.

Over the following years, writers began pushing back more forcefully against the Novotny regime. The demand for freedom of literary expression was the leading edge of a call for greater liberalization. In 1965, an increasingly restless student body had made Allen Ginsberg the "King of May" at their traditional May Day bacchanal. The shaggy-haired Beat poet paraded around Prague wearing a crown, much to the delight of the student body, many of whom had read his experimental and explicit poem "Howl" in translation. The Czechoslovak police kicked Ginsberg out of the country the following week, but a symbolic victory had been won.

In June 1967, the Fourth Congress of Czechoslovak Writers had turned into a scene of unexpected rebellion. The novelist Ludvik Vaculik led the charge, pointing out that the only reason they were assembled was that the Communist Party willed it to be so. He made the heretical claim that art and power should be kept separate. Another novelist, Milan Kundera, supported Vaculik and demanded to know why it was that the "guarding of frontiers was still more valued than the crossing of them."[53] After the conference, the writers who had shown dissent, including Ivan Klíma, Pavel Kohout, and the young playwright Václav Havel, were either kicked out of the writers' union or threatened with a ban on publication.

At a meeting of the student union later that year, groups of radical students expressed their solidarity with the writers who had spoken out. On October 31, the electricity failed at one of the largest student dorms, and while this was a frequent occurrence, this time the residents poured out into the street carrying candles and began to march through Prague chanting, "We want light! We want to study!" They were met by police who decided to put an end to the impromptu protests with a combination of tear gas and clubs. Dubcek, a reform-minded politician who had been secretary of the Party in Slovakia, called for an inquiry, and Novotny found his support dwindling rapidly. He resigned and was replaced by Dubcek, who, after a slow start, began instituting a series of reforms that dramatically opened up the country. "The Czechoslovaks were sincere," Spender wrote, "in wanting to combine the utmost freedom of the individual (by which they meant, precisely, *our* freedom) with Communist government."[54]

The end of censorship prompted an explosion of creative work in art, film, and literature, and previously banned work came back into circulation. As if this was not enough to alarm the Soviet Union, the Dubcek regime began weeding out Soviet agents in its police and security forces and began an inquiry into crimes committed in the purges that followed the 1948 Communist coup. Such was the success of these reforms that people demanded more. In an essay entitled "On the Subject of Opposition," Havel argued that the only way to guarantee the future of democratic socialism in the country was to institute a two-party structure and free elections. Dubcek remained a committed Communist and realized the need to check the speed of liberalization, especially as Brezhnev was presiding over an ideological hardening back in the Soviet Union. But it was already too late. The warnings from Moscow began coming thick and fast, and with a Party congress approaching in which the remaining Novotny loyalists were expected to be kicked out, Brezhnev decided to act.

On the night of August 20, a huge Soviet force, supported by Warsaw Pact allies, crossed into Czechoslovakia. The next morning two planes carrying Russian commandos landed at Prague airport. Tanks rolled onto Wenceslas Square in the center of Prague, and Dubcek and his political allies were arrested and flown to Moscow. There was scattered resistance, but such was the show of force by the Russians that any kind of concerted fight back was futile. Instead Czechoslovaks began a campaign of nonviolent resistance against the occupiers. The actions of the Soviet Union were met with outrage around the world, even among the European Communist Parties, some of which broke with the Kremlin permanently over the issue. When Dubcek returned to Prague, he was a beaten man and while he was allowed to stay on until he was replaced by Gustáv Husák the following year, his reforms were gradually reversed in a process known as "normalization." For the Czechoslovak writers, the Soviet suppression of the Prague Spring was a devastating blow. Some, like Kundera, went into exile while others were silenced. Their resistance was far from over, however. Led by the example of Havel, writers found new ways to fight back, circulating texts in samizdat and organizing the Czechoslovak underground. They had lost the battle but were still fighting the war.

Perhaps the most remarkable protest against the Soviet invasion took place in Moscow itself, where a group of seven courageous dissidents, including Larisa Bogoraz, the wife of Yulii Daniel, waved placards in a protest on Red Square. With the Brezhnev regime continuing to crack down on any form of local dissidence, they were swiftly arrested. By that time, Bogoraz and Pavel Litvinov, a physicist and dissident, were already known to Spender. After Alexander Ginzburg and his collaborators on *The White Book* were sent to labor camps in January 1968, Bogoraz and Litvinov wrote "An Appeal to World Public Opinion," an open letter that was published in newspapers in the West. Spender saw it in the *Times* and rallied writers and intellectuals including W. H. Auden, Cecil Day-Lewis, Mary McCarthy, Sonia Orwell, and Bertrand Russell to issue a statement of solidarity that was immediately distributed to the world press. Litvinov learned about the statement from foreign correspondents in Moscow and wrote to Spender urging him and his friends to create an organization that would champion the cause of writers who were subject to censorship or persecution around the world, a literary ancillary to the human rights organizations that were growing in influence. Shortly afterward, Bogoraz and Litvinov were themselves arrested for staging their protest in Red Square against the crushing of the Prague Spring. They were sentenced to exile in Siberia.

Spender ran with Litvinov's suggestion. Perhaps he saw in it a chance for redemption, an opportunity for an honorable return to the Cold War fray. With advice from Amnesty International and in collaboration with David Astor, Stuart Hampshire, and Edward Crankshaw, Spender formed Writers and Scholars International, a charitable trust that, in 1972, launched a new magazine, *Index on Censorship*, under the editorship of Michael Scammell.[55] The magazine became, and remains, a respected forum in which oppressed writers can find a home for their work. Among its most important successes was helping to continue the work of its founding protesters, that is, keeping alive the spirit of the Prague Spring. It was in *Index on Censorship* that the English translation of Charter 77 first appeared. This manifesto, authored by Václav Havel among others, was a rallying point for the Czechoslovakian resistance, and its authors went on to play instrumental roles in the Velvet Revolution. From deep within the ethical murk of the cultural Cold War, Spender had found a light leading toward a clearer path.

TWENTY-EIGHT
McCarthy

PARIS, SAIGON & HANOI, 1965-1972

ON MARCH 3, 1965, Mary McCarthy was on her way to her local bakery in the sixth arrondissement of Paris, near the Luxem-
bourg Gardens, when she saw the newspaper headlines on the
Metro kiosk. What she had feared for weeks had finally come
to pass: the bombing of North Vietnam had begun. She later
recalled that she "just stood there, swallowing and deep breathing."[1] She had convinced herself that it wasn't going to happen.
"This would surely be one of those crises—like the Cuban missile confrontation, like the Berlin Wall—that would somehow
pass," she wrote.[2] The sense of mounting horror on that Paris
morning took her back to another morning, on Cape Cod, when
she first saw a newspaper headline announcing the bombing
of Hiroshima. When she returned to her apartment on Rue de
Rennes, she felt the overpowering need to act. McCarthy did
not know it at the time, but she was already set on a course that
would take her into the path of those American bombs tumbling
on North Vietnam.

The aerial assault escalated quickly into Operation Rolling
Thunder, in which more tons of American bombs were dropped
than in either the Pacific Theater of the Second World War or in
the Korean War. The idea was to push what President Lyndon
Johnson privately called a "damned little pissant country" to its
breaking point.[3] It was a strategy designed not only to severely

damage North Vietnam's infrastructure and morale, but also to lift the spirits of South Vietnam amid fears that it was on the brink of collapse.

The United States was resolutely (and, it turned out, recklessly) determined that South Vietnam, in which it had invested vast sums of money, would not fail. The Vietnamese Army (the ARVN) had struggled to contain the communist insurgency that had erupted across the south in 1960, its soldiers outmatched by the forces of the National Liberation Front (NLF), known to the Americans as the Viet Cong. This insurgency was supported by troops from the north (and with weapons and supplies from the Chinese and the Soviet Union), who flowed down across the Seventeenth Parallel via a network of secret routes through Laos, known as the Ho Chi Minh Trail.

By 1963, American helicopters were operating in the south and American military advisors were working with the ARVN, but the situation swiftly destabilized when Ngo Dinh Diem, the leader the U.S. had helped install after the Geneva Accords and the withdrawal of French colonial forces, was overthrown by high-ranking military figures—a coup that the Americans were aware of and did nothing to stop. Diem and his brother, Ngo Dinh Nhu, the loathed head of the secret police, were brutally murdered in the back of an armored personnel carrier. This led to a period of intense political instability in Saigon, as leaders without a mandate staged coup after coup.

McCarthy was in Chicago later that year, taking a break from her duties promoting *The Group,* a novel enjoying enormous commercial success, and was staying with her friend Hannah Arendt. When she heard that President Kennedy had been assassinated, she struggled to make sense of the killing (later she would read the Warren Commission Report cover to cover). It was clear that the change in leadership would have consequences for Vietnam. Kennedy had been an aggressive anti-Communist, but he had been wary of committing American troops on the ground in Vietnam. He had a better understanding of the complexity of the situation in Vietnam, having visited Saigon while a congressman in the early 1950s (he stayed in the same hotel that Graham Greene used when he was in the city), and he feared direct military involvement could spiral out of control. His successor had a different perspective, however, and was more concerned with exhibiting strength—he was convinced that the United States needed to hold the line in the face of Communist aggression. Johnson was an adherent of the "Domino Theory" that the French had used in securing American backing for their war on the Viet Minh; if Vietnam fell under Communist control, then the rest of Southeast Asia would follow. The president was also very aware that any sign of weakness would be pounced upon by his opponents in the Republican Party.

As was later revealed in the leaked Pentagon Papers, Johnson was preparing to expand American commitment in Vietnam even though he had claimed, during his 1964 presidential campaign, that he was opposed to just such a policy. In March 1965, shortly after the bombing of North Vietnam began, the first American marines waded ashore to protect the airfield at Da Nang. From then, troop numbers would escalate dramatically from 184,300 at the end of 1965, to 385,300 at the end of 1966, to 485,600 by the end of 1967.

With the bombing of North Vietnam and the commitment of ground troops, protest against the war gathered momentum on campuses across the United States. From Paris, McCarthy followed the stories about demonstrations and teach-ins and sought any information from her friends stateside about opposition to the war. In June, McCarthy's longtime friend Robert Lowell refused an invitation from Johnson to participate in an arts festival (McCarthy and other intellectuals put their names on a telegram of support for Lowell, which was published on the cover of the *New York Times*); John Hersey, who did attend, made his protest by reading from his reportage about Hiroshima. The same month a collection writers and artists, including James Baldwin, Allen Ginsberg, Martha Gellhorn, LeRoi Jones, Howard Fast, Norman Mailer, Dwight Macdonald, Grace Paley, and Philip Roth, took out a full-page advertisement in the *New York Times* exhorting its readers to "End Your Silence" about "a foreign policy grown more nakedly inhuman with every passing day."[4]

The war in Vietnam invigorated intellectuals into political action in a manner reminiscent of the 1930s, when the Moscow Trials and the Spanish Civil War demanded writers take a public stand. In November 1966, Bertrand Russell and Jean-Paul Sartre convened a tribunal to investigate American war crimes in Vietnam. The following year, its members, distinguished leftist intellectuals from around the world, met in Stockholm and Roskilde, where they heard evidence from victims of napalm attacks, North and South Vietnamese fighters, and American military personnel. The tribunal unanimously decided—the verdict had never been in doubt—that the United States was guilty of a number of crimes in its prosecution of the war, including genocide against the Vietnamese people.

In the United Kingdom, editors John Bagguley and Cecil Woolf sent out a questionnaire to famous authors around the world to ask where they stood on Vietnam. This project was a conscious imitation of *Authors Take Sides on the Spanish War*, a survey circulated by Nancy Cunard, W. H Auden, Louis Aragon, and Stephen Spender in 1937 (which had prompted a vituperative response from Orwell). In response to this latest appeal, Auden wondered whether writers should even be asked such questions bearing in mind that "literary talent and political common sense are rarely found together," but nevertheless went on to say that the United States needed to stay in the fight until a negotiated peace was possible.[5] Spender, acknowledging the limitations of his expertise, declared himself opposed and demanded a stop to the bombing as it involved "paying too heavy a price in blood and misery." He, too, hoped for a negotiated settlement with North Vietnam.[6] Unsurprisingly, the majority of the respondents opposed the war. Susan Sontag declared that the United States "had become a criminal, sinister country," while Graham Greene wrote that he saw "no excuse whatever for the presence of foreign troops on the soil of this country."[7] James Baldwin suggested the problem could be resolved only by going to the United Nations. Others, including Anthony Powell and William Styron, shared Auden's skepticism about the value of literary opinion on the matter.

Some of the more hardened anti-Communists were more supportive of intervention. Perhaps most surprising was the position taken by John Updike, who had become one of America's most celebrated literary novelists. He responded saying that he did not believe "the Vietcong and Ho Chi Minh have the moral edge over us, nor do I believe that great powers can always avoid using their power. I am for our intervention if it does some good."[8] This earned him the dubious title, conferred by the *New York Times,* of being the only American writer "unequivocally for" the war in Vietnam. Updike responded with a letter to the newspaper saying that since filling in the questionnaire in August 1966, he had become convinced that the war was doing no good and that the bombing was "futile as well as brutal and should be stopped." (He made clear, however, that he believed the Johnson administration to be acting "with good faith and some good sense.")[9]

Living in Paris with James West, her diplomat husband, McCarthy felt isolated from much of this collective action. She had met West in Warsaw, where, along with Saul Bellow, she was part of a cultural diplomacy initiative to take American writers behind the Iron Curtain. West was the cultural attaché, and there had been chemistry between the pair from the moment they met. McCarthy left Bowden Broadwater, her third husband, and settled with West in Paris, where he had been seconded to the Organisation for Economic Co-operation and Development. Despite her distance from the United States, she obsessed about the war and what she could do to help stop it. McCarthy contemplated the idea of getting a group of prestigious American figures to band together and refuse to pay their income taxes but struggled to convince others to commit. She tried to use her contacts to reach senior figures in the administration to plead her case. The war took over everything; she could not think or write about anything else and even had dreams in which she had "Portia-like audiences" with Robert McNamara, the secretary of defense, who McCarthy had heard opposed the war even as he orchestrated it.

In the summer of 1966 McCarthy made her first major public statement about Vietnam in a TV interview. She expressed her frustration with the ineffectiveness of the manifestos and protest letters written by intellectuals, believing it was time for more radical action. "I think if we don't do something more serious and this whole thing continues on its course, unarrested, if somehow we aren't able to reach the political conscience of Washington, that we will really not be much better off than the German people under the Nazis," she said.[10]

It is perhaps surprising, then, that she initially turned down the chance to visit Vietnam and write about the war. In the spring of 1966, Bob Silvers at *The New York Review of Books* asked her if she wanted to go; the magazine had become a rallying point for American intellectuals opposed to the war but had not yet carried reportage from the front lines. McCarthy was an odd choice in some respects; she had no substantive experience as a reporter, and the magazine had been the venue in which

Norman Mailer had recently savaged *The Group*. But that novel had been wildly successful (it had gone to the top of the best seller list in October 1963 and stayed there until the following February, when it was displaced by John le Carré's *The Spy Who Came In from the Cold)* and that doubtless played into Silvers's decision: McCarthy was a writer with a large readership and strong opinions, and her lack of reporting experience might be a virtue if it brought fresh perspective on the subject. That she declined was due to her husband's work: West felt that if McCarthy went to Vietnam and criticized the war, his position at the OECD (and his future as a diplomat) would be jeopardized.

A frustrated McCarthy watched as the war continued to escalate, with more troops deployed and the scope of the bombing campaign expanded. In January 1967, Silvers tried again. McCarthy and West debated the consequences of her taking the assignment: he had concerns for her safety; she still worried he'd lose his job. On an auspiciously bright sunny winter's morning, West called McCarthy from work and asked her to meet him at the Deux Magots cafe. Over coffee he told her that he thought she should go. What of his job? "They'll have to fire me," he said. McCarthy could not contain her excitement as a year's worth of pent-up emotion poured out; she would finally get the chance to write about the subject that had obsessed her for the previous two years.

Even though West was supportive, her friends urged her not to go, citing the dangers and her lack of professional competence as a war correspondent. "I would only, they insisted, make a fool of myself and do more harm than good to the liberal opposition by making it look silly, too," she wrote. In response, she pointed out that John Steinbeck was "making a fool of himself but did not appear to be creating any disarray in the pro-war forces on whose behalf he was traveling."[11] Steinbeck, sixty-four, had been in Southeast Asia as a correspondent for *Newsday* since

December 1966 and in his articles, many of which had been written from combat zones, he staunchly championed American involvement in the war. As a writer who made his name in the 1930s drawing the nation's attention to the poor and the dispossessed of the Great Depression, his position on the war felt like a betrayal to intellectuals on the American left. Even back then, though, he had been more of a New Deal Democrat than a hard-left radical, and while on a trip to the Soviet Union after the Second World War, his anti-Communism had hardened into antipathy. Not only did he prize his loyalty to Johnson, whom he knew personally, and to the Democratic Party, but his sons, John and Thomas, both served in the conflict.[12] This did not, for McCarthy, justify his swallowing whole the official line on the war.

McCarthy did not have the mien of a hardened correspondent (she packed a full set of luggage and made sure to bring her Chanel suit), but she believed she had something unique to offer. "I could not write about our involvement in Vietnam unless I went there," she later explained. "Besides, why should anybody want to read a thoughtful essay by me on Vietnam? There were other essays of that kind available that were surely better and more persuasive than anything that would come off my typewriter. But I had one asset that the writers of those essays didn't have. And that reporters didn't have either. My readers. Not the millions—it must be by now—in America that bought or borrowed *The Group*, but some of them. It was unlikely that they kept up with all my writings, yet they would want to know about a month I spent in Vietnam." (She was not exaggerating: more than five million copies of her book were published in hardcover and paperback.)[13] McCarthy was expressing an element of defiance here about the importance of literature and those who produced it. "I had the conviction (which still refuses to change)," she recalled, "that readers put perhaps not more trust but a different kind of trust in the perceptions of writers they know as novelists from what they give to the press's 'objective' reporting or political scientists' documented and figure-buttressed analyses."[14]

She began the work of securing visas and credentials, making an appointment to see Chip Bohlen. He tried to dissuade her but, once he realized her determination, was very helpful. He told her to get a new passport in her own name rather than travel on the diplomatic passport she had secured through her husband; if she went to North Vietnam, as she hoped to, a diplomatic passport would make officials in Hanoi think she was a spy. A second official, a Vietnam specialist, then briefed her on North Vietnamese infiltration of the south and Viet Cong crimes, much of which McCarthy claimed to have read before. Bohlen gave her written introductions to officials in Saigon. With everything set for her trip, she sat down to make her will, appointing West and her writer friend Elizabeth Hardwick as co-executors. In February she flew to Saigon.

SWEEPING OVER THE MEKONG DELTA in a U.S. army helicopter, McCarthy saw the plumes of smoke, markers of that morning's bombing raids. She noticed a plane circling above that suddenly "plunged, dropped its bombs, and was away in a graceful movement, having hit the target again; there was a flash of flame, and fresh, blacker smoke poured out."[15] This was as close as McCarthy got to combat, having promised West she wouldn't do any frontline reporting nor go on patrol in the jungle; the risks were real on such excursions, even for journalists. Indeed, on that first trip to Saigon, McCarthy befriended Bernard Fall, an experienced reporter and expert on the region, who, not long after their meeting, was killed after treading on a land mine. On returning to Saigon, she attended the military's daily press briefing only for the airstrike she had witnessed to go unmentioned.

"Too trivial," explained one of the other journalists when she asked why. There was a brutal logic to this—so many sorties were being flown, and so many bombs being dropped that it was almost impossible to keep track; destruction had become routine. Still McCarthy was stunned.

McCarthy, who admitted she could "hardly tell a grenade from a pomegranate,"[16] was looking for her subject "not on the battlefront, which would be no different from battlefronts in any other war, but among the people, theirs and ours, in hamlets, hospitals, and refugee camps, on the one hand, in offices and field huts, on the other."[17] And people she knew. *The Group* was just the latest example of McCarthy's ability to expose the complexity and conflict in her characters' motivations. The novel, which followed the lives of eight women in the years after they graduate from Vassar, was finely tuned to the petty hypocrisies and small self-deceptions that shape human behavior. Now she wanted to turn her sharp novelist's eye on the people making the moral case for American intervention in Vietnam. "What we *can* do, perhaps better than the next man, is smell a rat," she argued.[18]

That she was looking for rats was clear from the first sentence of her first dispatch for *The New York Review of Books,* in which she confessed to going to Vietnam "looking for material damaging to the American interest."[19] Her essays exuded revulsion at what she had seen. From the moment of landing she found the sheer scale of the American presence "overwhelming"; Saigon appeared to her like an American city—"a very shoddy West Coast one"—so thoroughly had it been transformed by the occupation.[20] The streets were clogged with foreign cars and military vehicles, the shops catered almost exclusively to the American clientele, and there were "white men everywhere, in sports shirts and drip-dry pants."[21] By day, the city appeared to McCarthy like a "gigantic PX," but by night, with its array of restaurants and clubs competing for U.S. dollars, it seemed like a "World's Fair or Exposition in some hick American city."[22] McCarthy saw the marks of this material excess everywhere; in the countryside around Saigon it was expressed in the accumulation of trash: "It was this indestructible mass-production garbage floating in swamps and creeks, lying about in fields and along the roadside, which made the country, which must once have been beautiful, hideous."[23] During her stay there was a circus in town; the metaphors were realizing themselves.

McCarthy's arrival, in February 1967, came immediately after one of the most ambitious efforts by U.S. and South Vietnamese forces of the war. Operation Cedar Falls was an attempt to break NLF resistance in the forty-square miles of jungle known as the "Iron Triangle," an enemy stronghold northwest of Saigon, near the Cambodian border. The idea was that this vast search-and-destroy mission would not only inflict damaging casualties on the enemy but also deprive them of a key strategic base.

As it turned out, the operation was largely frustrating for the U.S. forces, as most Viet Cong troops either fled into Cambodia or hid in the network of bunkers and tunnels they had built (one tunnel was reputed to be twelve miles long). Meanwhile, the American troops forcibly removed and relocated the local civilian population and used vast amounts of defoliant to destroy swaths of jungle. As a result, instead of securing a morale-boosting victory, Operation Cedar Falls only succeeded in exacerbating a growing refugee crisis. McCarthy visited some of the camps in which these refugees were held. U.S. officials took her to a large camp near Phu Cuong, where she saw Vietnamese subsistence farmers from the Iron Triangle being taught "free enterprise." "We're trying to wean them away from the old barter economy and show them a market economy," one U.S. official told her.[24] This camp, at least, had a fresh water supply and was equipped with latrines. She met German volunteers with the Catholic

Knights of Malta who offered to take her to a more representative example of what refugee camps were like. In a camp in the north of the country, outside Hoi An, McCarthy was confronted by "misery and squalor" that she found "hard to convey." Some seven hundred people were using a stagnant duck pond for their drinking and washing water, and it was clear that many were suffering from malnutrition and that disease was rampant. The camp had been running for six months.

Driving in an army jeep past another refugee camp, she noticed a banner that somebody had set above the entrance, which read, "Refugees from Communism." "Who was the hard sell aimed at?" she wondered; the refugees themselves could not read English, nor would any journalists be persuaded by it. Everywhere she went, McCarthy met American officials and soldiers who were persuading themselves that they were doing good work. The most surprising thing to her was "the general unawareness, almost innocence, of how what 'we' are doing could look to an outsider."[25] She saw marines tossing candy to children injured by American bombs, something she dubbed "pharisee virtue." Some officials spoke about the American commitment to education, to freeing a young generation from Communist indoctrination through schools that were being rebuilt across the country. Steinbeck had written admiringly about just such a school in Rach Kien, in the Mekong Delta. But when McCarthy visited, a month after Steinbeck, she found work stalled for lack of materials. "In this hamlet," she wrote, "everything seemed to have halted, as in 'The Sleeping Beauty,' the enchanted day Steinbeck left."[26]

There was an evident disconnect between the reality of what she was seeing and the official language used to describe it. Instead of saying that Operation Cedar Falls involved burning down villages and forcing their inhabitants to move to refugee camps, officials called it "pacification" and "cleansing." The weapon used to roast its victims alive was not napalm but "in-cinderjell." Chemical defoliants, like Agent Orange, used to de-stroy Vietnam's flora, were domesticated as "weed killer." The Phu Cuong camp was a "pilot project," not a "showcase"—or, to use McCarthy's term, a "concentration camp."[27] "This resort to euphemism," she wrote, "denotes, no doubt, a guilty conscience or—the same thing nowadays—a twinge in the public relations nerve." As a writer, McCarthy was particularly alert to the way language could be manipulated to deflect and obscure the truth about power and violence. The deployment of sanitizing rheto-ric was something she had been fighting since the 1930s, when she had pushed back against the Communist Party line on the Moscow Show Trials. In "Politics and the English Language," Orwell argued that in the twentieth century political speech, whether about British conduct in India, the Russian camps, or the dropping of atomic bombs on Japan, had become "largely the defence of the indefensible." Authorities had resorted to "euphemism, question-begging and sheer cloudy vagueness" in order to occlude their own motives and to disguise their use of violence to achieve their aims. Orwell had shown this at work in his depiction of Squealer, the pig in *Animal Farm* whose sil-ver tongue persuades the animals to readjust their perception of reality in accordance with Napoleon's desires. In *Nineteen Eighty-Four*, he had given this insidious, pervasive propaganda a name: Newspeak. And to McCarthy's disgust, the United States was succumbing to its consoling self-deceptions in Vietnam. "In the Stalinist days we used to detest a vocabulary that had to be read in terms of antonyms—'volunteers' denoting conscripts, 'democracy,' tyranny, and so on. Insensibly, in Vietnam, start-ing with the little word 'advisers,' we have adopted this slippery Aesopian language ourselves."[28] It was, she bitterly concluded, a language constructed to allow those using it to live with them-selves.

Who were the orchestrators of this? McCarthy accused the CIA. The connections between the intellectual community and the spies were beginning to come to light. From 1955 to 1962 Michigan State University had been involved in helping the Diem regime in "state-building" but was exposed, in *Ramparts* in 1966, as having collaborated with the CIA, who trained a "special security unit" of the Vietnamese police. Her trip to Vietnam coincided with *Ramparts's* exposes on the CIA's secret backing of an array of American cultural institutions. Exhibitions, conferences, journals, and associations were revealed to have been secretly supported by Langley. McCarthy had attended many of these conferences and had been a contributor to *Encounter*, her most recent piece having been published the previous November. McCarthy was close friends with Spender and offered advice as he negotiated the fallout from the *Encounter* revelations. Similarly, another good friend, Nicola Chiaromonte, was plunged into crisis, having discovered that the magazine he edited, *Tempo Presente*, received CIA money.

What McCarthy truly knew in advance of this is not clear, although she hints, in her first essay about Vietnam, that she was in the know. "The ties that have come to light between the CIA and the intellectual community in the United States," she wrote, "have surprising parallels in Vietnam—surprising, at least, to anyone who has not observed the gradual and typically modern fusion of intelligence with 'intelligence.'"[29] There are many reasons why McCarthy might have known more than she let on, not least that her husband worked for the foreign service.[30]

And in Vietnam, she had seen the CIA everywhere she looked and wondered about the full scope of their influence. It was, she remarked, "more catholic in its patronage than other government agencies."[31] She wondered how many books on the war were secretly funded by the CIA. "It *likes* intellectuals, which is natural, first because they are walking repositories of information, and second because the CIA sees itself as a lonely mastermind, the poet and unacknowledged legislator of the government," she wrote.[32] Of course it was involved in much more sinister activity than the clandestine support of scholars and political theorists, though: the successor to Lansdale's schemes was the controversial Phoenix Program, which was in operation while McCarthy was in the country. Drawing on a network of interrogation centers, the program was an effort to hit more specific, high-value targets within the Viet Cong.[33] The CIA called this an "integrated, organized attack on VC infrastructure."[34] This involved abductions and assassinations (dubbed "neutralization") of Viet Cong officers by CIA-trained Vietnamese units, and in some cases it resulted in atrocities, including torture and decapitation of captured Viet Cong. All of these operations, as per CIA policy, were conducted under the "principle of plausible denial."

After returning to Paris and publishing her first round of dispatches, McCarthy faced an accusation of complicity from another direction. In an exchange in *The New York Review of Books*, Diana Trilling accused McCarthy of having been "taken in" by the Communist line on Vietnam, especially in her contention that the only solution to the conflict was unilateral American withdrawal. In her response, McCarthy assured Trilling that even if Vietnam were lost, and Communism spread around the globe, "[S]ome sort of life will continue, as Pasternak, Solzhenitsyn, Sinyavsky, Daniel, have discovered, and I would rather be on their letterhead, if they would allow me, than on that of the American Committee for Cultural Freedom." The invocation of Russian literary dissidents—and Sinyavsky and Daniel in particular—was pointed. Back in the late forties, McCarthy and Trilling had been united in the non-Communist left's opposition to Stalinist cultural policy and had railed against the disappearance of a generation of writers. To cling to an absolute anti-Communism, as she believed Trilling did, carried with it risks of a far greater complicity. McCarthy would rather be a dissident in the Communist system than complicit with American imperialism. The anti-Communist left, she argued, had forgotten how to tell truth to power, and Sinyavsky's defiance was a model for how this should be done.

And challenging American power was something she had done successfully in South Vietnam. Despite the relative brevity of her time in Saigon, and her lack of experience as a reporter, McCarthy's essays painted a vivid, and often perceptive picture of an American force that conspired in deluding itself to the consequences of its actions. "A discovery I have made in Vietnam is that those who seek to project an 'image' are unaware of how they look," she wrote. "The truth they are revealing has become invisible to them."[35] She did not buy the jargon, or the pilot projects, or positive spin about "pacification" and plans for reform. Her skepticism kept her sharp—all of which made the failures of her reporting from North Vietnam the following year the more surprising.

ON MARCH 19, 1968, McCarthy landed at Hanoi's Gia Lam Airport after dark and was pleasantly surprised to be presented with a bouquet of flowers from the Vietnamese Peace Commission delegate who greeted her on the tarmac. Her arrival followed some of the most intense fighting of the war. On the day of the Tet holiday—the celebration of the Vietnamese new year—the Viet Cong and the North Vietnamese army launched a huge, coordinated surprise attack across the country, having spent the preceding days and weeks infiltrating South Vietnamese cities. In Saigon, a small group of Viet Cong sappers scored a symbolic victory by blowing a hole in the wall of the U.S. Embassy and occupying part of the grounds for six hours, until American reinforcements could be landed on the roof. The Viet Cong successfully captured the historic city of Hué, and it took a brutal monthlong battle to retake it, during which much of the city was destroyed. In military terms, the Tet Offensive resulted in a defeat for the Communist forces—cities and territory were retaken and significant casualties inflicted—but the damage to American morale was substantial. There were renewed questions in the United States about the conduct of the war and the long-term strategy for ending it.

Fighting around the U.S. base at Khe Sanh was still going on when McCarthy landed. As such she arrived in Hanoi understandably nervous. The journey had been long and frustrating. The only way to get in was on a plane belonging to the International Control Commission (the commission was a neutral body that had been established to implement the Geneva Accords and oversee the subsequent cease-fire), a nonpressurized Convair, which flew only once every two weeks. The plane was held up due to bad weather, and she spent three days stuck in Cambodia and another four days in Laos. With little to occupy her as she waited, the reality of what McCarthy was doing hit her. It was the sight of the front page of the *Bangkok Post,* which carried a story about the deployment of the new American F111a bombers in Thailand, that brought home the danger in which she was putting herself.[36] McCarthy grimly recognized that she would soon be in their target zone. In her Vientiane hotel, she became certain she was going to die in Hanoi. "I paced around my small room," she wrote. "I sat on my bed. I cried. I got hold of myself and tried to read. A wave of panic would hit me and I would moan. It hurt, like a real pain."[37]

Now, sitting in the back of the car driving her into Hanoi, with the bouquet still clutched in her lap, McCarthy got her first taste of life under American bombs. The radio broadcast a warning that U.S. planes were sixty kilometers away and closing. The driver promptly pulled over, killed the lights, switched off the

engine, and went in search of the nearest bomb shelter. Mc-
Carthy later recalled, with understatement, "feeling quite apprehensive."[38] In the dark they made their way past the bombed
ruins of a building to the shelter. This time it was not needed—
after an anxious wait, and the news that the bombers were no
longer heading in their direction, they all climbed back into
the car and were on their way.

What had started as a source of great anxiety swiftly became part of the daily routine. At the height of the bombing,
there were six alerts inside twenty-four hours. First came the
announcement over the loudspeaker of approaching bombers,
followed by the scream of a siren when the attack was imminent, then the dull thud of the bombs' impact heard from the
shelter. McCarthy never got accustomed to the night attacks,
though. At the "shrilling of the siren" she "would jerk up from
the pillow with my heart pounding, grope my way out of the mosquito netting, find the flashlight in the dark, slippers, dressing
gown, et cetera, and stumble, still unnerved, down the stairs
and out through the hotel garden, pointing my flashlight down,
searching for the entrance to the shelter."[39]

There was a reason McCarthy was prepared to take such risks:
very few reporters had managed to secure access to North Vietnam. She was intrigued by what she would find and knew that
it represented a significant journalistic coup for herself and *The
New York Review of Books*. Harrison Salisbury, of the *New York
Times*, had been the first journalist to report from north of the
Seventeenth Parallel, in late 1966, but McCarthy, as in Saigon,
wanted to bring her readers something different from conventional reporting. Yet if they expected that same sharp, novelistic
eye that had seen through the official obfuscation in Saigon, they
were to be disappointed.

McCarthy's reportage from Hanoi was adulatory and, at
times, credulous. In Saigon she had challenged the official rhet-

oric about the prosecution of the war, but here she took at face value what she was told by the North Vietnamese government— and she was granted access to a number of important officials, including Prime Minister Pham Van Dong. Where South Vietnam was clogged with trash, the North was pristine, and she extolled the cleanliness of Hanoi. She marveled at the ingenuity and courage of the North Vietnamese she met, and in an essay she fittingly entitled "North Vietnamese Bucolic," wrote rapturously about the schools, workshops, and makeshift hospitals she found in the countryside. While she admitted seeing convoys of trucks and other military equipment, she said she did not want to ask awkward questions out of considerations of politeness and because "she did not want to feel like a spy."[40] Everywhere she went, she was escorted by an official. Even when she went to the toilet in the countryside, an official would appear at her side with toilet paper. McCarthy took this as a sign that she was being looked after, not that she was being closely monitored.

Part of her official tour included a visit to the Museum of War Crimes, the exhibits of which she described in detail:

The museum, unlike that at Auschwitz, is strictly contemporary. There were cluster bombs—guavas and pineapples [these were the North Vietnamese names]—some of the delayed action type, regarded as the most fiendish, ordinary placid TNT bombs of varying weights, ranging from babies of 200 to big daddies of 3,000 pounds, rockets, an assortment of missiles, crop-spraying powders (with the results in a bottle), tear gases, front and rear views of a patient hit by a spray of pellets from the "mother" bomb, X rays of pellets in human skulls, photos of napalm and phosphorous victims (napalm has not been used in the vicinity of Hanoi and Haiphong, or, as the Vietnamese say, not yet), quite a collection of exhibits.[41]

She noticed a woman shuffling through these exhibits and was told by museum staff that she had lost her son to an American bomb. A plant to secure the sympathy of a liberal Westerner? McCarthy thought not, as the staff seemed irritated at this woman's presence.

As the tour wound up, the museum staff invited McCarthy to join them for tea. No sooner had it been poured than "there was a long-drawn-out, shrill, banshee-like, shrieking noise, succeeded by a shattering explosion." McCarthy glimpsed the U.S. plane through the window before the museum director rushed her to the shelter in the garden. The early warning system had failed, and three bombs and a "Shrike" anti-radar missile had been launched, most likely targeting a nearby bridge. The attack completed, the group returned to their now cold tea, during which the director informed McCarthy there would be a parting ceremony in which they were to present her with gifts.

The first gift was a ring, inscribed with the date August 1, 1966, and the initials H. Y. (for Hun Yeng province). The second gift was a metal comb. McCarthy was informed that both items were made from the wreckage of U.S. planes that had been shot down. "*Merci beaucoup*," she murmured. The delegation watched her expectantly as she tried on the ring "hurriedly, like one rapidly swallowing medicine." Feeling uncomfortable, she then "instantly slid it off and dropped it into my handbag."[42] She prepared an excuse in case they asked why she wasn't wearing it— "it was a man's ring too big"—and, back in the hotel, put it away in the drawer of her desk. Yet she could not forget the ring: "it kept troubling my mind, making me toss at night, like an unsettled score."[43] Why did she accept it in the first place? "Perhaps, if I had the courage, I might have declined to take the ring, handed it back to the Vietnamese as soon as I realized what it was," she wrote. "As my grandmother tried to teach me, one need never be afraid to say no. But from their point of view, it was a symbol of friendship, a medal pinned on my chest. They were proud to bestow it."[44] The comb bothered her less, but she admitted she never once used it.

Accepting these gifts denoted a kind of symbolic complicity, which only made her subsequent actions in North Vietnam look even worse. At a villa in Hanoi, she was given the opportunity to interview two captive American pilots. Ahead of the meeting, Vietnamese officials told McCarthy they had been surprised by the prisoners' "low mental attainments," and McCarthy wrote that she, too, "was taken aback . . . by a stiffness of phraseology and naive rote-thinking, childish, like the handwriting on the envelopes the Vietnamese officer emptied from a sack for me to mail on my return for other captive pilots." For McCarthy, the limits of these pilots' intellect could only be explained by their having been "robotized," first by the American education system and then by the army.[45] As was revealed after their eventual release, though, there was another explanation for why these men might have appeared listless or vacant: they had been tortured.

To compound this failure in judgment, McCarthy unwittingly exposed the prisoners to more suffering. One of the pilots, Robbie Risner, whom McCarthy described as "gaunt" and "squirrel-faced," later claimed that during the interview McCarthy had rapped her knuckles on the desk—she had been "knocking on wood," hoping for an early end to the war—and that as a consequence he had been subjected to hours of interrogation, the captors mistaking the gesture for some kind of secret signal. "I sometimes wondered if Mrs. McCarthy was playing a dual role," Risner wrote. "I know I suffered because of her request to see me, and to my knowledge she did absolutely nothing to help our cause."[46]

Fixated in her opposition to America's involvement in the war, McCarthy had fallen prey to the very weakness she had diagnosed on her trip to Saigon: a failure to see beneath the officially mandated surface.[47] It was like the ardent anti-fascists who went to the Spanish Civil War and turned a blind eye to the crimes being perpetrated in the name of the Republic. She had been among the small band of American intellectuals in the 1930s who had refused to ignore the Stalinist purges taking place in Barcelona, Madrid, and Moscow. Accepting what the North Vietnamese government told her, even when they continued to hang portraits of Stalin on their wall, was just as credulous as Steinbeck swallowing the official U.S. Army rhetoric about pacification. This was a dereliction of the novelist's duty. It was a failure to read.

IN THE SPRING OF 1968, polls showed that after the Tet Offensive, opposition to the war was widespread in the United States. On April 1, the bombing stopped. The previous night, McCarthy listened on Voice of America as Johnson announced the end of the aerial bombardment of North Vietnam and that he would not be standing for reelection in 1968. Domestic dissent had worn down the Johnson administration. In October 1967, one hundred thousand protesters had gathered at the Lincoln Memorial in Washington, and roughly thirty thousand of these marched on the Pentagon. By the time McCarthy returned to Paris from Hanoi, the war had a different complexion; an end to the conflict appeared much more probable, and it seemed inevitable that U.S. troops would be withdrawn in the near future.

McCarthy had heard the news of Martin Luther King's assassination while she was in Hanoi but only managed to read about the full scale of rioting that followed once she was back in Paris. West had saved the newspapers for her. More tragedy was to follow. Eugene McCarthy and Robert Kennedy tussled for the presidential nomination of the Democratic Party on an antiwar platform but Kennedy, too, was assassinated. At the Democratic National Convention in Chicago that summer, the police cracked down violently on protesters, all of it broadcast live on television. When the Republican nominee, Richard Nixon, eventually defeated Democrat Hubert Humphrey, he did so on the promise of an "honorable end" to the Vietnam War. That end, though, was hardly imminent. Nixon had sabotaged Johnson's efforts to secure a peace deal in Paris in October 1968, fearing it would give his Democratic rival a boost, a so-called "peace bump." Using a secret back channel, Nixon told the South Vietnamese, led by Nguyen Van Thieu, to end negotiations as he could secure them a better deal.

Amid this unrest, McCarthy's dispatches failed to make the impact she had hoped for. The millions who had read *The Group* did not follow her to Saigon and Hanoi. McCarthy's essays in *The New York Review of Books* caused a stir in American intellectual circles, but the resulting pamphlets—*Vietnam* (1967) and *Hanoi* (1968)—were indifferently reviewed and sold poorly. The reasons were unclear but possibly numerous. Perhaps it was the unusual pamphlet format, which was difficult to market and sell. Perhaps it was the charges of anti-Americanism that the essays unsurprisingly elicited (even though McCarthy argued that it was *patriotism* that made her go).[48] Perhaps it was the perception of her as a dilettante compared, say, to her friend Frances FitzGerald, whose deeply researched book about Vietnam, *Fire in the Lake*, went on to win the Pulitzer Prize and the National Book Award. A younger generation was dismissive of writers whose liberal anti-Communism, they argued, made them complicit in American Cold War propaganda. Those who had participated in the activities of the Congress for Cultural Freedom, or published in its magazines, had become tarnished by their association with the CIA, no matter if they had been unaware of the fact. Students wanted more radical heroes, finding them in the likes of Joan Baez, Bob Dylan, Audre Lorde, Norman Mailer, Ken Kesey, and Allen Ginsberg.

In the months to come, Nixon sought to negotiate with the Soviet Union and then China as a way of putting pressure on North Vietnam, playing the Communist rivals off each other. He tried to intimidate and unsettle Hanoi with his "madman theory" of foreign policy, giving the impression he was capable of anything, and tried, just like his predecessors, to push the North Vietnamese to the breaking point. As well as mining Haiphong Harbor (which foreign ships used to resupply the North), his administration broached the idea of bombing the dikes in the Red River Delta to cause mass flooding, and even the use of nuclear weapons.[49] Rather than coming to an end, the war expanded into Cambodia, officially neutral until Prince Si-hanouk was overthrown in a military coup by the pro-American Lon Nol in March 1970. Nixon sent aid to Nol in his war with the Communist Khmer Rouge and, with the country no longer neutral, ordered the invasion of Cambodia in order to destroy Viet Cong and North Vietnamese bases across the border.

As a result, protests intensified in the United States. Two million people across the United States had taken part in the Moratorium protest in October 1969 and, with the Cambodian invasion, another round of campus demonstrations took place in May. At Kent State University, in Ohio, the police opened fire on unarmed protesters, killing four. Nixon, meanwhile, ordered the FBI and the CIA to intensify their attacks on the antiwar movement. The following year, the leak of the Pentagon Papers made clear how the Johnson government had deliberately misled the public about American entry into the war.

In the summer of 1971, McCarthy, having stepped back from the fray to finishing writing a novel, *Birds of America,* asked William Shawn, editor of *The New Yorker,* if she could go to Fort

McPherson in Georgia to cover the court-martial of Ernest Medina. In March 1968, in the aftermath of the Tet Offensive, U.S. infantrymen had been sent on a search-and-destroy mission to the village of Son My (called My Lai by the Americans), where they murdered between 347 and 505 unarmed Vietnamese civilians, including infants and young children, using machine guns, grenades, and bayonets. Women and girls were raped. The village was burned down. The army had sought to cover up the massacre, but the dogged reporting of investigative journalist Seymour Hersh had revealed the truth. William Calley, a platoon leader, had been found guilty of murdering twenty-two civilians and sentenced to life in prison the previous March (his sentence was soon reduced and he was eventually released in 1974). In his defense, Calley claimed to have been only following the orders he had been given by Medina, his commanding officer.

McCarthy was the granddaughter of a celebrated lawyer, and her analysis of the Medina trial displayed an acuity in handling legal arguments. She sensed the futility of the exercise from the beginning, with the prosecution poorly prepared and the defense, led by the flamboyant F. Lee Bailey, indulged. She took note not only of the general sense of boredom in the courtroom but also the general lack of interest from the press and the wider public. Part of the problem, she argued, was that the prowar right wanted the issue to go away and the antiwar left felt the junior officers were being scapegoated when the higher-ups should be on trial.[50] McCarthy was, of course, opposed to the war and the way it was being prosecuted, but she also believed men like Calley and Medina should be held responsible for their actions as individuals. She believed Medina's acquittal was preordained. "The idea that there was a conspiracy to let Medina get home free was hard to avoid at Fort Mac," she wrote. The court-martial stirred her to renewed anger at the perceived moral atrophy of the country both in Vietnam and on the home front. "The result is now visible," she wrote. "Medina and Henderson [another accused officer] off the hook, Calley's sentence reduced, others not tried, several identified and unidentified mass murderers welcomed back into the population. Now any member of the armed forces in Indochina can, if he so desires, slaughter a reasonable number of babies, confident that the public will acquit him a) because they support the war and the Army or b) because they don't."[51]

With Henry Kissinger, Nixon's National Security Advisor, seeking a "decent interval" solution, whereby Thieu's South Vietnamese government might be propped up long enough to save American face, the war, at least America's involvement in it, entered one last spasm. In March 1972, the North launched the Nguyen Hue offensive, an ambitious assault across the Seventeenth Parallel, and Nixon responded with a resumption of the bombing of North Vietnam. That summer, Kissinger thought a deal had been agreed for American withdrawal but Thieu, fearing his government—and South Vietnam as a whole—was simply being abandoned, refused to play ball. Nixon decided to side with Thieu and, that winter, redoubled the bombing of the North, for the first time using B-52s, with their huge payloads, to pummel Hanoi and Haiphong.

McCarthy was distraught at this resumption and came up with a scheme by which she would travel to Hanoi with a group of prominent intellectuals and authors to try to act as a deterrent to American bombing. She drew up a list of people she might ask, including fellow novelists Baldwin, James Jones, Mailer, and Styron. To add political heft, she wanted to approach Eugene McCarthy and Coretta King, Martin Luther King Jr.'s widow. While she was in the process of formulating the list, she received a call from Spender, offering sympathy and to do what he could. McCarthy told him about the plan to travel to Hanoi and he signed up on the spot. She thought "a poet would be good, especially one who looked like an archangel."⁵² However, the North Vietnamese were less enthusiastic about a large band of American martyrs heading to Hanoi; the airport had been badly damaged in the bombing and there was already a party of Americans, including Baez and Jane Fonda, in the country. McCarthy's planning was for naught.

The Christmas bombings were the last major American assault in the war. In January 1973, a peace deal was negotiated, along much the same lines as the previous summer's proposal. The U.S. military began its withdrawal, and the North Vietnamese released all American POWs. While some fighting continued, North Vietnamese and Viet Cong forces bided their time before launching a large final assault to take control of the whole country, wary of sucking the Americans back into the war. With Nixon's resignation in August 1974, as a consequence of the Watergate scandal, the Hanoi regime sensed their moment and attacked Saigon. All remaining Americans were airlifted out of the city, as well as some Vietnamese who had worked closely with U.S. agencies and the military. Soviet-made tanks burst through the walls of the Independence Palace on April 30, 1975, to signal the conclusion of the war.

It was far from the end of the suffering in Indochina, though. With the United States gone and the South Vietnamese army defeated, the Communists took control. In Cambodia, the Khmer Rouge seized Phnom Penh, began the systematic slaughter of perceived subversives, instituted agricultural reform that resulted in widespread famine, and sought to eradicate ethnic minorities. It is estimated that as many as 3 million Cambodians were killed. By December 1975 the Communist Pathet Lao abolished the monarchy and declared Laos a People's Republic. They, too, persecuted political enemies and minorities who had fought alongside the United States, including the Hmong people. The North Vietnamese enacted brutal purges, with an estimated sixty-five thousand southerners executed.[53] A further one million fled political persecution and poverty, often in precarious journeys by boat. McCarthy watched this unfold and did nothing. In a 1979 interview she said she had thought about "writing a real letter to Pham Van Dong," to ask "can't you stop this, how is it possible for men like you to permit what's going on?"[54] McCarthy continued to count the prime minister as her friend (he sent her a Christmas card every year). But the letter was never sent.

Part Eight

UNRAVELING

TWENTY-NINE
Solzhenitsyn

MOSCOW, FRANKFURT & WASHINGTON, 1968–1974

HARD AT WORK on the revisions to his novel *Cancer Ward*, Aleksandr Solzhenitsyn was disturbed by ominous rumbling. His summer house—little more than a wooden shack with a corrugated iron roof—was in the village of Rozhdestvo, fifty miles southwest of Moscow and located on a plot of land that afforded him relative privacy. At home in Ryazan, or when he stayed with friends in Moscow, the eyes and ears of the KGB were everywhere, but out here in the countryside he could follow his ascetic work routine—sixteen-hour days interrupted only by quick meals of tinned food—without distraction. The rumbling persisted. Hundreds of heavy vehicles were moving down the road near Solzhenitsyn's shack. He tried his best to prevent the noise from distracting him, even as it spilled into the following days. It was only when he tuned in to the BBC Russian service on his transistor radio on the morning of August 21 that he discovered that the tanks had been heading straight for Prague.[1]

"Since I did not regard *our masters* as out-and-out lunatics, I had not thought they would go to the length of occupying the country," he wrote in his memoir *The Oak and the Calf*. "For days and nights on end, tanks, trucks and service vehicles poured southward along the highroad a hundred meters from my dacha, but still I supposed our leaders were doing it only to frighten the

Czechs, that these were just maneuvers. But they 'entered' the country and successfully crushed it."[2]

The suppression of the Prague Spring sent an unambiguous message to intellectuals and dissidents at home and abroad: the road to reform was closed and the Soviet Union was going back into the ideological deep freeze. This was the final confirmation of the bad news that Solzhenitsyn had seen coming ever since Khrushchev had been ousted in October 1964, two years after the Soviet leader allowed him to publish *One Day in the Life of Ivan Denisovich*. This short novel of life in the camps, which Khrushchev had read in manuscript and personally approved for publication, was a huge success when it first appeared in *Novy Mir*, with readers waiting in line for hours in the hope of getting a copy. Solzhenitsyn's debut served as a reckoning with the unspoken past of purges and camps, and it made his reputation as a major writer. It also made him a target.[3] With Khrushchev gone, Solzhenitsyn had long felt the chill carried on the wind blowing his way. With the invasion of Prague, the Kremlin had confirmed that winter was coming.

FOR SOLZHENITSYN his priority was making sure his work survived. It took priority, even over his personal safety and that of his family. "[E]very scrap of my work was in the Soviet Union, and could be suppressed," he wrote.[4] The example of Vasily Grossman's *Life and Fate* haunted him; on learning of the existence of the novel the KGB had confiscated manuscripts, carbons, and notebooks, and Grossman was told his work would never be published.[5] To Solzhenitsyn that kind of erasure was unthinkable. As a result, when Khrushchev fell, he made sure to conceal multiple copies of his work with friends and, with the help of the writer Vadim Andreyev, who worked at the Soviet mission in Geneva, smuggled out a copy of his next novel, *The*

First Circle, on three rolls of microfilm.[6] "I felt a lot easier," he wrote of hearing that it had arrived safely. "They could shoot me now if they liked!"[7]

Still he had not taken enough care. No sooner had he learned of the arrests of Andrei Sinyavsky and Yulii Daniel in September 1965 than he discovered to his horror that the KGB had raided the home of his friend Venjamin Teush, where they had discovered a hidden archive of Solzhenitsyn's work, which included explicitly anti-Soviet material.[8]

Solzhenitsyn had fully expected to be arrested when his work had appeared in the West. Already a series of miniature stories had been published in *Encounter.*[9] But Solzhenitsyn described the seizure of his archive as "the greatest misfortune in all my forty-seven years. For some months I felt it as though it were a real, unhealing physical wound—a javelin wound right through the breast, with the tip so firmly lodged that it could not be pulled out."[10]

The fear was not just that what he had written would be suppressed, but that, if he were imprisoned or arrested, his future work would also be in danger. He felt he had jeopardized "the dying wishes of the millions whose last whisper, last moan, had been cut short on some hut floor in some prison camp. I had not carried out their behests, I had betrayed them, had shown myself unworthy of them. It had been given to me, almost alone, to crawl to safety; the hopes once held in all those skulls buried now in common graves in the camps had been set on me and I had collapsed, and their hopes had slipped from my hands."[11] The only thing that reassured him was that he had smuggled out *The First Circle,* his novel about the inmates of a *sharashka,* a camp on the outskirts of Moscow, in which skilled prisoners, including academics, engineers, and mathematicians, were made to do technical support work for the state security apparatus. When he had tried to have it published in Moscow, it was rejected, possibly because it depicted scenes in which the *zeks* (the slang term for gulag inmates) staged nonviolent protests against the captors. Solzhenitsyn mentally prepared himself for arrest.

Yet the KGB, for unclear reasons, had missed a trick. As they raided the homes of various writers and intellectuals in Moscow, they left Solzhenitsyn's summer house in Rozhdestvo untouched. It was a remarkable stroke of luck, because lying on his desk was the most explosive manuscript of all, that of the *Gulag Archipelago*. Solzhenitsyn realized that his history of the camps, built out of his own experiences and interviews with 277 other *zeks*, needed to be hidden away. "My precious notes and part of the completed first draft existed only in single copies, and were as dangerous as atom bombs," he wrote.[12] Using trusted friends, among them some former *zeks*, he managed to smuggle the manuscript to his "Hiding Place," a secret location deep in the countryside. When he wanted to work on it, he would shave off his beard and disappear there for weeks at a time.[13] It was while he was holed up in his Hiding Place that he had listened intently to radio updates of the Sinyavsky-Daniel trial in February 1966.

With pressure mounting on dissidents at home, the cultural liberalization taking place in Czechoslovakia became a beacon of progress. Solzhenitsyn was a hero to many of the Czech and Slovak writers who were at the heart of the Prague Spring. At the Fourth Soviet Writers' Congress in May 1967, Solzhenitsyn had scandalized the authorities by circulating an open letter that called for an end to censorship. The following month, when the Czechoslovak Writers' Union held their own congress, Pavel Kohout, the playwright and future member of Charter 77, daringly read the letter out to the audience. Plans had been made for the publication of *Cancer Ward*, a novel set in a hospital in Central Asia in which the patients, two years after Stalin's death grapple with the legacy of the Great Terror; stocks of the novel were sitting in a warehouse in Bratislava ready to be sent out when the Soviet tanks rolled in.[14]

That summer Solzhenitsyn had taken a further precaution regarding *Gulag Archipelago*. Having finished his work on the book, he had it copied onto microfilm and, as he had done with *The First Circle*, Andreyev smuggled it out to Geneva. This time the stakes were higher: the contents of the book were incendiary, and the Kremlin was in a punitive mood. Solzhenitsyn hid in a safe house in Moscow and waited anxiously until the call came that *Gulag Archipelago* was safely in Switzerland.[15]

The crackdown on dissidents continued apace. Alexander Ginzburg was imprisoned for his work on *The White Book*, which contained documents relating to the Sinyavsky-Daniel trial. When Larisa Bogoraz and her allies boldly staged their Red Square protest against the Warsaw Pact invasion of Czechoslovakia, they too were arrested. Despite his preference to operate as a lone wolf, Solzhenitsyn had got to know many of them personally and admired their determination.[16] But while his single-mindedness and his courage were formidable, he feared that if he protested the crushing of the Prague Spring he would follow the others to jail—and if he was imprisoned he would not be able to protect his work. The decision did not sit easily with him, but he resolved to keep his powder dry for the fight to come. He did not have to wait long.

THE MONTH AFTER THE TANKS ROLLED INTO PRAGUE two of his novels, both of which had been refused publication through official channels in Moscow, were published in the West. It was part of Solzhenitsyn's strategy to submit his work and test the boundaries of what was permissible, to show what the state was afraid of (other writers were understandably nervous about giving the authorities ammunition with which to attack them). *The First*

Circle and *Cancer Ward* were the first works by Solzhenitsyn to appear in over two years, and the sensation they caused—*The First Circle* was a best seller and Book of the Month Club choice in the United States—was exactly what Solzhenitsyn wanted.[17] It was a brazen move. Rather than trying to hide, Solzhenitsyn decided to leverage his profile, to use the fame he had accrued through the publication of *One Day in the Life of Ivan Denisovich* as a shield. He was not like the other dissidents, whose work circulated in samizdat among an urban, cultivated elite. The 1962 issue of *Novy Mir* that carried *One Day in the Life of Ivan Denisovich* had become a collector's item so quickly that its 95,000 copies sold out, and the novel was reissued first in a popular journal, *Roman-Gazeta* (750,000 copies), and then in book form in 100,000 copies by the state publisher—and even these had not come close to matching reader demand for the book. Hundreds of letters had poured in to the *Novy Mir* offices from all corners of the Soviet Union to thank Solzhenitsyn for what he had written.[18] As a consequence, the aging, conservative Politburo was wary of making him into a martyr. Solzhenitsyn gambled on the idea that his arrest and imprisonment would cause them more trouble than it was worth. It was a dangerous game in which he needed to maintain pressure on the government but not force them into taking drastic action against him.

The Kremlin's response was to try to discredit him through drip-fed misinformation. The KGB spread rumors that he drank heavily—laughable to those who knew him for the puritan he was.[19] Another more pernicious and persistent rumor was that he had collaborated with the Gestapo during the Second World War.

In November 1969, while back home in Ryazan, working on a historical novel, *August 1914*, he was unexpectedly summoned to a local meeting of the Writers' Union and summarily expelled, just as Anna Akhmatova, Boris Pasternak, and Andrei Sinyavsky had been before him.[20] This had tangible consequences for Solzhenitsyn: he would effectively be unemployed, be denied his pension, his medical insurance, and access to libraries. But if the government hoped by doing the deed in the provincial town of Ryazan, some 130 miles southwest of Moscow, they might subdue the subsequent publicity, they were mistaken. Solzhenitsyn released his version of the expulsion hearing in samizdat, and the BBC Russian service broadcast reports of the events back into the Soviet Union. The news prompted writers around the world to rally to Solzhenitsyn's corner. Letters of protest poured into the Kremlin, including one signed by writers with as varied politics as Heinrich Böll, Truman Capote, Günter Grass, Carlos Fuentes, Arthur Miller, Yukio Mishima, Jean-Paul Sartre, and John Updike. A letter published in the London *Times,* signed by Graham Greene and W. H. Auden among others, called Solzhenitsyn's expulsion a "crime against civilization," and demanded an "international cultural boycott" of the Soviet Union until it ended the "barbaric treatment of its artists and writers."[21] The Politburo simply ignored these protests and waited for the outrage to die down. No such luck.

In July 1970, François Mauriac, supported by roughly 50 other French writers, nominated Solzhenitsyn for the Nobel Prize in Literature, the award Solzhenitsyn coveted above all others. In his memoir he wrote that he had first heard of the prize while in the gulag and thought that it was "just what I needed to make my great breakthrough when the time came."[22] He kept a list of winners in his writing desk that he updated each year, and he knew full well the kind of platform the prize might give him. He admitted he was envious when Pasternak was awarded the prize in 1958 but "writhed with shame for him as though for myself," when the poet was bullied into turning it down. He was determined, if he won, to put up more of a scrap.[23] "No, oh no," he wrote, "if you are challenged to fight, and in such superb conditions, pick up the gage, fight for Russia!"[24] International PEN, the writers' association, lobbied on Solzhenitsyn's behalf, urging the Swedish academy to pick him. The Soviet Union responded by putting diplomatic pressure on Sweden and preparing a delegation of writers to argue against the nomination.

Two weeks before the award was supposed to be announced, Solzhenitsyn received a call from a Norwegian journalist, Per Egil Hegge, telling him he was the winner. Solzhenitsyn was rattled by the timing and initially skeptical. In the event of his winning the award, he had planned to wait a week to see how the Politburo reacted, but Hegge pushed him for a comment. Solzhenitsyn relented and wrote out a brief statement. "I am grateful for the award," he told Hegge. "I accept the prize. I intend to come and receive it on the traditional day insofar as this depends on me. I am well. The state of my health is no obstacle to my making the trip."[25] It was carefully phrased: with his history of poor health he suspected the authorities would claim he was not fit for travel. He assumed, rightly, that the Kremlin would do everything in their power to prevent him taking the podium in Stockholm.

Solzhenitsyn's win was reported on the front pages of newspapers in the United States and Europe.[26] Even the Communist Parties of France and Italy celebrated the award. In Moscow, the criticism was predictably fierce. The Union of Writers issued a statement saying that it was "deplorable that the Nobel committee allowed itself to be drawn into an unseemly game," while *Pravda* denounced Solzhenitsyn as being in league with "reactionary circles in the West."[27] This was the message that was repeated day after day in Soviet propaganda outlets: the award was not about literature, it was about the Cold War.

In the end it was not Solzhenitsyn's ability to travel to Sweden that was the problem, so much as whether he would be allowed back into Russia afterward. Years before he had considered this a price possibly worth paying, but now Solzhenitsyn was working on a cycle of epic historical novels, known as the *Red Wheel*, of which *August 1914* was but the first, and losing access to Russia and its archives would prevent him from completing what he increasingly saw as the most important work of his life.

There were also compelling personal reasons for his staying in the country. For some time, Solzhenitsyn's relationship with his wife, Natalia Reshetovskaya, had been disintegrating. They had first married in 1940, while Solzhenitsyn was a student, but the following year he had left for the front, where he had been arrested and sent to the gulag. Being married to a prisoner was punitive, and the couple divorced in 1952. Natalia began a new relationship with Vsevolod Somov but, after his release from the camps, Solzhenitsyn wooed her again, persuading her to leave Somov, and they were remarried in 1957. She supported his absolute commitment to his work and remained loyal to him even as the evidence of his infidelities mounted. By the time of the Nobel award, Solzhenitsyn was having an affair with Natalia Svetlova, a brilliant young mathematician who mixed in dissident circles.[28]

When Reshetovskaya found out that Svetlova was pregnant by her husband she suffered a breakdown. In the flat they shared in Moscow, Reshetovskaya wrote "я" (the Cyrillic letter for "I") in her blood on the bedsheets and then crossed it out.[29] The message she was sending to Solzhenitsyn about her sense of erasure was clear. The news of the Nobel Prize win actually prompted a temporary reconciliation, but as it became clear that Solzhenitsyn envisioned his future with Svetlova, Reshetovskaya fell into despair. They slept in separate beds and when she did not rise at her usual time one morning, Solzhenitsyn went into her bedroom to find her unconscious and drooling. She had taken an overdose of painkillers and avoided dying only because the drugs had paralyzed her esophagus and prevented her swallowing more. She was in a coma for twenty-four hours before coming around and, amid much secrecy, was transferred to a psychiatric ward. Solzhenitsyn feared the scandal would be used against him. Only after eleven days had passed did he agree to meet her, and she consented to a divorce.[30] Amid this emotional turmoil and impending fatherhood, Solzhenitsyn decided not to travel to Stockholm. He composed a statement to be read in his absence, pointing out the felicitous fact that the ceremony was to take place on Human Rights Day. "Nobel Prize winners are bound to feel that this coincidence places a responsibility upon them," he wrote. "Everybody present in the Stockholm City Hall must see a symbolic meaning in this. So let none at this festive table forget that political prisoners are on hunger-strike this very day in defense of rights that have been curtailed or trampled underfoot."[31] The Soviet Union and its allies boycotted the ceremony in any case.

As the authorities continued to look for leverage over him, he continued to work, and *August 1914* was smuggled out and published in the West in the summer of 1971. Once again, the book received adulatory reviews, including from Mary McCarthy, but was met with official silence in the Soviet Union.

Not that the KGB was finished with Solzhenitsyn. On a particularly hot day that summer Solzhenitsyn suffered heatstroke. Incapacitated and needing a spare part for his car, he sent a student friend, Alexander Gorlov, to pick it up from his summer house outside the city. When Gorlov arrived, he was stunned to find two men going over the house. Seeing him, they jumped Gorlov, wrestled his arms behind his back, and hit him across the back of the head. He came around to find himself being dragged toward the woods. Fearing he was about to be shot, he shouted that he was a foreigner and that there would be hell to pay if he were killed. Taking advantage of their hesitation he wriggled free and ran, only to be tackled and wrestled to the ground by another group. He was punched and kicked repeatedly, and when he cried out for help his assailants grabbed his mouth so forcefully that its corners were torn. The noise attracted locals, who challenged the attackers. Only then did one of them produce the badge of a KGB captain.[32] The attackers took Gorlov to the local police station, where the KGB officer warned him that if Solzhenitsyn found out about what had happened, not only would he be kicked off his Ph.D. program but his wife and son would also be in danger.

Nevertheless, Gorlov relayed everything to Solzhenitsyn, who was outraged and not a little rattled. The KGB had presumably been searching the house for incriminating material and doubtless bugged it for good measure. Solzhenitsyn did what he did best: he counterpunched. He wrote an open letter, published in samizdat, addressed to Yuri Andropov, the head of the KGB. "For many years," he wrote, "I have borne in silence the lawlessness of your employees: the inspection of all my correspondence, the confiscation of half of it, the tracking down of my correspondents, their persecution at work and by state agencies, the spying around my house, the shadowing of visitors, the tapping of telephone conversations, the drilling of holes in ceilings. . . . But after the raid yesterday I will no longer be silent." Solzhenitsyn challenged Andropov to arrest those who had burgled his house. "Otherwise," he wrote, "I can only conclude that they were sent by *you*."[33]

There had been plenty of writers who had shown great courage in defying the state, from Isaac Babel to Anna Akhmatova, from Boris Pasternak to Andrei Sinyavsky. But nobody had quite so brazenly called out the KGB. How was Solzhenitsyn able to avoid being slung into the Lubyanka? A large part of the answer was the change in climate in the Cold War.

THE SUPPRESSION OF THE PRAGUE SPRING was a reassertion of the Cold War status quo. Some in the West mistakenly inter-

preted it as a provocation, an escalation of hostility on the part of
the Soviet Union. To those Czechoslovaks who faced the tanks
rolling into Prague, it was clearly an act of aggression. But in
the larger Cold War picture, it was a fundamentally defensive
move, seeking to reinforce the hard border between East and
West in Europe at a time when it threatened to crack. The Soviet
Union made it clear that it was determined to preserve stability
and was willing to use force to do so. In Vietnam, the Americans
feared the domino effect of nations falling to Communism—yet
the Soviets also subscribed to their own version of that theory.
If the Czechs and Slovaks managed to liberalize their country,
the Kremlin feared other Warsaw Pact states would follow. Tell-
ingly, there was no substantive response to the invasion on the
part of the United States and its allies.

The lack of interest in confronting the Soviet Union over
Czechoslovakia was part of a wider Cold War exhaustion. Twice
the superpowers had played brinkmanship in the early sixties—
first in Berlin, then in Cuba—and twice they had found a way to
back down. There was no appetite to return to crisis. The Johnson administration was enmeshed in a war in Vietnam that was
deeply unpopular with its own citizens, a conflict that its own
intelligence services told them (although the White House kept
this knowledge secret) would be nearly impossible to win. The
Soviet Union had its own problems. At the time of the Prague
Spring, relations with China, which had already been poor, took
an ominous turn when fighting erupted along the disputed territory of the Ussuri River. The Soviets viewed the Chinese, in the
throes of the Cultural Revolution, as being dangerously ideological and lacking rationality in their apocalyptic approach to
remaking their society.[34] In turn, the Chinese thought the Soviets to be "socio-imperialists" who cared only about preserving
their own preeminence in the Communist hierarchy.

For these reasons, by the end of the 1960s, both the United

States and the Soviet Union welcomed the idea of détente. While Kennedy and Johnson had laid the groundwork for this mutual cooling off, it was a policy only fully embraced by Richard Nixon, who was elected in November 1968. Together with Henry Kissinger, his National Security Advisor (and also eventually secretary of state), Nixon set about capitalizing on the tension between the Soviet Union and China by opening up to the latter, using Pakistan as an intermediary. The idea was that this pressure would result in the Soviet Union coming to the negotiating table to talk about arms reduction. Nixon made his historic visit to Beijing in February 1972, with a follow-up visit to Moscow planned for May.

Solzhenitsyn, who listened avidly to these developments through the BBC Russian service on his transistor radio, launched into action. He was staunchly opposed to détente, as in the long term it would allow the Kremlin to consolidate its power and suppress internal critics like himself. Ironically, in the short term it also served to protect him, as the Soviet Union did not want to cause an embarrassing scandal that would jeopardize ongoing talks. In the weeks before Nixon arrived in Moscow, Solzhenitsyn ramped up his attacks, employing what he called his "cascade" strategy. First, he gave a joint interview to the *New York Times* and the *Washington Post* in which he detailed the ways he had been harassed and abused, including the confiscation of his archive.[35] To add to the provocation he arranged a private ceremony in Moscow at which he would belatedly receive the Nobel Prize. Even Solzhenitsyn, who had nerves of steel, felt anxious ahead of delivering the lecture he had written for the occasion, as it constituted his most direct and comprehensive attack on the Soviet system.

In his speech, he told how he had only managed to ascend to the platform of winning the Nobel Prize by climbing the "unyielding, precipitous, frozen steps, leading out of the darkness and cold where it was my fate to survive, while others—perhaps with a greater gift and stronger than I—have perished." He spoke, using the image for the first time in public, of an "archipelago" of gulags that had claimed a whole generation of Russian writers who never got the chance to write the work locked inside them. "A whole national literature" was lost, he said, "cast into oblivion not only without a grave, but without even underclothes, naked, with a number tagged on to its toe." That this was disastrous for Russia was because literature constituted, in Solzhenitsyn's words, "the living memory of the nation." The silencing of Russia's writers presented a danger to the nation itself. He called upon the solidarity of writers around the world—the very solidarity that had rallied around him when he was ejected from the Writers' Union—to keep fighting at this "white-hot hour" in the history of the world. Their task, Solzhenitsyn claimed, was nothing less than to "conquer falsehood."[36]

As it transpired, the publication of the lecture had to wait until later in the year. The Politburo could not live with the idea of Solzhenitsyn staging his own ceremony the month before Nixon arrived, but instead of taking action against the writer, they simply denied Karl Gierow, the permanent secretary of the Swedish Academy, a visa. Solzhenitsyn dashed off another angry open letter into samizdat in response, but the moment had been lost.

Nixon's visit to Moscow was a success for détente. The president's "new diplomacy" resulted in the successful negotiation of the SALT-1 agreement and the Anti-Ballistic Missile Treaty, putting the brakes on the arms race. There was also optimism on both sides about building new trade relationships. The fear among dissidents was that this new realpolitik would come at the cost of the burgeoning human rights movement. It was an apprehension with foundation: just before the visit many dissidents were arrested on petty charges or ordered to take additional military training to ensure there were no unseemly protests; after the treaties were signed, the Brezhnev regime continued to squeeze the dissident groups.[37]

Solzhenitsyn recognized that this was a perilous moment and, despite preferring to operate alone, he threw his lot in with other dissidents, joining the Moscow Human Rights Committee, which had been founded by a group of dissidents in 1970 (Esenin-Volpin and Litvinov were members). In the summer of 1973, he met Andrei Sinyavsky, and they walked in the woods, away from unwelcome eyes and ears, to talk literature, politics, and the future of Russia. Sinyavsky's health had degraded badly in his six years in the camps, and he was unemployed after being released. It had been communicated to Sinyavsky that if he wanted to leave the Soviet Union he could, and he was already planning to move to Paris. Solzhenitsyn wanted to stay and fight.[38]

At this time Solzhenitsyn also began to coordinate his efforts with Andrei Sakharov, a nuclear physicist who had worked on the Soviet Union's atomic weapons program before becoming a vocal activist for civil liberties. To the West, this pair became the faces of the dissident movement as they used their celebrity to push back against détente. On August 21, 1973—a date chosen because it was the fifth anniversary of the invasion of Czechoslovakia—Sakharov held a press conference. "Détente without democratization, détente in which the West in effect accepts the Soviet rules of the game would be dangerous," he said. "It would mean cultivating a closed country where everything that happens may be shielded from outside eyes, a country wearing a mask that hides its true face."[39] Then, abruptly, Solzhenitsyn ripped that mask off.

IN SEPTEMBER 1973, Solzhenitsyn received the shocking news that his former typist, Elizaveta Voronyanskaya, had taken her own life. The sixty-seven-year-old had been arrested and during five days of interrogation at KGB headquarters in Leningrad, eventually divulged that a copy of *Gulag Archipelago* was buried in the garden of a former *zek* in Luga. They wasted no time in digging it up.[40] With the book in the hands of the KGB, Solzhenitsyn knew confrontation was inevitable. He imagined what it must have been like as the manuscript made its way up the Lubyanka food chain to the head of the KGB, Yuri Andropov. "The blood must have turned to ice in their veins," he wrote; "its publication might be fateful to the system."[41] Solzhenitsyn drew up a list of possible sanctions. The worst was that they might take away his young children and keep them as hostages. He also feared their using agents operating under cover in the West to steal copies of the manuscript—although that seemed improbable. He was sure that the smear campaign against him would intensify. One other option, which he dared to hope for, was that they would seek to negotiate with him.

In a strange way, that's what seemed to happen, at least by Solzhenitsyn's account. After discovering that *Gulag Archipelago* was in KGB hands, he received a message that Natalia Reshetovskaya wanted to meet with him, not for another round of recriminations, but on a professional matter. At Moscow Kazansky train station, his ex-wife told him that the powers that be had let it be known that they were willing to publish some of his work in the Soviet Union, perhaps *Cancer Ward*. In return, she suggested, he could promise not to publish any new work for twenty years—by which she clearly meant *Gulag Archipelago*. She later claimed that she had sought out a deal with the authorities on her own, motivated by the desire to be reunited with Solzhenitsyn, hoping to show her value to him. Solzhenitsyn's account is more sinister. He believed she was being manipulated by the KGB and was convinced that plainclothes agents were monitoring them from the train platform. He rejected the proposal and made it known that *Gulag Archipelago* was to be published as soon as possible.[42]

By this stage Solzhenitsyn was staying with a friend at the writers' colony in Peredelkino. In order to throw off surveillance to meet with allies and friends in Moscow, he would sneak out through the garden, climb the back wall, and then hike through the countryside to the next train station down the line. In the depths of the Russian winter he listened to the radio, hoping for some news. On December 28 it came: *Gulag Archipelago* had been published in Russian in Paris.

Solzhenitsyn had referred to his book as containing the power of an atom bomb. Now it went off. The historian Tony Judt argues that the publication of *Gulag Archipelago* was a symbolic moment, "a hinge on which postwar Europe's self-understanding turned."[43] The idea of "real existing Socialism" was, in Judt's words, exposed as "a barbaric fraud, a totalitarian dictatorship resting upon a foundation of slave labor and mass murder." The existence of the labor camps was known—although in some cases willfully downplayed—but here, in weighty slabs of biting and bitter prose, Solzhenitsyn documented their history, from the immediate aftermath of the revolution to the height of the Great Terror. He brought to life the voices of those who had disappeared into mass graves in Siberia, a chorus of condemnation. In Western Europe, many on the left still harbored illusions about reforming Communism while others had been sympathetic to the Soviet Union as a direct reaction to the fervency of American anti-Communism and the foreign policy that it entailed, but *Gulag Archipelago* made equivocation impossible. It was the kind of blow to the Communist project that, on the surface, did not seem lethal, but the damage it caused ran deep, a slow internal bleed that, once begun, was impossible to stop.

ON JANUARY 7, 1974, the Soviet leadership convened a special meeting to decide what was to be done about Solzhenitsyn and *Gulag Archipelago*. These gatherings were hardly dynamic affairs. By this stage Brezhnev was an obese alcoholic in rapidly deteriorating health; he only worked a few hours a day and spoke with a slur, possibly as a result of suffering a stroke. He began the meeting by informing the group that *Gulag Archipelago* had been published and that a "debunking operation" had begun. But Brezhnev wanted more. "We have to determine what to do about Solzhenitsyn," he said. "By law, we have every basis for putting him in jail. He has tried to undermine all we hold sacred: Lenin, the Soviet system, Soviet power—everything dear to us . . . This hooligan Solzhenitsyn is out of control."[44]

Brezhnev was not wrong about *Gulag Archipelago*. It was a devastating indictment of the penal system that had underpinned Soviet society. Over seven volumes (only the first of which had so far been published), it drew on a wide range of sources, including firsthand accounts of inmates, diaries, bureaucratic and legal documents, letters, and, of course, the author's own experience. Written with bitter irony and black humor, it combined detailed historical research with vivid descriptions of life in the camps. One of the big myths that the book shattered was the idea that the gulag was an aberration of Stalinism, confined to the late 1930s. As Solzhenitsyn showed, the secret police, arbitrary imprisonment and execution, and systematic forced labor traced their origins to the immediate aftermath of the revolution, that mass incarceration and slave labor were baked into Soviet Communism.

Andropov had a suggestion. "I think Solzhenitsyn should be deported from the country without his consent," he said. "Trotsky was deported in his time without getting his agreement. . . . Everyone is watching us to see what we will do with Solzhenitsyn— if we will mete out punishment to him or if we will just leave him alone . . . I maintain that we must take legal action and bring the full force of Soviet law against him." The Politburo decided this was the best option of a bad bunch: it would punish Solzhenitsyn but not in a way that would seem excessively punitive to the West. As West German Chancellor Willy Brandt offered to take Solzhenitsyn in the event of his deportation, everything was set. But in order to prevent any resistance on Solzhenitsyn's part this had to come as a surprise. Andropov took personal responsibility for planning the operation, minute by minute.

The opening salvo was a renewed press campaign. Under the headline "Death of a Traitor," *Pravda* accused him of deliberately seeking to sabotage détente. He was, the article claimed, anti-Russian, pro-German, and only interested in making money. The rest of the Soviet press followed suit, accusing him of collaborating with "the most rabid reactionaries and cold warriors" in the West. He was no better than a "reptile" and "in daylight all reptiles look disgusting."[45] His home phone was bombarded with anonymous threatening phone calls and letters. The KGB approached people from his past, even childhood friends, and tried to blackmail them into slandering him.

Amid this assault, the public prosecutor summoned him to his office for what Solzhenitsyn assumed would be a routine dressing down (he'd been through this before). Used to these attacks, he countered by giving an interview with *Time* in which he denied wanting to blow up détente and reignite the Cold War but warned that the West must not pay for peace by propping up an oppressive society. *Gulag Archipelago,* he argued, was a call for a historical reckoning. Furthermore, he gave an interview to Western newspaper correspondents in which he revealed that there was safely locked away a hitherto secret seventh volume of *Gulag Archipelago* that dealt with the crimes of 1956 to the present—another provocation.

On February 12, 1974, two men appeared at the door of

Svetlova's Moscow apartment asking for Solzhenitsyn, claiming to want to "clear something up." When Solzhenitsyn took the door off the chain, the two men burst in, followed rapidly by six others. Despite the years spent planning for this moment, always keeping a prison bag packed, the moment took him totally by surprise. "I was in a state of witless shock," he later wrote, "as though flames had suddenly enwrapped and paralyzed me." He wondered what had happened to his "wolfish prison ways," acquired over the years in the gulag. He had even left his prison bag in Peredelkino.

He was whisked over to Lefortovo Prison, where he was stripped and searched "like a cow standing stock still waiting to be milked." He had planned to refuse to cooperate in any way but suddenly found himself meekly following orders. He was subject to a medical examination and forced to hand over all his belongings, including his crucifix. Half expecting to be met by senior KGB officials, Solzhenitsyn was surprised to be slung into a cell with two currency speculators.

An hour later he was taken to see Mikhail Malyarov, the deputy prosecutor general, who told him he was charged with treason, which carried with it a sentence ranging from ten years in prison to execution. Solzhenitsyn refused to sign any documentation. "I shall take no part in either your investigation or your trial," he told the prosecutor. He was taken back to his cell, where he spent an uncomfortable night. The next morning, he had a further, more comprehensive medical exam and was given medicine for high blood pressure. The guards presented him with a suit, shirt, tie, and new shoes. This, Solzhenitsyn assumed, could only mean one thing: he was going to see the Politburo.

Instead he was taken back to see Malyarov in his office. The prosecutor read a short statement: "By decree of the Presidium of the Supreme Soviet of the U.S.S.R. for the systemic execution of actions incompatible with Soviet citizenship and harmful to the U.S.S.R., Solzhenitsyn A. I. is to be deprived of Soviet citizenship and evicted beyond the borders of the Soviet Union, today 13 February 1974."[46] Keeping his composure, Solzhenitsyn demanded his family be allowed to go with him but was told they could only follow later.

He was driven by limousine to Sheremetyevo Airport and, along with seven plainclothes KGB officers, boarded an Aeroflot flight to Frankfurt. This was a regular scheduled flight and the rest of the passengers were told the three-hour delay had been for fog. The flight took two and a half hours, and on landing Solzhenitsyn was told to wait. When he finally emerged from the plane, one of the KGB agents thrust 500 marks into his hand and ushered him toward a group of German officials waiting on the tarmac. After being formally greeted by the German foreign minister he was again ushered into a limousine and accompanied by a police escort, driven to the Langenbroich home of the German novelist Heinrich Böll.

Solzhenitsyn's deportation was front-page news around the world and reporters in the hundreds descended on Langenbroich. Others camped out at Svetlova's Moscow apartment. The media furor only intensified when Solzhenitsyn refused to give any more than a perfunctory statement. He decided to base himself in Zurich, where his lawyer, Fritz Heeb, had managed his affairs in the West since being retained via intermediaries in 1970. However, he refused to fly, and when his car made for Cologne train station, all the reporters and members of the various film crews followed in a giant motorcade. More than two hundred journalists boarded the train with him at Cologne and more got on at every stop. In Zurich, they laid siege to the home of his lawyer, with whom he was staying. When two particularly tenacious members of the paparazzi refused to leave him alone, he roared at them, "You are worse than the KGB!"

Frustrated by the relentless press intrusion in Switzerland,

Solzhenitsyn decided to try his luck in Norway, which had long offered him asylum and which he hoped might remind him of Russia. As he traveled north, the Solzhenitsyn road show was greeted by big crowds in Copenhagen and Oslo. It was the start of a nomadic existence for Solzhenitsyn that would culminate in his setting down in a fenced-off property in rural Vermont.

The big question was what impact the deportation would have on détente. The Politburo had gambled on the move not warranting a dramatic response. Sure enough, Henry Kissinger, choosing his words carefully, explained that the "necessity for détente does not reflect approbation of the Soviet domestic structure." When Solzhenitsyn's family was allowed to leave the Soviet Union at the end of March to join him in Zurich, some of the intensity had gone out of the criticism of the Soviet Union's actions. To the Politburo's delight, they had removed a long and painful thorn from their side, although if they thought the wound would be quick to heal, they were mistaken.

SOLZHENITSYN WAS NOT EVERYTHING the West had expected. His irascible interactions with the press in the days and weeks after his deportation presaged his uncompromising stance on political subjects. Being an enemy of the Soviet Union did not necessarily make him a friend of the West. He showed little interest in living a Western lifestyle or in spending some of his newfound wealth (his books, after all, were best sellers).[47] He expressed rather disturbing opinions about Russia not being ready for democracy and needing at least a period of authoritarian rule. He was repulsed by the social and cultural liberalism of the West and banged the drum for good old-fashioned religious values. Rock and roll? The movies? They were "manure."

Where previous presidents might have sought to make Cold War capital out of Solzhenitsyn, the Nixon administration did their best to ignore him. At the time of the deportation, Nixon was fighting for his political life, with new revelations about the Watergate scandal coming by the week. In an effort to head off the investigations into his conduct, Nixon repeatedly warned that these imperiled the successes of his foreign policy. A visit to Moscow had been planned for the end of June 1974, and Nixon and Kissinger were determined that the Solzhenitsyn situation not jeopardize the gains of détente. At the Conference on Security and Co-operation in Europe in Geneva—the meetings that lead to the Helsinki Accords the following year—Solzhenitsyn's name was not mentioned once by delegates of the United States.

Not that Solzhenitsyn was content to drift into the background. He kept up his public attacks against the Brezhnev regime and its persecution of dissidents while also critiquing United States foreign policy. When U.S. Congressmen Donald Fraser and Benjamin Rosenthal sought his opinion on détente, he told them that the only way forward would be a reciprocal negotiation in which the Soviet Union made commitments over human rights. What the Nixon administration was negotiating with Brezhnev's Politburo was, in his words, "a pseudo-détente," by which the Soviet Union made few tangible concessions.[48]

Over the following year the United States was thrown into crisis. Facing impeachment, Nixon resigned in August 1974 and was replaced by Gerald Ford. The credibility of American Cold War policy had already been severely damaged by the publication of the Pentagon Papers in 1971, which revealed that three different presidential administrations had lied repeatedly to the American people about the prosecution of the Vietnam War and the possibility of winning it. In December 1974, Seymour Hersh, the reporter who had exposed the My Lai atrocity, revealed that under Nixon the CIA had been conducting a vast illegal spying operation on U.S. citizens. This prompted an investigation into the CIA by a Senate select committee chaired by Frank Church.

Among the many revelations of the committee's reports was that the CIA had attempted to assassinate foreign leaders, including Patrice Lumumba of the Democratic Republic of Congo, Ngo Dinh Diem of South Vietnam, and Fidel Castro of Cuba. The Church Committee also confirmed that the CIA tried to rig foreign elections, including spending $14 million to influence the 1964 election in Chile.

With the American economy still reeling from the OPEC crisis, Ford cut a besieged figure. There were a number of foreign policy hangovers he had to deal with. The Paris Peace Accords of 1973 had supposedly brought peace to Vietnam, but in December 1974 the North invaded the South and swiftly made progress toward Saigon. With Congress refusing any aid to South Vietnam, Ford announced that the war was finally over, and the evacuation of American citizens and South Vietnamese who had worked with them began. Saigon fell on April 30 and was renamed Ho Chi Minh City. Another headache was the Middle East. Kissinger's so-called shuttle diplomacy during the October War of 1973 had been much celebrated, as not only had he placated Israel but had also managed to "flip" Egypt from being a Soviet ally to an American one. Yet now Israel was getting restive, and relationships between the two countries were deteriorating.

Still, Ford clung to détente—one of the few foreign policy initiatives that seemed to be working—as a way of avoiding further conflict and rebuilding the economy. In the summer of 1975 final negotiations were taking place over the Helsinki Accords, and plans were made for an important symbolic meeting between American astronauts and Soviet cosmonauts in space. That summer Solzhenitsyn visited the United States. Ford had stated, soon after Solzhenitsyn's arrival, that he would happily meet with him if he were ever in Washington. But on July 2 he announced that this was no longer the case and that the invitation was withdrawn "on advice from the National Security Council."[49] Kissinger had sent a memo to Ford in which he described Solzhenitsyn's political views as "an embarrassment even to his fellow-dissidents" and recommend he not be received. Any such meeting would, Kissinger argued, "offend the Soviets." The decision made Ford look weak and Senators Jesse Helms and Henry Jackson invited Solzhenitsyn to meet members of both houses of Congress instead. Rattled by his mistake, Ford compounded it: he let it be known that he would welcome Solzhenitsyn at the White House after all. Solzhenitsyn declined the invitation (privately, Ford apparently called Solzhenitsyn a "god-damn horse's ass" who simply wanted to use a meeting with him to promote his books).[50]

It was an expensive mistake. His name now well known to an American public taking increasing interest in Russian dissidents, Solzhenitsyn became, in the words of *The New Yorker*, "the world's foremost opponent of détente."[51] He reserved particular ire for the Helsinki Accords. As part of this agreement, signed in August 1975, the Soviet Union's territorial gains after the Second World War were consolidated. It was a formal ratification of the status quo and one that, he believed, favored the Soviet Union. Solzhenitsyn attacked Ford for agreeing to these terms, saying they constituted the "betrayal of Eastern Europe" and that the United States was officially acknowledging its "slavery forever." There were also human rights provisions written into the Helsinki Accords, but Solzhenitsyn was convinced the Kremlin could just ignore them. The Politburo shared this opinion.

Partly as a result of such criticisms, détente was losing its luster, and the Kissinger-inspired Cold War realpolitik came under attack from left and right. Jimmy Carter, who won the 1976 presidential election, made a point of campaigning on the need to reintroduce moral considerations to foreign policy and, in the months after his election, he met with Russian dissidents. In the early months of 1977, he lambasted the Czechoslovakian government for its repression of Charter 77, a human rights collective that included the influential dissident writers Pavel Kohout and Václav Havel. Carter also shifted U.S. policy in Latin America, withdrawing or reducing aid to authoritarian regimes in Argentina, Brazil, Chile, and Nicaragua that had previously been cultivated for their anti-Communism.

The knockout blow came from the right, however. During his primary campaign against Gerald Ford ahead of the 1976 election, Ronald Reagan spoke of détente as being little more than appeasement, and the White House's refusal to meet with Solzhenitsyn as symptomatic of this cowardice. At the Republican National Convention, Reagan and his allies succeeded in getting an endorsement for Solzhenitsyn into the election platform (much to Kissinger's vocal disgust). Reagan failed to secure the nomination back then, but in 1980 he not only secured the nomination but also defeated Carter in a landslide. Détente was well and truly dead; the Cold War was heating up again.

THIRTY

Belli

NICARAGUA, 1975–1990

As Gioconda Belli rounded the curve in the road, her eyes flicked to the rearview mirror and saw a red car pull out behind her. It was early evening in Managua traffic, and she experienced a cold shock of recognition: she had seen the car earlier that day. Then it had roused her suspicion, but she had easily shaken it off by taking a detour, wondering if she was just being paranoid. But there was no mistaking what was happening now. She had been trained in how to recognize a tail and had spent two months the previous year under surveillance by state security services. In the mirror she could make out four men in the vehicle. "They're following us," she said.

Sitting in the passenger seat was Charlotte Baltodano, who in Belli's words was "a small pretty woman in a low-cut top, with a look that was somewhere between sensual and innocent, like an actress from a Roger Vadim film."[1] Baltodano was anything but innocent: she was a highly sought-after fugitive, a member of the Sandinista commando unit that had staged an audacious raid on a Christmas Party given for the American ambassador on December 27, 1974. While the ambassador had left earlier in the evening, the guerrillas took a number of high-profile hostages, members of the Nicaraguan elite close to President Anastasio Somoza Debayle. The Sandinistas secured the freedom of fourteen political prisoners, including the guerrilla leader Daniel

Ortega, in negotiating the release of the hostages. They also secured a $1 million payment and an agreement that the first San-
dinista communiqué would be published. It was a very public
embarrassment for Somoza, and he responded by instituting
martial law and unleashing a reign of terror against anyone connected to the Sandinistas. He ordered his security services to
ruthlessly hunt down everyone who had been involved.[2]

Now his agents had Belli and Baltodano trapped. Moving
slowly and methodically, Baltodano reached for her backpack,
pulled out a pair of sneakers, and replaced her high heels. She
continued to rummage through her bag and pulled out two
guns, laying one in Belli's lap. "Do you know how to use this?"
Belli nodded. That had also been part of her training: an experienced guerrilla had taught her to shoot. "They won't catch
us alive, do you agree?" Baltodano asked. Again, Belli nodded.
Four against two, the pair stood no chance. But being captured
was worse than being gunned down for anyone connected to the
Christmas Party raid.

That included Belli, although the authorities did not know
that yet. As a member of the Nicaraguan upper class and a distinguished poet she was not exactly first on the list of potential
suspects. She was educated at an elite Spanish boarding school
and got married to Mariano Downing at her parents' country
club in 1967, at the age of nineteen. That same year the couple
celebrated the birth of their first child; her life seemed mapped
out. Belli's first job, though, was at an advertising agency where
a colleague, an aspiring poet, introduced her to the bohemians
and radicals of Managua's café culture. Poets were venerated in
Nicaragua, in part due to the legacy of Ruben Darío, the father
of Latin American modernism. "To be known as a poet in my
country is to enjoy one of the highest, most cherished status
symbols in society," she wrote.[3] She began writing poems herself and when she published her first verses in 1970, at the age

of twenty-one, their sexually frank content caused a scandal in high society. Her work was defended by established poets, however, including José Coronel, Pablo Antonio Cuadra, and Carlos Martínez Rivas. As she forged relationships with writers and painters she also began to mix with revolutionaries. In fact, many of these artists *were* revolutionaries. She read the work of Frantz Fanon, Eduardo Galeano, Herbert Marcuse, and Che Guevara. "I felt like I had been hit over the head with a rock," she later recalled.[4] She saw the poverty of Nicaragua with fresh eyes. Energized and radicalized, she was recruited by Camilo Ortega, brother of Daniel, and introduced to Managua's underground network of Sandinistas. She read the group's literature, familiarizing herself with its ideology, which was shaped by Marxism but resistant to Soviet Communist orthodoxy. In 1973, she was formally sworn in, toward the end of her second pregnancy. She tried to protect her husband by keeping him in the dark about her clandestine work, using her job in advertising to collect information about the wealthy business elite that supported the regime and helped out as a courier. When her first collection of poems, *Sobre la Grama,* won a prestigious prize, she secretly donated the winnings to the cause.

Along the way she had become romantically involved with "Marcos" (nom de guerre of Eduardo Contreras), who had planned the hostage operation; Belli's role was to scope out potential targets. Using her status as a celebrated poet as cover, glamorously dressed, she visited cultural attachés at the various embassies in Managua ostensibly to talk about literary projects. Later she would sketch out floor plans from memory.

When the time of the Christmas Party operation approached, Marcos told her to leave the country to prevent being swept up in the police crackdown that would inevitably follow. She saw news of the raid in an Italian café after a day visiting Pompeii.

On her return to Nicaragua, Belli somehow avoided being

arrested. She suspected her privilege worked in her favor. Reconnecting with her network, Belli began work for the Sandinistas again. Despite the risks, she agreed to hide Baltodano at her home for one night. It was the following day that they found themselves being followed on the streets of Managua, trapped by the rush hour traffic.

Belli knew she had to do something as there would be military jeeps farther up the road. "I felt no fear, only a rush of adrenaline," she recalled. "Time was moving in slow motion but my mind was working with astonishing speed and precision."[5] She saw a junction ahead that led into a low-lying residential area that was a warren of alleys. She hit the gas and sped out into the opposite lane, forcing the oncoming cars to swerve out of the way. Reaching the junction, amid honking and shouting, she darted through traffic and into the dense residential streets, weaving her way through to a dirt road that led upward to the other side of the valley. When they stopped at the end of that road, there was no red car in sight. Belli's legs were shaking uncontrollably. But her bold move had saved them, at least for the moment.

Still, Belli knew her card was marked. Not long after that escape she saw the car again. This time it was parked outside the clinic of Jacobo Marcos, a psychiatrist who had been Belli's most recent handler. He was a veteran of the organization and had recruited Marcos, his namesake and Belli's lover. She managed to get a message of warning to Jacobo, but he did not appreciate the seriousness of his position. When he was arrested, Belli was instructed by the Sandinista hierarchy to get out of the country. The organization's code was if captured one was supposed to hold out for at least a week in order to give those in the compromised cell, like Belli in this case, the chance to escape. Somoza's security forces soon got to work on Jacobo. They buried him up to his neck in a yard and left him there under the brutal sun, kicking him and dousing him in trash and urine in an effort to break him. He held out long enough for Belli to escape into exile to Mexico, forced to leave her husband and children behind her. Three days after she left, the police raided her office and tore it apart.[6] She would continue to fight for the revolution from outside the country. From exile she would write a defiant poem, "Me seguían" ("They followed me"), about the "sick dogs" who had chased her out of the country:

> With each dawn I felt a more ferocious hatred
> spawning guts within me
> in which to reside
> and I who had never thought I was brave
> felt a growing courage, a growing strength
> to keep fighting.

BELLI AND HER COMPAÑEROS were playing a dangerous game with Somoza and his National Guard—all the more so because the game was rigged; standing behind the dictatorship, propping it up with economic and military support, was the most powerful country in the world, the United States. This support had a long history, dating back to American intervention in the nineteenth century, but had intensified during the Cold War as Somoza cleverly played on American anxieties about the potential spread of Communism in Latin America. As Somoza secured his position through his relationship with Washington, resentment among the Nicaraguan population built, eventually expressing itself in the formation of the Sandinistas. The very name adopted by the Sandinistas signaled their opposition to American interference in Nicaragua: in the 1920s and 1930s, when U.S. Marines occupied Nicaragua, Augusto Sandino, a general in the Nicaraguan army, took to the northern hills with a band of thirty men, who managed to resist the best efforts of the Marines to defeat them.[7] Indeed, such was Sandino's success that, for fear of losing more American casualties, the U.S. government helped with the creation and training of the Nicaraguan National Guard to take over the fight. The man who ended up running the National Guard, at the behest of the U.S. government, was Somoza's father, Anastasio Somoza Garcia. Sandino was eventually ambushed and executed by the National Guard in 1934; Somoza Garcia became president in a rigged election three years later.

From that point on the Somoza dynasty enjoyed almost unbroken backing from Washington, despite their authoritarian methods. "He may be a son of a bitch," Franklin Delano Roosevelt supposedly said, "but he's our son of a bitch."[8] When the relationship turned frosty under Harry Truman, Somoza exploited the dynamics of the emerging Cold War to regain American favor. In 1954, when the CIA staged a coup to replace the democratically elected Guatemalan president Jacobo Arbenz, suspecting him of being in the thrall of Communists, Nicaragua provided the United States with training bases and logistical support.

In 1956 Rigoberto López Pérez, a poet and supporter of Nicaragua's Liberal Party, shot and killed Somoza Garcia at a party before being gunned down by the dictator's bodyguards. Luis Somoza, the eldest son, took over, and quickly sought a closer relationship with the United States. American anxieties in the region had been sharpened by the Cuban Revolution, and Luis Somoza ingratiated himself to newly inaugurated President Kennedy by providing bases for the paramilitaries to use in the failed Bay of Pigs invasion. Shortly after this, the Frente Sandinista de Liberación Nacional (FSLN) was formed to fight back against the Somoza dictatorship.

Luis Somoza was in fact more liberal than his father and introduced some modernizing reforms, but on his death in 1967, his brother, Anastasio, head of the National Guard, effectively took over, bringing a return to their patriarch's authoritarian methods. A graduate of West Point and enthusiastically backed by Richard Nixon, he felt he had free rein to rule as he pleased. Particularly egregious was the way he and his circle exploited the 1972 earthquake that destroyed much of Managua for financial gain, siphoning off aid and corruptly distributing contracts.

During these years, the Sandinistas grew in numbers and influence, even if some of its members, like Belli, frequently had to operate from exile. Having escaped the security services, she was tried in absentia. Her lawyer read some of her patriotic poems in court, after which she was sentenced to seven years in prison.

Belli's time in Mexico was one of intense artistic inspiration and she wrote the bulk of the poems that made up her most celebrated collection, *Línea de Fuego*, in those first months of exile.[9] Still, not knowing when she would be reunited with her two daughters, Belli was despondent. The exile community rallied around her, and to her delight she was reunited with her lover, Marcos. But Belli did not want to remain abroad; she wanted to return home, even if it meant taking the risks of going underground.

Her colleagues persuaded her that this was a foolish enterprise: it would not take long for someone to recognize her. She was told she would be most effective working out of Costa Rica, where the government was sympathetic to their cause and offered shelter to guerrillas making raids across the border. Her husband, Mariano, visited her in Mexico, where they decided to split for good.

Belli's plan was to have her children join her in Costa Rica when she got settled. Not long after Marcos told her he was in a serious relationship with another woman and that their affair needed to end. The revolution being more important than romance, Belli met with Marcos for a last time in a bar on the Zocalo frequented by old exiles from the Spanish Civil War. "They were gaunt, somber men, figures out of a Goya painting," she wrote, "wearing a look of determination under black Basque berets." Marcos was full of admiration for these veterans, still holding out for the fall of fascism in Spain. Their perseverance should be an example to us, he told Belli. The next time she saw him was a picture of his corpse in the newspaper, gunned down in the streets of Managua, not far from where she had shaken off Somoza's agents in her car.

IN COSTA RICA Belli got a job with a local advertising agency and settled into the bohemian artistic milieu of San José, hanging out with the Argentine novelist Julio Cortázar and posing for the Nicaraguan painter Armando Morales.[10] At this time she fell in love with a Brazilian radical, Sergio de Castro, with whom she had a son. She began working with the Sandinista network in the city and met many of the most influential exiled opponents of the Somoza regime. She befriended Sergio Ramirez, an essayist and novelist, who was the leader of the Group of Twelve, a collection influential intellectuals, politicians, and priests who pledged their support to the Sandinistas (he kept his membership in the FSLN secret). Belli helped him as he worked on a screenplay about the life of Sandino. She also met Jaime Wheelock, one of the most important intellectuals of the Sandinista movement (a copy of his *Imperialism and Dictatorship* was found by the police in her desk after she fled and was used as evidence against her at her trial).[11] With these influential contacts, Belli was privy to the growing tension within the Sandinista movement, in which different factions pushed for their preferred strategies. Those proposed by Humberto Ortega troubled her. He and his brother, Daniel, seemed too ready to make accommodations and compromises and were too eager to welcome dubious allies, so long as they helped speed the path to revolution.

The Ortegas believed the moment to strike was imminent, and the Sandinistas began ramping up their training. Belli's home was converted into a temporary military school, and a veteran guerrilla came to instruct them. There they assembled and disassembled M-16s, Garands, and Galils, and studied the working of hand grenades. They lay on Belli's carpet with rifles to practice marksmanship, shooting imaginary bullets at paper targets. On October 12, Ramirez came to Belli's house to tell her that an ambitious new assault on the regime was planned for the next day and that they needed her help. They had a truck full of guns that needed running to the Nicaraguan border. A jeep would meet them in Liberia on the Costa Rican side and lead them to a crossing point where the weapons would be collected. "It sounded easy enough," Belli wrote, "that is, until I got a look at the pile of weapons we were supposed to load into my tiny, canary-yellow Toyota."[12] There were eight bags stuffed with weapons, and the car was packed to the brim. There was still one bag left. One of the guerrillas put it in the well of the front seat and told them not to smoke—the bag was packed with grenades.

Belli, accompanied by her husband, Sergio, took off into the night, driving down to the Pacific coastal road. By 2 A.M. they reached Liberia. "The meeting place was empty," she wrote. "No jeep, nobody in sight. I began to fume." Feeling conspicuous, they made for a late-night café and drank Cokes, pretending to be on a date. A Rural Guard patrol car pulled up, but the officer did not think anything untoward about the couple kissing and whispering at the table by the side of the highway. Finally, a jeep appeared on the road, flashing its lights as a signal to follow. Belli and Sergio, silent and tense, delivered the guns by moonlight.

While the attempt to launch coordinated attacks across the country failed, largely due to disorganized planning, the timing was ripe for an insurrection. The Carter administration had succeeded in getting Somoza to lift censorship limits, and the Nicaraguan opposition found its voice. Bodies of political prisoners were being exhumed to show evidence of torture. And to cap it all, Somoza was in Miami, recovering from a heart attack.

When Pedro Joaquín Chamorro, the fearless newspaper editor of *La Prensa* and vociferous opponent of the Somoza dynasty, was murdered, his body was carried through the streets of Managua. He had been a friend of the Belli family, and his death—in which Somoza's son was implicated—shocked the country.[13] Riots erupted and attacks on the National Guard increased.

Guerrillas returning from the front line used Belli's house in San José as a meeting point and weapons dump (the bazookas were stored in the attic). She worked as a courier, smuggling documents, letters, and forged passports between Costa Rica, Panama, and Honduras, often sewing them up in children's toys. Sometimes she would go to an airline gate and pick up a briefcase left for her by another operative not even knowing what was inside. On one occasion she smuggled more than $100,000 into Panama by pretending she was going to a wedding and hiding the notes amid tissue paper in a dress box (even then she needed help from a sympathetic Panamanian official).

At this time Belli shifted her allegiances within the factions of the Sandinista movement. The group led by the Ortega brothers advocated aggressive military action to provoke responses from Somoza as a way to keep the country polarized. They also continued to advocate a kind of popular front policy by which they allied themselves with any group opposed to Somoza, even if these groups were anti-Communists, and claimed they would run a consensus government should they be victorious. Belli knew this was opportunism, and worried that the means no longer justified the ends. Instead she sided with the faction that advocated forging strong links with rural laborers, modeling their strategy on that of Ho Chi Minh in Vietnam. One of the leaders of this faction was a hard-line guerrilla, "Modesto," who had been educated at Patrice Lumumba University in Moscow, and had spent many months fighting in the jungles of northern Nicaragua.[14] Belli and Modesto soon became lovers.

In the summer of 1978, the insurgency intensified. In a daring mission, Sandinista commandos infiltrated the National Palace and took members of the Congress hostage, securing the release of political prisoners and a $1 million ransom. A general strike followed, barricades were built, and attacks on the National Guard increased. Somoza responded by using his army, equipped by the United States and Israel, to try to crush the rebels. His forces dropped white phosphorous and napalm on rebel positions; the rebels fought back, taking on tanks with little more than Molotov cocktails. Despite the initial futility of such response, the anti-Somoza momentum grew. "The rebellion in Nicaragua advanced like a hurricane that builds spirals of clouds and wind far out to sea before hitting land with colossal force," Belli wrote.[15]

As the revolutionary storm gathered force, Belli won the Casa de las Américas prize, the most prestigious literary award in Latin America. Celebrating a Sandinista poet in the midst of their uprising, it was both a political statement and a validation of Belli's poetic talent. "Up to that point, politics not poetry was my central preoccupation. My basic identity was that of a Sandinista; being a poet was a convenient addition, a valuable talent that was useful to the political cause. My poems then were a mixture—often chaotic—of the erotic and the patriotic, two things that reflected the experience of my everyday life." Now Belli could put her increased profile to use, traveling abroad to secure support for her faction and the Sandinistas in general, ahead of the last push.

ON A COOL JANUARY MORNING IN 1979, Belli fired round after round from an AK-47 at a target while Fidel Castro watched. "With each shot I fired my body shuddered," she wrote, "the impact reverberating through every last joint, leaving an unbearable ringing in my head, sharp and disturbing."[16] Belli had picked out the gun from the vast and well-stocked munitions warehouse of the Cuban military, but she hated shooting it— she was a revolutionary, yes, but not a killer. Still, she knew that in the coming months, with the Sandinistas pushing for victory, she might find herself in combat. She switched weapons, opting for a .50-caliber machine gun. There was less recoil and firing it was less disorienting. Castro took note.

Belli was in Cuba for the celebrations of the twentieth anniversary of the revolution, invited as a representative of the GPP, the faction (or tendency, as they were known) of the Sandinistas to which she now belonged. It was her first time in the country, and it offered a vision of what a socialist Nicaragua might look like. She found Havana, strangled by the American economic embargo, run-down and drab, but she marveled at its citizens. "I was impressed by how even the youngest, simplest people were so well versed in politics," she wrote. "There was a special quality about those people, separated from consumerism, forced by their circumstances to focus their lives on different values, spiritual values like education, solidarity, love of country and community. The Cubans bemoaned all their hardships, but they got by cheerfully, with an epic sense of who they were."[17]

The anniversary celebrations were spectacular, with military parades and fly-bys by squadrons of Soviet-built MiG fighters. Guerrillas, left-wing politicians, and radical intellectuals arrived from all over the world, as far afield as Palestine, South Africa, and Vietnam. Writers were invited, too, and Belli struck up a friendship with the Colombian novelist Gabriel García Márquez and met Uruguayan poet Mario Benedetti. Márquez was a champion of the Sandinista cause, having helped broker support for the group from Panama and Venezuela in the late 1970s.

Belli had met Castro for the first time at a huge party at the modernist Palace of Conventions. After shaking his hand, he asked her where the Sandinistas had been hiding her. Belli was starstruck. "The material of his formal, impeccable olive-green uniform looked brand-new," she recalled. "His shoes gleamed. Everything about him exuded an air of authority, confidence, awareness that he was the most important person in the room." Castro moved on, and Belli was left to wonder if that would be her only meeting with the "secular Moses" of the Latin American left. She did not have to wonder for long. The next day, at a more intimate reception, she was introduced to him, this time by Benedetti, as a winner of the Casa prize. "And what do I have to do to read your book?" Castro asked. She assured him she could get him a copy. "But I want you to write me a dedication," he said. She assured the *comandante* she'd be happy to oblige. "And how can I get to see you?" he asked. "Going to your hotel would be difficult. I am too well known around here." She laughed it off but later that evening, over dessert, an official approached her and told her Castro wanted to speak with her privately.

Belli had cause to be nervous. On a recent mission she took to Panama, General Omar Torrijos repeatedly refused to accept no for an answer, taking Belli to his beach house, bullying her into writing a poem for his daughter, and, when she refused to join him in bed, made her sleep in a mildew-ridden outhouse. Belli made sure to lock herself in, and left Torrijos's place the following morning with a sense of great relief. Fidel was different, though. He was waiting for her in a softly lit room with green wallpaper and gold-framed paintings. With him was Manuel Piñeiro (nicknamed "Barbarroja"), another of the heroes of the Sierra Maestra. After some small talk about her background and her family, Belli and Fidel began discussing Nicaragua. She asked him why he supported the Ortega brothers and their tendency at the expense of the others. She argued that their politics were "unscrupulous and would be dangerous to the Sandinista cause in the long run." Fidel almost lost his temper, raising his voice, before lowering it dramatically. "How can you doubt my intentions? I have been a staunch advocate of Sandinista unity. I have spent entire nights with your leaders, trying to get them to agree." Belli pushed her point home, though, asking why he provided the Ortegas with more equipment and weapons than the other factions if he felt that way. The situation was getting heated and was only defused when Belli backed down, after realizing that Fidel "wasn't there to listen but to be heard."

The truth was that Castro's foreign policy had evolved, and this included the way he supported the Sandinistas. In the sixties, he had supported *foquismo,* the idea that small bands of insurgents could foster revolution through guerrilla warfare as in Cuba. Che Guevara had tried to export *foquismo* to Congo, fighting alongside anti-Mobutu rebels, but was forced to give up after a series of defeats and a bout of dysentery. Guevara tried again in Bolivia, but his band was ambushed by the Bolivian military and he was executed. The failure of *foquismo* was followed, in Castro's eyes, by the failure of a nonviolent social democratic approach. In Chile, Salvador Allende succeeded in winning the 1970 election despite the best efforts of the CIA to prevent him gaining power, but he never got the chance to fully implement his progressive agenda before being ousted in a CIA-backed military coup in 1973. To Castro and many others on the Latin American left, this made it clear that the United States would not permit a socialist state to be created through the democratic process. "The Chilean example teaches us the lesson that it is impossible to make the revolution with the people alone," he said. "Weapons are also necessary!"[18]

By the end of the 1970s Castro came to the conclusion that he needed to play a more sophisticated game. Cuba became a much more vocal member of the Non-Aligned Movement and avoided direct provocation of the United States, even exploring the potential for a degree of rapprochement.[19] This certainly did not connote timidity—after all, in 1975 he had sent Cuban troops to fight in the Angolan Civil War while both the Soviet Union and the United States avoided getting directly involved, fearful of damaging the policy of détente. With Nicaragua, Castro had, until January 1979, supported a traditional "foco" strategy being pursued by Belli's faction, the GPP, but the success that the Ortegas and Ramirez were achieving with their Popular Front strategy made him rethink. Castro realized that the Sandinistas needed to avoid becoming the site of another proxy conflict in the Cold War. What was required, he believed, was to present themselves as freedom fighters seeking to topple a dictator on behalf of a broad political consensus, not as Marxist insurgents seeking to create a new Cuba. The United States did not want to get into another war like Vietnam, but if the Sandinistas indulged in anti-American revolutionary rhetoric, the provocation might prove too much. In an interesting way, he actually served as a moderating influence. In strategic terms, he wanted the Sandinistas to engage Somoza's forces from fixed positions in the south in order to draw troops away from the north and leave them vulnerable to guerrilla columns. "It disturbed me to see that Fidel was so inclined to meddle," Belli wrote, "so intent on playing a leading role in our revolution."

In March 1979, two months after Belli's visit, the leaders of the different Sandinista tendencies met in Havana and, under Castro's guidance, agreed to put their differences aside as they made a final push toward seizing control. Modesto, Belli's lover, joined the new nine-man National Directorate, and Belli herself traveled extensively on fund-raising missions to Europe, seeking the help of socialist parties and other sympathetic figures. A sense of the inevitable mounted, as Sandinista forces seized town after town, and Belli began developing task forces to create policy for when the Sandinistas finally took control.

On June 20, 1979, as the guerrillas closed in on Managua, an American journalist, Bill Stewart of ABC News, was stopped at a National Guard checkpoint and ordered out of his van. Despite having all the relevant credentials, Stewart and his interpreter, Juan Francisco Espinosa, were executed with bullets to the head. His cameraman, Jack Clark, filmed the killing from inside the press van and smuggled the footage out of the country. When it was broadcast on the major news networks, any vestiges of support in Washington for the Somoza regime evaporated. "I will never forget the spine-chilling image of the soldier, and the absolute ease with which he pointed and fired," Belli wrote. "This was the hard evidence of what the Nicaraguan people were living with, day in, day out."[20]

Politically isolated and facing military defeat, Somoza fled to Miami, taking the exhumed remains of his father and brother with him. (He would not elude the Sandinistas for long; a commando team tracked him down to a Paraguayan hideaway the following year and blew up his Mercedes with a rocket-propelled grenade, killing him.) Belli and her comrades heard the news of Somoza's escape on the radio. "I don't know who began crying first," she wrote, "or how the tears spread from one person to another, but suddenly the tiny apartment was filled with wails and sobs." Belli's thoughts turned to all the friends she had lost in the war. "From a remote reservoir hidden deep inside of me, a wave of buried tears spilled forth," she wrote. "So many lives, too many lives, had been given up to hear that news flash, that short little sentence: 'Somoza left.'"[21] As the emotions roiled, one joyous truth cut through it all: Belli was going home.

ON JULY 20, 1979, Belli arrived in Managua aboard a DC-3 military plane packed with forty thousand copies of *Patria Libre,* the first edition of a newspaper heralding the triumph of the revolution. Belli and her husband, Sergio, had put together the paper themselves in Costa Rica, knowing that Somoza had bombed the offices of *La Prensa* in Managua. Belli's job was to lead the team who would distribute copies among the liberated populace. As the plane bumped down onto the tarmac, Belli felt a rush of recognition: "My senses were jubilant with the welcome heat, the smells, the clouds." The airport was strangely quiet; Belli's team loaded up a waiting truck and set out for the center of Managua. As they got closer to the city, they began driving through a crowd of people that got thicker by the mile, all of them returning from a celebration in the central plaza. Belli began handing out newspapers. As she did so she cried "Freedom!" and the crowd replied, "Or death!" completing the Sandinista slogan. "That slow truck ride reminded me of childbirth, of the joy after pain," she wrote. "I was witnessing the birth of my country."[22]

The victory of the Sandinistas was the first time a left-wing insurgency had succeeded in seizing power in Latin America since the Cuban Revolution in 1959. There had been unsuccessful attempts to overthrow authoritarian rulers in almost every other country in the region, and what made the Sandinista success so remarkable was how it had overcome a regime that had entrenched itself over decades. One of the explanations for this success was that the insurgency had built a coalition that included the Catholic Church, non-Marxist liberals, private interests, and people across social classes. Belli, the daughter of a prestigious Managua family, was a perfect example of how the

Sandinista appeal had reached across the strata of Nicaraguan society.

That this was a revolution of poets also mattered. When the novelist Salman Rushdie visited the country years later, Daniel Ortega told him, "In Nicaragua everybody is considered to be a poet until he proves to the contrary."[23] Rushdie's experiences on that trip certainly did not disabuse him of that notion: he had never seen a people "who valued poetry as much as the Nicaraguans."[24] (Rushdie attended a recital by Belli, whose work he described as "at once extremely sensual and politically direct.")[25] That so many of the revolutionaries were also poets burnished the image of the Sandinistas as romantic rebels, whose humanism was cultured and open in a way that made it different from the totalitarian aspects of the Soviet regime. This attracted the support of intellectuals and writers around the world, among them Carlos Fuentes, Graham Greene, and William Styron.[26] Greene donated half of his considerable royalties for his novel *Monsignor Quixote* (1982) to the Sandinista cause and, through his friendship with Tomás Borge, traveled to Managua to witness the aftermath of the revolution.[27] (For Greene's support of the Sandinistas, he was honored with the Ruben Darío medal in 1987.) In a world in which left-wing regimes were perceived to be oppressing literature, these qualities were important. That it was Belli, a celebrated poet, leading those chants on the road to Managua, and that she later wrote a poem ("The Blood of Others") about that experience, was evidence that the Sandinistas promised a different kind of socialism.[28]

In the center of Managua, Belli's squad pulled up to the National Guard headquarters, which was being gleefully looted by Sandinista soldiers. Belli helped herself to military uniforms and a machine gun, which she slung over her shoulder. This was not just to look the part: there were still National Guards hiding out in the city, attacking the Sandinistas under cover of darkness and shooting up checkpoints from speeding cars.

The Sandinista leadership was installed in "El Bunker." This had served as Somoza's headquarters and he had rarely left its luxurious, bombproof security in the final weeks of the war. After the revolution it became the nerve center of the new government. The United States had sought to negotiate a power-sharing arrangement, with some element of the military establishment involved, but even had the Sandinistas been open to such a plan, the National Guard had all but disbanded. The guerrillas had become governors.

Among these new leaders was Modesto. He now seemed different to Belli, cold and distant. He told her she would be working to set up the country's media. "About you and me," he said. "We can't go on like before." He said that even if she left her husband, they would have to live apart. He was, he said, a loner. They argued angrily but "ended up on the carpet, making love tangled in chair legs underneath Somoza's conference table."[29]

The affair with Modesto was one of "raw, electrifying passion, blind madness," and Belli, by her own admission, let it cloud her judgment. She separated from Sergio and began spending as much time with Modesto as possible. With so much work to do, that time was limited. Drawing on her experience in advertising, Belli was in charge of the new TV station, which involved writing scripts for the nightly news and digging up movies from the archives. She assigned herself to interview Sandinista leaders, to give her an excuse to visit Modesto in El Bunker. When he asked her to be his assistant and give up her work at the TV station, she assented, against her better judgment. "My rational mind clearly told me that following Modesto would hurt me in the long run," she wrote. "I knew my power rested in affirming myself through my own means, not in staying at Modesto's side."[30]

With Modesto she traveled around the world as Nicaragua sought to foster the relationships that would secure its future. In September she returned to Havana, where Nicaragua applied to join the Non-Aligned Movement. However, they were wary about allowing Castro too much influence. Belli wrote that, for all of their respect for Cuba and the Soviet Union, "we had different dreams for Nicaragua, we wanted a new kind of socialism— Nicaraguan, libertarian." To avoid the kind of Cold War isolation suffered by Cuba, they knew they needed a relationship with the United States. The Carter administration sent a delegation to Managua and $75 million in reconstruction aid. But back in Washington, the revolution continued to be described as a Communist threat, and Carter authorized the CIA to support non-Sandinista elements in the new government.[31] The Sandinistas, meanwhile, could barely conceal their skepticism about American intervention. In their anthem, after all, they pledged to fight the "Yanqui," the "enemy of humanity."[32] Furthermore, with victory assured, they started being less ideologically coy, and their professed social democracy began to evaporate.

In October and November 1979, the new regime gave their enemies in the United States more ammunition by sending a delegation on a "socialist tour." Belli and Modesto were part of the five-strong delegation that visited the Soviet Union, East Germany, Bulgaria, and Algeria. The idea behind the trip was to learn from functioning socialist states and to cement allegiances that would help protect Nicaragua in the event of American aggression. In Moscow they attended anniversary celebrations of the Bolshevik revolution and listened to Brezhnev speak at a session of the Central Committee of the Communist Party. Belli was exhilarated by the revolutionary pageantry but, as the days wore on, she grew "uncomfortable with the omnipresent specter of the Party, that patriarchal authority that seemed to follow everyone to the grave."[33]

In Algiers they witnessed another celebration: the twenty-fifth anniversary of the Algerian revolution. After watching the military parade, Belli and Modesto attended an official function at a hotel on the seafront. In a suite with a balcony overlooking the Mediterranean, Belli recognized Raúl Castro and Gabriel García Márquez talking to Vo Nguyen Giap, the Vietnamese general who had defeated the French at Dien Bien Phu and led the North Vietnamese army so successfully against the might of the U.S. military. "Dressed in a khaki military uniform with red stripes, he looked like the benign grandfather of a children's fairy tale," Belli wrote. Later, Giap quizzed Belli and Modesto about Nicaragua and they told him of the litany of problems they faced, not least of which was an economy on its knees. These, Giap replied, are the problems of victory. "If you hadn't won, you wouldn't have them," he said.[34]

There was, however, a new problem on the horizon, one that promised to overshadow any attempts by the new Nicaraguan regime to rebuild their newly liberated country. Its name was Ronald Reagan.

REAGAN WAS ELECTED in November 1980 promising to restore America's potency on the world stage. He argued that the Carter administration had left the United States humiliated and weak, and that the Soviet Union—the "evil empire" as he called it—had taken advantage of such impotency. The invasion of Afghanistan the previous year was the most brazen example of Soviet aggression, but Reagan was more concerned about matters closer to home. The Republican Party electoral platform accused the Carter administration of standing by "while Castro's totalitarian Cuba, financed, directed and supplied by the Soviet Union, aggressively trains, arms, and supports forces of warfare and revolution in the Western hemisphere." In Reagan's mind,

those forces of warfare were embodied in Nicaragua—the Sandinista revolution threatened to topple the Central American
dominoes and leave the United States exposed to a new Communist front to the south. "We deplore the Marxist Sandinista
takeover of Nicaragua and the Marxist attempts to destabilize
El Salvador, Guatemala, and Honduras," the Republican platform declared.[35]

As soon as he took office, Reagan began withdrawing loans
that Carter had promised Nicaragua. More ominous, Reagan
was insistent that the United States needed to purge itself of the
"Vietnam syndrome" and be prepared to launch military intervention should the need arise. The government of El Salvador
was fighting a guerrilla insurgency, and Reagan resolved not to
allow it to fall under Communist influence. Reagan's secretary
of state, Alexander Haig, suggested the best plan was to blockade or even attack Cuba. ("Give me the word and I'll turn that
island into a fucking parking lot," Haig said.)[36] Reagan instead
opted to back the El Salvadoran regime directly, offering huge
military support in exchange for a commitment toward democratic reforms, hoping this would curb some of the brutality by
the regime's death squads.[37] The problem was that the guerrillas
were also getting outside help. The Soviet Union recognized that
fostering revolutions in Central America could confer a huge
strategic advantage as the Cold War intensified. "The entire region is boiling like a cauldron," said Andrei Gromyko, minister
of foreign affairs.[38] The Kremlin arranged for more than $1 bil-
lion in military equipment to be sent to Cuba from North Korea
and Vietnam, and from there to Nicaragua and then into El
Salvador.[39]

The United States came up with a new strategy, working with
the Argentine junta to equip and train former Nicaraguan National Guards exiled in Honduras. These counterrevolutionaries,
dubbed Contras, infiltrated the northern border of Nicaragua to

try to stop arms from being smuggled to El Salvador but soon began working their way deeper into Nicaraguan territory. This suited the Reagan administration well.

Fearing the end point of this dramatic escalation, Belli realized something had to be done. She suggested a delegation be sent to talk to members of Congress and was appointed head of the Sandinista information office in 1982. She understood that the Sandinista leadership had a "moral obligation" to help the Salvadoran rebels and that "solidarity among guerrilla movements took precedence over caution."[40] However, she was frustrated with the provocative rhetoric adopted by Daniel Ortega, knowing that it played into Reagan's hands. She found that even Reagan's most committed opponents on Capitol Hill "raked us over the coals in a mild-mannered affable way."

In a joint session of Congress on April 27, 1983, Reagan signaled a renewed focus on Nicaragua. "The Sandinista revolution in Nicaragua turned out to be just an exchange of one set of autocratic rulers for another, and the people still have no freedom, no democratic rights, and more poverty," he said. "Even worse than its predecessor, it is helping Cuba and the Soviets to destabilize our hemisphere. . . . The national security of all the Americas is at stake in Central America. If we cannot defend ourselves there, we cannot expect to prevail elsewhere. Our credibility would collapse, our alliances crumble, and the safety of our homeland would be put in jeopardy."[41]

This was alarmist rhetoric, and Congress did not buy it. Legislation was passed between 1982 and 1984 preventing the United States from supporting the overthrow of the new Nicaraguan government and placing limits on funding for the Contras. Still, the Contras (whom Reagan referred to as "freedom fighters") continued to launch attacks, pushing Nicaragua effectively back into a state of civil war. The CIA offered clandestine support for the intervention, mining harbors and destroying fuel tanks to damage the country's oil reserve. The irony of the situation was not lost on Belli. "After many years of a one-man authoritarian rule in our country we were supposed to build a perfectly functioning democracy—at gunpoint."[42]

Another irony was that war with the Contras encouraged the very authoritarian tendencies that the United States was supposedly invested in stifling. In their first years in charge, the Sandinistas had combined progressive social policies regarding education, health, and women's rights with policies designed to tighten their grip on political power. There were some worrying signs of the direction in which the government was headed: some of the "Leninist" policies they instituted were much more hard-line than promised; there was armed conflict with the Miskito Indians in the northeast and tension with the Catholic Church. With the advent of the Reagan administration, the Sandinista leadership tacked more closely toward the Soviet Union; in 1981, Humberto Ortega and Tomas Borge traveled to Moscow to ask for more help, much of which was provided through Warsaw Pact states. (East Germany helped train the secret service, Poland provided helicopters, Bulgaria helped train pilots, and Czechoslovakia gave money.)[43] Now the Sandinista military and secret police began to crack down on anyone perceived as sympathizing with the Contras, often without any respect for due process. These authoritarian strategies combined with chronic food shortages eroded support for the regime.

Belli had her own encounter with the regime's darker side. After a painful split with Modesto, she had met an American journalist, Charlie Castaldi, in Washington. Castaldi worked for National Public Radio covering Central America and when he came to Nicaragua, they began a relationship. While he criticized many of the regime's policies, especially its censorship of the press, he was broadly sympathetic with the reforming goals of the revolution. Yet he was an American, and as the war with the Contras intensified, he fell under suspicion. Eventually, Belli, who was working on strategy for the 1984 elections, was called to the office of Tomás Borge, an old friend and one of the founding members of the FSLN. He told her to drop the relationship, fearing that Castaldi was either a CIA agent or working for them. A stunned Belli initially agreed, but without there being any evidence against Castaldi, she changed her mind, even if that meant she was edged away from the Sandinista inner circle. Not much later, Castaldi was accused by officials working for the U.S. State Department of distributing "Sandinista propaganda" in his reports.[44] The paranoia of the Cold War was bipolar.

ON OCTOBER 5, 1986, in the jungle of southern Nicaragua, a nineteen-year-old Nicaraguan soldier, José Fernando Canales, raised a Soviet-issue rocket launcher to his shoulder, aimed at the C-123 cargo plane, and fired. The heat-seeking missile arced through the sky and slammed into the plane's right wing. Three crew members—two American, one Nicaraguan—were killed in the subsequent crash, but one survived, having leapt from the flaming plane and engaged his parachute. Eugene Hasenfus, a former Marine from Wisconsin, was picked up by Sandinista forces shortly thereafter, sleeping in a hammock made from the canopy of his chute. In the wreckage of the plane were weapons, boots, and other supplies intended for the Contras. More damning were the logbooks detailing previous flights, itineraries of the equipment dropped, and paperwork tracing the operation back to Oliver North, who sat on Reagan's National Security Council.[45]

At his trial, Hasenfus freely confessed to having worked for the CIA's "Air America" in Southeast Asia and to knowing that the plane he was on contained military equipment destined for the Contras. He asked for leniency as he was only a "kicker," who loaded the plane and then pushed the cargo out of the hold at the right moment. Hasenfus further explained that he was not a CIA agent or a member of the military, but a private citizen who was hired at a rate of $3,000 per month.

This was embarrassing stuff for the Americans and public confirmation of what the Sandinistas had long been claiming: that the Reagan administration was illegally funding the Contras in their war on Nicaragua. But how were they paying for it? The Boland Amendment of 1982 prevented the United States from assisting the Contras in the overthrow of the Nicaraguan government. The answer was extraordinary.

On November 3, 1986, while Hasenfus was on trial in Managua, a story broke in Lebanese magazine *Ash-Shiraa* that the United States had been secretly selling missiles to the Islamic Republic of Iran, despite the virulent anti-Americanism of Ayatollah Ruhollah Khomeini. The Reagan administration was seeking the release of hostages being held in Lebanon by Hezbollah, over which Iran had considerable influence; Israel operated as the middleman to try to disguise the American hand in the sales. Reagan was forced to deliver a broadcast from the Oval Office to deny that he was exchanging arms for hostages. There was more to come. Attorney General Edwin Meese, investigating the arms deal, discovered that only $12 million of the $30 million was accounted for. Oliver North later admitted to a joint congressional committee that he had previously lied about what was done with the money and that it had been siphoned off to pay the Contras.

The scandal damaged Reagan badly—he suffered the single biggest approval rating drop of any president—but it did not destroy his presidency. Five members of his administration were found guilty of charges relating to the scandal but were later pardoned by George H. W. Bush (former Defense Secretary Casper Weinberger was also pardoned ahead of his trial). The United

States' global reputation was also damaged, both for its seeming willingness to negotiate with the terrorists of Hezbollah and for the underhanded support of the Contras. However, Reagan's appetite for regime change in Nicaragua abated. "Aid to the Contras stopped," Belli wrote, "and the Sandinista army gained ground, pushing large contingents of the rebel forces back to their camps in Honduras. With the Nicaraguan economy in shambles and the threat of diplomatic isolation over their heads, after the failure of a number of peace initiatives, the Sandinista leadership began talks with the Contras in Sapoá, near the Costa Rica border. Peace was desperately needed. We were all exhausted after so many years of war."[46]

Belli's own disenchantment with the Sandinistas continued to grow. It was a feeling many of her compatriots shared, especially those women, like Belli, who had been given leadership roles during the revolution but were now being marginalized. Daniel Ortega agreed to hold elections in 1989, and Belli was drafted in to work on the Sandinista electoral campaign. She wrote a proposal urging the party to make a plan in the event of defeat, but she was ignored. She was deemed a contrarian and, after one clash too many with the leadership, Ortega had her dismissed. She watched appalled as they staged a "bright, cheerful, Coca-Cola-style campaign" that jarred with the suffering of ordinary Nicaraguan people.[47] The Sandinistas lost the election and the revolution came to an end. The regime had survived being a pawn in the Cold War, manipulated and attacked on a number of fronts, only to be defeated by the votes of their own people.

THIRTY-ONE

Havel

PRAGUE, 1976–1990

ON MARCH 16, 1976, the secret police arrested nineteen people associated with Czechoslovakia's music underground, including all members of the psychedelic rock group the Plastic People of the Universe. Formed in the aftermath of the Warsaw Pact invasion of Czechoslovakia in August 1968, the band had become the leading light of a raucous underground music scene in Prague, with some of their songs set to the poetry of the iconic dissident Egon Bondy.[1] The band was named after a Frank Zappa song and took inspiration from experimental music of Captain Beefheart, Soft Machine, and Pink Floyd. The biggest influence, though, was the Velvet Underground, and just as the Velvets had Andy Warhol, so the Plastics took artistic direction from Ivan "Magor" Jirous, an art historian who believed the best way to fight back against the stultifying policies of the Communist regime of Gustáv Husák was to create a vibrant "second culture" that rejected the mainstream "permitted" culture.

Official hostility to the band increased throughout the seventies, with the police breaking up concerts and a documentary on state television claiming the group participated in drug-fueled orgies and animal sacrifices and, bizarrely, played the drums with dead rats.[2] The arrests—not just of members of the Plastics but other musicians, too—were not a huge surprise, with those detained accused of "disturbing the peace." The Czech authorities hoped the crackdown would be treated as criminal, rather than political, believing that the longhairs, with their eccentric clothes, hairstyles, and drug taking, would elicit little sympathy from the larger populace.[3] They had failed to reckon with one man, however. That was Václav Havel.

While the protests in response to the arrests involved many people, Havel was at the hub. To many observers, not least the secret police (the StB), the thirty-nine-year-old playwright was an unexpected ally. Sure, the bohemians he mixed with were no strangers to sexual adventure and hard drinking, but that did not stop him being associated with high culture; his plays were staged in theaters in Paris, London, and New York. He had heard some of the wild rumors about the lifestyles of this younger generation and was skeptical about their seriousness as a force of dissent. But a couple of weeks before the arrests, Havel had met with Jirous in Prague, listening to recordings of the band on a beat-up tape recorder and drinking and talking until 5 A.M. He came away convinced there was a "disturbing magic" to their music, a "profoundly authentic expression of the sense of life among these people."[4] It was a fateful encounter, bringing together the leaders of the literary and musical undergrounds. Jirous invited Havel to see the Plastics play live. Before the gig could take place, however, the band was locked up in prison.

Havel heard about the arrests while at Hrádecek, the countryside retreat where he sought respite from harassment by the authorities. While he was no longhair, he felt a sense of solidarity with these rebels and made straight for Prague, spurred on by the need to do something. Unlike many others in his circle, he felt the arrests were a sign that the regime had dramatically upped the stakes. "This case had nothing whatsoever to do with a struggle between two competing political cliques," he wrote. "It was something far worse: an attack by the totalitarian system on life itself, on the very essence of human freedom and integrity."

This was not, Havel concluded, just another crackdown on a political group deliberately provoking those in power—it carried much larger implications. "They were simply young people who wanted to live in their own way, to make music they liked, to sing what they wanted to sing, to live in harmony with themselves, and to express themselves in a truthful way," he wrote. "A judicial attack against them, especially one that went unnoticed, could become the precedent for something truly evil; the regime could well start locking up everyone who thought independently and who expressed himself independently, even if he did so only in private."[5]

Havel began organizing support, trying to combat the regime's propaganda in the state-controlled media, which depicted the defendants as alcoholics, drug addicts, and hooligans. "Perhaps a musical solo on a carpenter's plane, banging on cymbals tied together with a lady's bra, beating a car exhaust or splitting wood and throwing the logs to the mostly young audience is considered art in the West," one of these articles read. "Here, however, we are not interested."[6] To counter this narrative, Havel arranged both for a private appeal to Husák by leading intellectuals followed by a public statement warning of the risks posed to freedom of expression by the upcoming trial. Along with the novelists Pavel Kohout, Ivan Klíma, Ludvík Vaculík, and the poet Jaroslav Seifert, Havel wrote an open letter to Heinrich Böll, the German writer who two years before had taken in Aleksandr Solzhenitsyn after his deportation from the Soviet Union. The letter, and Böll's supportive response, were published in the West German newspaper *Frankfurter Allgemeine Zeitung*, and national newspapers in the United States and the United Kingdom soon picked up on the story.[7]

The public pressure appeared to have an effect; charges against most of those arrested were dropped, with only four going to trial: Pavel Zajicek, of the rock band DG 307; Svatopluk Kárasek, a Protestant minister and folk singer; Vratislav Brabenec, the saxophonist with the Plastics; and Jirous. The trial began on September 21, and Havel managed to get himself into the courtroom to observe the proceedings. He wrote up his experience in an essay, "The Trial," which circulated widely in samizdat. To Havel the playwright, the premeditated verdict gave the trial the air of a theatrical performance, but one that was not going the way it was supposed to go. The authorities were determined to show that this was a criminal trial like any other, crowding the defendants with police officers and keeping them in handcuffs even as they went to the bathroom. "The players in this spectacle found themselves in a paradoxical situation," Havel recounted. "The more candidly they played their role, the more clearly they revealed its unpremeditated significance, and thus they gradually became co-creators of a drama utterly different to the one they were playing in, or wanted to play in."[8] The proceedings veered from the agonizing to the absurd, and Havel on several occasions had to check the desire to shout in outrage. As expected, the defendants were found guilty, although not sentenced as harshly as the prosecutor demanded; Jirous got eighteen months, Zajicek got a year, Kárasek and Brabanec got eight months each.

For all the depressing predictability of the guilty verdicts, the trial had an extraordinary galvanizing effect on the opposition. What Havel called a "very special, improvised community" came together in the hallways of the district court. During breaks in proceedings the rockers and the intellectuals would retreat to the Malá Strana Café down the road to talk and make plans, followed there by gaggles of plainclothes police ("identifiable at once"). "Everyone seemed to feel that at a time when all the chips are down," Havel wrote, "there are only two things you can do: gamble everything, or throw in the cards." Havel and his allies chose to gamble.

HAVEL WAS BORN INTO A WEALTHY FAMILY, his paternal grandfather having made a fortune in property, including an entertainment complex in central Prague. His father, Václav Maria, took over the property business while his uncle, Miloš, established the biggest studio in the fledgling Czech film industry. His maternal grandfather was an engineer, a diplomat, a journalist, and a politician.[9] Havel's mother, Bozena, employed private tutors and supervised his education and that of his younger brother, Ivan. To preserve the family idyll, the families retreated to a country house during the Nazi occupation and, when the war ended, he was sent to an elite school housed in a thirteenth-century castle.[10]

At the end of the war, the Czechoslovak government had enjoyed good relations with Moscow. Unlike in other East and Central European nations, the Red Army had withdrawn, in November 1945. Free and fair elections were held in May 1946, in which the Communist Party enjoyed a number of electoral successes (Party membership had swelled from 50,000 to 1,220,000 in a year).[11] In 1947, at Moscow's request, Czechoslovakia rejected Marshall Plan aid, and the following February, at Stalin's behest, the Communist Party staged a political coup and seized control of the country. This was bad news for the Havels. Miloš was investigated because the Nazis had used his studios to make propaganda films; he was acquitted but because of his wealth and his homosexuality he was deemed "morally unfit" to work in the film industry. His studios were nationalized in 1949, and he spent two years in prison after trying to flee the country while awaiting trial. In 1952, with the help of American troops, he finally made it out via Vienna and settled in Munich.[12] Václav

Maria stuck it out in Prague but lost much of his business during the wave of nationalization.

Under Communist rule, Havel's school was closed. On returning to Prague, he discovered he had been labeled a "bourgeois element" and was no longer eligible for formal education beyond the age of fourteen. He spent his teenage years reading banned books and living through the anxiety of the Stalinist purges that resulted in hundreds of his countrymen being executed and tens of thousands imprisoned. In 1959, after having performed odd jobs and completed his military service, Havel became a stagehand and discovered his vocation. He worked his way up the hierarchy of jobs in the theater until, in 1963, his first play, *The Garden Party*, premiered at the Balustrade.

In Czechoslovakia, writers had far more freedom than in the Soviet Union or East Germany, and pushing the boundaries of what was acceptable to the authorities was a challenge artists like Havel embraced. *The Garden Party* was a revelation. Packed audiences were reduced to fits of laughter by the relentless satire of Communist bureaucracy and, despite the final line instructing the audience to leave ("And now, without sort of much ado—go home!"), they stayed and gave the cast round after round of applause.[13] Those who had seen it dragged along their friends to subsequent performances, and as *The Garden Party*'s reputation grew, fans would wait in line through the night to get tickets when the monthly box office opened.[14] The plot, such as it was, concerned a family sending out their son to a garden party of the Liquidation Office to secure himself a job, only for him to get into nonsensical and circular conversations with the functionaries he meets (and at one point he becomes responsible for the liquidating office deciding to liquidate itself). The recursive patterns resonated with a generation asphyxiated by layers of state bureaucracy, and people appropriated Havel's invented idioms and parodies of official jargon as catchphrases. The Balustrade also staged performances of plays by Samuel Beckett, Eugene Ionesco, and Alfred Jarry at the time, and Havel emerged as their impish Czech cousin.

The news that a major new playwright was at work in Prague soon spread. His next play, *The Memorandum*, performed at the Balustrade in 1965, attracted international attention. Like *The Garden Party*, it used absurdity to tackle the subject of totalitarian bureaucracy, only this time the satire was darker, springing from Havel's invented "scientific" language, "Ptydepe," analogous to Orwell's Newspeak. The play opens with Gross reading aloud a document (the memorandum of the title) written in what he takes to be gibberish—"Ra ko hutu d dekotu ely trebomu emusohe"—only to be informed that it is in fact the new "office language."[15] As we learn when Gross attends "Ptydepe Class," it is designed to make language less messy and more rational (getting rid of homonyms is one priority) and seeks efficiency through commonly used words having fewer letters (for example, "gh" means "whatever," apparently the most commonly used word). But because of a rule by which all words of the same length must differ from each other in at least 60 percent of their letters, the language descends swiftly into the absurd, as increasingly longer words need to be created (in the English translation, the Ptydepe instructor tells his class the longest word is "wombat," which is made up of 319 letters). By 1968 *The Memorandum* was playing at Joseph Papp's Public Theater in New York, in a translation by Vera Blackwell, a Czech émigré living in the UK.

At the height of the student protests in the city, Havel traveled to New York to see his play performed and hung out with Czech exiles, including his former schoolmate, the film director Milos Forman. He soaked up the atmosphere of a city in ferment and added a lot of new records to his musical collection, not least of which was *The Velvet Underground & Nico*. He gave interviews in which he called for an end to censorship and expressed hope for more cultural freedom back home.

When the Warsaw Pact forces invaded at the end of the summer, Havel was holed up in Liberec near the Polish border. "I saw Soviet tanks smash down arcades on the main square and bury several people in the rubble," he later recalled. "I saw a tank commander start shooting wildly into the crowd."[16] He had not been a particular vocal champion of Dubcek and his allies because he felt reforming Communism was not the answer—he argued instead for the introduction of a democratic party to compete with the Communist one in elections. But he certainly felt the country had been heading in the right direction, and when the Soviets intervened he threw himself into resistance work. In Liberec he helped produce radio and TV broadcasts, wrote speeches, and helped coordinate spontaneous actions to confuse the invaders. Havel was even responsible for an appeal to the writers of the world to unite in protest.[17] The invasion, Havel knew, was more than just another ideological crackdown; it was "the end of an era; the disintegration of a spiritual and social climate; a profound mental dislocation."[18]

Havel's work was banned by the Husák regime but while others, including the novelist Milan Kundera, went into exile, he stayed in Czechoslovakia and decided to publish in samizdat. The shift from being a satirical playwright to a dissident polemicist came with the open letter he wrote to Gustáv Husák in 1975, in which he accused the leader and his allies of having "chosen the easy way out for yourselves, and the most dangerous road for society: the path of inner decay for the sake of outward appearances; of deadening life for the sake of increasing uniformity; of deepening the spiritual and moral crisis of our society, and ceaselessly degrading human dignity, for the puny sake of protecting your own power."[19] It was not the kind of letter written in expectation of a friendly reply.

Through his dissidence, the countercultural kudos Havel had attained in the relatively liberal cultural atmosphere of the 1960s intensified. People read the letter to Husák, copied it, and passed it on. It soon found its way abroad, too, and was published first in—of all places—*Encounter.* The same year, Havel came up with creative ways of performing plays when he was banned from the theater. He wrote *Audience,* a one-act play for two actors, about his experience working as a casual laborer in a brewery (to be out of work risked being charged with social parasitism, so one took what work was available). During the course of the play Vanek, a disgraced playwright very much like Havel, is summoned to a meeting with his boss at the brewery who ends up, through much circular conversation, asking him to effectively inform on himself, all while progressively getting more and more drunk ("Want a beer?"). The play ends with Vanek coming back in and the meeting starting all over again, only this time, instead of telling the foreman he's fine, he tells him, "It's all a bloody mess."[20]

Havel had the idea to record a performance of *Audience* with him playing Vanek and his friend Pavel Landovsky, the flamboyant, brilliant, and blacklisted actor, as the brewery foreman. A recording was made in Prague and then smuggled out to Sweden, where it was released by the Safran record label, which was run by a group of Czech émigrés. Copies of the LP were then smuggled back into Czechoslovakia, where they circulated like a precious bootleg recording of a legendary gig. To his delight, Havel realized that people were reading or listening to his plays even if they could no longer see them performed in the theater. "I once picked up a hitchhiker and, without knowing who I was, he began to quote passages from that play," he recalled. "Or I'd be sitting in a pub and I'd hear young people shouting lines from the play to each other across the room."[21]

There was one public performance of a Havel play in November of that year, though. He had freely adapted John Gay's 1728 play *A Beggar's Opera*, and a group of amateurs planned to stage it in a restaurant in the eastern suburbs of Prague. Perhaps thinking the play was the original, or that it was Bertolt Brecht's adaptation (*The Threepenny Opera*), or just from sheer ineptitude, the local authorities gave the green light. "The performance was marvelous," Havel recalled, "the laughter and delight of the audience seemed endless, and for a moment I was back again in the atmosphere of the Theater on the Balustrade in the 1960s."[22] Embarrassed, the government cracked down hard on the theater community, promising more stringent censorship going forward. The fight was very much on.

THE PLASTIC PEOPLE TRIAL had helped unify different strands of cultural and political dissent. At clandestine meetings, some of the leading intellectuals of this emboldened movement began discussions that, by December, evolved into the drafting of a document that offered a defense of human rights and civic freedom, anchored in the Helsinki Accords, to which Czechoslovakia was a signatory. Havel authored the first draft of what became known as Charter 77 on December 16, 1976. It went through three further drafts, and three spokesmen for the declaration were nominated: Jirí Hájek, who had been foreign minister at the time of the Soviet-led invasion in 1968, the philosopher Jan Patocka, and Havel. The group, later known as the Chartists, began surreptitiously circulating the document, seeking the signatures of sympathizers.

They were careful about how they collected signatures. Rather than risk having one master document that might be confiscated at any moment, each contributor was asked to write out a short statement ("I agree with the Charter 77 declaration of Jan 1

1977") on a slip of paper and to add their address, occupation, and signature. For each signatory, this clarity made it obvious what they were getting into and much trickier to retract. In order to disguise their movements, the group decided to collect signatures between Christmas and New Year as the number of holiday parties would provide cover for their going all over town.

The plan proved successful at first, but when the secret police arrived, they did so in force. On December 10 one of their listening devices picked up a conversation between Havel and Kohout discussing a suspicious-sounding meeting between dissident figures, but it was not until January 5 that their surveillance discovered that documents of some kind were going to be transported the following day. The secret police launched an "emergency operation" with over a hundred uniformed and undercover officers, placing all of the suspects under surveillance.

In the chill of the morning of January 6, 1977, Havel tried and failed to start his Mercedes, not realizing that the StB had sabotaged it during the night by cutting the hydraulic lines.[23] He marched through the snowbound streets to the flat the group were using as a rendezvous. In another part of town, in the shadow of Prague Castle, Landovsky arrived at Kohout's apartment to pick up the signed documents. He spotted the plainclothes policemen as he approached. Kohout, too, realized he was being watched. Gesturing wildly, he communicated to Landovsky that he had hidden the materials in a toolbox in the communal landing of the building. Concealing the documents under his coat, Landovsky got into his car, a rusted-out old Saab, and drove to meet Havel, unexpectedly accompanied by Ludvík Vaculík, the writer, who had asked for a lift because he needed to visit a cobbler.

The plan had been to mail every signatory a copy of the Charter. As a result, the group had to lick and attach over 240 stamps to envelopes, which they would then stuff in different mailboxes in order to avoid arousing the suspicion of the postal services. As they made their final preparations, the conspirators were consumed with fits of nervous giggles. Heading back out into the cold, Landovsky spotted an Alfa Romeo that he suspected to be a secret police vehicle. The group piled into the rusty Saab, with Havel in the front passenger seat. It was his job to jump out and stuff envelopes into the mailboxes.

According to Landovsky, as soon as he pulled away in the Saab he realized he was being followed by a fleet of unmarked Skodas driven by the secret police.[24] He hit the gas and they sped into central Prague, hitting 70 mph. More cars joined the pursuit, their identities given away by the long antennas sticking out of them. Landovsky swerved down a side road, and two of the pursuers lost control in their attempt to follow and crashed into each other. Taking advantage of the confusion, Havel leapt out and crammed some forty letters into a mailbox. He dove back into the passenger seat just as the police approached and Landovsky sped off again, running a red light to get back onto the main thoroughfare of Lenin Street. They darted down another side street, but Landovsky was forced to break sharply when two police cars blocked the road. Before he could reverse, another two cars came up behind and blocked the exit. They were trapped.

"In a moment there were maybe eight cars in the street and about twenty guys rushed out of them at us," Landovsky later recalled. "I just locked all the doors from inside, so they couldn't get to us so easily." He turned to Havel and told him at least this way the police would waste some of their energy pounding on the car rather than beating them. "What a way to start a struggle for human rights!" Havel replied. The police, realizing they could not force their way in, slapped their StB ID cards on the windshield. Havel, convinced they had done nothing wrong—excepting the traffic offenses of course—decided to unlock his door. "They grabbed him and pulled him out like a rolled-up carpet, like a piece of pipe," Landovsky said. "All I saw were the shoes."[25] The other passengers were gathered up just as efficiently.

The situation then took a turn for the absurd, fit for one of Havel's plays. Landovsky was determined not to be taken quietly. He wrapped his arms around the steering wheel, clinging to it "like a leech," screaming (according to the police record of the incident) threats at the police the whole time.[26] A crowd began to assemble, attracted by all the noise. One of the police officers was filming the arrests on a camera, and when members of the public recognized the famous actor Landovsky they assumed they had stumbled onto a movie shoot. Realizing that the situation was spinning out of control, one of the officers got into the passenger seat and pulled his gun on the actor, ordering him to follow the police car ahead. "Holy shit, this is really screwed up!" the young police officer said. "We have been on alert since 2 A.M. What did you guys do, rob a bank or something?"[27] From the point of view of Husák and the Communist Party, they had done something much worse.

While the police managed to confiscate most of the copies of the Charter from Landovsky's vehicle, the majority of those that Havel had stuffed into the mailbox reached their recipients. Furthermore, thanks to the help of a press attaché at the West Germany Embassy, copies of Charter 77 made their way out to national newspapers in Britain, Germany, France, Italy, and the United States.[28] Despite the Charter spokesmen claiming the group was not an organization or a base for a political opposition, it became the center of gravity around which various dissident individuals and groups began to cohere. It also built bridges with the outside world. The publication was seized upon by President Carter, and the State Department issued a statement saying it "must strongly deplore" any violations of rights or freedoms.[29] Czechoslovakia was therefore the first country the

United States publicly criticized for failing to abide by the Helsinki Accords.

HAVEL KNEW THAT HUSÁK and his government would not accept the publication of Charter 77 meekly, and he steeled himself for their response. Within twenty-four hours of the car chase the Czech Politburo met and declared the Charter an "anti-state, counter-revolutionary document" and vowed to initiate criminal and "administrative" proceedings against the signatories. A wave of arrests, interrogations, and searches followed, and many Chartists lost their jobs. The government organized a televised event at the National Theater, at which actors, directors, and playwrights were coerced into signing a document condemning "the renegades and traitors" of the movement.[30] Havel, after a punishing series of StB interrogations, was finally arrested and charged with subversion on January 16. The arrest sparked international outrage, with some speculating that Moscow had ordered the apprehension as a way of sending a message to East European dissidents.

Such began a grueling period in Havel's life in which he was either in prison or, when outside, harassed by surveillance, arbitrary arrests, and interrogations. Havel had helped persuade Patocka, the philosopher, to become one of the Charter's three spokesmen but, at seventy, he struggled to withstand the rounds of interrogation. After one eleven-hour ordeal he complained of feeling unwell and died not long after of a heart attack. Havel felt culpable. He struggled to adapt to life in prison and was naive when it came to interrogation. The StB tricked him into thinking large numbers of signatories had abandoned the Charter and that the movement had collapsed. They applied further pressure by indicting him not for his work on the Charter but for smuggling literature out of Czechoslovakia. In a moment of weakness, he petitioned the prosecutor for his release, claiming that the Charter's purpose had been distorted by the foreign media and that he would henceforth refrain from engaging in political activity.[31] When he was released from pretrial custody in May, the entreaty was gleefully published by the state press.

Having realized his mistake and fueled by his shame at having failed to stand strong, he redoubled his efforts in the dissident cause. In April 1978, to advocate for those jailed after the publication of the Charter, those still at liberty established the Committee for the Unjustly Persecuted (VONS). Havel joined the sixteen-strong committee and participated in clandestine meetings with Polish dissidents at secret locations near the border between the two countries. One of these gatherings was raided by the secret police on both sides, but Havel escaped, once again accompanied by Landovsky, by hiding in the woods and navigating back to the local town by a cable-car track.[32]

Despite such efforts by the authorities, the movement was making connections and growing. Havel sensed that this movement needed galvanizing. In the summer of 1978 Havel retreated to his summer house and began to write. The result was not a play but a long essay-manifesto: "The Power of the Powerless." "A specter is haunting Eastern Europe," Havel wrote, "the specter of what in the west is called 'dissent.'"[33] It was a bold opening for two reasons. First, it deliberately and provocatively evoked the opening line of the *Communist Manifesto;* second, it was addressed not just to the Czechoslovak people but to all Eastern Europeans. But what, Havel asked in a barrage of rhetorical questions, is this "dissent"? Who are the dissidents? Where do they come from? He culminated with the key question of the whole essay: "Can they actually change anything?"

Clarifying these terms was crucial to Havel. He believed that dissidents *could* change things, but only if the definition of *dissent* were more broadly applied than it had been. In the West, dissidents were largely understood as celebrated individuals or small groups of intellectual activists, but this type of opposition, Havel argued, would change nothing in a place like Czechoslovakia. Under Husák, he explained, the country had become a "post-totalitarian system," by which Havel did not mean it had ceased to be totalitarian, just that it was totalitarian in a different way to the traditional formulation of dictatorship.[34] In this system the oppression was less immediately obvious but almost totally pervasive, largely because the people themselves had been coerced into maintaining its protocols. To dissent therefore meant throwing off the conditioned behavior that infiltrated everyday life and demanded participation in the construction of a statewide fiction. Ordinary people needed to become dissidents.

His famous example was that of the grocer who places in his shop window, among his vegetables, a sign that reads, "Workers of the world, unite!" Havel argued that the grocer did it not because he believed in the slogan but because it was easier to do it than to not. "If he were to refuse," Havel wrote, "there would be trouble."[35] By placing the sign in his shop front, the grocer is effectively saying, "I am afraid and therefore unquestioningly obedient."[36] But if he refused, Havel argued, he would be "living within the truth" and, as a consequence, would peel back the facade and expose the weak struts erected to prop up the post-totalitarian society.

Both the Plastic People of the Universe and Charter 77 were examples of people trying to live "within the truth."[37] It was clear that the regime feared anyone who behaved in this way and acted swiftly to suppress them. "Why was Solzhenitsyn driven out of his own country?" Havel wrote. "Certainly not because he represented a unit of real power, that is, not because any of the regime's representatives felt he might unseat them and take his place in government. Solzhenitsyn's expulsion was something else: a desperate attempt to plug up the wellspring of truth, a truth which might cause incalculable transformations in social consciousness, which in turn might one day produce political debacles unpredictable in their consequences."[38] If with *Gulag Archipelago* Solzhenitsyn had documented the great crime of the Communist regime in the Soviet Union, with "The Power of the Powerless," Havel spoke about fighting back against the small crimes, the everyday oppression in "normalized" Communist society. What both had in common was that they threatened to unravel their respective regimes by pulling persistently on the truth.

There were only two possibilities for the future, Havel declared. Either the post-totalitarian system would persist and evolve and result in "some dreadful Orwellian vision of a world of absolute manipulation," or the "independent life of society" would continue to grow in strength until society changed.[39] It was an argument that empowered its readers, giving value to their small acts of dissidence.

Even as he was writing the essay, the authorities ramped up their harassment. He was followed everywhere by the police, and the road to his summer house was blocked by a pile of gravel and a sign that read "No Entry." Police officers stationed on the road leading to Havel's property warned visitors that they entered "at their own risk."[40] The police even sabotaged the home's plumbing and heating pipes. One night, Landovsky, visiting his friend, discovered a wire the police had fed into the house, presumably for eavesdropping. Under cover of dark, he and Havel gleefully rolled it up and sold it at a local market the following morning.[41] When the Havels visited Prague, they discovered the police camped on the landing outside their apartment, preventing anyone from going in and out. The situation was too much for Havel to bear, and the couple returned to the countryside. By Christmas the authorities had erected a watchtower overlooking

Havel's house. He nicknamed it "Lunokhod," because it looked like the lunar rover the Soviets landed on the moon.

The escalating harassment reached its logical end point in May 1979. As ever, the police were dogged by embarrassing ineptitude as they sought his arrest. Havel and his wife, Olga, had an unconventional relationship by this stage, something like an open marriage, and when the police kicked down the door of Havel's Prague apartment he was nowhere to be found. Another group raided his country house but found only his wife, Olga. It took them hours to track him down at the flat of his lover, Anna Kohoutova, ex-wife of his fellow Chartist Pavel Kohout. (The arrest came as no surprise; like Solzhenitsyn, Havel traveled with a "prison bag" of essential supplies, including the Czech translation of Ken Kesey's *One Flew Over the Cuckoo's Nest*.)[42]

It was a brutally hot summer, and conditions in the prison were miserable. As he awaited trial, Havel went on hunger strike, but it had no effect except to make him weaker. Still, there was a possible way out. The Czechoslovak government knew that a trial would attract international outrage and tried to avoid the scandal by offering Havel the opportunity of going to New York for a year on a theatrical fellowship (something instigated by the Czech film director Milos Forman and negotiated between the U.S. State Department and the Czech Foreign Ministry; it was unclear what would happen when he tried to return). After consultation with Olga, he turned it down.

The trial took place in October and lasted just two days. Havel and five other members of VONS were found guilty of subversion. He was sentenced to four and a half years in jail. After a failed appeal, Havel was taken to Hermanice prison in Ostrava in the east of the country, near the Polish border.

Sure enough, there was an outpouring of support for Havel, including diplomatic protests. The U.S. government denounced the verdict and the sentences and accused the Husák regime of violating the Helsinki Accords. Condemnation came from the governments of Britain, France, and Sweden, and even from the Communist Parties of Italy, France, and Spain. The U.S. withdrew its ambassador, and the French foreign minister canceled a scheduled visit, as did envoys from Italy and Sweden. Pope John Paul II also condemned the convictions. There were protests by students outside the Czech cultural center in Warsaw, and Polish dissidents expressed their solidarity with the jailed Chartists. Nevertheless, despite fearing the economic consequences of becoming a pariah state, the StB continued to arrest people associated with Charter 77.

To Havel, the most meaningful support came from his fellow writers. E. L. Doctorow, Arthur Miller, and Kurt Vonnegut led a protest in front of the Czechoslovak mission to the United Nations, and the case was taken up by the American branch of PEN. Another writers' organization, the Authors League of America, sent Husák a letter of protest, signed by Edward Albee, Donald Barthelme, Ralph Ellison, Allen Ginsberg, and William Styron, among others. Playwrights were particular supportive of Havel, including Samuel Beckett and Harold Pinter. In Germany, Heinrich Böll and Günter Grass banged the drum.

Among Havel's most dedicated and vocal supporters was the British playwright Tom Stoppard, who was born in Prague to Czech parents. A fan of Havel's plays and himself already interested in the suppression of writers behind the Iron Curtain through his work with Amnesty International, Stoppard was prompted by Havel's initial arrest in January 1977 to write *Professional Foul*, a television script about an exiled Czech professor who returns to Prague and becomes involved with student dissidents. The resulting show was screened on the BBC three times in the months leading up to Havel's trial and won numerous awards; in his promotional work Stoppard drew public attention to Havel's plight. Stoppard even acted in a dramatization of the Charter trial, staged in Munich in 1980.[43] The pair became friends, and Stoppard dedicated *Rock and Roll*, a play inspired by the Plastic People trial, to Havel.

From his earlier taste of it, Havel knew that prison life would be tough. He was forced to work as a welder and perform other strenuous jobs that, as a forty-three-year-old playwright, he was not used to dealing with. In Hermanice he was bullied by a sadistic warden and, after one fifteen-day stint in solitary confinement, fell seriously ill and had to be transferred to a prison hospital. Fearing that Havel's death would cause a scandal, the authorities moved him to a prison near Pilsen, where he was given a comparatively cushy job in the laundry room.[44]

After 1,351 days, Havel was granted an early release after being landed back in the hospital with a severe chest infection. Once again, the authorities were anxious that Havel might die on their watch. When he emerged from prison on March 4, 1983, he was weak and exhausted. Husák and his Politburo hoped that incarceration was his final curtain, that he would have finally realized that his dissident ambition had overreached itself; perhaps he would retreat to his country house and start writing plays again.

They were mistaken. Havel had suffered and there had been moments when he felt like giving up and fleeing abroad, but he had survived those tests. The authorities had misjudged: this was only the beginning of the third act. And it was not the downfall of Havel that was driving the plot.

IN APRIL 1987, Havel left his apartment in central Prague and took his dog for a walk. The streets were packed with "endless rows of parked limousines and a vast number of policemen" and, as he made his way toward the National Theater, the crowd began to thicken. Pulled along by the dog, he made his way through the crowd until he got to the entrance to the theater. There he waited. After only a few minutes, the limousines started up their engines and bodyguards appeared. From the theater emerged Mikhail Gorbachev.

The atmosphere changed. Havel had been amused to hear the crowd winding up the secret policemen charged with keeping the peace, but no sooner had Gorbachev come into view than they were cheering enthusiastically. "I feel sad," Havel wrote, "this nation of ours never learns. How many times has it put all its faith in some external force which, it believed, would solve all its problems?" Gorbachev made his way slowly to the waiting car, waving to those shouting his name. And then suddenly he was right by Havel. He was, to Havel's mind, "rather short and stocky, a cuddly ball-like figure hemmed in by his gigantic bodyguards."[45] To Havel's surprise, he found his contempt replaced by pity: he felt sorry for the Soviet leader. Havel recalled chastising himself for going soft like that—after all, Gorbachev had just recently praised the very Husák regime that had crushed the life out of Czechoslovakia for almost two decades. Then Havel was caught off guard again. "Gorbachev [. . .] is walking just a few yards away from me," Havel wrote, "waving and smiling his friendly smile—and suddenly he seems to be waving and smiling at *me*." Before he even realized what he was doing, Havel waved back. Neither man could have known that they would meet again in very different circumstances.[46]

The reason the crowd was so enthused by Gorbachev came down to two words: *perestroika* and *glasnost*. The literal meaning of *perestroika* is "restructuring" and it was used as a blanket term to cover the reforms that Gorbachev had instituted since becoming general secretary in 1985. The translation of *glasnost* was "openness," and it was in this spirit that the reforms of pere-stroika were being undertaken. After years of a musty, gray haze, Gorbachev was throwing open the Soviet blinds.

UNDER BREZHNEV the Soviet Union had been run by a para-noid gerontocracy that, in the words of the historian Robert Service, was "locked into a condition of collective denial."[47] It was an era of economic, cultural, and social stagnation at home, and the country was mired in a disastrous war in Afghanistan. After Brezhnev, Yuri Andropov, the former head of the KGB, took over. While he was responsible for a more reform-minded agenda than Brezhnev (and even helped promote Gorbachev), he lasted just over a year before dying of renal failure at sixty-nine. Andropov looked positively sprightly compared to his successor, Konstantin Chernenko, whom historian John Lewis Gaddis described as an "enfeebled geriatric so zombie-like as to be beyond assessing intelligence reports, alarming or not."[48] He also lasted just over a year but spent most of that time in the hospital before succumbing to a cocktail of emphysema, heart disease, and cirrhosis (so decrepit was the Soviet leadership throughout the seventies and early eighties that they installed an escalator to the beach at the holiday dacha on the Black Sea coast).[49]

On March 11, 1985, Mikhail Gorbachev was elected unan-imously by the Politburo to become general secretary of the Communist Party of the Soviet Union. After Chernenko, this was a new type of leader: Gorbachev was, by Politburo standards, a youthful fifty-six, cultivated, well traveled, full of energy and new ideas.[50] And new ideas were needed. Indeed, the Soviet state was in no better health than Chernenko had been. Gor-bachev inherited an empire in crisis: an already stagnant econ-omy was put under severe pressure by the dramatic drop in price of raw material exports; these problems were exacerbated by the amount of money being spent on the military and propping up foreign allies; relations with other world powers had regressed.[51] During the seventies, the OPEC crisis had driven up the price of oil, allowing the Soviet Union to mask its economic problems by drawing on its petroleum reserves. With global oil prices stabilizing and the reserves dwindling, those days were coming to an end, and KGB analyses painted a bleak picture of what was ahead. The more Gorbachev learned, the more he believed the Politburo failed to grasp the true scale of the problem. If the Soviet Union was to be saved, it needed to be reformed.

With no time to lose, Gorbachev and his allies initiated a program of perestroika designed to liberalize both the economic and political system. To make sure these reforms worked and to bring an end to rampant corruption, there needed to be a cultural change, hence glasnost. Gorbachev wanted to encourage accountability and transparency in government, in part by ending censorship and persecution of dissenting opinions. In order to surmount the problems facing the Soviet Union, he believed the people needed to know the truth about what these problems were.

What crystallized the growing crisis was the war in Afghanistan. The invasion of Afghanistan had finished off an already enfeebled détente; relations with the United States and its Western European allies were once more hostile, and those with China and Japan were little better. Furthermore, to many in the Third World, it looked like a return to Soviet belligerence and neo-imperial regime change. And it was not as if this international isolation was a price worth paying for a necessary war. Soviet military spending was 25 percent of GDP compared to 6.25 percent in the United States, and therefore perpetuating conflict had a direct impact on standards of living at home. Despite the best efforts of the propaganda organs it was clear that the Afghanistan war was not going well. The Red Army was stuck in a bloody stalemate with guerrilla forces that were well equipped and knew the hostile territory inside out. The human costs were hard to calculate. By the end of the war it was estimated that there were 1.3 million Afghan dead, 2 million internally displaced, and 5 million fled as refugees.[52] The Red Army lost 14,500 men, with more than twice as many wounded (although these numbers were long kept from the public). Corruption was rife and war crimes common. Many of those soldiers that came back suffered from PTSD and addiction.

If Gorbachev wanted to dial down the intensity of the Cold War and set the Soviet Union on the path of domestic reform, he needed to end the war in Afghanistan. Just three days after Chernenko's funeral, Gorbachev met with Afghan President Babrak Karmal and told him that (according to Lenin) a revolution had to be able to defend itself, and therefore Soviet forces could not remain in Afghanistan indefinitely.[53] The message was clear. To sweeten the pill, Gorbachev offered a short-term surge in military forces and a boost to financial aid but only as tied to a scaled withdrawal.[54]

By the spring of 1986, Gorbachev told the Twenty-Seventh Congress of the Communist Party that the war was a "bleeding wound," and by the end of the year he told the Politburo that the new surge strategy was not working and that they needed to get their troops out by 1988 at the latest.[55] Still, as determined as he was to end the conflict, Gorbachev feared the domestic ramifications of admitting defeat. "A million of our soldiers went through Afghanistan," he said in February 1987. "And we will not be able to explain to our people why we did not complete [the war]. We suffered such terrible losses. For what? We undermined the prestige of our country, brought about so much bitterness. Why did we lose all those boys?"[56]

Nevertheless, by then, Gorbachev was resolved in his determination to pivot away from interventionist foreign policy so as to focus on domestic perestroika. The Warsaw Pact states were all deep in debt to Western banks and with little prospect of stimulating their economies. As a result, resentment was building against the ruling Communist parties and, by extension, the Soviet Union. The change in policy was so dramatic it was hard to credit. In December 1986, Gorbachev went to India to meet with Prime Minister Rajiv Gandhi and, in the Delhi Declaration, made a commitment to national self-determination that would have been heresy under previous rulers.[57] Previous attempts by nations in the Soviet Bloc to assert autonomy (most notably in Hungary in 1956 and Czechoslovakia in 1968) had been crushed under the tracks of Soviet tanks, but Gorbachev was determined that those days were over. The ramifications were huge.

These changes in Moscow brought hope for those in Eastern Europe seeking reform. In August 1980, Lech Wałęsa, a young Polish electrician, led a strike against rising food prices at the Lenin shipyard in Gdansk, which swiftly spread to factories around the country. In negotiating the end of the strike, the Polish government agreed to the legalization of an independent trade union: Solidarity. The following year, the union had almost 10 million members. Under huge pressure from the Soviet Union and members of the Warsaw Pact, including the threat of invasion, the Polish government, led by General Wojciech Jaruzelski, introduced martial law and arrested five thousand influential members of Solidarity.[58] With the policies of perestroika taking effect in the Soviet Union, Jaruzelski's government was painted into a corner. The economy was in a desperate state, with productivity flat and debt payments growing ever more unaffordable. Despite modest efforts at reform, Polish workers again went on strike in 1988.

In Hungary, which in the previous decades had been the most

liberal of the Warsaw Pact governments, the possibility of far-reaching changes were debated with relative freedom, and the aging János Kádár was replaced with the reform-minded Károly Grósz. Even in East Germany, where the Stasi employed ninety thousand full-time employees and more than one hundred thousand unofficial informants, an opposition movement was growing around the Protestant churches, unified around issues of human rights and nuclear disarmament.[59]

Yet in Czechoslovakia there appeared nothing but stasis. Gorbachev's visit raised hopes, but he merely offered support to the Husák regime, and it was not until December 1987 that there was any kind of concession on the part of the government that the climate was changing. Milos Jakes replaced Husák as general secretary, but he was hardly an improvement: the regime appeared to be sticking to its policy of stagnant normalization. Even worse, the secret police drew up plans to have thousands of dissidents arrested—with Havel's name prominent.[60]

In the face of government inaction, dissident groups mobilized. What Havel called the "parallel structure" or "second culture" was flourishing in the theater, at art exhibitions, and in music concerts. More writers, performers, and artists were taking risks. Czechs were speaking their mind in public and not just those associated with the Charter or VONS. People were beginning to live in truth—and Havel was there to see it. He attended as many relevant events as he could manage, and he was frequently greeted as a hero. At one music festival in Bohemia, he was invited onstage to speak between sets and was treated with as much adulation as the rock stars, including being chased for his autograph.[61] He was still writing plays and thought of himself as a literary person but, whether he liked it or not, the rapidly growing democratic opposition viewed him differently. They saw someone who had spoken up when others did not have the will or the courage. They saw someone who, by having that courage, had landed himself in prison. They saw a man who had articulated what it would take to bring down the corrupt and stagnant system. They saw a different kind of politician. They saw a leader.

THE DENOUEMENT HAPPENED FAST. As unrest grew, protests were planned for symbolic anniversaries. On August 21, 1988, the twentieth anniversary of the Soviet suppression of the Prague Spring, some ten thousand people marched into Wenceslas Square. On October 28, the seventieth anniversary of the independence of Czechoslovakia, another ten-thousand-strong crowd marched through central Prague, this time greeted by police with dogs, riot shields, and water cannons. Havel was not among them, having been detained by the authorities as a precaution the previous day. He was also arrested immediately after opening the "Czechoslovakia 88" symposium, a gathering organized by Charter 77 in collaboration with other activist groups to discuss human rights. It was clear those in power feared him.

On December 10 came the fortieth anniversary of the signing of the Universal Declaration of Human Rights. Opposition groups were denied the opportunity to host their rally in Wenceslas Square but were allowed to stage it in a less central part of Prague. Approximately a thousand people showed up and heard Havel, released after his most recent arrest, declare through a megaphone that the country "was beginning to recover from its long slumber."[62] Not only did the authorities allow this smaller rally to take place, but the security services did not break it up. Was this a sign they were ready to tolerate dissent? Was it a sign of weakness?

On January 16, 1989, the Chartists helped organize a protest to commemorate the anniversary of the death of Jan Palach, a student who had burned himself to death in 1969 under the statue of St. Wenceslas in protest at the suppression of the Prague Spring. Havel was twice arrested in the lead-up to the anniversary and was warned of dire consequences should any protests take place. Despite the police doing their best to cordon off the square, some five thousand protesters made it through and were violently dispersed. As they were attacked, they chanted, "Long live Havel."

The following day, some demonstrators returned and were swiftly dealt with by the police. Havel was among those arrested. The day after that, twice as many people showed up. The police redoubled their efforts and began beating the protesters with violent excess. Still they came back every day of that week. Havel, meanwhile, was sentenced to nine months for incitement; a petition for his release rapidly garnered three thousand signatures.[63] With pressure from its own citizens and foreign governments, the authorities lost their nerve, and in May Havel was released early for good behavior. Within weeks he coauthored a set of demands under the title "A Few Sentences" that attracted forty thousand signatures of support.

Havel's star was ascendant. When Joan Baez played a gig at a music festival in Bratislava in June, she dedicated a song to Charter 77 and introduced Havel, who was in the audience. (Havel had taught her how to say this in phonetic Czech.) Moments later the secret police cut the power and killed the TV feed.[64] In October, the police again sought to arrest Havel, fearing he might lead a rally on Independence Day, but found him home sick. He was transferred to a local hospital and, when the news spread, crowds gathered outside chanting his name. The rally went ahead in his absence and, in Prague's Realistické theater, excerpts from *The Garden Party* were included in the independence commemorations.

By then, the pressure on the Czechoslovak government was mounting, as it was across Eastern Europe. Gorbachev had decided that the Warsaw Pact countries were to be granted "unconditional independence, full equality, strict non-interference in internal affairs, and rectification of deformities and mistakes linked with earlier periods in the history of socialism."[65] If he was to be trusted, then there would be no repeat of 1968 in terms of Soviet intervention.

It was not just in Eastern Europe that a young generation was pushing back against the Communist state. In April, student demonstrations demanding democratic reform spread to all the major cities of China. In Beijing, protesters occupied the central Tiananmen Square. When Gorbachev arrived in May—the first visit of a Soviet leader in thirty years—he could hear his name being chanted outside the Great Hall of the People. After Gorbachev returned to Moscow, Chinese leader Deng Xiaoping ordered the military to forcefully break up the demonstration. On June 4, the military moved in, killing hundreds of protesters; thousands of others were imprisoned or went into exile. The dream of political reform died, but Deng continued on a path of economic reform. There was no cultural glasnost in China, only perestroika in the marketplace.

The same day that the tanks rolled into Tiananmen Square, Poland was heading to the polls. For the first time since the beginning of the Cold War, the country held multiparty elections and, of the 161 contested parliamentary seats, Solidarity won 160. The Communist Party tried to cling to power, but the defeat was comprehensive, and, by the end of August, Poland had a non-Communist government. Gorbachev made it clear that he would not intervene in Polish domestic affairs.

Later that month the Hungarian authorities staged the reburial of Imre Nagy, the leader of the 1956 revolution, in a symbolic break with the past, clearly nationalist and anti-Soviet

(Nagy had been executed after the Soviet invasion) in intent. Gorbachev did not object. At the funeral, Viktor Orban, a member of the Fidesz movement, gave a speech demanding the withdrawal of Soviet troops and democratic elections.

In East Germany, Erich Honecker sought to stem the tide. He berated Hungary and Czechoslovakia for letting East Germans use their borders to cross into West Germany and was publicly critical of Gorbachev's reform policies. When Honecker made the decision to close the borders to other Warsaw Pact countries, anger among the trapped population began to swell. The situation came to a head on October 9 in Leipzig, where a large protest had been planned. The police were equipped with live rounds, and the hospitals were primed for mass casualties. That it did not turn into a German version of Tiananmen was due to the discipline of the more than seventy thousand supporters, who ensured they kept the march around the Leipzig ring road peaceful, and to Helmut Hackenberg, the Leipzig party secretary, defying orders to "choke off" the protest and instead ordering the security forces to take up a defensive position.[66]

The following week 120,000 East Germans marched in Leipzig; the week after, 300,000. The Central Committee, realizing that something had to be done, voted Honecker out. The new general secretary, Egon Krenz, promised to negotiate with representatives of the opposition movement and to open up the borders, including adopting a more liberal policy toward travel.

On the morning of November 9, some especially eager bureaucrats exceeded their brief and came up with a reformed travel law that opened all borders, including the one running through divided Berlin. The law was passed by the Politburo during a smoking break and then it took just eight minutes for the Central Committee to approve it, with nobody actually bothering to read it. The new law also stated that the policy change would immediately go into effect. A confused Krenz claimed the law had received approval from Moscow when in fact only a draft had been approved. Furthermore, a distracted Krenz handed the announcement of the new law to Günther Schabowski, the most senior government spokesman, instead of the junior spokesman who was supposed to release the news at 4 A.M. the next morning. Schabowski promptly took it with him to a televised press conference.[67] When he read the law for the first time—live on air—the disbelieving reporters began shouting out questions. Schabowski confirmed that the law was to come into effect "immediately, forthwith," then fled the room.[68] Tom Brokaw, the American broadcaster, heard his German sound technician say it was the end of the Cold War.

The news spread rapidly. Crowds of East Berliners made their way to the border crossings and demanded to be let through (among them a young Angela Merkel). At midnight a veteran border guard at the Bornholmer Street crossing opened the gate.[69] As the people flowed into West Berlin, other barriers opened at checkpoints along the wall. By the next morning, Germans on both sides began dismantling the wall and with it, the most potent symbol of the Cold War in Europe.

THE FALL OF THE BERLIN WALL accelerated the protests in Prague. A large rally was planned for December, and Havel retreated to his country house to gather his strength. On November 17, however, a march organized by student groups refused to follow the official course and, chanting pro-Havel and antigovernment slogans, was brutally attacked by the police. A rumor went around that one of the students had been killed and, despite there being no truth to the story, it was soon being broadcast as fact around the country.

Havel rushed to Prague. With the secret police swarming the streets, the opposition leadership needed a place to meet. They decided, fittingly enough, on a theater. On the stage of the Actors' Studio, Havel presided over a meeting of leading activists at which the Civic Forum was born. The new group's declaration (which Havel had drafted that morning) demanded the resignation of the Communist leadership, an investigation into the violence used against protesters, and the freeing of all political prisoners. The declaration also picked up on one of the student demands: a national strike for the following week.

A day later, Monday, November 21, people poured into the streets as the Velvet Revolution entered its endgame (the name, which connoted the nonviolent nature of the uprising, was coined by Rita Klímová, the movement's English translator). Some 150,000 packed Wenceslas Square. Havel and his allies realized they needed to act before the government did anything stupid, and used their connections to secure a balcony overlooking the square. Havel's friends in the rock and roll world helped secure a rig to broadcast the speeches. Havel understood what an audience wanted, and he made sure to create a popular set alternating political speeches with performances by previously banned musicians. Eventually the festivities had to be moved to Letná Park in the north of the city to accommodate the more than one million people who wanted to attend.

On November 24 the leadership of the Communist Party resigned. The following day, to the delight of the crowd on Wenceslas Square, Alexander Dubcek, the popular leader of the Prague Spring, appeared on the balcony alongside Havel. Here were the two most credible candidates to lead a new Czechoslovakia. Dubcek was desperate to get a second chance at running his country, but after several private meetings with Havel, including one in the dressing room of the Laterna Magika theater, he somewhat reluctantly agreed to let the younger man take on the presidency on the understanding that it would be his turn next.[70] The Civic Forum had already begun negotiating a peaceful transfer of power with the Communist Party, and the Federal Assembly voted to introduce multiparty democracy. On December 29, 1989, amid a carnival atmosphere in Prague, Dubcek formally nominated Havel as president. The banned playwright became head of state.

IT WAS IMMEDIATELY APPARENT that the Havel regime was going to bring a totally different approach to government. His unorthodox cabinet—nicknamed the "bag of fleas"—was made up of an assortment of actors, directors, and writers. The new head of foreign intelligence, Oldrich Cerny, a former film translator, was selected in part because of his fondness for the work of John le Carré.[71] Havel ordered the decor of his offices in Prague Castle to be revamped and asked Theodor Pistek, who had won an Oscar for costume design on Milos Forman's *Amadeus,* to come up with a new uniform for the Castle Guard.[72]

Havel was swamped by well-wishers from around the world. Lou Reed came to interview him for *Rolling Stone* but forgot to switch on the tape recorder. Paul Simon performed to a crowd in Old Town Square. Havel flew the Rolling Stones in on his presidential plane to play a gig to one hundred thousand fans in Prague. Mick Jagger told Havel he was a big fan of his work, especially the "Letter to Husák," and the band appeared alongside the new leader on the presidential balcony. Frank Zappa, the inspiration for the Plastic People of the Universe, arrived on the invitation of Havel and left as "the roving Czechoslovak envoy plenipotentiary in matters cultural and commercial."[73]

Amid the partying, Havel was doing his best to keep up with the demands of governing. He issued a vast amnesty by which twenty-three thousand prisoners were released from jail (all but the most violent offenders) and had to persuade the populace that building for the future, rather than retribution for crimes of the past, was a priority. Also rumbling along was the issue of potential Slovakian independence. Just as pressing was the need to forge new relationships between Czechoslovakia and the rest of the world. That meant trips to both Washington and Moscow.

Having been invited by President George H. W. Bush, Havel arrived at the White House on February 20. He asked for political, but not economic, support, spoke of the need to disband the Cold War power blocs of the Warsaw Pact and NATO, and encouraged Bush to back both the reunification of Germany and democratic reform in Russia.[74] The following day he addressed a joint session of Congress and received rapturous applause before flying down to New York City, ditching the suit for jeans and a sweater and hitting up the legendary rock club CBGB. At the various receptions and parties held in his honor, Havel was treated like a rock star himself. American writers came out to pay their respects, including Edward Albee, Norman Mailer, Arthur Miller, William Styron, and Kurt Vonnegut.[75] At one particularly raucous event at the Czechoslovak Embassy in Washington, Havel was presented with a ceremonial pipe by a representative of a Native American tribe.[76]

After a brief stopover back in Prague, Havel headed for Moscow. On the flight Havel and his team, over bottles of beer, drafted a joint declaration with felt pen. The priority was to get the garrisons of the Red Army—some seventy thousand troops—to leave Czechoslovakia. At the Kremlin, Havel was taken aback by how cooperative Gorbachev proved. He read the drafted declaration and approved the withdrawal of troops, but asked that in return there be no retribution taken against members of the Communist Party. It was agreed that, going forward, both countries would respect each other's sovereignty. Havel then proposed celebrating their new agreement by lighting up the pipe he had brought back from the United States. "Mr. President," Havel said, after telling the story of how he had acquired it, "it occurred to me right there and then that I should bring this pipe to Moscow and that the two of us should smoke it together as a pipe of peace." Gorbachev, after all a child of the humorless Kremlin, was baffled. "But I . . . I don't smoke."

More solemn was the visit Havel paid to the outskirts of Moscow, to the grave of Andrei Sakharov, surrounded by birches and pines. The great dissident had died in December 1989 and Havel wanted to pay his respects to both Sakharov's fight for democratic reform within the Soviet Union and for his having declared support for Charter 77 back when it was dangerous to do so. He was accompanied on this pilgrimage by Larisa Bogoraz, the Russian dissident who had fought the cause of her husband, Yulii Daniel, and his friend, Andrei Sinyavsky, so courageously back in 1966. She was also one of the "group of six" who had dared to protest the invasion of Czechoslovakia in 1968 in Red Square.

The dissidents had won. Poland and Hungary were now multiparty democracies. Germany was on the path to reunification. Other countries had less peaceful transitions. In Bulgaria the Communist Party won the first free elections when they were held in June 1990, in part by appealing to nationalist, anti-Islamic sentiments among voters.[77] In Romania, the independent-minded Nicolae Ceauşescu was not prepared to go easily. After growing protests around the country that focused on Romania's economic crisis, violence erupted in Bucharest and hundreds were killed. Ceauşescu escaped by helicopter before the protesters could get hold of him, but he was arrested northwest of the city, and executed on Christmas Day 1989. The Iron Curtain was drawn back, and Central and Eastern Europe emerged blinking into a new era. On July 1, 1991, the Warsaw Pact was formally disbanded.

THIRTY-TWO

Greene, Solzhenitsyn & Le Carré

MOSCOW, 1986–1991

THERE WAS NO CLEARER SIGNAL of the end of the Cold War than the return of the books. With the Soviet Union teetering between liberal reform and existential crisis, the shelves of bookshops began to fill with previously banned literature. To ordinary Russian readers it was an extraordinary bounty, as if the great writers of the previous century had all decided to publish their best work within the space of a couple of years of each other. Between 1986 and 1988, masterpiece after masterpiece emerged from special locked archives into the light. The war on books, codified by Stalin's functionaries at the Soviet Writers' Congress in 1934 and ruthlessly waged by the secret police for the following fifty years, was finally coming to an end, and Zhivago's insurgent guerrillas were winning.

Even in the times of darkest Stalinist oppression, Russian readers had devoured the meagre offerings available in the state-run bookshops. Now they were confronted by a feast of almost unimaginable richness. Anna Akhmatova's *Requiem*, the poetry of her first husband Nikolai Gumilev, Joseph Brodsky's poems, Mikhail Bulgakov's *Heart of a Dog*, Andrei Platonov's *Chevengur*, Anatoly Rybakov's *Children of the Arbat*, Yevgeny Zamyatin's

We, and Vasily Grossman's epic novel *Life and Fate* finally appeared.[1] In March 1987, a conference was held in Denmark at which Soviet and exiled writers met to discuss literature; among the exiles was Andrei Sinyavsky. The meeting began fractiously before the Soviet historian Yuri Afanasiev made an appeal to their shared *Russian* cultural identity. It was a milestone moment.[2] Yulii Daniel, living in Kaluga after his release, had the satisfaction of seeing poems he had written on scraps of paper in the camps published in *Novy Mir* and *Ogonyok.* (He died the following year.) Controversial works by emigres and foreigners also found their way to the bookstands. In 1987 a Moscow court prosecuted a reader for owning a copy of Vladimir Nabokov's *Lolita,* claiming it was pornography. The case was dismissed, clearing the way for *Lolita* to be published. Nabokov's other works were released in Russia for the first time since he fled the revolution. Books previously banned for their explicit criticism of Communism were also published. Among them was the book that had been the West's most effective weapon in the cultural Cold War: George Orwell's *Nineteen Eighty-Four.*

At the beginning of 1988, Pasternak's *Doctor Zhivago* was serialized in *Novy Mir,* and the following May his dacha at Peredelkino was transformed into a museum. Dissidents and others with good connections had read these books in illicit or samizdat editions, but now the general population had access. David Remnick, the Moscow correspondent of the *Washington Post,* recalled how incredible it was to "ride the subways and see ordinary people reading Pasternak in their sky-blue copies of *Novy Mir.*"[3] Literary magazines, their circulations soaring, were so prized that lines would form in the early hours of the morning ahead of the publication of a new issue, and many readers rebound them to keep them from falling apart as they passed from hand to hand.[4] Samizdat had gone mainstream.[5]

For those who had fought censorship and demanded the freedom for writers to express themselves, it was a victory earned through great sacrifice. Akhmatova's forbearance, Pasternak's courage, and Solzhenitsyn's defiance had not been in vain. The determined optimism of the small band of protesters that had gathered in support of Daniel and Sinyavsky had not been misplaced.

WHEN SHE HAD FIRST MET HIM back in December 1984, Margaret Thatcher had famously declared: "I like Mr. Gorbachev. We can do business together." He had substantive discussions of policy with foreign leaders in a way that previous leaders had been either unwilling or incapable of doing. He was in earnest in wanting to denuclearize and reduce tensions with the West. And his economic reforms made clear that he was willing to make previously unthinkable changes to the Soviet command economy. But what about glasnost? In the early months of his leadership, it was not clear what this meant for Soviet society. Gorbachev was not an outsider; he had come up through the hierarchies of the Party and knew that while he had support from some younger reformists, much power was still concentrated in the hands of ideologues. As such, his public declarations were often careful and seemed to promise incremental change, rather than radical cultural liberalization. He demanded that writers and intellectuals look to the future rather than criticizing the past and cautioned against fixating on the crimes of Stalinism.[6] Any public discussion of the true scale of the Yezhov terror or the vastness of the gulag remained powerfully taboo, as was criticism of the war in Afghanistan. Those who had lived through the Khrushchev Thaw, and Brezhnev's subsequent ideological crackdown, had every reason to be skeptical about Gorbachev's commitment to openness. Then Reactor 4 in the Chernobyl nuclear power plant exploded.

THE FIRST INSTINCT of the Soviet bureaucracy was to cover up the disaster. By this stage it was hardwired into the system: bad news was dangerous, bad news got buried. The problem was that Swedish scientists were detecting alarming levels of radio-activity in the atmosphere, evidence that something terrible had happened. Gorbachev might well have chosen to suppress the truth or at least mitigate the impact, but instead he directed the media to report the disaster honestly.[7] That meant admitting that Chernobyl had been poorly built and maintained and that disaster could have been avoided if warnings had been listened to, including ones issued seven years previously by the KGB. The press reported on Chernobyl in a way that no other event had been covered. The reporting was honest and critical—which opened a door that could not easily be shut again. If Chernobyl was being covered honestly, then why not be open about the state of the economy? Or the disastrous war in Afghanistan?

After Chernobyl, glasnost became real. Readers learned the truth about the cost, in every sense of the word, of nuclear fallout in Ukraine, and they began to learn about how badly the war in Afghanistan was going. In the early years of the war, there was little reporting on combat and instead a focus on how Soviet sol-diers were helping develop the country's infrastructure by, for example, building schools.[8] In 1987 and 1988 Artyom Borovik filed reports from the front lines of the war, taking as his model Michael Herr's account of Vietnam in *Dispatches*. Svetlana Alex-ievich, who later won the Nobel Prize, began collecting first-hand accounts of the war from veterans, which she eventually published as *Zinky Boys* in 1990. These accounts depicted a bru-tal, futile war. By February 1989, Gorbachev had his wish and the last Soviet soldier returned home.

If the Soviet Union was to come to terms with its present, it also needed to come to terms with its past, filling what Gorbachev called the "blank spots" in its history. A population deceived by state-mandated history textbooks now learned about the reality of what had happened under Stalin and during the Great Patriotic War.[9] In institutions around the country archives documenting torture, false imprisonment, and executions began to see the light of day. The paperwork in such files was not the only evidence: the Russian soil contained its own archives, mass graves of those murdered by Stalin's executioners.

GORBACHEV RECOGNIZED that he needed to sell glasnost to both his own people and to the rest of the world. He was, compared to his predecessors, a cultivated man with cosmopolitan tastes, and in 1986 had established the Soviet Cultural Foundation to help fund artistic projects.[10] In February 1987, he hosted a three-day International Forum for a Non-Nuclear World and the Survival of Humanity in Moscow as a means of simultaneously reducing Cold War tension and inviting thousands of delegates—including scientists, entrepreneurs, film stars, intellectuals, and, of course, writers—to see for themselves the reforms that had taken place. The celebrities that attended included actors Gregory Peck, Claudia Cardinale, Kris Kristofferson, Paul Newman, and the artist Yoko Ono. The invited writers tended to be, if not sympathetic to Communism, at least staunch critics of the United States and its foreign policy; Gore Vidal and Norman Mailer were the best-known American writers there, and they even put aside their personal enmity to dine together. The star literary guest, though, was Graham Greene, who was to give one of the closing speeches.[11]

The most important delegate, though, was the nuclear physicist and dissident Andrei Sakharov. Since 1980 the sixty-five-year-old had been living in internal exile in the town of Gorky,

punished for his outspoken opposition to the war in Afghanistan. Several months previously, however, a KGB agent arrived
to tell him they needed to install a telephone. When that phone
rang, Gorbachev was on the other end, telling Sakharov his exile
was over and that he could return to his apartment in Moscow.
Sakharov overcame his skepticism and anger—he apparently
hung up on Gorbachev in that first conversation—to participate in the forum in the hope of helping the superpowers resolve
their impasse over denuclearization. At a summit in Reykjavik
in 1986, Reagan and Gorbachev had come close to agreeing a
deal only for it to founder on the issue of the Strategic Defense
Initiative (SDI), the proposed missile defense system that was
popularly dubbed "Star Wars." The Russians wanted the Americans to abandon SDI as part of any deal, a demand met by flat
refusal. At the forum, Sakharov urged Gorbachev to decouple
SDI from disarmament negotiations, helping prompt a policy
shift that resulted in the Intermediate-Range Nuclear Forces
Treaty the following December.[12] This debate aside, the forum
was more about optics than policy. Sakharov's presence signaled
more about the seriousness of glasnost than anything else.

Greene, seventy-eight, was a relatively safe choice as prestige
delegate. He had expressed broad sympathy with Communist
regimes, especially in Latin America, although his attitude was
as much about an antipathy toward American imperialism.
His position regarding the Soviet Union itself was more complicated. He was vehemently opposed to the Kremlin's cultural
policies and the way that writers had been suppressed. He had
been a prominent critic of the Sinyavsky-Daniel trial, and in a
letter to the London *Times* he not only protested their imprisonment but demanded that his Soviet royalties be given to Maria Rozanova and Larisa Bogoraz, who continued to campaign
while their husbands were in the camps.[13] He swore he would

never return to Moscow, which he had visited in 1961, unless there was a change in the state's treatment of writers.

Greene's presence, therefore, was an indication that under Gorbachev the Soviet writer's lot had improved. "I have great admiration for what Gorbachev has done," he told a reporter from the *Washington Post*. "He's got great courage, and I admire him for it."[14] Groups of delegates met in hotel rooms and conference venues to discuss denuclearization and other pertinent subjects, but Greene had only one issue he cared about: the unlikely alliance between Communism and Catholicism.

At the closing ceremony, hosted at the Kremlin Palace, where the Supreme Soviet would normally meet, Greene gave a speech calling for closer relations between the Vatican and Moscow. "We are fighting together against the death squads in El Salvador," he said. "We are fighting together against the *Contras* in Nicaragua. We are fighting together against General Pinochet in Chile." At the end of his speech Greene looked at Gorbachev and said that "the dream before I die is that there'll be an ambassador of the U.S.S.R. at the Vatican giving good advice." By Greene's account, Gorbachev smiled warmly at this peroration.[15] Fay Weldon, a British writer in attendance, was bemused by Greene's speech, with its fanciful claims to Communist-Catholic solidarity. "He had been drinking," she noted. There was one British listener who *was* impressed, however: Kim Philby.

BACK IN 1967, when Greene published his letter protesting the imprisonment of Sinyavsky and Daniel, he received an unexpected response. A letter arrived for him with Moscow stamps. It was from Philby. Perhaps surprisingly, he wrote to say he found Greene's position on the writers "just and honourable" and hoped that in the future conditions in the Soviet Union

might change so that there might be "some unexpected grati-
fication, some meal together, for instance, when we could talk
like in old times."[16] That same year, the KGB decided that it
would be a good idea for Philby to publish a memoir. (His KGB
debriefing notes were effectively a rough draft.) When *My Silent War* came out the following year, it had an introduction by
Greene, which, while noting "the sharp touch of the icicle in the
heart," praised the book as both a gripping thriller and a "dignified statement of his beliefs and motives."[17] "I was flabbergasted
when I read it," Philby said. "He understood what I had done
and why I had done it."[18] Unlike almost everyone else who had
worked with Philby, Greene did not seem to hold his betrayal
against him, and the old friends began to correspond regularly.
Greene even asked Philby to read the manuscript of *The Human
Factor*, his novel about a spy who defects to Moscow, for authenticity.[19]

Glasnost offered the prospect of Greene returning to Moscow and he and Philby having that meal together. Greene was
invited by the Union of Soviet Writers—possibly at Philby's
instigation—to visit in September 1986, the first of four visits
to the Soviet Union in the next two years, including his attendance at the forum. Philby claimed these trips were gratifying
to Greene because in Russian eyes he was the greatest living
British writer while back home in the UK his stock had fallen
somewhat. He was the subject of a TV documentary and hit by a
barrage of interview requests. "He hardly had a moment to himself the whole time he was here," Philby said.

The writer and the spy met for the first time since their days in
SIS at Philby's flat near Pushkin Square in Moscow. "No questions, Graham," Philby said by way of his opening gambit. "I've
only one question. How's your Russian?" Greene replied. They
then broke into a bottle of Stolichnaya and reminisced about old
times. The meeting only happened because the KGB willed it

to, and the conversation, as both Greene and Philby would have known, was bugged.

According to Genrikh Borovik, an aspiring spy novelist and Writers' Union official, it was his contacts that enabled the meeting to go ahead (the KGB had vetoed previous requests).[20] However, as ever with Philby, other rumors swirled, especially in the halls of Moscow Center. Was Philby being somehow sounded out about a return to Britain? Would MI6 seek to portray him as, in fact, a triple agent? Paranoia, for sure, but then they did have cause to fear for Philby's loyalty—he had hardly been treated well since his defection.

To the outside world Philby had been welcomed to Moscow as a hero. In 1965, two years after escaping SIS's agents by jumping on a tanker in Beirut, Philby was awarded the Order of Lenin. Three years later came the KGB-approved memoir in which he claimed to have "no doubt about the verdict of history" despite the crimes of Stalin. "As I look over Moscow from my study window," he wrote, "I can see the solid foundations for the future I glimpsed at Cambridge."[21] Over the following decades he doggedly reiterated his faith in "the Communist idea."

The truth was that in his early years in Moscow, Philby was profoundly unhappy.[22] After his defection Philby expected to take a senior position at Moscow Center but instead was put into quasi retirement, his phones tapped, his apartment bugged, and his correspondence read. The KGB did not trust their defector and maintained disproportionate fears that he might be an SIS plant (this was a long-standing issue: when he was relaying his most valuable information as a spy, some in the Center worried it was *too* good). Philby believed he had done his cause harm by his behavior in Moscow, as he ran off with Melinda, the wife of his fellow Cambridge spy Donald Maclean. That relationship soon foundered, and Philby was isolated and angry. Always a heavy drinker, he now embarked on "suicidal drinking bouts."[23] He suffered from insomnia and, at one stage, attempted to cut his own wrists.[24] His life was saved by Rufina Pukhova, a copy editor he met in 1971, and who, after they got married, succeeded in restricting his drinking and smoking.

Toward the end of the seventies he was invited to speak at Moscow Center. "In the course of my career," he told the assembled KGB operatives, "I have visited the headquarters of some of the world's leading intelligence services. And now, at last, after fourteen years in Moscow, I am visiting yours for the first time."[25] The KGB, having been on the front foot so long in the Cold War, were suddenly finding themselves exposed. A series of arrests of Scandinavian agents made Moscow Center suspect a traitor in their midst. They gave Philby the file of the case and he was convinced that a high-ranking KGB officer was responsible. He was not wrong: Oleg Gordievsky, an SIS double agent who rivaled Philby in terms of the damage he did to the agency he worked for, was in the room when Philby's report was analysed by the KGB leadership.

After Greene, seemingly unhampered by the vodka, left that first meeting, Philby turned to Rufina and said: "He is burdened by doubt as well."[26] This was hardly a revelatory remark to make about Greene: his best novels were intense explorations of the impossible search for certainty, often anguished narratives about the struggle to maintain an improbable faith. For Greene, doubt was a condition of his faith; he had little time for the dogmatism of the zealot. The remark, though, does reveal something about Philby. Despite his years of discipline and loyalty, he was not blind to the fact that the Soviet Union was buckling at the knees. His faith was shaken, too.

The pair met again the following year, when Greene attended Gorbachev's forum, but Philby's health was deteriorating. "You and I are suffering from the same incurable disease—old age," Greene said.[27] Philby died on May 11, 1988, in a Moscow hospital. His funeral was a grand affair, with a full KGB guard of honor. It was a last piece of triumphalism by a Soviet state whose own health was deteriorating rapidly, too. In hindsight it might have looked like Philby had, as usual, timed his exit well. But he died with things unsaid, truths untold.

GREENE WAS NOT THE ONLY BRITISH WRITER Philby sought out in those days of glasnost. Perhaps it was his physical decline, perhaps it was the need to unburden himself, perhaps it was simply a desire to be back at the center of things, but in 1987 he thought about publishing a second volume of his memoirs. It is not clear whether this was conceived as a sequel, detailing his escape from Beirut and life in the Soviet Union, or whether this would be a franker account of his time as a double agent, this time with less editorial control on the part of the KGB. What is known is the man he wanted for the job: John le Carré.

On the surface, at least, it was a perfect fit. Philby was an avid reader of le Carré's novels, which lined the bookshelves of his Moscow apartment. And of course le Carré was clearly fascinated by Philby, having brilliantly reimagined the story of his betrayal of SIS in *Tinker, Tailor, Soldier, Spy*. That novel told the story of George Smiley's pursuit of Bill Haydon, the mole at the top of the Circus whose personal charm masked his ruthless ideological conviction. Haydon, though, is captured by Smiley while Philby had escaped (although whether he had been allowed to get away was another matter). The possibility of le Carré telling Philby's story was tantalizing. There was just one problem: le Carré did not even want to meet with Philby.

Le Carré visited the Soviet Union in May 1987. Ever since the publication of *The Spy Who Came In from the Cold* in 1963, he had been attacked in the Soviet literary press for glamorizing the role of British intelligence, and previous efforts to secure a visa had been rebuffed.[28] His success on this occasion was due to a friendship with Bryan Cartledge, the ambassador to Moscow, dating back to their time in the officer cadets, and the intervention of Gorbachev's wife, Raisa. That the KGB was less than happy about this arrangement became apparent when his suitcase was "lost" in transit (returned after having been thoroughly rifled), his hotel room was obviously searched, and his every move was tailed by two watchers (whom he dubbed "Muttski and Jeffski").[29] And le Carré was getting around: he was planning to set his next novel in Russia and, looking for material, attended numerous functions and was treated as an honored guest, even as his KGB tail waited patiently outside.

It was at one of these functions, a meeting of the Union of Soviet Writers in his honor, that le Carré was approached by Genrikh Borovik to broker a meeting with Philby for the following evening. Le Carré was due to attend a reception by the ambassador the following night and told Borovik he could hardly "sup with the Queen's representative one night and the Queen's traitor the next."[30] He later revealed he felt a "spurt of hatred" at the request. "I felt, 'If he wants me, he can't have me.' I didn't want to give him comfort."[31] He later admitted that he regretted not meeting with him out of curiosity. "I now have it on pretty good authority that Philby knew he was dying and was hoping I would collaborate with him on his second volume of memoirs," le Carré wrote.[32] He was not to know Philby had less than a year left to live.

Not that the Soviet Union had much longer; le Carré felt the only people that could not see the end coming were the CIA. On a second trip to the Soviet Union, in September, he met with Sakharov at the only cooperative restaurant in Leningrad. The dignity of the man was in contrast to the infantile KGB agents who, pretending to be reporters, swarmed around their table setting off flashbulbs. Despite the distraction, Sakharov told the story of Gorbachev calling him to return from exile. The harassment of the KGB was futile in the face of the unfolding power of glasnost.

Even while le Carré was in town, there was a further lurch toward liberalization. Having planned a visit to Lenin's tomb, le Carré found Red Square closed, and it took the rest of the day for news to filter through that a nineteen-year-old German, Mathias Rust, had flown his Cessna through Soviet air defenses and landed it next to the Kremlin. The scandal gave Gorbachev the opportunity to get rid of his opponents. Sergei Sokolov, the hard-line defense minister, was forced to resign, and high-ranking military officers who opposed Gorbachev's reforms were sacked. The next time le Carré visited Russia, the Soviet Union was history.

THE ENEMIES OF GLASNOST did not go down without a fight, however, and, once again, literature was a battleground. In March 1988, the conservative newspaper *Sovetskaya Rossiya* published a letter from an outraged reader. Under the headline "I Cannot Forsake My Principles" and taking up the whole of the third page, Nina Andreyeva, a professor of chemistry at the Polytechnic Institute in Leningrad and a self-defined Stalinist, launched a vicious attack on *Onward, Onward, Onward,* a play published two months previously. The author of the play was Mikhail Shatrov, the son of a Bolshevik murdered during the Stalin purges, who had hitched his relatively mediocre talents to the wagon of Gorbachev's reforms. The play made the argument that the cause of Communism had been thrown off course by Lenin's death and that had he lived, he would have championed a version of socialism that looked an awful lot like what Gorbachev was trying to achieve with perestroika.[33] To Andreyeva the play represented all that was wrong with glasnost, undermining as it did the glories of Soviet history.

Before running it, the editor of *Sovetskaya Rossiya*, Valentin Chikin, forwarded the letter to Yegor Ligachev, the most powerful conservative on the Central Committee. Ligachev returned the letter with his annotations and "advised" Chikin to print it; a journalist was sent to help Andreyeva "improve" it. The Stalin purges had been "blown out of all proportion" and works of literature "blackened" Soviet history. "They try to make us believe that the country's past was nothing but mistakes and crimes," she wrote, "keeping silent about the greatest achievements of the past and the present."[34] Some of the uglier passages had been removed; Andreyeva was typical of the nationalists whose opposition to Gorbachev's reforms often included an ample serving of anti-Semitism. In her original letter she warned that the reforms were a repeat of the Prague Spring, which, she wrote, "began, too, with the congress of writers and with [Jews]. And how did that end?"[35] The irony was that Gorbachev *did* look to the Prague Spring as a model.[36]

Hiding behind Andreyeva, Ligachev was seeking to rally opponents of glasnost and pressure Gorbachev to rein in his reforms—in Remnick's phrase, a "soft coup." The publication of the letter was timed as Gorbachev left the country for a summit in Belgrade, and in his absence Ligachev called a meeting of newspaper editors at which he extolled the document's virtues. Provincial newspapers were encouraged to reprint Andreyeva's polemic, and it was also published in the official government newspaper in East Germany. For three weeks the liberal intelligentsia was in a state of disarray bordering on panic. Had the ideological wind changed? There was considerable infighting in the Politburo but Gorbachev, on his return to Moscow, prevailed. An article was published in *Pravda* attacking those who indulged in "nostalgia" and wanted to "put the brakes" on perestroika.[37] The message to the conservatives was unambiguous.

In the end, Andreyeva's letter effectively accelerated glasnost by bringing the issues to a head. In the carefully crafted riposte, orchestrated by Gorbachev, it was proclaimed that there should be "freedom of cultural and intellectual pursuits." It was effectively the Kremlin declaring an end to hostility against literature even if the formal dissolution of the censorship laws wasn't accomplished until two years later.[38] In the summer of 1988, the first nongovernment newspapers began to circulate, and by the autumn jamming of Western radio ceased. The momentum of glasnost appeared irreversible. The Russian public was ready to embrace the last Soviet pariah: Solzhenitsyn.

FOR THE CONSERVATIVE FIGURES IN THE KREMLIN, Solzhenitsyn was their glasnost red line. Akhmatova and Pasternak could be allowed, and even works of malign foreigners like Orwell might be permitted. But Solzhenitsyn was a step too far. In *Gulag Archipelago*, Solzhenitsyn did not just critique the camps and the purges under Stalin, he argued that they had their roots in the revolution and Lenin's policies. Terror was, he wrote, built into the Soviet system and it began with Lenin. Ligachev, the orchestrator of the Andreyeva affair, wrote a report for the Politburo after reviewing all of Solzhenitsyn's published works and concluded that he was unpublishable; the denigration of Lenin was a heresy too far.[39] In November 1988 the man who succeeded Ligachev as Party ideologist, Vadim Medvedev, declared that there was no way the Kremlin would permit the publication of Solzhenitsyn.[40] Such a decision, Medvedev claimed, would "undermine the foundations on which our present life rests."[41] Soviet certainty, though, was not what it used to be, and those foundations were crumbling.

In August 1988, an intellectual weekly, *Book Review,* published an article by Yelena Chukovskaya demanding that Solzhenitsyn, who was still living in exile in Vermont, be returned his citizenship. It was a courageous move on the part of Chukovskaya, whose mother, Lydia, had sheltered Solzhenitsyn at her dacha at Peredelkino during the height of his persecution. The article provoked a deluge of correspondence, as readers wrote to Chukovskaya, *Book Review,* and the Central Committee insisting that Solzhenitsyn be rehabilitated.

In October 1988, Solzhenitsyn's manifesto-essay "Live Not by a Lie" was published in an obscure newsletter for Ukrainian railway workers.[42] Early the following year it appeared in newspapers in Lithuania and Latvia, and a Russian journal, *Twentieth Century Peace,* published the same essay the following May. The editorial board of *Novy Mir* followed these developments closely. They had been responsible for publishing the sensational *One Day in the Life of Ivan Denisovich* back in 1962, and they wanted to reintroduce Solzhenitsyn to the wider reading public. From the summer of 1988 they were in contact with Solzhenitsyn about publishing his work and felt it would be politic to begin with some of his less controversial works, suggesting serializing *The First Circle* and *Cancer Ward,* the novels he had smuggled to the West on microfilm in the sixties. Solzhenitsyn, though, was a master of managing the impact of his work and insisted that the first of his works to be published was the most uncompromising: *Gulag Archipelago.*[43] Solzhenitsyn won out, and in October *Novy Mir* prepared an announcement that they would publish his work in 1989. Informers leaked the news to the authorities, and agents from the ideological department of the Central Committee intercepted the issue carrying this announcement at the printers. More than a million copies were ordered pulped and a new edition, without reference to Solzhenitsyn, was run.[44]

Novy Mir counterattacked. For every edition that was sent

to the censors, they included Solzhenitsyn's Nobel Prize acceptance speech. Every time, the censors removed it. The editor-
in-chief, Sergei Zalygin, appealed directly to Gorbachev. This
went on for months until, in June 1989, the pressure finally told.
Gorbachev wanted to keep up the momentum of his reforms,
and publishing Solzhenitsyn would certainly do that, but he did
not want to alienate the party. So the decision was handed off to
the Union of Soviet Writers—the organization that had led the
official attacks on Solzhenitsyn before he was deported—who
announced that his work was no longer banned.

In July 1989, the galleys of *Novy Mir* came back from the censor
with the Nobel Prize lecture still in place. The following month,
the first installment of *Gulag Archipelago* was published, with further installments following in subsequent issues, and the magazine's circulation grew by an estimated one million.[45] The state
publisher, Sovetsky Pisatel, announced that a collected edition of
his work was in production. In November, those Russians who
found themselves being able to read Solzhenitsyn's searing and
comprehensive history of the camps learned about the fall of the
Berlin Wall. In a society that had been conditioned to think of the
Soviet Union as a permanent state, anything seemed possible.[46]

IN THE SUMMER OF 1990, the Soviet Union appeared to be heading toward an existential crisis. Gorbachev had begun talks with
Boris Yeltsin about devolving political power to the fifteen different republics (the Baltic states, the Central Asian Republics, and
those, including Ukraine, on Russia's western and southwestern
borders), most of which sought at least a measure of autonomy,
if not full independence. Yeltsin was a charismatic politician
who, having demanded that perestroika be more radical in its
agenda, had been sidelined by the Kremlin. Undaunted, he had
exploited new democratic reforms and his personal popularity

to get elected to the Congress of People's Deputies of Russia. In May 1990, he had been elected Chairman of the Presidium of the Supreme Soviet of the Russian Republic. From this position of power, he backed Gorbachev into a corner by declaring Russian sovereignty in June and resigning from the Communist Party in July.

It was into this turbulent political moment that Solzhénitsyn dropped another literary bomb. On September 18, *Komsomolskaya Pravda,* a newspaper with a circulation of more than 25 million readers, published a sixteen-page essay by Solzhenitsyn titled "How to Revitalize Russia." Solzhenitsyn clearly sought to make an impact: the next day excerpts of the essay were published in the *New York Times.* "The death knell has sounded for Communism," he declared in the essay's opening lines. "But the concrete structure has not yet toppled, and we face the danger of being crushed by the debris instead of finding freedom."[47] He argued that all Soviet republics should be granted their independence immediately, with the exception of Ukraine and Belarus, which would join Russia in a Slavic union. "We do not have the energy to deal with the periphery, either economically or spiritually," he wrote. "We do not have the energy to run an Empire! And we do not need it, let us shrug it off: It is crushing us, it is draining us, and it is accelerating our demise."[48] When asked about Solzhenitsyn's proposal, Gorbachev said that, while he was an "undoubtedly great person," his vision was one taken from the past, "the Russia of old, the czarist monarchy. This is not acceptable to me."

Solzhenitsyn's vision was not acceptable to the right, either. These hard-liners, with support in the hierarchy of the military, did not want to see Russian imperial power dissolved and, in rhetoric dripping with nationalism and anti-Semitism, demanded a return to authoritarian rule. The *Military-Historical Journal,* for example, saw its circulation increase dramatically as it warned of the apocalyptic future that faced the nation if perestroika and glasnost were allowed to continue, and published excerpts from *Mein Kampf* and the anti-Semitic forgery *The Protocols of the Elders of Zion*.[49] This was not just the work of reactionary cranks—it was the leading edge of a conservative political backlash being orchestrated by powerful figures in the Kremlin, including Vladimir Kryuchkov, the chairman of the KGB, and Dmitri Yazov, the minister of defense. Despite the warnings of reformist allies like Eduard Shevardnadze and Alexander Yakovlev, Gorbachev dismissed the idea of a coup. Even a direct warning from President George H. W. Bush, who had been informed by the CIA that a plot was in the works, failed to convince Gorbachev that he was in peril.

In August 1991, Gorbachev went on vacation in Foros, Crimea, having agreed to the terms of a New Union Treaty that would have replaced the Soviet Union with a less centralized federal system. To Kryuchkov and his allies, it was now or never; they had to strike before Gorbachev returned and signed the treaty. On August 17, the plotters met in a KGB compound on the outskirts of Moscow and finalized plans for their coup.

Gorbachev knew something was wrong when the phone lines went down—even the line reserved for emergencies. A delegation arrived and told him he had to either support the state of emergency or resign. Despite being pressured and threatened, he refused to play ball; it was an inauspicious start to a rebellion that soon began to descend into farce. Back in Moscow, the news of the coup was broadcast on state television at 6 A.M. as tanks rumbled into the outskirts of the city. By 9 A.M., these forces had surrounded key locations, including TV and radio stations and the White House, home of the Russian parliament. But the plotters had made a catastrophic error: they had forgotten to arrest Yeltsin.

Over breakfast, Yeltsin heard what had happened and, realizing time was short, strapped on a bulletproof vest underneath his shirt and sped off toward the center of Moscow. At the White House, Yeltsin gathered his allies around him in the war room and planned his counterattack, issuing statements over the radio, urging people to take to the streets. In an iconic moment, at around noon, he came out of the building and, ignoring the snipers positioned on the hotel roof opposite, clambered up onto one of the tanks and addressed the crowd of onlookers. "We are dealing with a right-wing, reactionary, anti-constitutional coup d'état," he said. "Accordingly, we proclaim all decisions and decrees of this committee illegal." A mixture of veterans from the Afghanistan War and students arrived to defend the White House while first hundreds then thousands began to gather outside. The plotters made desperate plans to storm the building but, with Yeltsin having seized the initiative, what little support they had was dwindling. Within seventy-two hours of its inception, the coup had been defeated, the plotters arrested, and Gorbachev returned to Moscow.

On August 24, Gorbachev resigned as general secretary of the Communist Party, while remaining president—for a few months at least. The same day the statue of Felix Dzerzhinsky, the founder of the Cheka, which stood outside the KGB's Lubyanka headquarters, was taken down—a symbolic break with the authoritarian past. Over the following months, the Soviet Union was dismantled, and the republics all declared their independence. Gorbachev had hoped that he could find a way to reform Communism, but the people of the Soviet Union wanted a more radical break with the past than he could offer. On Christmas Day 1991, Gorbachev went on television to announce that he was resigning as Soviet president and that all powers, including the nuclear codes, were to be handed over to Yeltsin, the president of what was now known as the Russian Federation. That night, the Soviet flag, with its distinctive hammer and sickle, was lowered for the last time over the Kremlin, and replaced with the Russian tricolor. The Soviet Union had ceased to exist.

EPILOGUE

JOHN LE CARRÉ RETURNED TO RUSSIA in the summer of 1993 to see what had happened to the country after the Cold War. "I wanted to get a taste of the new order," he wrote. "Were the new crime bosses the old ones in new clothes? Was the KGB really being disbanded by Yeltsin, or had it been, as so often in the past, merely reconstituted under another name?" On arrival in Moscow, he found the city in thrall to Western materialism, or at least those that could afford it: expensive foreign cars parked outside stores selling luxury goods, even with the country's economy in free fall. Yeltsin, so heroic in resisting the August coup, was already embattled as he tried to push through his radical economic reforms, and parliament had narrowly lost a fight to impeach him. He had already begun privatizing Russia state assets, a program that in the years to come would be exploited by a small number of businessmen to accrue fantastic personal wealth. Increasingly drink addled, and having suffered a number of heart attacks, Yeltsin helped create an oligarchy.

For le Carré this was a nightmare foretold. In 1990, he had published *The Secret Pilgrim*, a book in which he was "determined to make a last farewell of the Cold War."[1] The premise involved "Ned," an agent of the Circus in charge of training new recruits, inviting George Smiley out of retirement to address the latest graduating class. Prompted by Smiley's reflections on his life in the service, Ned reminisces about his own experiences as a spy, although not with nostalgia: he remembers failed missions, incompetent agents, grubby compromises, and hollow sacrifices.

It is far from a triumphalist account of the clandestine Cold War. In the final chapter, Ned remembers going to see a Sir Anthony Bradshaw, a boorish English businessman whose dubious offshore companies had been used in the past by the Circus in a murky operation, a relationship of convenience that had come back to haunt them. Bradshaw has since become an arms dealer, selling guns in the Balkans and Central Africa, but when Ned tells him the government would like him to desist from such damaging activities, Sir Anthony tells him, in a foul-mouthed, racist rant, exactly where to get off. As he leaves, Ned remembers "Smiley's aphorism, about the right people losing the Cold War and the wrong people winning it."[2]

The wrong people were certainly winning in Russia. On his previous visit, le Carré's delighted Moscow publisher had greeted him with vodka and ambitious publication plans; this time he let him in only after ascertaining his identity through a peephole in a steel door replete with a battery of locks, all there to try to keep out the gangsters operating a protection racket. Such was the state of play in the Wild East.

Through Mikhail Lyubimov, a former KGB colonel he knew, le Carré secured a meeting with a gang boss, whom he called "Dima."[3] They met at the nightclub Dima owned. The outside was guarded by doormen with submachine guns while inside Dima was protected by ex–special forces soldiers, some presumably veterans of the Afghan War. Through an interpreter, le Carré asked Dima if he might ever consider reinvesting some of his wealth in the community, buying hospitals and schools and such like, just as the American robber barons had done as they got older. Dima delivered a long answer—to much laughter from his hangers-on. "Mr. David," the interpreter said, "I regret to tell you, Mr. Dima says fuck off."[4] It is a request to which le Carré wisely acceded—a year later he read that Dima had been arrested after two rival businessmen were discovered chained in his basement.

With the rise of Gorbachev, le Carré had dared to be optimistic about the future of Russia and its relations with the West. He had been in New York in 1988 when the Soviet leader had addressed the United Nations and came away convinced that it was "the beginning of a spiritual and positive revolution in politics."[5] Many in the West were also optimistic about the future, but for different reasons. In the summer of 1989, Francis Fukuyama, a Soviet expert with the U.S. State Department, had written an influential essay entitled "The End of History?" in which he made the case that with the imminent defeat of Communism, there were no more rival ideologies left to compete with liberal democracy.[6]

On his return from his second visit to Moscow, though, le Carré's optimism had soured. "We have squandered the peace that we've won in the Cold War," he said in an interview with *Time*. In his novels of the Circus and the Center, Smiley justified making compromises and sacrifices because they were made in the service of defeating the larger enemy in the Kremlin, but in *The Secret Pilgrim* he wondered if the price paid in the process might have been too high. "Now that the West had dealt with rogue forms of communism," le Carré asked, "how was it going to deal with rogue forms of capitalism?" This became the urgent subjects of his next novels: gangster capitalism in the post-Soviet world; big pharma exploiting postcolonial Africa; Western arms dealers enriching themselves in a developing world scarred by conflict.

Le Carré also began writing about the so-called war on terror, the battle against Islamic fundamentalist groups that intensified dramatically after the attacks of 9/11. Here was another accounting with the legacies of the Cold War: when the Soviet

Union was fighting its war in Afghanistan in the 1980s, the Reagan administration had provided $3.2 billion for the Afghan forces, including weapons sourced by the CIA. (Ironically the weapons were purchased via intermediaries from Soviet countries to hide their origins. The funds and weapons were funneled through Pakistan.) Among the indirect recipients of American largesse were the future fighters of Osama bin Laden's Al Qaeda. Bin Laden was the son of a Saudi Arabian construction magnate, and one of his most important contributions to the war in Afghanistan was the construction of a base for mujahedeen soldiers in the Tora Bora cave complex near the border with Pakistan. It was there that the American military went looking for him after the attacks on the Twin Towers.[7]

IN THE SECRET PILGRIM, Smiley warned his audience that the West needed to be careful how it handled its defeated enemy. "Do we leave the Bear to rot?" he asked; "encourage him to become resentful, backward, an over-armed nation outside our camp?" Over the last decades, under the leadership of Vladimir Putin, the Russian Bear has awoken from hibernation and has begun to bare its claws. The 2014 annexation of Crimea and Russia's support of separatist fighters in Eastern Ukraine are perhaps the most obvious examples of Moscow's challenge to the West. A return to sinister Cold War intrigue has been evoked by the fatal poisoning of FSB defector Alexander Litvinenko in a London sushi bar in 2006—his killers using the highly radioactive polonium-210—and by the attempted assassination in Britain of Sergei Skripal, a military intelligence officer who worked for British intelligence, through the use of Novichok, a nerve agent developed by the Soviet Union in the last decades of the Cold War.

The relationship with the West has deteriorated to such a degree that some commentators are claiming that we have returned to the conditions of the Cold War.[8] (Others claim that the adversarial relationship between the United States and China is either heading toward "Cold War 2.0" or is already there.)[9] Among those to warn against a return to hostilities has been Mikhail Gorbachev himself.[10] Others argue that viewing tensions between the United States and its rivals in this way is reductive. Historian Odd Arne Westad has warned against describing the complexity of current geopolitical relations in the terms of the Cold War, arguing that this constitutes a kind of "terminological laziness."[11] However, what is indisputable is that Russia's hostile relations with the United States and the European Union are a legacy of the Cold War and its aftermath.

The reversion began well before Putin took power. In the summer of 1992, Andrei Sinyavsky went to Russia and was "horrified" by what he saw.[12] The "shock therapy" reforms implemented by Yegor Gaidar, Yeltsin's most trusted adviser on economic affairs, had resulted in "a drastic split in the social stratification of the country."[13] He saw the streets of Moscow lined with designer stores whose products were far too expensive for the average Russian to dream of affording. As a small minority accrued incredible wealth through privatizing state industries, the rest of the country was forced, in Sinyavsky's words, to live with a "parody of capitalism," thoroughly demoralized by corruption, income inequality, hyperinflation, and financial uncertainty.[14]

It was not just the economic picture that worried Sinyavsky; he was seriously concerned about how quickly Yeltsin had slid back to an authoritarian approach. In 1993, the country entered a state of constitutional crisis as Yeltsin's relationship with parliament devolved into deadlock. Protesters who supported Yeltsin's parliamentary opponents occupied the White House in Moscow, and to resolve the crisis the president ordered in the military, who shelled the White House before storming it. To

Sinyavsky's disbelief, many among the Russian intelligentsia supported Yeltsin because the protesters included members of the Communist Party. The end of the Cold War had promised freedoms and a better quality of life, but to many Russians, their lives seemed worse. "In the eyes of the people, democracy became synonymous with poverty, embezzlement of public funds, and theft," Sinyavsky wrote.[15] In writing about the new Russia, Sinyavsky intended to "frighten" his readers: in this new democratic Russia "power is being controlled and administered not by society but by the criminal world."[16] He died shortly after.

After he was elected to a second term in 1996, Yeltsin's health deteriorated (he had suffered a number of heart attacks and drank heavily), his popularity crashed, and in 1998 Russia defaulted on its debts. It was clear that a new leader was needed and the wealthy group of oligarchs around Yeltsin, foremost among them Boris Berezovsky, went in search of a candidate. They settled on Putin, a former KGB colonel, who in 1990 had embarked on a political career in St. Petersburg, rising to be deputy mayor (seemingly enriching himself in the process), before becoming part of the Yeltsin regime in Moscow.[17] In the summer of 1998, Yeltsin had appointed him director of the FSB, the security service that had replaced the KGB. In the summer of 1999, Yeltsin appointed Putin acting prime minister and announced to Russia that he wanted the new man to be his heir as president. Amid a series of horrific apartment bombings that left the population shaken, Putin promised to rule with strength.[18] When Yeltsin resigned on New Year's Eve 1999, Putin became acting president and duly won the elections the following March. Putin proved far less malleable than some of his high-profile political supporters had anticipated, and he soon went about consolidating his power and isolating his perceived enemies. The Bear was coming out of hibernation.

Putin had served on the front lines of the Cold War and was dismayed and angered by Russia's reduced standing in the world since the collapse of the Soviet Union. He was the son of a soldier who had fought in a special NKVD unit during the siege of Leningrad during the Second World War, and had grown up dreaming of joining the secret service, a desire fueled by a popular novel that was published when he was twelve, *The Shield and the Sword,* and was adapted into a four-part TV miniseries three years later.[19] Written by Vadim Kozhevnikov, the book was about a Soviet spy who infiltrated Nazi intelligence shortly before the invasion of the Soviet Union and whose exploits undermined the German forces from within. An otherwise ordinary student, known for his bouts of violent temper, Putin managed to get himself into the KGB and, after going to officer school and learning German, was posted to Dresden in East Germany, where he was assigned to Directorate S, which dealt with "illegals."

Then his world began to fall apart. In 1989, he claimed to have been in a crowd that ransacked the Stasi headquarters in Dresden. The protesters soon moved on to the KGB building, where, according to his own account, he managed to persuade the crowd not to storm the building. (Other accounts claim KGB officers fired shots into the air.) All the while, the agents were phoning the military to intervene, but the army could not do so without orders from the Kremlin and nobody in Moscow seemed prepared to give them.[20]

Putin was no Communist ideologue (when the hard-liners staged their coup in 1991, Putin backed Gorbachev), but there was much about the Soviet Union that he believed ought to be restored. He began to centralize power by eroding democratic processes, weaponizing bureaucracy, and restructuring local governance. In terms of foreign policy, he presided over a brutal war in Chechnya and spoke forcefully of Russia's return to power and influence on the world stage. Journalists and political opponents who dared to criticize him ended up in prison or in exile, or died in suspicious circumstances. The Soviet-era national anthem was restored (with new lyrics).[21]

In 2003, Russia faced a potential turning point. Mikhail Khodorkovsky, who had become the richest of the post-Soviet oligarchs after acquiring the Yukos oil conglomerate, decided he was going to reinvest some of his wealth into the country. He began funding political parties, NGOs, universities, training for journalists, and Internet cafes all around the country. He also began cleaning up Yukos, seeking to purge corruption from his business and use that as a model for a wider cleaning up of the Russian economy.[22] Le Carré's question in that Moscow nightclub had not been so naive after all: here was a former robber baron growing a conscience and investing in civil society. This was a direct challenge to the direction Russia was heading under Putin, and not even his vast wealth could protect Khodorkovsky. In 2005, he was found guilty of six charges, including fraud and tax evasion, and went on to spend eight years in prison, most of it served in a former Soviet prison camp near the border with China.

THE TREATMENT OF KHODORKOVSKY was one factor among many in a deteriorating relationship with the West. In the early years of his rule, Putin had presented himself as an ally in the "war on terror," but the barely concealed corruption, the arrests or suspicious deaths of prominent critics, and the increasing belligerence in foreign policy (including in Ukraine and Syria) resulted in a souring of relations, to the point where the United States has imposed more than sixty rounds of sanctions on Russian individuals and government agencies. The Kremlin has imposed sanctions of its own, and its intelligence agencies have been accused of taking "active measures" to interfere in elections in the West (most prominently the 2016 presidential election).[23] The decision by President Donald Trump's administration to withdraw from the Intermediate Nuclear Forces Treaty in February 2019, and Putin's decision to follow suit, makes it understandable why people claim the world is returning to a state of Cold War.

There is, though, a fundamental difference: ideology. I began this book by recounting how the idea of dropping novels on the enemy by weather balloon seems absurd to our eyes—and it is not just for reasons of technological change. Literature is no longer conceived of as a weapon to be deployed in cultural warfare: it is hard to imagine the publication of a novel precipitating a geopolitical crisis in the manner of *Doctor Zhivago* or *The Gulag Archipelago*. One of the reasons for this is that both sides are no longer trying to sell each other on their social, economic, and political systems. All the major players in world politics are capitalist, on a scale from the social democratic to the authoritarian. As Westad puts it, in the conflict between the United States and Russia (and China), "ideology is no longer the main determinant," as it was in the Cold War.[24]

The specific circumstances of the Cold War will never be repeated, and the idea of literature being deployed by governments on a vast scale is no longer credible.[25] However, this does not mean that literature has lost a role. At the time of writing, the Putin regime was introducing new censorship laws, and wherever there are authoritarian regimes, writers will be silenced, imprisoned, or worse.[26] A brief look through PEN International's annual case lists demonstrates how writers are still feared enough to be censored, harassed, locked up, and murdered all over the world. (In 2017, it monitored 218 attacks against writers.)[27] And in societies where there is no state censorship, literature remains one of the best ways of confronting the past and imagining a different future, a role that has gathered urgency as populist nationalism gains power across what used to be called the Western Bloc. The story of the literary Cold War is one of complicity, in which writers were manipulated and co-opted, often without their knowledge or consent. It is a story of novels, poems, and plays being weaponized by the state as propaganda. But it is also the story of what happens when writers resist, when they fight back, when they take the risk of choosing, in Havel's words, "to live within the truth."

ACKNOWLEDGMENTS

I want to start by thanking my literary agent, Euan Thorney-croft, for believing in this project when it was a tangled mess of notes and ideas. With patience and necessary good humor, Euan nudged and cajoled me along every step of this process, and this book certainly would not exist without him. I am immensely lucky to have such a great editor in Geoff Shandler and I'm deeply grateful for his faith in me. I want to thank Tim Whiting for all of his generosity and support; with one insight Tim changed the whole direction of this book—and it is much the better for it. I also want to thank George Lucas at Inkwell for his belief in the project, and his invaluable help and advice along the way. Receiving the Royal Society of Literature's Jerwood Award for Non-Fiction was a moment of spirit-lifting validation, and I am grateful to the judges—Jonathan Beckman, Jonathan Keates, and Kate Summerscale—and to the Royal Society of Literature for their support.

This book is built on the strong foundations laid by other books and their authors. I could not possibly count the number of times I have returned to Tony Judt's *Postwar* and Odd Arne Westad's *The Cold War: A World History*. One could not wish for a better guide through the shadowy realm of espionage history than Christopher Andrew. Ben Macintyre's books were a source of inspiration and pleasure. A literary history like this is inconceivable without the work of biographers, and I leaned particularly heavily on Christopher Barnes, Carol Brightman, Bernard Crick, Frances Kiernan, Roberta Reeder, Hazel Rowley, Michael Scammell, Norman Sherry, Adam Sisman, Gerald Sorin, John Sutherland, and D. J. Taylor (among many others). Similarly, I am indebted to the painstaking archival work of scholars of the cultural Cold War, including that of Greg Barnhisel, Katerina

Clark, David Caute, Evgeny Dobrenko, Peter Finn and Petra Couvée, Patrick Iber, Vitaly Shentalinsky, Giles Scott-Smith, James Smith, Frances Stonor Saunders, Joel Whitney, Hugh Wilford, and Vladislav Zubok. There are of course many other scholars whose work has helped me in the writing of this book, both directly and indirectly, and I hope they will forgive me for not listing them by name.

I want to thank everyone who over the last five years has offered advice, heard me out, or kicked around ideas with me. Carol Dougherty and my colleagues at the Newhouse Center for the Humanities at Wellesley College gave me feedback on the very earliest drafts. Eric Naiman and the English, Comparative Literature, and Slavic Literature faculties at the University of California–Berkeley let me talk about my project at length and offered helpful feedback. Anne Applebaum, Martin Brody, Luke Menand, and Will Norman helped me think about the Cold War in different ways. Mateo Jarquin kindly lent his expertise on Nicaragua. My editors on the *Telegraph* books pages have made me a better writer, especially Lorna Bradbury, Iona McLaren, and Gabby Wood. I continue to benefit from the generous mentoring of David Bethea, Paul Giles, Jane Grayson, and Michael Wood. Like all writers, I am forever in the debt of librarians, and particularly those of the Widener and Lamont libraries at Harvard; the British Library; the Bodleian Library at Oxford; and the Arlington, Cambridge, and Lexington public libraries. Thanks also to Vedika Khanna for keeping me organized in the homestretch, Mark Steven Long for his insightful copy editing, and the design team at Custom House for making such a handsome book.

Much of this book was written while working at the History & Literature department at Harvard, and I want to thank all of my colleagues for their help over the years, especially Angela Allan, Jenni Brady, René Carrasco, Mike D'Alessandro, Lauren

Kaminsky, Emily Laase, Alan Niles, and Jessica Shires. Extra gratitude to Alan and Angela for reading sections of the manuscript with the deadline looming. Nick Donofrio lent me books, heard me out, and helped me track down two key photos. A special mention goes to Paul Adler, who read most of this manuscript when it was in rough draft, offered countless brilliant editorial suggestions, and weaponized his enthusiasm when my own was flagging (all errors that remain are, of course, mine). And I am grateful to all of my students for reminding me every day that to teach is to learn.

For moral support and friendship: Yambazi Banda, Ben Berlyn, Brendan Cooper, Peter Crosby, Jon Day, Christian Dickman, Alex Feldman, Richard Fletcher, John Gaston, Nicki Goh, Gid Habel, Paul Harrington, Tim Inman, Adam Kelly, Neelu Kumar, Jon McIntosh, Katie Murphy, Jonathan Northcroft, Alex Orquiza, Clint Sieunarine, Matt Sperling, Richard Tacon, Ed Vainker, Steve Vainker, Jimmy Wallenstein, and Sally Whitehill. The respective clans of Gauthier-Tintocalis and Bekarian-Mack have been stalwarts. Many of the writers in this book showed extraordinary courage, but even they could take a lesson in grit from Elise.

Finally, I want to thank my family for their love and support: my in-laws, Jill and Les; my parents, John and Wendy; my brothers, Tom and Ian (and their families); my children, Bella and Luke; and, above all, my wife, Eden. I don't have the words to express how much I owe her.

NOTES

INTRODUCTION

1. Alfred A. Reisch, *Hot Books in the Cold War* (New York: Central European University Press, 2013), 10; Richard Cummings, *Cold War Radio: The Dangerous History of American Broadcasting in Europe* (Jefferson, NC: McFarland & Co., 2009), 45.
2. See Herbert Freidman online collection of FEP leaflets and other propaganda material sent across by balloon into the Iron Curtain, http://www.psywarrior .com/RadioFreeEurope.html.
3. Kenneth Osgood, *Total Cold War: Eisenhower's Secret Propaganda Battle at Home and Abroad* (Lawrence: University Press of Kansas, 2006), 2.
4. *Book Publishing in Soviet Russia,* trans. Helen Lambert Shadick (Washington, D.C.: Public Affairs Press, 1948), 1–2.
5. David Priestland, *The Red Flag: Communism and the Making of the Modern World* (London: Allen Lane, 2009), xx.
6. Kevin McDermott and Jeremy Agnew, *The Comintern: A History of International Communism from Lenin to Stalin* (London: Macmillan, 1996), 1–27.
7. Sean McMeekin, *The Red Millionaire: A Political Biography of Willi Münzenberg, Moscow's Secret Propaganda Tsar in the West* (New Haven, CT: Yale University Press, 2003), 1.
8. McDermott and Agnew, *The Comintern,* 22.
9. Quoted in Kristin L. Matthews, *Reading America: Citizenship, Democracy and Cold War Literature* (Boston: University of Massachusetts Press, 2016), 3.
10. Ibid., 21.
11. Molly Guptill Manning, *When Books Went to War: The Stories That Helped Us Win World War II* (Boston, MA: Houghton Mifflin Harcourt, 2014), 81.
12. See John B. Hench, *Books as Weapons: Propaganda, Publishing, and the Battle for Global Markets in the Era of World War II* (Ithaca, NY: Cornell University Press, 2010), 109–30.
13. Ibid., 123.
14. Ibid., 90–91, 103.
15. Ibid., 70.
16. Quoted in Greg Barnhisel, *Cold War Modernists: Art, Literature, and American Cultural Diplomacy* (New York: Columbia University Press, 2015), 101.
17. Gregory Walker, *Soviet Book Publishing Policy* (Cambridge, UK: Cambridge University Press, 1978), 1.
18. Barnhisel, *Cold War Modernists,* 101.
19. Walker, *Soviet Book Publishing Policy,* 104. One subgenre produced by the Soviet Union was socialist-realist fiction commissioned by the Main Political Directorate of the Soviet military in order to raise troop morale. See Mark T. Hooker, *The Military Uses of Literature: Fiction and the Armed Forces in the Soviet Union* (Westport, CT: Praeger, 1996).

20. Barnhisel, *Cold War Modernists,* 104–5.
21. Ibid., 106.
22. See Mary L. Dudziak, *Cold War Civil Rights: Race and the Image of American Democracy* (Princeton, NJ: Princeton University Press, 2000).
23. In the later phases of the Cold War, prestige was also contested through cultural exchange programs, as both superpowers tried to impress each other with delegations of celebrated writers. See Yale Richmond, *Cultural Exchange and the Cold War* (University Park: Pennsylvania State University Press, 2003).
24. Quoted in ibid., 96. This line of thinking extended even into American creative writing programs. See Eric Bennett, *Workshops of Empire: Stegner, Engle, and American Creative Writing During the Cold War* (Iowa City: University of Iowa Press, 2015).
25. Dwight D. Eisenhower, "Freedom of the Arts," *The Bulletin of the Museum of Modern Art,* 22/2–1 (1954), 3.
26. The list of writers who wrote for *Encounter* while it was being secretly funded by the CIA through the CCF included James Agee, Kingsley Amis, W. H. Auden, James Baldwin, Saul Bellow, John Berryman, Malcolm Bradbury, Anthony Burgess, E. E. Cummings, T. S. Eliot, William Faulkner, Elizabeth Hardwick, Ernest Hemingway, Thom Gunn, Ted Hughes, Aldous Huxley, Jack Kerouac, Arthur Koestler, Robert Lowell, Louis MacNeice, Mary McCarthy, Nancy Mitford, Marianne Moore, Iris Murdoch, Vladimir Nabokov, Eugene O'Neill, Sylvia Plath, J. B. Priestley, Theodore Roethke, Dylan Thomas, R. S. Thomas, Lionel Trilling, Gore Vidal, Evelyn Waugh, Edmund Wilson, P. G. Wodehouse, and Richard Wright. This is intended as a sample of quite how wide a range of writers wrote for the magazine (some more political than others). Many of the major American writers who did not contribute to *Encounter*—a group that would include Truman Capote, John dos Passos, Ralph Ellison, Norman Mailer, Bernard Malamud, Philip Roth, Susan Sontag, and Tennessee Williams—contributed to *Partisan Review* in a period when Hugh Wilford tells us it was in receipt of CIA funding. See *The Mighty Wurlitzer: How the CIA Played America* (Cambridge, MA: Harvard University Press, 2008), 103–4.
27. Some of the inner workings of the Kremlin's cultural policies were revealed when archives began to open during Mikhail Gorbachev's policy of perestroika. Even more became available to researchers after the collapse of the Soviet Union in 1991. As Katerina Clark and Evgeny Dobrenko point out, these archives revealed just how important cultural policy was at the highest levels of the Kremlin, with Stalin personally making many of the decisions about the fate of Soviet writers. Some researchers even secured access to the KGB archives—although that access was often limited and temporary. The writer Vitaly Shentalinsky, for example, managed to gain access to the NKVD files of many writers who disappeared during Stalin's purges of the 1930s. Defectors from the KGB, among them Oleg Gordievsky and Vasili Mitrokhin, have provided invaluable insight into the way the security services policed the production of literature.

What we know about how the cultural Cold War was fought by the West is due to journalists and historians finding ways around the fact that many of the most important archives remain closed. While the CIA have released some materials, the files relating to their secret funding of cultural institutions have not been declassified. If anything, Britain's SIS is even more secretive. It is only thanks to the research of journalists like Frances Stonor Saunders and Joel Whitney, and of historians like Greg Barnhisel, Volker Berghahn, David Caute, Patrick Iber, Giles Scott-Smith, James Smith, and Hugh Wilford (among many others), that we have such a good understanding of how intelligence agencies and government departments conceived of literature as either a threat to be suppressed or a weapon to be deployed.

28. Stephen Spender, *The Thirties and After* (London: Macmillan, 1978), 160.

29. See Giles Scott-Smith, *The Politics of Apolitical Culture: The Congress for Cultural Freedom, the CIA, and Postwar American Hegemony* (New York: Routledge, 2002).

ONE

1. Frank Frankford, another ILP volunteer, remembers it differently. According to him, Orwell was regaling his men with stories of his experiences in Parisian brothels when he was shot. Frankford, from a Barcelona prison, went on to denounce the POUM and claim Kopp had been involved in receiving weapons from the fascist lines. See Bernard Crick, *George Orwell: A Life* (London: Penguin, 1992), 223, 233.

2. George Orwell, *Orwell in Spain*, ed. Peter Davison (London: Penguin, 2001), 131. This edition includes *Homage to Catalonia* and various other letters, reviews, and essays pertaining to Orwell's time in Spain.

3. Gordon Bowker, *George Orwell* (London: Little, Brown, 2003), 221.

4. Orwell, *Orwell in Spain*, 132.

5. Ibid., 133.

6. Ibid., 132.

7. Crick, *George Orwell*, 208.

8. For my account of the Spanish Civil War, I draw from Paul Preston's work, especially *The Spanish Civil War: Reaction, Revolution, Revenge* (New York: Harper Perennial, 2006), from Burnett Bolloten's *The Spanish Civil War: Revolution and Counterrevolution* (Chapel Hill: University of North Carolina Press, 1991), and from Antony Beevor's *The Battle for Spain* (London: Weidenfeld & Nicolson, 2006).

9. The Falange was a fascist group, founded by José Primo de Rivera, the son of Miguel Primo de Rivera, who had ruled Spain as a dictator between 1923 and 1930 after staging a military coup in 1923. They sought to sow public disorder through acts of terror in the years leading up to the war, and their forces perpetrated many atrocities during the fighting. The Carlists, based in the north, were archconservative defenders of Spanish Catholicism, who believed that a "judeo-marxist-masonic" conspiracy was going to "turn Spain into a colony of the Soviet Union" (Beevor, *The Battle for Spain*, 42).

10. Preston, *The Spanish Civil War*, 118.

11. Ibid., 134.
12. Orwell, *Orwell in Spain*, 170.
13. Orwell apparently chose the name after the River Orwell in Suffolk, along which he would go walking with his father. See Peter Davison, *George Orwell: A Literary Life* (New York: St. Martin's Press, 1996), 33.
14. John Rodden, *George Orwell: The Politics of Literary Reputation* (New York: Oxford University Press, 1989), 42.
15. The ILP was founded in 1893 with the goal of supplying more working-class candidates to a Parliament dominated by the conservatives and the liberals. They initially affiliated with the Labour Party, but after conflict about the pace of reform (the ILP favored a radical approach; the Labour Party sought incremental change) they disaffiliated in 1932. The ILP also had a complicated relationship with the Communist International, with which they declined to affiliate.
16. Crick, *George Orwell*, 208.
17. Orwell, *Orwell in Spain*, 32.
18. Ibid.
19. Ibid., 169.
20. Ibid., 5.
21. Quoted in Crick, *George Orwell*, 210.
22. Orwell's guide in the POUM was Victor Alba, who went on to write one of the most important histories of the group, *Spanish Marxism Versus Soviet Communism: A History of the POUM in the Spanish Civil War*.
23. Orwell's presence on the front was announced in the February 3, 1937, edition of the *Spanish Revolution*, the POUM's fortnightly bulletin.
24. Boris Volodarsky, *Stalin's Agent: The Life and Death of Alexander Orlov* (Oxford: Oxford University Press, 2015), 155.
25. Orlov, the son of a Jewish timber merchant from Belarus, had fought for the Russian army in the First World War. After the Revolution, he joined the Cheka, Lenin's secret police. During the Russian Civil War he worked as a saboteur behind the White Army lines in Ukraine and developed a reputation as a spy catcher, apprehending the American agent Xenophon Kalamatiano, who smuggled out his coded reports in a hollowed-out walking cane. Orlov's work caught the attention of Felix Dzerzhinsky, the head of the Cheka, and from the midtwenties to the midthirties Orlov was posted to France, Britain, Austria, and the United States on espionage assignments. Before heading out to Spain he played an instrumental role in initiating the Great Terror. Unlike many of his colleagues, he managed to avoid being purged himself. He twice saw through efforts on Moscow's part to have him taken back to Russia and managed to escape, via France and Canada, to the United States, where he gave evidence to the security services.
26. Christopher Andrew and Vasili Mitrokhin, *The Sword and the Shield: The Mitrokhin Archive and the History of the KGB* (New York: Basic Books, 1999), 59–60.
27. For a meticulous documentary account of Soviet intervention in the war, see Ronald Radosh, Mary R. Habeck, and Grigory Sevostianov, eds., *Spain*

Betrayed: The Soviet Union in the Spanish Civil War (New Haven, CT: Yale University Press, 2001).

28. See ibid., xvii. For Mexican support see Patrick Iber, *Neither Peace Nor Freedom: The Cultural Cold War in Latin America* (Cambridge, MA: Harvard University Press, 2015), 32–33.
29. Volodarsky, *Stalin's Agent*, 166.
30. Andrew and Mitrokhin, *The Sword and the Shield*, 72.
31. Andrés Nin had briefly been Trotsky's secretary, but the POUM had broken with Trotsky in 1935.
32. Volodarsky, *Stalin's Agent*, 176–77.
33. John Costello and Oleg Tsaraev, *Deadly Illusions* (London: Crown, 1993), 281.
34. Quoted in Volodarksy, *Stalin's Agent*, 177.
35. Crick, *George Orwell*, 212.
36. Kopp was a self-mythologizer who lied about his background and apparently tried it on with Eileen. Despite this, his friendship with Orwell seems to have been genuine. For an account of Kopp's life see Marc Wildemeersch, *George Orwell's Commander in Spain: The Enigma of Georges Kopp* (London: Thames River Press, 2013).
37. Orwell, *Orwell in Spain*, 69.
38. Edwards originally delivered this account in a 1960 BBC documentary about Orwell. The quotation here is from Crick, *George Orwell*, 215–16.
39. Orwell, *Orwell in Spain*, 85.
40. Ibid., 94.
41. Orwell had not joined the POUM because he was committed to their revolutionary politics. It had been a pragmatic decision. He now agreed with the Communist line that victory in the war over Franco had to take precedence over the revolution. Subsequent events revealed he was wrong to think the Communists were being merely practical.
42. Christopher Andrew and Oleg Gordievsky, *KGB: The Inside Story of its Foreign Operations from Lenin to Gorbachev* (New York: HarperCollins, 1990), 161. See also Radosh, Habeck, and Sevostianov, eds., *Spain Betrayed*, 32–54.
43. Orwell, *Orwell in Spain*, 101.
44. Ibid.
45. Ibid., 197.
46. Ibid., 104.
47. Ibid., 109.
48. Ibid., 111.
49. Ibid., 119.
50. Ibid.
51. Ibid., 175.
52. Ibid., 127.
53. The evidence from *Spain Betrayed* indicates that Orwell was right: had the Republican forces secured victory, the Communists were planning to change Spain into a satellite state, like the People's Democracies after the Second World War.
54. Orwell, *Orwell in Spain*, 133–35.

55. Ibid., 138.
56. Ibid., 141.
57. Ibid., 139.

TWO

1. Arthur Koestler, *Spanish Testament* (London: Victor Gollancz, 1937), 209.
2. Ibid., 212.
3. Paul Preston, *The Spanish Civil War: Reaction, Revolution, Revenge* (New York: Harper Perennial, 2006), 108.
4. Approximately four thousand Republicans were executed in Malaga. See ibid., 194.
5. Arthur Koestler, *The Invisible Writing: The Second Volume of an Autobiography* (London: Hutchinson, 1969), 391.
6. Ibid., 392.
7. The account of this episode is taken from ibid., 381–93.
8. Koestler, *Spanish Testament*, 225.
9. Ibid., 224–25.
10. Ibid., 226.
11. Ibid., 227–28.
12. Ibid., 228.
13. Ibid., 233.
14. Ibid.

THREE

1. Stephen Spender, *World Within World* (Berkeley: University of California Press, 1966), 131.
2. Ibid., 192.
3. Ibid., 202. Spender's memoir is at times beautifully written and in its sexual frankness a work of courage. The chronology, however, is all over the place, so in determining the order of events in this period I have placed more credence in the letters written to and by Spender at the time and in John Sutherland's meticulous biography.
4. In *Forward from Liberalism* Spender is critical of many aspects of Soviet orthodoxy, but his claim that the Soviet Union was moving "beyond terror" was most unfortunate in its timing, as Stalin's Great Terror was in full swing.
5. Spender, *World Within World*, 210.
6. The article announcing his joining the Communist Party is republished in Stephen Spender, *The Thirties and After* (London: Macmillan, 1978), 80–82.
7. John Sutherland, *Stephen Spender: A Literary Life* (New York: Oxford University Press, 2005), 209.
8. Spender, *World Within World*, 214.
9. Worsley recorded these experiences in *Fellow Travellers: A Memoir of the Thirties* (London: London Magazine Editions, 1971).
10. Sutherland, *Stephen Spender*, 151.
11. Spender, *World Within World*, 183.
12. Ibid., 214.
13. Sutherland, *Stephen Spender*, 210.

14. Spender, *World Within World*, 214.
15. Paul Preston, *The Spanish Civil War: Reaction, Revolution, Revenge* (New York: Harper Perennial, 2006), 195.
16. This is Hyndman's account in *The Distant Drum*, ed. Philip Toynbee (London: Sidgwick & Jackson, 1976), 127.
17. Sutherland, *Stephen Spender*, 213.
18. Richard Davenport-Hines, *Auden* (New York: Pantheon, 1995), 163.
19. Spender, *World Within World*, 222.
20. Ibid., 221.
21. Ibid.
22. Ibid., 222.
23. Ibid., 229.
24. Sutherland, *Stephen Spender*, 218.
25. Spender, *World Within World*, 228.

FOUR

1. The Republican government's secret police were known as the Servicio de Información Militar, or the SIM for short.
2. George Orwell, *Orwell in Spain*, ed. Peter Davison (London: Penguin, 2001), 146.
3. Information about David Crook's life is taken from the online biography hosted at http://www.davidcrook.net.
4. In his biography of Orwell, Gordon Bowker writes that Crook was trained by Ramon Mercader, who would go on to assassinate Trotsky, but it is not clear what evidence there is for this. See Gordon Bowker, *George Orwell* (London: Little, Brown, 2003), 213.
5. Wickes remains something of an enigma. Evidence for his working for the NKVD can be found in Boris Volodarsky, *Stalin's Agent: The Life and Death of Alexander Orlov* (Oxford: Oxford University Press, 2015), 494.
6. The evidence points to this being the *News Chronicle*.
7. Bowker, *George Orwell*, 219.
8. Bernard Crick argues that there is no evidence for the affair; see *George Orwell: A Life* (London: Penguin, 1992), 592. D. J. Taylor discovered letters from Eileen to friends that offer evidence of there having been intimacy of some sort. See "George Orwell: Another Piece of the Puzzle," *Guardian*, December 10, 2005.
9. Bowker, *George Orwell*, 219.
10. Christopher Andrew and Oleg Gordievsky, *KGB: The Inside Story of Its Foreign Operations from Lenin to Gorbachev* (New York: HarperCollins, 1990), 160.
11. Bowker, *George Orwell*, 223.
12. Orwell, *Orwell in Spain*, 153.
13. Ibid., 154.
14. Ibid., 154–55, 162–63.
15. Ibid., 154–55.
16. Ibid., 156.
17. Bowker, *George Orwell*, 224.
18. Orwell, *Orwell in Spain*, 164.
19. Ibid.

20. Ibid., 325.
21. Crick, *George Orwell,* 373. Kopp went on to fight for the French Foreign Legion in the Second World War. In a curious twist, Kopp ended up working for British Naval Intelligence in Marseille. In a further twist, his MI5 case officer was Anthony Blunt. Orwell left £250 to Kopp in his will.
22. Orwell, *Orwell in Spain,* 157.
23. Ibid., 165.
24. Ibid., 26.
25. Peter Davison, Sheila Davison, and Ian Angus, eds., *The Complete Works of George Orwell,* Vol. 11 (London: Secker & Warburg, 1998), 53.

FIVE

1. Arthur Koestler, *The God That Failed,* ed. Richard Crossman (New York: Harper, 1950), 17.
2. Ibid., 19.
3. Ibid., 23.
4. Ibid., 44.
5. Ibid., 60.
6. Arthur Koestler, *The Invisible Writing: The Second Volume of an Autobiography* (London: Hutchinson, 1969), 387.
7. Ibid., 403.
8. Paul Preston, *The Spanish Civil War: Reaction, Revolution, Revenge* (New York: Harper Perennial, 2006), 195; Arthur Koestler, *Spanish Testament* (London: Victor Gollancz, 1937), 254. Koestler claimed five thousand were shot in Malaga, but Preston claims nearly four thousand.
9. Koestler, *Spanish Testament,* 258.
10. Ibid., 266.
11. Ibid., 68.
12. Ibid., 273.
13. Ibid., 286.
14. Ibid., 288.
15. Ibid., 290.
16. Ibid., 309.
17. Koestler, *Invisible Writing,* 468.
18. Koestler, *Spanish Testament,* 364.
19. Ibid., 368.
20. Ibid., 376.

SIX

1. Quoted in John Sutherland, *Stephen Spender: A Literary Life* (New York: Oxford University Press, 2005), 221.
2. This is Philip Toynbee's memory of the situation; Spender had gone for lunch with him straight after meeting with Pollitt. Quoted in ibid.
3. Ibid., 223. Churchill did not send the ship but pressured the International Brigade to take Romilly off the front line. He then deserted so as to ensure he would be sent into battle as punishment, fighting heroically at the battle of Brunete.

4. Stephen Spender, *The Still Centre* (London: Faber & Faber, 1939), 10.
5. Ibid., 71.
6. Ibid., 73.
7. Robert Thornberry, "Writers Take Sides, Stalinists Take Control: The Second International Congress for the Defense of Culture," *Historian* (March 2000): 590.
8. Hughes, Bertolt Brecht, and Heinrich Mann attended only sessions of the Congress in France because they were unable to get papers to enter Spain.
9. Stephen Spender, *World Within World* (Berkeley: University of California Press, 1966), 239.
10. André Gide, *Return from the U.S.S.R.*, trans. Dorothy Bussy (New York: A. A. Knopf), 41–42.
11. Spender, *World Within World*, 240.
12. See Thornberry, "Writers Take Sides," 600–601.
13. Spender, *World Within World*, 243.
14. Ibid., 244.
15. That did not mean abandoning the Republican cause, however. Together with John Lehmann, he began to put together *Poems for Spain*, an anthology of work by those poets who had volunteered to fight in the conflict. The collection included poems by John Cornford and Charles Connolly, both killed in the fighting, and by Tom Wintringham, who had been seriously wounded at Jarama. In the introduction, Spender argued that the contributors were compelled to risk their lives in the war. "Unless they both fight and write," he writes, "there will be a future in which they are spiritually dead." Stephen Spender, "Introduction," *Poems for Spain*, eds. Stephen Spender and John Lehmann (London: Hogarth, 1939), 8.
16. See Peter Davison, Sheila Davison, and Ian Angus, eds., *The Complete Works of George Orwell*, Vol. 11 (London: Secker & Warburg, 1998), 54–60.
17. Ibid., 51–52.
18. Quoted in Bernard Crick, *George Orwell: A Life* (London: Penguin, 1992), 341–42.
19. See Davison, Davison, and Angus, eds., *The Complete Works of George Orwell*, Vol. 11, 41–46.
20. Quoted in Crick, *George Orwell*, 343.
21. Ibid., 344.
22. Quoted in Michael Shelden, *Orwell: The Authorized Biography* (New York: HarperCollins, 1991), 306.
23. Davison, Davison, and Angus, eds., *The Complete Works of George Orwell*, Vol. 11, 67.
24. *Authors Take Sides on the Spanish War* (London: Left Review, 1937).
25. Davison, Davison, and Angus, eds., *The Complete Works of George Orwell*, Vol. 11, 67.
26. Crick, *George Orwell*, 363.
27. George Orwell, *Orwell in Spain*, ed. Peter Davison (London: Penguin, 2001), 190.
28. Davison, Davison, and Angus, eds., *The Complete Works of George Orwell*, Vol. 11, 113.

29. Arthur Koestler, *The Invisible Writing: The Second Volume of an Autobiography* (London: Hutchinson, 1969), 468.
30. Ibid., 448.
31. Ibid., 451.
32. Ibid., 461.
33. Ibid., 465.
34. Ibid., 467.
35. Ibid., 468.
36. Ibid., 445.
37. Michael Scammell, *Koestler: The Literary and Political Odyssey of a Twentieth-Century Skeptic* (New York: Random House, 2009), 161.
38. Quoted in ibid., 162.
39. For the Nazi-Soviet Pact, see Ronald Grigor Suny, ed., *The Structure of Soviet History: Essays and Documents* (Oxford: Oxford University Press, 2014), 336–42.
40. Koestler, *Invisible Writing*, 480.
41. Ibid.
42. Ibid., 479.
43. Scammell, *Koestler*, 180–81.
44. Ibid., 194.
45. Quoted in ibid.
46. The publisher had rejected the original title of *The Vicious Circle*, and Hardy had suggested *Darkness at Noon* as an alternative (a fact she initially concealed from Koestler, fearing his temper).
47. Davison, Davison, and Angus, eds., *The Complete Works of George Orwell*, Vol. 12, 359.
48. Quoted in Scammell, *Koestler*, 246.

SEVEN

1. Andy McSmith, *Fear and the Muse Kept Watch* (New York: New Press, 2015), 117–18.
2. Gleb Struve, *25 Years of Soviet Literature* (London: G. Routledge & Sons, 1944), 208–9.
3. Pilnyak's *Mahogany* was published in Berlin in 1929, and the same year a shortened version of Zamyatin's *We* was published in *Volya Rossii* in Prague.
4. See Katerina Clark and Evgeny Dobrenko, *Soviet Culture and Power: A History in Documents* (New Haven, CT: Yale University Press, 2007), 139–40.
5. Radek was an "Old Bolshevik" who had allied himself with Trotsky during the power struggle after Lenin's death. He eventually defected to Stalin's side when it became clear that Trotsky had lost. Having previously been in charge of running the Comintern's activities in Germany, including the failed attempt at revolution in 1923, Radek had been reduced to the role of a newspaper editor. However, Hitler's ascent to power made Radek's knowledge of Germany valuable; his influence increased again, and he became a foreign policy spokesman in 1933. Warren Lerner, *Karl Radek: The Last Internationalist* (Stanford, CA: Stanford University Press, 1970), 156.
6. Kevin Birmingham, *The Most Dangerous Book: The Battle for James Joyce's "Ulysses"* (New York: Penguin, 2014), 331.

7. H. G. Scott, ed., *Problems of Soviet Literature* (New York: International Publishers, 1935), 152.

8. Ibid., 97.

9. Ibid., 113.

10. Ibid., 154.

11. Ibid., 97.

12. Ibid., 142.

13. Andy McSmith also points to the publication of Max Eastman's *Artists in Uniform* (1934), which drew unwelcome attention to the fate of dissident writers in the Soviet Union, as something that could have contributed to the decision not to execute Mandelstam. After serving a period in exile, Mandelstam was arrested a second time in May 1938 and sent to a labor camp, where he died, officially of illness.

14. Isaac Babel, *Complete Works,* ed. Nathalie Babel, trans. Peter Constantine (New York: Norton, 2002), 681.

15. Gregory Freidin, "Timeline," in ibid., 1054.

16. Stalin, in an article published years later, called Eastman a "gangster of the pen"; Eastman was falsely accused of being a British agent during the show trials. See Alan Wald, *The New York Intellectuals* (Chapel Hill: North Carolina University Press, 1987), 114.

17. Max Eastman, *Artists in Uniform* (New York: Knopf, 1934), 101.

18. Ibid., 102.

19. Babel, *Collected Works,* 4–5.

20. A. N. Pirozhkova, *At His Side: The Last Years of Issac Babel* (South Royalton, VT: Steerforth Press, 1996), 64.

21. Quoted in McSmith, *Fear and the Muse Kept Watch,* 125.

22. R. W. Davies, ed., *The Stalin-Kaganovich Correspondence 1931–36,* trans. Steven Shabad (New Haven, CT: Yale University Press, 1993), 143.

23. Ibid., 124.

24. Matthew Lenoe, *The Kirov Murder and Soviet History* (New Haven, CT: Yale University Press, 2010), 2.

25. Robert Conquest in *The Great Terror* and *Stalin and the Kirov Murder* made the most famous case for Stalin's culpability. Amy Knight makes a similar case in *Who Killed Kirov? The Kremlin's Greatest Mystery.* Matthew Lenoe, using documents declassified after the fall of the Soviet Union, painstakingly demonstrates the lack of evidence for Stalin's direct involvement in the Kirov killing.

26. Robert Conquest, *The Great Terror: A Reassessment* (London: Hutchinson, 1990), 14.

27. Babel and Pirozhkova were never formally married but, as was common at the time, lived as husband and wife and were considered such by the state after his death. See Pirozhkova, *At His Side,* 13.

28. Gregory Freidin, "Two Babels—Two Aphrodites," in *The Enigma of Isaac Babel: Biography History, Context* (Stanford, CA: Stanford University Press, 2009), 51–52.

29. Maxim Gorky, *Selected Letters* (New York: Oxford University Press, 1997), 365–67.

30. Freidin, "Two Babels—Two Aphrodites," 47–48.
31. Gorky, *Selected Letters*, 347.
32. When his film work became too high profile he was immediately attacked. He collaborated with Sergei Eisenstein on *Bezhin Meadow*, at the great director's behest, only for both men to be denounced for the work in February 1937. See Freidin, "Two Babels—Two Aphrodites," 52.
33. Pirozhkova, *At His Side*, 103.
34. Ibid.
35. Conquest, *The Great Terror*, 93.
36. Freidin, "Two Babels—Two Aphrodites," 52.
37. Conquest, *The Great Terror*, 297.
38. While he could not be described as a Trotskyist, he had met Trotsky at a literary salon in the 1920s and was privately admiring of his "charm and the strength of his influence." See Clark and Dobrenko, *Soviet Culture and Power*, 310.
39. McSmith, *Fear and the Muse Kept Watch*, 126.
40. Paul Gregory, *Women of the Gulag* (Stanford, CA: Hoover Institution Press, 2013), 113.
41. J. Arch Getty and Oleg Naumov, *Yezhov: The Rise of Stalin's "Iron Fist"* (New Haven, CT: Yale University Press, 2008), 204.
42. Gregory, *Women of the Gulag*, 37–43.
43. This, at least, is what Babel is supposed to have told his interrogators. Vitali Shentalinsky, *The KGB's Literary Archive* (London: Harvill, 1995), 44.

EIGHT

1. The review was published in the March 1934 edition of *Common Sense*.
2. Mary McCarthy, "My Confession," *Encounter* (February 1954): 53.
3. Ibid., 58.
4. Norman Thomas was a presidential candidate for the Socialist Party of America who worked with the Communist Party of the USA during the Popular Front period but later became an important figure in the anti-Stalinist left.
5. McCarthy fictionalized some of her early experiences in New York, including her marriage to Johnsrud, in *The Group*, her hugely successful 1964 novel.
6. McCarthy, "My Confession," 51.
7. Ibid.
8. Ibid.
9. For reasons relating to citizenship, Trotsky officially took on the name of his wife, Natalia Sedova, when they were married (even if he never used it publicly or privately), hence their son was Lev Sedov.
10. Mary McCarthy, *Intellectual Memoirs* (New York: Harcourt, Brace, Jovanovich, 1992), 61.
11. McCarthy, "My Confession," 54.
12. Frances Kiernan, *Seeing Mary Plain: A Life of Mary McCarthy* (New York: Norton, 2000), 118.
13. Quoted in ibid., 118–19.
14. McCarthy, *Intellectual Memoirs*, 62.

15. McCarthy, "My Confession," 23.
16. Alan Wald, *The New York Intellectuals* (Chapel Hill: North Carolina University Press, 1987), 131.
17. Ibid., 136.
18. Carol Brightman, *Writing Dangerously: Mary McCarthy and Her World* (New York: Potter, 1992), 146.
19. Wald, *The New York Intellectuals,* 78, 79.
20. McCarthy, *Intellectual Memoirs,* 61.
21. Mary V. Dearborn, *Ernest Hemingway: A Biography* (New York: Alfred A. Knopf, 2017), 372.
22. That same year Clark traveled to Mexico and became a translator for Trotsky; he was briefly married to one of his secretaries. *New York Times,* Obituary, February 19, 1996.
23. Robert K. Landers, *An Honest Writer: The Life and Times of James T. Farrell* (San Francisco: Encounter Books, 2004), 201.
24. McCarthy, *Intellectual Memoirs,* 86.
25. Mary McCarthy, *Theater Chronicles* (New York: Farrar, Straus, 1963), vii.
26. Editorial, *Partisan Review* (December 1937): 3.
27. McCarthy, *Theater Chronicles,* viii.
28. *Partisan Review* (December 1937): 32.
29. McCarthy, *Theater Chronicles,* viii.
30. *Partisan Review* (December 1937): 4. In the first iteration of their "Ripostes" feature, which closed the issue, they wittily dismissed the attacks of Communist cultural commissar V. J. Jerome, who had equated them with the murderers of Kirov (an insult dripping with historical irony).
31. Serge, a former Bolshevik, had been arrested in 1933. His incarceration had been protested at the International Congress for the Defense of Culture in Paris in 1935. It had been Serge who had warned his friend Gide to keep his eyes open when visiting the Soviet Union. That he was released was down to international pressure, but even in exile, agents of the NKVD pursued him.
32. Mary-Kay Wilmers, *The Eitingons: A Twentieth-Century Story* (London: Faber & Faber, 2009), 286.
33. Ibid., 273–75.
34. Ibid., 299.
35. Ibid., 303. Volodarsky believes the most plausible explanation is that he was bribed. See Boris Volodarsky, *Stalin's Agent: The Life and Death of Alexander Orlov* (Oxford: Oxford University Press, 2015), 364.
36. Wilmers, *The Eitingons,* 305.
37. *Partisan Review* (Fall 1939): 8–9.

NINE

1. Later that day the NKVD gathered a further 15 folders of manuscripts, 18 notebooks, 517 letters, postcards, and telegrams, and 245 loose sheets of paper from Babel's Moscow apartment. See Vitali Shentalinsky, *The KGB's Literary Archive* (London: Harvill, 1995), 23.
2. The account of Babel's arrest is from A. N. Pirozhkova, *At His Side: The Last Years of Issac Babel* (South Royalton, VT: Steerforth Press, 1996), 112–14.

3. Katerina Clark and Evgeny Dobrenko, *Soviet Culture and Power: A History in Documents* (New Haven, CT: Yale University Press, 2007), 310.
4. Ibid.
5. Simon Sebag Montefiore, *Stalin: The Court of The Red Tsar* (London: Weidenfeld & Nicolson, 2003), 179.
6. Quoted in ibid., 194.
7. Ibid., 208.
8. Ibid., 210.
9. Ibid., 204.
10. Robert Conquest, *The Great Terror: A Reassessment* (London: Hutchinson, 1990), 297.
11. Perhaps in order to try to protect him, Yevgenia stopped inviting Babel to her house in the summer of 1936. See Shentalinsky, *The KGB's Literary Archive*, 44.
12. Montefiore, *Stalin*, 241.
13. Ibid., 248.
14. Paul Gregory, *Women of the Gulag* (Stanford, CA: Hoover Institution Press, 2013), 170.
15. Pirozhkova, *At His Side*, 105.
16. Montefiore, *Stalin*, 252.
17. Ibid., 263.
18. Pirozhkova, *At His Side*, 63.
19. Montefiore, *Stalin*, 196.
20. Shentalinsky, *The KGB's Literary Archive*, 24.
21. As Shentalinsky points out, Babel's interrogators would have had only the vaguest notions of who he was beyond being a writer. See ibid., 27.
22. Ibid., 30.
23. Ibid., 31.
24. Ibid., 37.
25. Pirozhkova, *At His Side*, 103.
26. Montefiore, *Stalin*, 218.
27. Shentalinsky, *The KGB's Literary Archive*, 43.
28. Ibid., 44.
29. Ibid., 53.
30. Ibid., 61.
31. Ibid., 62.
32. Ibid., 66.
33. Ibid., 68–69.
34. Marc Jansen, *Stalin's Loyal Executioner* (Stanford, CA: Hoover Institution Press, 2002), 189.

TEN

1. The account of Philby's arrest is taken from his memoir *My Silent War* (London: MacGibbon & Kee, 1968), xiii–xv.
2. Ibid., xxv.
3. Suschitsky was married to Alex Tudor-Hart, a British doctor. Both had been recruited by Deutsch. See Christopher Andrew and Vasili Mitrokhin, *The*

Sword and the Shield: The Mitrokhin Archive and the History of the KGB (New York: Basic Books, 1999), 58.
4. Genrikh Borovik, *The Philby Files* (London: Little, Brown, 1994), 29.
5. Ibid., 28.
6. In German this is an affectionate term that might be translated as "Little Son" or "Sonny." It is possible that this nickname derived from the fact that the NKVD were interested in his father, St. John Philby.
7. Andrew Lownie, *Stalin's Englishman: The Lives of Guy Burgess* (London: Hodder & Stoughton, 2015), 47–48, 53.
8. Borovik, *The Philby Files*, 59.
9. Phillip Knightley, *Philby: The Life and Views of a K.G.B. Masterspy* (London: Deutsch, 1988), 56.
10. Different sources give different accounts of how Philby learned his mission. This is taken from Borovik. Volodarsky makes the case that Maly informed him of his mission before he even left for Spain. See Boris Volodarsky, *Stalin's Agent: The Life and Death of Alexander Orlov* (Oxford: Oxford University Press, 2015), 207. Either way Philby was instructed to assassinate Franco.
11. Borovik, *The Philby Files*, 89.
12. Ibid., 112.
13. Ibid., 146.
14. Philby later claimed the journalist Esther Marsdon-Smedley played an important role. He met her as he was leaving France with the BEF, and he later found out she worked for Section D of SIS. See ibid., 158–62.
15. Burgess was remarkably promiscuous and loved nothing better than "rough trade." This caught up with him in 1937 when he was hospitalized with syphilis. See Lownie, *Stalin's Englishman*, 84.
16. Burgess and Blunt also helped recruit the wealthy American Michael Straight, a member of the Apostles who had traveled to the Soviet Union with Blunt in 1935. It is disputed whether or not they recruited Goronwy Rees and, if they did, whether he was any more than just an informant. See ibid., 77–78.
17. Ibid., 89.

ELEVEN

1. Quoted in Norman Sherry, *The Life of Graham Greene*, Vol. 2 (London: Cape, 1995), 120. Greene was perhaps referring to one of the Bissagos Islands, such as Bubaque, that sit off the coast near Bissau.
2. Quoted in ibid. Greene remembered the scheme being rejected for a different reason: he was told that the French intelligence services had too much control over brothels.
3. Greene later claimed that despite all the searches, never once were diamonds discovered. See Graham Greene, "The Soupsweet Land," in *Collected Essays* (London: Vintage, 1999), 460.
4. Quoted in Sherry, *The Life of Graham Greene*, Vol. 2, 130.
5. Keith Jeffrey, *MI6: The History of the Secret Intelligence Service 1909–1949* (London: Bloomsbury, 2010), 412, 427.
6. Norman Sherry, *The Life of Graham Greene*, Vol. 1 (London: Cape, 1989), 161.

7. Graham Greene, *Graham Greene: A Life in Letters*, ed. Richard Greene (New York: Norton, 2008), 110.

8. Sherry, *The Life of Graham Greene*, Vol. 2, 85.

9. Quoted in ibid., 92.

10. In 1935, he had embarked on a trip to Liberia, ostensibly to write a travel book about his explorations in the interior. He had an ulterior motive, however, which was to acquire information for the Anti-Slavery Society about atrocities being committed by the government's Frontier Force on the Kru tribe, and he carried a letter of introduction to their leader, Juah Nimley. The name might sound benign, but the society's motives were paternalistic at best—it seems an annexation of parts of Liberia into Sierra Leone, a British colony, was one of the reasons for provoking an intervention. As it worked out, Greene never got to Nimley, finding in his path the leader of the Frontier Force, Colonel T. Elwood Davis, who had supposedly ordered the worst atrocities.

11. Quoted in Sherry, *The Life of Graham Greene*, Vol. 2, 98.

12. Greene, "The Soupsweet Land," 456.

13. Ibid.

14. Quoted in Sherry, *The Life of Graham Greene*, Vol. 2, 104.

15. Greene, "The Soupsweet Land," 459.

16. Quoted in Sherry, *The Life of Graham Greene*, Vol. 2, 113.

17. Greene, "The Soupsweet Land," 459.

18. Quoted in Sherry, *The Life of Graham Greene*, Vol. 2, 114.

19. Ibid., 119.

20. See ibid., 119–20.

21. In Sherry's biography the Lagos agent is named as Alexis Forter. He is "at the last stage of his career" and is described as a "sick man totally unacquainted with Africa." See ibid., 122. This does not match with Alexis Forter the MI6 agent, who was supposedly the model for John le Carré's lead character in the *The Honourable Schoolboy* and who was station chief in Paris as late as 1982.

22. Graham Greene, *Ways of Escape* (Toronto: L&OD, 2007), 121. In the same book he expresses his distaste for interrogation, which he considered "MI5 work."

23. Sherry, *The Life of Graham Greene*, Vol. 2, 127.

24. This assessment might be taken with a pinch of salt: Philby became Greene's friend and Dennys became his brother-in-law.

25. *The Heart of the Matter* went through three editions in the first month after publication. Due to the supposedly blasphemous suicide of its main character, Captain Scobie, the book was banned in Ireland and Greene was threatened with excommunication. See Sherry, *The Life of Graham Greene*, Vol. 2, 303.

26. Masterman's references were quite involved. "If in the double-cross world 'Snow' was the W. G. Grace of the early period, then 'Garbo' was certainly the Bradman of the later years," he wrote. Snow was Arthur Owens, a shift Welshman, who appeared at times to be spying for both MI5 and the Abwehr. Garbo was a double agent of a different order.

27. Quoted in Ben Macintyre, *Agent Zigzag* (New York: Harmony Books, 2007), 187.

28. Graham Greene, "Kim Philby," in Kim Philby, *My Silent War* (London: MacGibbon & Kee, 1968), viii.

29. Phillip Knightley, *Philby: The Life and Views of a K.G.B. Masterspy* (London: Deutsch, 1988), 121.
30. Philby, *My Silent War*, 27, 58; and Sherry, *The Life of Graham Greene*, Vol. 2, 168.
31. Knightley, *Philby*, 119.
32. Sherry, *The Life of Graham Greene*, Vol. 2, 169.
33. Tim Milne, *Kim Philby: The Unknown Story of the KGB's Master Spy* (London: Biteback, 2014), 124.
34. Ibid., 123.
35. Quoted in Sherry, *The Life of Graham Greene*, Vol. 2, 172.
36. Ben Macintyre, *Double Cross* (London: Bloomsbury, 2012), 184.
37. Greene describes the first idea for *Our Man in Havana* in *Ways of Escape*, 246.
38. Robin W. Winks, *Cloak & Gown: Scholars in the Secret War, 1939–61* (New York: Morrow, 1987), 247.
39. Pearson got H.D.'s daughter, Perdita, a job as his secretary. She had previously worked at Bletchley Park.
40. Philby, *My Silent War*, 55.
41. Michael Shelden, *Graham Greene: The Enemy Within* (New York: Random House, 1994), 254–55. Shelden does not provide a source for this anecdote, so it is not clear where he got it from.
42. Michael Holzman, *James Jesus Angleton, the CIA, and the Craft of Counterintelligence* (Amherst: University of Massachusetts Press, 2008), 49.
43. Philby, *My Silent War*, 34.
44. Milne, *Kim Philby*, 139.

TWELVE

1. As with all stories about Hemingway, there are several versions. In another telling, Hemingway, Pelkey, and Capa jumped off the motorbike after Pelkey took a wrong turn and drove into the path of the antitank gun. Either way, Hemingway banged his head badly. See Mary V. Dearborn, *Ernest Hemingway: A Biography* (New York: Alfred A. Knopf, 2017), 447.
2. Michael Reynolds, *Hemingway: The Final Years* (New York: W. W. Norton, 1999), 94.
3. Ibid., 99.
4. Ernest Hemingway, *Hemingway on War* (New York: Scribner, 2003), 333.
5. Reynolds, *Hemingway: The Final Years*, 105.
6. Richard Harris Smith, *OSS: The Secret History of America's First Central Intelligence Agency* (Guilford, CT: Lyons, 2005), 178. A number of Hemingway biographers state that Hemingway and Bruce were friends from his days at the American Embassy in Havana, but Bruce did not begin his diplomatic career until after the war.
7. Frances Stonor Saunders, *The Cultural Cold War* (New York: New Press, 1999), 34–35.
8. OSS had also been penetrated by Soviet intelligence. Donovan's assistant, Duncan Lee, was working for the NKVD.
9. Douglas C. Waller, *Wild Bill Donovan* (New York: Free Press, 2011), 235.
10. Ibid., 247.

11. Nicholas Reynolds, *Writer, Sailor, Soldier, Spy: Ernest Hemingway's Secret Adventures, 1935–1961* (New York: Morrow, 2017), 43–44.

12. Hemingway's NKVD file was seen by Russian journalist Alexander Vassiliev, who was commissioned to write a book about Soviet espionage in America during the early 1990s, when the SVR (the successor agency to the KGB) opened its archives to selected journalists. When the SVR changed its mind, Vassiliev fled to the West, taking his notes with him. See John Earle Haynes, Harvey Klehr, and Alexander Vassiliev, *Spies: The Rise and Fall of the KGB in America* (New Haven, CT: Yale University Press, 2009). Vassiliev remains the only source for Hemingway's NKVD file.

13. An NKVD agent met with Hemingway in Cuba in 1943, but after that the relationship seems to have fizzled out.

14. Reynolds, *Writer, Sailor, Soldier, Spy,* 145.

15. Quoted in ibid., 155.

16. Donald Sturrock, *Storyteller: The Life of Roald Dahl* (London: HarperPress, 2010), 226.

17. Nelson D. Lankford, *The Last American Aristocrat: The Biography of David K. E. Bruce* (Boston: Little, Brown 1996), 21, 24.

18. Quoted in Reynolds, *Hemingway: The Final Years,* 107.

19. David Bruce, *OSS Against the Reich,* ed. Nelson D. Lankford (Kent, OH: Kent State University Press, 1991), 166.

20. Hemingway, *Hemingway on War,* 327.

21. Ibid., 329.

22. Ibid.

23. Bruce, *OSS Against the Reich,* 170.

24. Hemingway, *Hemingway on War,* 333.

25. Ibid., 334.

26. Bruce, *OSS Against the Reich,* 171.

27. Ibid., 173.

28. Ibid., 174.

29. Antony Beevor and Artemis Cooper, *Paris After the Liberation, 1944–49* (London: Penguin, 2004), 59.

30. Ibid., 75.

31. Waller, *Wild Bill Donovan,* 305, 431.

32. Quoted in Lankford, *The Last American Aristocrat,* 129.

33. Harris Smith, *OSS,* 3.

34. The NKVD courier Elizabeth Bentley (run by "Golos") named twenty-eight Soviet informants in the U.S. government when she defected in 1945. Five of these were former OSS operatives, including Donovan's trusted assistant, Duncan Lee.

35. Roosevelt did not read Park's report before he died, but it is hard to imagine he would have backed Donovan in the face of such a damning assessment of his agency.

36. The FBI kept files on any writer associated with left-wing groups, or with civil rights organizations, including James Agee, Nelson Algren, Amiri Bakara, James Baldwin, Pearl Buck, Theodore Dreiser, Howard Fast, William Faulkner, Allen Ginsberg, Dashiell Hammett, Lilian Hellmann, Sinclair

Lewis, Norman Mailer, Arthur Miller, Dorothy Parker, Irwin Shaw, John Steinbeck, Thornton Wilder, and Richard Wright among others. Hoover was particularly obsessed with Hemingway because the writer had the temerity to call the Bureau an "American Gestapo." See Herbert Mitgang, *Dangerous Dossiers: Exposing the Secret War Against America's Greatest Authors* (New York: Donald I. Fine, 1988) and Natalie Robins, *Alien Ink: The FBI's War on Freedom of Expression* (New York: Morrow, 1992).

THIRTEEN

1.   Paul Potts, *Dante Called You Beatrice* (London: Eyre & Spottiswode, 1960), 82.
2.   Jeffrey Meyers, *Orwell: Life and Art* (Urbana: University of Illinois Press), 416.
3.   Quoted in John Rodden and John Rossi, "The Mysterious (Un)Meeting of George Orwell and Ernest Hemingway," *Kenyon Review* 31, no. 4 (Fall 2009): 4. I have relied on Rodden and Rossi's brilliant forensic investigation into the veracity of this anecdote.
4.   Ernest Hemingway, *True at First Light* (New York: Scribner, 1999), 139.
5.   Gordon Bowker, *George Orwell* (London: Little, Brown, 2003), 330–31.
6.   Quoted in Bernard Crick, *George Orwell: A Life* (London: Penguin, 1992), 392.
7.   Ibid., 381.
8.   John J. Ross, "Tuberculosis, Brocnhiectasis, and Infertility: What Ailed George Orwell?" *Clinical Infectious Diseases* 41, no. 11 (December 1, 2005): 1600.
9.   Crick, *George Orwell,* 500.
10.   Richard Cockett, *David Astor and the Observer* (London: Deutsch, 1991), 92.
11.   Peter Davison, Sheila Davison, and Ian Angus, eds., *The Complete Works of George Orwell,* Vol. 13 (London: Secker & Warburg, 1998), 351.
12.   Cockett, *David Astor and the Observer,* 102.
13.   This is from a letter by Smollett to Astor. See Jeremy Lewis, *David Astor* (London: Jonathan Cape, 2016), 122.
14.   Michael Scammell, *Koestler: The Literary and Political Odyssey of a Twentieth-Century Skeptic* (New York: Random House, 2009), 208.
15.   Quoted in ibid., 249.
16.   Crossman also helped him get Daphne Hardy a job at the Ministry of Information.
17.   Quoted in Scammell, *Koestler,* 219.
18.   Ibid., 209.
19.   Ibid., 239.
20.   Ibid.
21.   Quoted in ibid., 246.
22.   Quoted in Crick, *George Orwell,* 450.
23.   The exact dating of the writing and publication of this essay are not clear. See Peter Davison's note in Davison, Davison, and Angus, eds., *The Complete Works of George Orwell,* Vol. 13, 497.
24.   Peter Davison, Sheila Davison, and Ian Angus, eds., *The Complete Works of George Orwell,* Vol. 16, 18.
25.   George Orwell, *Animal Farm,* in Peter Davison, ed., *The Complete Works of George Orwell,* Vol. 8, 15.

26. Ibid., 31.
27. Ibid., 48.
28. Ibid., 55–56.
29. Ibid., 90.
30. Ibid., 95.
31. Davison, Davison, and Angus, eds., *The Complete Works of George Orwell*, Vol. 16, 59.
32. Ibid., 127.
33. Quoted in Crick, *George Orwell*, 454.
34. Davison, Davison, and Angus, eds., *The Complete Works of George Orwell*, Vol. 16, 229.
35. Quoted in Crick, *George Orwell*, 455.
36. Quoted in Davison, Davison, and Angus, eds., *The Complete Works of George Orwell*, Vol. 16, 282.
37. Christopher Andrew and Oleg Gordievsky, *KGB: The Inside Story of Its Foreign Operations from Lenin to Gorbachev* (New York: HarperCollins, 1990), 325.
38. Genrikh Borovik, *The Philby Files* (London: Little, Brown, 1994), 138.
39. In a strange twist, Greene got to know Smolka—going by the name Peter Smollett—after the war. Smolka was a consultant on *The Third Man*, a film set in postwar Vienna that Greene wrote and Carol Reed directed. It is not certain how many of Smolka's stories found their way into the final script, but it is speculated that Harry Lime's famous use of the Vienna sewers to escape capture was based on Philby's own adventures in Vienna during the February uprising. See Michael Shelden, *Graham Greene: The Enemy Within* (New York: Random House, 1994), 266.
40. This is embellished, according to George Woodcock—the messenger actually arrived by taxi and wore a bowler hat. See Crick, *George Orwell*, 492.
41. George Orwell, *Orwell and Politics,* ed. Peter Davison (London: Penguin, 2001), 228–29.
42. Davison, Davison, and Angus, eds., *The Complete Works of George Orwell*, Vol. 20, 227.
43. Davison, Davison, and Angus, eds., *The Complete Works of George Orwell*, Vol. 16, 393.
44. Ibid.
45. Quoted in Scammell, *Koestler,* 247.
46. This was Eric Bentley in *The Sewanee Review*. Quoted in ibid., 248–49.
47. Crick, *George Orwell,* 476.
48. Quoted in ibid., 498.

FOURTEEN

1. Bernard Crick, *George Orwell: A Life* (London: Penguin, 1992), 449–51.
2. George Orwell, *Nineteen Eighty-Four* (New York: Knopf, 1992), 33.
3. Ibid., 21.
4. Ibid.
5. Ibid., 196.
6. Not long after Tehran, Orwell began seriously reading the work of James Burnham, an American philosopher and political theorist, who wrote a

several books predicting that the world would be divided after the war by vast states run by powerful oligarchies. Burnham had been a radical in the 1930s, a friend of Leon Trotsky and, along with Sidney Hook, a prominent figure in the American Workers Party. Burnham grew disillusioned with left-wing politics, however, and, after a series of factional fights with Trotsky and his allies, renounced Marxism. In 1941, he published *The Managerial Revolution*, a hugely influential work that argued capitalism was dying and that socialism would not replace it. Instead, Burnham wrote, the future was "managerial society," by which super-states were run by oligarchies of "managers" (bureaucrats, financiers, scientists, technicians). Despite its bland name, managerialism was a form of totalitarianism, which Burnham felt had been most closely "approximated" by Nazi Germany and the Soviet Union (and to a lesser degree by New Deal America). Orwell had a lot of fun exposing the fallacies in many of Burnham's theories (and *Nineteen Eighty-Four* in part satirizes Burnham), but he believed that Burnham was right about the coming rise of oligarchical power in large states.

7. Peter Davison, Sheila Davison, and Ian Angus, eds., *The Complete Works of George Orwell*, Vol. 17 (London: Secker & Warburg, 1998), 320.

8. Ibid., 321.

9. See Sir John Balfour's message to the Foreign Office from the Moscow embassy. Quoted in Jussi Hanhimäki and Odd Arne Westad, eds., *The Cold War: A History in Documents and Eyewitness Accounts* (New York: Oxford University Press, 2002), 31. As well as creating a buffer zone of allied states on his western border, Stalin wanted to keep those lands that had been seized while the Soviet Union was aligned in its nonaggression pact with the Nazis between 1939 and 1941 (including Western Ukraine, Belarus, and the Baltic states).

10. Tony Judt, *Postwar: A History of Europe Since 1945* (New York: Penguin, 2005), 40.

11. Quoted in Hanhimäki and Westad, eds., *The Cold War*, 47–48.

12. Ibid., 108–9.

13. Ibid., 117–18.

14. Ibid., 122.

15. Ibid., 126–27.

16. Ibid., 129.

17. Quoted in Crick, *George Orwell*, 551.

18. Crick, *George Orwell*, 563.

19. Orwell, *Nineteen Eighty-Four*, 266.

20. Ibid., 28.

21. For Orwell's interest in the Lysenko case see Peter Davison, ed., *The Lost Orwell* (London: Timewell, 2006), 130.

22. Orwell, *Nineteen Eighty-Four*, 101.

23. Ibid., 136. The idea that lowbrow culture was instrumental to totalitarianism had become an intellectual cornerstone of the anti-Communist left cultural politics of *Partisan Review* (perhaps most famously expressed in Clement Greenberg's essay "Avant-Garde and Kitsch"). In *Nineteen Eighty-Four*, the "proles" are given newspapers that contain nothing but "sport, crime and

astrology," films "oozing with sex," pornography, cheap novelettes, and sentimental songs mechanically composed (ibid., 46).

24. Ibid., 56.
25. Davison, Davison, and Angus, eds., *The Complete Works of George Orwell*, Vol. 16, 99.
26. Davison, Davison, and Angus, eds., *The Complete Works of George Orwell*, Vol. 19, 88.
27. Orwell thought 1,500 copies had been seized, later revising that up to 3,000 copies. Secker & Warburg said 5,000 were seized. See ibid., 472, and Davison, Davison, and Angus, eds., *The Complete Works of George Orwell*, Vol. 20, 151.
28. Davison, Davison, and Angus, eds., *The Complete Works of George Orwell*, Vol. 19, 207.
29. Ibid., 392.
30. Ibid., 473.
31. Davison, Davison, and Angus, eds., *The Complete Works of George Orwell*, Vol. 20, 148.
32. Quoted in Crick, *George Orwell*, 492.
33. Quoted in John Rodden, *George Orwell: The Politics of Literary Reputation* (New Brunswick, NJ: Transaction, 2002), 24.
34. George Orwell, "Why I Write," in Davison, Davison, and Angus, eds., *The Complete Works of George Orwell*, Vol. 18, 319.
35. Rodden, *George Orwell*, 27.
36. Crick, *George Orwell*, 519.
37. Davison, Davison, and Angus, eds., *The Complete Works of George Orwell*, Vol. 20, 135.
38. Quoted in Crick, *George Orwell*, 567.
39. Ibid., 406.
40. The cult of youth and physical fitness in *Nineteen Eighty-Four* is clearly taken from National Socialism. The "Spies" are a version of the Hitlerjugend.
41. Orwell, *Nineteen Eighty-Four*, 211.
42. Quoted in Rodden, *George Orwell*, 25.
43. Ibid., 26.
44. Davison, Davison, and Angus, eds., *The Complete Works of George Orwell*, Vol. 20, 102.
45. Giles Scott-Smith. "'A Radical Democratic Political Offensive': Melvin J. Lasky, *Der Monat*, and the Congress for Cultural Freedom," *Journal of Contemporary History* 35, no. 2 (April 2000): 269–72.
46. Davison, Davison, and Angus, eds., *The Complete Works of George Orwell*, Vol. 20, 148.
47. Orwell, *Nineteen Eighty-Four*, 283.
48. Davison, Davison, and Angus, eds., *The Complete Works of George Orwell*, Vol. 20, 241.
49. Ibid., 319.
50. Hugh Wilford, *The CIA, the British Left, and the Cold War* (London: Frank Cass, 2003), 58–59. Wilford includes a series of panels from the graphic novel.
51. Ibid., 103.

52. Ibid., 255.
53. Ibid. As well as being homophobic in annotating his list, Orwell noted down that Paul Robeson was black and listed the fact that many of his "suspects" were Jewish.
54. Davison is excellent in establishing the context for Orwell's list. See ibid., 325. Davison was also told that Soviet intelligence was monitoring Orwell and kept a file on him, which would not be surprising.
55. Quoted in Michael Shelden, *Graham Greene: The Enemy Within* (New York: Random House, 1994), 482.
56. Hilary Spurling, *The Girl from the Fiction Department: A Portrait of Sonia Orwell* (New York: Counterpoint, 2003), 67.
57. D. J. Taylor, *Orwell* (London: Chatto & Windus, 2003), 365.
58. Michael Scammell, *Koestler: The Literary and Political Odyssey of a Twentieth-Century Skeptic* (New York: Random House, 2009), 301.
59. Spurling, *The Girl from the Fiction Department*, 91.
60. Quoted in Taylor, *Orwell*, 415.

FIFTEEN

1. "Review of the Scientific and Cultural Conference for World Peace," Committee on House Un-American Activities, House of Representatives, Washington, D.C., April 19, 1949, 1.
2. Robbie Lieberman, *The Strangest Dream: Communism, Anticommunism, and the U.S. Peace Movement 1945–1963* (New York: Syracuse University Press, 2000), 68.
3. Quoted in Frances Kiernan, *Seeing Mary Plain: A Life of Mary McCarthy* (New York: Norton, 2000), 284.
4. Quoted in Carol Brightman, *Writing Dangerously: Mary McCarthy and her World* (New York: Potter, 1992), 326.
5. Ibid., 151.
6. Quoted in ibid., 218.
7. Ibid.
8. Quoted in ibid., 251.
9. Ibid., 256.
10. Mary McCarthy, "I Was There but I Didn't See It Happen," *The New Republic* (November 4, 1940): 633–34.
11. See *Partisan Review* (Fall 1939): 126.
12. Quoted in Brightman, *Writing Dangerously*, 212.
13. Ibid., 271.
14. Kiernan, *Seeing Mary Plain*, 289.
15. Quoted in ibid., 308.
16. Vincent Giroud, *Nicolas Nabokov: A Life in Freedom and Music* (Oxford: Oxford University Press, 2015), 217.
17. See *Partisan Review* (January 1949): 4.
18. Babel's work was undergoing a New York revival. Back in the late 1920s the *Menorah Journal* had published five of his stories even before the first English translation of *Red Cavalry* had been published and a young Lionel Trilling, who was a regular contributor, became a champion of Babel. The enthusiasm

for Babel's work again began in magazines that promoted Jewish culture: in 1947 and 1948 *Commentary* published three of Babel's stories. Also in 1948, Avram Yarmolinsky, the head of the Slavonic Division of the New York Public Library, edited a new edition of Babel's stories.

19. "Global Unity Call Cheered By 18,000," *New York Times*, March 28, 1949, 3.

20. Quoted in Giroud, *Nicolas Nabokov*, 219.

21. "Our Way Defended to 2,000 Opening 'Culture' Meeting," *New York Times*, March 26, 1949, 1.

22. Quoted in Giroud, *Nicolas Nabokov*, 218.

23. William Phillips, *A Partisan View: Five Decades in the Politics of Literature* (New Brunswick, NJ: Transaction, 2005), 149.

24. Neil Jumonville, *Critical Crossings: The New York Intellectuals in Postwar America* (Berkeley: University of California Press), 30–31.

25. Quoted in Kiernan, *Seeing Mary Plain*, 309.

26. Ibid., 310.

27. "Shostakovich Bids All Artists Lead War on New 'Fascists,'" *New York Times*, March 28, 1949, 1.

28. Dwight Macdonald, "The Waldorf Conference," *Horizon* (May 1949): 317.

29. Ibid., 324.

30. Ibid., 325.

31. Frances Stonor Saunders, *The Cultural Cold War* (New York: New Press, 1999), 40–41, 55.

SIXTEEN

1. Quoted in Vladimir Pechatnov, "The Soviet Union and the World 1944–53," in Melvin P. Leffler and Odd Arne West, eds., *The Cambridge History of the Cold War*, Vol. 1, *Origins* (Cambridge, UK: Cambridge University Press, 2010), 98.

2. Pechatnov, "The Soviet Union," 90.

3. Quoted in Andy McSmith, *Fear and the Muse Kept Watch* (New York: New Press, 2015), 257.

4. Clare Cavanagh, *Lyric Poetry and Modern Politics: Russia, Poland and the West* (New Haven, CT: Yale University Press, 2009), 112.

5. Lazar Fleischman, *Boris Pasternak: The Poet and his Politics* (Cambridge, MA: Harvard University Press, 1990), 238–40.

6. See Christopher Barnes, *Boris Pasternak: A Literary Biography*, Vol. 2 (New York: Cambridge University Press, 1998), 216.

7. Elaine Feinstein, *Anna of All the Russias: A Life of Anna Akhmatova* (New York: Knopf, 2006), 196.

8. Ibid., 209.

9. It is important to note here that, as Katerina Clark and Evgeny Dobrenko argue, it was not the case that there was a widespread liberalization of culture in the war, rather that it was focused on popular patriotism, and that after the war there was no dissent by intellectuals. See Katerina Clark and Evgeny Dobrenko, *Soviet Culture and Power: A History in Documents* (New Haven, CT: Yale University Press, 2007), 349–51.

10. Akhmatova had actually published a collection called *From Six Books* in

1940, but that was soon taken out of circulation for being "a collection of ideologically harmful, religious-mystical verse" (quoted in ibid., 365).

11. The remark may be apocryphal. It circulated among writers at the time. Nadezhda Mandelstam writes in her second memoir, *Hope Abandoned*, that she heard it from Zoshchenko. See McSmith, *Fear and the Muse Kept Watch*, 257.

12. Quoted in Roberta Reeder, *Anna Akhmatova: Poet and Prophet* (New York: Picador, 1995), 291.

13. Quoted in Clark and Dobrenko, *Soviet Culture and Power*, 422–23.

14. Ibid., 421.

15. Quoted in Reeder, *Anna Akhmatova*, 293.

16. Ibid., 293.

17. See Clark and Dobrenko, *Soviet Culture and Power*, 351.

18. Ibid., 424.

19. Michael Ignatieff, *Isaiah Berlin: A Life* (New York: Metropolitan Books, 1998), 136–37, 142–48.

20. Ibid., 139.

21. Isaiah Berlin, "Conversations with Akhmatova and Pasternak," in Henry Hardy, ed., *The Soviet Mind* (Washington, D.C.: Brookings, 2003), 67.

22. Ignatieff, *Isaiah Berlin*, 151.

23. Gyorgy Dalos has dedicated a whole book to the meeting and its consequences, *The Guest from the Future*, trans. Anthony Wood (London: John Murray, 1998).

24. Ignatieff, *Isaiah Berlin*, 160.

25. Berlin, "Conversations," 71.

26. Anna Akhmatova, *Selected Poems*, trans. Walter Arndt (Ann Arbor, MI: Ardis), 142–48. Akhmatova also included Berlin in other work. At her second meeting with Berlin, on January 5, 1946, she gave him a collection of her poems, with a new one handwritten on the flyleaf. Later he discovered that this poem was to form the second part of the cycle of poems she titled *Cinque*.

27. Quoted in Jussi Hanhimäki and Odd Arne Westad, eds., *The Cold War: A History in Documents and Eyewitness Accounts* (New York: Oxford University Press, 2002), 110.

28. Isaiah Berlin, "The Arts in Russia Under Stalin: 1945," in *The Soviet Mind*, ed. Henry Hardy (Washington, D.C.: Brookings, 2003), 13.

29. The memorandum is reproduced in ibid., 11.

30. Gyorgy Dalos includes as an appendix to *The Guest from the Future* a document from the Leningrad branch of the Ministry of State Security, dated August 15, 1946, and addressed to Zhdanov, which shows that the security service carefully monitored Berlin's visits and felt they merited "special attention." See Dalos, *The Guest from the Future*, 212.

31. Quoted in Reeder, *Anna Akhmatova*, 288.

32. Ibid., 289.

33. Fleischman, *Boris Pasternak*, 247.

34. Pechatnov, "The Soviet Union," 102.

35. David Priestland, "Cold War Mobilization and Domestic Politics," in Melvin P. Leffler and Odd Arne West, eds., *The Cambridge History of the Cold War*, Vol. 1, *Origins* (Cambridge, UK: Cambridge University Press, 2010), 454; and

Nikolai Krementsov, *Stalinist Science* (Princeton, NJ: Princeton University Press, 1997), 137.
36. Reeder, *Anna Akhmatova,* 293.
37. Fleischman, *Boris Pasternak,* 250.
38. Reeder, *Anna Akhmatova,* 296.
39. Pechatnov, "The Soviet Union," 104.
40. See Tony Judt, *Postwar: A History of Europe Since 1945* (New York: Penguin, 2005), 143.
41. Ibid., 137.
42. Ibid., 135. Tito's Yugoslavia, which had not needed the help of the Red Army to defeat their German occupiers, was expelled from the Cominform in 1948 for refusing to toe the Moscow line.
43. Ibid., 178–80.
44. Ibid., 145.
45. Stalin's hostility to ethnic minorities was hardly new. During the war he had ordered the forcible displacement of minorities from the Crimea and Caucasus regions to Siberia or Central Asia. He feared they were an enemy within, who might side with the invading Germans.
46. Quoted in Reeder, *Anna Akhmatova,* 294.

SEVENTEEN

1. Quoted in Peter Coleman, *The Liberal Conspiracy: The Congress for Cultural Freedom and the Struggle for the Mind of Postwar Europe* (New York: Free Press, 1989), 1. Coleman was a member of the CCF in Australia, and his book is, at least in part, a defense of the organization as a necessary intellectual buffer against the threat of Communism.
2. Hugh Trevor-Roper, "Ex-Communist vs Communist," *Manchester Guardian,* July 10, 1950, 4.
3. On the final day of the Congress East Berlin cut off power supply to the West, forcing the use of a new power station, the building of which had begun during the airlift. See *New York Times,* June 30, 1950.
4. This list was decided on by Raymond Aron, James Burnham, and Arthur Koestler. See Sarah Miller Harris, *The CIA and the Congress for Cultural Freedom in the Early Cold War* (New York: Routledge, 2016), 81. In 1948, Jaspers had left Germany for Switzerland, where he took citizenship.
5. Quoted in Michael Scammell, *Koestler: The Literary and Political Odyssey of a Twentieth-Century Skeptic* (New York: Random House, 2009), 357.
6. Peter De Mendelssohn, "Berlin Congress," *New Statesman and Nation,* July 15, 1950, 62; Frances Stonor Saunders, *The Cultural Cold War* (New York: New Press, 1999), 79.
7. Harold Williams, "Koestler, at Anti-Communist Congress, Bars Neutrality," *Baltimore Sun,* June 26, 1950, 14.
8. Quoted in Coleman, *The Liberal Conspiracy,* 251.
9. Ibid., 24.
10. Quoted in David Caute, *Politics and the Novel During the Cold War* (New Brunswick, NJ: Transaction, 2010), 103.
11. The anti-Americanism of the Left Bank intellectuals became a subject of

fascination for American writers. In 1952, Mary McCarthy wrote of Beauvoir that she saw America as being "a gelid eternity of drugstores, jukeboxes, smiles, refrigerators, and 'fascism.'" Mary McCarthy, *A Bolt from the Blue and Other Essays* (New York: New York Review of Books Editions, 2002), 240.

12. Scammell, *Koestler,* 287.
13. Ibid., 288.
14. Quoted in ibid., 299.
15. Ibid., 306.
16. Ibid., 307.
17. Ibid., 314.
18. Quoted in Carol Brightman, *Writing Dangerously: Mary McCarthy and Her World* (New York: Potter, 1992), 301.
19. Quoted in Scammell, *Koestler,* 318.
20. Ibid., 342.
21. Ibid., 347.
22. David Cesarani, *Arthur Koestler: The Homeless Mind* (New York: Free Press, 1999), 349.
23. Scammell, *Koestler,* 351–52.
24. Sean McMeekin, *The Red Millionaire: A Political Biography of Willi Münzenberg* (New Haven, CT: Yale University Press, 2005), 305–6.
25. Quoted in Scammell, *Koestler,* 353.
26. Ibid., 364. Bohlen was a senior official, not the Ambassador (that was David Bruce).
27. Ibid., 109.
28. Tim Weiner, *Legacy of Ashes: The History of the CIA* (New York: Doubleday, 2007), 20.
29. Ibid., 27.
30. "National Security Council Directive on Office of Special Projects," NSC-10/2, Washington, D.C., June 18, 1948.
31. Weiner, *Legacy of Ashes,* 28.
32. Ibid., 32.
33. Ibid., 36.
34. The files on Operation QKOPERA remain classified.
35. Miller Harris, *The CIA and the Congress,* 60.
36. "Origins of the Congress for Cultural Freedom, 1949–50," Central Intelligence Agency, Center for the Study of Intelligence, Washington, D.C., 2007.
37. Quoted in Scammell, *Koestler,* 354.
38. Peter De Mendelssohn, "Berlin Congress," *New Statesman and Nation,* July 15, 1950, 63.
39. Trevor-Roper, "Ex-Communist vs Communist," 4.
40. Scammell, *Koestler,* 367.
41. Hugh Wilford, *The CIA, the British Left, and the Cold War* (London: Frank Cass, 2003), 57.
42. Quoted in Saunders, *The Cultural Cold War,* 61.
43. Quoted in Scammell, *Koestler,* 367.
44. Ibid., 368.
45. Quoted in ibid., 375.

46. Ibid., 382.
47. Quoted in ibid., 372.
48. According to Scammell, Koestler was "contemptuous that [the CIA's] officials were so bad at keeping a secret" (ibid.).
49. Miller Harris, *The CIA and the Congress*, 81, 91.
50. Quoted in ibid., 83.
51. Quoted in Scammell, *Koestler,* 384.
52. Ibid., 424.

EIGHTEEN

1. See Henry Louis Gates, *The African-American Century* (New York: Free Press, 2000), 146. Martin Duberman, in his biography of Robeson, points out that the singer was misquoted.
2. Gerald Sorin, *Howard Fast: Life and Literature in the Left Lane* (Bloomington: Indiana University Press, 2012), 56.
3. Ibid., 2.
4. Ibid., 185.
5. *New York Times,* September 6, 1949, 23.
6. Quoted in Sorin, *Howard Fast,* 188.
7. Howard Fast, *Literature and Reality* (New York: International Publishers, 1950), 9.
8. Ibid., 97.
9. Ibid., 9.
10. Quoted in Sorin, *Howard Fast,* 187.
11. In *Not Without Honor* (New York: Free Press, 1995), Richard Gid Powers documents the history of the anti-Communist movement and argues that depictions of it as merely a hysterical witch hunt are reductive.
12. Sorin, *Howard Fast,* 130.
13. Quoted in ibid., 130.
14. Ibid., 143.
15. Ibid., 131.
16. Ellen Schrecker, *Many Are the Crimes: McCarthyism in America* (Boston: Little, Brown, 1998), 211.
17. Robert Justin Goldstein, *Political Repression in Modern America, 1870–1976* (Urbana: University of Illinois Press, 2001), 303.
18. Sorin, *Howard Fast,* 136.
19. Schrecker, *Many Are the Crimes,* 320.
20. Ibid., 324.
21. Ibid., 327.
22. *New York Times,* June 8, 1950, 1. Fast was right that the United States was cultivating Spain as an ally. Trade grew rapidly between the two nations in this period. Three years later, under Eisenhower, the United States signed the Pact of Madrid with Franco's government, guaranteeing aid in exchange for permission to build naval and air bases in Spain.
23. Howard Fast, *Being Red* (Boston: Houghton Mifflin, 1990), 249.
24. Ibid., 249–50.

25. Internal Security Act, 1950, http://uscode.house.gov/view.xhtml?path =/prelim@title50/chapter23&edition=prelim.

26. David Caute, *The Great Fear* (New York: Simon & Schuster, 1978), 38–39.

27. *New York Times*, November 8, 1950, 2.

28. The letter was quoted in the *New York Times*, June 11, 1950.

29. Quoted in Frances Kiernan, *Seeing Mary Plain: A Life of Mary McCarthy* (New York: Norton, 2000), 338.

30. Ibid.

31. Michael Wreszin, *A Rebel in Defense of Tradition: The Life and Politics of Dwight Macdonald* (New York: Basic Books, 1994), 273.

32. McCarthy later recalled that of the group of intellectuals associated with *Partisan Review,* Philip Rahv alone "came out, in print, with an unequivocal condemnation and contemptuous dismissal" of McCarthyism. See Mary McCarthy, *A Bolt from the Blue and Other Essays* (New York: New York Review of Books Editions, 2002), 345.

33. William Fulton, "20 Top Writers Push Pension Russia's Praise," *Chicago Daily Tribune,* April 2, 1950, 8.

34. Quoted in Sorin, *Howard Fast,* 204.

35. Fast, *Being Red,* 276.

36. Howard Fast, *Spartacus* (Armonk, NY: North Castle Books, 1996), 363.

37. Quoted in Sorin, *Howard Fast,* 235.

38. Ibid.

39. Phillip Deery, *Red Apple: Communism and McCarthyism in Cold War New York* (New York: Fordham University Press, 2014), 45.

40. Fast, *Being Red,* 290.

41. Sorin, *Howard Fast,* 237.

42. Sorin claims this was actually a $2.50 edition.

43. Sorin, *Howard Fast,* 237–38.

44. Deery, *Red Apple,* 48.

45. Fast estimated that it was brought out in more than two hundred editions worldwide.

NINETEEN

1. Stephen Spender, *Journals 1939–83,* ed. John Goldsmith (New York: Random House, 1986), 95.

2. Accounts of Burgess's phone calls vary. Some sources say there was only one call, others say Burgess called Spender the next morning rather than the same evening as the first call. What is agreed is that Burgess and Spender had a significant conversation and that a message was given for Auden.

3. "Two British Diplomats Vanish," *New York Herald,* June 7, 1951.

4. Ibid., 1. Maclean certainly had suffered a breakdown, driven by his despair at the double life he was leading. Having asked to stop working for Moscow, and having been ignored, Maclean went on a drunken rampage in Cairo, where he was stationed, smashing up a flat belonging to two women who worked for the U.S. Embassy. He was given the summer off and sent to a psychologist. He was eventually adjudged to have recovered and made head of the Foreign

Office American desk. See Christopher Andrew, *The Defence of the Realm: The Authorized History of MI5* (New York: Allen Lane, 2009), 421.

5. "On Binge in Paris?" *Globe and Mail,* June 9, 1951, 7.

6. Andrew, *The Defence of the Realm,* 422.

7. *New York Times,* June 10, 1951, 14.

8. Ibid.

9. Ibid.

10. John Sutherland, *Stephen Spender: A Literary Life* (New York: Oxford University Press, 2005), 358.

11. *Manchester Guardian,* June 11, 1951, 5.

12. Quoted in Humphrey Carpenter, *W. H. Auden: A Biography* (London: George Allen & Unwin, 1981), 369–70.

13. Quoted in James Smith, *British Writers and MI5 Surveillance, 1930–1960* (New York: Cambridge University Press, 2013), 62.

14. Quoted in Christopher Andrew and Vasili Mitrokhin, *The Sword and the Shield: The Mitrokhin Archive and the History of the KGB* (New York: Basic Books, 1999), 81.

15. Ibid., 85.

16. Spender, *Journals 1939–83,* 96.

17. Quoted in Sutherland, *Stephen Spender: A Literary Life,* 361.

18. Smith, *British Writers,* 63.

19. Ibid., 65. MI5 also tapped the phone of Philip Toynbee, a friend of Maclean's, and overhead Cyril Connolly talking about how he had met Burgess on May 10 and told Burgess that Auden was in town (Connolly had dined with him and Spender the night before). He was also overheard talking to Lehmann, speculating the Americans had discovered Burgess and Maclean and they had made a run for it. Lehmann repeated that he had "evidence" of Burgess being a spy but was careful not to use Rosamond's name or describe the "evidence" itself.

20. Quoted in ibid., 67.

21. "Letter to the Editor," *Times Literary Supplement,* March 14, 1980, 294.

22. This included Peter Pollock, Jack Hewit, and Gerald Hamilton.

23. Smith, *British Writers,* 68.

24. Quoted in ibid., 67.

25. David K. Johnson, *The Lavender Scare: The Cold War Persecution of Gays and Lesbians in the Federal Government* (Chicago: University of Chicago Press, 2004), 16–17.

26. "Perverts Called Government Peril," *New York Times,* April 19, 1950, 25.

27. Johnson, *The Lavender Scare,* 34–35.

28. Andrew, *The Defence of the Realm,* 423.

29. S. J. Hamrick writes: "Among Angleton's Mad Hatter notions was his belief that the Sino-Soviet split was a deception; that British prime minister Howard Wilson was a Soviet agent; that CIA director William Colby's profile was that of a KGB sleeper; and that the Church Committee's 1975 investigation of the CIA was a plot masterminded from Moscow by Kim Philby." See S. J. Hamrick, *Deceiving the Deceivers* (New Haven, CT: Yale University Press, 2004), 193–94.

30. Kim Philby, *My Silent War* (London: MacGibbon & Kee, 1968), 116.
31. Ibid., 117.
32. Yuri Modin, who was London resident at the time, credits Philby with sabotaging the Albania operation, but Hamrick argues that this is at best fanciful. Hamrick, *Deceiving the Deceivers*, 201–3.
33. Philby, *My Silent War*, 126.
34. Philby did not trust the Washington residency and, before Burgess moved to Washington, was sending his reports to Burgess by mail so that he could deliver them to Yuri Modin, the London resident. See Andrew, *The Defence of the Realm*, 422–23.
35. Burgess's biographer Andrew Lownie disputes Philby's argument and contends that Burgess's recall was an accident that they then exploited. See Andrew Lownie, *Stalin's Englishman: The Lives of Guy Burgess* (London: Hodder & Stoughton, 2015), 220.
36. Yuri Modin, *My Five Cambridge Friends*, trans. Anthony Roberts (New York: Farrar, Straus & Giroux, 1994), 204.
37. Andrew, *The Defence of the Realm*, 423.
38. Philby, *My Silent War*, 131.
39. Ben Macintyre, *A Spy Among Friends* (New York: Crown, 2014), 160–61.
40. Ibid., 167.
41. Philby, *My Silent War*, 141.
42. Ibid.
43. Macintyre, *A Spy Among Friends*, 170–71.
44. See Andrew, *The Defence of the Realm*, 427. There was little concrete evidence against the other members of the Five. Burgess had got a message to Anthony Blunt before defecting, allowing Blunt to sweep Burgess's flat for incriminating material. He destroyed everything but some notes that implicated John Cairncross. While Blunt bluffed his way through interrogation, the circumstantial evidence against Cairncross was strong, and he was forced to resign from his job at the Treasury.
45. Quoted in Smith, *British Writers*, 68.
46. In 1956, Burgess claimed, in an interview with Tom Driberg in Moscow, that if he'd been able to get hold of Auden and make definite plans for a holiday in Ischia, he would "probably have gone straight on there after dropping Donald to Prague." He also claimed they had defected "on a whim." This interview should be taken with a pinch of salt. Not only was it vetted by the KGB, bur Driberg had been blackmailed into working for Moscow on that very trip, having been photographed having sex with an agent in a public toilet behind the Metropole. See Andrew and Mitrokhin, *The Sword and the Shield*, 400–401. When Spender met Burgess in Moscow many years later, he told Spender the same story. See Spender, *Journals 1939–83*, 95.
47. Smith, *British Writers*, 38–39.
48. Ibid., 42.
49. Spender was sufficiently trusted to be given intelligence work during the war. In his published journals, Spender wrote that he had researched Italian fascism for a "subsidiary branch of Political Intelligence." This work, he wrote, involved "[n]othing secret," but his MI5 file reveals that he was in fact working

for the clandestine Political Warfare Executive, employees of which used the more benign department of Political Intelligence as cover. As early as November 1943, the PWE consulted MI5 about employing Spender and they found no reasons to object, adjudging him to have broken with Communism. He was hired in August 1944. This did not mean he did not research Italian fascism; he very likely did. The difference was the ends to which this work was put: the PWE was charged with covert "black" propaganda. Spender also traveled to liberated Europe in 1945 as part of the Allied Control Commission, working on the cultural aspects of de-Nazification. While there he met up with his old friend Richard Crossman, head of the PWE's German section. See Smith, *British Writers*, 56–57.

50. As previously discussed, the creation of *Der Monat* not only preceded the founding of the CCF but actually played an important role in that process. For a clear account of *Der Monat*'s complex relationship with the U.S. military and the CIA, please see Michael Hochgeschwender, "*Der Monat* and the Congress for Cultural Freedom: The High Tide of the Intellectual Cold War, 1948–71," *Campaigning Culture and the Global Cold War: The Journals of the Congress for Cultural Freedom*, eds. Giles Scott-Smith and Charlotte Lerg (London: Palgrave Macmillan, 2017), 71–89.

51. Frances Stonor Saunders, *The Cultural Cold War* (New York: New Press, 1999), 169.

52. Tosco Fyvel, who had collaborated with Orwell during the war and worked for the IRD, was also involved in the planning of *Encounter*.

53. Woodhouse's cover was enhanced by his being a member of the Royal Society of Literature. He later went on to write a foreword to a 1956 Signet paperback edition of *Animal Farm*, which is often cited as an example of the way Orwell's work was repositioned to serve the ends of the Cold War. In that edition he quoted Orwell's famous claim: "Every line of serious work that I have written since 1936 has been written, directly or indirectly, against totalitarianism and for democratic socialism, as I understand it." Woodhouse, however, cut the final two clauses so it read as if Orwell's only purpose was fighting totalitarianism. See John Rodden, *George Orwell: The Politics of Literary Reputation* (New York: Oxford University Press, 1989), 212.

54. Spender, *Journals 1939–83*, 125. Josselson had sounded out Spender the previous month, saying he wanted him to edit "an English edition of *Preuves*" (quoted in Saunders, *The Cultural Cold War*, 173).

55. The CCF had first reached out to Spender in 1950 and the following year he became the inaugural chair of the British Society for Cultural Freedom and the British representative on the CCF's executive committee. See Hugh Wilford, *The CIA, the British Left, and the Cold War* (London: Frank Cass, 2003), 195–206.

56. In fact, the magazine had first been conceived as a way to reach intellectuals in India and East Asia (the CCF's second major conference had been held in Bombay [now Mumbai] in 1951), but the British intellectuals involved in the planning pushed for it to take a transatlantic approach. See Wilford, *The CIA, the British Left, and the Cold War*, 263–64. This did not mean that the CCF lost interest in India. *Encounter* was promoted there and two journals, *Quest*

and Freedom First, were funded by the CCF to combat perceived Communist influence.

57. Wilford, *The CIA, the British Left, and the Cold War,* 266.
58. For a brilliant account of the short life of *Perspectives USA,* see Greg Barnhisel, *Cold War Modernists: Art, Literature, and American Cultural Diplomacy* (New York: Columbia University Press, 2015), 179–216.
59. "A Postscript to the Rosenberg Case," *Encounter* (October 1953): 18–19.
60. Quoted in Saunders, *The Cultural Cold War,* 186.
61. "After the Apocalypse," *Encounter* (October 1953): 1.
62. Quoted in Saunders, *The Cultural Cold War,* 187.
63. Spender, *Journals 1939–83,* 442.

TWENTY

1. See Norman Sherry, *The Life of Graham Greene,* Vol. 2 (London: Cape, 1995), 356.
2. Quoted in ibid.
3. Graham Greene, *Ways of Escape* (Toronto: L&OD, 2007), 153–54.
4. Ibid., 146.
5. Sherry, *The Life of Graham Greene,* Vol. 2, 251.
6. Richard Stubbs, *Hearts and Minds in Guerrilla Warfare: The Malayan Emergency 1948–60* (New York: Oxford University Press, 1989), 61.
7. Greene, *Ways of Escape,* 158.
8. The example of the massacre at Batang Kali is particularly grim. See Piers Brendon, *The Decline and Fall of the British Empire, 1781–1997* (London: Jonathan Cape, 2007), 454.
9. Greene, *Ways of Escape,* 159.
10. Ibid., 147–48.
11. Quoted in Sherry, *The Life of Graham Greene,* Vol. 2, 352.
12. Greene, *Ways of Escape,* 147; Brandon, 455.
13. Quoted in Sherry, *The Life of Graham Greene,* Vol. 2, 357.
14. Graham Greene, *The Quiet American* (London: Penguin Books, 1991), 88.
15. Ibid., 25.
16. Greene, *Ways of Escape,* 161.
17. Fredrik Logevall, *Embers of War: The Fall of an Empire and the Making of America's Vietnam* (New York: Random House, 2012), 261.
18. Greene, *Ways of Escape,* 163.
19. Logevall, *Embers of War,* 18.
20. Ibid., 270.
21. Ibid.
22. Quoted in Logevall, *Embers of War,* 263.
23. Quoted in Sherry, *The Life of Graham Greene,* Vol. 2, 375.
24. Greene, *The Quiet American,* 51–52.
25. Ibid., 53.
26. Greene, *Ways of Escape,* 170. Greene does not identify the American in the passage, but Norman Sherry later discovered that it was Hochstetter. See Sherry, *The Life of Graham Greene,* Vol. 2, 418–19.
27. "A Bomb Makes a Shambles of a Sunny Saigon Square," *Life* (January 28, 1952): 19.

28. Greene, *Ways of Escape,* 171.
29. Mark Atwood Lawrence, *The Vietnam War: A Concise International History* (New York: Oxford University Press, 2008), 40.
30. Ibid., 46.
31. Ibid., 56.
32. A. J. Liebling, "A Talkative Something-or-Other," *The New Yorker* (April 7, 1956): 154.
33. Logevall, *Embers of War,* 635.
34. Quoted in Martin F. Nolan, "Graham Greene's Unquiet Novel," *New York Times,* January 30, 2003.

TWENTY-ONE

1. Michael Scammell, *Solzhenitsyn: A Biography* (New York: Norton, 1984), 278.
2. For a comprehensive account of the network of camps and prisons and how they worked, see Anne Applebaum, *Gulag: A History* (New York: Random House, 2003).
3. Ibid., 285.
4. Ibid., 284.
5. Aleksandr Solzhenitsyn, *One Day in the Life of Ivan Denisovich,* trans. Ralph Parker (New York: Dutton, 1963), 34.
6. Scammell, *Solzhenitsyn,* 283.
7. For a description of these strikes see ibid., 295–97.
8. Odd Arne Westad, *The Cold War: A World History* (New York: Basic Books, 2017), 192.
9. Scammell, *Solzhenitsyn,* 301.
10. Elaine Feinstein, *Anna of All the Russias: A Life of Anna Akhmatova* (New York: Knopf, 2006), 226.
11. As Clare Cavanagh notes, one part of the poem was published as "Sentence" in 1940 but given the deliberately misleading date of composition of 1934. The poem was actually written in 1939 after Lev's arrest. The whole poem was not published until long after her death. See Clare Cavanagh, *Lyric Poetry and Modern Politics: Russia, Poland and the West* (New Haven, CT: Yale University Press, 2009), 24–25.
12. Roberta Reeder, *Anna Akhmatova: Poet and Prophet* (New York: Picador, 1995), 307.
13. Joshua Rubenstein, *The Last Days of Stalin* (New Haven, CT: Yale University Press, 2016), 36–37.
14. This "myth of encirclement" was a major feature of late Stalinism. See Tobias Rupprecht, *Soviet Internationalism After Stalin: Interaction and Exchange Between the USSR and Latin America During the Cold War* (Cambridge, UK: Cambridge University Press, 2015), 1.
15. Rubenstein, *The Last Days of Stalin,* 72.
16. This is Khrushchev's account of what happened. For the discrepancies between different accounts see ibid., 1–34.
17. Westad, *The Cold War,* 192.
18. Tony Judt, *Postwar: A History of Europe Since 1945* (New York: Penguin, 2005), 310.

19. Quoted in Reeder, *Anna Akhmatova*, 318.

20. Amanda Haight, *Anna Akhmatova: A Poetic Pilgrimage* (Oxford: Oxford University Press, 1990), 162.

21. George Gibian, *Interval of Freedom* (Minneapolis: University of Minnesota Press, 1960), 10.

22. For a transcript of the "Secret Speech," see Ronald Grigor Suny, ed., *The Structure of Soviet History: Essays and Documents* (Oxford: Oxford University Press, 2014), 393–403.

23. Rupprecht, *Soviet Internationalism After Stalin*, 6.

24. Ibid., 55–58.

25. As a poet, her road to official rehabilitation was gradual and uneven. In 1958 the first volume of her poems since the Zhdanov resolution was published, with a more substantive collection following three years later. She had outlasted Stalin, even if it came at a terrible cost. See Haight, *Anna Akhmatova*, 173.

26. Gerald Sorin, *Howard Fast: Life and Literature in the Left Lane* (Bloomington: Indiana University Press, 2012), 263–64.

27. *New York Times*, February 19, 1953, 1.

28. *Baltimore Sun*, February 19, 1953, 1.

29. Maurice Friedberg, *A Decade of Euphoria: Western Literature in Post-Stalin Russia, 1954–1965* (Bloomington: Indiana University Press, 1977), 11; and Deming Brown, *Soviet Attitudes Toward American Writing* (Princeton, NJ: Princeton University Press, 1962), 281.

30. Howard Fast, *Being Red* (Boston: Houghton Mifflin, 1990), 349–50.

31. Sorin, *Howard Fast*, 174–75.

32. Ibid., 176.

33. Ibid., 316.

34. Quoted in ibid., 341.

35. John Merony and Sean Coons, "How Kirk Douglas Overstated His Role in Breaking the Hollywood Blacklist," *The Atlantic* (July 5, 2012).

36. Scammell, *Solzhenitsyn*, 317.

37. Tony Judt, *Postwar: A History of Europe Since 1945* (New York: Penguin, 2005), 310.

38. These were published first in English translation in 1966.

39. Reeder, *Anna Akhmatova*, 318.

40. Isaiah Berlin, "The Arts in Russia Under Stalin: 1945," in *The Soviet Mind*, ed. Henry Hardy (Washington, D.C.: Brookings, 2003), 23.

TWENTY-TWO

1. Richard Wright, *The Color Curtain: A Report on the Bandung Conference* (Cleveland, OH: World Publishing, 1956), 11.

2. Quoted in Hazel Rowley, *Richard Wright: The Life and Times* (Chicago: University of Chicago Press, 2008), 330.

3. Controversial books could get published in Paris when it was impossible elsewhere; James Joyce's *Ulysses*, Henry Miller's *Tropic of Cancer*, Vladimir Nabokov's *Lolita*, and William Burroughs's *Naked Lunch* were all published first in the city. Sylvia Beach, who brought out the first edition of *Ulysses*, was a frequent help to the Wrights.

4. Rowley, *Richard Wright*, 326.
5. Quoted in ibid., 373.
6. Ibid., 352.
7. Wright, *Color Curtain*, 12.
8. Ibid., 15.
9. Richard Wright, *Black Boy* (New York: Perennial Classics, 1998), 294.
10. Ibid., 315–16.
11. Ibid., 318.
12. Ibid., 332.
13. Rowley, *Richard Wright*, 93.
14. Wright, *Black Boy*, 332.
15. Quoted in Rowley, *Richard Wright*, 99.
16. Ibid., 126.
17. Quoted in ibid., 180.
18. Ibid., 158.
19. Ibid., 154.
20. Ibid., 183. Wright was not alone in being subjected to these kinds of pressures. Langston Hughes was pressured into dropping an essay on W. E. B. DuBois from his collection *Famous American Negroes* because of DuBois's support for Communist causes. See Stephen J. Whitfield, *The Culture of the Cold War* (Baltimore, MD: Johns Hopkins University Press, 1996), 4.
21. Ibid., 182.
22. Ibid., 191.
23. Wright had previously been married to Dhima Rose Meidman, born in Odessa to Russian-Jewish parents. She was into modern dance and had even been to Moscow to train Russians in the art. The marriage did not last long. See ibid., 176.
24. Quoted in Rowley, *Richard Wright*, 260.
25. Wright originally called his memoir *American Hunger* but ended up changing the title to *Black Boy* after the Book of the Month Club pressured him into dropping the second part of the book, concerning his struggles with the Communist Party in Chicago. The idea was that he might publish this as a separate volume. See ibid., 287.
26. Ibid., 371.
27. Odd Arne Westad, *The Cold War: A World History* (New York: Basic Books, 2017), 266.
28. Ibid., 269.
29. It was coined by the French historian Alfred Sauvy in 1952. Ibid., 261.
30. Rowley, *Richard Wright*, 363.
31. Ibid., 389.
32. Ibid., 390.
33. James Campbell, *Exiled in Paris* (New York: Scribner, 1995), 99.
34. Quoted in Rowley, *Richard Wright*, 398.
35. Ibid., 420.
36. Ibid., 426.
37. Kwame Nkrumah, "The Motion of Destiny," in *The Penguin Book of Twentieth-Century Speeches*, ed. Brian MacArthur (New York: Penguin, 1999), 255.

38. Quoted in Rowley, *Richard Wright*, 427.
39. Ibid., 429.
40. The irony here, of course, was that Nkrumah did become more and more dictatorial the longer he remained in office, until he was ousted by a coup in February 1966.
41. Rowley, *Richard Wright*, 436.
42. Quoted in ibid., 436–37.
43. Wright, *Color Curtain*, 76.
44. Ibid., 77.
45. Ibid., 79–80.
46. Ibid., 81.
47. Ibid., 82.
48. Ibid., 76.
49. Ibid., 92–93.
50. Ibid., 93.
51. Ibid., 94.
52. See Brian Russell Roberts and Keith Foulcher's *Indonesian Notebook: A Sourcebook on Richard Wright and the Bandung Conference* (Durham, NC: Duke University Press, 2016) for a comprehensive account of his activities in Indonesia.
53. Quoted in Rowley, *Richard Wright*, 465.
54. Wright, *Color Curtain*, 130.
55. Ibid., 132.
56. Ibid., 134–35.
57. Quoted in Odd Arne Westad, *The Global Cold War: Third World Interventions and the Making of Our Times* (New York: Cambridge University Press, 2007), 100.
58. Ibid., 101.
59. Wright, *Color Curtain*, 172.
60. Ibid., 158.
61. In this he participated in creating the "myth" of Bandung, which grew in power over the years that followed, a myth that did not map onto the events and speeches of the conference itself. One such example is the tenacious assertion that Kwame Nkrumah was among the delegates when he was not. See Roberts and Foulcher, *Indonesian Notebook*, 4–5.
62. Wright, *Color Curtain*, 207–8.
63. Quoted in Rowley, *Richard Wright*, 466.
64. Wright, *Color Curtain*, 220.
65. Westad, *The Global Cold War*, 99.
66. The concept of the Non-Aligned Movement is credited to Indian statesman V. K. Krishna Menon.
67. Westad's *The Global Cold War* is a brilliant and definitive account of the way the Cold War played out in the Third World.
68. Westad, *The Global Cold War*, 91.
69. Ibid., 102.
70. Quoted in Joel Whitney, *Finks* (New York: OR Books, 2016), 39.
71. Whitney gives a fascinating account of how the CIA was involved in founding *The Paris Review* see ibid., 1–46.

72. Quoted in Rowley, *Richard Wright*, 494.
73. Addison Gayle, *Richard Wright: Ordeal of a Native Son* (Garden City, NY: Doubleday, 1980), xv.
74. Natalie Robins claims it is 181 pages long; James Campbell says it runs to more than 250 pages. Either way, it is substantive.
75. Natalie Robins, *Alien Ink: The FBI's War on Freedom of Expression* (New York: Morrow, 1992), 284–85.
76. Quoted in Rowley, *Richard Wright*, 474.
77. James Baldwin, "Letter from Paris," *Encounter* (January 1957): 52.
78. Quoted in Rowley, *Richard Wright*, 478.
79. Quoted in Campbell, *Exiled in Paris*, 191.
80. DuBois was involved in organizing pan-African conferences between the wars. See Westad, *The Global Cold War,* 98.
81. Wright also gave an airing to his dubious opinion that leaders of newly independent countries should be allowed to employ authoritarian methods in order to ensure a transition to democracy. See Baldwin, "Letter from Paris," 59.
82. Rowley, *Richard Wright*, 480.
83. Ibid., 495–96.
84. Hazel Rowley, in her biography, writes that it is not clear how this happened— there is no smoking gun letter or document—but Wright certainly believed it. Perhaps the most plausible explanation is that a combination of his own paranoia and rumors about the CCF had ended up landing him at the truth. See ibid., 519–20.
85. Ibid., 452. Michael Josselson, executive director of the CCF, felt strongly that the congress's magazines should cover Bandung, and Wright must have seemed a perfect choice. Josselson was keen to promote the "decolonization without Communim" approach that George Padmore was popularizing, and Wright's anti-Communism made him an ideal candidate for the job. See Whitney, *Finks*, 90.
86. For a fascinating account of Wright and his relations to AMSAC, see Hugh Wilford, *The Mighty Wurlitzer: How the CIA Played America* (Cambridge, MA: Harvard University Press, 2008), 197–224.
87. Quoted in Whitney, *Finks*, 117.
88. As Brian Russell Roberts and Keith Foulcher point out in *Indonesian Notebook,* Josselson and the CCF had arranged for Wright to meet with Mochtar Lubis, himself a delegate at previous CCF conferences, and that the talks he gave in Jakarta were essentially cultural diplomacy in a country whose future was an important part of the American Cold War calculus. Lubis, who was later imprisoned for criticizing the regime, was freed in 1965 after Suharto's coup, and the following year, he began editing *Horison,* a Jakarta-based magazine funded by the CCF.
89. Rowley, *Richard Wright*, 520.
90. He claimed that William Gardner Smith and Richard Gibson, two black American journalists, were working for the CIA. For an excellent account of the "Gibson Affair" see Campbell, *Exiled in Paris*, 200–205.
91. The letter has not been found. See ibid., 243.
92. Ibid., 245. Biographer Addison Gayle, who revealed how Wright was being

harassed by the FBI and other agencies, found no evidence that they played a role in his death.

93. Quoted in ibid.
94. Rowley, *Richard Wright*, 522.

TWENTY-THREE

1. Alexander Fadeyev, "Suicide Note of A. A. Fadeyev," Sovlit.com, https://www.sovlit.net/fadeevsuicide.
2. There is certainly evidence that he helped Anna Akhmatova. In 1956 Fadeyev interceded on her behalf, appealing to the Prosecutor's Office that her son be released. See Robert Conquest, *The Great Terror: A Reassessment* (London: Hutchinson, 1990), 263.
3. Vitali Shentalinsky, *The KGB's Literary Archive* (London: Harvill, 1995), 159.
4. Lazar Fleischman, *Boris Pasternak: The Poet and His Politics* (Cambridge, MA: Harvard University Press, 1990), 249–50.
5. Andy McSmith, *Fear and the Muse Kept Watch* (New York: New Press, 2015), 279.
6. Fleischman, *Boris Pasternak*, 250.
7. Ibid., 254.
8. Quoted in Christopher Barnes, *Boris Pasternak: A Literary Biography*, Vol. 2 (New York: Cambridge University Press, 1998), 302.
9. Quoted in Peter Finn and Petra Couvée, *The Zhivago Affair: The Kremlin, the CIA, and the Battle over a Forbidden Book* (New York: Pantheon, 2014), 83.
10. Barnes, *Boris Pasternak*, 313.
11. Finn and Couvée, *The Zhivago Affair*, 92.
12. Quoted in ibid., 95. As added insurance, Pasternak sent copies out with two other friends, both of whom were Oxford professors. The first, Isaiah Berlin, promised to have the book published but felt it would be safer for Pasternak to wait until the situation was less perilous. The second, George Katkov, pushed ahead with plans for quick publication and gave the manuscript to translator Max Hayward.
13. Barnes, *Boris Pasternak*, 326.
14. Shentalinsky, *The KGB's Literary Archive*, 156.
15. Zuoyue Wang, *In Sputnik's Shadow* (New Brunswick, NJ: Rutgers University Press, 2008), 71.
16. Quoted in Finn and Couvée, *The Zhivago Affair*, 127.
17. These are not official figures (information on the Bedford Publishing Company has not been released) but an estimate from what is known. See Alfred A. Reisch, *Hot Books in the Cold War* (New York: Central European University Press, 2013), 507.
18. Quoted in Finn and Couvée, *The Zhivago Affair*, 125.
19. Ibid., 115.
20. Ibid., 131.
21. Finn and Couvée quote an early memo, sent just after *Zhivago*'s publication in Italy, in which the Nobel Prize is a stated aim (ibid., 116).
22. Finn and Couvée, *The Zhivago Affair*, 144.
23. It transpired that the firm, Mouton, did not have a deal in place with Feltrinelli, and when he discovered copies of the novel were being distributed

in Brussels, he hired a lawyer and detective, prompting much dissembling by everyone involved. Mouton eventually settled with Feltrinelli but not before the affair caused rumors of CIA involvement to circulate. See ibid.

24. Quoted in ibid., 156.
25. Barnes, *Boris Pasternak*, 343.
26. Quoted in ibid.
27. Ibid., 345.
28. According to Matthew Spender, Melvin Lasky tried to pressure his father into publishing these letters in *Encounter* as means of attacking the Soviet Union. Spender refused, fearing that such a move would cause Pasternak trouble. See Matthew Spender, Preface to *Campaigning Culture and the Global Cold War: The Journals of the Congress for Cultural Freedom*, eds. Giles Scott-Smith and Charlotte Lerg (London: Palgrave Macmillan, 2017), viii. The letters were published in the magazine after Pasternak's death. See Boris Pasternak, "Three Letters," *Encounter* 15, no. 2 (August 1960): 3–6.
29. Priscilla Johnson, "Death of a Writer," *Harper's Magazine* (May 1, 1961): 143.
30. Johnson's role in Russia during this period has been the subject of much speculation. The previous years she had interviewed an American defector by the name of Lee Harvey Oswald, and after JFK's assassination it was suggested that Johnson was working in some capacity for American intelligence. The North American Newspaper Alliance was owned by Ernest Cuneo, who had served as a White House liaison for the OSS during the Second World War.
31. Quoted in Finn and Couvée, *The Zhivago Affair*, 238.
32. Johnson, "Death of a Writer," 143.
33. Ibid., 144.
34. Ibid.

TWENTY-FOUR

1. Graham Greene, *Ways of Escape* (Toronto: L&OD, 2007), 248.
2. Ibid.
3. Ibid., 252.
4. Ibid., 252–53.
5. Graham Greene, *Our Man in Havana* (London: Penguin, 1979), 25.
6. Ibid., 36.
7. Greene, *Ways of Escape*, 257.
8. Norman Sherry, *The Life of Graham Greene*, Vol. 3 (London: Cape, 2004), 140. Greene's biographer, Norman Sherry, floated the theory that by being critical of the West's conduct in the Cold War, Greene was trying to lure out Kim Philby. The problem was that while MI5 and the Americans remained convinced of his guilt, at this stage Philby was technically in the clear and enjoyed the continued support of many of his former SIS colleagues.
9. John le Carré remembers MI5's lawyer telling him Greene had crossed a line by drawing on actual operations in his book, although the decision was made not to prosecute. See Adam Sisman, *John le Carré: The Biography* (London: Bloomsbury, 2015), 202.
10. Karl Marx, *The Marx Reader*, ed. Christopher Pierson (Cambridge, UK: Polity Press, 1997), 156.

11. Greene, *Our Man in Havana*, 9.
12. Ibid., 31.
13. Ibid., 28.
14. Ibid., 141.
15. At this time the Fair Play for Cuba Committee was established in New York City, with James Baldwin, Truman Capote, Allen Ginsberg, Norman Mailer, and Jean-Paul Sartre all early supporters. In response, J. Edgar Hoover ordered the FBI to write up summaries of all members for their files.
16. That the mission began in Guatemala is itself symbolic: in 1954 the CIA helped engineer the coup by which the left-wing reformist government of Jacobo Arbenz was replaced by the military dictatorship of Carlos Castillo Armas. In fact, it was the ease with which the CIA toppled the Arbenz regime that made them confident of replicating that success in Cuba.
17. Julia E. Sweig, *Cuba: What Everyone Needs to Know* (New York: Oxford University Press, 2009), 83.
18. Michael Dobbs, *One Minute to Midnight* (New York: Knopf, 2008), 10.
19. Ibid., 12.
20. Greene, *Our Man in Havana*, 72–73.
21. Ibid., 74.
22. Ibid., 146.
23. Ibid., 150.
24. Graham Greene, "Return to Cuba," *Reflections* (London: Vintage, 2014), 256.
25. Ibid., 258.

TWENTY-FIVE

1. Fred Taylor, *The Berlin Wall* (London: Bloomsbury, 2006), 147.
2. There were, however, a number of reports from agents of American, French, and German intelligence that made it clear a large-scale operation was imminent. See ibid., 154.
3. Quoted in John Lewis Gaddis, *The Cold War: A New History* (New York: Penguin, 2005), 71.
4. Quoted in Taylor, *The Berlin Wall*, 133.
5. Ibid., 134.
6. As Taylor points out, this meant Khrushchev keeping the belligerent Ulbricht on a "short leash"—refusing, for example, to agree to his plan to plant barrage balloons over West Berlin's airport to prevent flights leaving for West Germany. See ibid., 146.
7. John le Carré, *Conversations with John le Carré*, eds. Matthew J. Bruccoli and Judith S. Baughman (Jackson: University of Mississippi Press, 2004), 159.
8. John le Carré, Introduction to *The Spy Who Came In from the Cold* (New York: Pocket Books, 2001), viii.
9. Le Carré, *Conversations with John le Carré*, 98.
10. Le Carré, Introduction, viii–ix.
11. Ibid., x.
12. John le Carré, "I Was a Secret Even to Myself," *Guardian*, April 12, 2013.
13. Adam Sisman points out that another possible reason for Cornwell leaving is the story that he punched a housemaster who made inappropriate advances.

See Adam Sisman, *John le Carré: The Biography* (London: Bloomsbury, 2015), 69.

14. John le Carré, *The Pigeon Tunnel: Stories from My Life* (New York: Viking, 2016), 4.
15. Ibid.
16. Sisman, *John le Carré*, 104.
17. Henry Hemming, *Agent M: The Lives and Spies of MI5's Maxwell Knight* (New York: Public Affairs, 2017), 281–82.
18. Quoted in ibid., 184.
19. John le Carré, "Now You See It, Now You Don't," *Times*, August 7, 1993, 12.
20. Ibid.
21. John le Carré, "Babes and Yarns: My Good Old Days in the Mysterious MI5," *Washington Post*, August 8, 1993, C4. Angleton claimed to have figured out that Philby was a spy long before his defection from Beirut, but Ben Macintyre is skeptical of this, arguing that if this were the case, the CIA would have been monitoring Philby in Beirut (see Ben Macintyre, *A Spy Among Friends* [New York: Crown, 2014], 226). This would suggest that le Carré was mistaken in judging Philby's betrayal being the humiliating motivation for Angleton's witch hunts.
22. See le Carré, *The Pigeon Tunnel*, 21.
23. Sisman, *John le Carré*, 198.
24. Le Carré, *The Pigeon Tunnel*, 20.
25. Introduction to John le Carré, *Call for the Dead* (New York: Penguin, 2012), ix.
26. Ibid., xiii.
27. Sisman, *John le Carré*, 208.
28. Ibid., 209.
29. Ibid., 216.
30. Ibid., 214.
31. Ibid., 215.
32. Le Carré, *The Spy Who Came In from the Cold*, 5.
33. Le Carré, *Conversations with John le Carré*, 98, and Sisman, *John le Carré*, 238. Sisman points out that le Carré was still working on *A Murder of Quality* until January 1962, so his writing of *The Spy Who Came In from the Cold* must have been more gradual.
34. Le Carré, *Conversations with John le Carré*, 149.
35. See le Carré, *The Pigeon Tunnel*, 22.
36. Christopher Andrew and Vasili Mitrokhin, *The Sword and the Shield: The Mitrokhin Archive and the History of the KGB* (New York: Basic Books, 1999), 398.
37. There is some speculation that he was already on the path to Communism before his capture, having become increasingly anti-American.
38. Andrew and Mitrokhin, *The Sword and the Shield*, 399.
39. Ben Macintyre, *A Spy Among Friends* (New York: Crown, 2014), 235.
40. Blake managed to escape from prison after only five years, loosening one of the bars on the window and sliding down the roof before dropping to the ground. He climbed the outer perimeter with the help of a nylon ladder, thrown over by Sean Bourke, an Irish inmate he had befriended. This pair then escaped to

the Soviet Union via East Berlin. See Andrew and Mitrokhin, *The Sword and the Shield*, 400.

41. For an analogous compromise, in which U.S. intelligence recruited Nazi scientists, see Annie Jacobsen, *Operation Paperclip: The Secret Intelligence Program That Brought Nazi Scientists to America* (New York: Little, Brown, 2014).

42. Guy Walters, *Hunting Evil* (London: Bantam, 2009), 240.

43. It was officially attached to the Federal Chancellery in 1956. Andrew and Mitrokhin, *The Sword and the Shield*, 438.

44. In 2003, le Carré visited Pullach and was disgusted to discover that Gehlen lived in Martin Bormann's old house. See le Carré, *The Pigeon Tunnel*, 59.

45. Ibid., 57.

46. Le Carré, "I Was a Secret Even to Myself."

47. Le Carré, "Now You See It, Now You Don't," 12.

48. Quoted in Macintyre, *A Spy Among Friends*, 255.

49. Le Carré, "Afterword," in ibid., 295.

50. Ibid., 241.

51. Ibid., 261–67.

52. Le Carré, *The Pigeon Tunnel*, 22.

53. Angleton later claimed that he had known about Philby's deception before his defection but the files relating to his meetings with Philby disappeared.

54. Phillip Knightley, *Philby: The Life and Views of a K.G.B. Masterspy* (London: Deutsch, 1988), 215–16.

55. Hugh Sidey, "The President's Voracious Reading Habits," *Life* (March 17, 1961): 59.

56. In October 1962, Cornwell, while finishing his novel, watched the Cuban Missile Crisis unfold, fearful for his family.

57. Le Carré, "I was a Secret Even to Myself."

58. Sisman, *John le Carré*, 247.

59. Thomas Powers, *The Man Who Kept Secrets: Richard Helms and the CIA* (New York: Knopf, 1979), 55.

60. Quoted in Frances Stonor Saunders, *The Cultural Cold War* (New York: New Press, 1999), 359.

61. Sisman, *John le Carré*, 253.

62. Quoted in ibid., 255.

63. Le Carré, "I Was a Secret Even to Myself."

64. Le Carré, *The Pigeon Tunnel*, 22.

TWENTY-SIX

1. My account of the KGB's pursuit of Tertz is drawn from Christopher Andrew and Vasili Mitrokhin, *The Sword and the Shield: The Mitrokhin Archive and the History of the KGB* (New York: Basic Books, 1999). In 1992, Vasili Mitrokhin was exfiltrated from the Soviet Union with six cases of documents detailing KGB operations, Operation Epigoni among them.

2. *Kultura* also published *Fantastic Stories,* a new collection by Tertz, in 1961, which was translated and published by Pantheon in the United States, and Collins and Harvill in London in 1963. That year another Tertz novella

appeared: *Lyubimov* was first published in Polish and Russian before being translated as *The Makepeace Experiment* when it was put out by Pantheon and Harvill in 1965.

3. Arzhak/Daniel's novella *Hands* was published by *Kultura* in January 1961. Russian-language editions of *This Is Moscow Calling* (1962), *Hands* (1963), *Man from MINAP* (1963), and *Atonement* (1964) were published by Inter-Language Literary Associates, which was run by Russian émigré Boris Filippov.

4. "On Socialist Realism" first appeared in February 1959 in the French progressive Catholic journal *L'Esprit*, edited by Jean-Marie Domenach. The essay was published in the UK by *Soviet Survey*, another journal funded by the CCF. The editor of the journal, Leopold Labedz, a Polish anti-Communist who had spent time in the gulag, also wrote an endnote to *The Trial Begins* in *Encounter*. "On Socialist Realism" was then published by the American magazine *Dissent*, in their Winter 1960 issue. It was splashed on their front cover with the headline "A Major Document from Russia."

5. Sinyavsky continued to champion Pasternak even after the *Zhivago* scandal. In 1962 Sinyavsky took on the commission to write an introduction to the first comprehensive collection of Pasternak's poetry since his death. For three years Sinyavsky fought with the editorial board of *Biblioteka poeta* to get his version through with as few changes as possible. In the meantime, he wrote articles about Pablo Picasso and Robert Frost, and sprang to the defense of the controversial young poet Andrei Voznesensky (who was very publicly denounced by Khrushchev in 1963).

6. Lauren Weiner, "Sympathy for the Devil," *New Criterion* (April 1990).

7. The following year she married the Polish sculptor August Zamoyski and is referred to in the Mitrokhin files as Hélène Zamoyska.

8. Abram Tertz, *Goodnight!*, trans. Richard Lourie (New York: Viking, 1989), 1.

9. Alfred A. Reisch, *Hot Books in the Cold War* (New York: Central European University Press, 2013), 8.

10. The signatories to the letter were Edward Albee, Hannah Arendt, W. H. Auden, Saul Bellow, Michael Harrington, Lillian Hellman, John Hersey, Robert Lowell, Norman Mailer, Lewis Mumford, Dwight Macdonald, Reinhold Niebuhr, Philip Rahv, Philip Roth, Meyer Schapiro, William Styron, Lionel Trilling, and Robert Penn Warren.

11. Lyudmila Alexeyeva, *Soviet Dissent: Contemporary Movements for National, Religious, and Human Rights* (Middletown, CT: Wesleyan University Press, 1985), 269–82.

12. Abram Tertz, "On Socialist Realism," trans. George Dennis, *Dissent* (Winter 1960): 40. Andrei Zhdanov had been responsible for the purges of writers in the aftermath of the Second World War while the novelist Maxim Gorky, who had come in and out of official favor before his death in 1936, was the founder of socialist realism.

13. Ibid., 45.

14. Ibid., 66.

15. Abram Tertz, *The Trial Begins*, trans. Max Hayward (New York: Pantheon, 1960), 8.

16. Ibid., 9.

17. Michael Frayn, "Lightning over Moscow," *Guardian*, April 29, 1960.
18. "Socialist Surrealism," *Time* (October 3, 1960).
19. Brodsky eventually emigrated to the United States in 1972 and won the Nobel Prize for Literature in 1987.
20. Tarsis wrote about his experiences in *Ward 7* and managed to defect to Britain while ostensibly on a lecture tour in London.
21. For a recent account of samizdat literature, see Ann Komaromi, *Uncensored: Samizdat Novels and the Quest for Autonomy in Soviet Dissidence* (Evanston, IL: Northwestern University Press, 2015).
22. Quoted in David Caute, *Politics and the Novel in the Cold War* (New Brunswick, NJ: Transaction, 2010), 223.
23. Quoted in Catharine Theimer Nepomnyashchy, *Abram Tertz and the Poetics of Crime* (New Haven, CT: Yale University Press, 1995), 10.
24. The letter, sent on February 1, was signed by the following: France: Maurice Blanchot, André Breton, Jean Cassou, Marguerite Duras, Pierre Emmanuel, André Frenaud, Jean Guehenno, François Mauriac. West Germany: Heinrich Böll, Günter Grass, Uwe Johnson, Hans Magnus Enzensberger, Klaus Haupprecht, Martin Walser. Italy: Libero Bigiaretti, Italo Calvino, Diego Fabbri, Alberto Moravia, Ignazio Silone, Giancarlo Vigorelli. United States: Hannah Arendt, W. H. Auden, Saul Bellow, Michael Harrington, Alfred Kazin, Mary McCarthy, Dwight Macdonald, Arthur Miller, Philip Rahv, Philip Roth, Meyer Schapiro, William Styron. Britain: A. Alvarez, A. J. Ayer, David Carver, Brian Glanville, Graham Greene, Julian Huxley, Rosamond Lehmann, Doris Lessing, Iris Murdoch, Herbert Read, Clancy Sigal, Muriel Spark, Philip Toynbee, John Wain, Bernard Wall, C. V. Wedgwood, Rebecca West.
25. "The Trial of Sinyavsky and Daniel," *New York Times*, April 17, 1966.
26. Quoted in Walter F. Kolonosky, *Literary Insinuations: Sorting Out Sinyavsky's Irreverence* (Lanham, MD: Lexington Books, 2003), 13.
27. Copies of books by Tertz and Daniel had never been more potent as weapons of cultural propaganda. A recently declassified CIA file, from December 1966, shows a company called International Book Exchange (a CIA front) ordering 300 copies of Arzhak's books, 500 copies of Tertz's books, and 200 copies of Max Hayward's book about the Daniel-Sinyavsky trial from Inter-Language Literary Associates, presumably for distribution behind the Iron Curtain. The smuggled-out transcript of the trial was published by Harper & Row as *On Trial: The Soviet State Versus "Abram Tertz" and "Nikolai Arzhak."* In January 1967 a theatrical adaptation of the trial transcript was televised, and the following month a radio play on the subject, entitled *The Crime of Fantasy*, was read by Theodore Bikel for radio WEVD.
28. Andrew and Mitrokhin, *The Sword and the Shield*, 310.
29. Quoted in *New York Times*, February 15, 1966, 8.

TWENTY-SEVEN

1. "Foundations as 'Fronts,'" Editorial, *The Nation* (September 14, 1964).
2. Jason Epstein, "The CIA and the Intellectuals," *The New York Review of Books* (April 20, 1967).

3. Quoted in John Sutherland, *Stephen Spender: A Literary Life* (New York: Oxford University Press, 2005), 429.

4. Stephen Spender, *The Thirties and After* (London: Macmillan, 1978), 163.

5. Peter Coleman, *The Liberal Conspiracy: The Congress for Cultural Freedom and the Struggle for the Mind of Postwar Europe* (New York: Free Press, 1989), 222.

6. Letter to the Editor, *New York Times*, May 9, 1966. O'Brien had long been a critic of the magazine. In 1963 he reviewed an anthology of articles from *Encounter* in the *New Statesman*, and he took issue with the idea that it was a *journal de combat* and pointed out that it failed to criticize U.S. Cold War foreign policy in supporting dictators in Cuba, Vietnam, Guatemala, Nicaragua, and South Korea.

7. Quoted in Conor Cruise O'Brien, "International Episodes," *The New York Review of Books* (September 29, 1983). Schlesinger responded to rebut aspects of O'Brien's account in the November 10 issue of *The New York Review of Books* but did not dispute the quotation attributed to him.

8. Jason Harding, "'Our Greatest Asset': *Encounter* Magazine and the Congress for Cultural Freedom," *Campaigning Culture and the Global Cold War: The Journals of the Congress for Cultural Freedom*, eds. Giles Scott-Smith and Charlotte Lerg (London: Palgrave Macmillan, 2017), 118.

9. Quoted in Sutherland, *Stephen Spender*, 439.

10. Quoted in Conor Cruise O'Brien, "Encounters with the Culturally Free," *New Left Review* (July–August 1967).

11. "Column by R," *Encounter* (August 1966).

12. This was a second visit to the Garrick with Josselson for Kermode, who tried to resign in September but was talked out of it.

13. Spender claimed this call took place in April 1967, but that was after *Ramparts* had gone to press with its allegations about the CIA. Sutherland claims the call took place in February, which seems much more likely. In Stephen Spender, *Journals 1939–83* (New York: Random House, 1986), 257.

14. Spender, *Journals 1939–83*, 257.

15. Frances Stonor Saunders, *The Cultural Cold War* (New York: New Press, 1999), 381.

16. Letter to the Editor, *New York Times*, March 27, 1967.

17. Quoted in Saunders, *The Cultural Cold War*, 383.

18. Frank Kermode, *Not Entitled: A Memoir* (New York: Farrar, Straus, Giroux, 1995), 236.

19. Quoted in Sutherland, *Stephen Spender*, 451.

20. Ibid. According to Kermode, he, Spender, Isaiah Berlin, and Stuart Hampshire discussed launching a rival magazine called *Counter-Encounter* if the trustees did not follow through. See Kermode, *Not Entitled*, 236.

21. Ibid., 452.

22. Braden had been working on the article since March with the politically connected journalist Stewart Alsop. The CIA knew about the article before it was published, and Richard Helms, the director, made President Lyndon Johnson aware that it was forthcoming. See Saunders, *The Cultural Cold War*, 401–2.

23. Braden was succeeded in the role by Cord Meyer, whose CIA career had

interrupted his literary aspirations. Meyer appointed John Clinton Hunt, an Oklahoma novelist turned CIA agent, to work in the field with the CCF. Hunt succeeded Josselson as executive director of the CCF when Josselson retired to Geneva. Meyer also appointed Robie Macauley, a novelist and editor, to the International Organizations Division of the CIA. Hunt and Meyer knew each other from the Iowa Writers' Workshop. See Giles Scott-Smith and Charlotte Lerg, "Introduction: Journals of Freedom?," in *Campaigning Culture and the Global Cold War: The Journals of the Congress for Cultural Freedom*, eds. Giles Scott-Smith and Charlotte Lerg (London: Palgrave Macmillan, 2017), 4.

24. The following year Kristol claimed to know that the CIA did plan to approach him, but that he failed a security check due to the radical politics of his youth. See Irving Kristol, "Memoirs of a Cold Warrior," *New York Times*, February 11, 1968.

25. Sylvan Fox, "Stephen Spender Quits Encounter," *New York Times*, May 8, 1967, 1.

26. *Forum* (Austria) and *Cuadernos* (Latin America) were spared the worst of this, having both ceased production in 1965.

27. *Mundo Nuevo* folded in 1971. For a fascinating account of the role of CCF journals in Latin America during the Cold War, see Patrick Iber, *Neither Peace Nor Freedom* (Cambridge, MA: Harvard University Press, 2015).

28. Eric Pullin, "*Quest*: Twenty Years of Cultural Politics," in *Campaigning Culture and the Global Cold War*, 296.

29. Elizabeth M. Holt, "Cold War in the Arabic Press: *Hiwar* (Beirut, 1962–67) and the Congress for Cultural Freedom," in *Campaigning Culture and the Global Cold War*, 234–35.

30. The situation with Black Orpheus, based in Nigeria, was less dramatic, although the loss of CCF funding meant it was only published irregularly in the years that followed. For the CCF's African journals see Asha Rogers, "*Black Orpheus* and the African Magazines of the Congress for Cultural Freedom," in *Campaigning Culture and the Global Cold War*, 243–59.

31. Coleman, *The Liberal Conspiracy*, 229. *Jiyu* lasted longer than most journals tainted by the scandal, only stopping publication in 2009. *Quadrant* (Australia), *Freedom First* (India), *Horison* (Indonesia), and *New African*, based in London, continue to publish to this day.

32. Quoted in Sutherland, *Stephen Spender*, 454.

33. Norman Mailer, *Armies of the Night* (New York: New American Library, 1968), 85.

34. "Statement on the CIA," *Partisan Review* (Summer 1967).

35. See Saunders, *The Cultural Cold War*, 335–40, and Hugh Wilford, *The Mighty Wurlitzer: How the CIA Played America* (Cambridge, MA: Harvard University Press, 2008), 103–4.

36. Frank Kermode used similar language to describe the CFF, writing in his memoir that it was "a well-known gravy train"; Kermode, *Not Entitled: A Memoir*, 225.

37. Jason Epstein, "The CIA and the Intellectuals," *The New York Review of Books* (April 20, 1967).

38. Christopher Lasch, "The Cultural Cold War," *The Nation* (September 11, 1967).

39. Quoted in Scott-Smith and Lerg, "Introduction: Journals of Freedom?," 14.
40. Matthew Spender, Preface, *Campaigning Culture and the Global Cold War,* viii.
41. Saunders, *The Cultural Cold War,* 315–21.
42. See ibid., 324. How much direct control the CIA exercised over *Encounter* and other CCF journals remains a source of contestation. Joel Whitney cites an interview with Saunders in which she said she found between twenty and thirty cases of editorial intervention of some sort; see Joel Whitney, "On *Finks,* Who Paid the Piper, and the CIA's Literary Legacy," *Guernica* (January 19, 2017). Whitney also argues that the way John Berger's 1958 novel *A Painter of Our Time* was withdrawn by Secker & Warburg after attacks from CCF intellectuals seems suspicious, especially because of the publisher's link to the founding of *Encounter,* see Whitney, *Finks,* 97–98. On the other side, Greg Barnhisel, Jason Harding, and Hugh Wilford point to evidence of how difficult the CIA found exercising control over intellectuals and that, rather than conceiving of the agency as all-powerful puppet masters, it is important to also understand the way intellectuals exploited the CIA to their own ends.
43. Spender, *The Thirties and After,* 163.
44. Ibid., 164. James Smith has questioned Spender's claims to ignorance in *British Writers and MI5 Surveillance, 1930–1960* (New York: Cambridge University Press, 2013).
45. Quoted in Saunders, *The Cultural Cold War,* 425.
46. Mary McCarthy and Hannah Arendt, *Between Friends,* ed. Carol Brightman (New York: Harcourt Brace Jovanovich, 1995), 220.
47. Stephen Spender, *The Year of the Young Rebels* (New York: Random House, 1969), 40.
48. Ibid.
49. Ibid., 46–47.
50. Ibid., 49.
51. Ibid., 50–51.
52. Quoted in Annie Cohen-Solal, *Sartre: A Life* (New York: Pantheon, 1987), 463.
53. Quoted in David Caute, *Sixty-Eight: The Year of the Barricades* (London: Hamilton, 1988), 161.
54. Spender, *Young Rebels,* 64.
55. Stephen Spender, *Journals 1939–83,* 258–59.

TWENTY-EIGHT

1. Mary McCarthy, *The Seventeenth Degree* (New York: Harcourt Brace Jovanovich, 1974), 8.
2. Ibid., 7.
3. Quoted in Mark Atwood Lawrence, *The Vietnam War: A Concise International History* (New York: Oxford University Press, 2008), 99.
4. "End Your Silence," *New York Times,* June 27, 1965.
5. Cecil Woolf and John Bagguley, *Authors Take Sides on Vietnam* (London: Owen, 1967), 18.
6. Ibid., 70.
7. Ibid., 37.

8. Ibid., 73.
9. John Updike, "Writer's Opinion on Vietnam," *New York Times,* September 24, 1967.
10. Quoted in Frances Kiernan, *Seeing Mary Plain: A Life of Mary McCarthy* (New York: Norton, 2000), 575.
11. McCarthy, *The Seventeenth Degree,* 22.
12. Thomas E. Braden, "Introduction," in *Steinbeck in Vietnam* (Charlottesville: University of Virginia Press, 2012), xi–xvi.
13. Mary McCarthy and Hannah Arendt, *Between Friends,* ed. Carol Brightman (New York: Harcourt Brace Jovanovich, 1995), 144.
14. McCarthy, *The Seventeenth Degree,* 27. McCarthy's argument is perhaps bolstered by the fact that so much excellent literary reportage and fiction came out of the Vietnam War. Philip Caputo, Le Ly Hayslip, Michael Herr, Bao Ninh, Tim O'Brien, Susan Sontag, Truong Nhu Thang, and Tobias Wolff all offer fascinating ways of thinking about the war.
15. Ibid., 91.
16. Ibid., 22.
17. Ibid., 20–21.
18. Ibid., 187.
19. Ibid., 63.
20. Ibid., 64.
21. Ibid., 66.
22. Ibid.
23. Ibid., 109.
24. Ibid., 79.
25. Ibid., 63.
26. Ibid.
27. Ibid., 101.
28. Ibid., 283.
29. Ibid., 135.
30. In her biography of McCarthy, Carol Brightman claims that Jim West told McCarthy back in 1961 that the Congress for Cultural Freedom "did not appear on state department dockets." See Carol Brightman, *Writing Dangerously: Mary McCarthy and Her World* (New York: Potter, 1992), 500.
31. McCarthy, *The Seventeenth Degree,* 135.
32. Ibid., 136.
33. Thomas Ahern, *Vietnam Declassified* (Lexington: University Press of Kentucky, 2010), 260.
34. Ibid., 262.
35. McCarthy, *The Seventeenth Degree,* 115.
36. Frances Kiernan, *Seeing Mary Plain: A Life of Mary McCarthy* (New York: Norton, 2000), 588.
37. McCarthy, *The Seventeenth Degree,* 35.
38. Ibid., 192.
39. Ibid., 205.
40. Ibid., 214.

41. Ibid., 209.
42. Ibid., 211.
43. Ibid.
44. Ibid.
45. Ibid., 299.
46. Quoted in Kiernan, *Seeing Mary Plain*, 602.
47. McCarthy was at least partly aware that this was happening. "I counted on the public to believe me, as it had believed Harrison Salisbury [of the *New York Times*], when all earlier reports had been discounted as coming from suspicious sources. Yet after a few days with those single-minded North Vietnamese, I found my claim to being a disinterested party starting not exactly to disappear, but to shrink from showing itself, as if ashamed. The Vietnamese, beginning with peasants eagerly showing you where their fields had been bombed, had an earnest disarming conviction that you would give them total credence. To question facts, figures, catch small discrepancies would be to abuse this open, naive (from a Western point of view) trust." McCarthy, *The Seventeenth Degree*, 312.
48. Ibid., 317.
49. Lawrence, *The Vietnam War*, 145.
50. McCarthy, *The Seventeenth Degree*, 365.
51. Ibid., 404–5.
52. Ibid., 46.
53. Lawrence, *The Vietnam War*, 168.
54. Quoted in Kiernan, *Seeing Mary Plain*, 607.

TWENTY-NINE

1. Michael Scammell, *Solzhenitsyn: A Biography* (New York: Norton, 1984), 637.
2. Aleksandr I. Solzhenitsyn, *The Oak and the Calf: Sketches of Literary Life in the Soviet Union*, trans. Harry Willetts (New York: Harper & Row, 1980), 220.
3. Scammell points out that copies of *One Day in the Life of Ivan Denisovich* were being secretly withdrawn from libraries. See Scammell, *Solzhenitsyn*, 596. David Remnick writes that the censors went so far as to use razor blades to cut the pages of the novel out of bound copies of *Novy Mir* being held in libraries. See David Remnick, *Lenin's Tomb: The Last Days of the Soviet Empire* (New York: Random House, 1993), 27.
4. Solzhenitsyn, *The Oak and the Calf*, 90.
5. Unbeknownst to Solzhenitsyn, Grossman, who died in 1964, had managed to secrete at least two manuscript copies of the novel, one of which was microfilmed and smuggled out to the West in 1974. *Life and Fate* was published in English translation in 1980.
6. Scammell, *Solzhenitsyn*, 509–10.
7. Solzhenitsyn, *The Oak and the Calf*, 90.
8. Teusch, a mathematics professor, had also given some of the archive to one of his disciples, Ilya Zilberberg, for safe keeping. He was raided, too. Ibid., 101–2.
9. Aleksandr Solzhenitsyn, "Breathing," *Encounter* (March 1965): 3–8.

10. Solzhenitsyn, *The Oak and the Calf*, 103.
11. Ibid., 104.
12. Ibid., 105.
13. Scammell, *Solzhenitsyn*, 548.
14. Ibid., 626.
15. Ibid., 630.
16. Ibid., 636.
17. The short story "Zakhar the Pouch" was published in January 1967.
18. Denis Kozlov, *The Readers of Novy Mir* (Cambridge, MA: Harvard University Press, 2013), 209.
19. Scammell, *Solzhenitsyn*, 664–65.
20. Ibid., 664.
21. Ibid., 683.
22. Solzhenitsyn, *The Oak and the Calf*, 290.
23. Ibid., 292.
24. Ibid.
25. Quoted in Scammell, *Solzhenitsyn*, 702.
26. See, for example, *New York Times*, October 9, 1970, 1.
27. *New York Times*, October 10, 1970, 1, 8.
28. Scammell, *Solzhenitsyn*, 660–61.
29. Ibid., 710.
30. Ibid., 710–11.
31. Quoted in ibid., 717.
32. Ibid., 739.
33. Quoted in ibid., 741–42.
34. Jussi Hanhimäki, *The Rise and Fall of Détente* (Washington, D.C.: Potomac Books, 2013), 50.
35. Scammell, *Solzhenitsyn*, 758–63.
36. Alexander Solzhenitsyn, "Nobel Lecture" (1970), https://www.nobelprize.org/prizes/literature/1970/solzhenitsyn/lecture.
37. Scammell, *Solzhenitsyn*, 797.
38. Ibid., 802.
39. Quoted in Robert Horvath, *Legacy of Soviet Dissent* (London: Routledge, 2013), 50.
40. Scammell, *Solzhenitsyn*, 815.
41. Quoted in ibid., 817.
42. Ibid., 820–22.
43. Tony Judt, *Postwar: A History of Europe Since 1945* (New York: Penguin, 2005), 559.
44. Quoted in David Remnick, "The Exile Returns," *The New Yorker* (February 14, 1994): 64.
45. Quoted in Scammell, *Solzhenitsyn*, 829–30.
46. Ibid., 840.
47. The profits from *Gulag Archipelago* were invested in a charity to help political prisoners and their families. See ibid., 874.
48. Ibid., 875.

49. Ibid., 917.
50. Ibid., 925; Remnick, "The Exile Returns," 72.
51. "Talk of the Town," *The New Yorker* (July 21, 1975): 19.

THIRTY

1. Gioconda Belli, *The Country Under My Skin: A Memoir of Love and War* (New York: Knopf, 2002), 114.
2. Victor Bulmer-Thomas, "Nicaragua Since 1930," in Leslie Bethell, ed., *Cambridge History of Latin America* (Cambridge, UK: Cambridge University Press, 1990), 349.
3. Belli, *The Country Under My Skin*, 38.
4. Quoted in Margaret Randall, *Sandino's Daughters Revisited: Feminism in Nicaragua* (New Brunswick, NJ: Rutgers University Press, 1994), 172.
5. Belli, *The Country Under My Skin*, 115.
6. Randall, *Sandino's Daughters Revisited*, 174.
7. The Marines had been sent in to protect American interests regarding the planned construction of a Nicaraguan canal to connect the Atlantic to the Pacific, which was eventually constructed in Panama.
8. The line is now thought to be apocryphal but continues to circulate nevertheless, largely because it so pithily sums up the attitude of Washington to the military dictators it supported.
9. Belli, *The Country Under My Skin*, 128.
10. Ibid., 140.
11. Ibid., 141.
12. Ibid., 165.
13. Bulmer-Thomas, "Nicaragua Since 1930," 350.
14. The university was founded in 1960 with the goal of educating politically sympathetic students from developing countries.
15. Belli, *The Country Under My Skin*, 196.
16. Ibid., 1.
17. Ibid., 217.
18. Quoted in Hal Brands, *Latin America's Cold War* (Cambridge, MA: Harvard University Press, 2010), 181.
19. Ibid.
20. Belli, *The Country Under My Skin*, 235.
21. Ibid., 239–40.
22. Ibid., 247.
23. Salman Rushdie, *The Jaguar's Smile: A Nicaraguan Journey* (New York: Viking, 1987), 35–36.
24. Ibid., 40.
25. Ibid., 41.
26. Stephen Kinzer, "For Sandinista a Strong Literary Escort," *New York Times*, January 16, 1988, 4.
27. Greene gives a brief account of this 1980 trip in his book about his friendsip with Panamanian ruler Omar Torrijos. See Graham Greene, *Getting to Know the General* (London: Bodley Head, 1984), 163–72.

28. This poem appears in Gioconda Belli, *From Eve's Rib,* trans. Steven F. White (Willimantic, CT: Curbstone Press, 1989), 49.
29. Belli, *The Country Under My Skin;* ibid., 252.
30. Ibid., 264.
31. Brands, *Latin America's Cold War,* 186.
32. Belli, *The Country Under My Skin,* 276.
33. Ibid., 280.
34. Ibid., 282.
35. Republican Party Platform of 1980, https://www.presidency.ucsb.edu /documents/republican-party-platform-1980.
36. Brands, *Latin America's Cold War,* 199.
37. For a typically brilliant account of what this looked like from the ground, see Joan Didion, *Salvador* (New York: Vintage, 1994).
38. Quoted in ibid., 196.
39. Ibid., 198.
40. Belli, *The Country Under My Skin,* 292.
41. Reagan to Joint Session of Congress, April 27, 1983, https://www.reaganlibrary .gov/research/speeches/42783d.
42. Belli, *The Country Under My Skin,* 299.
43. Tobias Rupprecht, *Soviet Internationalism After Stalin: Interaction and Exchnage Between the USSR and Latin America During the Cold War* (Cambridge, UK: Cambridge University Press, 2015), 276.
44. Belli, *The Country Under My Skin,* 326.
45. Stephen Kinzer, *Blood of Brothers* (New York: Putnam, 1991), 309–11.
46. Belli, *The Country Under My Skin,* 353.
47. Ibid., 354.

THIRTY-ONE

1. Although, as Jonathan Bolton points out, the Plastics were not initially political. See Jonathan Bolton, *Worlds of Dissent: Charter 77, The Plastic People of the Universe, and Czech Culture Under Communism* (Cambridge, MA: Harvard University Press, 2012), 118.
2. Bolton, *Worlds of Dissent,* 133.
3. The term *Vlasatec* ("longhair") became a semiofficial designation used in police reports and other documents. See ibid., 121.
4. Václav Havel, *Disturbing the Peace,* trans. Paul Wilson (New York: Knopf, 1990), 126.
5. Ibid., 128.
6. Quoted in Michael Zantovsky, *Havel: A Life* (New York: Grove Press, 2014), 164.
7. See ibid., 164–65. The *Washington Post* and the *Observer* also covered the story.
8. Václav Havel, *Open Letters,* ed. Paul Wilson (New York: Vintage, 1992), 103.
9. John Keane, *Václav Havel: A Political Tragedy in Six Acts* (London: Bloomsbury, 1999), 84.
10. Zantovsky, *Havel,* 28.
11. Tony Judt, *Postwar: A History of Europe Since 1945* (New York: Penguin, 2005), 138.

12. For an account of Miloš's difficulty with the Nazi occupation see Keane, *Václav Havel*, 55–61.
13. Václav Havel, *The Garden Party*, in *Selected Plays 1963–83* (London: Faber & Faber, 1992), 51.
14. Zantovsky, *Havel*, 69.
15. Václav Havel, *The Memorandum*, in *Selected Plays 1963–83*, 54–56.
16. Havel, *Disturbing the Peace*, 107.
17. Zantovsky, *Havel*, 116.
18. Havel, "Second Wind," in *Open Letters*, 8.
19. Havel, "Dear Dr. Husak," in *Open Letters*, 82–83.
20. Havel, *Audience*, in *Selected Plays: 1963–83*, 211.
21. Havel, *Disturbing the Peace*, 123–24.
22. Ibid., 124.
23. Zantovsky, *Havel*, 175.
24. As Bolton points out, Landovsky was "a brilliant raconteur" whose stories were not without embellishment. He told the story many different ways, with conflicting details, but the essential train of events is consistent. The different versions of the story became inscribed into the Charter 77 legend. See Bolton, *Worlds of Dissent*, 149.
25. Quoted in ibid., 149–50.
26. Zantovsky, *Havel*, 176–77.
27. Bolton, *Worlds of Dissent*, 150.
28. It was published in the *New York Times* on January 27, 1977, having been first published in the *New Leader*.
29. *New York Times*, January 27, 1977, 1.
30. Zantovsky, *Havel*, 178–80.
31. Ibid., 186.
32. Ibid., 197–98.
33. Havel, "Power of the Powerless," in *Open Letters*, 127.
34. Ibid., 131.
35. Ibid., 132.
36. Ibid., 133.
37. Ibid., 154.
38. Ibid., 150.
39. Ibid., 204.
40. Zantovsky, *Havel*, 207.
41. "A Thoroughly Politicized Czech Playwright," *New York Times*, October 25, 1979, A3.
42. Zantovsky, *Havel*, 210–12.
43. *Washington Post*, March 4, 1980, B1.
44. Zantovsky, *Havel*, 233. To keep himself sane, Havel wrote long, philosophical letters to Olga, which were subsequently published. They revealed little of life in prison, and Havel never publicly gave an account of how he had suffered there.
45. Havel, "Meeting Gorbachev," in *Open Letters*, 352–53.
46. Ibid., 353.
47. Robert Service, *The End of the Cold War: 1985–1991* (London: Macmillan, 2015), 101.

48. John Lewis Gaddis, *The Cold War: A New History* (New York: Penguin, 2005), 30.
49. Service, *The End of the Cold War*, 54.
50. Vladislav Zubok, *Zhivago's Children: The Last Russian Intelligentsia* (Cambridge, MA: Harvard University Press, 2009), 336.
51. For the Soviet Union's problems with exports see Odd Arne Westad, *The Cold War: A World History* (New York: Basic Books, 2017), 379.
52. Gregory Feifer, *The Great Gamble: The Soviet War in Afghanistan* (New York: Harper, 2009), 255.
53. Archie Brown, "The Gorbachev Revolution and the End of the Cold War," in Melvin P. Leffler and Odd Arne Westad, eds., *The Cambridge History of the Cold War*, Vol. 3, *Endings* (Cambridge, UK: Cambridge University Press, 2010), 255.
54. Westad, *The Cold War*, 367.
55. Ibid., 371, 375.
56. Quoted in ibid., 372.
57. Brown, "The Gorbachev Revolution," 254.
58. Westad, *The Cold War*, 512.
59. Mary Elise Sarotte, *The Collapse: The Accidental Opening of the Berlin Wall* (New York: Basic Books, 2014), 9.
60. Zantovsky, *Havel*, 272.
61. Ibid., 278.
62. Quoted in ibid., 280.
63. Ibid., 283.
64. Ibid., 293.
65. Quoted in Westad, *The Cold War*, 586.
66. Sarotte, *The Collapse*, 74.
67. Ibid., 118.
68. Westad, *The Cold War*, 591.
69. Sarotte, *The Collapse*, 136–37.
70. Zantovsky, *Havel*, 314–15.
71. Ibid., 328. Havel's biographer also tells the story of how one General Tomecek secured the job of head of the military office because at his interview he said he was reading *Catch-22*.
72. Ibid., 345.
73. Ibid., 347.
74. Ibid., 355.
75. Ibid., 359.
76. Ibid., 356.
77. Westad, *The Cold War*, 596.

THIRTY-TWO

1. See "Once More Unto the Breach! Ink-Stained Warriors Rush the Citadel Anew," *New York Times*, January 28, 1988; and David Remnick, *Lenin's Tomb: The Last Days of the Soviet Empire* (New York: Random House, 1993), 59.
2. Vladislav Zubok, *Zhivago's Children: The Last Russian Intelligentsia* (Cambridge, MA: Harvard University Press, 2009), 336–37.

3. Remnick, *Lenin's Tomb*, 59.
4. Alexei Yurchak, *Everything Was Forever Until It Was No More* (Princeton, NJ: Princeton University Press, 2006), 3.
5. Glasnost operated across all cultural spheres. One of the most influential works of this period was the film *Repentance*, directed by the Georgian filmmaker Tengiz Abuladze, which was a satirical attack on Stalinism and its legacy and which was seen by millions after its release.
6. Remnick, *Lenin's Tomb*, 36.
7. As Service points out, the KGB had warned the Kremlin about the state of the plant seven years earlier. Robert Service, *The End of the Cold War: 1985–1991* (London: Macmillan, 2015), 185.
8. Holly Myers, "Svetlana Aleksievich's Changing Narrative of the Soviet-Afghan War in *Zinky Boys*," *Canadian Slavonic Papers*, October 2017, 332.
9. Anatoly Pristavkin, for example, published a novel about the forced deportation of the Chechen people during the war. See Zubok, *Zhivago's Children*, 340.
10. Ibid., 338.
11. Michael G. Brennan, *Graham Greene: Political Writer* (New York: Palgrave, 2016), 168.
12. Archie Brown, "The Gorbachev Revolution and the End of the Cold War," in Melvin P. Leffler and Odd Arne Westad, eds., *The Cambridge History of the Cold War*, Vol. 3, *Endings* (Cambridge, UK: Cambridge University Press, 2010), 262.
13. Norman Sherry, *The Life of Graham Greene*, Vol. 3 (London: Cape, 2004), 744. For a copy of the letter see 855–56.
14. *Washington Post*, February 17, 1987.
15. *Washington Post*, September 20, 1988.
16. Sherry, *The Life of Graham Greene*, Vol. 3, 744.
17. Graham Greene, "Kim Philby," in *My Silent War* (London: MacGibbon & Kee, 1968), vii–ix.
18. Quoted in Phillip Knightley, *Philby: The Life and Views of a K.G.B. Masterspy* (London: Deutsch, 1988), 232.
19. The letters were mostly personal. Greene said that Philby knew anything of intelligence value would be passed by Greene straight on to SIS. See ibid., 245.
20. See Genrikh Borovik, *The Philby Files* (London: Little, Brown, 1994), 370–72. Borovik was the father of Artyom Borovik, the journalist reporting from the front lines of the war.
21. Philby, *My Silent War*, xviii.
22. Rufina Philby, *The Private Life of Kim Philby* (London: St. Ermin's, 1999), 173–77.
23. Christopher Andrew and Oleg Gordievsky, *KGB: The Inside Story of Its Foreign Operations from Lenin to Gorbachev* (New York: HarperCollins, 1990), 6.
24. Ben Macintyre, *A Spy Among Friends* (New York: Crown, 2014), 291.
25. Quoted in Andrew and Gordievsky, *KGB*, 5.
26. Philby, *The Private Life*, 175.
27. Sherry, *The Life of Graham Greene*, Vol. 3, 745.

28. Only two of his books had been published in the Soviet Union: *A Murder of Quality* and *A Small Town in Germany*.
29. Adam Sisman, *John le Carré: The Biography* (London: Bloomsbury, 2015); and John le Carré, *The Pigeon Tunnel: Stories from My Life* (New York: Viking, 2016), 115.
30. Sisman, *John le Carré*, 455.
31. Quoted in Sarah Lyall, "Spies Like Us: A Conversation with John le Carré and Ben Macintyre," *New York Times*, August 25, 2017.
32. Le Carré, *The Pigeon Tunnel*, 187.
33. Remnick, *Lenin's Tomb*, 71.
34. Quoted in ibid., 75.
35. Quoted in Zubok, *Zhivago's Children*, 425. A translation of the Andreyeva's article "I Cannot Give Up My Principles" can be found in Ronald Grigor Suny, ed., *The Structure of Soviet History: Essays and Documents* (Oxford: Oxford University Press, 2014), 503–11.
36. Ibid., 343.
37. Quoted in Remnick, *Lenin's Tomb*, 85.
38. Zubok, *Zhivago's Children*, 342–43.
39. Remnick, *Lenin's Tomb*, 265.
40. Ibid., 61.
41. Quoted in ibid., 267.
42. Ibid., 266.
43. D. M. Thomas, *Alexander Solzhenitsyn: A Century in His Life* (New York: St. Martin's Press, 1998), 498.
44. Remnick, *Lenin's Tomb*, 267.
45. Thomas, *Alexander Solzhenitsyn*, 498.
46. For a nuanced approach to the idea of the permanence of the socialist state and what happened when it collapsed, see Yurchak, *Everything Was Forever Until It Was No More*.
47. Excerpts from Aleksandr Solzhenitsyn, "How to Revitalize Russia," *New York Times*, September 19, 1990.
48. Quoted in Remnick, *Lenin's Tomb*, 369.
49. Ibid., 435.

EPILOGUE

1. John le Carré, *Secret Pilgrim* (New York: Ballantine, 2017), 381.
2. Ibid., 378.
3. Sisman, *John le Carré*, 499.
4. Le Carré, *The Pigeon Tunnel*, 131.
5. John le Carré, *Conversations with John le Carré*, eds. Matthew J. Bruccoli and Judith S. Baughman (Jackson: University of Mississippi Press, 2004), 126.
6. Francis Fukuyama, "The End of History?" *The National Interest*, no. 16 (Summer 1989): 3–18. For a series of explorations of the theme of Cold War triumphalism, including responses to Fukuyama's article, see Ellen Schrecker, ed., *Cold War Triumphalism: The Misuse of History After the Fall of Communism* (New York: New Press, 2004).

7. Gregory Feifer, *The Great Gamble: The Soviet War in Afghanistan* (New York: Harper, 2009) 132.

8. A few examples: Mark MacKinnon, *The New Cold War* (New York: Carroll & Graf, 2007); Edward Lucas, *The New Cold War: The Future of Russia and the Threat to the West* (New York: Palgrave Macmillan, 2008); Patrick Wintour, Luke Harding, and Julian Borger, "Cold War 2.0: How Russia and the West Reheated a Historic Struggle," *Guardian*, October 24, 2016; Stephen F. Cohen, "New Cold War Dangers," *The Nation*, December 5, 2018.

9. A couple of examples: Editorial Board, "The U.S. and China Are on the Brink of Cold War 2.0. This Is How to Avoid It," *Washington Post*, November 29, 2018; Robert D. Kaplan, "A New Cold War Has Begun," *Foreign Policy* (January 7, 2019).

10. Tom Balmforth, "Frail Mikhail Gorbachev Warns Against Return to the Cold War," Reuters, November 8, 2018.

11. Odd Arne Westad, "Has a New Cold War Really Begun?" *Foreign Affairs* (March 27, 2018).

12. Andrei Sinyavsky, *The Russian Intelligentsia,* trans. Lynn Visson (New York: Columbia University Press, 1997), 30.

13. Ibid., 5.

14. Ibid., 15.

15. Ibid., 29.

16. Ibid., 79–80.

17. See Masha Gessem, *The Man Without a Face: The Unlikely Rise of Vladimir Putin* (New York: Penguin, 2012), 101–5, 118–25.

18. As Gessem makes clear, while the government claimed the perpetrators of these bombings were Chechen terrorists, there are many unanswered questions about these attacks, many of which indicate FSB involvement; see ibid., 23–42.

19. Gessem, *The Man Without a Face,* 52.

20. Ibid., 68–69.

21. Ibid., 180.

22. Ibid., 237–38.

23. Matt Apuzzo and Sharon LaFraniere, "13 Russians Indicted as Mueller Reveals Effort to Aid Trump Campaign," *New York Times*, February 16, 2018.

24. Westad, "Has a New Cold War Really Begun?"

25. It is tempting to claim that this is the result of changes in technology, the rise of TV and the Internet, and a fundamental change in our reading habits, but in recent years, publishers have been reporting a rise in the number of people buying books, including fiction. See Danuta Kean, "Book Sales Boom but Authors Report Shrinking Incomes," *Guardian,* July 19, 2018.

26. Emily Tamkin, "With Putin's Signature, 'Fake News' Bill Becomes Law," *Washington Post,* March 18, 2019.

27. "The PEN International Case List 2017," PEN International, https://pen -international.org/app/uploads/PEN-CaseList_2017-FULL-v2-1UP.pdf.

INDEX